FAYETTE COUNTY, PENNSYLVANIA BIOGRAPHIES

EDITORIALLY MANAGED BY
JOHN M. GRESHAM

ASSISTED IN THE COMPILATION BY
SAMUEL T. WILEY

CLEARFIELD

Originally published
as pages 127–602 of
Biographical and Portrait Cyclopedia of Fayette County, Pennsylvania
Chicago, Illinois, 1889

Reprinted for
Clearfield Company, Inc. by
Genealogical Publishing Co., Inc.
Baltimore, Maryland
1997

International Standard Book Number: 0-8063-4750-3

PREFACE

BUT till recently little attention has been given to the preservation of biography except in so far as it pertained to persons who have been prominent in governmental affairs, or distinguished in their profession or calling, or by some accident of fortune made in a manner conspicuous before the public, and requiring that more than usual should be known of the individual. Within the last decade, however, there has been a growing demand for the preservation of not only biography but for genealogy of families; not altogether for its immediate worth but for its future value; and a laudable and commendable pride in its preservation. This medium then serves more than a single purpose: while it secures biography it records history that would be lost in any other way. This will be most strikingly illustrated by reference in these sketches to the period of the War of the Rebellion.

Of the necessity of preserving biography and genealogy in permanent form, one needs the experience of a collector of material for work of this character, as in a majority of cases nearly all trace of ancestry is lost back of grandfather and grandmother, even in families where intelligence and prominence would seem to guarantee better things. In many other instances the material composing the sketches of this volume has been secured from those immediately interested; and was afterwards submitted to them through the mails in typewritten form, so that all errors might disappear.

THE PUBLISHER.

....CONTENTS....

BROWNSVILLE AND BRIDGEPORT.

FRANKLIN.

WASHINGTON.

TYRONE.

MENALLEN.

ILLUSTRATIONS.

Fayette County . . . .

Biographies

. . . . UNIONTOWN, North and South Union.

CHARLES EDMUND BOYLE. By the space allowed by the plan of this work it is impossible to do justice to the memory of this remarkable man: yet we deem it most appropriate that a record of the salient points of his life should be given in the Biographical Cyclopedia of Fayette County.

Charles E. Boyle. As calm and unbiased judgment of a man's life is most likely to be rendered when its labors are ended and its ambitions and rivalries can no longer affect the award; and as the time is now here the historian should render such judgment in making record of the life of the Hon. Charles E. Boyle, a distinguished lawyer, statesman and jurist. The rightful measure of distinction to which he is entitled is both local and national: as it was honorably and justly won it should be freely accorded space on the Biographical page.

Charles E. Boyle was born at Uniontown, Fayette county, Pennsylvania, February 4, 1836; and was the youngest of a family of four children. His father was Bernard Boyle, who came from Ireland and died near New Market, Virginia, 1839.

Charles E. Boyle received his education in the common schools (which, at that time, were merely ushered into existence in Pennsylvania), afterwards pursued his studies at Madison College, and ended his school life with a course at Waynesburg College. While yet at school, he spent his spare moments in a printing office, and at the age of nine years he had picked up the art of setting type. Leaving college, he engaged as printer in the office of the *Genius of Liberty.* He soon passed from the type-setter's case to the editorial chair and the proprietorship of the paper; and the unceasing toil of the boy gave unerring promise of high position to be won through the earnest labors of the man. In 1861, he sold the paper to Colonel E. G. Roddy in order to engage in his chosen life pursuit, that of the law. While proprietor of the *Genius* his leisure hours were devoted to reading law with the late Hon. Daniel Kaine, and was admitted to the bar December 2, 1861. He at once entered upon the practice, in partnership with his preceptor, which lasted until 1865. Mr. Boyle, in 1862, was elected and served for three years as District Attorney of Fayette county. At the bar he developed and matured professional attainments and intellectual powers that won him respect as a lawyer and member of Congress, and subsequently as Chief Justice of Washington Territory.

As a lawyer his comprehensive mind was peculiarly fitted to grapple with the difficult questions arising out of a complicated case at law. His clear statement of the facts and relevant points of his case, his strong and convincing arguments, his logical conclusions, his comprehensive summary of evidence and his masterly exposition of the law, made him one of the foremost lawyers of Pennsylvania. After a most careful and exhaustive study of his cases—so when called in court for trial, he was generally successful in winning them. His political career began in 1865, when he was elected by his party—the democrats—as Representative to the Assembly, and re-elected in 1866, and was placed on several important committees. In the last session of which he was a member, he at once assumed leadership of his party in the House, and his course of action was so acceptable to his democratic fellow-members that they presented him at the close of the session with a costly service of silver. He was elected president of the Democratic State Convention of 1867 over Judge Jere. Black, and in the following year was the democratic candidate for Auditor General of the State. Intellectual attainments, mature mind and nearly twenty years of useful public life, amply qualified him to enter a wider field of activity and usefulness, and accordingly his name was presented by his friends in 1872, 1874, 1876, 1878 and 1880 as a candidate for Congress from the twenty-first district before the democratic convention. In each of these years his native county increased her majority for him, but he failed each time in the nomination, it going to men in one or the other counties of the district. After an acrimonious contest in 1882, he was nominated and elected to Congress by a handsome majority over the late popular Charles S. Seaton; and was re-elected in 1884 by a very flattering vote over the Hon. J. W. Ray. While serving his second term, he was chairman of the Pan-electric Committee, and made one of the ablest reports ever sent out from a committee room. He was a candidate for President Judge in 1887 of the Fourteenth Judicial District, composed of the counties of Fayette and Greene: Receiving the nomination of his party for that office in Fayette, but as there was in the county an independent democratic candidate for the same office, divided the democratic vote so that the republican candidate was elected. He was well qualified for the office, and would have made an able, learned and most excellent Judge. He held various offices of trust and responsibility: Director of the First National Bank and Vestryman of St Peter's Protestant Episcopal church. From 1871 to 1880, he operated largely in coke. He was solicitor of the B. & O. R. R. Co. and retained counsel of nearly all the large coke and furnace companies of Southwestern Pennsylvania. In the Democratic conventions of 1876 and '80 as a delegate, he strongly advocated the nomination of General Hancock for President. From his speeches and reports in Congress, he acquired National reputation, and without solicitation upon his part, the President appointed him 1888 Chief Justice of Washington Territory. Just before leaving to assume the duties of this important office, however, he was given a banquet at his home and every member of the Fayette County bar was present. Soon after receiving this flattering testimony of good will and esteem from his legal associates, he left for Washington Territory, where he arrived November 18th: publicly installed on the 22d of the same month and immediately entered upon the important duties of

C. E. Boyle

his office as the Chief Justice of the territory. Only a few short days and Charles E. Boyle, who so well graced the Bench and so ably discharged the duties of his high office, was stricken down by the hand of death, in the midst of what promised to be a long life of honor and usefulness. He died on the evening of December 15th, 1888, Occidental Hotel, Seattle, Washington Territory, of pneumonia, contracted while in the discharge of his judicial duties. Of Washington Territory and of Pennsylvania, his friends alike were surprised and grieved at his sudden and unexpected death. Many of the leading citizens of Washington Territory mingled with their aspirations of Statehood the hope of sending Judge Boyle, when the star of Washington as a State should be placed on the flag of the Nation, to represent her interests and protect her rights on the floor of the United States Senate.

"The Cayuse" of Seattle, Washington Territory, the leading literary journal of the Pacific Slope, spoke as follows of Judge Boyle: "The sudden death of Chief Justice Boyle cast a gloom over this whole community. Leaving his home in a distant State, where a long life in an honorable profession had brought him distinction, he came to our young Territory to fill her highest office. Only one month of service was allowed him by the decrees of Providence. Yet in that brief space, all who had the pleasure of his acquaintance learned of the broadness and greatness of his mind and intellect. * * * * He identified himself with the interests of Washington Territory and devoted his abilities to her advancement. * * * * The renown of his noble character belongs to us as well as Pennsylvania, and will live with us as long as there is a reverence for greatness in the State of Washington."

The Bar of Seattle, Washington Territory, in its resolutions of respect to the memory of Judge Boyle, closed with the following well deserved tribute: "That he won the esteem, regard and confidence of the Bar, and of the general public; and that the people of Washington Territory have by his death suffered the loss of a learned, able, upright and dignified Chief Justice."

The press of Fayette county, of Washington Territory, and all the leading papers of the land, spoke in fitting terms of the distinguished life and valuable services of Judge Boyle. The Pittsburg *Leader*, in extended mention of him, said he was "A figure which had become honorably conspicuous in the politics of Western Pennsylvania." The Pittsburg *Post*, in concluding a long and able article on the death of Judge Boyle, stated that "C. E. Boyle's attainments were solid rather than showy, while his personal integrity and sense of honor were striking traits of a well-rounded character."

He was married to Miss Mary Hendrickson of Uniontown, February 7, 1858. They had seven children: Lucy (dead), John, Edgar, George, Charles E., Frances and Florence.

A friend of Mr. Boyle's speaks of his domestic life thus: born and reared at Uniontown, and was one of the most familiar forms to be seen on the streets. As a boy he was slight in size but possessed a bright, thoughtful and intelligent face, manly bearing, courteous in intercourse and sustained an irreproachable character. On his reaching manhood he was still slight and below the average height. His complexion was dark and pale with rather an unhealthy look, and at no time had a strong and vigorous vitality; but for the last fifteen years of his life he became healthier and more robust in appearance. His portly form, high and well-shaped forehead, strongly marked face closely shaved, except a heavy mustache, gave him a commanding appearance. His domestic life was charming, and his elegant home,

"Oak Hill," commanding as it does one of the most extensive and varied landscape views of the beautiful valley of the Redstone, and the bold outlines of Chestnut Ridge of the Alleghany system can be seen for a distance of thirty miles. His home, a model of elegance and refinement, furnished a worthy retreat for his highly cultivated tastes: its extensive library of history, biography, geography, physical sciences, poetry of America and England, were the source from which he drew his varied intellectual food. It was here, surrounded by his family, that he appeared to many at his best.

Under the benign influences of our republican institutions, the successful and honorable career of Charles E. Boyle clearly illustrates the fact that a trinity of massive intellect, indomitable will and ceaseless labor will lift their possessor to the very pinnacle of fame and fortune without the fictitious aids of wealth and power, which too frequently stand sponsors at the baptism of great men so called, in the old world.

He died in the land of sunset skies where oceanward rolls the mighty Columbia. He sleeps in the beautiful and historic valley of the Monongahela where riverward flows the gentle Redstone. But his fame is not in keeping of either the East or the West but has passed into the possession of a nation. *Requiescat in pace.*

ZACHARIAH BALL (deceased) was a highly respective citizen of North Union township. He was a son of John and Rachel Ball and was born in Dunbar township, Fayette county, Pennsylvania, April 3, 1819, and died in North Union township, March 11, 1886.

Zachariah Ball left the subscription schools of Dunbar township at an early age to engage in farming. About 1844 he purchased the well known Craig farm and erected thereon a large barn and fine brick residence, which were blown down a few years later by a severe wind storm. Mr. Ball and his family were sleeping at the time, in a lower room, which was the only part of the house left standing. He rebuilt the house and in a few years sold his farm, that cost him $30 per acre, for $150 per acre, and purchased the Swan farm in North Union township, near the county home, and where he resided until his death.

On November 2, 1841, he married Miss Lydia Longanecker. They had three children: Sarah E., died November 16, 1863; Jacob E., died July 17, 1868, and Joseph L., born August 11, 1844, married Clarissa Barricklow and has three children: Sarah E., wife of J. N. Hibbs, George W. and Altha. Joseph L. Ball owns 150 acres of fine land. Mrs. Lydia Ball's father was Joseph Longanecker, son of John Longanecker, a prosperous farmer and leading member of the Mennonite church. He was married to Sarah Mack, now an active old lady in the ninety-first year of her age.

Zachariah Ball was a school director in Dunbar township. After his removal to North Union township, he devoted all his time to the improvement and cultivation of his farm, and died enjoying the good will and respect of all who knew him.

JOSEPH BARTON is a son of William and Hannah (Collins Foster) Barton. He was born in the house where he now resides, in South Union township, Fayette county, Pennsylvania, December 16, 1833.

His father, William Barton, was a native of Bucks county, Pennsylvania, born September 13, 1795, and died November 6, 1865. He was a son of William Barton, Sr., died November 30, 1826, of Quaker faith and English lineage, the latter a native of New Jersey, and came to German township, Fayette county, when William Barton was about twelve years of age. William Barton was well educated, and was employed in early life as a clerk and furnace manager. November 28, 1824, he was united in marriage to Mrs. Hannah (Collins) Foster, widow of Captain John Foster (the last named a soldier of the War of 1812) and daughter of Colonel Thomas Collins, of Uniontown. Colonel Thomas Collins married Miss Mary, sister of Dr. Daugherty, of Morgantown, West Virginia. They had two children: Ann and Hannah.

He was born near Winchester, Virginia, in 1741, and died at Uniontown, November 3, 1813. His father was John Collins, a native of Ireland.

Unto their union were born four children, all now dead except Joseph Barton. Mrs. Barton was born October 28, 1795, and married to John Foster. By this marriage she had two daughters: Jane married Joseph Gray, Elizabeth married Samuel Yarnell. Her father, Thomas Collins, was a colonel in the War of 1812, sheriff of Fayette county from 1796 to 1799, and a very popular man in his time. He died November 8, 1827.

William Barton removed to the old Collins farm in South Union, where he engaged in farming, stock-raising and operating a distillery. He was a whig and afterward a republican—was a school director for years, and a man of strictest integrity in business.

Joseph Barton attended the common schools of South Union township, and was a student at Madison College for several terms.

He enlisted, 22d of June, 1861, at the outbreak of the late war, in Company A, First West Virginia Cavalry, commanded by Captain William West, and served until September 12, 1864. The principal engagements he participated in were Carnifex Ferry, South Mountain and Antietam.

Mr. Barton has been twice married. His first wife was Miss Ruth (daughter of Basil Brownfield), to whom he was married January 1, 1857; she was born October 23, 1834, and died January 10, 1884. They had six children, four of whom are living: William, married to Laura Todd; Priscilla, Harriet and Josephine. On September 21, 1884, he again married, his second wife being Miss Florence, daughter of George Shanabarger, of Georges township.

Mr. Barton was one of the founders of A. E. Wilson Lodge, No. 208, K. of P. He is a member of Fort Necessity Lodge, No. 254, I. O. of O. F., P. O. S. A., and the Grand Army of the Republic. He has always been an active Republican and has filled the various township offices. He is intelligent, patriotic and an agreeable gentleman, and is the possessor of a large tract of well improved land.

MAX BAUM, a leading merchant of Uniontown, was born in Germany February 3, 1842, and came to the United States in 1865 and located first in Cumberland, Maryland, where he remained for one year—thence to Baltimore, where he remained but six months, when he returned to Cumberland, and on August 5, 1867, came to Uniontown, Pennsylvania, and engaged in the clothing business. In January, 1879, he removed to his present stand at the corner of Main and Morgantown streets.

Mr. Baum is the oldest merchant clothier at Uniontown, and has by close attention to business, never failing courtesy and the strictest honesty, gained a host of friends and the good will of all who know him, and has established the best and the largest trade in his line in the county. His store is an emporium, which contains a large assortment of the choicest clothing and the best of goods for manufacturing clothes, and all of the appurtenances to the complete outfit of a gentleman's toilet.

Mr. Baum is thoroughly Americanized in manner, speech and feeling. When he offered himself as a candidate for the legislature he carried a great many of the districts of the county almost unanimously. He is especially popular with the farmers.

He was married in 1869 to Miss Sarah Rosenbaum, of Cumberland, Maryland, and has five living children: Rachel, Mattie, William, Simon and Isaac.

Rachel is married to Louis Hirsch, of Cumberland; who is engaged in the wool and hide business. The other children are at home. Mr. Baum is a member of the Free and Accepted Masonic society.

L. C. BEAL, M. D., was born in Franklin township, Fayette county, Pennsylvania, December 26, 1850.

His boyhood days were spent on the farm, and his early education was received at the public schools of his native township. He graduated at the Southwestern Normal School in 1886, and for eleven years was engaged in teaching in the public schools of Fayette and Washington counties; and was in the meantime principal of the West Brownsville and Burgettstown public schools, of Washington county: he also conducted a summer normal at Ohio Pyle, Fayette county, for two years.

He subsequently graduated from the medical department of the Western Reserve University, at Cleveland, Ohio, and began the practice of medicine at Farmington, Fayette county, Pennsylvania, where he continued in successful practice until the 1st of April, 1889, when he removed to Uniontown; and in connection with his professional duties opened a drug store, at No. 621, Main street.

The only office he ever held was secretary (for three years) of the School Board of Wharton township, Fayette county, Pennsylvania.

He is a son of John and Jane Beal, both natives of Fayette county, Pennsylvania, and were members of the Flat Wood Baptist church.

JACOB M. BEESON, a responsible and substantial business man, and a descendant of one of the pioneer families of Fayette county, is a son of Strauther and Mary M. (Miller) Beeson. He was born at South Bend, Indiana, April 2, 1847, and came to this county at an early age.

His grandfather, Jacob Beeson, was a brother of Henry Beeson, the founder of Uniontown. Both came from Virgiania between 1765 and 1769. Jacob Beeson purchased of Henry Beeson 236 acres of land west of what is now Morgantown street, Uniontown, paying £85 for the same. Jacob Beeson afterwards received the patent for this tract, which was called Mt. Vernon. On this same tract he platted and laid out two additions to Uniontown, known as Jacob's addition and Jacob's second addition.

His father, Strauther Beeson, was born at Uniontown, and died in December, 1878. He was a prosperous business man, a real estate speculator, and a lawyer by profession. His wife was Miss Mary M., daughter of Hiram Miller, the latter a whig, a Cumberland Presbyterian, and a successful farmer of South Union township.

Jacob M. Beeson was educated in the common schools and at Madison College, under Professors Lewis and Mercer. He is at present engaged in farming.

On December 16, 1874, he was united in marriage to Miss Jennie, daughter of William Barton, of South Union township. Of this union is one living child: William Barton Beeson, born June 29, 1877. Mrs. Beeson was a member of the Cumberland Presbyterian church, and died January 25, 1880.

Mr. Beeson is an ardent and influential re-

Everhart Biser.

publican. He served two terms as school director, and has filled various other township offices, and is a well-liked and public-spirited citizen of South Union township.

EVERHART BIERER (deceased). The Buehrer family—or, as the name is Anglicised, Bierer—is an old one, and traces its ancestry, who were mainly residents of the Kingdom of Wurtemberg, Empire of Germany, back several centuries. They were mostly farmers, merchants and tradesmen, though some of them were prominent in the military and civil annals of Germany.

The subject of this sketch, Everhart Bierer, was born January 6, 1795, in the town of Wiernsheim, district of Maulbronn—Duchy of Wurtemberg—and was the youngest of a family of three sons.

His father, John Bierer, was a farmer in good circumstances. His mother's maiden name was Barbara Muller of Brackenfeldt Castle—situated in a beautiful valley of the river Neckar—a tributary of the Rhine. Wiernsheim is in the same valley—forty to fifty miles from Heidelburg, the seat of the famous German University. In 1803 the Duke of Wurtemberg became an ally of the Great Napoleon. In consequence of this alliance Napoleon extended the dominions of Wurtemberg and made the duke a king, and his descendants as kings yet occupy the throne of Wurtemberg.

In May, 1804, John Bierer migrated with his family, taking shipping at Amsterdam for the United States. The voyage occupied nearly five months, the vessel having been carried by storms to the region of the West Indies, and was there becalmed several weeks; during which time a tropic fever broke out on shipboard and many of the passengers died, among whom was the father of Everhart Bierer, the latter then a boy of nearly ten years of age. The vessel in the latter part of September or early in October, 1804, landed at Baltimore, Maryland, and his widowed mother and her three sons traveled across the mountains and settled at Greensburg, Westmoreland county, Pennsylvania.

There the subject of this sketch grew up to manhood. He had but limited opportunities of education, as the expenses of the migration to this country—coupled with the loss of a large part of their means—through the villainy of a trusted friend of their father, left the widow and her children with scanty funds. This trusted friend had been authorized to receive and remit the deferred payments, amounting to about one-half of the price of the German homestead, but instead of remitting the money or bringing it over to the family in this country, embezzled and kept it. But the three boys thus thrown upon their own resources, proved equal to the emergency, and in after years rose to wealth and influence. Two of them, John and Frederick Bierer, died many years ago, near Greensburg, Pennsylvania.

On the 15th of April, 1816, at Greensburg, Pennsylvania, Everhart Bierer married Catherine Margaretta Rukenbrod, who was born October 28, 1798, in the village of Malmsheim, Wurtemberg—a few miles distant from the birthplace of her husband—and who, with her parents, George David Rukenbrod and his wife Catherine, had also migrated to the United States in 1804, but not in the same vessel that brought the Bierers over. Soon after their marriage the young couple moved to Pittsburgh, Pennsylvania, and thence in the spring of 1817 to Uniontown, Pennsylvania, where he followed the occupation of cattle dealer and butcher up to the fall of 1849. He was also engaged in farming from 1828. In 1854 he sold the Gilmore farm, adjoining Uniontown, and in 1855 moved on the farm still owned by his family, where in 1861 he virtually retired from active business.

Eleven children, seven sons and four daughters, were born to them, and raised to maturity: Frederick, Barbara A., David, John, Catharine E., Everhard, George W., Jacob, Daniel, Rebecca T. and Eliza J. The mother was lovely in amiability, refinement and devotion to her husband and children, and the father was a man of great individuality and force of character. The names of both were synonymous among their large circle of acquaintances for virtue and integrity. Both were members, from early youth, of the Lutheran church, and he remained a member of that church all his life. Mrs. Bierer, as there was no Lutheran congregation at Uniontown, united herself, about 1855, with the Protestant Episcopal church.

By industry and economy, combined with good judgment in both, they secured not only competence but riches. His wife, Margaretta Bierer, died July 15, 1858. Everhart Bierer died August 2, 1876. All their children are living except Barbara A., who died March 27, 1883, and Jacob, who died January 7, 1885.

On January 2, 1862, Everhart Bierer married his second wife, Mrs. Ruth Shaw, a widow, by whom he had no children, and who survived him until June, 1888.

Everhart Bierer was always an enterprising and public spirited citizen, and though not a politician, was an active democrat most of his life, and was honored by his fellow-citizens with several public positions. For a number of terms in succession he was elected one of the directors of the Poor of Fayette county, and from 1858 to 1862 was superintendent of the Eastern Division of the Cumberland or National road. He was one of the board of directors of the Bank of Fayette County—now National Bank of Fayette county—from its organization in 1858 to his death in 1876.

During the Civil War he was unflinching in his loyalty to the Union cause, and became an ardent supporter of Lincoln's administration. Two of his sons, John and Everhard Bierer, served in the Union army, and none rejoiced more than he over the suppression of the rebellion and a reunited country.

His remains with those of his wife Margaretta rest in Oak Grove cemetery near Uniontown.

COLONEL EVERHARD BIERER, who won distinction as an officer on the field battle and later in the forum as a lawyer, is now successfully engaged in the practice of his profession at Hiawatha, Kansas. He is a son of Everhart and Catherine Margaretta Bierer, and was born at Uniontown, Pennsylvania, January 9, 1827. He received a good education at the private schools and at Madison College in his native town. Leaving college in 1845, he commenced the study of the law in the office of Joshua B. Howell, Esq. (afterwards, colonel of the Eighty-fifth Pennsylvania Volunteers, who was killed by a fall of his horse before Richmond, Virginia, in 1864),and was admitted to the bar March, 1848. After two years in traveling through the West and in some desultory literary and educational work, he returned to his native town and entered upon the practice of his profession. In October, 1850, he was elected the first district attorney of Fayette county,—the office having previously been appointive. He performed the duties of the office during the term of three years and successfully continued the practice of his profession until April 23, 1861, when he left his office and raised the first company of Volunteers, in Fayette county, in the war for the Union. His company afterwards became Company F of the Eleventh Regiment Pennsylvania Reserved Corps; he continued in command

Everhard Biezer.

of it until September 14, 1862. He served mostly in the Army of the Potomac, and was in the battles of Drainesville, Mechanicsville and Gaines Hill or Cold Harbor before Richmond, where he was surrounded and captured with his command June 27, 1862. With his company, he made, it is believed, the last desperate resistance on that bloody field. He and the survivors were taken to Libby Prison and Belle Island, from which they were released by exchange, August 14, 1862. Six days afterward, he returned to Washington, where he was granted, by Secretary Stanton, a twenty-days' leave of absence on account of ill health, and went home; but learning by telegram of the impending battle of Second Bull Run, he returned to the army and joined his command on the day of the last battle, August 30, 1862. He was also in the battle of South Mountain, September 14, 1862, where he was severely wounded in the left arm, the ball fracturing the arm and passing through the elbow joint and lodging there, from which it was not extracted until November 25th, following. Having become convalescent, on October 24, 1862, he was appointed commandant of Camp Curtin at Harrisburg, Pennsylvania, with the rank of colonel, where he organized the One Hundred and Seventy-first, One Hundred and Seventy-second, One Hundred and Seventy-third, One Hundred and Seventy sixth, One Hundred and Seventy-seventh and One Hundred and Seventy-eighth regiments of infantry; and on November 18, 1862, was commissioned colonel of the One Hundred and Seventy-first. After service in southeastern Virginia, with headquarters at Suffolk, his regiment was ordered to New Berne, North Carolina, marching overland to Ballard's Landing, on the Chowan river, there taking shipping. From there he was engaged in several expeditions and several skirmishes in the interior of that State. Subsequently he was ordered to Washington, North Carolina, on Pamlico river, in April, 1863. In the months of May and June, he was in commmand of the Military District of the Pamlico and part of the time in command of General Henry Prince's division, Eighteenth Army Corps. He was in an engagement at Blount's creek, near Washington, North Carolina, April 7, 1863, commanding a brigrade under General F. B. Spinola (now a member of congress from Brooklyn, New York). Spinola's forces were obliged to retire before superior numbers under the rebel General Hill. To Colonel Bierer was assigned the command of the rear guard, the enemy following in heavy force. The duty was critical. Spending the entire night in the midst of intense darkness, though pine forests and cypress swamps, the march was conducted. He finally succeeded in bringing off the column with the train, artillery and all the wounded.

July 1, 1863, Colonel Bierer returned with his regiment to Virginia, going with General Dix on his expedition to Richmond, while Lee with the Rebel army was in Pennsylvania. The expedition marched from White House landing on the Pamunkey river to within eight or ten miles of Richmond, destined as was then supposed, for an attack upon the rebel capital. Dix had a large force and the Rebel force around Richmond was small. After some skirmishing with the Rebels, Dix ordered the expedition to return to Fortress Monroe, much to the surprise and disappointment of Colonel Bierer and many other officers.

Colonel Bierer, with his regiment, went on to Washington and thence to Boonsville, Maryland, via Harper's Ferry, where he joined General Meade, and on the 7th of July was given a brigade command and afterwards assigned to duty as commander of western Maryland, with headquarters at Frederick City. September 26, 1863, he was mustered out; the regiment's term of service having expired. During the winter of 1863 and 1864, Colonel Bierer served in the Veteran Reserve Corps, but in March, 1864, on account of illness and suffering from his wound, resigned. October, 1865, after the close of the war, he migrated with his family to Kansas. Settling on a beautiful farm one mile east of Hiawatha in Brown county, resuming the practice of law.

April 8, 1852, at Brownsville, Pennsylvania, he married Ellen, daughter of Samuel and Elizabeth Smouse, a lady of extensive family connections in Alleghany county, Maryland and in Somerset and Bedford counties, Pennsylvania. They have eight children, all living: the eldest son, Everhard, graduated from Kansas University, at Lawrence, in the class of 1877, and has been for nearly eight years engaged in various departments in Washington, District of Columbia, now on the Board of Re-review in the Pension Bureau. One son, Andrew G. Curtain Bierer, is engaged in the practice of law at Garden City, Kansas. The youngest son, Bion. B. Bierer, is a cadet at the United States Naval Academy, Annapolis, Maryland. The others are engaged in mercantile pursuits and farming.

The Colonel was originally a democrat, and, as the nominee of that party, he was elected district attorney of Fayette county in 1850. His opposition to the repeal of the Missouri Compromise and the extension of slavery, caused him to support Fremont for President in 1856. In 1860 and 1864 he supported Lincoln, and in the latter campaign he was elected one of the presidential electors of Pennsylvania. In 1867 he was elected representative from Brown county, Kansas, to the legislature of Kansas. In 1868 he supported Grant for president, but with considerable misgivings on account of the financial policy and the reconstruction measures of the republican party, which he bitterly opposed. He was thoroughly disgusted with the carpet-bag policy at the South, and with the administration of Grant generally; and believing as he did that the republican party had abandoned its early principles, and was no longer the party of 1856 and the war: he with such men as Seward, Chase, Curtin, Sumner, Fessenden, Trumbull, Julian, Palmer and nearly all the old founders of the republican party, supported Greeley for the presidency, in opposition to Grant, in 1872. Colonel Bierer has supported all the democratic nominees for the presidency since.

He became a member of Fort Necessity Lodge, No. 254, Independent Order of Odd Fellows, at Uniontown, in February, 1852: subsequently he joined the Encampment branch, has been district deputy grand master and district deputy grand patriarch of the order in Fayette county, and member of the Grand Lodge and Grand Encampment of Pennsylvania. He also became a Mason at Uniontown, and is versed in all the mysteries of the Blue Lodge, Royal Arch Chapter, Commandery and historical degrees of Masonry.

Colonel Bierer has been all his life a careful student of the Bible, and is well acquainted with the other religious systems of the world, especially Buddhism, Mohammedanism and Confucianism. He believes in the inspiration of the moral and religious teachings of the Bible, the divine Sonship of Jesus and the efficacy of His life and teachings for the purposes of redemption; but he does not believe in the doctrines of the Trinity, vicarious sacrifice and eternal punishment. He accepts a salvation by conduct as well as belief, and includes all in the family of the Universal Father, who act according to their highest conceptions of life, right and duty, whatever may be their creed or religious belief.

John Boyd

A. D. BOYD. What a man makes of himself, and not what he is made by the aid of family or the influence of friends, is a record that he can proudly leave behind him for the inspection of the world; and the field of action in which a life career of activity or usefulness may be carved out, need not be national in its dimensions. Such has been the fortune of the subject of this sketch. He has won for himself the position in life he now holds, through his own efforts.

Albert D. Boyd is a native of Menallen Township, and was born December 31, 1845, and is the son of William and Jane (Burgess) Boyd. His grandfather, Robert Boyd, was a native of Fayette County, Pennsylvania, and served one term as associate judge. His great grandfather Boyd came to the Shenandoah Valley, Virginia—thence he removed and settled near Connellsville. William Boyd, his son, and A. D. Boyd's father was raised a farmer, and followed that pursuit for a livelihood. William Boyd died in 1880. His wife, Jane Burgess Boyd, was born in Maryland.

Albert D. Boyd was raised on a farm, and educated in the common schools, and attended an academy for a few sessions. He read law with Judge Willson, and was admitted to the bar March 1, 1869. He was elected district attorney and served as such from 1871 to 1874. He was twice chairman of the democratic central committee of Fayette county. With his splendid executive ability, energy and push, his appointments were generally designated as "the right man in the right place."

He was married in 1872 to Miss Annie E., daughter of Robert Patterson, a native of Ireland, from whence he emigrated in about 1815. Mr. Boyd has five children: Alpheus E., Samuel P., Albert D., Wallace B. and Mary E.

A. D. Boyd is a good lawyer, a good speaker, is making a fine record, and is rapidly rising toward the head of his profession. He enjoys a large practice, and is highly respected at the bar.

DR. JOHN BOYD is of a family that has produced a number of eminent, professional men as well as men of note, gentlemen and scholars. His grandfather, William Boyd, came from Kilmarnock, Scotland, and brought a grant for several hundred acres of land, covering the present site of the City of Halifax. This grant bore the seal of James VI., King of England; but his sympathy for the American colonists, during the War of the Revolution, caused the forfeiture of his lands to the crown. His father, Rev. Eben L. Boyd, was a noted preacher in South Berwick for many years. His eldest son, Dr. Eben L. Boyd, was a graduate of Cambridge, Massachusetts, and had an extended reputation throughout the Eastern States as an able physician and surgeon: having performed some very wonderful surgical operations in his day. He died at Wilkesbarre, Pennsylvania.

Dr. John Boyd was a man of considerable reputation, not only as a physician and surgeon, but as a preacher of the Word of God. He was born in South Berwick, Maine, July 11, 1817, and was a son of Rev. Eben L. and Sarah Frazier. He was married to Maria A., a daughter of Joseph Stevens, of Boston. For eighteen years, and was at the time of his death, inspector at the Custom House at Boston. His wife, Clarissa Cushing, was a lineal descendant of Caleb Cushing, the latter coming over in the Mayflower, and whose potrait can be seen at the Independence Hall Museum, Philadelphia.

Dr. John Boyd was educated in the schools at South Berwick; and afterwards read medicine with Dr. Charles Trafton, of the same place. In 1835 Dr. Boyd had a call to the ministry at Haverhill, Massachusetts, and subsequently preached at Portsmouth, New Hampshire, Hampton and Kennebunk, Maine. He was a strong advocate of temperance and delivered lectures through Maine in the interests of her first prohibition laws. In 1848, on account of his failing health, he accepted an agency for the America and Foreign Bible Society for the State of Pennsylvania; and visited and preached at many of the principal Baptist churches throughout the State. He was the pastor at Wilkesbarre for about five years, and later for about the same length of time pastor of the Baptist church at Washington, Pennsylvania. He came to Uniontown in 1864, and devoted himself to the practice of medicine, and built up a lucrative practice. He continued to preach at Uniontown up to the time of his death. He was endowed by nature with a strong mind, was a hard student, great reader, well versed in literature, and a good thinker. For fifty-six years he was a devout Christian and his faith in the promises of God was firm and secure, and died in full trust and hope in them. He was full of love and charity for his fellow-men. In his library are some of the oldest books extant: a priestly Bible published in 1634, Oyer and Terminer, of the city of London, published in 1730; Court of the Gentiles, published in 1674, and some very valuable medical works. He kept a hand-book of his practice of medicine, and registered every dose of medicine that he ever gave. He also kept a register of all the patients he ever treated: giving a full history of each case in all its different stages. The pension officials at Washington would often come to Dr. Boyd for dates and facts in the history of applications for pensions. He was made a life member of the American Baptist Missionary Union, Boston, September 30, 1846. He had in his possession the family coat of arms, which is several hundred years old. The children of Dr. Boyd are five in number: John, who died soon after the war at the age of twenty-two years; Eben L., died in infancy; Sarah F., died November 4, 1882, at the age of twenty-seven; Mrs. Maria F. Gribble, and Mrs. Clara B. Johnson, are the living children, and both reside with their mother at Uniontown. Dr. Boyd spent the last moments of his life in helping the sick: having gone out at 4:30 A. M. to see a patient, returning home at 9:30 A. M., and with a severe attack of hemorrhage passed away February 27, 1889: "full of years and full of honors." His remains rest with those of other members of the family at Newburyport, Massachusetts.

JOHN BOYLE, one of the young and successful lawyers of the Fayette County bar, is a son of the late Hon. Charles E. and Mary (Hendrickson) Boyle, and was born at Uniontown, Fayette county, Pennsylvania, November 22, 1858.

He attended the Uniontown public schools, and completed his education at St. James' Episcopal College, Washington county, Maryland. He read law with his father, and was admitted to the Fayette County bar, December 5, 1881. Five years later he became a partner with his father and S. L. Mestrezat. After the death of his father, he continued in partnership with Mestrezat until August 13, 1889, when he opened an office on his own account, and is now successfully engaged in the practice of his profession. April 12, 1882, he was married to Miss Ella L. Litman, daughter of George W. Litman, a former editor of the *Genius of Liberty*. Mr. Boyle's practice is of the largest among the young attorneys of the county.

In political opinion, he follows in the footsteps of his illustrious father. He has a large and lucrative practice, to which he devotes his whole time and attention.

CLARK BREADING—a stanch republican, Masonic Knight Templar, successful farmer and a large stock dealer—was born in Luzerne township, Fayette county, Pennsylvania, March 9, 1806, and died April 12, 1883.

He grew to man's estate on his father's farm, and walked over four miles to school that ran but three months in the year, with the speller as its only text-book. With these limited opportunities he fitted himself well for business, and was successful in whatever he undertook. He engaged in farming, in which he continued till 1865. In 1865 he purchased the property on the corner of Main street and Mount Vernon avenue, in which he resided until his death. He was a large and well known stock dealer, and was for many years in the drug business.

The ancestry of the Breading family is as follows: David Breading, of Scotch descent, was born in Ireland, and came to Lancaster county, Pennsylvania, in 1728; accompanying him was his son James. James had two sons: Judge Nathaniel Breading, who served under Washington, married Ann, daughter of General Ewing. Judge Breading was born 1751, in Lancaster county, and died, 1822, in Fayette county, Pennsylvania. David Breading was born in Lancaster county, Pennsylvania, in 1756; he also served under Washington, was at the battle of Monmouth, and a witness to Washington's severe reprimand of General Lee. David Breading, Jr., married Elizabeth Clark, November 17, 1785, came to Fayette county, Pa., in 1794, followed farming, and died in 1844, aged eighty-six years and thirteen days; and was followed by his faithful helpmeet on March 27, 1855.

Clark Breading, son of David Breading, Jr., had one brother and three sisters, who died of cholera in 1835, at Troyhurst, Indiana, namely: James, Eliza, Jane, wife of William Scott; Nancy, wife of William Lagow.

Clark Breading was united in marriage to Miss Mary Craft, of the county, on May 1, 1827. By this marriage he had one child: Margaret, married Dr. O. E. Newton, May 10, 1849, and who now resides at Cincinnati, Ohio.

Mr. Breading's wife died June 2, 1828: he was again married the second time, September 10, 1834, to Miss Hettie Jane, daughter of William Roberts, a farmer of this county, the latter born August 25, 1795. She died January 10, 1868. Of this second marriage, one child, John C. Breading, was born, August 5, 1851. He attended the Tuscarora Academy: leaving school, he came home to engage with his father in the drug business in 1872. In 1879 he sold out his store and bought a farm near Uniontown. In 1885 he returned to Uniontown and again engaged in the mercantile business. He was married, in 1873, to Miss Ella Brownfield, daughter of Nathaniel Brownfield, one of Uniontown's oldest and best known citizens. They have four living children, three boys and one girl: Clark, Hettie, Frank and Nathaniel.

John C. Breading is regarded as one of the safe and solid business men of Uniontown, as was his father before him. He is of that class that gives to a place whatever of business reputation it possesses.

NOAH BROWN is descended from one of the pioneer families of Fayette county. He is a son of Emanuel and Sarah (Franks) Brown, and was born in South Union township, April 10, 1833. His great-grandfather was Wendel Brown, one of the earliest settlers of Fayette county. An account of the part he took in the French and Indian War is too lengthy for insertion in a sketch of this character; but can be found in the Fayette County History and Veech's "Monongahela of Old." One of his grandsons, Abraham Brown, was born in 1764, and married Mary, sister of Col. Ben. Brownfield. They had fourteen children, one of whom was Emanuel, father of Noah Brown. Emanuel Brown was born in 1800, in Georges Township, where he afterwards owned three hundred acres of good land — he was a farmer and died in 1859. In politics he was a democrat, and served as Poor House Director. He married Miss Sarah, daughter of Michael Franks, of German Township. Noah Brown was raised on a farm, received his education in the subscription schools, and engaged in farming as his life pursuit. October 2, 1864, he married Miss Eliza Jane Lawrence. They have seven children: Alfred C., born October 7, 1865; Benjamin F., August 17, 1866; Martha V., February 20, 1870; John C., November 4, 1871; Ada Osceola, July 21, 1875; Wade Hampton, December 1, 1877; Lulu Olive, September 16, 1881. Mrs. Brown is a member of the Lutheran church, and she is a daughter of Caleb Lawrence, born 1799, and a grand-daughter of Jacob and Barbara (Walser) Lawrence. Jacob Lawrence was taken prisoner by the Indians during the French and Indian War. After two years of captivity, he succeeded in making his escape. Mr. Brown has a good farm of 327 acres of land in the township; is a democrat of the "old school;" is a member of the Knights of Pythias; and is a good citizen and an intelligent farmer.

FRANCIS MARION BROWNFIELD, a descendant of one of the old pioneer families of Fayette county, is a son of Elmer and Mary Jane (Douglas) Brownfield, and was born in South Union township, Fayette county, Pennsylvania, December 17, 1854.

Charles Brownfield, great-great-grandfather, was born in Scotland and came to Winchester, Virginia, but soon after joined the pioneer stream of emigration to the fertile lands of the Ohio Valley. In 1760 he arrived in what is now South Union township, where he located on three hundred acres of land. Warrant number 3456, dated June 14, 1769, was issued to him for this tract. In 1783 Charles Brownfield sold this farm to his son, Benjamin Brownfield, and removed to the "Dark and Bloody" hunting grounds of Kentucky.

Benjamin Brownfield, great-grandfather, was born May 1, 1755, and died December 20, 1823.

Col. Benjamin Brownfield, grandfather, was one of Fayette county's centenarians. He inherited the homestead farm on which he was born March 28, 1780, and died October 7, 1880. Colonel Brownfield, March, 1804, married Miss Ruth Sutton, born December 7, 1783. He was a farmer and stock raiser, and a very successful business man. His real estate consisted of several hundred acres in Missouri, four hundred acres in Ohio and one thousand acres of coal land in Fayette county. His mind was active up to the hour of his death.

Elmer Brownfield, father, was born on the farm, June 27, 1826. He was educated in the subscription schools and afterwards engaged in farming. March 7, 1854, he married Miss Mary Jane, daughter of James Douglas. He was a democrat, as was his father before him, and was a faithful member of the Baptist church, at Uniontown.

Francis Marion Brownfield was educated in the common schools. Leaving school, he turned his attention to farming. January 10, 1878, he married Miss Nancy H. Thomas, born June 15, 1851. She is a daughter of Thomas Thomas, of South Union township. They have had two children: George W., born November 21, 1878, and Bessie Ellen, born August 26, 1881.

Mr. Brownfield is a conservative democrat. He owns the home farm, which is well

Dr. Hugh Campbell

cultivated and very productive, and it is underlaid with coal. He is an unassuming but intelligent and prosperous farmer. He is a member of the Patriotic Order Sons of America, Knights of Pythias and Odd Fellows fraternities.

JUDGE EDWARD CAMPBELL, a leading lawyer of Western Pennsylvania, is a son of Dr. Hugh Campbell, (whose portrait appears opposite this sketch). Dr. Campbell was born at Uniontown, May 1, 1795; and was educated at Jefferson College, Cannonsburg, Pennsylvania, afterwards read medicine and was graduated from the Medical Department of the University of Pennsylvania in 1818. From 1815 to 1840 he was located at Uniontown in the practice of medicine and was one of the leading physicians of Fayette county. He was a fine scholar, a good linguist; ordained elder of the Presbyterian church at Uniontown and was until his death regarded as one of the pillars of that church. Dr. Campbell, Rev. A. G. Fairchild, Jesse Evans and Judge Nathaniel Ewing, were the pioneers of the temperance movement of sixty years ago in Fayette county which banished whiskey from the merchant's counter, the side-board and the harvest field. In 1860 he retired from the active practice of medicine, and from 1865 to 1868 was Warden of the Western Penitentiary at Allegheny City. His father, Benjamin Campbell, was from the famed highlands of Scotland—a silversmith by trade, who came to Uniontown in 1780. A clock made by himself over a hundred years ago, is now in his grandson's law office. The maiden name of Dr. Campbell's wife was Rachel Lyon, a native of Baltimore, a daughter of Samuel Lyon, born at Carlisle, Pennsylvania, and the latter's father came to this country from Ireland.

Judge Edward Campbell, born at Uniontown, July 24, 1838, was a law student of Judge Nathaniel Ewing, and admitted to the Fayette County bar September 5, 1859. He received his education at John Lyon's Academy and Madison College at Uniontown. When Beauregard's circling batteries opened fire upon Fort Sumter in 1861 and the country realizing the fact that a terrible war was at hand, among the first who responded to the call of the Federal government for troops, was Judge Campbell. He volunteered as a private in April, 1861, and served in camp only during that summer. At the expiration of this time he enlisted as a private in the 85th Pennsylvania, was promoted October 21, 1861, to second lieutenant, to captain May 15, 1862, major September 6, 1862, became lieutenant-colonel of his regiment October 16, 1863, and was honorably discharged from the service November 22, 1864. He served three and a half years in the war and won an enviable war record that reflected no discredit on the firmness and bravery of that wonderful Scotch-Irish race of which he is descended. At the close of the war, he returned to Uniontown, opened an office for the practice of law, where he has acquired a large and lucrative practice and is recognized as an able lawyer.

On the death of Judge Gilmore in May, 1873, Governor Hartranft appointed him President Judge of the District for the short period of less than one year. He left the Bench carrying with him the good will and respect of all for his kindness and courtesy in discharge of his high duties as Judge. His speeches made in important cases are of characteristic force and ability and as a constitutional lawyer he stands in the front rank of leading lawyers of Pennsylvania. Courtly, suave in manner, pure in conversation and firm in his convictions of right, he is regarded deservedly high as a Christian gentleman and scholar.

JOHN MORGAN CAMPBELL was born June 15, 1850, in Dunbar township, Fayette county, Pennsylvania, and is the son of Emmanuel and Lydia (Morgan) Campbell.

Emmanuel Campbell was born May 9, 1824, in Georges township, and was married to Miss Lydia Morgan, the daughter of Morris Morgan.

David Campbell was the name of the paternal grandfather of John Morgan Campbell.

Morris Morgan was his maternal grandfather; he was a blacksmith by trade, and an old time democrat in politics. At an exciting election, in 1812, a Tory cried, "Hurrah for King George;" no sooner had he uttered the shout than he was knocked down by the brawny fist of Morris Morgan. He was afterwards a soldier in the War of 1812–15 against England. He was a brother of Colonel John Morgan, who represented this county in the legislature for several terms. Morris Morgan married Susan Stentz, of this county.

John Morgan Campbell was reared on the farm, and was educated in the common schools of Menallen township and at Waynesburg College, Pennsylvania. His first business was that of tanning and farming, and was a scientific farmer. He engaged in school teaching for ten terms, a part of that time he taught in Illinois, the remainder of it in the schools of the county. He came to Hopwood in the year 1881, and engaged in the tanning business and continued in the same for four years, when he embarked in the general mercantile business, in which he has been successfully engaged ever since.

He is energetic and enterprising, a good citizen, and is an active member of the Patriotic Order of Sons of America, of the United States Benevolent Fraternity, and has been a Good Templar. He joined the Cumberland Presbyterian church, of Pleasant View, and was superintendent of the Sabbath School, at that place, a number of years, and served as trustee of that church. He is now a member of the same denomination at Uniontown, and has been the superintendent of the Sabbath-school there. He is a democrat in politics, and has held township offices almost ever since he became a voter, although not an office seeker. He was appointed postmaster at Hopwood by President Cleveland.

He was married to Miss Lydia Miller, September 20, 1877, by Rev. J. P. Fulton, pastor of Dunlap's Creek church. She was born February 5, 1854, and her father, Warwick Miller, was born December 5, 1811. He married Mary Moore, daughter of Aaron Moore, of German township, and died at the advanced age of ninety-six years.

To the marriage of J. M. Campbell and Lydia Miller have been born four children, Ira Fulton, born August 29, 1878; Rolla Miller, March 11, 1880; Mary Frances, December 1, 1882, and Clarence Danley, February 10, 1888.

Mrs. Campbell is a member of the Cumberland Presbyterian church at Uniontown.

JOHN RICHEY CAROTHERS was born April 23, 1855, in Sewickly township (near West Newton), Westmoreland county, Pennsylvania, and is the son of William E. and Caroline (Taylor) Carothers, the latter a daughter of Isaac Taylor, of Allegheny county, who had been an old hotel keeper and farmer on the National road.

William E. Carothers, subject's father, was born on the homestead farm in Westmoreland county, and removed, in 1865, to the well known James Veech farm in Fayette county, which he purchased, and where he now resides. This farm, containing 200 acres, is underlaid with a nine-foot vein of coking coal. He also owns a farm of 286 acres in North Strebane township, Washington county.

He is a farmer and stock dealer to some extent, a strong republican and a much respected member of the Presbyterian church.

Samuel Carothers, subject's grandfather, was an old and reliable citizen of Westmoreland county, where he was born.

John R. Carothers, was reared on a farm, and was educated in the common township and Uniontown public schools.

On December 8, 1881, he married Miss Anna M., daughter of 'Squire James W. and Caroline E. Craft. 'Squire Craft was a son of David Craft and grandson of George Craft, who came to Redstone township in 1771, and purchased the old Craft homestead, one mile east of Merrittstown.

James W. Craft was born February 13, 1807, and died February 20, 1880. He married his cousin, Caroline E. Craft, in 1847. They had nine children, seven of whom are living: Ellen L., wife of Samuel Colvin; Loretta, wife of Sheriff Joseph O. Miller; Hester B., wife of Dr. H. W. Brashear; Richard N., married to Rebecca Nutt; Hayden R., married to Laura B. Colley; Annie M., wife of subject, born September 17, 1860, and Jesse Benton. Mr. Craft was a justice of the peace for thirty years, and was greatly missed after his death.

J. R. Carothers is engaged in farming and stock dealing. He is a prosperous farmer, an intelligent citizen and an active republican worker. He served two terms as school director in South Union township, and was elected poor house director in 1888, on the republican ticket, for a term of three years.

HARVEY COBURN, a prominent citizen of Fayette county, and a gallant soldier of the War of the Rebellion, is a son of Captain James and Sarah (Moody) Coburn, and was born near Kingwood, Preston county, Virginia (now West Virginia), August 19, 1823.

Captain James Coburn was a brave and efficient officer, and commanded a company that rendered good service in the War of 1812. After the close of that war he married Miss Sarah Moody, daughter of Robert Moody, of Harrison county, West Virginia. Captain Coburn was an energetic business man, engaged in various business enterprises, and was a member of the old and highly respected Cobun family so widely settled about Masontown, Preston county, West Virginia (West Virginia family spell their name Cobun). The Cobuns came to western Virginia prior to 1790.

Harvey Coburn was educated in the old log school-houses under the Primary School System of Virginia. His first business in life was farming, which he abandoned temporarily for a clerkship in his father's store at Fairfield, Harrison county, Virginia.

Later he removed to Fayette county and engaged in farming.

October 1, 1850, he was married by Rev. H. A. Hunter to Miss Susan, daughter of Nathan Jeffries. She was born June 26, 1822, and is a member of the Methodist Episcopal church. They have had six children, four of whom are living, namely: Mary, born April 22, 1852, wife of William G. Freeman; Sarah E., born September 24, 1854, has been a successful teacher for sixteen years, and is now teaching in Dunbar Borough; Millard F., born September 22, 1856, and Samuel H., born December 27, 1862.

Harvey Coburn enlisted February 8, 1864, in Company K., or Battery K, 112th Regiment, Pennsylvania Line or Second Heavy Artillery. He did his duty faithfully as soldier until May 20, 1864, when he was caught and crushed between two logs at Fort Ethan Allen. The surgeons told him that he could not live, but, having a wonderfully strong constitution and a determined will, he survived his injuries, and got well. He is a successful farmer, a good citizen, and has been a member of the Methodist Episcopal church for many years. Politically, Mr. Coburn is a stanch democrat, and, although living in a republican township, and never asking for an office, has been twice elected road supervisor.

MARK MORDECAI COCHRAN. Among those who have cast their fortunes with their native county, and who might worthily be placed in the van of the young professional men of the county is Mark M. Cochran, a rising young lawyer of the Fayette county bar. He is a son of Mordecai and Susanna (Welsh) Cochran, and was born at the old Cochran homestead, Tyrone township, Fayette county, Pennsylvania, July 13, 1854; and is the youngest of a family of thirteen children, of whom three died in infancy, three after middle age, and seven who are now living.

His father, Mordecai Cochran, was born at the old Cochran homestead in Tyrone township, October 8, 1797, where he lived until his death, December 29, 1880. He was among the first to engage in the manufacture of Connellsville coke, and the first to introduce it in the Cincinnati market. In 1843, he, with his two nephews, Sample and James Cochran, floated two boats loaded with coke to Cincinnati, and after a favorable test sold the same to Miles Greenwood, a prominent foundryman of that city. It was the first Connellsville coke ever sold for money, and being thus enthusiastically reassured of the value of this product, he and his nephews returned home, determined to push forward the industry, which they afterward did most successfully. They and their sons became prominent in the business, and so remain up to the present time.

Samuel Cochran, the paternal grandfather of M. M. Cochran, was born in Chester county, Pennsylvania, August 24, 1750, and was a son of John Cochran, a Scotch-Irish Presbyterian, who had emigrated from the north of Ireland, and settled in Chester county, in about 1745.

February 12, 1776, as a private soldier, Samuel Cochran enlisted in the War of the Revolution, in a company commanded by Captain Samuel Hay; his company belonged to the Sixth Pennsylvania Battalion. He re-enlisted in the following year with Captain Hay, this time with the Seventh Pennsylvania Regiment. He did hard service at Paola, Brandywine, Germantown and Valley Forge. At the close of the war, he went to Chamberburg, Pennsylvania, and there married Esther, daughter of Daniel John, the latter a prominent Quaker, and the grandfather of Gideon John, the last named elected sheriff of Fayette county in 1832.

Samuel Cochran came "West" and located in Fayette county in 1789, for a while in the "Washington Bottoms" near the present site of Perryopolis, remaining there until the spring of 1792, when he removed to Tyrone township and purchased a farm of Captain Joseph Huston, of 300 acres. On this tract of land he built a primitive log cabin, but he soon replaced it by a more commodious structure, and in 1811 he erected the large stone barn recently rebuilt by his grandson, Lutellas Cochran. Besides being a splendid farmer, Samuel Cochran was a practical surveyor, and a consistent member of the Tyrone Presbyterian church up to his death, July 2, 1837. His children were: Samuel, Jr., James, John, Thomas, Isaac, Mordecai and Esther (wife of John Strickler), the latter an only child by a second marriage. He devised his farm to his two sons, Mordecai and James. The other sons of Mordecai Cochran were: James W. (known as Big Jim), Alexander C. and Lutellas. They all engaged early in making coke with their

M M Cochran

father, and boated it down the river. In 1867 they purchased their father's plant on the Youghiogheny river, and afterwards entered into partnership with W. H. Brown, of Pittsburgh, enlarging their original plant "Sterling," and in 1871 built a large coke plant on Hickman Run, called Jimtown, in honor of the managing partner, James W. Cochran. This firm of Brown & Cochran were the largest coke producers, at that time, in the State; but in 1873, the partnership dissolved, on account of the death of two of its members, W. H. Brown and Alexander C. Cochran. The affairs, in a few years thereafter, were settled by the surviving members of the firm.

M. M. Cochran grew to man's estate on the old farm in Tyrone township. He was educated at Bethany College, West Virginia, from where he graduated in 1875. He immediately entered the law office of Hon. C. E. Boyle as a student-at-law, and was admitted to the bar June 5, 1877, and has successfully continued in the practice of law ever since. In 1883, he was elected by his party—the democrats—district attorney of Fayette county, the duties of which responsible office he discharged with fidelity to the interests of the people, and with honor to himself for a term of three years. In 1881 he was elected a member of the board of trustees of Bethany College, his alma mater, and in this position he has ever since continued to serve. January 1, 1879, he was married to Miss Emma J. Whitsett, daughter of Dr. James Estep Whitsett, of Bethany, West Virginia, but now of Perry township, this county. Two children have blessed their union: Percy B. and Emma. In 1880 Mr. Cochran, with his two brothers, James W. and Lutellas, and H. S. Darsie, purchased a fine field of coking coal in Georges township, and are the present proprietors of the same.

He took a leading part in the construction of the excellent bridge at Dawson, that spans the Youghiogheny river, being one of the original corporators and directors of the company. Mr. Cochran is mild and unassuming in manner, yet firm and determined in whatever he undertakes. He neglects nothing which tends toward developing the material resources of old Fayette.

COLONEL JOHN COLLINS, one of the prominent and popular attorneys of the Fayette county bar, is the gentleman whose name stands at the head of this sketch. His career has been a long life of public service and public usefulness. He is a good citizen, a safe lawyer and Christian gentleman.

Colonel John Collins was born in Connellsville, December 7, 1815. He is the son of James and Huldah (Tharp) Collins. Colonel Collins' father was a native of Westmoreland county, a tailor by trade, who came to Connellsville in 1814 and did a large business until his death in 1841. His grandfather Collins was from Ireland, and was a Westmoreland county farmer until his death. His mother's maiden name was Huldah Tharp. Her father, Moses Tharp, stopped in Fayette county on his way from New Jersey to the Miami country in Ohio. He died after being in this county about one year.

Colonel Collins was raised in Connellsville, and received a common school education. He learned the tailor trade and continued that business some time after his father's death. He had a natural disposition to the law, and a strong inclination for it, but before he was ready to pursue the study of the legal profession, he was elected register and recorder of the orphan's court of Fayette county, Pennsylvania, overcoming a large standing democratic majority. He served as register and recorder from 1854 to 1857, the duties of which responsible office he discharged with fidelity to the interests of the people, and with honor to himself.

In 1857 he was admitted to the bar, and after practicing two years he was taken up by the republican party and elected to the lower house of the State legislature. He served two terms, serving as chairman of the committee on railroads, and during his second term was on the judiciary committee.

He was elected a member of the Pennsylvania constitutional convention of 1872. His popularity enabled his political party (although in the minority) to elect him as hereinbefore stated.

When quite a young man he was commissioned colonel of a Fayette county militia regiment, by Governor David R. Porter. The command of this regiment, he held for nearly seven years.

Colonel John Collins was united in marriage in 1840, to Miss Eliza McDonald, of Brownsville, who died in 1852. Her father, Hugh McDonald, was a weaver by trade, and came from Ireland. He was married again in 1855 to Elizabeth Caldwell, who is still living.

Colonel Collins has six children living, namely: Mrs. Sally Ann Bryson, James and David F. Collins, Mrs. Belle Mouck, Mrs. Lide Reisinger and Mrs. Mary Mitchell.

He owns fifty acres of land adjoining the Borough of Uniontown, and was acquired by honesty and judicious management such a sum as to be well fixed in life in his old days.

R. PORTER CRAIG is the son of John S. and Jane (Springer) Craig. John S. Craig, the father of the subject of the sketch, was of Irish descent. He was born in East Liberty, on the west side of the Youghiogheny river, opposite to what is now Dawson borough, April 4, 1800. He lived seven years with his grandfather, Hon. John Smilie, at Dawson, and eight years with his uncle, Joseph Huston, two miles north of Uniontown. In 1816–17 he was at the Union Rolling Mill, and in charge of the works for over one year. In 1818 he went to the old Forge, two miles north of Uniontown, which he assisted in running until he was married. On April 4, 1822, he was married to Miss Jane Springer, daughter of John Springer. One week after his marriage he removed to the old Redstone Furnace, and acted as manager there of the same till 1824. He commenced farming about 1824, and continued to farm until his death. He died February 2, 1887. In April, 1856, he went West and returned in September and bought the farm in North Union township, where he lived and died.

William Craig, grandfather of R. Porter Craig, came from Ireland in the latter part of the eighteenth century, and settled in Fayette county.

Jane (Springer) Craig was born June 13, 1804.

R. Porter Craig was born October 2, 1836, in Menallen township, Fayette county, Pa. He was raised on a farm, and has been a farmer all of his life, and is now a producer of grains and small fruits. He was educated in the common schools of North Union township, and one of his old teachers was James Springer.

He was married February 24, 1863, to Catherine M. Springer, by Rev. Sinsabau, a Methodist pastor. To this union were born three children, named: Albert R., born January 2, 1865; he is a farmer, married to Fannie Rankin, of South Union township; Charles H., born September 5, 1867, living at home; Walter C., born June 8, 1869, living at home.

Mr. Craig has been a member of the Baptist church since 1855, and has held the office of deacon for many years. Mrs. Craig is a member of the same church. Mr. Craig is a member of the Masonic order. He is a pleasant gentleman, and is of quiet, easy manners, and is highly respected by his neighbors.

E B Dawson

Dennis Springer, the father of Mrs. Craig, was born February 3, 1787, in North Union township. He was a farmer. He married Miss Sarah Brownfield, daughter of Thomas and Elizabeth Brownfield. She was born September 25, 1797, and came to this county in 1805 with her parents from near Winchester, Va.

ELLIS BAILY DAWSON. One of the old and well-established families of Fayette county, is the Dawson family founded in North Union township, in the pioneer era of privation and bloodshed by Nicholas Dawson; and among the many worthy and honorable descendants of that daring old pioneer and Revolutionary hero, is Ellis Baily Dawson, one of the most upright and public spirited citizens of Fayette county; and is a son of Judge John and Ann (Baily) Dawson, and was born at Uniontown, Fayette county, Pennsylvania, October 29, 1820.

Nicholas Dawson was born near the site of Washington City and came with his father, George Dawson, to near the site of Youngstown coke works, in 1768, and settled there. They were planters and brought their slaves with them. Nicholas Dawson was with Washington in 1764 and served with him during the Revolutionary War. He was in Crawford's defeat and barely escaped capture that he might save a bewildered soldier from being captured by the Indians. His wife was Violet Littleton, of Fairfax county, Virginia. He removed to the "Pan Handle" of West Virginia, where his son, Judge John Dawson, was born July 13, 1788; and at twenty years of age, John Dawson removed to Uniontown, read law with Gen. Thomas Meason and Judge John Kennedy; and was admitted to the Fayette county bar, August 17, 1813. He practiced law most successfully for over thirty years; and was appointed associate judge in 1851, and died January 16, 1875. He was a sound lawyer, a safe counselor, an agreeable companion and a popular judge. He married Miss Ann, the only daughter of Ellis Baily.

Ellis Baily Dawson was reared in Uniontown, attended the excellent schools and Madison College of the same place, and was graduated from Washington College in the class of 1839. He studied law with his father, and was admitted to the practice of law in the courts of Fayette county, June 6, 1843, and in the Supreme Court of the State in 1846. E. B. Dawson pursued the practice of his profession successfully for several years, but subsequently had to abandon professional work on account of his business interests that required his personal attention. Although retired from active practice, he has not given up his interests in legal affairs or his participation in matters of general interest, or in State and national politics. In all that has concerned the advancement and prosperity of his native place and county, he has always taken a lively interest and an active part.

Though he never sought public office, yet in 1862, upon solicitation by Governor Curtin, he accepted "commissioner of the draft" for Fayette county. It was an arduous and delicate post as matters then stood; but he fulfilled the trust with impartiality and success, and the full quota of Fayette county's 2,500 men were added to the State troops for the National service. He has always been studious, and his leisure time has always been occupied with the perusal of history, biography and literature. Within the last year he has evinced anew his interest in his native place by donating five acres or more of highly valuable ground for the erection of a large glass-works, which establishment is now completed and in successful operation. Mr. Dawson stands high as a citizen and gentleman. Hopeful and ever alert for the mental and material development of his native county, he is always ready to aid any enterprise calculated to attain either or both of these objects.

HON. JOHN LITTLETON DAWSON was a son of George and Mary Kennedy Dawson, and was born at Uniontown, Fayette county, Pa., February 7, 1813. When quite young he removed to Brownsville, which was his residence during the greater part of his subsequent life. He was educated in Washington College, Pa., and immediately after being graduated from that institution began to read law with his uncle, John Dawson, at Uniontown. He was admitted to the Fayette county bar September 9, 1835, and immediately entered upon the active practice of the law. He was a good lawyer, an able counsellor and a brilliant pleader before a jury. Having carefully studied the science of government and the great political issues of Jackson's and Van Buren's administrations, at an early age he entered the political arena: his ample and comprehensive mind grasped the bearings of the great public issues that divided the political parties of that day. Specially fitted by nature, observation and study, no wonder that the young and rising democratic attorney soon passed to a respectable position in the political affairs of Western Pennsylvania. The first office he filled was that of deputy attorney-general for Fayette county. His faithful and able discharge of the duties of this office commended him as possessing unusual elements of successful leadership. United with this he had a gift of eloquence which made his name a fireside recollection in the homes of Western Pennsylvania. President Polk, in 1845, appointed him United States district attorney for the western district of Pennsylvania, and he held the office during the whole of Polk's administration. He discharged the duties of this important office in a most satisfactory manner to the president and to the people of the district. John L. Dawson was not long in being recognized as one of the ablest and most talented leaders of Pennsylvania democracy. In 1848 he was put forth as the democratic nominee for member of congress in the district composed of Fayette, Greene and Somerset counties, but was defeated. He was renominated in 1850, and was elected. In 1852 he represented in congress the district composed of the counties of Fayette, Washington and Greene. At the end of his second term he declined a renomination, but in 1862 allowed the use of his name and was triumphantly elected and re-elected in 1864, the last time from the district composed of Fayette, Westmoreland and Indiana counties. Mr. Dawson signalized his entrance into congress and engaged the thoughts of our people by his resurrection and re-introduction of the Homestead bill, which had been previously introduced and defeated. Orignating and adding several important provisions to this celebrated bill, he eloquently and ably advocated it until it became a law of the land, opening millions of homes upon the broad prairies of the West to actual settlers, and wonderfully accelerating the progress of the country in her many Western fields of wealth and promise. This one act of his political career entitles him to rank as an able statesman and a public benefactor.

Mr. Dawson married Miss Mary Clark, of Brownsville, daughter of Robert Clark, merchant of Brownsville. Unto this union were born four children—three daughters and one son: Sarah, married Charles Spears, of Pittsburgh, Pennsylvania, and Mary married Hon. Chauncey Forward Black, son of Judge Jere Black, ex-Lieutenant-Governor of Pennsylvania.

John L. Dawson retired from public life 1867, after four terms of honorable and distinguished services in the interest of his country. From 1867 he resided with his family on the estate known as "Friendship Hill" (the former residence of Albert Gallatin) until his death, September 18, 1870, in the 58th year of his age. At his death the Cincinnati *Enquirer* gave the following deserved tribute to his memory:

"He belonged to a school of great, good and useful men, but a few of whom linger now to adorn and serve a country whose name their genius contributed so much to make glorious, and whose prosperity and happiness their wisdom and integrity ever sought to promote. Among political philosophers and practical statesmen, he was one of our profoundest thinkers. As an orator, whether on the mission of persuasion or conviction, he had but few rivals; and as a private citizen, his exalted character was without a blemish. His career in congress was in every respect brilliant. The private friendships he there contracted, even in the face of the bitterest prejudices, the lapse of years served only to strengthen and brighten, and the public record that he made is a proud heritage for his family and a shining example for future statesmen, and must grow brighter and brighter as time reveals—as reveal more and more each revolving year it surely will — the soundness of his judgment, the breadth of his comprehension, the clearness of his foresight, and the truth of his predictions. Always dignified, debonair and dispassionate in debate, no eruptions of temper ever ruffled the calm surface of his vigorous intellect. Endowed with an impressive and imposing presence, and those rare and peculiar gifts so prominently adapted to *ad captandum* discussion, he was not more honored by his own party as a leader than he was dreaded by the opposition as an adversary. The loss of such a man as John L. Dawson amounts to a national calamity."

John L. Dawson saw at a glance the true relations of things, the exact bearing of current events; what was proper to be done, and how to do it; and the force, the energy of his will bore him forward in its immediate and successful execution. He had great decision of character. He never stopped to speculate or doubt; and no leader ever should while he continues the contest, for uncertainty and hesitancy palsy the arm in its attempt to execute. As a general truth, it may be asserted that none but the sincere, believing, earnest men will efficiently, or can successfully, struggle with difficulties. It was the possession in a high degree of the qualities above mentioned that drew upon Dawson, by common consent, the leadership among those with whom he might be; for the wavering and timid always follow the decided and brave. And it was those qualities, also, that gave him such distinguished success as a politician and leader.

NATHAN DIVVENS, a soldier in the War of the Rebellion, was born in Westmoreland county, Pennsylvania, March 1, 1841. Reared and educated in Pittsburgh, where his parents removed when he was but seven years of age. Leaving school he learned the trade of tobacco manufacturer, working at his trade up to the breaking out of the war. August 7, 1862, he volunteered as a private in the One Hundred and Thirty-ninth Regiment Pennsylvania Volunteers, with Judge Collier, of Pittsburgh, colonel of the regiment. Mr. Divvens was in the battles of Bull Run, Gettysburg, three fights at Fredericksburg, and in numerous other battles. At the battle of Spottsylvania—on the 12th day of May, 1864—he was wounded and lost his right arm, and was discharged from the service at Pittsburgh, March 16, 1865.

In April, 1867, he came to Uniontown

and engaged in the manufacture of cigars, and has continued successfully in this business ever since. He has built up a large and extensive business, making a specialty of the manufacture and sale of the Toby cigar.

In 1866 he was married to Miss Susan E. Emerick, of Sharpsburg, Pennsylvania, daughter of John Emerick, the latter killed in the war; and they are the parents of five children, two boys and three girls: Lillie, Nathan, Pearl, Herbert and Edna.

Nathan Divvens' parents, Jacob and Elizabeth R. (Miller) Divvens, were natives of Bedford county, Pennsylvania. His father died in 1884 at his home in Pittsburgh, and his mother died in 1865, at the age of fifty-seven years.

JAMES R. DORAN, a popular liveryman and proprietor of the Keystone livery stable of Uniontown, is a son of William and Louisa (Hyde) Doran, and was born at Uniontown, Fayette county, Pennsylvania, July 31, 1854.

William Doran is a carpenter, and was born near Uniontown in 1819. He has been engaged at his trade for nearly fifty years in Uniontown, and has served as councilman. He is a republican, and married Miss Louisa Hyde, born in 1824, and her death occurred in 1884. Mrs. Doran's father, Edward Hyde, was a native of Birmingham, England, emigrated in early life to Uniontown, was a bricklayer and contractor on brickwork.

James R. Doran attended the Uniontown public schools until fifteen years of age. He learned the trade of carpenter with his father, pursued it for twelve years, and then engaged as warehouseman at the Baltimore & Ohio depot for some time. In 1883 he bought a few teams and engaged in the express business, which he followed for two years. In November, 1885, he engaged in his present livery business.

In 1875 he was married to Miss Amanda, a daughter of Frederick Cupp. They have five living children: Charlie, Nellie, Jessie, Hellen and Ollie.

James R. Doran is a member of the Odd Fellows, Knights of Pythias, and Haptasophs. His Keystone livery stables are substantially constructed and advantageously located near the Southwest depot. He has a splendidly selected assortment of handsome carriages and buggies and a large stock of excellent and carefully chosen saddle and harness horses. Mr. Doran gives careful attention to the wants of his numerous patrons, is a popular liveryman and a man of good business ability.

JOHN S. DOUGLAS, an energetic young business man of Uniontown, was born in West Newton, Westmoreland county, Pennsylvania, February 11, 1856, and is a son of Robert and Harriet (Wimer) Douglas. His grandfather, Robert Douglas, was one of seven brothers that came from Scotland and located near what is now Douglas Station, on the Pittsburgh and McKeesport railroad. He was the father of Robert Douglas, a teamster on the old National road, and was afterwards a farmer. Robert Douglas was a prominent member of the Salem Baptist church, in Westmoreland county. His wife was a daughter of David Wimer.

John S. Douglas was educated in the common schools of Westmoreland county. His first employment, after starting in life for himself, was the management of his father's farm. In the spring of 1882 he came to Uniontown and engaged in the agricultural implement business until 1887, when, in that year, he became a traveling salesman for William Deering and Company, of Chicago, with whom he remained for two years. In the spring of 1889, he associated

Daniel Downer

himself with Captain J. S. Horn, in the insurance business in Uniontown. October 14, 1880, he was married to Miss Lulu, daughter of William and Rachel (Masters) Norcross, of near Brownsville.

In politics he has always adhered to the principles of the democratic party, being an active worker in that organization, and is always anxious for his party's civil supremacy and complete success. His devotion to his party's interest has won him a host of friends. He is a Heptasoph and a member of the Royal Arcanum. Mr. Douglas is a member of the Uniontown Baptist church, and is president of its board of trustees, and has also been treasurer of the same church for several years. He is an honest, capable, and is one of the thoroughly business young men of the county.

DANIEL DOWNER. One of the solid and substantial families of Fayette county, distinguished for over a century for moral standing and business ability, is the Downer family of Uniontown; and one of its highly respected representative members is Daniel Downer, a gentleman of stainless character, and a good lawyer of reputable standing at the Uniontown bar.

Daniel Downer was born in the house he now resides in, at Uniontown, Fayette county, Pennsylvania, November 27, 1820, and is a son of Levi and Elizabeth (Hall) Downer.

His great-grandfather, Jacob Downer, was a native of Germany, where he married Elizabeth Starner, and in 1778 came to Lancaster county, Pennsylvania. Two years later he removed to Fayette county: leaving his family here he went to seek a permanent home in Kentucky, where it is supposed he was killed by Indians, as he never returned or was heard of afterwards. His wife and family removed to Uniontown, where she lived to be 105 years of age. One of the sons, Jonathan Downer, was born in 1754, and died at seventy-nine years of age, a highly respected citizen of the county. He erected and successfully conducted a large tannery, married Miss Drusilla Springer and reared a family of thirteen children, of whom Levi Downer was one, the father of Daniel Downer. The former was born November 11, 1788, reared at Uniontown, and died there October 2, 1854. He was a quiet, industrious and successful business man, and one of the well and favorably known citizens of his native town, where he successfully operated the celebrated Downer Tannery. He married Miss Elizabeth Hall. Her father, Hugh Hall, was a native of Berkeley Springs, Virginia, and owned and resided on the Rankin farm in North Union township, near Uniontown, previous to 1812. Mr. and Mrs. Downer reared one of the most remarkable families in the history of the county. Ten children were born; none died under fifty years of age; all lived honorable, upright lives, and none of them were ever married. Daniel, Caroline A. and Eliza M. reside at Uniontown; Major James P. Downer served under Scott in Mexico, and was a commissioned officer of a Kansas regiment for four years during the late war; served two terms in Pennsylvania legislature, and now resides in Colorado; David resides in Colorado, and has been editor or proprietor of over thirteen newspapers; J. Allen died at Uniontown, July 24, 1882; William H. died at Uniontown, May 12, 1885; Lieutenant George W. Downer served through the Civil War, and was drowned at Brookville, Pennsylvania, September 21, 1885; Dr. Hugh H. Downer, of California, died at Uniontown, in 1888, and Jacob, a Uniontown merchant, died February 26, 1888. Mrs. Downer, of Scotch-Irish descent, was born February 24, 1792, and died April 5, 1868.

Daniel Downer was reared at Uniontown, attended Madison college, and was so well prepared for college that on entering Jefferson college in 1839, he was immediately promoted to the sophomore class, and was graduated from this renowned old institution of learning in 1842. While at Jefferson, he was a member of the celebrated Philo Literary Society, and was one of its most enthusiastic members. He read law with Judge John Dawson (then a prominent attorney of the Fayette county bar), and was admitted to the practice of law in the courts of Fayette county, September 2, 1845. Immediately after admission to the bar, he opened an office at Uniontown, and has continued successfully in the practice of law up to the present time—a period of over forty years.

Daniel Downer is attentive to all business matters entrusted to his care, and is always prompt in having them receive proper attention. His clients' interests are his own, and are carefully looked after while in his charge. He is a careful, learned and successful lawyer, and has enjoyed a large and remunerative practice. For the past two years, however, he has virtually retired from the active practice. He is not, and never was, a politician, always preferring to give attention to the duties of his profession rather than to enter the field of politics.

He is a gentleman of pleasing manner, strict integrity and unquestionable business ability, and enjoys the confidence and respect of the whole public and of his numerous acquaintances.

ASHBEL FAIRCHILD DOWNS, an active young attorney of the Uniontown bar, and at present the efficient treasurer of Fayette county, was born at New Geneva, Fayette county, Pennsylvania, September 7, 1854, and is a son of David Downs, whose biography appears in this volume. His mother's maiden name was Eleanor Thompson, born in County Down, Ireland. A. F. Downs attended the public schools of his native county, and at the age of seventeen years he entered the State university of West Virginia, at Morgantown, and was a student there for three years. While at college he displayed marked ability in literature and oratory, taking three prizes, the last of which was the Regents' prize for the best declaimer. Afterward he taught several school terms, and in 1876 he entered the Philadelphia school of elocution and oratory, and was graduated from there with class honors in 1877. (It may be well to remember that this is the only chartered school of its kind in the United States.) He has given many readings from Shakespeare and other poets, and has taken high rank as a recitationist. The late Professor J. W. Shoemaker has, over his own signature, spoken in most unbounded praise of Mr. Downs' talent as a delineator of the passions. A. F. Downs became a student at law in the office of the Hon. C. E. Boyle, and was admitted to the bar of Fayette county in August, 1880, and has been successfully practicing in the courts of the county much of the time ever since.

A. F. Downs has always adhered to the long established doctrines and principles of the democratic party, and has been most active and zealous in the support of that organization, particularly in the way of public address, having earned the deserved reputation of being one of the best political speakers in Western Pennsylvania. He showed exceptional moral courage during the great coke strike of 1886, boldly taking the platform and presenting throughout the region the grievances and demands of the strikers, while others, with calculating shrewdness, were watching the direction of the wind. And he is credited with having done more to achieve the victory won by the workingmen than any other one man, and when the passions of the hour had subsided,

A. F. Downs

his moderation and fairness and his great influence in preventing disorder were generally acknowledged.

In 1886 Mr. Downs received 2,171 votes at the democratic primaries for the nomination of district attorney, receiving next to the highest vote. The nomination for the same office at the next election was conceded to him, but he became the candidate on the regular Democratic ticket in 1887, for county treasurer, and was elected in a hotly contested campaign, in which most of the candidates on the same ticket were defeated. He has executed the duties of his office with all fidelity to the State and county, enforcing claims due in a way that to some seems severe, but which was demanded by his oath of office. In obedience to that oath, Mr. Downs knows no fear, favor, sect or party, and those of a domineering, dictatorial, scheming or greedy spirit have found him a rock in their pathway. They have at times vented their spleen and disappointment in harsh criticism, but have not injured him among honest and right thinking men.

He displayed a talent for literary work, early in life, which he has since cultivated, and at one time was offered a place in the list of lecturers, in a leading lyceum bureau. His forthcoming book, entitled: "Heroes and Heroic Deeds or Uncrowned Kings," now in the hands of his publishers, the Franklin Printing Company of Philadelphia, will, in adition to new matter, include some of his former productions: Notably, his "Robert Emmett," which has been highly commended by such men as the Hon. James G. Blaine and the Hon. Chauncey Black.

Mr. Downs is a married man, whose family consists of a wife and two boys.

WILLIAM BROWNFIELD DOWNS was born in Redstone township, Fayette county, Pennsylvania, May 27, 1824, and is the son of Johnathan and Mary (Miller) Downs.

Johnathan Downs was born in Redstone township in 1788, was a farmer, and died in 1844, aged fifty-six years. He was in active membership in the old regular Baptist church and was a republican.

The grandfather of W. B. Downs, Jeremiah Downs, was a native of England, and came to this country in the latter part of the last century and settled in Redstone township.

Mary Miller, the mother of William B. Downs, was the daughter of Peter Miller of Jefferson township; she was born in 1790, and died June 4, 1855, in the sixty-fifth year of her age.

Johnathan and Mary Downs had ten children: Lucinda, married to Thomas Stephens of Washington township; David lives at New Geneva, and is the father of A. F. Downs, county treasurer; Margaret Miller, married to John Master of Washington township; Joseph Miller lives in Knox county, Illinois; Alex. Campbell, lives in Pike county, Ohio; William B.; Johnathan resides in Noble county, Ohio; Caleb Bracken lives at Granville, Fairfield county, Ohio, and is a Presbyterian minister; Isaac Newton lives at West Newton, Westmoreland county, Pennsylvania, and Mary is matron in the Newsboys' Home, Columbus, Ohio.

William B. Downs was reared on the farm, and has been a farmer all of his life. He was educated in the subscription schools of Redstone township, and is a republican in politics. On March 24, 1848, he was married to Miss Rebecca M. Wells, by Rev. Thomas Martin. She was born August 12, 1828, and was the daughter of Joseph Wells, the latter for many years a worthy citizen of this county. They have two living children: John Allen, born March 12, 1853, married to Miss Alice J. Rittenhouse and lives in Franklin township; and they have two children: Mary T., born October 12, 1862, married to James Reid, of Uniontown.

Mr. Downs and wife are both members of the Presbyterian church, of Uniontown.

JUDGE JOHN KENNEDY EWING, the son of Judge Nathaniel Ewing, Sr., deceased, is a worthy scion of a noble stock, and a fit representative of a name that stands untarnished.

The name of Ewing is honorably and indelibly stamped upon the history of Pennsylvania: in the East, by eminent ministers and men of scientific knowledge; in the West, by able jurists and honorable legislators. One member of this widely extended family is Judge John Kennedy Ewing, only child of Judge Nathaniel and Jane (Kennedy) Ewing, and was born at Uniontown, Fayette county, Pennsylvania, December 15, 1823.

He is descended from the Ewings of York county, a widely known and well connected family of ability and influence, planted in Eastern Pennsylvania prior to the war of the Revolution.

His grandfather, William Ewing, was born in York county, Pennsylvania, May 19, 1769. He was a son of George Ewing and a nephew of Rev. Dr. John Ewing, of Philadelphia. Dr. Ewing was selected on account of his natural fitness and educational qualifications, companion and assistant of the illustrious Rittenhouse, "whose name is coextensive with scientific knowledge," to run the southern boundary line of Pennsylvania. William Ewing came to Fayette county as a surveyor of lands, in 1790 and located in Luzerne township, where he died in 1827. He was a gentleman of suave and accomplished manners, and one of the leading men in the early settlement of the county. In 1791 he married Miss Mary Conwell, a daughter of Jehu and Elizabeth (Stokely) Conwell: a woman of superior mind, marked individuality and a most devoted Presbyterian. Their children were: Judge Nathaniel, Sr., Hon. John H. Ewing, of Washington, Pennsylvania, born October 5, 1796; James, born April 18, 1807, of Dunlap's Creek; Hon. George Ewing, born February 27, 1797, of Houston, Texas; Mrs. Elizabeth Breading, born July 9, 1799; Mrs. Maria Veech, born August 22, 1811, of Emsworth; Mrs. Ellen J. E. Wallace, born January 23, 1819, of Allegheny City; Mrs. Louisa Willson, born March 8, 1802; Mrs. Mary Ann Mason, born February 24, 1816, of Muscatine, Iowa, and Caroline, born April 20, 1804 (the latter dying in infancy).

Judge Nathaniel Ewing, Sr., was born July 8, 1794, and February 14, 1874, he died. He received a thorough classical education, and was graduated from Washington College with the highest honors of his class. He read Latin, Greek and Hebrew with rapidity and ease. Subsequent to leaving college, he read law with Thomas McGiffin, of Washington, Pa., and was admitted to the Fayette county bar November 19, 1816. In 1817 he began the practice of law, and soon after became recognized and acknowledged as one of the leading lawyers of Pennsylvania. February 15, 1838, Governor Ritner appointed him president judge of the 14th Judicial District, composed of Washington, Fayette and Greene counties. For a period of ten years he served as judge of the district, without a stain on his judicial ermine, which could not more appropriately fit the person of any one.

He married Miss Jane, second daughter of Hon. John Kennedy, judge of the supreme court of Pennsylvania. Judge Kennedy was a native of Cumberland county, Pennsylvania; came to Fayette county as a soldier during the Whiskey Insurrection, and so pleased with the country he remained, and was admitted to the Uniontown bar in September, 1798. He was an able lawyer as

Jno. K. Ewing.

well as an excellent jurist and a graduate in the same class with Roger B. Taney at Dickinson College, and died in 1846. Nathaniel Ewing, Sr., February 3, 1833, was ordained an elder in the Presbyterian church, and for forty years was a tower of strength to the cause of Presbyterianism. Mrs. Jane Ewing was an estimable woman, and died at an early age, in 1825. Judge Nathaniel Ewing, Sr., was one of the ablest lawyers and finest jurists of Pennsylvania. Several times he obtained from the supreme court of the State a reversal of their previous decisions, and on this account was called the "law-giver of Western Pennsylvania."

Third in lineal descent from George Ewing of Eastern Pennsylvania, is Judge John Kennedy Ewing, who received a classical education, and was graduated from Washington College in the class of 1842. He applied himself assiduously to the study of the law under the instructions of his father, and was admitted to the Fayette county bar in March, 1846. By his diligence and ability he soon acquired a large law practice, and attained to eminence in his profession. In addition to having mastered the principles of law, he was fairly conversant with legal, political and constitutional history, and in the preparation of a case there was no phase of it in legal or historical point of view that escaped his attention. He relied for success on the clear, strong points of his case, carefully studied and concisely presented.

In November, 1864, he was appointed president judge of the Fourteenth Judicial District, comprising the counties of Washington, Greene and Fayette and served commendably until January, 1866, in filling out the unexpired term of Judge Lindsey, who died in 1864. Leaving the bench, he also retired from the active practice of the law, a step that he contemplated before going on the bench on account of his impaired health.

In 1847 he was married to Miss Ellen Willson, a woman of brilliant and superior intelligence and a sister of Judge A. E. Willson. (See his sketch.) Her death occurred January 4, 1884.

Judge Ewing, during his whole life, has had to contend against ill health; but by indomitable energy, perseverance and a strong will power, he has succeeded in accomplishing a great deal more than seemed possible for him to do. Leaving the bench, he has been largely interested in the coal and iron industries of Western Pennsylvania. He went West and invested in land, and since engaging in business has been signally successful. He is now the president of the National Bank of Fayette county.

On May 4, 1846, he united with the Presbyterian church of Uniontown and was ordained and installed as elder March 4, 1860. He was commissioner to the General Assembly which met in Pittsburgh in 1864 and also at Omaha in 1887, and has frequently been a delegate to synod and presbytery; and in the session of the Uniontown church his services have been invaluable. Judge Ewing is modest and retiring in manner; yet he is pleasing in address and courteous to everybody. He possesses unusual mental vigor, accurate and exhaustive information, entertains broad and liberal and enlightened views, and is strong in his convictions and earnest in his efforts. A Presbyterian, he loves his church and takes deepest interest in whatever concerns the church's welfare. There is nothing of the bigot in his disposition. His sympathies include all denominations and to all his assistance is freely given. A man of earnest piety and charitable disposition, his practice conforms to his professions and his example and counsel exert a commanding influence. Among Fayette county's honored sons none stand higher at home or elsewhere, wherever known for intellectual power and purity of character, than Judge Ewing. He never sought an office in his life, yet he is qualified to fill any office from judgeship to the presidency.

REV. THORNTON F. FARMER, D. D. S., is a native of Fayette county, Pa. He was reared on a farm, and attended the public schools. At the age of twenty-one he went to Meadville and studied at Allegheny College. In 1863 he began the study of dentistry with Dr. George Morris, of Morgantown, W. Va., and in the winter of 1871 was graduated at the Philadelphia Dental College. In the fall of 1872 he came to Uniontown and commenced the practice of his profession, where he has since resided, and has established a large and lucrative practice. He is the oldest practitioner at Uniontown, and has kept abreast with his profession in every department, having all of the improved instruments and appliances belonging to the art.

He was married in 1862 to Miss Emily Ross, of German township. She died in 1875, leaving one child, Hattie R., who died May 20, 1878.

He married a second time in 1876, to Nannie G. Hopwood, of Monroe, this county; she died in 1880, leaving two children: Hattie R. and Gaddis H. Gaddis H. died May 16, 1889, at the age of nine years.

Dr. Farmer was married, a third time, in 1881, to Maggie L. McIllree—the daughter of Henry and Louesil McIllree, of Fayette county; by this wife he has three children: Thornton F., Ulysses Simpson and Lou Byron. Dr. Farmer is the son of Daniel and Mary Ann (Gray) Farmer, both natives of Maryland, who came to the county in 1813. Their route to Fayette county was across the mountains by the road made by General (then Major) Washington in his advance to Fort Duquesne—now Pittsburgh—in the French and Indian War. They first settled near New Salem, but afterward in Springhill township—now Nicholson—where they died. Dr. Farmer's father died March 10, 1865, in the seventy-fifth year of his age. His mother died in September, 1878, in the eighty-third year of her age.

Dr. Farmer has been a member of the Methodist Episcopal church for thirty-five years, and a local preacher for twenty years; and has creditably filled many of the pulpits in the county, as well as in West Virginia. In his father's family were ten children—seven girls and three boys: John G. Farmer, the oldest, was born in 1811. He was a fine mathematician, and at his death in 1879, he was the oldest and most successful surveyor in the county. A. B. Farmer was the youngest child, born 5th day of April, 1834. When the War of the Rebellion broke out, he enlisted in Captain George Gilmore's company. Much of his time was spent among the bushwhackers of West Virginia, where many of the boys in blue were killed, and sleep in far off graves. A. B. has been a citizen of Indianapolis for many years.

CHARLES M. FLEMING, a prominent grocer of Uniontown, is a native of Dunbar township, Fayette county, Pa., and was born March 20, 1854. He is the son of Thomas J. and Mary Ann (Smiley) Fleming, both natives of this county. The mother died in 1879, and the father and two sisters reside at Uniontown.

C. M. Fleming was brought up on the farm until he attained his majority, when he engaged as a clerk for Markle, Sherrick & Co., coke operators, continuing with them for two years, and then took a position with the H. C. Frick Coke Company, with whom he remained for two and one-half years. He left Frick's store in 1881, and went to the Red Stone Coke Company as manager of their store. This position he held for over six years. In April, 1888, he came to Union-

Smith Fuller

town and bought out the grocery of O. P. Markle.

In Uniontown he has built up a flourishing trade, and is a popular young business man. He belongs to the Junior Order of American Mechanics, and is a member of the Methodist Episcopal church.

LUKE H. FRASHER comes of one of the old families of Fayette county. His great grandfather, Peter Frasher, came to Fayette county, from Winchester, Va., before the old National Road was made. His son Luke—the grandfather of Luke H—came with him and both were teamsters on that old thoroughfare, the principal artery for the commerce of the country in its day.

James Frasher, the father of Luke H. Frasher, was born in Fayette county, Pa., in 1814, and died in 1878 at the age of sixty-four years, and was a farmer by occupation. He married Miss Eliza J. Wheatley, a native of Fayette county, and who is now living on the farm in Franklin township. The Wheatley family is an early one to the county also. Luke H. Frasher is of the fourth generation of the Frasher family, in Fayette county.

He was born December 14, 1853, in Franklin township, Fayette county, Pa. He worked on the farm until he arrived at the age of seventeen years, and attended the common school of his neighborhood. In 1871 he entered the West Virginia University, at Morgantown, W. Va., where he remained for five years, and was graduated n the class of 1876. In 1878 he began the study of law in the office of W. H. Playford and was admitted to the bar at Uniontown in 1880. He immediately began the practice of his profession, and has been successfully engaged in it ever since. He has gained a prominent place at the bar, and has quite a large practice for a young man.

June 1, 1889, he was nominated by the democratic party, as their candidate for district attorney.

Prior to taking up the study of law, Mr. Frasher had taught several terms of district schools in this county: one term at Kingwood, as the principal of the public schools, and one term as principal of mathematics at the Commercial College, Wheeling, W. Va.

DR. SMITH FULLER has passed an epoch in the study and practice of medicine, which, measured by time, would cover but a small extent in the age of the medical science; but, counting the advance in the knowledge of diseases and their treatment, it covers more space than all of the previous centuries combined would do. In all of the departments of the profession, there has been but the one word—advance; and it now stands before the world as a science which is rapidly approaching a condition of comparative perfectness. Dr. Smith Fuller was born at Connellsville, Fayette county, Pa., February 3, 1818. He attended the common schools, and in about 1835 he went to Washington College, which at that time was one of the finest institutions of learning in the United States west of the Alleghenies. He remained at college three years, electing and successfully pursuing an irregular course. In 1838 he began the study of medicine at West Newton under Dr. John Hasson, a distinguished physician of Westmoreland county and a graduate of the University of Pennsylvania. Smith Fuller attended a regular course of lectures at Jefferson Medical College, Philadelphia, and located at Uniontown in the practice of medicine in the spring of 1840. His field of practice soon extended beyond Fayette into adjoining counties of Pennsylvania, Maryland and Virginia, twenty to thirty miles being no uncommon distance in many cases to reach his patients. He returned to Jefferson Medical College in 1846, took further courses of lectures under Dunglison & Pancoast, professors, of national reputation. He was graduated in 1847, and returned to Uniontown, and his Southwestern Pennsylvania field of practice, where he has earnestly and successfully labored up to the present time. Dr. Fuller is known among men as a man whose sterling worth, unaffected manners, generous impulses and active brain make him a leader in any community. His courteous bearing, his high sense of honor, his acknowledged ability and professional skill have secured for him an extended consultation practice. For nearly half a century he has not counted his own pleasures or enjoyment in order that he might be of service to others. In many a home there is an unwritten history of his medical skill and humane devotion to the interests of the sick, and this, if written, would be his highest tribute. Dr. Smith Fuller as a physician is recognized as wise, skillful and trustworthy His quiet firmness, his ability and skill make him an ideal physician. Originally he was a democrat, but identified himself with the national American party in 1856. He became a member of the republican party upon its birth, and in 1860 was a delegate to the republican national convention that nominated Abraham Lincoln. He was elected member of the State senate in 1860, and represented for three years the district composed of Fayette and Westmoreland counties, and was chairman of the committee on military affairs. His party in 1864 made him their candidate for congress in the district composed of Fayette, Indiana and Westmoreland counties. His opponent was John L. Dawson (see his sketch), who was declared elected by sixteen votes. Dr. Fuller contested the election, and spent five months at Washington, but was unsuccessful in securing the seat. He has been largely engaged in tanning for the wholesale trade in Georges township, of this county, and is a director of the National Bank of Fayette county. Dr. Fuller's grandfather, Daniel Fuller, was a native of Ireland, and at the age of fifteen was shipped as a hand on board a vessel for his passage across the Atlantic over one hundred years ago. He stopped for a time in a Quaker neighborhood, and, in a short time after, Daniel Fuller came out to Fayette county with a Mr. Bailey. Dr. Fuller's maternal grandfather, Dr. Bela B. Smith, was born at Hartford, Conn. Dr. Smith practiced medicine at West Newton, Westmoreland county, for about fifty years. He was of English descent, and was much esteemed as a physician. He accumulated a large landed estate, and died about 1837. Dr. Fuller's father, John Fuller, represented Fayette county in the legislature of Pennsylvania during three terms, and was a member of the Constitutional Convention of 1838. He was born in 1786, and died in 1865. The mother of Dr. Fuller was Harriet R. Smith, the daughter of Dr. Bela B. Smith, and the wife of John Fuller. In 1839 Dr. Smith Fuller married Miss Elvira Markle, of West Newton, who died in 1846. By her he had three children: John M., a physician, Harriet and Elizabeth. His second wife was Jane, daughter of William D. Beggs, of Uniontown, a prominent school teacher of his day. Dr. Fuller married Miss Jane Beggs in 1849, and they have three sons living of five born unto them: William B., a physician; Frank M., an attorney at law, and Smith, the youngest son, a physician.

ALBERT GADDIS was born May 30, 1849, in Franklin township, Fayette county, Pa., and was reared on a farm. He attended the common schools of the county, and the normal school at California, Pa. In 1868-69 he taught district schools, and in 1872 went to Monongahela City, and was engaged in the grocery business there for five years. In 1877 he engaged in farming, which he followed for nine years, in North Union township. In 1886 he removed to Uniontown and formed a partnership with A. G. Thomas in the milling business, the firm being Gaddis & Thomas. They bought the flouring mill opposite the Baltimore & Ohio depot, which burned July 9, 1886. In March, 1887, Thomas died, and Mr. Gaddis rented the mill and continued to run it alone, until it was also burned. In September, of same year, Mr. Gaddis formed a co-partnership with Barnard V. and Samuel W. Jones, under the firm of A. Gaddis & Co. They then built their present mill, of a splendid roller process, which they have successfully run ever since, built up a large trade and run day and night, making *sixty* barrels of flour a day.

Albert Gaddis was married in 1871, to Miss Ester V. Jones, daughter of John Jones, of North Union township. John Jones is one of the oldest men in North Union township, being in the eighty-sixth year of his age.

Mr. Gaddis has one child, Jennie C., born in 1873. He is a son of Robert and Sarah (Carter) Gaddis; the former was a prominent farmer and a native of North Union township, Fayette county, Pa., born in 1809. The grandfather of Albert Gaddis, John Gaddis, was also a native of Fayette county. The Gaddises were of the first to settle here. Albert Gaddis is a member of the Methodist Episcopal church, of the Independent Order of Odd Fellows, and of the Royal Arcanum.

JOHN GALLAGHER. James Gallagher, the paternal grandfather of John Gallagher, was born in County Donegal, Ireland, and came to this country and settled in what is now Fayette county, Pa., previous to 1775 (probably 1769). On March 20, 1786, he obtained a patent for 203 acres of land, with the allowance, adjoining the present site of Uniontown, then known as Beesontown. (The original patent for this land is now in the possession of his grandson, the subject of this sketch.) This was a part of a tract of land containing three hundred acres, that he had purchased from Aaron Robinson, January 25, 1775. He was one of the original lot holders or owners in the village of Beeson's Mill in 1776. The name of this place was afterwards changed to Beeson's Town, and then again to that of Union, and later to Uniontown. All of the "North Addition" to the present rapidly growing town is built upon what was once known as the "Gallagher property." Diana (Askren) Gallagher, wife of James Gallagher, was born in Harford county, Md.; her father, Thomas Askren, was a native of Yorkshire, England, and her mother, Martha (New) Askren, an American by birth.

The maternal grandparents of John Gallagher, Jacob and Catherine (Fletcher) Black, were of German descent but of American birth.

John Gallagher was born in North Union township, Fayette county, Pa., the place of his birth being now inside of the corporate limits of Uniontown; and was reared on the place where he now resides. He was educated in the schools of the borough and at Madison College. Leaving college he studied law for a short time with Hon. Andrew Stewart, and finished his studies with Judge John K. Ewing. He was admitted to the bar in 1859, and practiced law for about six years at Uniontown, and has been principally engaged in farming ever since.

His parents were John and Mary (Black) Gallagher, both natives of Fayette county, Pa. His father was a farmer and owned in addition to other lands, sixty-seven acres of ground that is now within the borough of Uniontown, situated partly west of, and including Redstone creek, extending eastward, including all of Lincoln, Maple and Walnut streets, and the southern part of North Gallatin avenue. He was a soldier in the War of 1812–15, was orderly sergeant of the company in which he served, and the adjutant of the regiment. He died January 1, 1869, in the eighty-fifth year of his age. His widow died February 26, 1872, in the seventy-sixth year of her age.

Their children: Evalina W., James M., Jane K., Elizabeth D., Jacob B., Mary L. and John, all reside in Pennsylvania; Jacob B., Mary L. and John live together at Uniontown, on a part of the original homestead. The Gallagher family is one of the oldest in the county.

ROBERT HAGAN was born July 3, 1831, on the old Hagan homestead in South Union township, Fayette county, Pa.

John Hagan, the father of Robert Hagan, was born in 1788, in County Derry, Ireland; and came to America in 1807. He married Margaret Grimes; and she was born near Hagerstown, Md., in about 1792. John Hagan was a contractor on the National Road, and received a contract to make a section of that road, in September, 1815. After the National Road was finished, he became a contractor upon the Erie Canal. He was superintendent upon the farm, which he afterwards bought, and where he spent the last years of his life. He was a democrat. He donated the ground on which the Catholic church is built, and died in 1869.

Robert Hagan was educated in the schools of South Union township, and started out in life in business as a merchant at Waynesburgh, Pa., where he remained two years, when he came to Uniontown and engaged in business with his brother John Hagan. From 1868 to 1871 he was engaged in buying and selling stock.

On January 9, 1853, he was married to Miss Ann Wood, the daughter of Josiah Wood. They had seven children: Alonzo (see his sketch), a member of the Uniontown bar; Margaret, born March 22, 1857, living at home; Harry, born June 20, 1860, civil engineer at Uniontown; Elizabeth, born in 1864; Mollie, Ida and Robert, the latter born November 22, 1875.

Robert Hagan is a democrat, was elected in 1871, as county commissioner and served as such for three years. He is now serving his tenth year as school director and takes considerable interest in educational matters. He is a good citizen and stands well in the community where he lives. He is a member of the Baptist church.

JACOB SIDWELL HACKNEY, M. D. is the youngest son of Hiram H. and Elizabeth S. Hackney. Hiram H. Hackney was born in Fayette county, Pa., in 1822, and was graduated from Madison College when that school was in the halcyon days of its existence. He was one of the world famed "'49ers" who crossed the "Great Plains" amid dangers and privations, to seek for the golden treasures buried in Pacific sands. J. S. Hackney's grandfather was the youngest son of Aaron Hackney, born in Luzerne township, Fayette county, Pa., on what is now known as the "Hackney Knob farm." The Hackneys were English, who emigrated to America in about 1650, from Hackneytown, a suburb then, but now a part of the city of London.

Dr. Hackney's mother was a daughter of Jacob and Hannah Wyly, of Carmichael's, Greene county, Pa. Her maiden name was Elizabeth Styne Wyly.

J. S. Hackney was born May 4, 1862, and grew to manhood on his father's farm, near New Salem, Menallen township, receiving such educational training as was afforded in the graded school of that place. At seventeen years of age he entered the Southwestern State Normal School, at California, Pa., and attended two summer sessions, when he secured a country school and taught for one winter. At the expiration of his first school he entered the Freshman class at Mt. Union College, Mt. Union, Ohio, and studied two years, taking principally the scientific branches. Having determined upon medicine as the vocation of his life, in July, 1882, he entered, as a student of medicine, the office of Dr. Smith Fuller, Sr., of Uniontown, and for the first year taught school near his home, and on Saturdays went to Uniontown to recite to his preceptor. In the fall of 1883 he entered the Jefferson Medical College, of Philadelphia, from which he was graduated two years later, April 2, 1885, standing third in scholarship in a class of 176. Instead of branching out in the practice of his profession at once, he wished further to prepare himself for actual practice, so he became an applicant for and was afterwards appointed (through a competitive examination) to the position of resident physician in the West Penn Hospital, at Pittsburgh. Serving one year at the hospital, he decided to locate at Uniontown for the further pursuance of his profession.

On June 7, 1887, he was married to Anna M., daughter of Dr. Henry and Mary Eastman, of Merrittstown. Dr. Eastman is one of the oldest and ablest physicians of Fayette county. (See his sketch.)

Dr. Hackney is an active member of the Fayette County Medical Society, and takes deep interest in its proceedings. Although young in the profession, he is fast building up a large and lucrative practice, and is at present the surgeon of the Columbia Iron and Steel Works, of Uniontown, which position he has held from the starting of the works.

ALONZO C. HAGAN, a young and rising attorney of the Fayette county bar, was born in South Union township, July 27, 1854, and is a son of Robert and Mary Ann (Wood) Hagan. Robert Hagan resides in South Union township. (See his sketch.)

Alonzo C. Hagan was reared on a farm and educated in the common schools, public schools of Uniontown and Waynesburg College, and attended the latter from 1872 till 1875. In 1876 he began reading law with W. H. Playford, and was admitted to the bar of Fayette county March 5, 1877. In the same year he located at Atchison, Kansas, in the practice of his profession, but, not pleased with Kansas, he returned to Fayette county in 1879, and opened a law office at Uniontown, where he has been continuously engaged successfully in the practice ever since. By prompt and strict attendence to business, he has built up a good and remunerative practice. He has been interested in many of the important cases, and is fast winning the reputation of a successful lawyer.

In October, 1880, he was married to Miss Mary M., daughter of Thomas D. Miller, of Monroe. She died April, 1889, while en route to Uniontown from Florida, where she had been for her health.

Mr. Hagan is a firm believer in the "time honored principles of the democratic party," and has always taken an active part in the political campaigns of the last fifteen years. He was chairman of the democratic central committee of Fayette county, and ably conducted the campaigns while chairman. He is a good lawyer and an honarable citizen.

DANIEL P. GIBSON. From the farm goes many a boy to win distinction or success in life, and among those who have become successful business men may be mentioned Daniel P. Gibson. He was born on a farm in Fayette county, Pa, April 20, 1827. He attended the public school and worked on the farm, until sixteen years of age, when he apprenticed himself to learn the harness and saddlery trade at Petersburgh, Somerset county, Pa., with John Morrow, with whom he remained five years. On attaining his majority he located at Upper Middletown and pursued the harness and saddlery business from 1848 to 1876—a period of twenty-eight years. He built up a large trade and acquired the reputation of being an honest and reliable business man. In 1876 he selected Uniontown as center for a wider field of operations and his subsequent success attests the wisdom of his selection. To his regular business he added, in 1876, that of handling buggies. He visited the factories inspected the materials and examined the process of construction in its every stage, thus securing himself and customers from imposition in the buggies he put upon the market. Mr. Gibson also engaged in farming, and was in the general mercantile business from about 1862 to 1879, running two general stores, one at Upper Middletown, the other at Searights. After locating at Uniontown he started a grocery and hardware store but sold it in 1881, on account of ill health. Success has marked his ventures in every field. He owns valuable property in Osceola, also in Clark county, Iowa. He has acquired quite an amount of improved real estate in Uniontown of houses and lots that return a handsome rental. He is a Master Mason and holds membership in the Independent Order of Odd Fellows, is a member of the Baptist church, and has been for many years one of the church's trustees. He is also one of the directors of the First National Bank of Uniontown.

Daniel P. Gibson is the son of Joseph and Rachel Gibson (neé Philips). Joseph Gibson was born in Fayette county, Pa., and was a farmer. He died in 1830, aged fifty years. He was the son of John Gibson, a native of Ireland. Rachel Philips Gibson was a native of New Jersey, and came with her parents when quite young to the county. Her father was Benjamin Philips and a farmer by occupation. Daniel P. Gibson was married in 1874 to Miss Hannah Jane, daughter of William Brown, a well-known and prominent Fayette county farmer, and has one child: Della Pearl. Mr. Gibson is a fine business man, possessed of good judgment, but plain and quiet in conducting his business. Losing no chances, missing no opportunities, making no rash ventures or wild speculations, and satisfied with small but certain profits. He is truly one of Fayette county's most successful business men.

WILLIAM HANDLIN was born December 28, 1844, in North Union township, Fayette county, Pa. His father, Daniel Handlin, was born near Hopwood, Fayette county, Pa., in 1814. His wife (Daniel's), Nancy White, was a daughter of John White, of Fayette county. To them were born five children: Jacob, Sarah H., Elizabeth H., John and William. The father and two sons were soldiers in the Civil War; although the father, Daniel Handlin, could have been exempted from duty on account of his age. He enlisted in 1862, in the One Hundred and Fortieth Pennsylvania Regiment, and was mustered out in April, 1864. William Handlin enlisted in 1864, as a private in the Fourteenth Pennsylvania Cavalry, under Captain Harrison's command, and J. M. Schoonmaker as his colonel. He joined this regiment at Martinsburg, was in the battles of Wythville Gap, and after the Union forces were defeated at Lynchburg Mr. Handlin was transferred to General Sheridan's command, and was with that renowned commander at Winchester, Fisher's Hill and

Cedar creek. He was promoted to corporal, and honorably discharged from the service November 22, 1865. He was a brave soldier, as was also his brother Jacob, the latter taken prisoner by the Confederates at New River and confined in Andersonville prison, and died while incarcerated there. Daniel Handlin is still living and in good health, at seventy-five years of age. Anthony Handlin is the father of Daniel Handlin. His wife's maiden name was Nancy Hunt.

William Handlin was married, June 11, 1877, to Susan Castell, daughter of James Castell, of North Union township. To this union have been born six children: Louis, Henry, Jennie, Nannie, Nellie and Bessie. He was educated in the common schools of the county. Leaving school, he learned the trade of stonemason under James Hanan, of North Union, and with whom he has been in business ever since, for the last fourteen years as partner. He is a democrat, and a member of the M. P. church, and is class-leader. He takes an active interest in educational affairs, believing the way to get good teachers is to pay good wages. He is one of the school directors of his township.

HARVEY HANDLEN was born near Smithfield, Georges township, Fayette county, Pa., November 22, 1821. His father, Daniel Handlen, was a native of Ireland, and came to this country when about thirteen years of age. He married Elizabeth Hunt, a daughter of Jacob Hunt. (For ancestry of the Hunt family, see sketch of William Hunt.) To their marriage were born ten children, of whom Harvey is the youngest. Daniel Handlen was a collier by trade. He died in 1833. William, the father of Daniel Handlen, was also a native of Ireland, and a farmer by occupation.

Harvey Handlen was married to Eliza M., a daughter of Greenberry Balsley, of North Union township, February 21, 1847, and have two children living: Greenberry, born September 22, 1855, was married to a daughter of James Darby, and has one child by her—Nancy. His second wife was Lydia, a daughter of William Holsing, of Uniontown, and by her has three children: Jessie, Sarah and Catherine. Harvey Handlen's other child, Ellen, was born August 10, 1848, and is now the wife of S. W. Means, of North Union. She is the mother of five children: Harvey, Thomas H., Ann Eliza, John and Greenberry.

Harvey Handlen was reared on the farm. Early in life he learned the trade of stonemason under William Hanan, and worked at it for many years. For the last twelve years he has been engaged in coal mining. He has always voted the democratic ticket, as did his father and grandfather before him. He is a member of the Knights of Labor, of the Sons of Temperance, a devoted member of the Methodist Protestant church, held the various offices in the church, and is at present one of the trustees of his church. His wife was also a member of the same church.

JOHN HANKINS was born on the old Hankins Homestead, North Union township, Fayette county, Pa., July 2, 1826. His father, James Hankins, born July 24, 1780, in North Carolina, was brought to Fayette county by his father, John Hankins, in 1783, who was born October 9, 1738, in North Carolina, and with his wife and children came to "Beesontown" in 1784. He was married to Rhoda Ireland, December 10, 1761. She was of Scotch-Irish origin, as are also the Hankins.

Mary Moreland, the mother of John Hankins, was a daughter of William Moreland, of near Connellsville. She was born below

Broad Ford, Fayette county, Pa., April 23, 1788, and was married to James Hankins in about 1817, and died August, 1864. James Hankins was a strong democrat. His father, John Hankins, voted for Washington for president. John Hankins purchased a piece of land where William Hankins now resides, previous to the War of the Revolution, and the deed bears the seal and name of King George III. This same property is still in possession of the Hankins family.

John Hankins, whose name heads this sketch, was married to Rachel Foster, daughter of John Foster, of North Union township, March 17, 1853. She was born February 14, 1835. To their marriage have been born seven children, three of whom are now living: John F., born August 11, 1861, and is married to Lida Rankin; Lucinda, born November 7, 1863, is the wife of Frank H. Rosboro, of Dawson, and Ella Margaret, born September 9, 1868.

John Hankins takes a deep interest in educational matters; being for the fifteen years past a school director. He is a strong democrat and a good citizen.

WILLIAM HENSHAW, one of South Union township's substantial citizens, is a son of James Smith and Ann (Gray) Henshaw, and was born on the farm taken up by his great-grandfather in North Union township, Fayette county, Pa., June 10, 1850.

Nicholas Henshaw (great-grandfather), who lies buried in the Presbyterian churchyard at Laurel Hill, came from Virginia, and patented 255 acres of land in 1789, where some of his descendants now live. He was the father of William Henshaw, who married Ann Parker, and one of whose sons, James S., is the father of William Henshaw.

James S. Henshaw was born November 20, 1809. He was a farmer—was a democrat—held various township offices and was a ruling elder in the Presbyterian church at Laurel Hill for a number of years. He was first married to Miss Ann, daughter of Jonathan Gray, May 24, 1848. She died October 31, 1850. They had two children: Jonathan G., deceased, and William. His second wife was Miss Harriet, daughter of George Chalfant; she died in 1866. They had six children, of whom three are now living: Clarissa F., married to Samuel W. Dunn; Elizabeth, married to Hiram Rankin, and Samuel W., married to Elizabeth Hankins. In 1860 he married Miss Maria Jane McDougle, who still survives him. They had two children, one of whom is now living: Mary Margaret, unmarried. He was a successful farmer and a steady, earnest man: he died October 20, 1878.

William Henshaw received his education in the common-schools of North Union township. Leaving school, he engaged in his present business of farming.

September 24, 1879, he married Miss Dorcas R., daughter of Moses and Caroline (Smith) Hazen. To this union have been born five children: Lulu Belle, Carrie Jane, James S., Thomas H. and Robert Walker. Mrs. Henshaw was born September 13, 1855.

William Henshaw is a democrat in politics and is a good farmer and citizen.

ISAAC CONDIT HAZLETT, M. D., is a native of Franklin township, Washington county, Pa., and was born February 20, 1840. His father, Samuel Hazlett, was a farmer, as was also his grandfather Hazlett who owned the Muse farm. Dr. Hazlett's mother was Mrs. Jemima Forsythe, widow of David Forsythe, before her marriage with Samuel Hazlett. She was born in Washington county, Pa., and a daughter of Jonas Condit, a native of New Jersey.

Dr. I. C. Hazlett married Miss Nancy

Ellen Jennings, of Hillsboro, in 1867. He obtained the elementary course taught in common schools, and afterwards studied Greek and Latin under the tutelage of Rev. N. B. Lyons of Washington county, Pa. He began to read medicine at the age of twenty-two years with Dr. E. F. Dodd, of Washington. He entered the University of Pennsylvania, and graduated from the same school in 1870. He practiced medicine before his graduation, however, first at Hillsboro, where he began his first practice April 26, 1866, thence to New Salem in 1867. After his graduation, in 1873 he removed to Belle Vernon, resided and practiced there till 1886, when he located at Uniontown. In 1881 he took the post graduate course at the University of Pennsylvania. His practice at Uniontown has doubled itself in the last year.

He is an active member of the Fayette county Medical Society, of which he was president in 1884, is a member of the State Medical Society and also holds membership in the American Medical Association. He wields a ready pen and contributes to the medical journals of the day. He is one of the most progressive members of the medical fraternity of Fayette county—is devoted to his profession and he always takes an interest in it that never flags or wearies.

ELLIS HOLLAND was born on the old Holland farm in North Union township, Fayette county, Pa., July 29, 1827, and on the same farm his father, James Holland, was also born in 1792. James Holland was married to Mary Ann Ellis, daughter of M. P. Ellis, who came to Fayette county from Maryland in early manhood. To their marriage seven daughters and one son (Ellis) were born. James Holland has been an active member of the Methodist Episcopal church since he was thirteen years of age. He was a member of the old whig party until it was supplanted by the republican party in 1856, when he became a republican. Ellis Holland's grandfather, Holland, was a native of Maryland, and came to Fayette county in an early day and bought the farm on which all of his children were born. Subsequently he sold the farm for thirteen dollars per acre. Ellis Holland was married to Rachel, daughter of James Hogsett, and a sister of Robert Hogsett, of Fayette county. She was born in Menallen township, April 17, 1831, and was married January 27, 1853. Seven children were born to this union: James W., born April 20, 1854; Elizabeth Ann, January 30, 1856; F. B.; Frank M., March 6, 1864; Charles S., August 14, 1866; Robt H., January 30, 1868, and John H., October 31, 1870. Ellis Holland was reared on a farm in North Union township, and learned the trade of cooper, but soon abandoned his trade and began farming. He is a stanch republican and in 1874 was appointed postmaster at Mt. Braddock by president Grant, and still holds the office.

DAVID M. HERTZOG, the present active and efficient district attorney of Fayette county, is a son of John and Margaret Hertzog, and was born March 30, 1852.

David M. Hertzog (for ancestry, see sketch of John Hertzog) was reared on a farm and was educated in the common schools of the county, Southwestern Pennsylvania Normal School and Mt. Union College, Ohio. At seventeen years of age, he began teaching in the common schools and continued in that line of work for several years: teaching in the winter and attending school during the summer. In 1875 he was registered as a law student at Uniontown. He read law with C. E. Boyle, and was admitted to the Fayette county bar September 2, 1878. In the same year he entered the law department of Michigan University, at Ann Arbor, and took a full course. May 1, 1879, he became a partner of Paoli S. Morrow, at Uniontown, where he has continued most successfully in the practice of law up to the present time. In 1886 he was the democratic candidate for district attorney of Fayette county and was elected, while the majority of the other democratic candidates of that year were defeated. In 1889 he was elected chairman of the constitutional amendment county committee and so ably directed the campaign that Fayette county rolled up an unexpected majority of 3,012 in favor of the prohibitory amendment to the State constitution.

David M. Hertzog was elected clerk of Great Bethel Regular Baptist churh in 1878 and has been superintendent of its Sabbath-school since 1880. He is a prominent attorner at the bar, a logical reasoner, an earnest, forcible speaker, and has well managed the many important cases he has been interested in since he began practice in the courts of Fayette county.

ROBERT F. HOPWOOD, one of the leading lawyers of the Uniontown bar for some years past, was born at Uniontown, Fayette county, Pa., July 24, 1856; and where he grew to manhood. He attended the public schools till at the age of twelve years, and from twelve to the age of eighteen he was a clerk in different stores of the place. Leaving school he attended night schools, and there took limited courses of Latin and higher mathematics. He has continued his studies till the present time, and is now possessed of one of the best libraries in the town, a glance at which shows his especial fondness for historical and poetical works. He can, at a moment's notice, turn to the page and paragraph in any of his books that has specially impressed him, and can quote copiously from them.

At the age of twenty he commenced the study of law with Charles E. Boyle, and was admitted to the Uniontown bar July 25, 1879. He immediately began the practice, has since continued, and now has a very large and lucrative practice. He was elected attorney for Uniontown in April, 1882, and has held the office ever since his first election.

In 1886 he was the republican candidate for District Attorney, and was only defeated forty-five votes out of a total of 12,000. He was the chairman of the republican county committee in 1883 and 1884, and for several years was secretary of the same committee. He has been secretary of the Fayette County Agricultural Association since 1881, and treasurer of the same association for several years past. The company was organized in 1879. In having the steel and glass works located at Uniontown, he was instrumental in soliciting the money to buy the ground upon which to locate the plants. He was also largely instrumental in the establishing the natural gas works at Uniontown, and sold four-fifths of the stock for the company. He has been the attorney for the Knights of Labor, of the Amalgamated Association for three years, and was their attorney in the Jimtown riot case. He has been engaged in a large number of criminal cases of more or less importance during the last few years. On the 27th of May, 1889, he was nominated by his party, the republicans, for district attorney.

He was married in June, 1880, to Miss Emma S. Miller, daughter of Mr. W. H. H. Miller. (See Miller's sketch.) They have five children: Samuel C., Ruth, Frank P., Edith M. and Elizabeth. He is a member of the Methodist Episcopal church, and is the superintendent of the Sabbath-school. At the time he became superintendent the attendance was about 150, and now the average attendance is about 300 children.

R. F. Hopwood is the son of Rice G. and Ruth (Jackson) Hopwood. His father was a lawyer, and died August 17, 1880, at the age of seventy-one years. His mother is still living. His two brothers, David J. and Frank P., reside in Minneapolis, Minnesota, connected with the wholesale dry goods house of Wyman, Mullen & Co., the largest house of the kind west of Chicago.

R. F. Hopwood is of the fifth generation of the Hopwood family in Fayette county. His great-great-grandfather, John Hopwood, came from Lancashire, England, to Fayette in 1761, located on a large tract of land and laid out the town of Hopwood. On the mother's side of the family Mr. Hopwood is of English and Scotch Irish extraction. The Jacksons have been in the county as long as the Hopwoods.

LEVI HUNTLEY was born near Smithfield, Georges township, Fayette county, Pa., January 18, 1834, and is a son of Robert and Mary (McKean) Huntley, the former a native of New Jersey. Mary McKean was a daughter of James McKean, the latter an early settler of, and probably the first manufacturer of iron in Fayette county.

Stoddard Huntley, the grandfather of Levi Huntley, came with the Connells early in life from New Jersey and settled near Connellsville. He was a shoemaker by trade, a strong democrat, and served in the official capacity of justice of the peace and constable for many years previous to his death, which occurred at the advanced age of ninety-one years.

Levi Huntley is the sixth of ten children born to his parents. On the 14th of August, 1861, he was married to Lavina Richards, daughter of Adam Richards, of Uniontown. To their marriage have been born five children, four boys and one girl: William Searight, born June 18, 1863; Orella, born December 4, 1864 (she was graduated from California State Normal School, and a teacher for eight years past); Thomas Allen, born January 4, 1866 (he is a blacksmith); Isaac Newton, born July 8, 1869 (he was educated at Madison College and is also a teacher); Robert Hogsett, born June 3, 1876.

Levi Huntley began life as a farmer; later, he learned the trade of blacksmith with Henry Nycum, of Uniontown, and has, excepting a short interval during the war, worked at it ever since. In March, 1864, he volunteered in the First Kentucky Regiment of Cavalry, which became a regiment of veterans, under the command of General Sherman. He fought at the battles of Kenesaw Mountain and around Atlanta, Ga., and was fighting Johnston when Sherman was making his famous march to the sea. He was principally engaged as a raider while in the service, and at the close of the war, in 1865, he was honorably discharged. He is a school director, and takes a deep interest in educational matters. In politics he is one of Jackson's strong adherents.

WILLIAM HUNT. There is a quiet, unassuming worth of character that often but slowly works its possessor into public notice. There are men who grasp not at high position in their initial efforts in the race of life, but who willingly and cheerfully accept the duties that come to them; and, quietly, yet faithfully and effectively discharge every duty that other more important ones are reposed in them. Such character is portrayed in William Hunt, born February 2, 1836, in Dunbar township, Fayette county, Pa. In 1850 he went to learn his trade with H. W. S. Rigdon, of Uniontown (now of Ottawa, Ill.), and at that time the leading jeweler of Southwestern Pennsylvania. He remained with this eminently practical workman for four and a half years, mastering every detail of the business, gaining the entire confidence and receiving the highest encomiums of his employer. In 1858 he engaged in business at Uniontown, and by close attention to business and honesty in his work, built up the largest trade and has the most extensive jewelry store in the county. His store is now located at 530 Main Street.

William Hunt is a prominent member of the Independent Order of Odd Fellows; of the Blue Lodge, Chapter and Commandery of the Ancient York Masonic fraternity; is Past officer in each, and holds membership in the Royal Arcanum. He was elected in January, 1886, as jury commission on the democratic ticket, and served for three years. Recognized as a man of sound financial views, he was appointed a director of the First National Bank of Uniontown, to fill the vacancy caused by the death of Charles E. Boyle. He is the son of Isaac L. and Hannah (Lincoln) Hunt. His father was a native of Fayette county, Pa., was an industrious farmer and shoemaker in Dunbar township, and at the time of his death, in 1836, was county commissioner. His grandfather, Jacob Hunt, was born in New Jersey, and came to Fayette county in 1790. His mother's father, Benjamin Lincoln, was a native of Reading, Pa., and came to Fayette county in 1790. Benjamin Lincoln was a first cousin of President Lincoln. Hannah (Lincoln) Hunt was born in 1795, in Fayette county, Pa., and died February 10, 1889, at the advanced age of ninety-four years. Her father was a civil engineer and was also a farmer to some extent. William Hunt was married in 1861 to Miss Margaret Simbower, a daughter of Mrs. Mary Simbower, of Uniontown, but a native of Maryland. Mr. Hunt has twelve children: Isaac, Robert W., Mary Frances, Ellen, Margaret, Hannah, Sarah, Lucy, Lottie, Elizabeth, Eve and Benjamin L.

HARVEY C. JEFFERIS was born near Barton's Mill, now the present site of the Chicago and Connellsville coke works, in South Union township, Fayette county, Pennsylvania, January 25, 1832. His father, Nathan Jefferis, was born on the Brandywine, at a point known now as Jefferis Ford, Chester county, Pennsylvania, December 28, 1790. He was a miller by trade, came to Fayette county in 1800 and enlisted in the War of '12 and '15, near its close. He was a member of the Methodist Episcopal church, and a whig in politics. In 1819 he married Mary Cloud, a daughter of Joel Cloud, of Greene county, Pa. She was born July 16, 1799, and is still living, has a remarkable memory and is now in the ninety-first year of her age. She is the mother of five children, two sons and three daughters, all of whom are living: Elizabeth, wife of W. T. Basser, of Urbana, Ohio; Susannah, wife of Harvey Coburn, of Uniontown, Pa.; Mary G., whose first husband was Captain Jacob G. Coburn, of W. Va., and after his death became the wife of James H. Lewis, of this county; Elias C., now of Clayton county, Iowa, and Harvey C. The grandfather, Elias Jefferis, was born about 1768, in Chester county, Pa., was a farmer and weaver, and came to Fayette county in 1800. He married Elizabeth Woodward, and had ten children.

Harvey C. Jefferis was married to Nancy, a daughter of Evan Morre, of South Union township, April 2, 1856, by Rev. W. F. Hamilton, of the Presbyterian church of Uniontown. To their union were born ten children: Mary Elizabeth, born 12th of January, 1857; Evan Morre, born January 1, 1859, married a daughter of Elijah Crossland; Susannah J., born September 8, 1860, wife of Thomas E. King; Elias Biddle, born January 31, 1862; Hannah Morre, born December 3, 1864, a teacher; Salina F., born December 11, 1866, a graduate of Uniontown

George B. Hutchinson.

public schools, and is a teacher; Blanche, born December 21, 1868; John W., born September 19, 1870; Mabel, born October 26, 1872, died February 18, 1885, and Nancy Etta, born November 2, 1877.

Mr. Jefferis is one of the highly respected and one of the substantial farmers of the county. Since 1852 he has been a devoted member of the Cumberland Presbyterian church, and is now one of the church's ruling elders. He has held several township offices, and for twelve years served on the school board, is a republican in politics and voted for the prohibitory amendment to the State constitution, in June, 1889.

GEORGE B. HUTCHINSON, a successful young lawyer of Uniontown, was born in South Union township, Fayette county, Pa., January 25, 1855, and is a son of Isaac and Mary (Brownfield) Hutchinson. His father, now in his seventy-second year, resides near Smithfield, and has been for the most of his life a miller by occupation, but quit that business in 1877 and bought the farm where he now resides. The flouring mill he owned was located in South Union township, known yet as Hutchinson mill, but is now abandoned. Isaac Hutchinson, the grandfather of George B., was a native of New Jersey, and, when at the age of nineteen years, came to Fayette county, and was one of the earliest settlers here.

George B. Hutchinson was reared principally in South Union township, and at the age of eighteen years (in 1873), he entered Waynesburg College, but in 1876 abandoned the full college course on account of his failing health. He entered the office of Robinson F. Downey, of Waynesburg, as a student-at-law, and was admitted to the bar to practice in the courts of Greene county, in June, 1878. In September, 1878, he came to Uniontown, and was admitted to practice in the courts of Fayette county and at once opened an office, and has been successfully engaged in the practice of law ever since. July 12, 1884, he formed a partnership with Thomas R. Wakefield, of Uniontown, the partnership expiring July 12, 1889.

George B. Hutchinson was married to Miss Mary M. Gorley, of Fayette county, and a daughter of Alfred M. and Lucinda Gorley, both natives of the county, June 24, 1879. To their union have been born five children: Howard S., Herschel, Della Pearl, Helen M. and Mary. He is a member of the Knights of Pythias, and on June 26, 1889, was elected by Madison Lodge, No. 419, Knights of Pythias, to represent it at its last sessions of the Grand Lodge, that met at Lancaster, Pa., August 20, 1889.

HENRY J. JENNINGS, proprietor of the Jennings House, was born November, 23, 1827, in Greene county, Pa., and was reared on a farm, and attended the common schools. He remained on the farm till the age of eighteen years, when he went to learn the blacksmith's trade, under James C. Neal, at Carmichael's, Greene county; and continued with him for three years and a half. In 1849 he started a shop for himself at Carmichael's, and worked at blacksmithing till 1857. In 1857 he engaged in keeping hotel, and for seventeen years ran a hotel at Carmichael's. In the spring of 1875 he came to Uniontown, and took the hotel he is now keeping—then known as the Seaton House—but the name was afterwards changed to the Jennings House.

He was married in 1851 to Miss Caroline Hart, daughter of Levi Hart, a farmer of Greene county, who resided near Pierceville, Pa. He has two living children: Salome J. and Mary. The former is the wife of James I. Feathers, of Uniontown. Henry J. Jennings is a son of Jeremiah and Jane (Ewart)

Jennings, natives of England and Ireland, respectively, and both came to America when quite small, with their parents. Jeremiah Jennings was a carpenter by trade, and died at Carmichael's in 1834. Jane Jennings died in the spring of 1875, at the age of ninety-three years.

Mr. Jennings has been quite a successful business man.

HON. DANIEL KAINE (deceased). Rising from an obscure position to a prominent station in life by sheer force of will, Daniel Kaine is presented as one of a distinguished class of men of intellect and indomitable will, who not only deserve success, but who win it.

He was born December 10, 1811, at Lebanon, Pa., and was the son of Daniel and Nancy (Little) Kaine, (the subject of this sketch changed the spelling from Kane to Kaine), both natives of Ireland, and were raised near the Giant's Causeway. Daniel Kaine, Sr., was a revolutionist in the rebellion of 1797 that sought to free Ireland, and was, for that reason, driven out of his native country. He came to Philadelphia, and thence he removed to Cornwall Iron Works, Lancaster county, now Lebanon county, Pa. Barely escaping with his life from Ireland, he was poor and accepted the first work that was offered him, and became a collier. He died in 1817, leaving his wife with several children, one of whom was Daniel Kaine, who came to Connellsville in 1820.

He learned the shoemaking trade under Joseph Herbert; after learning the trade he soon abandoned it, and engaged for a short time as a clerk in a store. He next engaged in the furnace business at Finley or Break Neck Furnace, and by the time he became well versed in the business, the company was dissolved.

He was a great student and acquired a good knowledge of French, Latin and Greek: learning without a teacher while on the shoebench in the store, and at the furnace.

Daniel Kaine began to read law with General Joshua B. Howell in 1839, and was admitted to the Fayette county bar March 18, 1842.

His political career commenced in 1837, when he was elected clerk of the State senate. Afterwards, in 1842, he was elected prothonotary of Fayette county. Near the close of his term of four years he was reelected and served until 1850. In 1850 he was a candidate for the democratic nomination for congress in the congressional district then composed of the counties of Fayette, Greene and Washington. He ran against the Hon. John L. Dawson and was unsuccessful. In 1861 he was elected a member of the house of representatives of Pennsylvania, and was made chairman of the judiciary committee, over such talented and eminent lawyers as Charles R. Buckalew and James Hopkins. Daniel Kaine was considered the finest lawyer in the house, was an active member, and an acknowledged leader. In 1863 he was chairman of the investigating committee, which considered the case of Hon. Simon Cameron, charged with bribing members of the Pennsylvania legislature to secure his election to the United States Senate.

Daniel Kaine was a candidate for president judge of this judicial district in 1865 but was defeated. He was elected a member of the Pennsylvania constitutional convention of 1872, served as chairman of the judiciary committee; and in this body his services were both conspicuous and useful. In 1874 he was a candidate for lieutenant-governor of the State but was defeated in convention assembled at Pittsburg.

In all these positions Mr. Kaine discharged his duties in a manner that was alike creditable to himself and his constituents. It may

R. P. Kennedy.

be truly said of him that in whatever position he was placed, whether in the legislative halls, in the constitutional conventions or in educational and councilmanic deliberations, he labored assiduously to advance the interests and elevate the condition of the people whom he served or represented. To the public spirit, energy and perseverance of Mr. Kaine, probably more than any other man, the citizens of Uniontown are indebted for one of the finest public school buildings and one of the best public schools in Western Pennsylvania. He always manifested a deep interest in the general welfare and prosperity of his adopted town, and ever took a leading part in every movement inaugurated for its improvement. His attainments as a legal counselor and attorney at law are well known and acknowledged, not only in this county, where he practiced for over forty years, but also in other counties as well as in the higher courts to which his practice extended.

He practiced law from 1850 to 1861, acquiring a large and lucrative practice, and applying the most of its proceeds to paying the debts of those whose paper he had previously indorsed. From 1861 to the time of his death in 1886, he acquired a large competency from his extensive law practice.

He was married in 1842 to Eliza Jane Irwin, a native of Wheeling, W. Va. (then Va.). He had seven children, three living and four dead: George B., Charles and Lyman P., living; William, Mary, Katie and Elisha Kent, deceased.

Daniel Kaine died in 1886, at Uniontown, Pa., aged seventy-four years. His life was one of activity and event. He was a self-made man; he enjoyed none of the educational advantages of the present era, nevertheless he was a man of scholarly attainments, a student of industry and research, the hewer out of his own fortune and the honest architect of his own fame.

ROBERT PLAYFORD KENNEDY is one of the most dashing and brilliant attorneys of Fayette county, or indeed, of Pennsylvania herself; and as a criminal lawyer is without a peer among the younger attorneys of the State, in his consummate skill and admirable tact in preparing and presenting a case to a jury. He is truly a fit representative of the professional young men of the day, whose future is bright before them. He is of Scotch-Irish and English extraction, and was born at Brownsville, Fayette county, Pa., August 14, 1856. His father, the Rev. Dr. David Kennedy, is a native of Paisley, Scotland, educated abroad, and received his collegiate and theological degrees in Scotland and Ireland. He came to this country when a young man, and while living in Philadelphia studied medicine and was graduated at Jefferson Medical College. Dr. Kennedy married Miss Caroline Playford, a daughter of Dr. Robert W. Playford, the latter a native of London, England, a graduate of Oxford University, and for many years, one of the most successful and able physicians of Western Pennsylvania.

Robert P. Kennedy was reared at Brownsville at the home of his grandparents, and received his rudimentary education in the schools of his native town. He became, as it were, one of his grandfather's family, and after the death of Dr. Playford in 1867, continued to make his home with his grandmother, Mrs. Margaret A. Playford, until he came to Uniontown in 1878, to finish his legal studies. In 1873 he entered Washington and Jefferson College, Washington, Pa., and for two years stood at the head of his classes, when he left and went to Lafayette College, Easton, Pa., where he graduated in 1877, receiving the degree of Bachelor of Arts. Three years later he had the honorary degree of Master of Arts conferred upon him by the same institution.

He read law at Uniontown with his uncle,

the Hon. Wm. H. Playford, one of the ablest and most eloquent jurists of the day; was admitted to the Fayette county bar in 1879, and immediately entered upon the active practice of his profession. On the retirement virtually, of Mr. Playford from professional work in 1883, Mr. Kennedy succeeded to much of his large and remunerative clientage, and of late years has been prominently identified with many of the most important cases tried in the county. His practice is not confined to the courts of Fayette alone, but in Philadelphia and Pittsburgh, as well as in counties adjacent to Fayette and other points in the State. He has successfully engaged in the trial or argument of causes, and whenever heard is recognized as one of the brightest exponent, of his profession. At home he has a large civil and criminal practice, and in the latter branch of the law may be safely said to be without a superior in Fayette county, where he has the largest criminal practice of any attorney at the bar. He has often defended with astonishing success, men and women who have had testimony submitted against them that seemed to warrant their conviction.

On August 14, 1883, Mr. Kennedy was married at Elizabeth, Pennsylvania, to Miss Ratie C. O'Neil, a daughter of Captain W. W. O'Neil, a prominent business man of Pittsburgh, and the president of the Marine Bank there. They have three children: O'Neil, Harold and Ralph.

In stature Mr. Kennedy is tall and commanding; of mind he is broad an liberal; by temperament he is genial, quick and sympathetic, which, infused into his clear cut, forcible and eloquent addresses, gives him great influence and power over his hearers. Sanguine and cheerful, free and unselfish, he is at once attractive and engaging. As an advocate he wins a case by a careful and searching examination of witnesses, followed by an earnest and masterly presentation of their testimony in his argument to the jury. His future is bright for continued honors in his chosen profession.

ROBERT JUNK is a prosperous farmer and estimable citizen of North Union township, where he was born February 12, 1818. He is a son of John and Sarah (Preston) Junk.

Thomas Junk was a native of Ireland, where he married Elizabeth Small, and had five children: Thomas, Robert, James, Mary and Elizabeth. Thomas Junk came from Ireland to New Jersey, and subsequently removed to North Union township.

John Junk was born in New Jersey, and, when twelve years old, with his father, came to North Union township. He married Miss Mary, daughter of Samuel Preston, a farmer of Dunbar and a native of Ireland. Unto this union were born: James (dead), Samuel (dead), Thomas (dead), Robert, Mary, Eliza, Margaret (dead) and Sarah J. John Junk was engaged in farming and stock raising until his death in 1869.

Robert Junk was educated in the subscription schools of his township. Leaving school he engaged in farming and stock raising on the same farm he now owns in North Union township.

He was married March 10, 1857 to Miss Rebecca Jane, daughter of Peter Humbert. To their union were born six children: John S., Louisa, wife of Albert Bryson, a farmer in North Union township; Mary Eliza, wife of J. J. Dixon, also a North Union farmer; Annie, Sarah and Catherine.

Mr. Junk has devoted his time and attention for years to farm and stock raising.

In politics he takes considerable interest, and is a prohibitionist. A law-abiding and order-loving citizen, he is interested in whatever benefits his township. His family are all members of the United Presbyterian church at Laurel Hill. His farm has been in possession of the Junk family for over 113 years.

THOMAS G. KING was born November 25, 1822, at Connellsville, Fayette county, Pa. He remained at home till the age of fourteen years, and attended the public schools. At fourteen years of age he came to Uniontown, and engaged to work for L. W. Stockton, proprietor of the blacksmith shops of the old stage yard. As Mr. King's father was a blacksmith, Thomas G. almost grew up in the shop, and naturally became an expert in a knowledge of the tools and their use.

He continued to work for the stage company as long as they ran on the road. He was one of the men who ironed the stage which General W. H. Harrison and family rode in from Wheeling to Cumberland, on Harrison's trip to Washington just previous to his inauguration as president. Mr. King went into business for himself long before the stage line went out of existence, but the stage men followed him up, however, and had him to do their work. He was working for the stage company when the great Dr. Bradley stage or mail robberies were committed at Uniontown. Mr. King has continued here ever since, has a large trade, and has accumulated considerable property.

In 1855 he was married to Miss Emily Marietta, of Connellsville, and five children have been born to them—three boys and two girls—Jennie, Ida, Frank, Edward and Thomas. Mr. King is a member of the Masons, of Fort Necessity Lodge, No. 254, of Odd Fellows; of the latter he became a member in 1847. During the war he did all he could in raising recruits for the Union service at Uniontown. His parents were Charles and Phebe (White) King. His father was a native of New Jersey, and came to this country to assist in starting a nail mill for a company below Connellsville, the first factory of the kind started in this section of the country. He was so pleased with the new country that he never returned East to live. He died at his home in Uniontown, in 1865, at the age of seventy-four. His wife died of the cholera in 1852.

JOSEPH HENRY KERR, the efficient, gentlemanly and accommodating cashier of the "Peoples Bank of Fayette County," was born at Mansfield, Allegheny county, Pa., December 13, 1853, and is a son of Rev. B. M. and Margaret A. (McKaig) Kerr.

Joseph H. Kerr is a lineal descendant of Sir Walter Kerr, who fled from Ireland to the United States on account of religious persecution. (For ancestry, see sketch of Rev. B. M. Kerr.) At fifteen years of age, Joseph H. Kerr entered a bank at Ebensburgh, Pa., where he remained for three years. Leaving the bank, he attended the graded schools of New Castle and Mercer, and in February, 1873, entered the banking house of Burd & McClure, of Mercer, Pa., with which he was connected for about three years. June 11, 1877, he was elected as cashier of the Clintonville Bank, and served acceptably until June 15, 1887, when he resigned to accept his present position as cashier of the "Peoples Bank of Fayette County." Its president is James A. Scaright, and teller, T. J. Kerr, the latter a brother of the subject of this sketch.

September 14, 1876, he was united in marriage to Miss Alice I. E. Van Name, of Mercer, Pa. They have three children: Lu Estelle, Alice Josephine and Joseph Henry.

Joseph H. Kerr is a member of the Presbyterian church, and is treasurer of the Grand Lodge of Pennsylvania, Knights and Ladies of Honor. Mr. Kerr is a good cashier, and is well qualified for that important position by natural ability, years of experience and a special aptitude for banking pursuits.

JOHN KIRK, although a son of Scotland, yet so intimately has he identified himself with the development of Fayette county that she claims him by right of adoption. He was born at Barrwick Scotland, January 24, 1845, and is a son of John and Agnes Kirk, both natives of Scotland.

John Kirk (father) was born at Dumfries, in the Midlands of Scotland and was a miner by occupation. In politics he was a chartist, in religion a Catholic, and was a man of sterling worth and integrity. He came to the United States in 1862 and located in Westmoreland county, Pa., where he remained till 1871, locating at Dunbar, in the same year, where he died in 1875. Agnes Kirk, was born in the Highlands of Scotland, and died at Dunbar, in 1878. She was originally a Protestant, but became a Catholic after marriage.

Their children consisted of three sons: James, Peter and John. James was a soldier in the English army; Peter was a private of Company H, One Hundred and First Pennsylvania Volunteer Infantry, in the late war, volunteered in 1863, served till the war ended and died six months afterward.

John Kirk, whose name heads this sketch, at the age of four years, with his parents, emigrated to Northumberland county, England, lived there until 1862, when he with his parents came to the United States. At the age of nineteen he entered the Union army as a private in Battery K, Second Pennsylvania Heavy Artillery, which belonged to Uniontown, and was commanded by Captain Amzi Fuller.

He was discharged from the service in February, 1866, at camp Cadwallader at Philadelphia; returning to Westmoreland county, he began mining, and continued to reside there till 1869, when he moved to Dunbar and took a contract with the Dunbar Furnace Company, to mine iron ore. He continued there till 1871, when he went to California, Nevada, Arizona, and spent about five years on the Pacific slope. In 1875 he returned to Dunbar, and was principally employed in mining ore for the same company. In 1887 he was elected county commissioner on the republican ticket and is now filling that office.

He was married in 1875 to Miss Celia Quinn, a native of Limeric, Ireland, and has six living children: Agnes M., Catherine, Lucy, Della, James E. (dead), Mary and Jane.

John Kirk's early education was of a limited character, attended school only a short time while he resided in England. But he has read and studied all of his life, and is now much above the average man in information obtained from books, and extensive travel.

He displays ability in the administration of the county business, going to the bottom of each case as presented to the board, and, by his strict honesty and close attention to business, is discharging the duties of his office acceptably to everybody.

JOHN H. KING, an "Old Pike" wagoner and a well-to-do farmer of South Union township, is a son of Upton and Polly (Bates) King, and was born on what is now the Colley farm in Menallen township, Fayette county, Pa., May 8, 1820.

Upton King was born near Georgetown, Md., October 11, 1797, and came to Fayette county about 1817, where he lived for many years on the Miller farm. For a long time he was a contractor on the "Old Pike." His wife was Polly Bates, born about 1797 or 1798. They had seven children.

John H. King on leaving home engaged in wagoning on the "Old Pike," a business he pursued for several years. His next employment was in the coal trade, in which he continued for some time. In 1859 he purchased his present farm of fifty acres in South Union township, and since then has given his time to its improvement and cultivation.

In 1844 he married Miss Nancy, daughter of John and Catherine (Grier) Byers, of Menallen township. Mr. and Mrs. King have had six children: Ann Eliza, born April 1, 1844, died May 7, 1862; Sarah M., May 27, 1849, wife of Johnson Rhoderick; Charles W., September 17, 1852, married Sarah A., daughter of John Williams; Darlington J., October 27, 1854, married Mary Hess; Thomas E. August 4, 1859, married Jennie Jeffries, and John A., September 12, 1862.

John H. King and his wife are consistent members of the Methodist Episcopal church at Uniontown. He has been all his life an active and hard working man.

JOHN N. LEWELLEN, a native of Monongalia county, W. Va., was born March 8, 1837. He remained in that county until at the age of eighteen years, working on a farm from childhood until he went to his trade. At the age of eighteen he came to Fayette county, Pa., and apprenticed himself to his uncle, James Lewellen, of Masontown, to learn the blacksmith's trade. At the expiration of his apprenticeship he was married to Miss Mary Ellen Bradley, of Masontown, daughter of James Bradley. He then went to near Morgantown and worked at his trade for three years, carrying on a shop of his own. From thence he removed to Mount Morris, Greene county, Pa., and continued work at his trade for twenty-three years. In 1866 he formed a partnership with his brother Colerman, and engaged in the manufacture of wagons, buggies, carriages, etc. The firm was Lewellen Brothers. They continued in business for sixteen years. In 1882 John N. Lewellen sold out his interest in the business to Ben Clovis, came to Uniontown and engaged in the carriage business, with his sons as partners. They still continue in the same business, and have built up a good trade, and are doing good business.

John N. Lewellen has been a member of the Methodist Episcopal church since his boyhood, and is now an officer in the church. He has five living children, two boys and three girls: Arabella, James W., Carrie, Frank E. and Myra. Frank E. is married and resides with his father. Carrie, the wife of B. F. Billingsley, and is now a resident of Minneapolis, Kansas. James W. married, and is also a resident of Minneapolis, Kansas.

John N. Lewellen is a son of William G. and Mary (Norris) Lewellen, both natives of Monongalia county, W. Va. His father was a farmer, and died in 1880, at the age of sixty-four years. His mother died in 1859, at the age of forty-eight years. She was a consistent Christian and an honorable and respected mother.

The subject of this sketch has been very successful in business. He started in life very poor, but now has a comfortable living and a good home. While at Mount Morris he continued the blacksmith business with his carriage factory. The firm name since coming to Uniontown has been Lewellen & Son. Their chief aim is to manufacture first-class carriage goods. They make a specialty in repairing in all the branches pertaining to the trade, such as wood-work, iron-work, painting and trimming. They have built up quite a reputation in Fayette and adjoining counties, and at present they have a large and commodious carriage shop in Uniontown, fronting on Main street eighty feet and extends back seventy-seven feet. They also own shop property, good residence property, on Mount Vernon and Berkley streets. The junior member, Frank, has been married about one year to Lillie Divvens.

REMEMBRANCE HUGHES LINDSEY, a leading lawyer of the Fayette county bar, is a son of John and Anna (Collins) Lindsey, and was born in Greene county, Pa., April 14, 1845.

His ancestry is traced back through that long-lived and wonderfully energetic Scotch-Irish race. Scotland being located as the birthplace of his paternal great-grandfather, who left that realm of titled classes and aristocratic privileges, and sought the shores of the new world, for a home in the land of free institutions and democratic principles. He landed in the Quaker province, and settled in Lancaster county, Pa., where Mr. Lindsey's paternal grandfather, James Lindsey, was born and reared. He was engaged in mercantile pursuits for a few years, and subsequently moved to Greene county, Pa. His wife was Miss Mary Hughes, a Greene county lady. Colonel Charles Swan, the maternal great-grandfather of Mr. Lindsey, was a prominent man, and a pioneer settler of Greene county, and located there as early as 1769. One of James Lindsey's sons, John Lindsey, was born in 1803, and died in 1865. He was a man of prominence and influence in Greene county, and served as prothonotary and sheriff. He married Miss Anna Collins, the father of whom was of Irish origin, and a native of Delaware. Their eldest son, the late Hon. James Lindsey, was president judge of the Fourteenth Judicial District, and died while in office, in 1864. Judge Lindsey was an able lawyer, a fine jurist and a most exemplary citizen, as well as one of the most popular judges that ever presided over the courts of the district. He had a host of most worthy friends, and his death was universally lamented by all.

Remembrance Hughes Lindsey, the youngest brother of Judge Lindsey, at the age of sixteen entered Waynesburg College, where he continued his studies until he received the appointment as cadet to West Point, and was graduated from West Point school with high distinction, and great credit to himself, in the class of 1869. Soon after his graduation he was promoted to second lieutenant in Third Artilley, United States Army, and served for only a short time, when he resigned. He stood high as an officer in the army, receiving a complimentary letter from General T. W. Sherman, on account of his faithful service as an officer, and his unbending integrity as a gentleman.

While in the army Mr. Lindsey pursued his law studies; returning home, he finished reading law at Waynesburg, sufficiently so, to be admitted to the bar to practice law in 1871. In 1872 he located at Uniontown, and began with remarkable success, the practice of his profession. As a lawyer at the bar, he is quiet and even in his temperament, courteous and polite to his witnesses; has a penetrating manner, and, added to this, he has a polished address and is one of the most finished speakers at the bar. In 1873 he was nominated by his party, the democrats, for the office of district attorney; and was elected by a large majority. He served until 1877, when he declined a re-nomination, and has since devoted his time most assiduously, to the interests of his many clients. He has built up a large and remunerative practice in the courts of Fayette, and his services are often in demand in the courts of adjoining counties.

On December 27, 1877, he was married to Miss Eliza Willson, daughter of the late Hon. Alpheus Willson. (See sketch of Judge Willson.)

The true life of a successful lawyer can never be fully and perfectly written, for some of his greatest efforts are made in his

R. H. Lindsey

library among his books and briefs and others replete with learning and eloquence delivered in the judicial forum are often only preserved in "naked verdicts of juries and formal decrees of courts." So in tracing Mr. Lindsey's career at the bar, as well as any other successful lawyer, we can only make record of a portion of his legal efforts. There is nothing of importance in a case that does not receive his whole attention and to the consideration of which he brings an intelligence and comprehension that always command respect.

WILLIAM McCLEARY is a son of Ewing and Katherine McCleary, and was born at Uniontown October 10, 1813. His father was a native of Adams county, Pa., and came to Uniontown when a young man to follow his trade of hatting.

His mother's maiden name was Katherine Brownfield, a daughter of Thomas Brownfield, who came to the county from Winchester, Va., in the early settlement of the county. Many years he kept the Swan hotel—a great and popular wagon stand in that day.

William McCleary attended Madison College when it was opened, and at the age of seventeen he apprenticed himself to William Crawford, of Uniontown, to learn the saddle and harness trade. He worked four years and four months, and in 1836 went to South Bend, Ind., and started in business for himself. He sold out in the same year, and returned to his native county and became a clerk for his uncle, Colonel Ewing Brownfield. He continued in the general mercantile business at Uniontown until 1845, when he removed to Smithfield, and for twenty-three years was a leading and successful merchant of that section. He sold out in 1868 and returned to Uniontown, and engaged in the same business. He next took an interest in the coke company of Ewing, Boyd & Company, and in this venture he was quite unsuccessful. In 1881 he accepted the position of teller in the People's Bank, and efficiently discharged its duties until the spring of 1889.

He was elected in 1843, captain, and held the office for several years, of the Uniontown volunteers. He served from 1879 to 1882 as jury commissioner of Fayette county, being elected by the people.

William McCleary has always been honest and straightforward in his business transactions, and possesses the confidence of all who trade or transact business with him. He has always held unswerving to the line of moral rectitude and practiced the principles of correct and fair dealings. He has a firm and abiding faith in the Christian religion, and has been a ruling elder in the Presbyterian church for nearly the third of a century.

He was married January 11th, 1838, to Miss Rebecca Swearingen, an estimable woman, and is held in kindliest remembrance by the poor and afflicted—many of whom received material aid and personal attention from her. Her father, William D. Swearingen, was a native of Wellsburg, Va., came to this county when a young man, followed farming and droving, and was known as "Drover Bill." Mr. McCleary has three children — one son and two daughters: Ewing has been engaged in the mercantile business for many years, is now located at Jefferson, Greene county, Pa.; Elizabeth D., wife of the Hon. Matthew G. Holmes, a member of the West Virginia legislature, and owns a large mercantile establishment at Clarksburg, W. Va. — he and his wife were residents for several years of the "Celestial Empire," where Mr. Holmes transacted and controlled a large American and English trade with the "Flowery Kingdom;" Kate, who married Warren W. Mitchell of Illinois. They reside in Washington City, where Mr. Mitchell holds an important position in the public printing office.

JOHN HENRY McCLELLAND was for over forty years one of the active and useful business men of Uniontown. He was a son of William and Rachel (McIntyre) McClelland, and was born at Uniontown, Fayette county, Pennsylvania, June 15, 1823.

His father, William McClelland, came from Washington county to Uniontown and erected the well known McClelland house.

John H. McClelland was reared at Uniontown, and educated in select schools and Madison College. He learned coach making but abandoned the trade shortly after completing his four years apprenticeship. He engaged in the drug business forming a partnership with Dr. Smith Fuller and W. H. Bailey. After some time, Mr. McClelland withdrew from the drug business and removed to Leavenworth, Kansas, where he was successfully engaged for nearly ten years in the general mercantile and drug business. He boated the balloon frame of his building from Cincinnati and witnessed at Leavenworth many terrible and tragic scenes of the Kansas Border Warfare.

About 1857 he returned to Uniontown and formed a partnership with W. H. Lewis, and for ten years engaged in the wholesale and retail grocery business. During the last fifteen years of his life, he was interested in the banks of Uniontown and Connellsville, and was one of the leading directors and was vice-president of the "National Bank of Fayette County" at the time of his death. He was one of the corporators of the "People's Bank of Fayette county," and was largely instrumental in founding the "First National Bank of Connellsville," of which he was a prominent director. His death occurred February 8, 1885.

December 23, 1867, he was married to Miss Margaret J., daughter of John and Jane (West) Brownfield. The former a prosperous farmer of Georges township and a son of Colonel Ben. Brownfield. (See the sketch of F. M. Brownfield.) The latter died on March 2, 1851, and was a daughter of Enos and Margaret (Snyder) West of Uniontown. Mr. West was a sober, industrious man and fine mechanic; his sister, Sarah West, married the celebrated Rev. William Brownfield. Mrs. West was a daughter of Peter Snyder and sister of ex-county commissioner James Snyder and ex-sheriff William Snyder. Mrs. McClelland is a woman of intelligence, culture and refinement, was educated under John G. Hertig and in the select school of Ethelbert Oliphant. She had two brothers: Ben. W., a successful architect in St. Louis, and Enos W., who went to Wichita, Kansas, in 1870, to invest in land, and was murdered for his money.

John H. McClelland was an Odd Fellow, a conservative republican, and for several years previous to his death was a consistent member of St. Peter's Episcopal church of Uniontown. He was a man of fine personal appearance, and the public, after his death, rendered universal testimony to his unswerving integrity, his spotless character and his generous impulses. He began life with no capital, but by his keen foresight, excellent management and honest dealing he amassed an estate worth $100,000; and was greatly missed in social and business circles.

WM. B. McCORMICK is of Irish descent, his father having come to America when only seven years of age. He was a weaver by trade, also a farmer and a school teacher, spending the greater part of his time in the latter calling. He died March 29, 1850, at the age of 62 years. The mother of W. B. McCormick was a native of New

Jersey, and died December 5, 1841. W. B. McCormick was born August 25, 1821, near Smithfield, Fayette county, Pa., and came to Uniontown with his parents in 1832. He was brought up in the vicinity of Uniontown on his father's farm, and attended Madison College. In 1840 he taught a select school in North Union township, and afterwards taught in the public schools at intervals for twenty years. He was principal and superintendent of the public schools of Uniontown from 1848 to 1860. At the commencement of the war he engaged in butchering at Uniontown, and continued till 1877, when he turned his business over to his son George. He was very successful in business, having one of the largest list of customers of the town. In 1877 he engaged in the grain business at Uniontown with his youngest son, Milton A. McCormick. In 1881 they removed to Fairchance, and, with the grain, added the lumber business, and have built up a paying business, conducted and principally managed by Milton A. McCormick. W. B. McCormick has retired from active business, and gives the greater part of his attention to his bees, and on this subject he is regarded as authority. He has served as a member of the town council for five or six years, has been a member of the Methodist Episcopal church ever since he was fifteen years of age, and a trustee of his church for a number of years. His parents were Noble and Ester (Hadden) McCormick. He is a Mason, Knight Templar, and has been treasurer of the Blue Lodge of the Chapter and Commandery for the past ten years. He is a director and secretary of the Uniontown Water Works Co., and was the instigator in starting this improvement in the borough, having advocated it for several years before the measure was adopted, and which is now acknowledged to be one of the greatest blessings of the town. He was married September 10, 1842, to Miss Susan Allen, daughter of Matthew Allen, who served as high sheriff of the county for two terms. He was first elected in 1837 and re-elected in 1850 on the democratic ticket. He was a native of this county, and died August 18, 1875. They have seven living children: Mary, George A., William C., Milton A., Ellen Jane, Lizzie and Sophia. George A. is the present nominee of the democratic party for sheriff of the county. Mary, married to Frank L. Brook, of Ohio, now of Uniontown, and is a dealer in agricultural implements. William C., engaged in the grain and feed business on Fayette street, and is a member of the town council. Ella Jane is married to William B. Thorndell, a native of Uniontown, and where he now resides. Lizzie and Sophia are single and at home.

W. B. McCormick is a good citizen, highly respected by all who know him, and is one to whom the people can go for advice and assistance without fear of rebuff. He is a man whose desire is to benefit his fellow-man and never to harm anybody.

FRANK W. McCRAY was born on the old McCray homestead in Menallen township, Fayette county, Pa., November 6, 1830. His father, John McCray, was also born in Menallen township, and was married to Margaret Duff, a native of Ireland, who came to America in 1810, at the age of twelve years.

Frank W. McCray was married to Mary Jane Miller, daughter of Warnick Miller, August 13, 1863. (For her ancestry see sketch of John Campbell.) To their union have been born five children, three of whom are living: Maggie M., wife of M. H. Hare; Ella R.; Warnick Miller, born February 26, 1867, and was drowned July 13, 1886, at West Point and his remains lie buried there, and where he has a fine monument erected by his comrades to his memory. It was a sudden ending of a young life, that seemed to be full of promise. His position in his class at West Point, although its youngest member, was most excellent. His character was clean and without a stain, and his mental capacity was beyond the average at his age. His death was mourned by every member of his class. His appointment was secured by C. E. Boyle, through a competitive examination. At West Point he stood 12th in a class of eighty-five members; George W. McCray, the youngest, was born April 21, 1877.

Frank W. McCray was educated in Menallen. His first teacher was William Beggs, who taught in an old log school house that stood on the present site of Grace church. For twenty years, Mr. McCray has been an Odd Fellow. For the past thirteen years he has been successfully engaged in mercantile business; five years at Uniontown and eight years at Hopwood.

SAMUEL McGIE, the enterprising and prosperous proprietor of the McGie livery, feed and sale stables, of Uniontown, is a son of George McGie and was born within one mile of Uniontown, September 19, 1855.

He received his education in the public schools of Uniontown. At nineteen years of age he entered a printing office, but that business not suiting him, he engaged in plastering for four or five years. Leaving plastering he engaged in his present successful livery business, at Uniontown.

In 1872 he was married to Miss Rosa Wilda, daughter of Nicholas Wilda, an emigrant from Germany to the United States in 1808. They have six children living: Melvina, Lelia, Eddie, Jacob, John and Fenia.

Samuel McGie has been extensively engaged at Uniontown in building and selling houses. He has built and owned 152 houses, and at the present time is the owner of thirty houses at that place. He has been surpassed by few in the number of houses that he has built. He is a quick, stirring trader, and is very beneficial to the business interests of Uniontown.

McGie's livery and feed stables are substantial, commodious and very conveniently arranged to accommodate a large and constantly increasing patronage. Excellent saddle horses and first-class teams are furnished promptly and at ordinary prices. He has a fine stock of carriages and buggies, and is accommodating and obliging to all.

HENRY McGLAUGHLIN, one of the industrious citizens of North Union township, is a son of Joseph and Mary (Moore) McGlaughlin, and was born near Evans Station, North Union township, Fayette county, Pa., October 8, 1840.

George McGlaughlin (grandfather) was a native of Ireland, and came to Fayette county early in life. He was a soldier in the War of 1812.

Joseph McGlaughlin (father) was born March 4, 1797, in Fayette county, where he died January 4, 1865. He married Miss Mary, daughter of Abraham Moore, of North Union township. They reared a family of seven sons and three daughters. Three of the sons were in the Civil War, where one (Hamilton) was taken prisoner and died soon after his release and return home.

Mrs. McGlaughlin, who now resides in Uniontown, was born January 30, 1803.

Henry McGlaughlin attended the common schools of North Union township, but at an early age left school and engaged in farming. After several years' experience as a farmer, he engaged in his present business of quarrying and coal mining.

February 11, 1869, he was married to Miss Ellen, daughter of William Hanan. (See his sketch.) They have had seven children, of whom three are living: Emma, born April 28, 1872; Laura Nettie, born September 23, 1874, and Harry Cannon, born August 26, 1877.

Henry McGlaughlin is a democrat and has served three years as school director. He and his wife are members of the Methodist Episcopal church. He is an industrious, temperate and persevering man, and has acquired by his own efforts a fair competency of material wealth.

STEPHEN LESLIE MESTREZAT was born at Mapletown, Greene county, Pa. He attended Waynesburg College, and graduated from there in 1869. He subsequently entered the celebrated Washington and Lee University at Lexington, Va., from whose portals he came forth with high honors as a law graduate in the class of 1871. In September, 1871, he was admitted to the bar at Waynesburg, where he had been previously registered as a student-at-law.

In 1871 he went west, but after an extended trip returned to Pennsylvania, and was admitted to the Fayette county bar December 7, 1872, and January 16, 1873, opened a law office at Uniontown. On April 1, 1875, he formed a partnership with the late Judge C. E. Boyle. The firm was Boyle & Mestrezat. The partnership lasted until in November, 1888. (See Boyle's sketch.) Boyle & Mestrezat were retained as counsel for all of the principal corporations of the county, and employed in all of the leading and celebrated criminal cases tried in the county: among others might be mentioned the famous Mollie Maguire cases in 1881, and the great Nutt and Duke case.

S. L. Mestrezat has always taken an active part in politics, and is a stanch democrat, has served several times as congressional conferee, and was chairman of the democratic county committee in 1884 and 1885. He was a delegate to the democratic state convention in 1882 and in 1886. In 1877 he received the nomination from his party for district attorney of Fayette county, was elected, and served from 1878 to 1881. He took an active and leading part in all the campaigns that Judge Boyle was engaged in during their partnership.

He is the son of Jean Louis Guillaume and Mary A. (Hartley) Mestrezat, both natives of Pennsylvania, and who now reside at Mapletown, Greene county, Pa.

His paternal grandfather, Charles Alexander Mestrezat, was a native of France, came to this country in 1795, and was engaged in the mercantile business at Mapletown up to his death in 1815. His maternal grandfather, Matthias Hartley, was a farmer of Greene county, and of English-Irish descent.

He was married on August 1, 1888, to Miss Eliza Willson Ewing, of Uniontown.

He is now the solicitor for the Baltimore & Ohio Railroad Company, has retained about all the practice of the old firm of Boyle & Mestrezat, and has acquired additional practice. Hard study and close application to business have given him the power to quickly scan a case, to thoroughly grasp its salient points and intricate bearings. He brings to his aid, in the presentation of his case to the jury, an eloquence in language and an earnestness in manner that in many instances has won success, where success seemed impossible.

WILLIAM H. H. MILLER. In the journalistic history of Fayette county, one of the papers that will never be forgotten was the old *American Standard.* The last editors of this paper were Jacob B. and William H. H. Miller.

William H. H. Miller was born at Rockford, Ill., December 27, 1837, brought to Uniontown when quite small, and attended Madison College. Leaving school, he learned "the art preservative of all arts" with his brother-in-law, John F. Beazell, who at that time was the editor of the *Pennsylvania Democrat*. Mr. Miller became the publisher of this paper in 1867, which was then called the *American Standard*. He published the paper from 1867 to 1879, when he sold it. The *Republican Standard* of to-day is the same paper.

In 1882 he engaged in his present dry goods business, has a large store, and enjoys a good and increasing trade.

He was elected school director in Uniontown in 1883, and served as such for six years. He is a member of the Presbyterian church, deacon in the church, and holds membership in the Royal Arcanum.

W. H. H. Miller has had business training as well as editorial experience; working on his uncle's farm in Washington county, Pa., from the twelfth to the sixteenth year of his age. In 1856 he went to Pittsburgh and engaged in the coal business, and boated coal down the Ohio and Mississippi to Cincinnati, Louisville and Memphis. He left the coal office for the editorial tripod in 1867, at a time when the local correspondence of the county press was generally of a political character; was one among the first editors of Southwestern Pennsylvania to establish a corps of regular local correspondents in the different sections of the county. He largely assisted in making Fayette county papers what they now are, and better home newspapers are nowhere to be found in the State.

He was married in 1858, to Miss Margaret Stewart, of Pittsburgh, a daughter of Hugh and Jane Stewart. Hugh Stewart was a manufacturer of carding machines. Mr. Miller has six living children: Emma, Elizabeth, Ada, James Todd, Edith and John Beazell. Two of his children died young: Frank and Jacob B.

W. H. H. Miller is a son of John and Mary Ann (Amos) Miller. His father was a native of Greenbrier county, W. Va., and carried on a large tannery at Uniontown; removed to Rockford, Ill., where he died in 1840. His mother was a native of Howard county, Md. (near Baltimore). She died at her home in Pittsburgh, in May, 1864, at the age of sixty-three years.

William H. H. Miller has never been idle; as a farm hand, coal dealer, clerk, printer, editor, and as a merchant; has always been honest and active, though not worrying or rushing. He is a self-made man, and whatever success he has achieved has been the work of his own brain and hands.

J. E. MOFFITT, D. D. S., the oldest practitioner of dentistry in Uniontown, was born in Canton, Ohio, May 5, 1838. He studied dentistry and commenced practice with an older brother (J. W.), in 1857, in Harrisburg, Pa. Dr. Moffitt first came to Uniontown in 1873, with his father, and engaged in the manufacture of teeth, on Fayette street. It was the first manufactory of that kind west of the Allegheny Mountains.

In the spring of 1876 he bought out Dr. Young, the first resident dentist of Uniontown, and resumed the practice of his profession in Uniontown, where he has been engaged in active practice ever since. He is unmarried, and resides in the house where his parents died, corner of Church and Redstone streets.

Dr. J. E. Moffitt is the son of Rev. John J. Moffitt, a worthy preacher of the Methodist Episcopal church.

Rev. John J. Moffitt, D. D., was born near Boundbrook, N. J., July 23, 1811. His family lived in New Jersey for three or four generations previous to his birth. In

P H Moore

1827 he came to Northumberland county, Pa., where an older brother resided, and with whom he remained till he reached manhood. In 1832 he was married in Cumberland county to Miss Charlotte Eppley. Her family had been settled in Dauphin, Cumberland and Lancaster counties, for several generations. Mrs. Moffitt was born October 25, 1809, and died in April, 1885, in the seventy-sixth year of her age.

In 1836 Rev. J. J. Moffitt went west and settled at Canton, Ohio. He entered the ministry in 1838, of the Methodist Episcopal church, and held the following appointments, consecutively: Sandyville, Carrollton and Richmond, Ohio; West Newton and Redstone, in Pa.; Ohio Circuit, W. Va.; Cadiz, Ohio; South Common, Allegheny City; and was elected to the General Conference in 1856, presiding elder of Cambridge, Barnesville and McConnellsville districts, in Ohio for ten years. He was then stationed at Salem, Ohio; McKeesport, Pa.; Uhrichsville, Ohio; Uniontown, Pa.; Dawson, Uniontown Mission, Marchland and Meyersdale. Meyersdale was his last regular appointment. At the conference of 1879 he took a superanuated relation and settled at Uniontown, where he lived until his death January 15, 1881, in the seventieth year of his age. At the conference of 1880 he was made a member of the court of appeals and received the honorary degree of doctor of divinity from Scio University, Ohio, in 1872.

No man ever lived and died at Uniontown who had more the respect of the people than Rev. Moffitt. His Christian bearing and courteous manner towards the entire community were such as to merit and to receive the commendation of all. He was first stationed at Uniontown in 1873, and for three years he was pastor of the church. Many additions were made to the church roll during his ministry. In 1879 he returned to Uniontown and made it his permanent home.

He was an able preacher, never enthusiastic, but always earnest, plain and strong; and was a man of good judgment and strong character.

PRESLEY H. MOORE, one of the leading operators in the manufacture of the world-renowned Connellsville coke, in Western Pennsylvania (the "workshop of the New World"), was born in Rostravor township, Westmoreland county, Pa., February 7, 1839. He is a son of Ebenezer and Nancy B. (Hurst) Moore.

His grandfather, Robert Moore, in early life (1780) removed from Cecil county, Md., and settled in Rostravor township. He was married in 1780, before leaving Maryland, to Miss Jane Power, a sister of Rev. James Power, D. D., the first Presbyterian to settle and to preach in the "Western Wilds." Dr. Power came from Eastern Pennsylvania and preached in Fayette and Westmoreland counties in 1774. Robert Moore erected a large two-story log house, into which he moved and lived during his life. He was one of that sturdy class of men who settled in the region of Dunlap's Creek, Rehoboth and Round Hill churches. They were decidedly Presbyterian and formed the nucleus for those churches which have stood so long and whose old members have left the impress of their lives upon the generations to follow them.

Ebenezer Moore, the youngest of Robert Moore's six children, was born August 3, 1793, and was the last of the family to marry, on account of remaining at home to care for his aged and feeble mother. In 1846 he removed to the old Blackstone farm, in Tyrone township, Fayette county, Pa. His wife had an inherited part in the farm, and he bought the interests of the other heirs and added to the farm by purchase, 150 acres of adjoining land. These two farms were heavily underlaid with coal, and it was here that the coke interest was started which has since been developed by his two younger sons, J. W. and P. H. Moore. Ebenezer Moore was six feet in height and weighed 190 pounds. He had a strong frame and a large, well shaped head. He kept his face smoothly shaved, was always genteel and respectable in appearance and was a fine looking man. Better than this he was a man of sterling integrity, was strictly honest, fair in his transactions and was a man of great kindness of heart, while his tenderness of feeling was one of his distinguishing characteristics. His attachments to his home and family were very strong, and he loved them with the greatest devotion. As a business man, he at times appeared rigid though always just, and seldom made mistakes.

He was a Presbyterian, was modest, unassuming, had a high regard for men, and was twice chosen elder in the church. He did not accept, however, on account of his lack of self confidence, yet he had mental powers that, with more self assurance, would have given him a high position in the church. Withal he loved to converse on Christian topics, and at his home ministers of the gospel were often found, were always welcome, and he loved their society. In politics he was an "old line whig," and was positive in his faith. He was an intelligent reader, and took a deep interest in the passing events of his time. He conversed with great earnestness and upon the political as well as upon religious issues of his day. In 1844 he represented Westmoreland county in the legislature, and it is an interesting fact that he received all the votes except five that were cast in his own township.

In May, 1833, Ebenezer Moore married Miss Nancy Blackstone Hurst, daughter of James and Sarah Hurst, of Mt. Pleasant township, Westmoreland county, Pa. They reared a family of six children in the house in which Mr. Moore was born. The old house is still standing. The farm is now owned by the eldest son, James H., and for 109 years has been in the possession of the family. Mrs. Moore was a granddaughter of James and Priscilla Blackstone, of Fayette county. They had six children: one died in infancy; Sarah Jane, died February 23, 1858, at thirteen years of age; the eldest son, James H., married Miss Amanda Thirkield, of Fayette City, and resides at Monongahela City; the second son, Rev. R. B. Moore, D. D., of the Presbyterian church, married Miss Louisa J., youngest daughter of James Paul, of Fayette county, but now of Tiffin, Ohio; the third son, John W., married Miss Elizabeth Stauffer, of Connellsville; was engaged for several years in buying and selling stock, and then engaged in the coke business, and now resides at Greensburg.

Presley H. Moore came with his parents to Tyrone township when six years of age, and was educated at the Mt. Pleasant Classical Institute and continued to work on his father's farm until 1879. In 1879 he removed to Uniontown and with his brother, J. W. Moore, engaged in the coke business, the name of the firm being "The Redstone Coke Company, Limited." In 1881 Col. J. S. Schoonmaker was admitted as a partner. In 1885 J. W. Moore retired from the firm, disposing of his interest to P. H. Moore and Colonel Schoonmaker. These works have been run most successfully since their establishment in 1880, up to the present time.

The Redstone Coke Works, now owned and operated by P. H. Moore, are situated three miles south of Uniontown, at Brownfield Station, on the S. W. P. R. R. The property embraces over nine hundred acres of coal land, with a frontage of two miles along the railroad. On May 1, 1881, there were only seventy-five ovens, now Moore & Co. have 450 ovens and employ about five hundred men. Two excellent stone-quarries have been opened near the ovens and quite a town is building on the property. A reservoir and a mountain stream afford an abundance of water for coke or other manufacturing purposes. These works are known as "Moore's Works."

Presley H. Moore is one of the prominent business men of Fayette county. For nearly ten years he has successfully conducted one of the large businesses of one of the great manufacturing industries in the United States.

SAMUEL MORRIS is a native of Greene county, Pa., and was born May 25, 1848. He is a son of Isaac A. and Nancy (Everly) Morris. Isaac Morris is of Welsh descent, and was born at Uniontown, near the present site of the S. W. P. R. R. depot, in 1812. He is now living, in his seventy-eighth year, in Greene county, Pa., near the West Virginia line. Nancy Everly Morris is of Scotch-Irish descent, and was born in Monongalia county, West Virginia (then Virginia), near the celebrated old Ft. Martin of Revolutionary days.

Samuel Morris was married in 1873 to Miss Annie V. Stewart, of Stewartstown, W. Va., who died in 1875. She left one child, a son, Isaac Stewart Morris. Samuel Morris's second wife was Miss Emma J. Doty, a daughter of Susan Doty, to whom he was married in 1882, and she is a native of Carmichaels, Greene county, Pa. By this marriage they had two children: Jessie B. and Kiser P.

Samuel Morris was brought up on a farm in Greene county, Pa.; he attended the common schools, and in 1876 engaged in the general mercantile business at Pt. Marion. He continued in business there for five years. He came to Uniontown January 2, 1881, and engaged as a clerk for L. Kuth, the confectioner, and sold goods on the road through Washington and Greene counties. In 1884, he took a position with Markle & Fulton, who at that time were doing the largest grocery business in Uniontown. In 1887 he left their employ and bought the grocery and business of W. B. Thorndell, No. 420, Main street.

He has built up a large trade and is an enterprising merchant. He stands well with the public and with all who know him.

SPRINGER A. MORRIS, county commissioner, was born at Perryopolis, Perry township, Fayette county, Pa., October 6, 1827. He was reared partly in his native township, and later removed to Uniontown, attending school at both places.

At the age of nineteen years he commenced to learn the trade of a carpenter with Charles D. Turner, of Uniontown. He completed his apprenticeship and worked at his trade till 1864. In 1864 he engaged in farming in North Union township, and has since followed farming, and owns a nice farm of sixty acres on Redstone creek, where he now resides.

In 1887 he was elected county commissioner on the republican ticket, and is now serving his time. He is president of the board, fills the position with honor to himself and with satisfaction to the other members of the board. He is a man of good judgment and strong common sense.

He was married, in 1851, to Miss Nancy J. Turner, the daughter of James D. Turner, of Uniontown. They have seven living children: William, Eliza, Charles, Milton, Emily, Rush and James.

William is now in Iowa, employed in farming. Eliza is married to Skiles Rutter, and is now living in Uniontown. Charles is in

Iowa, working at the carpenter trade. Milton is a carpenter in Uniontown. Emily is married to John White, who is a clerk in Uniontown, but lives in North Union township. Rush and James are single, and reside at home.

Springer A. Morris is the son of Dr. William and Eliza (Marchand) Morris. His father was a practicing physician of this county, a native of Uniontown, and died in 1828. The Morris family came originally from New Jersey to the county.

His mother was a native of Fayette county, Pa. She died in 1834, was the daughter of Dr. Daniel Marchand, who was a practicing physician of the county, and died many years ago. S. A. Morris was left an orphan at the age of seven years.

Rev. William Brownfield, who married Mr. Morris, performed the same ceremony for his father and grandfather. He is a good citizen, and held in high esteem by his friends and neighbors.

PAOLI SHEPPARD MORROW, a well established and successful member of the Fayette county bar, is a son of John C. and Elizabeth (Sheppard) Morrow, and was born in East Huntingdon township, Westmoreland county, Pa., March 8, 1848.

His great-grandfather, Samuel Morrow, emigrated from County Tyrone, Ireland, to Adams county, Pa., prior to the revolutionary war, and subsequently removed to Westmoreland county. Samuel Morrow, with several of his brothers who emigrated with him, were the ancestors of many of the Pennsylvania, Ohio, West Virginia, Iowa, Kentucky and California Morrows. One descendant was the well-known Rev. James Morrow, of Southern Ohio. Samuel Morrow had a son, James Morrow, the father of John C. Morrow. March 6, 1825, John C. Morrow was born; and on April 22, 1847, married Miss Elizabeth, daughter of Paoli and Catherine (Tarr) Sheppard. Paoli Sheppard was a soldier of the War of 1812, was named Paoli by his father, Henry L. Sheppard, a native of Massachusetts, and a soldier at the battle of that name. Catherine Sheppard, a woman of much intelligence, was a daughter of Hon. Gasper Tarr, son of a revolutionary soldier, and a relative of Christian Tarr, a Pennsylvania member of congress. The Tarr family was noted for their intelligence.

Paoli S. Morrow was reared on a farm, and educated in common and select schools and Mt. Union College, Ohio. He taught thirteen consecutive terms in the common schools of Fayette and Westmoreland counties, and afterwards he engaged in the practice of the law. He read law with ex-Lieutenant Governor John Latta, of Greensburg, and Hon. Charles E. Boyle, of Uniontown; and after passing a rigid examination was admitted to the Fayette county bar, September 2, 1878. In 1879 he entered into partnership with D. M. Hertzog, and has ever since enjoyed a constantly growing and lucrative practice. The firm of Morrow & Hertzog is sufficiently well known in Fayette county to need no comment. Mr. Morrow is also a member of the Westmoreland county bar, and of the supreme court of Pennsylvania.

December 25, 1878, he was married at Uniontown by Rev. S. S. Gilson, to Miss Catherine, daughter of Samuel N. Long, of Connellsville, and granddaughter of Robert Long, a well-known citizen of Fayette county. They have three living children: Helen J., born April 13, 1881; Samuel L., born September 23, 1883, and Katy, born February, 1885. Morrow & Hertzog, in addition to their other legal business, have been engaged in the settlement of as many estates, and have acted as counsel for as many trustees, guardians, executors and administrators as any other attorneys now at the Uniontown bar, and own as good a law library as is found in the county. Mr. Morrow makes little pretensions to oratory, is a plain unassuming speaker, and a cautious and safe counselor. He knows his books well, studies his cases carefully, and is well informed on both the statutes and the decisions of the supreme court. A pleasant and sociable gentleman, a well-read lawyer, a close student, and is deserving of the success he is achieving.

ANDREW J. MOSER, a prominent and successful merchant of Uniontown, is a native of Georges township, Fayette county, Pa. He was born August 26, 1844, and raised on the farm, where he remained till at the age of twenty-two years, and attended the schools of Smithfield. At the age of twenty-two years he engaged in the general mercantile business at Masontown, and remained there for two years, thence to McClellandtown, there continued in the same line for about three years. Returned to Masontown, engaged in the same business, and remained there four years longer. He then removed to Uniontown and formed a partnership with E. T. Walters, of Masontown, and engaged in the grocery business. Mr. Walters sold out to H. M. Kyle, of Smithfield, but this partnership lasted but a short time, when the firm became Moser & Brother. The firm of Moser & Brother is now one of the most enterprising grocery firms in the county. Ephraim F. Moser, the brother, lives on a farm, and Andrew J. Moser manages the business of the store. A. J. Moser was married in 1873, to Miss Mary E. Allebaugh, the daughter of Mr. James M. Allebaugh, of German township, who was a prominent farmer of that township, but is now a resident of Masontown. They have three living children, two boys and one girl: Howard Allen, Herman Lee and Elmira M. Mr. Moser is a member of the German Baptist church.

His parents were John and Amy (Sterling) Moser, both born in Fayette county, Pa. His father was a farmer of Georges township, and died in 1888, in his seventy-ninth year. His grandfather Moser was one of the early settlers of Fayette county. His maternal grandfather, John Sterling, was also a farmer of the county.

A. J. Moser was born and reared a democrat, and is rock-ribbed in his faith.

DAVID PORTER, M. D. One of the most eminent physicians of Southwestern Pennsylvania, distinguished alike by his classical learning and his medical skill, was Dr. David Porter, deceased. He was born in the city of Wheeling, W. Va., March 17, 1794.

His father, William Porter, was a fine teacher at Washington, Pa. He was quite prominent in the "Whiskey Insurrection," and removed to Wheeling, Va. (now W. Va.), in 1794, to escape arrest. He remained in Wheeling for four years, when he accompanied William Darby (author of Darby's Universal Gazetteer), to Louisiana. Mr. Darby was employed by the government to make a very important survey in Louisiana. William Porter accompanied him on his trip South and while there contracted yellow fever and passed away.

At the age of six years Dr. Porter was adopted and made heir by Capt. William Woolsey, who commanded a privateer during the Revolutionary War, and whose commission is now in the possession of Mrs. David Porter of Uniontown. Captain Woolsey was an old friend of Dr. Porter's father and owned a very fine farm in Rostraver township, Westmoreland county, near the Fayette county line. Dr. Porter received his knowledge of the languages under Gad Tower, an excellent classical scholar and a superior teacher of his day.

On attaining his majority Dr. Porter chose medicine as his life-vocation, and began its study under Dr. Louis Marchand, and subsequently attended lectures in Baltimore. Leaving Baltimore he practiced two years at home when he attended a course of lectures at Philadelphia, where he was taught by the celebrated Dr. Benjamin Rush, and was graduated from Jefferson Medical College. After graduating he practiced in Rostraver township, then at Brownsville, and from Brownsville he removed to Pittsburgh where he secured a large practice but soon left Pittsburgh on account of his wife's declining health: he returned to Rostraver. He practiced in Rostraver for thirty years, and in 1869 removed to Uniontown, where he died September 22, 1875, at the age of eighty-one years.

Dr. Porter was married to Miss Lucinda Jennings November 9, 1820. She was the daughter of Rev. Obadiah Jennings, of Washington, Pa. Unto this union were born three children: Obadiah Jennings Porter was a physician and died of consumption March 5, 1860; William Findlay Porter, who went to Texas in 1858 for his health, and died with consumption, and Margaret Woolsey Porter, who married Levi Johnson, June 5, 1845, died in April, 1888, near Belle Vernon, where they owned a country seat.

Dr. Porter was happily married a second time to Miss Rebecca Miller, a daughter of John Miller, deceased, an esteemed citizen of Uniontown. The result of this last marriage was one daughter: Ada A., who was a graduate of Mantua Seminary, Philadelphia. Returning to Rostraver, after her graduation, she brightened the home circle with her presence but a short time, when she passed away. The sadness brought over their threshold by her departure, was the cause of her parents leaving their beautiful Westmoreland home, and locating at Uniontown.

The opinion of Dr. John Dixon, an eminent physician of Pittsburgh, was that "Dr. Porter was fifty years in advance of his age," and the opinion was correct. He wrote ably on medical subjects before medical journals were common, and after they came into general use he contributed valuable articles to their columns. He always enjoyed a large practice, and was held in the highest esteem by all who knew him.

His judgment was clear and decisive, and the ablest physicians called him in consultation. Aside from his valuable professional labors, the virtues of his life, his superior mind, his intelligence and philanthropy fully entitle him to honorable and commendable mention in this work.

ANDREW PRENTICE. In 1817 the "National Road" was projected to cross the Alleghenies, to bind more closely the East to the West. It was built from Washington City west into Indiana. The road was commonly called the "Old Pike," and drivers on it were known as "Pike Boys."

Andrew Prentice, the oldest "Pike Boy" now living in Fayette county, was born on Chestnut street, in Philadelphia, Pa., September 11, 1815, and was brought from his native city by his parents to Uniontown in 1817. He attended Madison College, and at twenty years of age commenced driving a six-horse team from Uniontown to Baltimore. He afterward drove one of his father's teams from Cumberland, Md., to Wheeling, taking him nine days to make the trip. He hauled bacon from Wheeling to Cumberland, and often hauled tobacco from Little Washington on his trips to the East. His re-

Andrew Prentice

turn loads were chiefly made of store goods, and his Conestoga wagon generally bore from sixty-five to seventy-five hundred-weight of whatever he transported over the road. He was one of the best drivers on the "Old Pike," and after fourteen years' service, from night driving and great exposure, he was compelled to leave the road; but, during this period of time, he never lost anything, and never made but one mistake, for which he was docked $40. Leaving the Pike, he was next employed by Mrs. Seaton to take charge of the Seaton Hotel (now the Jennings House); and when she sold out four years later, Andy Prentice went to the National Hotel on Morgantown street, and for two years managed the National, also the stage office, for Colonel Samuel Elder, and remained in the same capacity for one year with his successor, Hon. Joshua Marsh.

Some of the "Old Pike boys" who are still living in the county, and associates of Mr. Prentice, are: Philip Johnson (colored), Wm. Worthington, John Snider, Peter Frasier, James Smith, Ellis Woodword and George McGlaughlin, aged ninety-eight, ninety-one, seventy-two, seventy-three, seventy-two, seventy-four and sixty-eight years, respectively.

In 1856 Mr. Prentice rented a store-room on Morgantown street, and carried on a grocery store for thirteen years, when he sold out and opened another grocery which he ran for seven years. He retired after twenty years of hard work in that business. As a driver, a hotel manager and a grocer, he was always known as being strictly temperate and honest. He was a successful business man, and accumulated considerable wealth.

Andrew Prentice has always helped the churches, the needy and worthy poor, and has aided in all good causes. When the country stood aghast at the Johnstown horror, and in the same moment rallied and poured in its contributions, Andrew Prentice headed Uniontown's list of contributors with $200, the largest individual contribution made in the county.

He has been for half a century on the subscription roll of the *Presbyterian Banner*, published at Pittsburgh; when he was in Pittsburgh, in 1887, the publishers of the *Banner* presented him with a nicely bound copy of a work entitled "The Gist of It, or a Philosophy of Human Life," by the Rev. Thomas E. Barr, A. B. The volume was given as an expressive token of esteem they held for Andy Prentice, and his long and earnest support of their paper.

He is a son of Thomas and Isabella (Laisk) Prentice. Thomas Prentice's father was a native of Scotland, and came to this country while yet a young man, and married in Philadelphia a young lady, native of that city. Thomas Prentice was a hard worker, a good business man and temperate and abstemious in his habits. He helped to make the National road, and kept two or three teams running all the time. He hauled a large amount of coal, and was engaged in the manufacture of brick, used in the construction of the older churches and brick buildings of Uniontown. Thomas Prentice's wife was a Presbyterian, and passed to the unseen world on February 27, 1842, at the early age of forty-two years. Thomas Prentice followed her in 1869, having reached his eighty-fifth mile stone along the rugged pathway of life.

Thomas and Isabella (Laisk) Prentice had six children, namely: Andrew, Elizabeth (died young); Isabella, wife of John Crossland; Jane, wife of W. K. Cooper, and dead; Thomas, married Elizabeth Brownfield, and Henry (dead). In 1825 he shook hands with La Fayette, when that renowned general was making his triumphant tour through the country; he has also shook hands with Andrew Jackson, at the time the general stopped over night at the Eagle

House with his slaves, on his way to Washington to be inaugurated president; of Henry Clay, Hayes, Curtin, Grant and Blaine; and he is thankful to his maker that he is as "true blue" republican as ever grew. He has been a commendable member of the Presbyterian church since June 1, 1841, joining under Rev. Joel Stoneroad, and is now one of the "landmarks" of Uniontown.

WILLIAM A. RANKIN, a comfortably situated farmer and a reliable citizen, is a son of John and Nancy Huston (Bryson) Rankin, and was born on the farm where he now resides in North Union township, Fayette county, Pa., February 11, 1858.

William Rankin, Sr., grandfather, was a native of Pennsylvania, married Miss Eliza Junk (see sketch of Robert Junk), and was a native of Fayette county.

John Rankin was born December 31, 1831, in Fayette county, Pa., and resides in North Union township. He was twice married; his first wife was Nancy Huston, daughter of Andrew Bryson. She died May 12, 1866, leaving five children. His second wife was Miss Margery, daughter of William Harper, of Dunbar. She is living, and they have three sons.

William A. Rankin was raised on a farm, and was educated in the common schools. Leaving the school, he engaged in farming. October 2, 1884, he was married to Miss Mollie L., daughter of William and Emily (Crossland) Craig. Mrs. Rankin was born September 29, 1866.

William A. Rankin is a democrat in politics, and is serving very creditably as assessor of North Union township. He is a member of the Presbyterian church at Laurel Hill, to which his wife also belongs. He and his brother own a valuable farm in North Union township, where he resides. He gives his attention principally to farming, and is well known and highly respected by his neighbors.

WILLIAM RANKIN was born February 20, 1841, in North Union township, Fayette county, Pa., on the old Rankin homestead, which has belonged to a Rankin by the name of William for four generations.

William Rankin, the father of the subject of this sketch, was born at the Rankin homestead September 25, 1800. He was a whig in his younger days, but became a democrat in 1856. He died March 27, 1877. His father and grandfather owned the present Rankin homestead.

Eliza Junk, daughter of John Junk, of North Union township, was the mother of the subject of this sketch. She was born April 13, 1807, and was married February, 1831, to William Rankin. They had four children: John, William, Samuel and Hugh.

John Junk, the father of Eliza Junk, was married to Sarah Preston. He was an elder in the U. P. church, was a prosperous farmer, and left large tracts of land to his children. He voted for General Washington for president.

The subject of this sketch was brought up on a farm, and was educated in the common schools of North Union township. His business is farming, which he has followed all of his life. He owns a finely improved farm, where he resides, and owns valuable property in Uniontown. On November 19, 1861, he was married to Miss Martha B. Hurst, by Rev. B. P. Ferguson. Mrs. Rankin was a daughter of Nathaniel G. Hurst, and was born April 1, 1843. They have six living children, two boys and four girls: Mary Eliza, born June 15, 1863, married to John F. Hankins, of Uniontown; William H., born February 18, 1865, engaged in teaching; Isaac, born May 4, 1867; Frances, born February 12, 1869, married to Albert R. Craig; Ida M., born January 21, 1873, attending school, living at home, and Daisy M., born December 16, 1880.

In politics Mr. Rankin is a stanch democrat, and is a strong temperance man. He holds the office of supervisor in a strong republican township.

SAMUEL C. PRICE, a prominent citizen of South Union, is a son of Joseph and Anna (Clemment) Price. He was born two and a half miles from Ohiopyle, in Stewart township, Fayette county, Pennsylvania, May 24, 1830.

His father, Joseph Price, was born near Fredericksburg, Virginia, in 1786. His occupation was teaming; he drove on the old Braddock road, afterwards for a while on the National road, but subsequently engaged in farming. His wife was Anna Clemment, a sister of Samuel M. Clemment. He was a strong whig, and was an ardent supporter of Andrew Stewart and a warm admirer of Henry Clay. His death occurred April 18, 1861.

Samuel C. Price spent his early years on a farm, educated in the common schools and in Dunlap's Creek Academy. He was married in 1877 to Miss Priscilla J., daughter of James Fearer, a farmer of Preston county, West Virginia. His son, Frank Price, was born August 6, 1858, and married Miss Emma Fearer. Unto this latter union was born two children: Charles Marion, born March, 1879, and Minnie Belle, born November, 1881.

Saumuel C. Price taught thirteen terms of school in Pennsylvania, and three terms in Illinois. He was a successful teacher, maintaining strict discipline and securing good progress. He next engaged in farming and in connection with his farming operated a large brick-yard. He takes considerable interest in educational matters and is a strong friend to the common schools. He is a republican from principle, and has held all of the various township offices. He is a member of the Cumberland Presbyterian church, and is a man of enterprise and energy, deserving of the success he has won.

FREDERICK CONVERSE ROBINSON, M. D. Uniontown has always been fortunate in having good and skillful physicians—men well read, of good judgment and extensive practice. Among the names of this class of physicians who have honored their calling will be found that of Dr. Frederick C. Robinson.

He was born in Saratoga county, N. Y., November 30, 1820, and is a son of Eleazer and Experience (Downer) Robinson (the latter born in 1776), both being of families of the old Puritan stock. Eleazer Robinson was a native of Vermont, born in 1782, and was by occupation a farmer. He died in 1826, in the Newark Valley, N. Y. His father, Eleazer Robinson, Sr., was born in 1736 (in New England), and died in 1820. He was also by occupation a farmer.

When Dr. Robinson was small, his parents removed to Newark Valley, Tioga county, N. Y., where the father died in very moderate circumstances. Dr. Robinson came to Erie county, Pa., in 1837, and from thence to Uniontown in 1840. He was educated in select schools and at Madison College. He read medicine at Uniontown, subsequently went to Ohio, there finished his studies, and after which he entered Jefferson Medical College and graduated in March, 1851. He began the practice of medicine in Harrison county, Ohio, in 1845, but returned to Uniontown in 1851, opened an office and built up a large practice. During the late war, he was the medical examiner for the twenty-first enrollment district. He was appointed pension surgeon in 1866, but resigned in 1879, not desiring to longer retain the position.

He was married to Susan Hollingsworth, of Harford county, Md., on the 11th of November, 1847. The Hollingsworths are of Quaker stock who trace their history back to 1200, in Cheshire, England, where an estate still belongs in the family. Valentine Hollingsworth, a worthy member of the "Society of Friends," came over with William Penn, and settled on the Brandywine. Dr. Robinson's wife is of the seventh generation from "honest old Valentine Hollingsworth."

Dr. Robinson has four children, namely: Ada Virginia, born August 17, 1848, and married to William K. Gillespie, a wholesale grocery merchant, of Pittsburgh; Henry E., born May 19, 1851, was graduated in the class of 1871, at West Point, and is a first lieutenant in the Fourth United States Infantry. He married Miss Sallie K. Gaddis of Uniontown; Charles C., born January 25, 1855, went West and is engaged in the mercantile business. He married Miss Elizabeth Scott, of Allegheny county, Pa.; Elizabeth H., born April 24, 1861, was married to First Lieutenant John Baxter, Jr., of the Ninth United States Infantry, November 11, 1885. He graduated at West Point in the class of 1877, and is now stationed as Military Instructor at the Normal University, Ada, Ohio.

Dr. Robinson having acquired a competency, he has virtually retired from the practice of medicine, after more than forty-four years of hard and efficient service as an active physician.

He was at one time president of the Fayette County Medical Association, and although retired, yet feels as deep an interest as ever in his profession and its advancements.

He resides in a delightful home on Morgantown street, where he has lived for more than thirty years. The old house is embowered in shade trees and surrounded by beautifully kept grounds, that in summer are rendered attractive by a profusion of flowers. His excellent wife who has been long noted for her taste and skill in the cultivation of roses has rendered the old house as attractive without as it is genial and hospitable within. The cheery voices of some of their numerous and ever welcome grandchildren almost constantly ring through the old house where their parents were reared and went forth thence to their life work. Old age is bringing a welcome serenity to the old home.

JESSE REID, the present Burgess of Uniontown, was born March 1, 1821, in Rostraver township, Westmoreland county, Pa. He was educated in the common schools, and at the age of eighteen learned the milling business in Webster, where he worked at the same business for about ten years. He was married in 1846 to Miss Sarah A. Carson of Webster. He came to Fayette county in 1847 where he followed milling the greater part of his time up to 1874. In 1874 he was elected county commissioner on the republican ticket, and was probably the first republican ever elected to that office in the county, overcoming a democratic majority of about 1,000 or 1,200. He was elected for three years; his term of office having expired he was engaged in farming till 1885, when he came to Uniontown, and in 1886 was elected Burgess. Re-elected in 1887–8 and 9.

He has been a member of the Methodist Episcopal church for about thirty-five years, and is stewart of the church. He joined the Odd Fellows in 1859, is about as high in the lodge as a member can go and has been twice representative to the Grand Lodge.

He has five living children: James H., Ann Maria, Samuel C., Martha Jane and William G. His parents were Samuel and Marie (Watson) Reid. The former a native of Washington county, Pa., and was a blacksmith by trade; his death occurred some fifteen years ago.

WILLIAM L. ROBINSON, is a son of Eleazer and Elizabeth J. (Wilson) Robinson, and was born at Uniontown, Fayette county, Pa., March 26, 1856.

Eleazer Robinson was born March 4, 1804, in Bethel, Windsor county, Vt. He was the son of Eleazer and Experience (Downer) Robinson, whose ancestors were of the Pilgrim band that came over in the Mayflower. Eleazer moved to New York, where Eleazer, Jr., was educated at an academy. The latter was well qualified for a civil engineer, but took up the study of the law, which he relinquished on the death of his father, and gave his attention to farming and school teaching, in order to provide for his father's helpless family. When free to do for himself, a great freshet swept away from him a fortune in the lumber business at Oswego, N. Y. He afterwards engaged in the drug business at Erie, Pa., where he made the acquaintance of Jonas Hathaway, the inventor of a stove. He obtained control of the "Hathaway Stove," so wonderfully popular forty years ago.

He removed to Pittsburgh and engaged in the manufacture of the stove, but his foundry was soon destroyed by fire. Undismayed by reverses, he came to Uniontown in 1837 and established another stove foundry; and here his business increased so rapidly that he was necessitated to start a branch foundry at Washington, Pa., as he also established agencies at Carlisle, Pa., and at several other points throughout Pennsylvania and Virginia. After thirty years of successful business life, Mr. Robinson retired from the stove business, in 1867. In 1872 he became proprietor or the Uniontown gas works, and was one of the orignal directors of the First National Bank of Uniontown.

He was married July 12, 1837, to Miss Cornelia Wells, of York, N. Y., who died in 1845. They had four children, of whom one, Mrs. Emma R. King, is now living. On November 6, 1846, he married Miss Mary Ann McClelland, of Uniontown, and she died in 1850, leaving no children.

He again married on November 24, 1852, Elizabeth J. Porter, daughter of James Wilson, Esq., of German township. She died April 29, 1881, at the age of sixty-eight years, leaving two children: William L. and Mary E.

William L. Robinson was educated in the public schools of Uniontown, but having the inclination to engage in business pursuits, he left school in 1872 and engaged with his father in the gas business. In 1876 he took entire charge of the business which he still conducts. He was elected by the republicans to the town council in 1883, in 1886 elected president of the council, and was elected a member of the school board in 1889. He is a prominent Free Mason, Knight Templar, and is a member of the Presbyterian church.

W. L. Robinson was married in 1882, to Miss Annie F. Oliphant, a native of Uniontown, but was a resident of Wampum, Lawrence county, Pa., at the time of her marriage. She is the grand-daughter of F. H. Oliphant; his father, Colonel John Oliphant, and grandfather, Andrew Olipant, came from Chester county, Pa. Fideleo Hughs Oliphant was born January 4, 1800, and died November 10, 1879.

He was a prominent iron manufacturer of Fayette county, and built the Fairchance and Oliphant furnaces.

He was a Presbyterian, honest, just, and a generous man.

HAROLD L. ROBINSON is the son of Dr. Jabez and Agnes (Cannon) Robinson. His father was a native of New England, was a practicing physician, and died in Montana Territory in 1866, at the age of fifty-two years. His mother was born in Fayette county, Pa., where her family have resided ever since the Revolutionary War. Her grandfather, Daniel Cannon, was an officer in the War of the Revolution. She is now residing in Uniontown. The Cannons came from Virginia, were among the first who settled in Fayette county, and who resided for many years in the Laurel Hill neighborhood.

Harold L. Robinson was born in Oregon City, Mo., July 25, 1864, and was graduated from the West Virginia University, at Morgantown, in 1884. He read law with James Darby, was admitted to the practice of law at the Uniontown bar in June, 1887, and immediately opened an office at Uniontown.

He is a member of the M. E. church, and is a member of Jr. O. U. A. M.

JOSEPH K. RITENOUR, a pleasant gentleman and a popular and efficient druggist of Uniontwon, was born in Preston county, Virginia (now West Virginia), November 28, 1854. He is a son of William M. and Elizabeth A (Shaw) Ritenour, the former was born in Rappahannock county, Virginia, and came to Uniontown in 1846. He was a commissioned officer during the late war and is now living in Florida, the latter is a native of Fayette county, Pennsylvania.

Joseph K. Ritenour was reared at Uniontown, where he was educated. In 1872 he engaged as a clerk in a drug store and continued as such for four years. In 1876 he formed a partnership with A. L. Moser and they were engaged successfully in the drug business up to 1882. In September, 1882, he dissolved partnership with Moser and purchased the drug store of Dr. S. Fuller & Sons on Broadway street. After operating this drug store successfully for three years, he removed to his present large and commodious building on Morgantown street. His room is of ample dimensions, well arranged, fully equipped with every facility and convenience for the transaction of his line of business. He has a large and excellent stock of pure and fresh drugs, medicines, chemicals, extracts, proprietary remedies, perfumery, toilet articles, fancy goods, and a large supply of school books and standard works of literature.

In 1877 he was married to Miss Kate Rodehaver, of near St. Louis, Missouri. They have three children: Joseph P., Altha M. and Margaret L.

Situated within a few steps of Main street, Mr. Ritenour's drug store is a very valuable and eligible business building. He does a fine business, retaining his many old patrons and constantly securing new ones. To fine business qualifications, he adds years of successful experience and stands high in Western Pennsylvania as a druggist. He is one of the live, enterprising citizens of Fayette county.

COLONEL THOMAS BROWNFIELD SEARIGHT. The oldest in active practice of the lawyers at the Uniontown bar, and one of the prominent and well known public men of Fayette county, is the gentleman whose name heads this sketch—a man of good legal attainments, fine literary ability, and extended political influence. Thomas Brownfield Searight is a son of William and Rachel (Brownfield) Searight and was born on the national road in Menallen township, Fayette county, Pa., February 20, 1827. (For history of ancestry see sketch of William Searight.)

Colonel T. B. Searight was reared on a farm and successfully prosecuted his academic studies at Dr. Wilson's Academy and Madison College at Uniontown. He entered

T. B. Searight

Washington and Jefferson College May 1, 1844, and was graduated from that famous old college in the class of 1848. One of his class-mates was Judge Slagle, of Pittsburgh, another was Hon. J. Murray Clark, and one of his warm and intimate friends while there was James G. Blaine, who graduated one year earlier. Leaving college, Colonel Searight read law under James Veech, a learned historian and able jurist, and was admitted to the Fayette county bar in 1850. In 1851, his father being the proprietor of the *Genius of Liberty*, the organ of the Fayette county democracy, Colonel Searight assumed charge of the paper as editor, and conducted it until the beginning of the war against the South. In 1857 he was elected prothonotary and in 1860 was re-elected. In 1863 he represented Fayette county in the house of representatives of the State legislature, and was re-elected in 1864. Two years later he was chosen State senator from the district composed of the counties of Greene, Fayette and Westmoreland. He was a leading member as well as one of the acknowledged leaders of his party on the floor of the house and senate, serving on many of the important committees, took a prominent part in all important legislation, and was generally successful in securing the passage of measures that he favored and advocated. Active in behalf of the people's interests of his district, he received many manifestations of regard from Governors Curtin and Geary; and on the proposition to ratify the fourteenth and fifteenth amendments to the Constitution of the United States, his speeches in all the debates arising thereon were both effective and conspicuous against their ratification by the legislature of Pennsylvania. He was delegate to the Pennsylvania democratic State convention of 1857 that nominated William F. Packer for governor, of 1860 that nominated Henry D. Foster, of 1863 that nominated Judge Woodward, of 1866 that nominated Heister Clymer, of 1869 that nominated A. H. Dill, and of 1882 that nominated Robert Emory Pattison. He was delegate to the National Democratic conventions at Chicago that nominated General George B. McClellan and Grover Cleveland, for the presidency, in 1864 and 1884. In all the political campaigns since 1848, he has taken an active and leading part in Fayette county, and at various other parts throughout the State. Without solicitation upon his part, he was appointed in 1873, by President Grant, surveyor general of Colorado, and served as such for for three years. In 1881 he was elected prothonotary for a third term, and three years later elected for a fourth term. In 1883 he received the democratic nomination for the judgeship of the Fourteenth Judicial District, but opposing influences in an adjoining county, and dissensions in his own party in Fayette county, prevented his election.

October 29, 1857, he was married to Miss Rose Flenniken, only daughter of Hon. Robert P. Flenniken. They have four children: Emily, William, Eliza, and Annie. Hon. Robert P. Flenniken was born in Greene county, Pa., in 1804, and died in San Francisco in 1879. He practiced law for many years at Uniontown, was an able lawyer, and served three terms in the Pennsylvania legislature, was appointed in 1845 Minister Extraordinary and Plenipotentiary to Denmark, under President Polk, and subsequently served as associate justice of the Territory of Utah, under President Buchanan.

At the close of his last term as prothonotary, Col. Searight again resumed the active practice of law, and has secured a large practice. For over thirty years he has almost continnously held important offices, and has always discharged the duties devolving upon him creditably to himself and satisfactorily to the public. Rev. J. S. Marquis, a fine scholar and able writer, has the following in a biography of Col. Searight, his college class-mate: Searight has made some valuable contributions to literature. His letters on States Rights are logical and evidently prepared with great care and research. His (forthcoming) history of 'The Old Pike' containing reminiscences, romance, accident and incident, and scenes along its thoroughfare in its earlier days, is a gem of that kind of writing." We quote the following sentences from the opening chapter of "The Old Pike" as illustrative of the style of the work: "The National Road was for many years the great highway of the nation, preceding the era of canals and railroads, and rivaling in grandeur the Appian Way that connected Ancient Rome with Southern Italy. Its numerous and magnificent stone bridges, with splendid, handsomely turned arches, and its iron mile posts, attest the skill of the workmen engaged in its construction, and remain enduring monuments of its grandeur and solidity."

Col. Searight is easily approached, is affable in manner and easy in conversation. His practice is before the courts of Fayette county, United States District court, State courts at Pittsburgh and the Supreme Court of Pennsylvania. In the field of politics he has ever steadfastly held to the principles founded by Jefferson, and afterward so ably espoused and powerfully enunciated by Jackson: having carefully studied the history and examined the principles of all the great political parties that have ever existed in the country, his early democratic principles have become his mature convictions.

JAMES ALLISON SEARIGHT. Among the many prominent and successful business men of Fayette county, none are more modest and unassuming, and yet more conscientious and useful, than James Allison Searight, who represents at Uniontown the leading and reliable insurance companies of both the Old and the New World. James Allison Searight, youngest son of William and Rachel Searight, was born on the old "Searight Homestead," Menallen township, Fayette county, Pa., September 13, 1836. (For his family genealogy, see sketch of his father, William Searight.)

Until at fourteen years of age he remained at home and attended the local schools of his neighborhood. In 1850 he began an academic course in Dunlap's Creek Presbyterian Academy—then in its most palmy days—and during his attendance there was instructed by Dr. Wilson (founder of the school), Dr. Black, and Professors Powers, Downs, Chalfant and Mercer. Leaving the academy, he spent some time in the banking house of John T. Hogg, at Brownsville, and from the bank he went and took a partial commercial course at Iron City College, Pittsburgh, Pa. In 1859 he entered the preparatory department of Kenyon College, Gambier, Ohio; after the first term he was admitted to the freshman class, and was graduated from there in 1863. One of his class-mates was E. L. Stanton, son of the great war secretary, E. M. Stanton. During his college course, the president of the institution resigned, raised a regiment for the army and it was not long until it was Mr. Searight's sad duty to help entomb the body of the soldier college president, near the old chapel of Kenyon College. At the close of his collegiate term in 1863 he became a student of Divinity under Dr. Ohl of Brownsville, Pa., and in the fall of 1865 entered the Philadelphia Divinity school. At the end of a year's close application to theological studies his health began to fail and he was compelled to abondon his chosen profession. Mr. Searight passed a couple of years in Washington City; and in 1871 he

J. A. Searight

came home and opened his present insurance and real estate agency.

He is a member of St. Peter's Protestant Episcopal church at Uniontown, and has frequently represented the church in its diocesan councils. He was a member of the diocesan council when the first division of the diocese of Pennsylvania was made, and was also a member when Dr. Kerfoot was elected bishop of the diocese of Pittsburgh. He was also a member of the diocesan convention that elected Dr. Whitehead, the present bishop, and served on the committee that notified him of his election. In 1873 Mr. Searight, with several others, applied for and obtained the charter of the "Peoples Bank of Fayette county," with a capital stock of $50,000. Shortly after its formation Mr. Searight was elected cashier, and upon the death of the president of the bank, Colonel Ewing Brownfield, in 1889, Mr. Searight was elected his successor, a position he now holds. He has spent considerable time and expense in securing facts and data for an accurate sketch to preserve for all time to come the memory of his family and ancestry. He has also taken a deep interest in the success of the Biographical Cyclopedia as the only sure way of preserving the ancestral history of Fayette county.

For nearly twenty years Mr. Searight has conducted a large and continually increasing insurance business. His agency represents nineteen of the largest fire, life and accident insurance companies of the world, and the Anchor and State lines of steamship companies. Represents the Ætna, North American, Hartford, National, Connecticut, Phenix Continental, Pennsylvania and farmers (U. S.); Royal, Phenix Guardian, London, Lancashire, and Queen (England) and Western (Canada) Travelers' Life, Travelers' Accident, Pennsylvania Life of Philadelphia and United States Plate Glass of same city. Altogether, he represents over fifty millions of capital.

WILLIAM E. SEAL, merchant tailor of Uniontown, was born in Belmont county, Ohio, September 23, 1863, and is a son of Richard and Nancy (Watters) Seal, the former born in Maryland, in 1826, the latter a native of Baltimore.

William E. Seal was educated in the public schools of Ohio. Leaving school, he removed to Wheeling, W. Va., where he learned the trade of a tailor with Thomas Hughes & Co. Desiring to perfect himself in his chosen trade, he attended Mitchell's Cutting School in New York City, and was graduated from there in 1886. From 1885 to 1887 he was a partner in the firm of Seal & Bro., engaged in fine tailoring at Bellaire, Ohio. June 2, 1887, he married Miss May, daughter of Captain Stephen Thompson, of Pittsburgh. Mrs. Seal is a native of Monroe county, Ohio, born June 20, 1863.

W.E.Seal came to Uniontown July 25,1887, and purchased the merchant tailoring stock of John Lynch, which he removed to his present rooms on Main street. He is the resident and managing partner of Seal Bros., merchant tailors, Main street, Uniontown, who constantly carry a large and valuable assortment of cloths and trimmings, directly imported from Europe. W. E. Seal is a practical cutter and merchant tailor, who personally attends to every department of his business, and is deserving of the large and flattering patronage he has built up for the firm in a comparatively short time.

THOMAS SEMANS, a Jacksonian democrat and a solid business man of Fayette county, is a son of Henry and Polly (Warren) Semans, and was born at the head of Morgantown street, in Uniontown, April 26, 1800.

Henry Semans came from New Jersey to Uniontown. He was a carpenter, and enlisted in the War of 1812, but was not called into active service, as peace was declared soon after his enlistment. His family consisted of three sons and five daughters.

Thomas Semans was educated in the subscription schools of South Union township and Uniontown. He learned the trade of tanner with John Miller, of Uniontown, and operated a tannery for forty-five years in South Union township, and made many improvements to save labor while he was engaged in that business. In addition to the tannery he conducted a shoe shop, carried on a general store at home for fifteen years, and owned an interest for several years in a Uniontown store.

In 1827 he married Miss Lydia, daughter of Jacob Johnson. They had five children: Francis M., merchant at Monroe; George W., of Morgantown, W. Va.; Eliza, wife of Samuel McDonald; Harriet, wife of Samuel Clark (dead); Mary Ann, wife of Henry Cassidy (dead). Mrs. Semans is dead. His second wife was Miss Margery Grant, whom he married in 1845. They were blessed with ten children, of whom but three are living: Ezra, in coal business; Sarah and Walter at home. After the death of his second wife, he married Miss Melicent, daughter of Thomas J. and Rebecca (Slagle) Foster, the latter a descendant from the famous Simpson family of Maryland.

Thomas Semans is a Royal Arch Mason, is prominent in lodge and chapter and served one term as District Deputy Grand Master to instruct the Masonic lodges of four counties. He has been a member for sixteen years of the Protestant Episcopal church, of Uniontown. He has served five years as tax collector, three terms as school director, two terms as justice of the peace, and two terms as poor house director. He is remarkably well preserved in both body and mind for a man verging on ninety years of age, and was engaged in binding grain in his harvest fields during the last summer. His first presidential vote was cast for Jackson, and for sixty-five succeeding years he has yielded unswerving allegiance to the political principles of Jackson.

PETER F. SMITH, M. D. The Smith family for the last three generations is one of pure American birth and rearing; and the ancestors were, with one exception, born and reared in Fayette county, Pa.

John T. Smith, paternal grandfather of Dr. Smith, was born in New Jersey, in 1811, and came to Fayette county, in 1849. He was a shoemaker by trade, but later in life he became a farmer and gardener. He was married to Miss Williams and they were the parents of two children: Robert H. and Francis. He married a second time to Miss Hadden, of South Union township, Fayette county, Pa., and they had three children: Thomas H., Annie and James B. James B. is a member of the faculty of the "California State Normal School of Pennsylvania."

Peter Humbert—Dr. Smith's grandfather on his mother's side—was born in 1808, in Fayette county, Pa., and was a farmer. He married Abby Hadden. They have six children: Joseph, Julian, Thomas, Smith, Jane, Eliza F. (the mother of Dr. Smith) and Mary.

Robert H. Smith, father of Dr. Smith, was born in 1833, in New Jersey, came to Fayette county with his father in 1849, and is now a farmer in Dunbar township. He married Eliza F. Humbert, the daughter of Peter Humbert, a farmer of North Union township. They are the parents of Peter F., S. Jennie, William W. and Charles H. S. Jennie graduated at the California State Normal School of Pennsylvania, in 1888, and taught one term before, and one term after her graduation. She married Clyde Kimball, of Dunbar township, and now lives on a farm near Dunbar borough. Charles H. graduated at the Central State

Normal School, at Lock Haven, Pa., in the class of 1886, taught school for two years and then entered upon the study of Pharmacy.

Dr. Peter F. Smith was born April 16, 1857, in North Union township, Fayette county, Pa. He was educated in the common schools of Dunbar, and for two years in the California State Normal school, entering this school in 1882. In the interval between the common school and the Normal school he worked upon a farm.

Leaving the normal school, he commenced the study of medicine in the office of R. W. Clark, of Dunbar. He entered the medical department of the University of Michigan, at Ann Arbor, in 1884 and graduated in 1887.

He is located in the practice of his profession at Percy, in Fayette county, where he has been in practice for two years.

Dr. Smith is a member of the Presbyterian church, of the Fayette County Medical Society, of the Jr. O. U. A. Mechanics, and of the Royal Arcanum.

Dr. Smith is a young physician of great promise, and has a glowing future before him, both as a professional man and as a citizen. It is to be hoped that his success will be equal to his ability and merit.

JOHN SNIDER, Sr., was born January 14, 1819, in Washington county, Md., and is a son of Andrew and Rachel (McCoy) Snider.

John Snider (subject's paternal grandfather) was born near Berlin, Prussia, and came to America in 1770. He was a wagonmaker. Enlisting in the Continental Army, he served under Washington from Long Island to Yorktown. After the Revolutionary War he removed from Pennsylvania to Maryland, was in the War of 1812, when Washington City was threatened, and volunteered to haul supplies to the nation's endangered capital, and did so until the city was captured. He died at his Maryland home. His wife was a Miss Elizabeth Armstrong, born in York county, Pa., in 1766, and died in 1837.

Andrew Snider (subject's father) was born January 6, 1792, in York county, Pa., and removed to Maryland in 1806, where he died July 5, 1865. He married Rachel McCoy. She was born in Washington county, Md., in 1767, and died April 12, 1832. Her father was Andrew McCoy, a Catholic, who came from Cork, Ireland, to Maryland, in 1775, where he died in 1827. His wife was a Scotch lady by the name of Mary Mountz, born in 1767.

John Snider, Sr., was raised on a farm, and on December 29, 1841, married Miss Margaret Pence. They have had nine children: Andrew, born April 6, 1844, died March 15, 1846; Mary, born September 8, 1846, living at home; William, born November 22, 1848, died February 16, 1889; married Olive Morris, December 26, 1868; two of his children, Margaret and Ellen, are school teachers. Henry, born March 10, 1851, died September 4, 1856; Elizabeth, born September 16, 1853, married Luke Patterson October 5, 1887, and has one child; John, Jr., born Februrry 2, 1854, married Belle Sampey December 21, 1880, and has three children: Josephine, born December 2, 1855; Lydia, born April 8, 1860, married John Dixon September 17, 1882, and has three children: Edward, born February 17, 1865, married Josephine Hustead, daughter of J. M. Hustead, March 31, 1886, and has two children.

John Snider, Sr., moved to Monroe, and followed teaming until 1852. He had control of two lines of "transporting" wagons from Wheeling to Cumberland. He received all moneys and paid all bills.

In 1852 he bought the Peter Skiles farm, in North Union township, and one year later purchased Redstone Furnace, which he ran for twelve years. In 1864 he purchased the Jeffries farm, where he now resides.

Mr. Snider's most important line of work is in railroad construction. As a railroad contractor he built in 1871 the bed of the railroad from Uniontown to Fairchance, and in '72 and '73 he built one fourth of the road from Greensburg to Connellsville. From '74 to '76 he built the S. W. P. R. W. from Connellsville to Uniontown, and in 1878 built an extension of the same road for H. C. Frick & Co.

He says the cares of a stage or wagon line on the "Pike" were as onerous as the management of a railroad is at the present time. He never had a manager, and scarcely ever needed a clerk. His memory is remarkably good, remembering past events and dates as though they were but of yesterday, and often did the clerical work of four men. He is a Free Mason, and a Calvinist in belief, though not a member of any church. His wife is a Protestant Methodist. She was born in Somerset county, Pa., November 15, 1821, and was the daughter of William Pence, a native of Eastern Pennsylvania, and who died at Cook's Mills (Tippecanoe) in 1858. His wife was Mary Shirer, a native of Somerset county.

John Snider is one of those men who believe in "wearing out" not "rusting out," as his long life of activity and toil well attest.

LEVI B. SPRINGER, one of the modest and retiring citizens of North Union township, as well as one of the township's most substantial farmers, was born in the old Springer homestead in North Union township, Fayette county, Pa., in 1832. His father, Denis Springer, was born February 1787, on the farm on which Levi B. Springer now resides. In 1821 he married Sarah Brownfield, a daughter of Thomas Brownfield. She was born at Pughtown. near Winchester, Va., September 26, 1797; she is still living, and is in good health. Denis Springer was a prosperous farmer in the early history of Fayette county, and had two brothers in the War of 1812. From 1812 to 1818 he followed flat-boating flour from Brownsville to New Orleans, and afterward bought the home farm, containing 386 acres. His death occurred in 1866. He was the father of five daughters and one son: Mary A., Elizabeth B. and Sarah are still living with their mother on the old homestead. Lydia S. married A. A. Rizer, of Cumberland, Md.; Catherine M. married R. P. Craig, of South Union township.

Levi B. Springer's grandfather, Levi Springer, was born in 1744, probably near Winchester, Va. His second wife (grandmother of Levi B.), was Mrs. Sarah Duke (*nee* Shepherd), whose father was Colonel Moses Shepherd, commander of the fort during the Colonial War at Wheeling, W. Va., where he died. His great-grandfather, Denis Springer, descended from the Wilmington Delaware branch of the Springer family. The founder of this family came from Sweden.

WILLIAM H. STURGEON has been for the last thirty years a well known and prominent physician of Uniontown and of Fayette county.

He is a native of Uniontown, and was born on the 24th day of January, 1826. He was brought up in his native town, attending Madison College, and afterwards entered and graduated from Jefferson College in 1847. He read medicine with Dr. Alex. Hamilton Campbell, of Uniontown, and attended lectures at Jefferson Medical College in 1848, and 1849. From 1849 to 1853 he practiced medicine in Uniontown, but in the latter year he accepted a clerkship in the United States mint, which position he held until 1861, when he retired with the democratic party.

In 1861 he returned to Uniontown and resumed the practice of medicine, which had engaged all his spare moments while in the mint. From 1861 to 1889 he has built up the large and lucrative practice which he now enjoys.

Dr. Sturgeon is a graduate of Jefferson Medical College, is a member of the Fayette County Medical Society and Pennsylvania State Medical Society. He is enrolled in the National Medical Society, and holds membership in the International Medical Society of the world. Dr. Sturgeon met with the last named medical society at its last session, in 1887, held in Washington City. In 1886 he was appointed member of the State Board of Lunacy, a position which he still holds.

Dr. Sturgeon is the son of Daniel and Nancy (Gregg) Sturgeon. His mother was a native of Fayette county, a daughter of James Gregg, a Scotchman, who was born in Ireland and came to this country when a young man, and was one of the early merchants of Uniontown. His wife, Nancy Gregg, reached the age of eighty-seven years.

His father was Daniel Sturgeon, known as the "Silent Senator." He was born in Adams county, Pa., October 27, 1789, was a son of William Sturgeon, a native and a farmer of that county and of English descent. William Sturgeon removed to Allegheny county, in about 1806. Senator Daniel Sturgeon, after his graduation from Jefferson College at Washington, Pa., came to Uniontown and read medicine with Dr. Stevens. He went to Greensboro, Greene county, Pa., to practice medicine; and after one year's practice there, and at the death of Dr. Stevens, he returned to Uniontown and took charge of Dr. Stevens' extensive practice.

Daniel Sturgeon soon left the ranks of the medical profession and entered the political arena, for which he was eminently fitted and especially qualified. Embarking in politics, he moved forward from post to post in the State, until he was sent to represent Pennsylvania, on the floor of the United States Senate. He discharged all the duties of his post with fidelity, firmness and prudence, reflecting credit alike on the State of his nativity and the county of his adoption.

Daniel Sturgeon was largely of Scotch-Irish origin, a wonderful race noted for its iron will, indomitable courage, and inflexible honesty of purpose. Andrew Jackson was an illustrious representative of this sturdy race; his iron will and energetic action in crushing out South Carolina nullification in the '30's was equaled in the same decade by Daniel Sturgeon as State treasurer, when he crushed out with an iron hand "the Buckshot War" of Pennsylvania by persistently refusing Gov. Ritner's order for $20,000, and by placing an armed force around the vaults of the treasury.

Daniel Sturgeon, although well read, of finished education, of polished manners, of extended observation, a pleasant conversationalist and a deep thinker; yet he never graced, as a public speaker, the stage of life upon which he was a prominent actor. He preferred to give his thoughts to the world in actions rather than words. Senator Sturgeon, like Andrew Jackson, illustrated one part of Goethe's maxim, that decision and patience are the king qualities of human nature. He had the decision of Jackson, but he never had the opportunity of exhibiting it on the national stage like Jackson. Senator Sturgeon was a magnificent specimen of physical manhood, whose brow was stamped with the seal of genius and whose appearance was majestic and impressive. At this time Pennsylvania was well represented in the United States Senate by the "Silent

Senator" and the "Sage of Wheatland," Sturgeon and Buchanan. Both were able, but, unhappily and unfortunately, Buchanan lacked some of the kingly virtue of decision, such as Sturgeon so largely possessed.

Daniel Sturgeon's political record spanned nearly forty years of his life, from 1819 to 1859. He represented Fayette county in the House of Representatives of Pennsylvania for three terms, from 1819 to 1825. He was then sent to the State senate of Pennsylvania for four terms, and was speaker of the house in 1828. Leaving the senate in 1829, he became auditor-general in 1830, and served six years in that position. He next became State treasurer, and served during 1838 and 1839. His continuous and efficient service for the State secured him the position of United States senator from Pennsylvania. He was elected in 1840 and re-elected in 1845, and served until 1851. In 1853 President Pierce appointed him treasurer of the United States mint at Philadelphia, and President Buchanan continued him in the same position, but he resigned in 1858, and retired to private life. He died July 2, 1878, lacking but a year of being ninety years old.

In 1814 Daniel Sturgeon married Nancy Gregg, of Uniontown. She was born in 1792 and died in 1836. The senator never remarried. He left four sons and one daughter, of whom but one son, the subject of this sketch, survives. One son, Lieutenant John Sturgeon, Company H, Second Pennsylvania Volunteers, died while in the service of the Mexican War.

Dr. W. H. Sturgeon was married in 1853 to Miss Emily V., daughter of John Dawson, a well-remembered lawyer of Uniontown. Their children living are two sons and three daughters: John D., a practicing physician of Uniontown; Daniel, an attorney at law, located at Uniontown; Mary E., Katharine B. and Ellen B.

ANDREW STEWART was one of the most distinguished public men Fayette county ever produced—a man of national reputation, whose name is indelibly stamped for all time to come on the political pages of American history. He was the oldest son of Abraham and Mary (Oliphant) Stewart, and was born in German township, Fayette county, Pa., June 11, 1791.

Abraham Stewart was a native of York county, Pa., and emigrated to German township in an early day. He served as justice of the peace and married Mary Oliphant, born in Chester county, Pa.

Andrew Stewart at an early age was thrown upon his own resources and worked upon a farm until he was eighteen years of age. By teaching school and working at a furnace, he secured sufficient means to take him through college and read law. After his graduation from Washington College, he came to Uniontown, read law and was admitted to the Fayette county bar January 9, 1815, and in the same year was elected to the Pennsylvania legislature and re-elected for a term of three years. He next offered himself as a candidate for the State senate but before the election withdrew from the canvass to accept an appointment of district attorney tendered him by President Polk. The office he subsequently resigned to take his seat in congress, to which he had previously been elected. For eighteen years he served as congressman from this district, and was a member of the Seventeenth, Twentieth, Twenty-second, Twenty-third, Twenty-sixth, Twenty-seventh, Twenty-eighth, Twenty-ninth and Thirtieth congresses of the United States. He became a member of congress in 1820, and his retirement from that body was in 1850, when he peremptorily declined to serve his constituents longer. In congress he was a contemporary with John Q. Adams, Andrew Jackson, Martin Van Buren, John Tyler, James Buchanan, Millard Fillmore, Franklin Pierce, Abraham Lincoln and Andrew Johnson. In 1848 he was a candidate for the vice-presidency before the Whig National Convention, at Philadelphia, and failed of the nomination through the blunder of the chairman of the Pennsylvania delegation. On the first ballot, Mr. Stewart received fourteen of the twenty-six votes cast, and would have gotten the unanimous vote on the second ballot, but the chairman hastened to report that the members of the Pennsylvania Delegation had failed to agree upon a man, and which proved to be the cause of the nomination of Mr. Fillmore who afterwards succeeded to the presidency on the death of Taylor. Thus by a mere blunder, Mr. Stewart failed to reach the presidential chair and Fayette county lost the honor of furnishing the eleventh president of the United States. He declined the treasury portfolio offered him by President Taylor. From 1850 up to his death, he gave most of his attention to his large and varied business interests, yet by his voice and pen took more or less active part in all the important political issues up to 1872. Andrew Stewart was a life-long advocate and able expounder of the tariff, internal improvements and other living questions of the day. He was known throughout the whole country as "Tariff Andy." That the industries and manufacturing interests of the country might be developed and fostered, he claimed the tariff was a necessity. He was a member of the democratic party till 1828, when he left that organization because of the stand it took on the tariff, and became a whig and afterwards one of the founders of the republican party. During his political career, he was idolized at home, and even after the change in his political faith was elected to congress by a majority of 235 votes, while Jackson's majority for president in the district was 2,800. In 1825 he married a daughter of David Shriver, of Cumberland, Maryland. Of his six children, one was the brave Lieutenant-Commodore W. F. Stewart, United States navy., lost on the Oneida that sank January 24, 1870, and whose last words were: "No, let others take the boat, my duty is on board my ship." In the eighty-second year of his age, Andrew Stewart died at Uniontown, July 16, 1872. He did as much as any one of his time for the material prosperity and development of Fayette county.

JASPER MARKLE THOMPSON was one of the men that Fayette county delighted to honor. He was one of that useful class of men in every State whose patriotism, integrity, intelligence and usefulness give stability to society, prosperity and progress to its business affairs.

He was born near Washington, Mason county, Kentucky, August 30, 1822, and was the youngest son of Andrew Finley and Leah (Markle) Thompson.

He is of Scotch-Irish and Pennsylvania Dutch ancestry. His ancestors on both sides fled from the "Old World" on account of their religious convictions, and found shelter in the colonial lands of Pennsylvania, early in the eighteenth century.

His paternal grandfather came from the Cumberland Valley to near Mt. Pleasant, Westmoreland county, Pa. He married Mary, daughter of John Jack, who was prominent in drafting the Hannastown Declaration of Independence, in 1775. He moved to Kentucky and was a comrade in arms of Boone. He died in Mason county of that State.

Andrew Finly Thompson was born in Kentucky in 1791, and served as a soldier with three of his brothers in the War of 1812. He was taken prisoner at Hull's disgraceful surrender, and after being released, traveled on foot from the wilds of Michigan to the home of his relatives in Westmoreland county, Pa. He wedded Miss Leah Markle, of Westmoreland county, the youngest of Gasper Markle's twenty-two children. Gasper Markle was a native of Berks county, and settled in Westmoreland county toward the close of the French and Indian War. His father, upon the revocation of the Edict of Nantes, fled from Alsace in 1686, and went to Amsterdam, where he engaged in business until 1703. In the same year he removed to Berks county, Pa.

A. F. Thompson, with his young bride, returned to Kentucky, where Mrs. Thompson died in 1823, and was soon followed to the grave by her husband. They were the parents of three children: William L., who died at twenty years of age; Mary, wife of J. P. Carothers, of this county, who died in 1865, and Jasper M.

Jasper M. Thompson, after his parents' death, when less than three years of age, was taken to Westmoreland county, and lived with his grandmother, Mary Markle, until her death in 1832, when he engaged with his cousin, General Cyrus P. Markle.

After twelve years of varied and useful experience in farming, clerking and bookkeeping, he removed, in 1850, to Redstone township. He purchased a part of the Walters farm, near New Salem, but in the same year bought and removed to a farm in Menallen township, two and one-half miles from Uniontown, where he farmed and dealt in live-stock until 1862.

President Lincoln appointed him collector of internal revenue for the Twenty-first district of Pennsylvania. After serving efficiently for four years, he resigned and retired from the office with the respect and good will of all with whom he came in contact.

He was one of the original stockholders (1863) of the First National Bank of Uniontown, and of which he was a director from 1863 to 1870, and president from 1870 until his death. He was also president of the Uniontown Building and Loan Association, a director in the Fayette County railroad, and president of the Fayette County Agricultural Association, a trustee of Washington and Jefferson College and a director in Western Theological Seminary at Allegheny City.

In 1873 the citizens of Fayette county elected him to the legislature by 1,031 majority on the republican ticket. The democratic majority in the county at that time was about 1,000. He was elected in 1868 as a republican presidential elector, and cast his vote for General Grant.

He was married, in 1846, to Miss Eliza, youngest daughter of Samuel Caruthers, of Sewickly township, Westmoreland county, Pa., ruling elder in the Presbyterian church. Mr. Caruthers' mother was a daughter of Lieutenant John Potter, and her brother, General James Potter, was a highly trusted friend of General Washington during the Revolutionary War.

Mr. Thompson had four children, two sons and two daughters: Ruth A., educated at the Female Seminary at Washington, Pa., and was married, in 1875, to Dr. J. T. Shepler, of Dunbar; Lenora M., educated at the same institution, and was married, in 1873, to John A. Niccolls, of Uniontown; William M. graduated from Washington and Jefferson College in 1871, and resides upon the home farm of over 650 acres; Josiah V. graduated from the same institution, and at the same time as his brother. He was chosen teller in the First National Bank of Uniontown, in 1872, was elected cashier in 1877, and became the president of the bank April 3, 1889.

The First National Bank of Uniontown was organized in 1863, commenced business May 1, 1864, with a capital stock of $60,000, and which was increased, in January, 1872, to $100,000. The bank has an average annual deposit of $480,000, and now has a surplus fund of $95,000. Its officers are, Josiah V. Thompson, president; Edgar S. Hackney, cashier; Francis M. Semans, Jr., teller. Its directors are H. H. Hackney, Joseph M. Campbell, D. P. Gibson, George W. Hess, William Hunt and J. V. Thompson.

Jasper M. Thompson died of pneumonia at his home in Menallen township, March 15, 1889. He had made a business trip to the South, in February, 1889, and while there contracted a cold which soon developed into symptoms of pneumonia. By traveling almost day and night he succeeded in reaching his home, where he died upon the evening of his arrival.

He attended the old subscription schools, but the more important school from which he received his education was the "great world of active life."

He was for nearly thirty years a ruling elder in the Presbyterian church at Uniontown, of which he was an honored member for forty years. The grand secret of his success was attention to business and devotion to duty. Christian consistency and true philanthropy was the cause of his popularity and the basis of his usefulness.

JOSEPH WHITE, a native of Claysville, Washington county, Pa., was born January 3, 1834, and was brought up in Claysville and learned the marble business. His father was engaged in the same business up to the time of his death, which occurred when his son Joseph was quite small. The elder brother took charge of the business, and Joseph worked for him till 1850. He was in Waynesburg, Pa., from 1850 until 1856. In 1856 he came to Uniontown and started in business for himself. He continued in business at Uniontown up to the commencement of the war, when he went into the army. He was in the quartermaster department, sick and confined in the quartermaster's hospital at Washington City for two months, when he was discharged and returned home.

His education was confined to the public schools of Claysville, as he had to work for his own living at the time many young men, more fortunate than himself, were finishing their education in the academies and colleges of the country.

In 1853 he married Miss Barbara Hager of Greene county, Pa., who died in 1854, leaving one child, Caroline.

In 1856 he married again, to Miss Margaret Hagan. She died in 1884, and was a daughter of John Hagan a farmer of the county. He died in 1869. By this marriage he has three children, living: Alice, William H. and Alexander.

In 1875 he again started in the marble business at Uniontown, and has successfully carried it on ever since. He has built up a large trade, and has made a host of friends.

He is a member of the Heptasophs, served in the council in 1878–79, and was elected on the republican ticket. He was elected a member of the school board in 1880, and is, at present a member of the board.

His parents were Alexander and Sarah (Carr) White. His father was of Scotch-Irish origin, came to this country in 1811, and died in 1848, at the age of fifty-seven years. His mother, Sarah (Carr) White, was a native of Washington county, Pa., and died in 1856, aged sixty-five years.

Her father, Alexander Carr, was born near Staunton, Virginia. He ran flatboats from Pittsburgh to New Orleans before the day of steamboats. He was drowned, which occurred by his hearing a cry from a lady in distress in a cabin on the bank near the mouth of the Ohio river. Starting to rescue her on a horse that he kept on the boat, he swam to the bank and rescued the lady and brought her to the boat in safety. He made a second trip for some of her apparel, but on his return to the boat the horse gave out and sank, and both were lost.

STEPHEN E. WADSWORTH, the efficient superintendent of the Schoonmaker Coke Works, at Brownfield, is a son of Walter M. and Sarah (Guy) Wadsworth, and was born in Madison county, Ohio, September 27, 1842.

Walter M. Wadsworth, son of Samuel Wadsworth, was born in Hartford, Conn., July 17, 1801. In 1825 he emigrated from the "land of steady habits" to Ohio, where he engaged at his trade of fancy and fine painting.

He married Sarah, daughter of Jacob Guy, a member of the Universalist church and a native of Montreal, Canada. Mr. Wadsworth was engaged in farming several years preceding his death on February 4, 1874.

Stephen E. Wadsworth was reared on a farm, and enjoyed the rural school privileges of Ohio. When the Civil War began he enlisted in Company H, Second Battalion, United States Infantry, August 9, 1861. His company was commanded by Captain Ten Eyck, and the battalion by Colonel Carrington, who at the time was adjutant-general of Ohio. Mr. Wadsworth was in the battles of Green River, Ky., Stone River, Chickamauga; and for strict attention to duty, both in the camp and on the field, he was promoted to first sergeant of his company. After four years of severe marching and hard fighting he was honorably discharged, August 9, 1865.

In 1868 he engaged as an engineer on the P. R. R., serving in this capacity until December, 1885. During this period of twenty years he never received an injury nor met with an accident of any kind. He left his position on the railroad to become superintendent of Colonel J. M. Schoonmaker's coke works (known as Moore's works), at Brownfield station.

On May 30, 1876, he was married, and has one child: Frederick G. Wadsworth.

Mr. Wadsworth married, October, 26, 1888, for his second wife, Mrs. Sallie R., (Brownfield) Brown, the widow of Isaac Brown. She received her education principally at Adrian College, Mich.

Mr. Wadsworth is a fearless and aggressive republican, but has never held any office. He has ably discharged the many important duties of his responsible position, and is an energetic, upright business man.

REV. JOHN ARMSTRONG WATERS, pastor of St. Paul's Evangelical Lutheran church, a popular young minister of Uniontown and a fearless divine in denouncing modern vices and home follies generally, is a son of Rev. Asa H. and Hannah C. (Steck) Waters, and was born in Butler county, Pa., July 16, 1857.

Rev. A. H. Waters retired from the school superintendency of Butler county, Pa., in May, 1866, and in the same month was requested by Hon. Thomas H. Burrowes, who was then organizing the system of Pennsylvania soldiers' orphan schools, to select a suitable location for a soldiers' orphan school somewhere in the western counties of Pennsylvania, that was not already furnished with a school of that kind. So on the 19th of September, 1866, he opened a soldiers' orphan school in Madison college, at Uniontown, and superintended it successfully for eight years. April 8, 1874, the school was moved to Dunbar's Camp, four miles and a half east of Uniontown, on Laurel Hill, where it has flourished and prospered until the present time, under the efficient supervision of the Rev. A. H. Waters. No finer or healthier location for a school can be found in the State, than Dunbar's Camp, where the health of the pupils has been universally good.

Rev. A. H. Waters is a native of Pittsburgh, and was married to Miss Hannah C. Steck of Greensburg, Westmoreland county, Pa. She is a daughter of the Rev. Michael J. Steck and a granddaughter of Rev. John Michael Steck, both pastors of the Lutheran church at Greensburg.

Rev. J. A. Waters came to Uniontown with his father in 1866, receiving his early education in the soldiers' orphan school, graduating from Thiel college, at Greenville in 1879, and from the Theological Seminary in Philadelphia in 1885. In the time intervening was principal of the Uniontown Soldiers' Orphan School. At the organization of the Lutheran church, December 18, 1885, at Uniontown, he became pastor of the church, and has served in this capacity faithfully and acceptably until the present time. He is courteous and pleasant in manner and conversation, but forcible and energetic in the pulpit in denouncing wrong and wrong doers. He stands deservedly high as a minister, a gentleman and a citizen.

WILLIAM H. WILHELM was born in Franklin township, Fayette county, Pa., February 27, 1840, was reared on a farm, and resided in Franklin township till he was eighteen years old. His education was obtained in the common schools of the township. At the age of fifteen he commenced his trade—blacksmith—with George Crop, and served with him for three years, when he came to Uniontown, and worked as journeyman for eighteen months. In 1861 he started in business for himself, and has continued ever since at the same location.

He built a new and better shop on the same place occupied by the old building. His principal business now is the manufacture of wagons, and selling agricultural implements. He has built up a large business at Uniontown.

He is the son of George and Lydia (Quaill) Wilhelm. His father was born in Fayette county, Pa., and was by occupation a farmer. He is now living at Hanover, Jefferson county, Ind.

George Wilhelm, grandfather of the subject of this sketch, was the first to discover iron ore in the mountains, and the place still goes by the name of "Wilhelm Ore Banks." He was a trapper and hunter of the mountains. Before the country was settled to any great extent, he transported fur and game to Baltimore on sleds.

He was once captured by the Indians, and made his escape at night by secreting himself in a hollow log, but was found and taken back to the Indian village. The second attempt he succeeded in making good his escape. He has been dead about seventy years.

JAMES B. WIGGINS, an intelligent and prosperous farmer of South Union, township, is a son of Isaac and Matilda (Brenton) Wiggins. He was born on the home farm in South Union township, January 17, 1835.

Isaac Wiggins was born in 1797 in Eastern Pennsylvania, and died in South Union township in 1866. He was an active Republican, an elder in the Cumberland Presbyterian church, and a director in the National Bank of Fayette county. He was fully trusted by his neighbors, and settled many estates in Fayette county. He married Miss Matilda, daughter of Joseph Brenton. Isaac Wiggins was a son of Basil Wiggins, who came from Eastern Pennsylvania, and kept the "old Moxley Stand," in early Pike days.

James B. Wiggins was educated in the common schools, and engaged in farming. He served as a soldier in the late war, enlisting in July, 1861, in Captain G. W. Gilmore's Cavalry Company from Fayette county, and was in the Kanawha Division of the Army of West Virginia. He served under Generals Averill, Rosecrans, Hunter, Cox and Hays, and was twice sent East. He was in the battles of Carnifex Ferry and Winchester, Wytheville and many others, did some hard marching and scouting, and was captured at Frederick City, Md., by J. E. B. Stuart's cavalry, a few days before the battle of Antietam, but he was soon paroled. He was promoted to a sergeant, and was honorably discharged at Wheeling, W. Va., September 10, 1865.

In 1869 he married Miss Elizabeth, daughter of John Freeman, of Georges township. She died in 1880. In 1885 he married his second wife, Miss Jennie, daughter of Jacob Downard, of Georges township. Unto the latter union have been born two children: I. B. and James Arthur.

Mr. Wiggins owns a fertile and beautiful farm, two miles west of the county seat, where he is engaged in farming. He succeeded the late Jasper M. Thompson as president of the Fayette County Agricultural Society, is a director in the National Bank of Fayette county, and is also a director of the Fayette Fuel and Gas Company. He is a very pleasant, intelligent gentleman, and is highly esteemed for his strict business integrity.

JOSIAH V. WILLIAMS was born September 17, 1848, at Uniontown, Fayette county, Pa., where he was reared and attended the public schools. His family for four generations have resided in Fayette county. His grandfather was a native of England and was one of the earliest settlers here. He was a shoemaker by trade, and, as it was the custom in those days, he went from house to house to do his work. His son, Isaac, a native of Fayette county Pa., and the father of J. V. Williams, was married to Martha Jane Lancaster, who was also born in Fayette county, Pa. Isaac Williams was engaged a great deal of his life in the manufacture of brick, until 1869, when he retired.

J. V. Williams took charge of the business, and has successfully conducted it ever since.

In 1889 he bought J. W. Miller's brickyard. He is now running both yards, is making 25,000 brick per day, and employs from sixteen to twenty hands. J. V. Williams was married September 17, 1871, to Ellen M. Derrick, a daughter of Joseph Derrick, a prominent farmer of South Union township.

To their marriage have been born three children: Allen D., Florence and Eliza. He is a member of the Methodist Episcopal church, and was elected assessor of South Union township on the republican ticket.

HON. ALPHEUS E. WILLSON. One of the ablest lawyers and one of the finest jurists that Fayette county ever had, was the distinguished judge whose name is mentioned at the head of this sketch. He was descended from one of the oldest, most polished, cultivated and influential families of old Virginia.

His grandfather, the Hon. Thomas Willson, read law with Judge Stuart of Staunton, admitted to the bar, and removed to Western Virginia where he was engaged in most all the important cases at Morgantown, besides doing considerable practice at Clarksburg and Wheeling. He was a member of congress during the War of 1812, and his son, Edgar Campbell Willson, represented the same district in the Twenty-third congress. Hon. Thomas Willson held high rank as a lawyer, and was a gentleman of polished manners and a man of unquestioned integrity.

His wife's maiden name was Mary Poage. He died in 1826, leaving behind him five sons and three daughters, all of whom were distinguished for their talent and ability.

Hon. Alpheus E. Willson died in Uniontown of consumption, at five o'clock, Tuesday morning, September 9, 1884. He was the son of the Hon. Alpheus Poage and Eliza (Evans) Willson, and was born at Rock Forge, on Decker's creek, in Monongalia county, Virginia (now West Virginia), October 24, 1828.

Hon. Alpheus Poage Willson was born March 2, 1794; he was drowned in the Monongahela river near Brownsville, February 10, 1832. He was an excellent lawyer, and served in the Virginia legislature in 1819 and 1820, and in the Virginia senate from 1821 to 1825. September 20, 1821, he married Miss Eliza Evans, daughter of Jesse and Mary Evans and a sister of the late Colonel Samuel Evans, who was one of Fayette county's prominent and honored citizens, and a son of Jesse Evans one of Pennsylvania's successful and leading iron manufacturers.

When the Hon. Alpheus E. Willson was four years old, his parents removed from Virginia to Uniontown. In Uniontown he prepared himself in the public and private schools for college and at the age of sixteen years entered the sophomore class at Priceton college, and graduated from that institution in the class of 1847.

He read law with the late Judge Nathaniel Ewing, admitted to the bar, June 3, 1850, and immediately opened a law office. After ten year's practice, he removed to London, Ohio, where he formed a law partnership with Judge Lincoln of that place. In August, 1863, he returned to Uniontown and resumed the practice of law. He at once "rose to the front rank in his profession, and was known throughout the county as a safe and learned counselor."

September 18, 1855, he was married to Miss Catherine H. Dawson, daughter of George and Mary Dawson of Brownsville, Pennsylvania, and sister of the late Hon. John L. Dawson. (See Dawson's sketch in Spring Hill township sketches.) Judge Willson left three daughters—Mrs. R. H. Lindsey, Mrs. Hazard and Miss Mary K. Willson. He was the only son of his parents; his youngest sister, Mrs. Judge John K. Ewing, died in January, 1884. His mother is still living at the advanced age of eighty-eight.

In 1873 he was nominated by the democracy of Fayette county for president judge of the fourteenth judicial district, composed of the counties of Fayette and Greene. His opponent was Hon. David Crawford, nominated by the Greene county democrats. The republicans of the district made no nomination, but supported Judge Willson, who was elected by a large majority. At the time of his election, he was president of the Dollar Savings Bank, of Uniontown, and a director of the S. W. R. R. Co., both of which positions he resigned before taking his seat upon the bench. He was also a member of the coke-manufacturing firm of Willson, Boyle & Playford, from which he retired in 1880, with fair profits as the result of successful management.

While on the bench Judge Willson discharged each and every duty of the high position with unquestioned probity, courage and ability for a period of ten years.

He took his seat as president judge of this district on the first of January, 1874, to find the business of the district quite a number of years behind owing to the protracted illness of his predecessor, the late Hon. Samuel A. Gilmore. This accumulated business was, of itself, almost enough to have occupied the time of his entire term, and done justice to himself, but, added to this was the immense and constantly increasing volume of current business of the most remarkable decade of our legal history. With a high purpose and an energy equaled only by that determination to execute his great trust faithfully and well that caused him to fall a martyr to an exalted conception of duty, he began the accomplishment of what was one of his ambitions—the disposal of the public business with such rapidity, consistent with care, as would leave the dockets at the end of his term entirely clear. To the casual reader this will seem no ordinary task, but it is only to those who were intimately associated with him in its undertaking that its Herculean proportions really appear; and yet this ambition was so nearly realized that he retired from the bench with the business of Greene county in such condition that a cause commenced at one term may be tried at the next succeeding one, and that of Fayette county not over one year behind, and this the fault of the attorneys who, through sympathy for his condition during the last year and a half, would insist upon continuing their causes from term to term against his most earnest protest. He began his labors by a revision of the rules, which he brought to such perfection as greatly to facilitate practice in the several courts, and aid in making a strong bar. His term was remarkable not alone for the great volume of its business, but for the importance of its individual causes as well. Knowing neither friend nor foe, with the cold neutrality of an impartial judge, he decided every cause upon its merits alone. Nor did he decide them upon general principles, but always, after a most careful and exhaustive reading of the authorities bearing in any possible degree upon the question involved; so that an opinion of a few pages might, and in most instances did, represent the result of hours of the most conscientious toil and careful reflection. The result was, a standing as a judge before the supreme court as well as the bench-at-large equaled by few, excelled by none, and worthy the emulation of all. In short, as a judge, no man was more universally beloved, honored and revered by the people of any judicial district, and few ever retired from the bench so much regretted.

He possessed in the highest degree that combination of rare qualities so essential to the successful discharge of the grave duties of that responsible position. The satisfaction with which his decisions as a judge were received was only equaled by the esteem in which he was held by the whole people as a gentleman. No one disputed his ability, none doubted his integrity.

In all his relations of life Judge Willson was scrupulously prompt in meeting his engagements, and, during his term of office, he was never one minute late at court, and during its sitting never left the bench but once in this county, and twice in Greene. It was close application to business and its consequent confinement that developed the disease with which he died. His friends thought they foresaw the impending danger and advised his retirement two years or more ago, but, thinking there was none, he declined to heed their good counsel, and the sad consequence was not unexpected. He was broad-minded and liberal, generous and charitable, without being ostentatious. When such a man dies, then have we indeed a time to mourn."

JAMES C. WORK was brought up a "farmer boy," and as the name indicates, is of Irish origin. He was born February 8, 1859, in Fayette county, Pa. His father, John Work, is an intelligent and prosperous farmer of the county, and owns quite a large tract of valuable land. He is a native of Harrison county, Ohio, coming to Fayette county with his parents, James and

Jno. D. Carr

Nancy Work, when he was only seven years old.

The maiden name of James C. Work's mother was Sarah McLaughlin, born in Fayette county, Pa., and a daughter of Charles and Mary McLaughlin. James C. Work attended the public schools of his native township. Leaving the common schools, he entered college at Waynesburg, Pa., and graduated with honor from that college in 1884. He immediately began the study of law, and in the same year entered the law department of the University of Michigan, Ann Arbor, where he prosecuted his law studies for nine months. In the fall of 1885 he went to Yale and graduated from the law department of that institution in June, 1886, with the degree of L. L. B. He was at once admitted to practice at the bar of the supreme court of Connecticut. In December, 1886, he was admitted to practice in the several courts of Fayette county, and immediately opened a law office at Uniontown, where he has been engaged in active practice ever since. In practice Mr. Work is careful and painstaking, and often discourages rather than encourages litigation. He looks upon the law as a science and not a mere trade by which to grind out a living.

JOHN D. CARR, one of the most enterprising and public spirited men of the county, was born near Recreation Park, Allegheny county, Pa., December 16, 1849. His father was the largest and most successful market gardener in his day, of Pittsburgh and Allegheny. The information that enables the envied steward of the county home to outdo all our farmers with farm products and vegetables, was gathered during his boyhood days on his father's extensive farm. "I have hoed the cabbage, cared for the corn and picked potatoes on the very ground now known as Recreation Park," remarked Mr. Carr recently, and his wonderful display at the late county fair would indicate that his early training had been improved by time.

On reaching man's estate, Mr. Carr was apprenticed to a marble cutter. He learned the trade thoroughly and was recognized as a skillful mechanic. He assumed the charge of, and became superintendent of the Pittsburgh Marble Works, of W. W. Wallace, the largest establishment of its kind in Pennsylvania. Holding this position until 1873. In the same year he came to Fayette City and started in the marble business on his own account. He met with great success, and his work was rapidly securing a reputation, when in October, 1884, his shops were destroyed by fire.

In January, 1885, he was elected steward of the County Home, his excellent management of this trust has been faithful, sensible and humane. His efforts have always been directed in the interests of the tax-payers of Fayette county, and no fair man of either political party has ever accused him of being dilatory in the discharge of his duties. His official career has ever been open to the most rigid investigation, and he has always been able to rise above party prejudice in the management of his important charge.

A more eloquent tribute to a faithful servant could not be written than the official letter appended:

STATE OF PENNSYLVANIA.
Committee on Lunacy, the Board of Public Charities.
Office, No. 1224 Chestnut St., Philadelphia.
A. J. OURT, M. D., Philadelphia, Secretary.
January 8, 1887.

JOHN D. CARR, Esq., Steward Fayette County Almshouse, Uniontown, Pa.:

My Dear Sir: I have just learned that some changes have been made in your Board of Directors. This, I hope, will not interfere with your re-appointment to the position you have so creditably filled. In my official visits to your county home or almshouse, I have observed with pleasure the tidy appearance of the inmates and their cheerful and contented disposition, indicative of the interest which you have always manifested in our several interviews for the welfare and comfort of the indigent poor under your charge.

The cleanliness of the apartments of the inmates, and of the institution in general, have not, I am sure, escaped the notice of the humane and Christian gentlemen who constitute your board, and will compare favorably with any almshouse in the State.

I have taken the liberty of writing you at this time these few lines of commendation as an expression of my appreciation of your unexceptionable abilities as a steward, and also to assure you it will give me pleasure to be informed of your re-election to a position the duties of which yourself and wife have conscientiously discharged.

Very truly yours, &c.,

ANDW. J. OURT.

The Pittsburgh *Times* of yesterday contains this notice: "It is expected that Governor Beaver will this week name the commission of three to revise the poor-laws of the State, in accordance with an act of the late legislature. There is considerable speculation regarding the make up of the commission. Already half a hundred names have been sent to His Excellency. A gentleman, one posted in charitable affairs, gave it as his opinion yesterday afternoon that the Commission will be composed of R. D. McGonnigle, of this city; John D. Carr, of Fayette county, and James Hall, of Northumberland county. The annual convention of poor directors of the State will be held in Altoona early next month, and it is probable the commission will hold their first meeting in that city at that time. McGonnigle and Carr are recognized as authority in poor house matters."

He was elected on the democratic ticket, and took charge of the asylum in April, 1885. As noticed previously, he was re-elected in 1889, and is the present incumbent. He served ten years as school director while at Fayette City; and was secretary of the board during that time, with the exception of one year. He served also as a member of the borough council for several years.

In 1871 he was married to Miss Amanda M. Cook, of Fayette City, and a daughter of James R. Cook, then a farmer of the county, who now resides in Michigan. They have seven children living: the eldest, Wooda N. Carr, for a few years past the brilliant young editor of the Uniontown *News*, was born February, 1871, and is now attending school preparatory to entering the profession of the law. The other children are: John D., Jr., Charles H., Walter Russell, Edna E., Ethel C. and Katie B.

John D. Carr's parents, Nicholas and Catherine Carr (*née* Burns), were natives of Ireland, who came to America when quite young, and were married in this country. Nicholas Carr was a man of strong mind and fine business qualifications. He did a large business as drover and cattle dealer, and died in 1879, at the age of sixty-nine years. His wife died in 1868, at the age of forty-five years.

John D. Carr is a member of the Masonic Order, Knights of Pythias and of the Royal Arcanum. He is P. M. of Masons, and member of the Grand Lodge of Pennsylvania.

John D. Carr possesses great force, energy and determination, and has that thorough-going disposition which takes right hold of great projects with both hands, and drives into thick and thin in spite of all obstacles and opposition, and generally accomplishes whatever he undertakes.

In politics he is truly democratic and solely a democrat from instinct. There is none of the demagogue in his nature, nor of the "rule or ruin policy." He believes in no "milk and water" politics, but, on the contrary, is aggressive, and favors hewing close to the line, letting the chips fall wherever they may. He is of that class of men who, whenever and wherever placed as representatives of the people's interests, are always true to the trusts reposed with them, regardless of consequences.

PROF. SOLOMON F. HOGUE, one of Pennsylvania's leading educators, is a son of Solomon and Rachel (Huss) Hogue, and was born at "Hogue's Mills," near Waynesburg, Greene county, Pennsylvania, April 1, 1848.

His grandfather, Solomon Hogue, was a consistent member of the Society of Friends. He was born at Winchester, Va., and came to the vicinity of Waynesburg in an early day. He was a farmer by occupation and a democrat in politics.

His father, Solomon Hogue, Jr., was born in 1803, and died in 1877. He learned the wagon-making trade at Winchester, Va., and engaged in that business for some time at Waynesburg. He next erected the first steam grist-mill in Greene county (now Lippincott's distillery), engaged extensively in manufacturing and exporting flour to Philadelphia and other important markets. With two others he built a steamboat to carry his flour to market on the "Western waters." His partners ran away with the boat and sold it. He married Miss Rachel, daughter of John Huss, a distiller, miller, democrat, and member of the Baptist church. John Huss married Miss Elizabeth Eaton, a distant relative of General R. E. Lee.

Mr. and Mrs. Hogue had eight children: John H., merchant at Waynesburg; Jacob, farmer; Asa B., merchant at Waynesburg; William H. R., farmer; Martha, dead, was the wife of William Ingraham, uncle of Judge Ingraham; Mary, wife of Benjamin Ruehart, a wealthy farmer; Elizabeth, wife of J. K. Scott, of Crow's Mills, and Professor S. F. Hogue.

Professor S. F. Hogue was educated in the common schools, Waynesburg College, and Edinboro Normal School, where he graduated in the class of 1872. He afterwards spent three years at Cornell University. He is also a graduate of Waynesburg College and the University of New York. He began teaching at the age of nineteen years, taught when not attending school in common and private schools until 1878, when he was elected county superintendent of common schools of Greene county, Pa.

"During his administration as county superintendent his county was one of the best managed in this part of the State, and his work was quoted as a specimen of what a faithful superintendent could do.

DR. GEO. P. HAYS,
Ex-President W. & J. College."

In 1881, upon solicitation, Professor Hogue became principal of the Tidioute Union and Normal School and there he built up the first industrial school in the State outside of the cities. In June, 1885, he resigned and became professor of Latin and higher mathematics at Edinboro Normal School, remained until February, 1886, when he accepted the presidency of Defiance Normal College, Ohio.

In May, 1887, he became principal of the training department of California Normal School. In July, 1888, he came to Uniontown and organized Redstone Academy, a select private school for young men and young ladies, and for boys and girls, in a suite of rooms in the First National Bank building; but owing to the growth and prospects of the school, larger and more suitable rooms have been secured for it in the new Commercial block, centrally located at the corner of Church and Morgantown streets.

The following is a just tribute to Professor Hogue:

"Professor S. F. Hogue is a most efficient instructor and educator.

DR. J. W. SCOTT."

Dr. Scott is President Harrison's father-in-law.

In 1875, Professor Hogue was married to Miss Etta Bell, a teacher in the high school of New Castle, and a native of Grove City. She died, and he was remarried in 1880 to Miss Emma Downey, teacher of French in Waynesburg College.

She died in 1881, and in 1886 he was married to Miss Lydia Lee Evans, of Tidioute. They have one child, Frank W. Hogue. Mrs. Hogue is a graduate of Chamberlain Institute, New York, Edinboro Normal School, and of the first class of the Chautauqua L. S. C.

Mrs. Hogue is now preceptress and teacher of French, English language, literature and gymnastics in Redstone Academy.

Professor and Mrs. Hogue are members of the Presbyterian church. He is a democrat in politics, is an efficient, active school worker, successful teacher, thorough scholar, and a polished gentleman.

BROWNSVILLE AND SPRINGHILL

CHARLES P. ACKLIN, of Brownsville, is a son of John and Rebecca (Cook) Acklin, and was born February 4, 1849, in Pittsburgh, Pa.

John Acklin (father) was born in Brownsville, Pa., is a glass-blower by trade, and belongs to the Methodist Episcopal church. He has served several terms as a member of the city council, elected on the democratic ticket. He was married to Miss Rebecca Cook, of Fayette City. Mr. Acklin is now seventy-three years of age, and his faithful wife is in her sixty-seventh year.

When Charles P. Acklin was only about two years old his parents removed from Pittsburgh to Brownsville. At Brownsville he attended the common schools till he was fourteen years old, when he engaged in the glass factory at Brownsville, and learned the trade of gathering. In four years he became a proficient glass-blower, working at Brownsville in the business until 1882, excepting a short time at Pittsburgh, and three years at Belle Vernon. In the spring of 1882 he embarked in the mercantile business, and opened out his present store, in which he carries a full line of dry-goods, groceries and queensware. He has been very successful in his mercantile calling, and has built up a large and lucrative business.

He is a democrat from instinct, but, in county or township elections, votes for the man, and does not always vote the regular ticket. In 1878 he married Miss Sarah Graham, a daughter of William Graham, the latter a carpenter of Brownsville, who is now in the seventy-sixth year of his age. Two children were born to their union—twins: William G. and Lizzie E. By economy and good management Mr. Acklin has achieved considerable success in business.

WILLIAM C. ARMSTRONG, of Bridgeport, is the son of Joshua and Lydia (Drum) Armstrong.

His father, Joshua Armstrong, was a native of New Jersey and came to Washington county, Pa., when about eighteen years of age. He remained there a short time, when he removed to Brownsville in 1818. He was a carpenter by trade, and built over one hundred houses in Brownsville and Bridgeport and vicinity. He was a prominent citizen of Bridgeport and died in 1881, eighty-three years of age.

The mother of W. C. Armstrong was a native of Maryland, and came to Fayette county with her parents when twelve years of age, and died September, 1875, at the age of seventy-two years. Her father came to the county in 1815, where he died in 1845.

William C. Armstrong was born at Bridgeport, October 14, 1835, and where he grew to manhood. He attended the common schools. On leaving school he apprenticed himself to Alexander Moffit to learn carriage blacksmithing, and remained there for four years. In 1856 he went on the river to learn steamboat engineering on the steamer J. M. Converse. This boat was sunk by the ice in 1857 at Ferry Island, Mississippi river. Mr. Armstrong was on the boat from the time of starting until she sank.

He remained upon packet boats as engineer until 1861, when he was made First Assistant Engineer on the Government boat Marmond, and took part in all of the principal naval battles along the Mississippi river and its tributaries. He was at the fight at Vicksburg when the canal was cut across the strip of land in front of that city. He served in the navy all through the war, and was honorably discharged at Mound City, Ill., in 1866. He next became engineer on a Missouri river boat plying from Sioux City to Fort Benton, and remained till 1873, when he received a position on a tow-boat at Pittsburgh, which he held until 1875. At this time he and others built a tow-boat called the Dauntless. He took charge of this boat as captain and pilot and ran the boat till 1883. He then left the river and settled at Bridgeport as manager of the large grocery and agricultural implement house, which he has successfully managed ever since and is still engaged in.

Mr. Armstrong was married in 1872 to Miss Ella Bugher, daughter of Captain Doyle Bugher, of Brownsville, who is an old steamboat captain. He is now a member of the council, having been elected on the democratic ticket against a republican majority of above one hundred votes in the borough.

THOMAS AUBREY, the proprietor of the well-known and extensive Retrieve Planing Mills, West Brownsville, was born in Jefferson township, Fayette county, Pa., February 15, 1827.

Thomas Aubrey was reared on a farm, educated in the subscription schools until at the age of seventeen years, when he went to Brownsville to learn the trade of a steamboat joiner and house carpenter. After serving an apprenticeship of three years with Noah Worcester, he was engaged at journey work for a period of twelve years. In 1859 he became a member of the firm of Aubrey, Cromlow & Coon. This firm erected and operated the Excelsior Planing Mill, the first of the kind in West Brownsville. The mill burned, and they erected another on the site of the John Gregg Distillery. In 1869 Mr. Aubrey withdrew from the firm and removed to Mahaska county, Iowa, where for two years he was engaged in farming. He returned to Bridgeport in 1872, and formed a partnership with his son, Robert L. Aubrey. They rented and operated the Excelsior Mill until June 30, 1883, when it burned, inflicting a loss of twelve thousand dollars. Undaunted by this loss, Thomas Aubrey immediately took steps to rebuild on a large scale. He erected the present Retrieve Planing Mills, in which are found all the latest improved machinery and modern inventions necessary in the planing mill business. These mills are the largest of the kind in Washington county. Aubrey & Son are manufacturers of first-class flooring, lath, shingles, sash and doors.

In 1848 Mr. Aubrey was married to Miss Maria Boyd, of Bridgeport. Unto their union were born seven children: James M. (of Washington county), Robert L., Mary C. (died September 30, 1887), Ella, John N., Oliver C. and Lina.

Mr. Aubrey is a democrat, has served as a member of the town council, and is now president of the Bridgeport board of school directors. He is a stockholder in the natural gas company of Bridgeport, a stockholder in the P. V. & C. R. R., and is a member of the I. O. O. F. He is a useful member of the M. P. church.

Mr. Aubrey has achieved an enviable career, beginning life as a carpenter; but he now stands in the front rank of our best business men in Southwestern Pennsylvania.

JAMES P. BAKER is a son of John and Catherine (Saddler) Baker, and was born near Morris Cross Roads, Springhill township, Fayette county, Pa., March 2, 1843; is descended from an old and worthy German family. His grandfather Baker was one of the earliest settlers of Fayette county.

John Baker (father) was born near Morris Cross Roads, on the 15th of September, 1807, and died September 23, 1853. He owned a farm of 240 acres of excellent, well-improved land, and devoted all his time to farming. He married Catherine Saddler, daughter of William Saddler, a farmer, and one of the earlier settlers. They had ten children: William, Jacob, Michael D., Mary, Joseph L., Daniel M., James P., John, Mattie and Margaret. All of these children are living except Jacob, who died while a soldier in the Union army.

James P. Baker worked on his father's farm, and attended the common schools until twenty years of age. Leaving school he engaged in farming with his father.

He rented the Everhart farm in 1875, and farmed it one year.

In 1876 he took charge of the celebrated "Friendship Hill" estate, the home of Albert Gallatin, and the "favorite seat of John L. Dawson, who ended here his brilliant and useful life."

Mr. Baker continued to manage "Friendship Hill" estate until 1884, when he bought a farm of sixty-five acres, and removed to it. He remained upon this farm until January 1, 1889, when he again took charge of the "Friendship Hill" estate, where he now resides.

James P. Baker was married November 7, 1867, to Elizabeth Everhart, daughter of Adolph Everhart, a Fayette county farmer. Their union has been blessed with five children: Lena, Ella, Mattie, Elizabeth and Eliza, all now living except Elizabeth, who died at nine months of age.

Mr. Baker is a democrat, and has always voted that ticket. He is a member of the Lutheran church at Morris Cross Roads, and is a man of good judgment, correct business habits, gives intelligent thought to his business, and has always been successfnl in whatever he has undertaken.

MICHAEL BAKER an old and respected citizen of Springhill township, is of German descent; and was born March 3, 1815. He is the son of Michael and Catherine (Everly) Baker, both natives of Maryland.

Michael Baker, Sr. (father), when a young man came to Springhill township with his father and mother. He bought a farm of 125 acres, which he improved and cultivated during the remainder of his life. He married Miss Catherine Everly, and unto them were born six sons and four daughters. He engaged in farming, and for many years employed a team in hauling goods from Cumberland, Md., to Fayette county. He was an honest and respected citizen, and by hard work accumulated considerable property. He died in 1859, being preceded twenty years to the tomb by his faithful wife.

Michael Baker was reared on a farm, and attended the subscription schools until seventeen years of age. He then engaged in farming; and after his father's death he purchased the home farm, where he resides to-day. He has erected a very fine residence and a large, commodious barn on the old homestead, where he is passing his last days in peace and plenty.

Mr. Baker was married April 28, 1845, to Miss Catherine, daughter of Richard Surgent. To their union were born seven children: Richard, Sarah, Elizabeth, Jefferson, Barbara, John and Margaret Ellen (dead). John and Sarah are still at home, while the others are married and have homes of their own. Mrs. Baker was a member of the Presbyterian church until her death, January 15, 1873.

Mr. Baker was admitted to membership, many years ago, in the Disciple church at Oak Grove.

He is a democrat of the Jeffersonian school, has served as judge of elections and supervisor of roads in Springhill township.

By intelligent management and honest labor, he has acquired a competency, lives surrounded by all the comforts of life, and enjoys the confidence and respect of those who know him.

JOSEPH LYONS BAKER is of German ancestry and a member of one of the prominent families of Springhill township. He is a son of John and Catherine (Saddler) Baker, and was born September 5, 1838, in Springhill township, Fayette county, Pa.

His grandfather, Michael Baker, was a native of Hagerstown, Md., and was one of the early settlers in Springhill township.

His father, John Baker, was born in Springhill township, and received a plain but practical education and engaged in farming as his life's pursuit. On arriving at man's estate, he married and immediately purchased his father-in-law's farm of 246 acres of land. He bought it on credit and by industry and prompt attention to his business paid every dollar of his indebtedness. He was married to Miss Catherine, daughter of William Saddler. To them were born ten children: William, Jacob, Michael, Joseph L., Daniel, James, John, Mary, Martha and Maggie, all living but Jacob, who died in the Federal Army. John Baker was a democrat and served as road supervisor and assessor. He was a kind father, a good citizen and died September 23, 1853. His venerable widow is now living with her daughters in Missouri.

Joseph Lyons Baker was reared on a farm, educated in the common schools, and the Millsboro Normal School, in Washington county, where he attended two terms. Leaving school, he engaged in teaching and taught three terms in the common schools of Fayette county, one term in Indiana and one term in Missouri.

During 1866 he returned to Springhill and engaged in farming on the homestead farm for three years. In 1869 he removed to his father-in-law's farm in Dunbar township, and remained there four years. In 1873 he purchased ninety-two acres of the home farm in Springhill township, and immediately removed there. He erected a fine dwelling and has greatly improved his farm by fencing, draining and liming.

He was married November 7, 1867, to Miss Rebecca, daughter of Nathaniel G. Hurst, a well known citizen of Fayette county. They have seven children: Jesse Hurst, Lilly May, Julia M., Katie Hurst, Beatrice, Isaac G. and Queenie.

Mr. Baker was a democrat until 1888. Being in favor of a high protective tariff, he left the democratic ranks in that year and voted with the republican party.

He has served one year as tax collector and is serving his fourth term as school director.

For two years he has been an elder in the Lutheran church at Morris Cross Roads, of which he and his wife have been members for several years.

GEORGE BAKER is of German origin, was born April 11, 1818, in Springhill township, Fayette county, Pa., and is a son of George and Julia Ann (Dick) Baker.

His paternal grandfather, Peter Baker, came from Maryland to Springhill township in 1802, and purchased a farm of 291¼ acres of land. He was a successful farmer in his day and kept an apiary.

George Baker, Sr. (father), was born near Boonsborough, Md., and received a very good education. He married Miss Julia Ann Dick, December 14, 1794; in 1800 moved across the mountains in wagons to Springhill, and settled upon his father's tract, of which he became heir to 141, acres, his brother receiving the remainder. He had six children: Elizabeth, Mary, Margaret, Thomas, Charlotte and George. George Baker, Sr., was a weaver by trade, and he and his wife were members of the Lutheran church. He died in 1839 at the age of seventy-five years, and in two months his wife, a native of Germany, passed away, aged sixty-nine years.

George Baker was reared on a farm, and attended the subscription school until eighteen years of age.

The home farm was willed to him on condition that he pay the other heirs a certain sum each, which he did. He has held the farm since his father's death in 1839, and has added greatly to its appearance and value by many valuable improvements, one of which was the erection of a large, tasteful and comfortable residence.

He was married October 7, 1844, to Miss Margaret, daughter of Richard Sergent. Their union has been blessed with seven children: Julia Ann, April 6, 1846; Sarah E., April 10, 1848; Oliver P., March 10, 1850; James, April 23, 1852; Emma C., July 15, 1854; William E., February 10, 1857; Joseph M., August 31, 1859, and two who died in infancy.

Mr. Baker is a Jacksonian Democrat, as was also his father, he has held the township offices of auditor, road supervisor and school director.

He is a prominent citizen of Springhill, and is a good farmer. His wife has spent half a century of her life in the membership and service of the Presbyterian church, and has been a faithful friend of the church to which her husband also belongs.

HUGH THOMPSON BOLEY is a merchant at Bridgeport, in Fayette county, Pa., and is a son of Daniel and Ruth (Thompson) Boley. His father was born and raised in Allegheny county, Pa., and was a pilot on the Ohio and Mississippi rivers. His home was at Sewickley, Allegheny county, where he died in 1853, at the age of forty-seven years. He was a democrat. Mrs. Boley was born and reared in Washington county, Pa., and died at Pekin, Ill., in 1855, at the age of seventy-eight years. Alexander is engaged in the ice business, and has been for the past twenty-five years, at Pekin.

Hugh Thompson Boley was born at Sewickley, July 14, 1845, where he was reared till at the age of fourteen years. At the age of fourteen he went on the river, at the age of sixteen was acting as mate on the Ohio and Mississippi rivers, and continued on the river in this capacity till 1874. He was in the government service throughout the entire war, was on the steamer Henry Clay on April 14, 1862, when she ran the blockade at Vicksburg and was sunk by the batteries of the city.

In 1874 he came to West Brownsville, and married Miss Belle Weaver, a daughter of Mr. Joseph Weaver, of the same place. In the same year he formed a partnership with his father-in-law (the firm name being Weaver & Boley), and engaged in the general mercantile business at Bridgeport. They have been very successful in building up a large trade and in doing good business. Mr. Weaver died on the 13th of February, 1889, at the age of seventy years. The business is still carried on in the old firm name. The establishment carries a nice stock of goods.

Mr. Boley resides in West Brownsville, while he carries on business at Bridgeport. He is a warm democrat, and has served several times as a member of the council, and as judge of the elections. He has no children.

JOHN WILSON BOWERS was born in Springhill township, Fayette county Pa., March 26, 1860 of pure German origin, and is the youngest son of Joseph and Julia Ann Bowers (née Brooks). Joseph Bowers, the grandfather of John W., was an early settler in the southern part of the county. He was a man of genius, and in the crude state of mechanical arts of that day and in that respect gained considerable reputation. He was an upright, liberal Christian gentleman. He owned a farm of one hundred acres; the land, due to its location, was rather unproductive, but by his energy and excellent management lived reasonably well, and raised a family of eleven children, who reached man and womanhood and occupied with honor and respect various positions in life.

Joseph Bowers, with his farming and other business, built a small distillery and made, whiskey and apple brandy.

In 1828, when the Women Temperance Society was founded, many of its members, unreasonably as it may appear, vehemently denounced the manufacture, sale and use of whiskey, in every form. They attacked Joseph Bowers and told him that if he did not cease making and selling whiskey his sons would be drunkards. His sons were all temperate and grew to be respectable men.

He died in 1846. Joseph Bowers, Jr., was born July 26, 1825, on the old homestead farm in Springhill township, Fayette county, Pa., and received his education in the schools of the township, becoming well learned in mathematics. In 1845 he was married to Julia Ann Brooks, a daughter of James Brooks (deceased). After marriage he began housekeeping on his father's farm. One year later his father died, and, by an order of the orphan's court, the farm was appraised at fifteen dollars an acre. Joseph Bowers bought and paid the other ten heirs their part in the estate in money. With a little over $100 he started in life; and for twenty-three years he remained on the home farm, and by the many improvements he made added much to the value of the farm. In 1868 he sold the farm and purchased the Alex. Ross farm, two miles north of Morris Cross Roads. This farm at that time was in a bad condition, the buildings and fences almost gone; but Mr. Bowers immediately after his purchase began to replace them with more substantial structures and improvements. The old buildings gave way to more modern and fashionable ones, and his barn and house are models of neatness and convenience. To their union were born three children: James P., George D. and John W.

John W. Bowers was married to Miss Anna E., daughter of Rev. William O. Wilson, D. D., March 13, 1888. In April of the same year he assumed the control and management of the homestead farm, where he now resides. He received his education in the common schools of the county, and at the Southwest Pennsylvania State Normal School. He never smoked a cigar nor drank a glass of whiskey in his life.

He is a consistent member of the Lutheran church, and has been from his early youth. He is now superintendent of the Lutheran Sabbath-school. His start in life would indicate a very promising future, and few men so young as he are as well situated in life. He is active, and a fit representative of the young democracy of his township. He has filled the office of township auditor for two terms, and served as member of the county central committee.

NELSON BLAIR BOWMAN is of a stock that represents three nations of people: United States, England and Germany: Requiring the bull-dog courage of English character, to conquer and hold the soil, the persistent frugality and industry of the German to develop the resources of the same, and the combination of the two races to establish the country which is rapidly developing into the strongest and greatest nation of the world.

The Bowman family settled in the County Cumberland, England, where they remained for many generations. When Robert Seymore Bowman, third son of Stephen Bowman, of Kirkoswald, was at the age of fifteen years, he was placed as a page in the household of Elizabeth, daughter of King James the First. In 1613, Elizabeth married Frederick the Fifth, Elector Palatine of Germany. Young Bowman continued in her service, going with her to Germany, where in 1618 he married and founded the German branch of the Bowman family. From this branch Nelson B. Bowman is descended. Simon Bowman, a descendant of Robert (or Rupert as the Germans have it), came to the United States the middle of the last century, and settled on a farm known as Big Spring, six miles from Hagerstown, Maryland. He married Mary Easter, and after the birth of his son, Jacob, removed into Hagerstown in 1764, and built the first stone house constructed in that town. His death occurred in 1802.

The second of this line, Jacob Bowman, the father of Nelson B. Bowman, was born at Big Spring in 1763. At the age of sixteen years he entered the store of Col. Robert Elliott, of Hagerstown, where he continued as a clerk till in the twenty-fourth year of his age, when he became partner with Col. Elliott, and in 1786 came to Brownsville, where he was one of the earliest merchants of that place. He acted as assistant commissary to the western army during Wayne's campaign against the Indians. During Washington's administration he was appointed postmaster at Brownsville, holding the office thirty years, or until Jackson became president, when he was removed for being an offensive partisan—a Washington Federalist. He was one of the founders of the Episcopal church at Brownsville, as well as one of its earliest, most useful and prominent members. He was a man of great mind, enterprise and industry, and died in 1847, leaving a large estate. His wife was Isabella Lowry, native of County Donegal, Ireland. In 1845 she passed away, at the age of seventy-eight years. She was the daughter of Major James Lowry, of Castle Finn, Ireland. The wife of the latter was Susan Blair, daughter of Rev. Arthur Blair, rector of Carnone. Major Lowry was descended from James Lowry, of Ballynagorry, who came to Ireland from Maxwelton, Dumfries, Scotland, in 1619, and died in Ireland in 1665. After the death of her parents, Isabella came to this country in 1784, with her guardian, Robert Nelson, a merchant of Baltimore, and a relative of her mother.

The present head of the Lowry family in Ireland is Somerst Richard Lowry, Earl of Belmore of Castle Coole, County Fermagh, with whom Mr. Bowman is in regular correspondence. The Countess of Belmore is a niece to the right Hon. William E. Gladstone, the late Premier of Great Britain.

Nelson Blair Bowman was born at Brownsville, July 8, 1807, and is the youngest son of a family of nine children; and of whom he is the only survivor. At twelve years of age, he entered Washington (now Washington and Jefferson College,) taking a four years' course. Leaving college, he engaged in the mercantile business and continued in the same with remarkable success up to 1855, when he retired from active business. He is now vice-president of the Monongahela Bank of Brownsville, one of the strongest and most reliable banks in the whole country, and one of the very few banks that did not suspend specie payment prior to the breaking out of the late Civil War.

Nelson B. Bowman's father was the first president of this bank in 1812, remaining as such until he handed in his resignation, just previous to his death. He was succeeded in the presidency of the same by his son James Lowry Bowman, who continued as president till his death in 1857. He was succeeded by his brother, Goodloe Harper Bowman, who acted in the same capacity till his death in 1874.

Nelson B. Bowman was married in 1856 to Miss Elizabeth L. Dunn, of Reading, Pennsylvania. To their union were born six children, two of whom are now living: Sara and Charles William. Mr. Bowman has never held any office, nor aspired to political honors of any kind. He is senior warden of Christ Episcopal church at Brownsville. He owns two beautiful farms near Brownsville, besides large tracts of land in the West, and is otherwise well fixed in life. He is a man of pleasant manners, and is well versed in literature, a good conversationalist, and takes special pride in entertaining his friends at his beautiful home, Nemacolin Towers, where he was born and where his father lived for sixty years, from his marriage to his death. The house is very extensive, castle shape, commands a magnificent view of the Monongahela, of the extensive suburbs of Bridgeport and West Brownsville. With its ample grounds, finely improved, it is considered by many to be the finest residence in Fayette county.

June 16, 1889, he mourned the loss of his excellent wife. The following concerning the same appeared in the *Genius of Liberty*, June 20, 1889: Mrs. Elizabeth L. Bowman, wife of Nelson B. Bowman, died at their home in Brownsville, Sunday June 16, 1889, in her sixty-second year. Mrs. Bowman was a woman possessed of many Christian graces and had many friends. With her husband, two children, a son and a daughter, mourn her death. She was a devoted member of Christ church in which her funeral rites were performed and in the churchyard near by her remains were interred on Tuesday the 18th.

GOODLOE HARPER BOWMAN. The late Goodloe Harper Bowman who died at Brownsville, January 30, 1874, was during his life pre-eminently one of the ablest and most highly respected business men of the county, and his life was without stain or blot. His family is an old and very respectable one (whose history in full is given in the sketch of Nelson B. Bowman). He was the third son of Jacob and Isabella (Lowry) Bowman, the former of English-German extraction and the latter of Scotch-Irish descent.

Goodloe H. Bowman was born in Brownsville, April 20, 1803, and his educational advantages were none of the best. He attended the subscription schools of Brownsville only a few terms before entering the store of his father, who carried on a general mercantile business at that time at Brownsville. Young Bowman soon developed an unusual talent for business, and formed a co-partnership with his brother, N. B. Bowman, on the retirement of their father (Jacob Bowman) from business. They continued in the general mercantile business from 1832 to 1855.

Goodloe Harper Bowman was elected cashier of the Monongahela Bank, of Brownsville, in September, 1830, and filled the position most acceptably for about twelve years, when he resigned on account of the passage of an act by the legislature of Pennsylvania, which prohibited a cashier from engaging in any other business; and he was not disposed to relinquish his mercantile business for the cashiership.

He became president of the Monongahela Bank, of Brownsville, in 1857, as the successor of his brother, James L. Bowman, who went in as president in 1843, as the successor of their father, Jacob Bowman, the first president of the bank. Under the administration of the Bowmans, the bank attained the fine reputation that it still possesses, as a reliable and prosperous institution.

Mr. Bowman, on January 9, 1840, married Miss Jane Correy Smith, of Reading, Berks county, Pa. He left five children, namely: Isabella Lowry (now Mrs. Leoser), James L., John Howard, Ann S. and William Robert. Jane Corry (Smith) Bowman, who died August, 1877, was the daughter of John Smith, of English descent, who married Elizabeth Bull, daughter of Colonel Bull, a native of Berks county, Pa. He was a highly respected and very prominent man in eastern Pennsylvania.

Mr. Bowman was for many years senior warden of Christ's Protestant Episcopal church, at Brownsville. He was a consistent church member, an able and honest business man, a kind husband, an affectionate father —a model man.

MICHAEL CAGEY, a well-to-do farmer of Springhill township, was born February 2, 1811, in German township, Fayette county, Pa. He is a son of Christian and Margaret (Wall) Cagey, both natives of German township and of German descent.

Christian Cagey (father), was born in 1780, and died in 1838, at the age of fifty-eight years. He was a farmer, and was a quiet and industrious citizen of Fayette county.

Michael Cagey, Sr. (paternal grandfather) came to his death while roofing a house, falling from the roof and was instantly killed. He left a wife and four children.

Elizabeth Wall Cagey (mother) was born in 1786, and died in 1869, at the advanced age of eighty-three years.

Michael Cagey worked on his father's farm, and attended the subscription schools of that day until twenty-one years of age.

He was married on February 17, 1842, to Miss Mary Bowers, daughter of Joseph Bowers, of Fayette county, Pa., he was a farmer and blacksmith.

Of this union six children were born: John, Joseph, Catherine, Harriet, Susan and Jonathan. Two of these children are dead, Joseph, died March 30, 1868, and Jonathan departed this life on June 6, 1876.

Mary (Bowers) Cagey was born December 21, 1810. She is still living, and is a consistent member of the Evangelical Lutheran church.

Michael Cagey has followed farming for an occupation. He owns a farm of eighty acres of well-improved land, and resides in a nice and comfortable house, which he built thirty-eight years ago. He is a member of the Lutheran church, at Morris Cross Roads, and is one of the worthy citizens of Springhill township.

WILLIAM CHATLAND, a worthy citizen of Brownsville, where he has resided for the last thirty-five years, and is one of the foremost business men of the place, having been engaged in the bakery business ever since he came to Brownsville in 1854. At present he is carrying on an extensive cracker manufactory, in partnership with his son-in-law, George W. Lenhart (see his sketch), under the firm name of Chatland & Lenhart. They have the reputation of making the best water cracker in the market.

William Chatland was born at Stratford-on-Avon, Warwickshire, England, June 9, 1811. His father, William Chatland, was a citizen of Meriden, a borough six miles north of the city of Coventry and in the same shire. He died in London, in 1819, in the forty-first year of his age. The mother of the subject was named Priscilla Green, a native of Brier Hill, Staffordshire, England. She died in 1814, when her son was but three years of age.

Mr. Chatland was given in charge of his grandmother, who died when he was ten years old. His uncle Joseph Chatland, a prosperous baker, then took charge of him till he was thirteen years old, when he was apprenticed to learn the trade of a baker with David Claridge, who was at that time a famous baker in the city of Coventry.

When through his apprenticeship, he spent and one-half years in London, where he was employed in two first-class houses. He then returned to Coventry, established himself in the baker's business and was married to Miss Elizabeth Manton, daughter of William Manton, a farmer of Berkswell, Warwickshire. He remained here about six years, when he migrated to the United States with his wife and three daughters, and arrived at New York, April 20, 1844.

Shortly after landing he left for Pittsburgh, on the old "Bingham Line," remained a short time in Pittsburgh, and finally settled at Washington, Pa., where he lived for about eight years and carried on the bakery and confectionery business. In 1852 he organized a company of fifteen persons, and went overland to California. In Sacramento, he bought out a bakery and operated it with success, but was compelled by sickness to quit the country. He now returned to Washington, Pa., where he had left his family, not being satisfied with the outlook for business at that place, he removed to Brownsville in 1854, and established himself in business in the full line of his trade. For eighteen years he continued alone in the business, when Mr. Lenhart became his partner.

Mrs. Elizabeth Chatland, his wife, died in Brownsville, January 28, 1874, in the sixty-first year of her age, leaving three daughters: Elizabeth, the eldest, married Theodore Bosler, a son of Dr. Bosler, of Mechanicsburg, Pa., now living at Dayton, Ohio; Miss Mary Ann, the second daughter, resides at home with her father; Sarah, is the wife of George W. Lenhart.

Mr. Chatland was raised in the faith of the Church of England, and he and his family are members of the Protestant Episcopal church. He is now vestryman in the church at Brownsville, and has been for many years past. Since 1848, Mr. Chatland has been a prominent member of the F. and A. M. He was District Deputy Grand Master for Pennsylvania, for fifteen years; District Deputy High Priest, for sixteen years; Eminent Commander of St. Omer's Commandery, No. 7, of Brownsville, for about eighteen years, and is proud of his record as a Mason.

JOHN A. CLARK was born January 29, 1842, near Morgantown, Monongalia county, W. Va., is the oldest son of William F. and Sarah A. (Batton) Clark, a daughter of John Batton, of Springhill township, who was a strong democrat and a good farmer.

His father, William F. Clark, was born in Virginia, March 21, 1814. He clerked in his father's store until he attained his majority, when he went to Mobile, Alabama, and engaged with his brother in the mercantile business. Six years later he came to Springhill township, leased a farm and engaged in farming, but soon removed to West Virginia, where he followed the same business for eleven years, and then returned to Springhill, where he purchased property. In 1870 he visited Missouri, and three years later removed to that State, but soon left and located in the Nemeha valley, Nebraska, where he now resides, and is engaged in the mercantile business. He is a well preserved old gentleman, needing neither glasses nor a cane. He was married to Sarah A. Batton. Their union was blessed with eight children. Mrs. Batton died in 1865. His paternal grandfather, Clark, was a Virginia merchant, and owned a large number of slaves.

John A. Clark attended the common schools of Springhill township, and spent some time in the subscription schools of Virginia. He took two courses in the Southwestern Pennsylvania Normal School, one in the summer of 1863, the other during the following summer, and followed teaching in the common schools for four years. From 1867 to 1871 he was engaged in cultivating his farm near Morris Cross Roads.

In 1871 he engaged in the lumber business, having a saw-mill near Morris Cross Roads. Eighteen months later he went into partnership with his father-in-law, and they erected a saw-mill at Crow's Ferry on Cheat river.

In 1874 he began the erection of a planing-mill at Point Marion. In 1881 he attached a saw-mill, and the whole structure was terribly wrecked by a cyclone that struck it on March 24, 1887. The next day he began to rebuild the mill and repair his dwelling-house, that had been badly damaged.

When rebuilt he operated the mill until the flood of July 10, 1888, came and swept his mill buildings of their foundations and badly damaged the machinery. He is now preparing to build a mill on the opposite side of the river on a site above high-water mark.

Mr. Clark was married, October 11, 1886, to Miss Martha Dillner, who died in 1875. Of this union three children were born: May, Charles, and an infant which is dead.

January 18, 1882, Mr. Clark was married a second time, to Miss Elizabeth Dunham, and by this marriage has one child, James Daniel Clark.

Mr. Clark, in politics, is a democrat, and in religious belief a Methodist Protestant. He is of German-French and Irish-Scotch descent.

WILLIAM COCK, one of the successful business men of Fayette county, and the efficient manager of the Eclipse Flouring Mills, is a son of John and Jane (Faucett) Cock, and was born in the borough of Bridgeport January 5, 1841.

John Cock was a native of Holme, County Westmoreland, England. He was apprenticed to John Davison March 16, 1824, by his father, H. Cock, to learn the trade of joiner, house carpenter, cabinet and wagon-maker. He served seven years as an apprentice. In 1832 he came to Albany, New York, and in the following year removed to Brownsville, where he engaged in a machine shop and foundry with his uncle, William Cock, the maker of the first iron plow manufactured west of the Allegheny Mountains.

John Cock, in 1846, entered into partnership with Leonard Lenhart, and engaged in building steamboats from 1846 to 1858, and during that period built over one hundred boats. He retired from active life in 1858, and died in 1875, aged sixty-six years. He was a member of the Episcopal church. His wife died in 1885, aged seventy-five years.

Thomas F. Cock, a fine mechanic and an extensive boat builder, was born at Bridgeport August 14, 1833. He was educated in the common schools of Bridgeport and West Brownsville. He learned the boat building business with Cock & Lenhart, and in 1858, in connection with D. D. Williams, bought out the firm. The new firm, Cock & Williams, continued till 1865, when they sold out. They built fifty-one boats. In 1872 Thomas F. Cock and his brother, H. B. Cock, bought out the firm of Cock, Hutchinson & Williams. They continued successfully in the boat building business until 1880. For the last nine years Thomas F. Cock has not been actively engaged in business beyond having an interest in the Brownsville & Geneva Packet Line.

In 1854 he was married to Miss Elizabeth, daughter of Henry Snyder, a ship carpenter of West Brownsville. They have four children: Jane, John W., Christian O. and Henry B. Thomas F. Cock served as captain of the steamboat Messenger in 1872. He is a member of the Masons, Odd Fellows, American Mechanics, and is a republican and a member of the Episcopal church. He is a prudent, watchful business man and a useful citizen. He resides in a comfortable and beautiful home in Bridgeport.

William Cock learned the trade of a machinist with John Snowdon & Sons. From 1863 to 1870 he was a member of the firm of J. Herbertson & Co., machinists and foundry men. From 1871 to 1887 was in the mercantile and grain business. In 1887 he became a partner in the Eclipse Milling Company, and is now its president and general manager.

These mills have the roller process and capacity of fifty barrels per day. He was married to Miss Harriet Lenhart, who died in 1869, leaving one child, a daughter, Jane. In 1872 he married again to Margaret, daughter of Harrison Mason. They have two children: Mary E. and William F., William Cock is a republican, has served thirteen years as a councilman and five years as a school director. He attends the Episcopal church, and is one of Bridgeport's enterprising business men.

JACOB CONN is of Scotch-Irish parentage and was born on Georges Creek, near Smithfield, Fayette county, Pa., December 5, 1811, and is a son of Isaac and Nancy (Zearley) Conn.

George Conn (paternal grandfather) was a ship carpenter; in 1759 came from Hagerstown, Md., and took up 400 acres of land on Georges Creek under what was known as a "Tomahawk right." About 1760 a man by the name of Powell settled on a part of this tract, and disputed the ownership of the same with Conn. They agreed to settle their quarrel by a fight. They fought near a spring; Conn was victorious and held the land. The spring has been known ever since as the "Powell Spring." His wife's maiden name was Lydia Flintham. They reared nine children, seven sons and two daughters.

Isaac Conn (father), a twin, was born in 1784, on Georges Creek, and was reared on his father's farm. He enjoyed but the scant educational privileges of that frontier day. He married Nancy Zearley, and they had ten children, four sons and six daughters. In 1838 he removed to Highland county, Ohio, and died there in 1869, in the eighty-fifth year of his age. His wife followed him to the portals of the tomb in a few years.

Jacob Conn was raised on a farm. Although school advantages of that day were meagre, he acquired a fair education and became an ordinary scholar.

In 1831 he worked for his uncle at seven dollars per month. From 1832 to 1834 he helped his father, who then resided in Virginia. He was married to Miss Sarah, daughter of John Weltner, April 3, 1838. Unto their union were born eleven children: Isaac Phillips, John W., Susan W., Rachel, Ann Elizabeth, Eliza Jane, Hannah W., George W., Sarah L., Thomas J. and Catherine.

From 1838 to 1843 he rented the Phillips

farm, afterwards leased a farm near Point Marion and cultivated it for five years.

In 1848 he bought 163 acres of the John McFarland farm and removed to it. He had but forty dollars of his own, but honesty and integrity linked to energy established a credit and he borrowed the money to pay for his purchase. Working very hard in a few years he discharged every dollar of his indebtedness.

The first barn he built was struck by lightning, and was consumed, together with a horse and wagon. In 1873 he erected a fine, large two story frame house, complete in all his equipments, in which he now resides.

He is a democrat. He has been since 1843 a member of the "Forks of Cheat" Baptist church, to which his wife and children belong.

Mr. Conn began life a poor boy and now owns a splendid and well-improved farm of 260 acres, partly underlaid with coal. Studying Franklin's maxims when a boy, he became a successful man, is now an honored and respected citizen, influential and a prosperous farmer of Springhill township.

ISAAC P. CONN was born January 5, 1839, near Anderson Cross Roads, Fayette county, Pa., and is of German and Scotch-Irish parentage. He is the son of Jacob Conn, Sr., and Sarah (Weltner) Conn. His father was born on Georges Creek, Fayette county, Pa., December 5, 1811. He was brought up on the farm and attended the subscription schools of his day; he acquired a fair education, and was considered a good scribe. He was married April 3, 1837, when he rented a farm and began life on his own account. He remained on this farm for five years; he then rented a farm in the "Forks of Cheat," remained on this farm for ten years, when he bought a farm of his own of 160 acres adjoining, and removed there. He has since added 120 acres to his farm, has of late built a new house and barn, is very comfortably situated, and has attained enough of this world's goods to enable him to live with ease and comfort the remainder of his life. He is a staunch democrat, a good citizen, and a member of the Baptist church at the "Forks of Cheat," West Virginia.

Mr. Conn's mother was born February 29, 1814. She is the mother of eleven children, seven of whom are still living. She is living, at the age of seventy-six years, is a member of the same church as her husband, and of her children.

Mr. Conn's grandfather was born on Georges Creek, Fayette county, was a farmer, and moved to Ohio in 1833, where he continued to farm until his death. He was a good citizen, and a religious man.

The great-grandfather of Isaac P. Conn came to Fayette county at an early day and settled on Georges Creek, where he took a "Tomahawk Claim" on a tract of land containing four hundred acres. He was one of the earliest blacksmiths in the county. (At one time he fought a man by the name of Powell for fifty acres of land, and won the fight and the land.)

Isaac P. Conn grew up on the farm till he was eighteen years of age. He attended the common schools; though his advantages for education were limited, he became a fair scholar. He remained on the home farm until 1879, when he removed to a farm of 163 acres he had previously bought in Springhill township, and where he now resides. Sixty-five acres of his land is underlaid with coal.

His farm is in a good state of cultivation, shows the care he has bestowed upon it, and also is proof that Mr. Conn is an excellent farmer. He deals considerably in live stock.

January 9, 1879, he was married to Miss

Arilda Lyons (daughter of Joseph Lyons, deceased). She is a member of the Lutheran church, while Mr. Conn is a member of the Baptist church at the "Forks of Cheat." In politics Mr. Conn is a prohibition democrat.

WILLIAM GANS CONN is of Irish-German parentage, and one of Springhill's prosperous farmers; is a son of John and Hannah (Gans) Conn, and was born in Monongalia county, Va. (now West Virginia). His great-grandfather, George Conn, came from Maryland to Georges Creek, and settled there in an early day.

His grandfather, Jacob Conn, was a native of Springhill township, was married to Eleanor Hartman, and removed from Georges Creek to Monongalia county, Va. They had six sons and four daughters, all of whom lived to an advanced age. Jacob Conn enlisted in the War of 1812, but his company on its third day's march toward Washington City received the news that a treaty of peace had been concluded. He died at eighty-four years of age, and his wife reached her ninetieth year.

W. G. Conn's father, John Conn, was born December 5, 1813, in Monongalia county, Va., on a farm, and received but three months' schooling, yet by dint of hard study at home he remedied his lack of school learning so far as reading, writing, and a practical knowledge of arithmetic was concerned. In 1834 he married Miss Hannah, daughter of Benjamin Gans, a native of Springhill township. John Conn removed from Jaco Farm, Va., to near Point Marion, where he purchased the Rudolph Saddler farm, containing 116 acres. On this land he erected a fine house, built a large barn, and made many valuable improvements. He purchased the farm for $750, and now it is valued at $10,000. He and his wife were members of the Baptist church from 1837 until the beginning of the war, when they left the Baptist denomination and united with the Disciple church at Oak Grove. During the war John Conn left the democratic party and became a republican. While serving as school director he was instrumental in securing the construction of a new school-house in the "Forks of Cheat." From his own lack he realized the importance of education, and accordingly educated all of his children, of whom four became teachers, and two still remain teachers.

William G. Conn was raised on the farm, received his education in the common schools, and in the Millsboro Normal School, where he attended two terms. Between his Normal courses he taught two terms of district school.

In 1863 he enlisted in Company B, Sixty-first Pennsylvania Infantry Volunteers, was in the battles of Rappahannock Station, Mine Run and the Wilderness. In one of the battles of the Wilderness he was struck in the shoulder by a minnie ball, which passed down into his side, where it still remains. After being wounded he was sent to Findlay Hospital, in Washington City, remained seven months, but he rejoined his regiment in December, before the walls of Petersburg. He was with the regiment in all its engagements until the legions of Lee grounded arms at Appomattox. After witnessing Lee's surrender his regiment was marched to Danville, Va., thence to Washington City.

He was discharged at Camp Reynolds, returned home, removed to the "Oil Regions" of West Virginia, where he engaged for ten years in the mercantile business and teaching school.

In 1885 he returned to Point Marion, where he has since been engaged in teaching and farming.

September 26, 1868, he was married to Miss Emily M., daughter of James and Sarah

J. (Hood) McGough, of Westmoreland county. They have five children: Lillian G., born July 26, 1870 (Wood county, W. Va.); Arthur, May 10, 1873 (Gales Fork); Helen E., May 26, 1877 (Richie county); Edith K., October 11, 1879 (Pennsylvania), and Harvey Raymond, June 28, 1889 (Pennsylvania).

He has been a deacon in the Church of Christ at Point Marion, ever since the church's organization.

He honors, by his prudence, thrift and intelligence, one of the old families of the county.

ALPHEUS S. CONN was born July 31, 1842, in Monongalia county, Va. (now W. Va.), is a son of Isaac and Eliza (Norris) Conn, and is of Scotch-Irish descent.

Isaac Conn was born on Georges creek, in 1811, and received the limited education of farmers' boys of that day. He remained on the home farm until 1854, when he rented a farm of his father and cultivated it for twenty-nine years. In 1883 he went to Pittsburgh and kept a hotel for one year. In 1884 he removed to Point Marion and bought property. Here, on July 3, 1889, he had a stroke of paralysis of the left side, from which he is slowly recovering. He married Eliza Norris, born in 1818, died in 1855, and had seven children: John I., William E., Amy E., Alpheus S., Jacob L., George H., Harriet E. He is an earnest member of the M. P. church at Stewartstown, W. Va., and is now in the seventy-eighth year of his age.

Jacob Conn (paternal grandfather) was born in Fayette county, and died in 1864. He was a son of George Conn, one of the pioneer settlers on Georges creek, and one of the three Georges from which it is said the township derived its name.

Alpheus S. Conn was reared on a farm, received the limited school advantages of his time until he was eighteen years of age, when he engaged with his brother, J. I. Conn, to learn the trade of a shoemaker.

But two years of his apprenticeship had passed until the Civil War began, when he enlisted as a volunteer in a company which disbanded before doing any service. He was afterward drafted, served in Company B, Sixty-second Pennsylvania Infantry, and was in the battles of the Wilderness, Spottsylvania Court House, where one-half of his right ear was cut off by a minnie ball. He was in the battles in front of Petersburg, was a prisoner for a few minutes at Five Forks, and witnessed Lee's surrender.

From the close of the war until 1871 pursued his trade at Point Marion, when he removed to Stewartstown, W. Va. In 1881 he sold his Stewartstown property, and removed to his present home near Morris Cross Roads.

He was married on March 10, 1866, to Miss Hannah, daughter of Michael Crow. They have four children: Charles S., taught one term of school; Frank L., Nellie G. and Chester A.

Mr. Conn is a republican, and has served as inspector of elections. He is a member of Post 180, G. A. R., at Uniontown.

He is a good tradesman and reliable citizen, is a member and trustee of the M. P. church, whose membership roll bears the names of his wife and two oldest children.

SEABORN CRAWFORD, undertaker and furniture dealer, of Brownsville, is a son of Nathan and Mary (Carlton) Crawford. He was born in West Pike Run township, Washington county, Pa., March 27, 1826.

Seaborn Crawford (grandfather) came from Maryland, and located in Washington county, Pa., and was a farmer and blacksmith.

Nathan Crawford (father) was born in West Pike Run township, March, 1804, and lived and farmed in that and Somerset township until about 1860, when he moved to Luzerne village, where he lived until 1884, and died in July of that year, aged eighty years. He married Mary Carlton, who died January 2, 1870. They had seven children: Samuel C., a lawyer, who died in Little Rock, Arkansas, January, 1857; Mark C., a carpenter, who died in Canton, Ohio; Richard, a carpenter; Beulah, widow of Caleb Odbert; Sarah F., wife of Thornton Rogers; Liddia, a twin sister of Sarah, died at the age of four months, and Seaborn.

Seaborn Crawford was reared on a farm, attended the subscription schools, until he was eighteen years of age, when he spent three years in learning the trade of a carpenter with Andrew Hopkins of Bridgport. He received board and washing and $100 in money for his labor.

In the fall of 1848 he went to Cincinnati to work at his trade, but finding little work in that city he engaged as a book agent with a Connecticut Yankee, and successfully solicited orders in western Ohio and eastern Indiana until the following spring. He returned home and continued or pursued his trade until 1850, when he caught the "gold fever" but possessing little money, he borrowed $500 of his friend Daniel P. Griffith. Leaving Pittsburgh April 10, 1850, Mr. Crawford and Gideon Allison, a medical student of Brownsville, traveled by boat to western Missouri; there they rigged out a mule team and started for California, traveling by the way of Fort Bridger and Salt Lake City. On their arrival at the base of the Sierra Nevada Mountains they cut up their wagon and made pack saddles, so as to enable them to carry their provisions and clothing across the mountains.

Mr. Crawford remained between two and three years in California, where he was engaged in operating a saw-mill and mining. He returned home by the way of the isthmus, spent a day in Acapulco, Mexico, and one day and night in Jamaica, and landed in Norfolk, Va., October, 1852.

In the winter of 1852-53, he attended school at Mt. Union, Ohio, and in the summer of 1853 he went to Illinois and invested in land in Bureau county.

In the fall of 1853 he returned to Brownsville and became a member of the dry goods firm, D. P. Griffith & Co., of Bridgeport. He remained in this firm until the winter of 1856. He was married to Miss Edith, daughter of John and Edith Riley, May 2, 1854.

In 1857 he removed to Clarke county, Iowa, with his wife and one child, and engaged for three years in the flouring and saw-mill business with Isaac and Loyd Bennett.

In 1860 he rented his mill interests, with his wife and two children he returned to Brownsville. He started on a second trip to the far West, and with an ox team and cow crossed the plains, entered the Rocky Mountains at the "Golden Gate," and arrived at Central City in June. He remained here for nearly two years, was engaged in erecting quartz mills, mining and prospecting. In the fall of 1861 he returned to Denver, and helped to erect the soldiers' barracks. From thence he returned to Brownsville, and engaged in carpenter work for two years. In 1864 he began merchandising in the "Neck" at Brownsville, continuing until 1882. In that year he engaged in the saw-mill, lumber and coal-boat siding business.

May 1, 1885, he engaged in his present furniture and undertaking business in Brownsville. He has in his warerooms such goods as will add to the elegance and comfort of any home. He also understands and practices successfully the art of cavity and arterial embalming. Mr. Crawford has three children: Charles S., attorney at law in Pittsburgh; Samuel C., in the furniture business; Luther L., a druggist.

M A Cox

Mr. Crawford was reared a Friend or Quaker, was an anti-slavery man, and is at present an ardent temperance advocate, and a member of the Cumberland Presbyterian church.

JOHN H. COULTER, a prominent merchant of Brownsville for many years, was born at Brownsville, Fayette county, Pa., May 10, 1839, attended the schools of his native place, and at the age of seventeen he began to learn the trade of tinsmith with James Slocum. After learning the trade and working at the same for six years, Mr. Slocum gave him a clerkship in the store, and put him in charge of the business. In 1885 he became Mr. Slocum's successor. By his zealous attention to business he has retained all of the business of his predecessor, and now has a very large and extensive trade. He has acquired all he possesses by means of his own exertions, and has the respect of the public as a straightforward business man.

He was married, in 1870, to Miss Mary E. Smith, a daughter of Wilson Smith; the latter died when she was quite young. Her mother was Virtue Smith. Mrs. Coulter was a native of West Wheeling, Belmont county, Ohio. They have four children: Charles W., Mary Eleanor, Florence E. and Emma V.

Mr. Coulter is a member of the Methodist Episcopal church, of which he is steward and trustee.

His parents were James N. and Rebecca (Van Horn) Coulter, both born in Fayette county, Pa. James N. Coulter was a blacksmith by trade. He died at Brownsville, in 1852, in the forty-fourth year of his age. He was a member of the Methodist Episcopal church, and of the order of Sons of Temperance.

John Coulter—the grandfather of the subject of this sketch—came to this county from Hagerstown, Md., and was a stone mason by trade. He was a Presbyterian and was of Scotch-Irish descent. He died in 1852.

Rebecca Coulter—the mother of J. H. Coulter—is living in Brownsville, in the eighty-second year of her age, and is remarkably well preserved. Her father, Bernard Van Horn, was one of a family of thirteen children, was born in 1770, in the eastern part of Pennsylvania, and came to Fayette county before the War of 1812. He was a farmer in Menallen township, where he owned a farm, and died in 1847, at the age of seventy-seven years.

CAPTAIN MICHAEL A. COX, of Brownsville, is one of the ablest as well as safest commanders that ever trod the deck of a steamboat, and is one of the oldest steamboat captains now in active service on the western rivers. He has commanded twenty-two different steamboats (being part owner in all of them), on the Monongahela, Ohio, Mississippi, Missouri, Arkansas and Cumberland rivers. He has also a pilot's license on all of these rivers. Transporting hundreds of thousands of passengers, moving millions of tons of freight, he has never had an accident by which a life was lost or any amount of property destroyed. The beginning of his long and so far distinguished career upon the "Western Waters" was in 1844 as clerk of the steamboat "Massachusetts," commanded by Captain Isaac Bennet. Captain Cox is now commanding the Adam Jacobs on the Monongahela river.

Captain M. A. Cox was born in Hampstead, Carroll county, Maryland, July 26, 1821, and is a son of Jacob and Keziah (Armacost) Cox, both natives of Carroll county, Maryland.

Jacob Cox came to Fayette county in 1825, and engaged in his life-long pursuit of farming near Brownsville. He died in 1836, and his wife passed away eighteen years later.

Captain Cox obtained his education in the country subscription schools of that time: his attendance was, however, limited to the winter sessions as he was employed on the farm during the summer.

At seventeen years of age, he turned his attention to the mercantile business. In order to properly qualify himself for that pursuit, he engaged as a clerk with James L. Bowman of Brownsville, with whom he remained for six years. He completed his experience in mercantile life with two years spent as a clerk for Jesse H. Duncan, in an iron and commission house in Brownsville.

He was united in marriage, May 7, 1850, to Miss Mary Ellen Krepps, a daughter of the Hon. Samuel J. Krepps; she died in 1880, leaving five children: Annie E., Samuel K., Solomon G., Michael A., Jr. and Mary E. Two of his sons (Samuel K. and Solomon G.) are successful business men of Chicago and the other (Michael A. Jr.) is a prosperous business man in St. Louis. One of his daughters, Mary E., married Mr. William J. Parshall, the other, Annie E., is single and has the care of her father's comfortable home in Brownsville.

In addition to his Brownsville possessions, Captain Cox owns a valuable body of land in West Virginia, besides other property. Thus he has accumulated enough of this world's goods to render him comfortable in his old age, and to give his children a fair start in life.

He is a man of fine and commanding presence. Politically he is a democrat. Although not connected with any church, his religious views are in accord with the teachings of the Protestant Episcopal church. The captain in forty-five consecutive years of service in navigating western rivers, has often piloted his own boats.

He is as spry and active as the general run of men who are his juniors in age by twenty years, and bids fair from his present appearance to tread the deck for a number of years to come.

The Captain has been a prominent member of the Masonic order for more than thirty years, and has been eminent commander of St. Omer's Commandery No. 7 at Brownsville for many years.

DR. WILLIAM STEVENS DUNCAN, of Bridgeport, a widely known and highly esteemed physician and surgeon, was born in Brownsville, May 24, 1834. He is a son of Judge Thomas and Priscilla (Stevens) Duncan.

Dr. Duncan's great-grandfather, Thomas Duncan, and his wife, emigrated from Scotland to County Donegal, Ireland, in 1775. They had four children (all born in Scotland): George, John, Arthur and a daughter, whose name there is a doubt whether it was Jane or Nancy. Arthur Duncan, when twenty years of age, engaged in the Irish Rebellion of 1792, and immediately after its suppression sought safety in flight from the English authorities. He was placed in a cask which was filled with straw, the head replaced, thus was smuggled on board a vessel bound for the United States, and landed at Philadelphia, January 10, 1793. In 1795 he joined Washington's troops that were sent out from the Capital to suppress the Whiskey Insurrection. After his discharge, he settled near "Plumsock," (now Upper Middletown) in September, 1802, and took out his naturalization papers. He married Sophia Wharton, a daughter of Arthur Wharton, of Franklin township. Arthur Duncan died at Moundsville, Virginia, in 1850, and his wife, in Pittsburgh, Pennsylvania, in 1845. They had ten children, namely: Thomas, George, Arthur, James, Benjamin, Enos, Mary Ann, Jane, Elizabeth and Nancy.

Judge Thomas Duncan was born in Franklin township, August 22, 1807, and received his early education in the Thorn Bottom School. He engaged in the Plumsock Rolling Mill for a time, but at eighteen years of age made arrangements to learn the trade of a cabinet-maker. He engaged with an expert mechanic, Thomas Hatfield, with whom he remained three years as an apprentice, and afterwards three years more as a partner. He then removed to Bridgeport, and has continued successfully in the same business. Judge Duncan was married in May, 1829, to Miss Priscilla, daughter of Dr. Benjamin Stevens, of Uniontown. Her father, Dr. Benjamin Stevens, was born in Maryland, February 20, 1737, read medicine with his father, Dr. Benjamin Stevens, and graduated at the Annapolis Medical School, Maryland. He came to "Plumsock," engaged in the practice of medicine, where he also owned and operated an iron forge and slitting-mill till his death in 1813.

Judge Duncan has held the more important offices of Bridgeport. He is a prominent democrat, and takes an active part in public affairs. He served as county commissioner from 1843 to 1845. In 1851 he was elected associate judge of Fayette county for a term of five years, and was re-elected in 1856.

He has been a bank director, and since 1834 has belonged to the Independent Order of Odd Fellows. He stands high in the Masonic Order of which he has been member for thirty-seven years; is now a Knight Templar of St. Omer's Commandery, No. 7, and has been a member of the Methodist Episcopal church for forty-eight years. Judge Duncan and wife have five children, three of whom are living: Mrs. Elizabeth Worrell, Dr. W. S. Duncan, both of Bridgeport, and Thomas J. Duncan, a practicing attorney at Washington, Pa. Judge Duncan assisted his father, Arthur Duncan, in 1822 in manufacturing the first coke made in the county, and no man has been more honorably prominent in Fayette county than Judge Duncan. He is now an octogenarian in years, and is in good health. Mrs. Duncan died in February, 1873, aged sixty-six years.

Dr. William Stevens Duncan received a thorough literary education in Mt. Union College, Ohio, read medicine with Dr. M. O. Jones, then of Brownsville, but now a resident of Pittsburgh. He attended two full courses of lectures in the University of Pennsylvania, and was graduated from there in the spring of 1858 with the degree of M. D. In June, 1858, he formed a copartnership with his preceptor in the practice, the partnership ending in 1861 by the removal of Dr. Jones to Pittsburgh. From 1861 to the present time Dr. Duncan has occupied the office in which he wrote his first prescription.

March 21st, 1861, Dr. Duncan married Miss Amanda, daughter of Benjamin and Mary (Berry) Leonard. They have one child, a daughter, Helen, a pupil in Lenna Female College at Pittsburgh.

He is a public-spirited citizen, and is always interested in the material welfare of his community. He has been a director of the Brownsville Dollar Savings Bank and was director of the Brownsville Railway Company, which he assisted to organize.

Dr. Duncan is a member of the Fayette County Medical Association, the Pennsylvania State Medical Society, the American Medical Association, the Rocky Mountain Medical Society, and an honorary member of the California State Medical Society. He owns one of the largest medical libraries in the State. He is a hard student and has contributed many able papers to the leading medical journals of the day, among which are: "Belladona as an Antidote to Opium Poisoning," (1862); "Medical Delusions," (a pamphlet, 1869); "Iliac Aneurism Cured by

Electrolysis," (1875); and the "Physiology of Death." He has in his practice skillfully and successfully treated difficult cases, as well as ably described such in the medical journals of the day. In surgery he has performed many important operations: for tracheotomy a number of times and trephining skull repeatedly, and excision of the head of the humerus and the lower half of the radius.

He served as a volunteer surgeon at the battle of Gettysburg, and was taken prisoner by the Confederates.

Dr. Duncan has but few equals, is well read, and a skillful physician and surgeon. As a medical author, he is broad and liberal in his treatment of subjects. As a citizen he is justly entitled to the high esteem in which he is held.

DANIEL DE LANEY, a courteous gentleman and a fine musician, was born in Leeds, Yorkshire, England, July 7th, 1833. He is a son of Daniel and Ann De Laney, was raised in Leeds, where he attended the pay schools of that place, and received musical instruction from a professor of some note.

He learned the trade of a baker; not pleased with this business he entered a machine shop and learned the trade of a machinist.

In June, 1853, he came to Brownsville, and as soon as the legal machinery of the court could act, he became a citizen of the United States.

He engaged in the machine shop of John Snowdon for a short time, when he accepted a position with John Herbertson, which he held for ten years.

In 1865 he formed a partnership with his brothers Henry and Samuel De Laney and Henry Drum under the firm name of Drum & De Laneys. They engaged in the manufacture of oil tools for the oil wells, and did a good business during the oil excitement in the Monongahela Valley from 1865 to 1866. In 1867 they admitted Thomas Fall into the firm, and the firm became Fall, Drum & De Laneys. This firm leased the old Faulls Foundry and machine shops in Bridgeport, and engaged in all kinds of work pertaining to a foundry or machine shop. They built several steam boats, erected stationary engines, made saw-mill machinery, and did all kinds of work in their line of business.

In 1872 the firm dissolved, and Mr. De Laney again engaged and is now employed on journey work for John Herbertson & Sons. He and his sons own a one-eighth interest in the Eclipse Flouring Mill.

He was married to Miss Berthia Redman, of Wheeling, W. Va., November 1st, 1860. They are the parents of seven children, five sons and two daughters: Benjamin E., who died at Martin's Ferry, Ohio, July 1st, 1889, aged twenty-eight years; John H., William W., Edward S., Charles, Mary M. and Ellen Elizabeth.

Mr. De Laney is a republican and has served as councilman, burgess and as school director for fourteen years successively.

In England he connected himself with the Episcopal church, and in that faith he grew to manhood. At Brownsville he has been warden of the Episcopal church and superintendent of the Sabbath-school.

He is a member of Brownsville Lodge, No. 51, I. O. O. F., member of Redstone Encampment, No. 70, of the same order, has been for over twenty years order secretary of the former, and scribe of the latter.

Mr. De Laney is a fine violin player, he has been an instructor of the Brownsville and other brass bands, and has always led the Brownsville orchestra. His children are all expert musicians; his daughters are excellent pianists and his sons play on almost every musical instrument in use.

Mr. De Laney is a skilled workmen in his line of business, an industrious citizen, and stands high in his community as a neighbor and gentleman.

THOMAS COUSER DUNHAM was born in Springhill township, Fayette, county, Pa., May, 30, 1829, and is of Irish descent. His parents were Jonas and Elizabeth (Couser) Dunham, both natives of Fayette county, Pa. Thomas C. Dunham was raised in a rural district, and received but little schooling, as he had no opportunity to attend any schools except the indifferent subscription schools then in existence in the State. Leaving school at nineteen years of age, he engaged in farming on a rented farm until 1871, when he purchased a farm of his own of forty-five acres.

Mr. Dunham was married October 19, 1849, to Miss Sarah O'Neil, daughter of Henry O'Neil, a native of this county, and a miller by trade.

Nine children were born to them: Henry, Francis V., Elizabeth, Emma, James, John R., William J., Zachariah T. and Minnie S., of whom six are living.

His wife died March 1, 1882, and was a very estimable woman. Soon after his wife's death he sold his farm, and purchased a house and a couple of acres of ground, where he now lives.

He is a worthy member of the Presbyterian church at Mt. Moriah. As a boy, he was industrious, and dutiful to his parents. As a man he has always been industrious and frugal. He has by his own hard work accumulated some property, and raised a large family of very respectable children.

ADOLPH M. EBERHART was born August 19, 1841, in Springhill township, Fayette county, Pa. He is a son of Adolph and Sarah (Beatty) Eberhart, both natives or Fayette county, Pa.

Adolph Eberhart, Sr., (subject's grandfather) came from Switzerland to Maryland. He came to Fayette county, Pa., when a young man, and learned the trade of glass blowing and glass cutting. He was an employe of the first glass factory west of the Allegheny Mountains, located on Georges Creek, near New Geneva.

He married Elizabeth Phillips, daughter of Col. Theophilus Phillips who came to Fayette county about 1760, and soon thereafter purchased a large tract of land in Springhill township, called "Phillips' Choice," containing about 480 acres. He died on board a ship *en route* from New Orleans to Philadelphia, and was buried at sea.

Adolph Eberhart, Jr., (subject's father) was born June 8, 1816, and was raised on his father's farm. He was married in 1839, was a farmer, and, at his father's death, in 1863, inherited one-half of the homestead farm of 480 acres (once "Phillips' Choice"). He erected a comfortable house on the land, and there he continued to farm till his death. From 1850 to 1852 he was engaged in the manufacture of glass at New Geneva, as a member of the firm of A. and M. Eberhart & Co. From 1852 he gave his attention to farming until his death, September 10, 1882. He was a prominent democrat during life, and served acceptably as a road commissioner and school director. His wife, Sarah (Beatty) Eberhart, was a daughter of Thomas Beatty, a farmer of Springhill, who was an earnest democrat, and was justice of the peace in Springhill for a number of years. He was a strict Presbyterian, and died in 1840. Adolph and Sarah (Beatty) Eberhart had eleven children, six sons and five daughters: Mary Jane, dead; Adolph M.; Eliza, dead; William, dead. Mrs. Eberhart was born in 1813, March 31st, and died May 14, 1877.

Adolph M. Eberhart worked on the farm

and attended the common schools until eighteen years of age, when he left school and engaged in farming on his father's land until 1887. In that year he bought eighty-six acres of the home farm, and lives in the homestead mansion.

He has on his farm a bed of potter's clay of the finest quality, and from this he realizes about $500 per year.

Mr. Eberhart has followed farming all his life. He is an ardent democrat, and proud of having cast his first ballot for Gen. George B. McClellan for president. He is of German-Irish descent, is a successful farmer, a careful manager and a good observer.

WILLIAM A. EDMISTON, cashier of the Monongahela Bank, at Brownsville, Pa., is the son of Samuel and Margaret (Bryce) Edmiston.

His father was a native of Fulton county, Pa., and was a chairmaker by trade. He came to Brownsville some time in about 1840, and opened a shop. He continued to work at his trade until his death, in 1856, in the forty-fifth year of his age. He was a Presbyterian, and was of Irish and Scotch descent. Of the paternal grandfather of the subject of this sketch the only facts to be gathered at this time are that he was born in Ireland and came to America and settled in Fulton county, Pa.

After the death of her husband the mother of W. A. Edmiston was married a second time, to George W. Harrison, of Washington county, Pa., and they still live on their farm in that county, three miles from Brownsville.

Andrew Bryce, maternal grandfather of W. A. Edmiston, was a native of Scotland, who came to this country in about 1820. He was a miller, and worked at that business all of his life. He died in the State of Indiana, while there on a visit.

William A. Edmiston was born at Brownsville, December 23, 1846, and attended the public schools of the town. Leaving school, he became a clerk in the drug store of John Wallace & Co., of Brownsville, for about one year, and afterwards he was for several years a clerk in different other stores. In 1856 he secured a position of second clerk on one of the steamboats that belonged to the Pittsburgh, Brownsville & Geneva Packet Company. Remained there as clerk for sixteen years, excepting the years of 1871 and 1872, engaged in the dry goods business at Brownsville. He was employed as first and second clerk while on the river, except during the last four years—from 1878 to 1882—he filled the place of captain of the steamboat Germania, which ran from Geneva to Pittsburgh.

In 1882 he was elected teller of the Monongahela Bank, in which position he continued until 1888, when he was elected cashier of the Monongahela Bank, which was organized in 1812, chartered in 1814, and now has a capital of $200,000 and an average deposit of $125,000, with a surplus of $50,000. The present officers of the bank are: Gibson Burns, president; William A. Edmiston, cashier. The directors are: Gibson Burns, James L. Bowman, M. A. Cox, H. W. Robinson, W. M. Ledwith, J. C. Woodward, Jacob Sawyer, N. B. Bowman, George E. Hogg, H. B. Cock, W. P. Searight, Eli J. Baily and W. J. Stewart.

Mr. Edmiston was for several years the clerk of town council, and is now the treasurer. He was twice elected, on the republican ticket, and served as a member of the school board and secretary of the board during the terms of his office—the first time in the year of 1883, and re-elected in 1886. He is a member of the Methodist Episcopal church at Brownsville, is the treasurer, trustee and steward of the same.

He was married in 1869 to Miss Virginia Beacon, daughter of the Rev. L. B. Beacon, of the Methodist Episcopal church. They have four living children: Clarence B., Bessie L., William R. and Helen V.

COONROD S. EMRY was born March 13, 1821, in Springhill township, Fayette county, Pa., and is of German and Scotch-Irish parentage. His parents were William and Margaret (Saddler) Emry. His father was born March 22, 1792, in New Jersey, and was brought up on a farm and received his education in the subscription schools taught three months in the year, and where the course of study was covered by the "three R's." He remained on the farm with his father until he was twenty-three years of age, when he came to Fayette county, Pa. He married the daughter of William Saddler, spent one year in weaving, and then rented a farm and turned his attention to farming; rented for thirteen years, when he bought a farm in German township, where he removed April 6, 1829, and lived there till he died, in 1874. He was a Jacksonian democrat.

The mother of Coonrod S. Emry was born June 8, 1795, in York county, Pa. She was the mother of seven children, six sons and one daughter, and died in 1868.

The paternal grandfather of Coonrod S. Emry came from New Jersey at an early day, and settled in Fayette county, Pa., where he remained for several years, and then removed to Ohio, where he died.

The maternal grandfather of the subject of our sketch was William Saddler, a farmer and a native of York county, Pa.; he came to Fayette county in 1805, and settled upon a farm in Springhill township, where he died. The maternal great-grandfather was Jacob Saddler, and his father was Frederick Saddler, who came from Germany.

Coonrod S. Emry was brought up on the farm, remained with his father till he was twenty-four years of age. He attended the subscription schools of his youth, received about two months' schooling a year untill he was seventeen. At the age of twenty-four he married Miss Mary Coffman, a daughter of Andrew Coffman, a farmer of this county, and son of Andrew Coffman. They immediately settled upon the farm upon which he was born. This farm he purchased afterward, which contains 110 acres of valuable land. On this farm he has erected a fine brick dwelling-house of two stories in height, a large and well-appointed barn, and other buildings all in the best of style, both as to appearance and utility.

To his marriage six sons and one daughter were born: Andrew J., Margaret Ann, William M., John H., George V., Oliver J. and Ira A., all living except the daughter, who died May 2, 1877. The sons are all married except one, and all are farmers.

Mr. Emry is a member of the Lutheran church at Morris Cross Roads, is one of the deacons; and has held the office of elder. Mrs. Emry was also a member of the Lutheran church. She died December 6, 1884. He is a democrat, and has held the positions of judge of elections, township assessor, director of the schools and auditor. He has been successful in life, and by his industry and frugality has accumulated a competency.

In 1882 he engaged in the saw-mill business, which he has since carried on.

ALLEN D. FRANKENBERRY, a native of Springhill township, Fayette county, was born August 13, 1841. He was brought up on a farm and attended the common schools of Springhill till he was twenty years of age, when he went to Waynesburg College, at Waynesburg, Greene county. He remained at college till August

20, 1862, he then enlisted as a volunteer in Company K, Fifteenth Pennsylvania Regiment of Cavalry, known as the Anderson Cavalry. He was engaged in the battles of Antietam, Md., Stone River, Tenn.; in May, 1863, was made an orderly at General Rosecrans, headquarters, and served in that position till October 14, 1863. He was disabled in September of that year, while carrying a dispatch from Bridgeport, Alabama, by way of Trenton, Ga., to General Stanley, near Rome, Ga. The journey in the intense heat brought on a disability from which he has never entirely recovered. Upon the successful delivery of this message depended the evacuation of Chattanooga—an almost impregnable position—by Bragg. His service was rendered on the 19th day of September, 1863; was so disabled, as to have to be sent to the hospital, where he remained until April, 1864, when he was transferred to the Signal Corps of the United States Army; and was detailed to the Fourteenth Army Corps at Ringgold, Ga. He participated in all of the engagements of Sherman's army, till the battle of Jonesboro, Ga., September 1, 1864, when he was ordered to Kenesaw Mountain, and was present when the famous message, "Hold the Fort," was sent from Sherman to General Corse at Allatoona. Mr. Frankenberry still has in his possession the signal flag by means of which this message was sent, and holds it as an invaluable relic of the war. He was mustered out of service on June 30, 1865, and returned to Pennsylvania, where he engaged in the lumbering business in 1867, in which he is still engaged at Point Marion, in the firm of Keyser & Frankenberry. He is a member of the Grand Army of Republic Post, No. 180, Uniontown, Pa.

Mr. Frankenberry was married in 1868 to Miss Carrie E. Conn. Of this union was born one daughter—Retta. Mrs. Frankenberry died September 12, 1874.

Mr. Frankenberry was afterwards married to Miss Mary A. Sheets. To this union were born three children: Harry, Howard and Garfield. Harry died in infancy.

Mr. Frankenberry is a member of the Church of the Disciples at Point Marion.

His parents, Samuel and Eliza (Dilliner) Frankenberry, were both natives of Fayette county, Pa., and live in Springhill township. His father was born in 1820, has always been and is still engaged in farming. The grandfather of Mr. Frankenberry was born in Maryland and was of German descent.

STEPHEN GADD, a highly respected citizen of Brownsville township, and a blacksmith by trade, was born in German township, Fayette county, Pa., March 7, 1824, is a son of Elijah and Mary (Haney) Gadd. His father was also a blacksmith by trade and a native of Redstone township, Fayette county, Pa. His mother, Mary Haney, a daughter of Samuel Haney, was born in German township, Fayette county, Pa., as was also Samuel Haney, who died there.

Joseph Gadd, an early settler of the county, was of Scotch-Irish extraction and was engaged in the business of farming and speculation in horses.

Stephen Gadd was educated in the schools of German township, and learned his trade with his father. He has been twice married. Elizabeth Balsinger, his first wife, was a daughter of William Balsinger, born near New Salem, Menallen township, and was married July 17, 1866; Mary A. Moss, his second wife, was the widow of Cunningham Moss, of Luzerne township, to whom he was married the 4th of June, 1868. He is the father of nine children, of whom six are living: Sarah, the wife of Wellington Reynolds; Mary, the wife of James Ball, Jr., of Luzerne township; Curtis, born in Menallen township, April 1, 1851; Jennie was born July 14, 1855; Stephen, Jr., born May 4, 1869, in Luzerne township, and Frank, born in the same township, July 31, 1873.

Stephen Gadd is a member, and is now treasurer, of Lodge No. 613, Independent Order of Odd Fellows, and is a strong democrat and an efficient worker in his party. In 1888 he was a candidate for poor house director, but was defeated on account of dissensions in his party. His father and grandfather were also substantial democrats.

ALBERT GALLATIN, a distinguished statesman of the United States and one of the illustrious citizens of Fayette county, was a native of Switzerland and a resident of Springhill township. He was born at Geneva, Switzerland, January 29, 1761, and was baptized on the 7th of February following by the name of Abraham Alfonse Albert Gallatin.

In 1755 his father, Jean Gallatin, married Sophie Albertine Rolaz du Rosey, of Rolle. They had two children: Albert and a daughter, who died young. Albert Gallatin was graduated in May, 1779, from the University of Geneva, first of his class in mathematics, natural philosophy and Latin translation. He declined the commission of lieutenant-colonel in a German command, and emigrated to America and landed at Cape Ann, Mass., July 14, 1780. In November of the same year he served his adopted country as commandant of a small fort at Machias, Maine; afterward taught the French language at Harvard University; soon removed to Richmond, Va., where he acted as interpreter for a commercial house. At Richmond he became acquainted with many eminent Virginians, and, acting upon their advice, purchased lands in the Valley of the Monongahela, became the proprietor of "Friendship Hill" and a resident of Springhill township, Fayette county, Pa.

In 1786 he purchased land, and in 1789 located here as a resident. He named the small village of New Geneva, in remembrance of his trans-Atlantic birthplace, and was largely engaged in the manufacture of glass.

In 1789 he was a member of the convention to revise the constitution of Pennsylvania, and served two terms as a member of the Pennsylvania assembly. In 1793 he was elected to the senate of the United States, but by a strict party vote was excluded on the ground of constitutional ineligibility, as he had not been a naturalized citizen of the United States for nine years. He became somewhat involved in the "Whiskey Insurrection," but fully acquitted himself of all intention to oppose the enforcement of the laws. From 1795 to 1800 he served as a member of congress, where he was recognized as the republican leader and regarded as a logical debator and a sound statesman.

May 14, 1801, President Jefferson appointed him secretary of the treasury. He successfully managed the financial affairs of the nation during Jefferson's administration, and under Madison's until 1813, when he resigned to accept service under his adopted country as minister in European courts.

In 1813 he was sent to St. Petersburg as one of the envoys to negotiate with Great Britain under the meditation of the Czar, and later was one of the commissioners who negotiated a treaty of peace with England in 1814, at Ghent. From 1816 to 1823 he was resident minister at the court of France, and during this period was employed successfully on important missions to Great Britain and the Netherlands. In diplomatic services he never lacked in skill and judgment, and was always successful in protecting the rights of America. President Madison offered him the secretaryship of State,

Monroe offered him the navy department, but Gallatin refused them both. In 1824 he refused the second highest office within the gift of the American people, by declining the nomination of vice-president of the United States offered him by the democratic party. In 1824 he returned to "Friendship Hill" and there received and entertained his warm friend, the Marquis de Lafayette. In 1826 he was sent as minister plenipotentiary to England. His mission to the court of St. James was successful, and was the close of his long, arduous and successful political career. It was also the termination of his thirty-three years of residence in Fayette county. In 1828 he became a resident of New York City, became president of a bank, assisted in founding the New York Historical Society, the American Ethnological Society, and, a few days before his death, was elected one of the first members of the Smithsonian Institute. His long and eventful life came to a close at Astoria, Long Island, on August 12, 1849, at the age of over eighty-eight years.

May 14, 1789, Albert Gallatin was united in marriage to Sophia Allegre, a beautiful young Italian lady of Richmond, Va. The marriage was consummated much against the wishes of the bride's mother. Gallatin returned to "Friendship Hill" immediately after his marriage, and three weeks later the spirit of his young bride fled from its tenement of clay. He was re-married November 11, 1793, to Miss Hannah Nicholson, daughter of Commodore James Nicholson, United States Navy. This marriage allied Gallatin with some of the first families of the land. Eighteen members of the Nicholson family had served as officers in the United States Navy.

He made the first move in Pennsylvania (1792) toward establishing normal schools, by his bill to locate an academy in each county for the training of teachers. His financial views were conservative and safe and the United States enjoyed prosperity under their enforcement for twelve years. "The Hamiltonian doctrine was that the United States should be a strong government, ready and able to maintain its dignity abroad and its authority at home by arms. Gallatin maintained that its dignity would protect itself if its resources were carefully used for self-development, while its domestic authority should rest only on consent." Which of these views is correct is still a subject of political agitation and debate.

AMEDIE J. GANS was born at Morris Cross Roads, Springhill township, Fayette county, Pennsylvania, November 7, 1852. He is of German descent, on his father's side; his mother is a descendant of an old Welsh and Irish family, and was born in Monongalia county, West Virginia. He was brought up in his native township, and attended the common schools until he was eighteen years of age. He then entered Georges Creek Academy, at Smithfield, Pennsylvania, assiduously pursued his studies for two years, acquiring a thorough and complete knowledge of the text-books in use in the schools. Leaving the academy, he engaged in teaching, and has continued in that profession for the last sixteen years. He is eminently successful and popular as a teacher; always commands the best wages given by the board of directors, and a premium by the district that secures his services. Mr. Gans holds a permanent certificate that entitles him to teach anywhere in the State. A. J. Gans is at present engaged as principal of a select school in Point Marion, Pennsylvania. During vacation he is employed as agent for the United States Life Insurance Company, of New York. A. J. Gans and Carrie L. Hall were married August 30, 1879. Mrs. Gans is a daughter of Isaac C. and Ann C.

Hall, both natives of Springhill township. Mr. and Mrs. Gans have two children: Nellie, eight years old, and Ray, ten months old. Mr. Gans is a member of the Mount Moriah Baptist congregation, at Smithfield, Pennsylvania, and adorns his profession by a chaste and correct life. He is a democrat in politics, and takes a lively interest in the success of his party. He owns a fine residence, lives comfortably and enjoys the society of his friends. He is industrious and frugal in his habits, and commands the re-respect of the community. His father, Jasper N. Gans, was born in Springhill township, July 17, 1823; is a shoemaker by trade, a democrat in politics, and a member of the Baptist church. He was drafted into the service of the United States in October, 1862, to serve for nine months; was mustered at Camp Howe, near Pittsburgh, Pennsylvania, in the One Hundred and Sixty-eighth P. D. M., under command of Col. Joseph Jack, but, before the expiration of his term of service, was honorably discharged, at Newberne, N. C., on account of disability.

DR. C. LEWIS GUMMERT, a prominent young physician and surgeon of Brownsville, is a son of Thomas C. and Amanda A. (Clemmer) Gummert, and was born in Brownsville February 5, 1860.

The ancestry of Dr. Gummert's family goes back to Revolutionary days, when Christian Gummert, his great-grandfather, left Germany on account of religious persecution, and landed at Richmond. Va. Entered the Continental Army, and served throughout the war. After his discharge he settled in Virginia, and died at Shepherd's church, that State, after seeing twelve birthdays in the second century of his life.

Christian P. Gummert, the grandfather of Dr. Gummert, was born in 1806, in Charlestown, Va., and came to Fayette county in 1820. He was a shoemaker, and secured a contract for making the shoes for the men then employed on the national road between Uniontown and Washington, Pa. In connection with his shoe business he did a profitable and successful banking business. He was one of the old members of Christ's Protestant Episcopal church. He married Miss Shutz, and then Miss Sheppard, of W. Va., and died in 1856. He was a prominent and influential Mason, and was one of the first officers of Brownsville Chapter, No. 164, R. A. M.; Gummert Lodge, No. 252, A. F. and M. Fayette City was named for him. He was for many years grand master of the Masonic Order of Pennsylvania, the most important office in that ancient order.

Thomas C. Gummert, the father of Dr. Gummert, was born in 1832, and died in 1883. He was engaged for a while with his father in the banking business, afterward he was with John T. Hogg in the banking business at Mt. Pleasant, Greensburg, Pittsburgh and Brownsville. In 1854 he became assistant cashier in the Bank of Louisiana, at New Orleans. In 1856 he returned home. In 1861 was employed in the United States commissary department during the war, and was stationed at Parkersburg, W. Va. In 1865 he became chief clerk for Westley Frost, United States revenue collector of the Twenty-second district. At Frost's death he became collector, and served as such until 1869, when the Twenty-second district was consolidated along with the Twenty-fourth. He was a democrat, and was once nominated by his party for register and recorder of Fayette county, but declined to run on account of his mercantile and other business at Brownsville. He was a member of the Episcopalian church, justice of the peace for sixteen years, a Knight Templar in Masonry, besides being a prominent member in five other secret orders. He was an active, useful, influential and an honorable citizen of the county.

Thomas C. Gummert was married in 1858 to Miss Amanda A. Clemmer, of Smithfield. They had three children: Thomas N., C. Lewis and John S. Mrs. Gummert was born in 1828, and died in 1879. Her father, Lewis Clemmer, was a native of Germany and a saddler by trade. His wife, Esther C. Clemmer, was a niece of the Hon. Benjamin Butler.

Dr. C. Lewis Gummert was educated in the public schools of Brownsville, and on leaving school engaged as a clerk in a store for four years.

He quit the store to read medicine with his uncle, the late Dr. U. L. Clemmer, attended lectures at the college of physicians and surgeons, Baltimore, Maryland. From this school he was graduated March 2, 1882, ranking eighth in a class of one hundred and eighty-four. In addition to his regular graduation, he received an honorary diploma for operative surgery.

In May, 1882, he came to Brownsville and began the practice of his profession, where he has practiced with great success ever since. He was appointed United States examining surgeon, August 4, 1885, and medical inspector to the State Board of Health in April, 1888. He is a member of the Fayette county Medical Society, the American Medical Association and the International Medical Congress. He is medical examiner for eight or ten secret order associations.

Dr. Gummert was married September 11, 1880, to Miss Mary Hastings of Browns ville. She was born in 1859 and died May 5, 1881.

He is a member of the I. O. O. F., I. O. R. M. and K. of L.

He is a solid democrat, a prominent citizen and an intelligent, skilled and careful physician.

JOHN HERBERTSON, of Bridgeport was born in Glasgow, Scotland, September 16, 1805, attended the common schools and listened to the scientific lectures of the famous Ure, until he was seventeen years of age. Leaving Scotland he arrived in New York City in July, 1823. He soon went to Marietta, Ohio, engaged in farm work until April, 1824, when he removed to Pittsburgh, and learned the trade of steam-engine building.

In 1829 he located at Brownsville as foreman of John Snowden's engine shop. Mr. Snowden took the contract for the erection of the Dunlap's creek iron bridge, which is believed to be the first iron bridge ever built in the world. Mr. Herbertson designed the bridge and supervised its construction.

From 1837 to 1842 he was engaged in the business of engine-building with Thomas Faull. Their works were known as the Fayette Foundry. In 1842 Thomas Faull withdrew and Mr. Herbertson continued the business until 1880, when he took his sons, George S. and William H. and two other parties into partnership under the name of J. Herbertson & Co. In a short time the firm became J. Herbertson & Sons, manufacturers of steam engines, and general supplies for coal mines.

In 1830 Mr. Herbertson was married to Miss Eliza, daughter of Peter and Sarah (Potts) Nimon of Pittsburgh. Twelve children were born to them, three of whom are living: John P., George S. and William H. Herbertson.

George S. Herbertson was born June 22, 1847, took a course at the Iron City business college and was married in 1874 to Miss Sarah, daughter of Jackson Bar of Fairmont, W. Va. She was raised by E. H. Bar, proprietor of the Bar house, and has two children: James and Edgar. G. S. Herbertson is a blacksmith by trade, has passed the chairs in the Odd Fellows, in Knights of Pythias, belongs to the Encampment, the Royal Arcanum and the United States Brotherhood of Firemen.

William H. Herbertson was born June 24, 1850, attended the common school, took a commercial course in the Iron City business college at Pittsburgh, and learned the trade of a pattern-maker. He was a member of the city council and is past chancellor in the Knights of Pythias.

John P. Herbertson was born July 1, 1839, and was married to Frances C. Marquis, March 9, 1862. He learned the trade of a machinist, and is at present a river engineer.

John Herbertson has filled orders for steamboat and mill engines from all parts of the United states and Mexico, but has taken no part in the foundry work for the last five years. His sons, who are skilled mechanics, are successfully running the machine shop and foundry, and are doing a large business.

John Herbertson was eighty-four years of age in September, 1889, and his excellent wife in years has spanned three-fourths of a century. He is a republican, but has never engaged in politics.

URIAH F. HIGINBOTHAM, one of the progressive young business men of Fayette county, was born in Redstone township, Fayette county, Pa., November 30, 1858. He is a son of Uriah and Tabitha (Edington) Higinbotham.

Samuel Higinbotham (paternal grandfather) was a merchant for many years at Mapletown, Greene county. He moved to Masontown, and continued merchandising there until 1860. He was a Methodist, and died in 1862.

Uriah Higinbotham (father) was born in Greene county, and was a well known farmer and stock-raiser of Redstone township. He married Miss Tabitha Edington. Uriah Higinbotham was a member of the Masonic fraternity, and was an elder in the Cumberland Presbyterian church. He died in 1888, aged fifty-eight years. His wife was born in 1821, is living, and very active for her age. She is a daughter of James Edington, who for many years was a merchant at Masontown, afterward a farmer, and died in 1872.

Uriah F. Higinbotham was reared on a farm, attended the common schools until the age of sixteen, when he entered the Southwestern Pennsylvania Normal School, and took a three years' course. Leaving school, he engaged in farming until 1884; the farm did not afford enough of business to keep him employed in a manner that he desired.

In 1884 he formed a partnership with A. G. Miller. They purchased 1,200 acres of land in Ottawa county, Kansas, and placed thereon 500 head of cattle; and after three years' residence on Western prairies, he returned to Bridgeport, and traded his interest in the Kansas cattle investment to W. H. Miller for the "Prospect Flouring Mills," of Bridgeport, and some adjoining land. He has operated these mills very successfully for the past year, and has secured a large trade.

He was married, in 1880, to Miss Emma V., daughter of Oliver Miller, a merchant of Bridgeport. They have two children: Ethel and Margaret. Mr. Higinbotham is a republican, and was elected by that party, in the spring of 1889, a member of the town council of Bridgeport. He is a member of the Free and Accepted Masons, and is an influential member of the Cumberland Presbyterian church.

He belongs to an old and highly respected family of Fayette county, and his own life, so far, has well sustained the record of honest industry left by his forefathers. He is active, intelligent and progressive, and is always ready to enlist in any enterprise that is beneficial to Bridgeport, or advantageous to its people.

JOHN HERTZOG, an industrious farmer and reputable citizen, was born in Spring hill township, Fayette county, Pa., February 11, 1806, and died July 24, 1870. He is a son of George and Margaret Hertzog.

George Hertzog came from Lancaster county when quite young. He learned the trade of gunsmith, at which he worked for several years, when he devoted the remaining portion of his life to farming. He was a valued member of the Mt. Moriah Baptist church, at Smithfield, and lived and died a respected citizen of Springhill.

John Hertzog's life until he attained his majority, was spent on a farm, and his education, received in the subscription schools, although necessarily limited, yet was practical, and good for his day.

He learned the trade of a tanner, and followed it successfully for several years; relinquishing tanning he turned his attention to farming, and was successfully engaged in that pursuit until the time of his death.

He was married March 23, 1843, to Miss Margaret, a daughter of Jacob Hertzog, who came from Lancaster county when only eight years of age. Jacob Hertzog was raised on a farm, received a fair education, and learned and pursued the trade of a blacksmith until his death in 1821. They had five children, three sons and two daughters: Elizabeth, George J., John A., D. Morgan, attorney at law (see sketch), Catherine (dead). Mrs. Hertzog was born December 4, 1811, and is still living.

John Hertzog was a prosperous farmer, and owned two hundred acres of land at the time of his death. He was one of the substantial citizens of Springhill, and for many years an earnest and faithful member of the Mt. Moriah Baptist church.

John A. Hertzog was born March 14, 1849, was reared on the farm, and educated in the common schools. On his father's death in 1870, he and his brother, George J., took charge of the home farm, and have increased its acreage until they now own 430 acres of fine farming and grazing land. About one hundred acres of this land is underlaid with a vein of coal. In connection with their farming interests they are now engaged extensively in stock-raising.

John A. Hertzog is a democrat, and has been a school director for six years. His amusement during some of his leisure hours consists in hunting and shooting. He is said to be a very fine marksman, and an adept in the use of the rifle.

R. W. HIGINBOTHAM was born August 27, 1849, at Point Marion, Fayette county, Pa., and is of English and Dutch descent. He is the son of Thomas H. and Malinda (Maple) Higinbotham.

Thomas H. Higinbotham was born in Carmichael's, Green county, Pa., December 7, 1824; was the son of a merchant, and brought up in a store. He attended the subscription schools of his county, and acquired a good edu tion in the lower branches of study. During vacations he clerked in his father's store. At the age of sixteen he engaged as a salesman in the mercantile establishment of Robert Maple, where he remained for nine years, on a salary of ten dollars per month, and saved five hundred dollars of his earnings. In 1848 he married Miss Malinda Maple, a native of Greene county, and the daughter of Robert Maple, of Mapletown, Greene county, Pa. He at once came to Point Marion, Fayette county, and opened a store, the first one of the place. He remained there until 1850, when he purchased a store at Ross' Cross

Roads, in Dunkard township, Greene county, where he remained until 1857, when he sold the store. He then purchased a farm of 120 acres of land in Redstone township Fayette county, on which he is at present located. At various times he has added to this farm and now has a farm of over six hundred acres. It is valuable land, underlaid with coal, and is well improved, having four good dwelling houses upon it, in which live himself, two sons, and one married daughter. He is still hale, and active, at the the of sixty-five years, and cultivates ninety acres of the farm himself. Malinda Maple, his mother, was born December 14, 1822, at Mapletown, Greene county, Pennsylvania, and is the mother of four sons and three daughters, all living except one son and one daughter. She is still living at the age of sixty-seven.

Samuel Higinbotham—the paternal grandfather of R. W., was born near Uniontown, Fayette county, March 2, 1789. He was a blacksmith by trade, and followed that business till his health failed him. He then went into the mercantile business at Carmichael's. He married Esther Cowden, August 8, 1810. He was an earnest Christian, and a member of the Methodist Episcopal church. He was tall and straight, and had a peculiar movement in walking, by which he was always readily recognized. He was successful in life and died March 19, 1861, at the age of seventy-two years.

Robert Maple, the grandfather of R. W., was born in New Jersey, August 1, 1780, and came to Pennsylvania in 1801. He married Jane Hall, daughter of William Hall, December 25, 1802. He traded cloth for land, giving one yard of cloth for one acre of ground until he had a farm of three hundred acres. He was a natural mechanic and followed the business of a wheelwright, a sickle-smith, and afterwards was a cooper. He manufactured linseed oil, and built a grist mill and a carding machine. It was upon his farm that the Dunkard Creek oil excitement of 1863-64 had its start. A town was built up in six months time containing five hotels. He sold one-eighth interest in one well for $10,000, and at one time was offered $250,-000 for his farm. He accumulated a large fortune, and died at the advanced age of ninety-two years.

Robert W. Higinbotham was brought up on a farm with his father, and had a great predilection for horses. He went to school but little before he was seventeen years old, after which time he attended constantly till he was twenty-one. Leaving the common schools he went to Waynesburg College for one term, and two terms to a select school. He then engaged in farming with his father.

October 28th, 1875, he was married to Miss Elizabeth Morgan, daughter of David and Caroline Morgan, of Springhill township.

Three children were born to them: Malinda A., Caroline and David Morgan, all living. He immediately moved upon his father's farm, and lived there till April 1st, 1880.

In January, 1880, the poor house directors selected him as the steward of the County Home, of which he took charge on April 1st, 1880, and remained in that position until 1885, declining the appointment for another term. While in charge of the Home he reduced the annual expenses of the place from $33,000 to $16,000. In 1883 he purchased the somewhat noted Tom Morris farm, near Morris X roads; April 1st, 1885, he removed, and is now residing there.

Mr. Higinbotham was born and reared a republican, and remained with that party till Horace Greely was nominated for president by the democrats in 1872. Being a great admirer of Mr. Greely he voted for him, and continued to vote the democratic ticket till 1888. He was an advocate for a high protective tariff, and voted for Harrison, and is again on the side of the Republican party.

GEORGE E. HOGG was born in Fayette county, Pa., September 7th, 1815, and is the son of George and Mary (Breading) Hogg, born respectively in Northumberland county, England, and in Fayette county, Pa. They were married in 1812, and raised a family of six children. Mrs. Hogg died in September, 1855, at the residence of her son, the subject of this sketch.

John Hogg, the grandfather of George E. Hogg, was born in Northumberland county, England, and came to the United States in about 1800, and settled in Licking county, Ohio, where he died about the year 1835. His wife was also a native of Northumberland county, England and died in Licking county, Ohio, in 1836.

George Hogg, the father of George E. Hogg, settled at Brownsville, Fayette county, Pa., in about 1804, and engaged in a general mercantile business, which he continued till 1843, when he moved to Allegheny City and lived there in retirement until his death in 1849. He was for many years one of the leading directors of the Monongahela Bank of Brownsville, and was warden of Christ's Episcopal church. He was a very successful business man, and a most useful and highly respected citizen.

George E. Hogg was educated and graduated at Kenyon College, Ohio, September 6, 1836. He returned to Fayette county, Pa., where he engaged in farming, which he has carried on extensively e er since. He has also been concerned in a general mercantile business at various times for over forty years. He was elected president of the Monongahela National Bank of Brownsville in March, 1874, which position he continued to hold for about fourteen years, when he resigned and was re-elected, but declined to accept on account of his private business requiring his whole attention and time. He is one of the most successful and public-spirited citizens that has ever lived in Brownsville.

He was married March 28, 1843, to Miss Sarah A. McClung of Brownsville, and has raised seven children: George, Mary, Sarah, Elizabeth, Nathaniel, Frank and Caroline.

He is still a very active man for one of his years.

FRANK T. HOGG is a native of Brownsville, Fayette county, Pa., and was born May 19, 1862. He was reared at Brownsville, and attended the public schools. He finished his classic education at LaFayette College, where he graduated in 1884, and took a subsequent course at the same college in mining and engineering.

Leaving college he formed a partnership with C. L. Snowdon of Brownsville, under the firm name of Snowdon & Hogg, and engaged in the coal mining business; they ship their coal to the lower river markets, Cincinnati, Louisville, Memphis and New Orleans.

They still continue in this business, and ship about two and one-half millions of bushels of coal, each year. They employ one hundred and fifty men at their works. Their mine is located one mile down the river from Brownsville, just below the mouth of Redstone creek, on the site of the old Albany Glassworks, and is called the Albany Mines. This firm owns the working parts of the mine, the ground and coal belongs to Mr. Geo. E. Hogg, the father of the subject of this sketch.

This firm also operates at times, coke ovens in connection with their other business. Their coke is pronounced, by the Edgar Thompson steel works, to be equal in quality to any other that they have ever used. Their slack and dust have preference in the Pittsburgh market.

He received the nomination for county surveyor, in June, 1889. He is a member of the Protestant Episcopal church, and is also a member of the vestry. He was married in 1887, to Miss Alice Bosler, of Dayton, Ohio. They have one child: Sarah Elizabeth.

Frank T. Hogg is the son of George E. Hogg. (See sketch.

His wife is the grand-daughter of Wm. Chatland. (See his sketch.)

MARTIN HOPE was born August 8, 1839, at Brush Creek, Beaver county, Pa., and is of German descent. He was brought up on a farm near Pittsburgh. Although his advantages for procuring an education were limited, yet he acquired sufficient education to transact all ordinary business. He lived on the farm until he was twenty-one years old, when he enlisted in the army under Captain C. T. Ewing, of Company G, First Virginia Light Artillery, at the first call for troops in 1861. He served in this company under Captain Ewing for three years, and fought in all of the engagements under McClellan and Rosecrans in Virginia in the early part of the war, and afterward in the Shenandoah Valley under Freemont and Pope. He was in the famous raid of General W. W. Averill, in which his company was kept within the Rebel lines almost a month. In getting out of their lines he had to cross a river seven times, and was badly frozen. In this raid he was eight days without provisions, and traveled two hundred miles in the midst of winter without pants or shoes. When he reached the Union lines, he was sent into the hospital at Grafton, where he remained till he fully recovered. He and seven others of his company were taken prisoners by the enemy. He broke through the enemy's lines, and was chased by them one mile across Jackson river, but fortunately he ran into a regiment of Union soldiers, and successfully made his escape. At the expiration of his term of enlistment he re-enlisted, in 1864, in the Eighty-eighth Regiment Pennsylvania Volunteers, under Lieutenant Robert Heron. During this year he did but little fighting, but a great deal of hard marching. He was present at the surrender of Lee's army at Appomattox Court House.

After four years' active service for his country, Mr. Hope was mustered out at the close of the war (1865) at Philadelphia. He returned to Greene county November 19, 1867, and was married to Miss Leah Keener, a daughter of David Keener, of Greene county. They are the parents of three children: Lora H., David M. and Leah M., all living and at home. His wife died August 30, 1874, and his oldest daughter is keeping house for him. In 1869 he removed to Fayette county and bought a farm of 112 acres of land, where he has since resided.

His parents were Casper and Elizabeth (Schaffer) Hope, both natives of Pennsylvania. His father was a musician in the garrison at Pittsburgh for several years. He died with cholera at New Orleans while on a Southern tour with a troupe. They had five sons, only two of whom are living.

J ALLEN HUBBS, M. D., of Bridgeport, is a gentleman in the fullest sense, and the word, as used in connection with his name, is not merely an idle term of complaisance, but one definitive of the man and of his character and life.

He is the son of William G. and Elizabeth (McFee) Hubbs. His father was a native of Baltimore, Md., born in 1811, and in 1818 he came with his father, Charles Hubbs, to Mt. Pleasant, Westmoreland county, Pa. Charles

Hubbs, M. D., was a native of New Jersey, born in 1767. He practiced medicine at Mt. Pleasant from the time he moved there till his death, in 1847. William G. read medicine with his father, practiced his profession at Fayette city from 1830 to 1867, and had a large and successful practice. In 1867 he removed to Bridgeport, and practiced medicine till April 6, 1881, when he died, at the age of seventy years. Since 1850 he had practiced the physio-medical system. He was a member of the Christian church.

The mother of the subject of this sketch was a native of Freeport (now Fayette City), and was born in 1818. She died at her home in Bridgeport, in 1881, at the age of sixty-three years.

J. Allen Hubbs was born in Fayette City, Fayette county, February 13, 1840. He commenced reading medicine with his father when he was sixteen years old, graduated at the Physio-Medical College of Cincinnati, Ohio, in the winter of 1857, and at the Physio-Medical Institute, Cincinnati, Ohio, in 1860. (This institute is now located at Chicago, Illinois.) In 1860 he commenced practice in Fairview, Greene county, Pa., where he continued till 1867, when he came to Bridgeport, and with his brother, M. G. Hubbs, engaged in the drug business, the firm being Dr. J. Allen Hubbs & Co. He continued successfully at this until the death of his father, when he commenced the practice of medicine again, and has followed it ever since. He is a general practitioner, but gives special attention to the treatment of diseases of the stomach and liver, also dropsy and female weakness, in which he has been very successful. He is a member of the American Association of Physio-Medical Physicians and Surgeons.

Dr. Hubbs was married, in 1861, to Miss Sarah J. Titus, daughter of Eli Titus, Greene county, Pa. She died in 1880, leaving one child, Cherrie T., now twelve years old. He married, the second time, Miss Maggie A. Adamson, of Greene county, daughter of Thomas Adamson, a farmer of that county. By this marriage he has no children living. The second wife died May 21, 1889.

Dr. Hubbs cast his first vote for Abraham Lincoln, and his last presidential vote for President Harrison.

HENRY HUNTER was born May 15, 1806, of German and Irish parentage, in Chester county, Pa., and is a son of Hiram and Margaret (Ashaphelter) Hunter. His father was a native of the same county. He was a stone mason, and followed the business all of his life. He was the father of seven children, four sons and three daughters, two of whom are now living. The father came to Fayette county in 1818, and remained until 1827. He then removed to Kentucky, where his wife died. After which he returned to Fayette county, Pa. He died at the age of seventy-five. Henry Hunter was brought up on a farm, his opportunities to obtain an education were very limited, having attended the old time subscription schools only about six months. He remained on the farm with his father until he was twenty-one years of age. He then commenced to work among strangers wherever he could obtain employment, at twenty-five cents a day. He early learned to save his earnings, small as they were. He soon became renowned as a careful, hard-working, prudent man, and commanded better wages. He was a lover of good horses, and became a skillful teamster. Being strictly honest himself, he reposed confidence in his follow-men, and loaned his money without requiring security, and lost all his hard earnings, after he had accumulated several thousand dollars. He bore his loss philosophically, and never ceased work. Before old age came upon him, however, by dint of industry and care, he replenished his fortune, and now has a competence and lives in comfort. Henry Hunter was never considered parsimonious, and his accumulations have been an enigma to many. He always dressed neatly and comfortably, and in company with his friends spent money liberally. He has lived a retired life for the last eight years. He never was married. At the age of eighty-three years, he reads without glasses and writes well and legibly, though he has had three paralytic strokes recently. It is pleasurable to say that it is the universal testimony of his neighbors and acquaintances that a more honest or upright man than Henry Hunter never lived, though not a member of any of the church organizations.

JAMES WITHRINGTON JEFFERIES, of English lineage and a highly respected citizen of Brownsville, the second son of Evan and Rebecca (Withrington) Jefferies, and was born in the city of Bristol, England, August 29, 1806.

Evan Jefferies was a native of the city of Cambridge, Glamorganshire, Wales, born February 2, 1766, and was a son of Evans Jefferies, of a family of the ancient Briton fathers. He married Miss Rebecca Withrington, of London, the latter born June 2d, 1787.

James Withrington Jefferies was reared in Bristol, England, receiving a good education in the schools of that city. He studied at the Mechanical Institute, and learned the trade of general painter. In March, 1832, he came to the United States. He first located in New York City, but remained only four months there on account of the prevalence of the cholera, and then removed to Pittsburgh. He remained eight years in the latter city in the successful prosecution of his trade. In 1840 he removed to Brownsville, and until he retired from active business in 1874 was successfully engaged in painting. On October 12, 1828, he was married in St. James' Episcopal church, Bristol, England, to Miss Sarah, daughter of John and Sarah (Sawyer) Case. Unto this union were born ten children: Ellen, Mary (deceased), Maria, Anna, Caroline, Isabella, George (deceased), Nelson, Charles and Frank.

Since twelve years of age Mr. Jefferies has been a consistent member of the Protestant Episcopal church. He has been a vestryman of Christ's church, Brownsville, for over forty-seven years.

For half a century he has been a prominent member of St. George's Society, also of the different orders of A. Y. M.

At eighty-four years of age, Mr. Jefferies is now as active in mind and body as most men of sixty. He has always been an upright and successful business man and an exemplary citizen, worthy of the esteem and respect which he enjoys.

ERASMUS KAISER, jeweler, at Brownsville, Pa., is the son of Erasmus and Margaret Kaiser. His father was a carpenter and contractor in Freiberg, Baden, Germany, where he died in 1843, at the age of forty-five years. The mother of the subject of our sketch died there in 1846, at the age of forty-six years. Mr. Kaiser left home early in life and does not know much of the ancestral history of his family.

Erasmus Kaiser is a native of Freiberg, Baden, Germany, and was born December 26, 1826. He was brought up there till at the age of fourteen, when he went to Lahr, Baden, to learn his trade—watch and clock making. He remained in Lahr, working at his trade till 1848, when he came to America.

He first located at Hollidaysburg, Pa., and there worked at his trade for a Mr. De Boyne until 1850, when he went to Greensburg, Westmoreland county, Pa., and engaged in the jewelry, watch and clock business. Not pleased with this location, he remained but a short time, when he removed from there to Brownsville, and commenced business in April, 1852, and has carried on a jeweler's store most successfully ever since.

He carries a large and assorted stock of all kinds of goods connected with a first-class jewelry house, and has one of the best appointed stores of his kind in western Pennsylvania. As a workmen his reputation and his work throughout southwestern Pennsylvania pronounce him to be of the first class.

He has built up a large trade at Brownsville and the surrounding country, and has at the same time made many warm personal friends. He stands high in the community where he lives, and is esteemed by all who know him.

He has served several terms as a member of the council in Brownsville, and has been twice elected as school director on the democratic ticket. He has been a member of the Presbyterian church for twenty-five years past, and is a deacon.

He was married at Greensburg, Pa., in 1850, to Miss Catherine Iftner. She is a native of Bavaria, Germany; came to this country in 1846, and located at Hollidaysburg, Pa., with her half-brother, Henry Iftner, who afterwards removed to Pittsfield, Ill. They have four children: Charles, Lizzie, Joseph and William F. Charles is engaged in the jewelry business in Hanover, York county, Pa. The others are all at home.

IRA H. KEYSER was born in Greene county, Pa., July 13, 1827, of German and Irish parentage, he is a son of John and Sarah (Dilliner) Keyser. His father was a native of Fayette county, Pa., and born in 1802. He was educated in the subscription schools of his day, when there were but three months in the year taught. He early manifested a disposition for the mechanical arts, and learned the millwright trade, possessing naturally a fine mathematical mind which peculiarly fitted him for the intricate duties of the profession of his choice. He was taciturn and unobtrusive in disposition and manner, strictly honest and conscientious in his dealings, which marked characteristics, together with his acknowledged ability as an artisan, commanded all the principal contracts in his line within the wide range of his acquaintance. He erected an elegant mansion on Cheat River at the point known then as McFarland's Ford.

His wife, Sarah Dilliner, was a daughter of George Dilliner, one of the early settlers of Greene county, who heard the war-whoop of the savage, and battled with the forces of nature in preparing the earth to yield her bounties for man's subsistence. He preempted a large tract of land on the Monongahela river, and by industry and frugality amassed a considerable fortune.

Mrs. Keyser died in September, 1841, leaving but one child, the subject of this sketch. John Keyser remained a widower for several years, then married Miss Esther Gans, an estimable and accomplished woman. Of this union four children were born, two sons and two daughters. After the children were grown to man and womanhood, they went West and settled near Bloomington, Illinois. The mother, true to her maternal instincts, wanted to be with her children, and induced her husband to leave the home he had built with his own skillful hands, for the new and untried society of strangers, much against his will. He lived but a short time after going West. He died in the winter of 1874.

Ira H. Keyser was educated in the common schools. He inherited, in an eminent degree, the leading traits in his father's character, and learned the same trade. At the age of nineteen he was so proficient and skillful in his profession that his father intrusted him with the superintendency of all his mill contracts. Before arriving at his majority he took the contract for building two large grist-mills in the State of Illinois, for a man by the name of Baily, who reposed so much confidence in him that he gave him $500 and instructed him to go to Pittsburgh, Pa., to purchase the necessary machinery for the mills. After completing the mills he returned to his native county.

He was married to Miss Hannah E. Morris, April 5th, 1852. Of this union there were born seven children, three sons and, four daughters: Louisa, Alva, Mary, Alice, William, Ida and John. The sons are all dead, the daughters all living, two of whom are married.

Mr. Keyser continued actively engaged in his profession until 1866, when Ambrose Dilliner, A. D. Frankenbery, B. R. Crow and he entered into co-partnership in the saw-mill, planing-mill and lumber business in Point Marion. Dilliner and Crow dissolved their connection with the company a few years ago, and the business, which is very extensive and lucrative, is carried on by Keyser & Frankenbery.

Mr. Keyser lives in the old homestead, which is a beautiful and picturesque place. Every summer the mansion is crowded with city boarders. He owns one hundred acres of land, lives comfortably, and enjoys, in the fullest sense, the confidence and esteem of his fellow-citizens.

Mr. Keyser is a member of the Disciple congregation at Point Marion, and takes a lively interest in all religious movements.

Ira H. Keyser is an excellent civil engineer and draughtsman, and one of the best mechanics in the county.

WILLIAM H. LE CLERE, a popular and prosperous merchant of Brownsville, is a son of John Lewis and Mary (Shunk) Le Clere, and was born in Brownsville, Fayette county, Pa., February 2, 1854.

John Lewis Le Clere was born in 1808 near Paris, France, and learned the trade of a weaver. He lived in Paris until 1831, when he came to Baltimore, and thence in 1832, he removed to near Brownsville. He engaged in farming until 1847, when he entered John Snowdon's foundry and worked for twenty-three years at boiler-making. In 1870 he retired from work, and since then has resided with his son, William H. Le Clere. J. L. Le Clere's first wife was Miss Barbara Rinecker, who died in 1845, leaving three children. He married again, and his second wife was Miss Mary Shunk, daughter of Simon Shunk. She died December 23, 1875, and left five children: John M., William H., Louis C., George A. and James B. He has been a member of the Methodist Episcopal church for forty years.

William H. Le Clere attended the common schools of Brownsville until he was fourteen years of age, when he entered the glass works and learned the trade of a glass flattener, which he still continues to pursue.

In July, 1883, he engaged in the grocery business at the old Gabler stand, corner of Market street and Hatter's Lane. He has a first-class grocery.

He established a furniture store in September, 1886. He carries a large stock of furniture and is doing a very fine business.

He was married, July 15, 1875, to Miss Eliza, daughter of George W. McClain of West Brownsville. Their union has been blessed with four children: Mary L., Harry M., Russel B. and William H., Jr.

He is a democrat, and served from 1885 to 1889 as a member of the town council. Mr. Le Clere is one of the live and successful business men of Brownsville. Thrown upon his own resources early in life, without a dollar of capital, he has by energy, perseverance, honesty and business tact built up a very prosperous business in his native town.

GEORGE W. LENHART was born April 25, 1842, in Bridgeport, Fayette county, Pennsylvania, and was reared in that town and attended the public schools. In the fall of 1862 he obtained the position of second clerk on one of the steamers belonging to the Pittsburgh, Brownsville & Geneva Packet Company, and held the position about eighteen months, when he was made clerk upon one of the Government boats running between Cincinnati, Ohio, and Nashville Tennessee, where he remained for about one year. He then left the river and, in 1865, engaged in the general merchandising business in Brownsville, and continued at that for about one year, when he sold out.

In 1866 he formed a partnership with William Chatland, in the manufacture of crackers, in Brownsville, the firm being "Chatland & Lenhart." Their factory has a capacity for making fifty barrels of crackers per day, and is well equipped with all the latest improved machinery.

In 1875 Mr. Lenhart was so unfortunate as to have his right arm caught in the cracker roller and so badly crushed that it had to be amputated above the elbow. After this he took up the "general insurance" business, in which he has been quite successful in building up a large patronage.

In 1887, when the natural gas was introduced in Brownsville, Mr. Lenhart was made secretary and treasurer of the company, and is at present holding that position.

He has been elected once as a member of the Borough Council, on the democratic ticket.

He is a member of the Episcopal church, and is a member of the vestry. He belongs to the Masonic Order, and to the Independent Order of Odd Fellows.

He was married, March 8, 1865, to Miss Sarah, daughter of Mr. William Chatland (his partner in the cracker factory). They have two children: William (now in the real estate and insurance business in Trinidad, Colorado) and Bessie.

He is the son of Leonard and Hannah (Baldwin) Lenhart, both born near Fayette City, Fayette county, Pennsylvania. His father was for many years a steamboat builder at West Brownsville, but removed to his farm in Redstone township, in 1860, where he now resides. Mr. Lenhart's mother died in 1858 at the age of forty-eight years.

Michael Lenhart, the grandfather of the subject of this sketch, was a native of Carlisle, Pennsylvania.

Mr. William Chatland, father of Mrs. Lenhart, was born at Stratford-on-Avon, Warwickshire, England, June 9, 1811. He was the son of William C. and Priscilla (Green) Chatland. His father was a native of Meriden, Warwickshire, England, and died in 1819. His mother was born at Brier Hill, Staffordshire, England, and died in 1814. At nine years of age he was left an orphan, and his grandmother took him to raise. She died when he was ten years old, and his uncle Joseph then took him till he was thirteen years of age, when he was apprenticed for seven years to Daniel Claridge, a baker of Coventry.

After he had learned his trade he went to London for three and one-half years, then returned to Coventry and established himself in business. While there he married Elizabeth Manton, the daughter of William Manton, a farmer of Berkwell. He came to the United States, arrived in New York City April 20, 1844, thence to Pittsburgh, from there to Washington county, where he remained till 1852, when he went to California, but was compelled to leave on account of bad health. He returned to Washington county, and thence to Brownsville in 1854, where he has since resided.

He is a prominent Mason, has been district deputy grand master for Pennsylvania for fifteen years; district deputy high priest for Pennsylvania for sixteen years; eminent commander of St. Omer commandery, No. 7, held at Brownsville for many years. He is a member of the Protestant Episcopal church, and a member of the vestry for a great many years.

JOHN ADAMS LYONS was born in Springhill township, Fayette county, Pennsylvania, July 10, 1824, and is of Scotch-Irish and Welsh parentage. He is a prominent member of one of the old and well-connected families of the southern part of the county. He is a son of Major Philip and Susan Lyons, the latter being a daughter of David Morgan, a well-to-do farmer of Fayette county, who died at the age of fifty-four years, February 14, 1787. Major Philip Lyons was a fine penman, a good mathematician, a successful farmer and stock-raiser. When twenty-six years of age he married Miss Susan Morgan, and unto their marriage were born nine children: George, Mary, Nancy, Elizabeth, William, Morgan, John A., Margaret and Samuel. Philip Lyons was a major in a militia regiment, was well and favorably known throughout the county, until his death in December, 1845.

William Lyons (grandfather) emigrated from New Jersey to Springhill township in 1787, which was then almost a wilderness. His capital for commencing business consisted of a few blacksmith tools, a good span of horses, and twelve and one-half cents in money. He was quiet, attentive to business, and, by half a century of hard labor and careful management, amassed a large estate. At seventy-one years of age he died, leaving to each of his six sons and three daughters a large and well-stocked farm.

John A. Lyons was educated in the old Grassy Run schoolhouse, of his native township, under the subscription school system of his day. In politics he is a republican. He and his wife are unassuming, useful members of the Lutheran church at Morris Cross Roads. In 1848 he cast his first presidential vote for Taylor, and in 1852 he voted for Pierce, the anti-whig candidate. In 1856 he voted for Fremont. He has voted for but two defeated presidential candidates in his life, Freemont and Blaine. He was elected tri-annual assessor for Springhill township in 1865, having been elected over a democrat in a township where his party was largely in the minority. He was also appointed to the same office by the county commissioners, and collected the township tax during the same year, having been appointed collector by the same authority. In 1868 he was nominated by his party for the office of county commissioner, but was defeated, owing to the county being overwhelmingly democratic. He was school director for his township for eight consecutive years, and has held several other township offices.

In the spring of 1845 he was elected first lieutenant of the Springhill militia; received his commission of Colonel Mustard, at Smithfield, which he resigned the same day and joined the Georges Creek Cavalry, serving with it for seven years. In 1847 his cavalry received a call from the government to join General Taylor's forces to help defeat the Mexicans. The company voted almost unanimously to do so, but before it was ready to start peace was declared.

John A. Lyons married Miss Margaret, daughter of Henry and Eliza (Showaters) Huhn, January 21, 1847. Of this union were born twelve children: William T.,

Susan (dead), an infant (dead); Henry H., married Eliza Rhodes; Amzi F., married Samantha Ganoe; Philip L., married Ollie J. Stentz; Alvin D., married Elma Hill; Estella, married Alvin J. Stentz; John C. (dead); Lou B., married Belford E. Lynn; Thomas and Benjamin F.

Mr. Lyons grew to manhood on his father's farm. After becoming of age he engaged in farming, and from 1845 to 1849 he rented his father's farm. In 1849 he purchased 130 acres of his present farm, near Morris Cross Roads, and removed there. Twelve years later he added twenty-six acres to his original purchase. In 1872 he built a large, handsome frame dwelling-house near the center of his farm, and four years later he erected a large barn near his residence.

Mr. Lyons has now almost retired from active business, lives in his beautiful residence near Morris Cross Roads, superintends his farm, and enjoys the confidence, good will and respect of his neighbors.

HENRY C. MADEIRA. The Madeira family was originally from Spain, from near the Madeira Islands. The ancestors of the American branch of the family migrated to Germany, and thence to this country.

"The coat of arms of the Madeira family is a blue shield, with three solid silver triangles to represent the three Madeira Islands. Helmet on the top is steel, finished in gold. Wreath on top of shield is silver and blue mountings, inside silver, outside blue. Three solid silver triangles above the helmet."

Nimrod Madeira, the father of the subject of this sketch, was born at Morgantown, W. Va., in 1815. He lived at Morgantown all his life, and died in March, 1888, at the age of seventy-three. He was a carpenter and contractor, and one of the best in that section of the country.

He married Miss Elvira Knox, a native of Morgantown. She was the daughter of Jacob Knox, a carpenter and contractor who came from Reading, Pa., and located at Morgantown. She died in 1847 at the age of forty years.

Henry C. Madeira was born January 26, 1838, in Morgantown, Va., and grew to manhood there. He attended the common schools of his native town.

In 1856 he came to Brownsville where he completed his apprenticeship as a molder, with John Herbertson, and at present resides at Brownsville. The molder's trade not agreeing with his health, he abandoned it, and learned that of a stone and brick mason. In this business he has prospered and is now a contractor.

In 1861 he was married to Miss Annie E. Cox, daughter of David and Elizabeth Cox, of Brownsville. David Cox was a bricklayer by trade, and died in 1864. The result of this marriage was four children: Ella, Norval, Howard and Maud, all living.

Norval was born July 26, 1867; he was reared in Brownsville, and attended the common schools there. For the last two years he has been studying electricity, and has become an expert electrician. He is also a watchmaker and a timer, having learned the former calling with J. S. Moorhead of Brownsville, and the latter with S. Vorhees, of Bridgeport. He is now in the hardware business, and carries on the other three vocations in connection with his hardware. He deserves credit for his success; very few have done as well so early in life.

ADOLPH GARDNER MINEHART was born November 8, 1825, at Bridgeport, Fayette county, Pennsylvania. He was educated in the schools of his native town. Being of an active turn of mind, at an early age, he assisted and worked at ruling paper. This was in the year 1835; also worked at paper making for Carter, and also for Herbertson & Faull, engine builders, in the capacity of engineer. He did all the drilling, lath and rail work that composed the upper work of the iron bridge, the second of the kind erected in the United States of America, spanning Dunlap's or Nemicolin creek, uniting Brownsville and Bridgeport. This bridge was built by the government, being a part of the National road, and was finished in 1838. He learned the trade of tailoring with H. Casson, and after serving four years, he finished his trade, crossed the Allegheny mountains on horseback with Robert Mitchell, who was going to Philadelphia with a drove of horses, and remained in the East until July, 1846, when he returned to Bridgeport to visit his parents expecting to return East, but his parents persuaded him to remain with them. He was married in Philadelphia to Miss Emma Selina Willits. She came to Pittsburgh, Pa., by canal and there joined her husband. She was a daughter of Jacob and Sarah Willits, and was born at Little Egg Harbor, N. J., whither her grandfather had moved from Long Island, N. Y., in the spring of 1847. He opened business in West Brownsville, Washington county, and in the next spring he moved over to Bridgeport and in 1852 to Brownsville, at which place he has remained ever since, and is the oldest merchant in the town. To their union have been born ten children: Samuel Hay, John Willits (dead), Charles Alexr., Emma Celeste (now Griffin), Mary E., Wm. H., A. G., Julia B., Thomas A. and Adelaide Lemy.

Adolph Minehart, Sr., came from Maryland with his father to New Geneva, and in the same year he learned glass-blowing at Albert Gallatin's glass factory. He was born in 1788 and died in 1854. After learning his trade he went to Pittsburgh and worked for Mr. Bakewell; his works were situated where the old B. & O. R. R. depot now stands. He married Miss Elizabeth Gardner, who was born in Baltimore, Maryland, on April 27, 1809. To their union were born eleven children: Julia A., Jacob C. Alexr. Hay, Eliza, Samuel, Mary, Mariah, A. G., Jno. R., David and William. Three of whom are living at this time: A. G., Mariah and Jno. R. He moved to Bridgeport to enter into a partnership in erecting and prosecuting the glass business; he sold out his stock, and in after years was engaged in merchandising. His wife died in the year 1875, being eighty-six years old at her death, having been born in the year 1789.

JOSEPH MOORE was born March 2, 1825, near Brownsville, Fayette county, is of Irish and German descent, and a son of William and Margaret (Coats) Moore.

William Moore (father) was born on February 24, 1792, at Winchester, Va. He attended school but little, yet he became a good penman and mathematician. At the age of seventeen he left home, and enlisted in the United States army for five years. He served his time under General Winfield Scott, and was at the battle of Lundy's Lane. He was in the company of Colonel Miller, who answered the question, "Can you take that battery?" by saying, "I'll try." He was in many skirmishes with the Indians on the frontier, and was through the entire War of 1812-15. When his enlistment expired he came to Pennsylvania and worked at his trade, that of a stone-splitter, which he followed up to his death in this county, August 1, 1847.

The grandfather of Joseph Moore was born in Virginia, and died from a wound inflicted by a mowing scythe.

Margaret (Coates) Moore died September 29, 1829, when her son Joseph was but little past three years old.

Soon after his mother's death Joseph was bound out to Philip Bourtner, with whom he remained until he arrived at the age of sixteen years. From Bourtner he received his board and clothes, and nine months' schooling. At sixteen years of age he was apprenticed for five years to James Barnes, to learn the trade of a millwright, and remained with him until he was twenty-one years of age. This man gave him five months' schooling, and a "freedom suit." From this time he worked at his trade up to 1881, when his health and eyesight failed him. He abandoned his trade and engaged in farming. He now owns a very valuable farm of 107 acres, where he at present resides.

In 1862 he volunteered under H. H. Cree, Company A, One Hundred and Sixty-eighth Regiment Pennsylvania Volunteer Infantry, commanded by Colonel Joseph Jack. He did little fighting, but a great deal of hard marching. He was mustered out August 1, 1863, and returned home to his family.

He was married December 24, 1848, to Miss Elizabeth Ann Johnson, of Greene county, Pa. Of this union two daughters were born: Susan Emily and an infant. This wife died December 25, 1851, at Carmichael's, Greene county. On March 16, 1853, he was again married, to Sarah Sams, daughter of Isaac Sams, of Greene county, Pa. They have the following children: Marsenna J., Elliamra, Harland, Gibson, Mary, Estella, Louvisa, Vienna, Lystra and Mazeppa, and are all living.

Mr. Moore reared all his children without having a doctor's assistance, or one cent's worth of medicine in his house. He is a republican in politics.

GEORGE L. MOORE is the son of William B. and Eliza (Sharp) Moore. William B. Moore is a native of Luzerne township, Fayette county, Pa., and is still living in that township. He is a millwright by trade. Eliza (Sharp) Moore was born in Washington county, Pa. John Moore, the grandfather of George L. Moore, was born in Luzerne township, and followed farming. John Moore, great-grandfather of the subject of this sketch, went with his father, Phillip Moore, from New Jersey, on the Delaware river between Easton and Philadelphia, to the neighborhood of Hagerstown, Md., about the time of the Revolutionary War. From Hagerstown he came to Fayette county, Pa.

George L. Moore is a native of Luzerne township, Fayette county, and was born October 30, 1843. At the age of twelve years he received a position as errand boy on a steamboat; continued in this capacity for five or six years, being employed on the boat during the summer, and attending school at home during the winter. He subsequently attended the State Normal school, located at that time at Millsboro, Washington county, but now at California, Pa. At the age of eighteen years Mr. Moore commenced to teach district school in Fayette county and continued to teach in the winter seasons for seven or eight years.

In 1868 Mr. Moore formed a partnership with his brother, at Millsboro, in a small line of country store business, in this he continued till 1873, when he sold out to his brother. He then came to Bridgeport and entered into partnership with Mr. C. W. Wanee, the firm name being Moore & Wanee, in the hardware and agricultural implement business, and ran this business till 1875, when Mr. Wanee died. He then bought out the interest in the store held by his estate, and has continued the business in his own name ever since. He has built up a good trade, has been deservedly successful in business, and now stands as one of the leading merchants of the place.

He was one of the prime movers in organizing the company to bore for natural gas at Bridgeport in 1885. Since then he has been interested in two other companies which operated at the same place. He has always taken an active interest in everything toward the advancement of the interests of his town. He is interested in the Eclipse Flouring Mills, which have the roller process. He was elected school director of Luzerne township on the republican ticket. He resides in what is known as Luzerne Township Village.

In 1873 he was married to Miss Emma F. Gibbons, daughter of E. P. Gibbons, of Luzerne township, who was one of the leading men of his township during his life. He died in 1886, aged fifty-eight years. Five children were born to this union: Guy G., Frank D., Charlie L., Carl F. and Elisha P. Mr. Moore is a member of the Cumberland Presbyterian church, and has been a deacon since 1869.

REV. JOSEPH GALLOWAY PATTON, the pastor of the Cumberland Presbyterian church, of Bridgeport, is a son of Stephen and Susanna P. (Galloway) Patton, natives of Washington township, Fayette county, Pa., the former born in 1805, now residing on his farm, two and one-half miles from Fayette city, Washington township, in the eighty-fifth year of his age. For sixty years he has been a devoted member of the Presbyterian church, a carpenter and cabinet-maker by trade, and has served as school director.

Rev. Patton's grandfather was by occupation a farmer, a native of Washington township, Fayette county, Pa. His father, a New Englander by birth, came to Fayette county and settled in Washington township in 1790, making the Patton family among the earliest here. Susanna P. Galloway died in the seventy-fourth year of her age. Her father, Robert Galloway, was a miller and farmer of Washington township, of Scotch-Irish extraction, and died at the age of forty-five.

Rev. Joseph G. Patton was born on a farm in Washington township, Fayette county, Pa., September 11, 1861, and at the age of sixteen years entered the normal school at California, Pa., which he attended for two years, and during vacations taught school in Tyrone township. In 1880 he went to Waynesburg College, was graduated in 1883, taking a classical course, and in 1886 he received from this college the degree of A. M. In the fall of 1883 he entered the Union Theological Seminary, New York City, and was graduated from there in May, 1886. During his term of theological study he did mission work at the Covenant Presbyterian chapel, Brick church, Presbyterian chapel, and the Home for Friendless Women. He preached in the Congregational church at Roxbury, New Hampshire, during first vacation in his seminary course, and during second vacation for the Cumberland Presbyterian mission, Connellsville, Pa. He was called to the Cumberland Presbyterian church at old Concord, Washington county, Pa., in the spring of 1886, and to the Cumberland Presbyterian church at Bridgeport, in the fall of 1888. Rev. Patton, besides attending to his duties as pastor, contributes as a writer to the *Cumberland Presbyterian Review*, *Sunday School Gem*, *Missionary Banner*, *Missionary Record*, and has just finished a life of Jesus: "In Thesi."

DANIEL H. PEARSALL is a son of Daniel and Sarah (Hingley) Pearsall. He was born at South Staffordshire, England, August 4, 1852.

Daniel Pearsall was a miner in England, where he died. His wife came to America in July, 1880, and eight years later died at Brownsville in the sixty-fourth year of her age.

Daniel H. Pearsall attended the pay schools of England until thirteen years of age, when he learned the trade of puddler. After five years experience as a puddler, he came to the United States, locating at Saw Mill Run in Allegheny county, and engaged in mining coal for seven years. In 1877 he removed to California, Washington county, and continued in coal mining for one year.

After eight years' hard labor, by prudence and economy he acquired a small sum of money. He invested this money, assisting to organize the Knob Coal Company. The Knob Coal Company was organized in February, 1878, leased and operated for five years. The coal bank is one mile north of West Brownsville. In 1882, with fifteen others, bought the bank and christened it "The Knob Coal Works." They are well equipped with the latest machinery for the mining, breaking, screening and shipping of coal. Daniel and Samuel Pearsall now own eleven of the sixteen shares. The company employ from 125 to 150 men, and their yearly output is about one million and a half bushels of coal. This coal is of a superior quality, and is principally shipped to Cincinnati, Louisville and New Orleans.

In 1882 he was elected by the company to take charge of their general store at Bridgeport, and as such he still continues.

His brother, Samuel H. Pearsall, now manages the coal works. He came from England in 1859, and resides in West Brownsville.

In 1872 D. H. Pearsall married Miss Tillie Leadbater of Sand Creek, Allegheny county. They have four children: Henrietta, Eva, Sarah and Minnie. He is a K. of P., a member of the Royal Arcanum and K. T.

The collieries are strong factors of American progress, and D. H. Pearsall is a notable example of a self-made man who has risen from a humble beginning to a prominent position in the colliery business of Pennsylvania.

REV. JOHN W. RIGHTER, minister of the Methodist Episcopal church at Brownsville, is the son of Lewis and Mariah J. (Myers) Righter. They were natives of Chester county, Pa. His father was a carriage manufacturer, and a resident of Salem, Ohio, at the time of his death, September 5, 1875, and was fifty years of age. He removed to Ohio in 1852, and was a member of the Methodist Episcopal church. Rev. Righter's mother died September 6, 1875, at the age of forty-five years. She was also a member of the Methodist Episcopal church, and the daughter of Rev. Daniel Myers. Rev. John W. Righter was born January 9, 1853, at Mt. Union, Ohio, and was brought up at Salem, Ohio. He attended the high schools of Salem; leaving school, he went into the printing office of the Salem *Republican*, where he learned the trade of printer, and worked at it consecutively for six years. At the age of sixteen years he was converted in the Methodist Episcopal church at Salem, Ohio. He studied for the ministry at his home under private teachers, and was licensed as a local preacher in February, 1873, in the Philadelphia conference. In March, 1874, he joined the Pittsburgh conference, and has continued in it ever since. He was first stationed on the New Galilee circuit, in Beaver county, Pa. He was next at Unionville and Concord, also in Beaver county; then at Harmony, Butler county; thence to Smith's Ferry, same county, and afterwards at Kittanning, in Armstrong county. In October, 1887, he came to Brownsville, and has since been the pastor of the first Methodist Episcopal church.

In 1875 he was married to Miss Achsa M. Early, of Darlington, Beaver county, Pa She is the daughter of Samuel and Lucinda (Grosvener) Early. They have three children: Edna C., Blanche E. and Frank P.

Mr. Righter is a member of the A. O. U. W.

ROBERT H. ROSS is a native of Fayette county, Pa.; was born at Masontown, April 22, 1824, and is of Scotch-Irish descent. He was brought up on his father's farm, and attended the schools of his youth, which were of the old class of subscription schools, the present common-school system not having been adopted in Pennsylvania till the year 1838.

Attaining his majority he commenced farming in company with his father, continuing to do so until October, 1861, when he enlisted as a volunteer in Company G, Eighty-fifth Regiment Pennsylvania Volunteer Infantry. He remained in the war two years and seven months, when he was mustered out on May 11, 1864. He was promoted to first sergeant while in the service.

Eight months of this time were spent in the hospital. He was wounded at Fort Sumter, S. C., by a shot through the left shoulder. The ball penetrated the lung, which almost entirely deprived him of the use of his left arm. He fought in the battle of Fair Oaks, Virginia, and was in several skirmishes.

Mustered out of the service, he returned to his home, and again engaged in farming, in which he has since continued.

By thrift and industry, he has succeeded in accumulating quite a considerable property, and owns one hundred acres of valuable land.

He is a member of the Presbyterian church at Georges Creek, and has been a ruling elder in the church since June, 1856. During his whole life he has been a pupil and a teacher in the Sabbath-school.

His father, Warwick Ross, was born near Masontown, Pa., June 7, 1797. His grandfather, Robert Ross, was one of the earliest settlers of Fayette county. He is a man of high standing in his neighborhood, and is esteemed as a good citizen and Christian.

GEORGE WASHINGTON ROSS was born February 2, 1847, in Monongalia county, Va. (now W. Va.), and is a son of Robert and Tabitha (Hoard) Ross.

His paternal grandfather came from Ireland, located at Uniontown, where he married Miss Evans, and then removed to Crawford county, where he remained until his nine children were grown to man and womanhood. He made his last removal to Monongalia county, Va., where he spent the remainder of his life reaching within ten years of the century mark.

Robert Ross (father) was a native of Crawford county, and came with his father to Monongalia county, Va. He had received a fair education for that day, and engaged in farming. In 1859 he bought a farm near Point Marion, where he resided till his death, June 9, 1878. He had five children: Elizabeth A., James L. (died), Francis M., George W. and William Miles (dead). His widow is still living in the seventy-eighth year of her age.

George W. Ross was educated in the common schools of Pennsylvania, and engaged in farming with his father until the death of the latter, when he removed to his present farm in Springhill township. He also owns a well improved farm of forty acres in West Virginia, one hundred acres of timber land in West Virginia, and a valuable house and lot in Point Marion.

He was married October 24, 1878, to Miss Lydia Jane, daughter of Thomas Campbell. They have two children: Isa Dora, born September 1, 1881, and Charles Franklin, born August 5, 1885.

In politics he is a democrat, and has served his township as assessor and collector of taxes.

He is a Methodist in religious belief, and his wife belongs to the Disciple church at Oak Grove.

He is one of the prosperous farmers of Springhill township.

JOHN C. RUBLE is a native of Monongalia county, W. Va., and was born January 7, 1845. His family is of German and Irish origin. His father William Ruble, was born June 2, 1818, in Monongalia county, W. Va.; he attended the schools of his day, and received a good education. He afterwards learned the trade of shoemaker with Jacob Tederick, and has followed it all of his life.

He was married in 1840 to Miss Elizabeth Wolfe. Six children have been born to their union: Jacob, one of the number, May 12, 1846, and Wm. R., physician at Mayfield, Ky., and Jacob is a Presbyterian minister. Elizabeth (Wolfe) Ruble, the mother, was born in 1817, and died in 1876. She was a member of the Presbyterian church, and a very devout Christian woman.

Jacob Ruble, the grandfather of the subject of the sketch, was a native of Virginia (now West Virginia), was a distiller, and became wealthy. He owned a large body of land, and at his death gave each of his eight children a valuable farm. He was a good citizen, and, notwithstanding his business, was a sober man. John C. Ruble's great-grandfather was one of the earliest settlers of Fayette county.

John C. Ruble was brought up on a farm, attended the common schools, winter and summer, till at the age of sixteen years, when he went into the war as a substitute, and remained nine months. He afterward enlisted as a volunteer in Company E, Fourteenth Pennsylvania Cavalry, under Captain Duncan, September 4, 1864, and remained till the close of the war. While scouting near White Post, W. Va., he was wounded by three balls —one entered below the shoulder blade and penetrated the lung, the other two entered the right side and still remain there. He was at once taken prisoner, and his wounds received no attention for two weeks. He was rescued, sent to the hospital at Baltimore, Md., recovered, and in two months he rejoined his regiment. He was mustered out of the service at Alexandria, Va., returned home, and engaged in drilling oil-wells for some time.

On December 1, 1866, he married Nancy L., daughter of Jacob Conn, and to their union were born six children: Dell, Harry J., Fred L., Frank C., Maggie A. and Russel Ray. All are living and at home but the oldest son, Dell, who was drowned in Cheat river June 16, 1888, in the twentieth year of his age. At the time he was employed in the lumber business.

J. C. Ruble learned the trade of shoemaker with his father, and after his marriage he worked at it for three years. He then went on a farm as a day hand, and in 1877 rented a farm. In 1879 he bought a farm of eighty-four acres, and is now doing well.

He is a republican, has been jury commissioner of his township, and is a member of G. A. R. Post, No. 180, at Uniontown. He gets a pension of six dollars per month.

CYRUS K. SADDLER, one of the substantial farmers of the county, is a native of Springhill township, Fayette county, Pa., and was born June 28, 1837, near Pt. Marion. He was brought up in his native township, and attended the common school until his twenty-second year.

He is a son of John and Hannah (Keiser) Saddler. John Saddler was a native of Fayette county, born at Pt. Marion, in 1810, and died May 28, 1861. He was a farmer and his father (C. K. Saddler's grandfather) Christian Saddler, was a native of Little York, Pa., came to Fayette county, Pa., in 1800 and settled in "The Forks of Cheat." He owned all the land where the pleasant town of Pt. Marion now stands. Here he engaged in farming and distilling, and died in 1840. Hannah (Keiser) Saddler was born in Greene county, Pa., in 1810, and died February 11, 1878.

Cyrus K. Saddler, leaving school, engaged in farming with his father at the old homestead, and has continued farming ever since. He now owns eighty acres of the old homestead that is well improved and productive. He has erected on his farm an elegant residence.

Mr. Saddler was never an office seeker, and is not a member of any secret society. He is a prominent member of the Disciple church, at Pt. Marion, and is a deacon. He has by prudence, economy, honesty and hard work, accumulated considerable property, and is one among the best farmers of Fayette county.

He was married in 1863, to Miss Susan G. Crow, a daughter of Michael Crow—a well-to-do farmer of the county. Of this marriage seven children were born: William, Evalena, Jennie, Plesie, Frank S., Zella, and Bessie, all of whom are single and at home, except Jennie, who is with an aunt at Hastings, Neb.

ACKISON M. SARGENT, of Bridgeport, and the proprietor of one of the finest liveries in Fayette county, is a son of James and Isabella Sargent. He was born January 10, 1860, in Zollersville, Washington county, Pa.

His parents were born near the same place. His father died before the subject of this sketch was born, and his mother when he was only thirteen years of age. Thus thrown upon the cold charities of the world as a friendless orphan, Ackison M. Sargent proceeded to manfully fight his own way through life, unaided by friends or influence. For four years he labored on a farm, and during the winter season worked for his board and the chance of attending the common schools.

At seventeen years of age he came to Fayette county, and engaged in farming on shares, in which he successfully continued for four years. In 1881 he came to Bridgeport, and engaged for two years in the grocery business. After selling his grocery he began teaming, at which he still continues.

In the spring of 1885 he engaged in the livery business, which was owned by E. H. Bar; it burned in 1886. In 1887 Mr. Sargent erected in Bridgeport a large livery stable, one hundred and thirty-eight feet long, thirty-two feet wide and sixteen feet in height to the square. In its construction fifty-three thousand feet of lumber was used. It is one of the finest livery stables in the county, is well stocked with a large lot of excellent horses, and is furnished with a large number of fine carriages and buggies. He is prompt to accommodate his patrons, and has a large and increasing trade.

Mr. Sargent was married, August 26, 1881, to Miss Ella, daughter of Oliver Allen, a farmer residing near Brownsville. They have one child, a daughter, Annie M. Sargent.

He is a republican, is attentive to his business, and is one of the self-made young men of Fayette county.

JOHN D. SEATON, merchant at Wymp's Gap, Springhill township, was born in Fayette county, Pa., March 15, 1834. He was reared on the farm, attended the schools of the neighborhood until he arrived at the age of nineteen years. On leaving school, he remained on his father's farm till he became of age, and then rented a farm and managed it on his own account up to 1863, when he removed to Preston county, W. Va. Here he ran a hotel for eighteen months, and thence he removed to Greene county, Pa. He was engaged in drilling oil wells in Greene county till 1877. In 1877 he began merchandising at Rosedale, where he remained till 1883, when he returned to Springhill township, engaged in the same business at Wymp's Gap, and where he is at present engaged. He was married October 12, 1854, to Sarah E., daughter of Solomon Elliot, the latter a farmer of the county. In politics Mr. Seaton is a sterling democrat, as is also his father. He was appointed by President Cleveland post master at Wymp's Gap, October 1, 1888 and is the present occupant of that office. He has a pleasant home in Springhill, and is doing a splendid mercantile business.

John D. Seaton's parents were Hiram and Mary (Fisher) Seaton. The former was born in 1800 and the latter in 1797. The mother died in October, 1883.

Hiram Seaton was born at Uniontown, where he received a very good education. At the age of eighteen he engaged in peddling goods, continued at it for two years, when he purchased 600 acres of land in Wharton township and engaged in farming.

He was married in 1821. In 1823 his wife died and he was again married in 1827. To this last union were born seven children, five sons and two daughters; all became men and women. Hiram Seaton was elected treasurer of Fayette county in 1855, and was popular with the people. A special act of assembly was passed by the legislature of Pennsylvania for the purpose of re-electing him as treasurer, for a second term, and after serving two terms as county treasurer most acceptable to the people, he retired to his farm in Wharton township. In 1869 he removed with his family to Pleasant Hill, Cass county, Mo., where he died October 28, 1870, in the seventieth year of his age.

Hiram Seaton's father was one of Uniontown's early settlers. He was the proprietor of the old Seaton House, which for many years, was the leading "tavern" at Uniontown for drovers and wagoners on the National road, and was run by Mr. Seaton during the palmiest days of the old road.

CAPTAIN JOHN SNOWDON (deceased). John Snowdon came to Brownsville, Fayette county, Pa., in 1818, from Yorkshire, England. He was a blacksmith by trade, and about all he possessed was a wife and two children. His household furniture was scanty, as we find in a sketch published of him in the Brownsville *Clipper* of July 24, 1867, his bed was the bare floor, his chair a block of wood and his table a store box.

He commenced work as a journeyman, in the shop of John Weaver, at one dollar a day, and was the first man who received so large an amount for wages as a blacksmith, at Brownsville. His first work, outside of the regular line in the shop, was to make an English oven or stove, for Mr. George Hogg. After that he made several more, which were probably the actual introduction of the use of the stove into this section of the country.

Mr. Hogg asked him why he did not start a shop of his own, the reply was, that he had not the means. Mr. Hogg furnished him with all of the necessaries of the trade for starting a small shop on Market street. He showed superiority in his work and added to his "shop," different departments of work, until he became proprietor of the foundry, machine and other works.

The "shop" was the nucleus around which was built a machine shop, then a foundry and pattern shop. At these works the engines were built for the steamer Monongahela, in 1827. In 1831 he built larger shops, and in them were built the engines of the iron-clads Manayunk and Umpqua. This plant stood where the rolling-mill now stands, and was destroyed by fire September, 1853. In 1853-54 he built the present "shops." In 1853 he built the rolling-mill, and operated it, individually, for some time, and later in connection with his sons, under the firm name of John Snowdon & Sons.

The following from a sketch of the life of

Captain John Snowdon, published in the Brownsville *Clipper*, of July 24, 1867, gives an epitome of the works of the man: "He established, as we at present see them, a foundry, machine and pattern shops, of an aggregate length of 685 feet, and in which have been employed on an average for the last five years, nearly 200 hands; he has built steamboats, or the iron portion of them, for the States of Georgia, Florida, Alabama, Texas, Michigan, California and other States, to the number of almost 300; having himself established the business in this place, and built one of the first two boats that ever navigated the Monongahela river; also, boats for the government, to run on the Rio Grande, during the Mexican War, as well as two gun-boats for the government during the late War of the Rebellion, at a contract price of $1,500,000, besides building an iron steamboat for a private party during the same time that the two government boats were in progress. He built the first boat that ever ran on the Sacramento river, and the iron bridge across the creek between Brownsville and Bridgeport, more than forty years ago was built by him, which is still standing as firm and substantial as ever, and as a specimen of bridge architecture, is embraced in the list of studies on engineering at West Point Military Academy. This is supposed to have been the first iron bridge built in America. He made the iron mile-posts for the National pike." From the same paper we also clip the following with reference to his losses in business: "He lost by the bankrupt law of 1841 more than $40,000. In 1853 his whole establishment, including machinery, patterns, etc., amounting to upwards of $80,000, was destroyed by fire, upon which there were only $5,000 insurance. He lost by the failure of the Southern contractors, in consequence of the rebellion, some $25,000, and these several sums by no means cover all the losses he has sustained since the day he sat upon a wooden block and took his meals from the cover of a store box."

In 1852 he took a trip to England, visiting the World's Fair; was presented to Queen Victoria by the Hon. James Buchanan, then minister plenipotentiary to the court of St. James, and afterward president of the United States.

In 1860 he took another trip to England, visiting his old home, his relatives and friends. He went as a passenger on the steamship Great Eastern on her first trip across the ocean. Upon his return home to Brownsville, he was received by the citizens with the ringing of bells and firing of guns. This in passing will give the esteem in which he was held by his fellow-citizens of his adopted country, and especially so by his friends and employes.

Captain John Snowdon was born at Martin, near Scarborough, Yorkshire, England, March 22, 1796. His early education was of a limited character; his trade was learned in England, and he was married there. In 1818 he migrated to the United States, and the remainder of his life and history belong to this country. His life and character was that of an upright man, full of kindness to his fellow-men, and bestowed much money in assisting the poor, helping the laboring man, and often carrying men on his pay-roll who were not needed in his works. He bestowed aid upon the widows and orphans of his former employes. As a citizen he stood high in the estimation of all of the community in which he lived. As an employer he was generous and just, gentle and careful of the feelings and condition of his men. Having gone through the path of the laboring man himself, he could sympathize with him. He appreciated the duty he owed to his men as fully as that which they owed to him. The result of this was that he had the full affection and respect of his men. As an instance of this, we cite the presentation of a very fine cane to him by the employes of Snowdon's foundry and machine shops, which took place on Saturday, July 13, 1867. The whole affair was gotten up by the men, and Captain Snowdon was not aware of the cause for which he had been called to the foundry, till John L. Snowdon presented to him a beautiful ebony stick heavily mounted with gold and bearing the inscription: "Presented to John Snowdon, by his employes, July, 1867."

Captain Snowdon was an F. and A. M. for many years before he died. He was married in 1816 to Miss Mary Smith. They had the following children: Ann, wife of Adam Jacobs, of Brownsville; Elizabeth, wife of Walter Smith, of Cincinnati, Ohio; Samuel S., of St. Louis, Mo.; I. W. S., of Brownsville, and Sarah M., wife of I. H. Roberts, of Allegheny, Pa.

Captain Snowdon did more to build up the business and wealth, and to advance the interests of Brownsville, during the fifty-seven years of his residence there, than any other man who ever lived in the town.

Captain Snowdon died at Brownsville on the 25th of January, 1875, universally mourned by all. His wife also died at Brownsville.

JOHN N. SNOWDON was born in Brownsville, October 15, 1827, and was brought up there; he attended the common schools of the borough. He was the son of Captain John Snowdon and Mary (Smith) Snowdon (see sketch of Captain Snowdon).

In 1845 he took a position as clerk in the forwarding and grocery house of George Cass, but remained there but a short time. In 1846 he went, as second clerk, on one of the packet boats, and remained on the river till 1854. During this time he had command of and owned several boats that were running on the Ohio river.

In 1854 he went into partnership, with his father and his brother Samuel, in the foundry and machine shops, and boat-building business; the firm name being J. Snowdon & Sons. This firm continued till 1860, when Samuel withdrew; the firm name then was changed to J. Snowdon & Son.

This firm built two gunboats for the government during the war (the Umpqua and Manayunk), at a contract price of over one million dollars. The latter was so great a favorite in the navy, that when the gunboats were sold off, at the close of the war, she was retained in the service, and her name was changed to Ajax.

The firm of J. Snowdon & Son, besides their works at Brownsville was running a foundry, machine shops and boat-yards at Pittsburgh, employing as many as two thousand men in the two towns; the two gunboats were built at Pittsburgh. In 1856 they turned out twenty-six steamboat engines. They took contracts to build and complete in all its parts, and to furnish an entire steamboat in sixty days, and finished and delivered it in forty-five days—fifteen days in advance of time. This firm continued till 1872.

In February, 1878, Mr. J. N. Snowdon was appointed postmaster of Brownsville, by President Hayes, and was re-appointed in 1882 by President Arthur. He held the office from February, 1878, to June, 1886, this being for a longer time than any other man, except Jacob Bowman, who was the first postmaster, and held the place for seventeen years; he is the only man, besides him, who has been appointed to succeed himself in the office of the borough.

At the time that the erection of the public school building was in question, Mr. Snowdon was a candidate for director and was elected, against strong opposition, as in favor of the building, and was made chairman of the board, and held that position for eight years.

At present Mr. Snowdon is in the office of his son, C. L. Snowdon, whose sketch is in another place in this work.

Mr. John N. Snowdon was married January 17, 1853, to Miss Eliza J. McSherry, daughter of James McSherry (who was a tailor of Brownsville). They have three children: Charles L., John Howard and Mary. John Howard is at home and clerks for his brother C. L. Mary is married to Walter Bare, who resides in Lancaster, where he is engaged in the tobacco business with J. Wolf & Co.

CHARLES L. SNOWDON is the son of John N. and Eliza J. (McSherry) Snowdon, and the grandson of Capt. John Snowdon. For family history, see the sketches of the father and grandfather, John N. and Capt. John Snowdon.

C. L. Snowdon was born June 25, 1854, in Brownsville, Pa., and was reared and educated there. He was afterwards employed as a clerk for several years, and from 1873 to 1877 acted as teller in the Dollar Savings Bank of Brownsville. In 1887 he went as first clerk of the steamer Geneva, that ran between Pittsburgh and Brownsville, and belonged to the Pittsburgh, Brownsville & Geneva Packet Co. He remained in this capacity for three years.

In January, 1880, he became interested in the Umpire Coal Works, of Cunningham & Co. The firm consisted of J. S. Cunningham, L. H. Abrams and C. L. Snowdon. They continued in business together till 1881, when J. S. Cunningham and L. H. Abrams drew out, and S. S. Graham and W. B. McCormick became interested, and the firm then became Graham, Snowdon & Co. In 1882 S. S. Graham sold his interest to N. B. Hogg, Jr., and the name was changed to C. L. Snowdon & Co. The mine is located just above the mouth of Redstone Creek, between the railroad bridge and Brownsville. The coal is of superior quality and is shipped by river to Pittsburgh, Cincinnati, Louisville and New Orleans. They shipped from this mine annually from one and one-half to two millions of bushels of coal, and employ on an average one hundred and twenty five men. The firm of C. L. Snowdon & Co. operate coke ovens in connection with their coal mining interests, and their coke is pronounced by the Edgar Thompson Steel Works to be equal to the Connellsville, or any other coke they have ever used. The slack and dust from this mine has preference in the Pittsburgh market.

In 1882 Mr. Snowdon opened the Oro Coal Works, on Water street opposite the glass works in Brownsville; he operates them to supply the home trade.

In 1885 Mr. Snowdon formed a partnership with Frank T. Hogg, and opened the Albany mine, located one mile down the river from Brownsville, near the mouth of Redstone creek, on the site of the old Albany Glass Works. The coal is of an excellent quality,and they ship from two millions to two and one half millions of bushels yearly.

As it will be seen, from the above recital of Mr. Snowdon's business ventures, he is a stiring, energetic, go-ahead business man.

On June 26, 1879, he was married to Miss Elizabeth Hogg, daughter of George E., of Brownsville (see his sketch). They have four children: Eliza, George Hogg, Caroline McClurg and Felix Brunot.

Mr. Snowdon is a member of the Protestant Episcopal church at Brownsville, and is a member of the vestry. He is a member of the borough council, having been twice elected; first in 1883, re-elected in 1887, and in 1889 he was elected as a member of the school board.

JOHN L. SNOWDON is the son of William and Mary (Lickas) Snowdon, both natives of Yorkshire, England.

His father was born in Yorkshire, England, in 1782, and learned the trade of blacksmithing. He was married in England to Miss Mary Lickas of Nunington, Yorkshire.

In 1833 he and his family took ship at Liverpool, sailed for the United States; after a voyage of eleven weeks, the officers of the ship having lost their reckoning, and after a circuitous route, they landed at New York City. From New York they traveled to Philadelphia by canal; thence to Baltimore; from there by stage to Brownsville. They came to Brownsville, or rather a part of the way, in a covered wagon; on account of the snow they were compelled to abandon the wagon for a sled, in which they finally reached Brownsville after many days of travel.

Having arrived at Brownsville, Mr. Snowdon engaged at work in the rolling-mill of Rev. Arthur Palmer, where he worked for four years. He then opened a shop for himself and continued to work at his trade, shoeing the stage horses for the company so long as the line continued to exist. He died at Brownsville in 1855, at the age of seventy-three years. He was a useful and consistent member of the Methodist Episcopal church. His wife died in Brownsville when eighty-four years old.

John L. Snowdon was born May 10, 1820, in Yorkshire, England, and came to Brownsville with his parents when thirteen years old. Soon after he arrived at Brownsville he went to Capt. John Snowdon's "shops," to learn the trade of machinist blacksmith, where he served six years' apprenticeship. At the expiration of his term, he commenced work in Capt. Snowdon's employ, and remained with him the greater part of the time till the death of Capt. Snowdon. In 1861 he went to Pittsburgh, South Side, and worked in the rolling mill of Zug & Painter for about one year; thence he removed to Pittsburgh, where he lived and worked for about three years, when he returned to Brownsville, to engage with Capt. Snowdon.

In 1870 he went to New Haven and took the position of foreman in the blacksmithing department of Messrs. Dawson & Bailey's locomotive shops, where he continued for three years, when he quit the business. He then returned to Brownsville and commenced business for himself in the old "Snowdon Shops."

John L. Snowdon, on account of his long connection with and intimate relations to Capt. John Snowdon, was selected by his fellow workmen, as the person best fitted to present the cane they gave as a testimony of their esteem to the captain. (See Capt. Snowdon's sketch.)

John L. Snowdon was married in Brownsville, 1845, to Miss Elizabeth Downs, a daughter of John Downs, who was a blacksmith in Brownsville. His wife died leaving seven children: William N., Mary Ann, John T., Arabella, Walter, Samuel A. and C. Loy. He was married the second time, to Miss Rebecca Downs, a sister of his first wife.

He is one of the old residents of Brownsville, and is a true democrat. For twenty-five years he was a member of I. O. O. F. but withdrew from the order during the war.

Mr. Snowdon is a good man, esteemed by the people of the borough generally, and beloved of those who are classed as his friends.

EDWARD SNOWDON, of Brownsville, Fayette county, Pa., is the son of William and Mary (Lickas) Snowdon. (For their history see sketch of John L. Snowdon.)

Edward Snowdon was born June 2, 1824, in Yorkshire, England, and came to Brownsville in 1833, with his parents. He learned the trade of blacksmith with his father, and continued to work for him until the subject of this sketch was of age.

In 1845 Edward Snowdon went on the river to learn steamboat engineering. He has since followed the river as engineer and pilot, and has boated on all the southern and western rivers. He is probably the oldest engineer and pilot now living in Brownsville. At the Pittsburgh custom house he is registered as having taken out one issue of license as steamboat engineer more than any other man whose name is found on the books.

Mr. Snowdon has displayed great ingenuity in the building of two miniature steamboats. These boats, which show great skill in their construction, can be seen at his residence.

John Snowdon was the father of Captain John Snowdon, and was the first of the Snowdon family that came to this country.

Edward Snowdon was married to Miss Sarah Ellis of Fayette county. She died leaving nine children: Maggie, Jennie, Alvin, Belle, Edward, Ellie, John and Dora. He married again, to Miss Eliza Warner, daughter of Philip Warner of Allegheny City. By this wife he has five living children: Ross, Francis, Nettie, Hester and Bertha.

Mr. Snowdon is a regular attendant at the Methodist Episcopal church, and is a demo crat.

WILLIAM C. STEELE, one of Brownsville's young business men, and a leading merchant, is a son of Samuel and Elizabeth A. (Conwell) Steele. He was born in Brownsville, May 23, 1857.

William C. Steele's great-great-grandparents came from Ireland to eastern Pennsylvania about 1740.

One of their sons, William Steele, the great-grandfather of William C. Steele, settled in Maryland, where he married and resided for a time. He removed, in 1784, from Maryland, and purchased a large tract of land on the old "Pack Horse Road," six miles east of Brownsville. At the beginning of the nineteenth century William Steele removed to Westmoreland county, where he died in 1806.

John Steele, the grandfather of William C., was born in Maryland in 1773, and died June 6, 1856. He married Agnes Happer, and they were the parents of eight children.

Samuel Steele, the father of William C., was born in Jefferson township, this county, June 15, 1814, and died August 3, 1886. He was a republican, and a member of the Presbyterian church. He spent three years in learning the trade of a tanner and currier, with Jesse Cunningham, of Brownsville. At the close of his apprenticeship he engaged with Mr. Cunningham, and remained until the latter's death in 1843, when he went into partnership with Mr. Cunningham's widow (his sister). In 1860 he withdrew from the firm, and erected a large tannery, which he operated alone until 1878, when he took in his son, William C. Steele. The firm being Samuel Steele & Son. This firm continued till the death of the senior partner in 1886. Samuel Steele was married February 11, 1852, to Miss Elizabeth A. Conwell, of Brownsville. To them were born eight children, four of whom are living. Mrs. Steele is living, and in her sixty-first year.

William C. Steele was educated in the public schools of Brownsville, with the exception of one year at Southwestern Normal School.

In 1878 he became junior partner with his father in the firm of Samuel Steele & Son. They used 150 cords of bark, and tanned 1,000 hides per year. They shipped their leather largely to Iowa and Minnesota. William C. Steele continued in the tanning business until 1888, when he closed up the affairs of the firm, and retired from the business.

In 1887 he engaged in mercantile business

in Brownsville. He is located on the Hogg corner in a commodious room, where he carries a large stock of boots, shoes, leather, hats and caps. He is accommodating, and is doing a fine business.

December 14, 1881, he married Miss Alice, daughter of Captain E. D. Abrams, a steamboat commander of thirty-five years' experience on the Western rivers. Mr. and Mrs. Steele have had three children: Bessie Abrams, who died in infancy, Helen J. and William C., Jr.

Mr. Steele is a prominent republican. He was elected a member of the town council in 1885, and was re-elected in 1888 for a term of three years.

He is one of the young, progressive and accommodating merchants of Brownsville. With his educational qualifications and business experience, he bids fair to achieve mercantile distinction in the future.

DR. ALPHEUS P. STEWART was born near Stewartstown, W. Va., January 16, 1820, and is the son of John Stewart and Susanna Stewart, both natives of Maryland. His father lost his eyesight by cataract soon after his marriage, and the sad fact is a matter of record that he never was permitted to look into the face of one of his children. His mother was an invalid for many years, and upon the doctor devolved the care of his afflicted parents.

Dr. Stewart's advantages for schooling were limited. His first lessons were studied by the light of the old fashioned fireplace. He worked at home on the farm until 1854, when he went to Stewartstown, and began the study of medicine. After a year's reading he attended the Eclectic School of Medicine at Cincinnati, Ohio. He returned to Stewartstown and followed the mercantile business until 1858, when he went to the mineral springs of West Virginia for his health. His health having partially improved, he located at Taylortown, Greene county, Pa., and engaged in the mercantile business, which he followed up to 1874. He practiced medicine in Illinois from 1874 to 1883. He opened an office in 1884 at Point Marion, where he has built up a large and lucrative practice.

Dr. Stewart was married in 1847 to Miss Eliza John, daughter of Owen and Elizabeth John. Of this union four children have been born: Virginia Helen, Josephine, Laura and Lebbeus P. All living except Virginia, who died at the age of thirty-six years.

Dr. Stewart is a self-made man and sets a worthy example of filial affection to the young and rising generation by the kind care he took of his parents.

JESSE E. STENTZ, one of the remarkably successful business men of Springhill township, is a son of Daniel and Elizabeth (Bowman) Stentz, and was born in Springhill township, Fayette county, Pa., Nov. 16, 1820.

Philip Stentz (grandfather) was a merchant in Little York, Pa. During the Revolution he became nearly bankrupted by the depreciation of the old Continental paper money. In order to better his fortunes he removed West and located in Springhill township, where he purchased land. He was a blacksmith by trade, but abandoned his trade after coming here, and gave his whole attention to farming.

Daniel Stentz (father) was born in Little York, Pa., May 19, 1779, and was a mere child when his parents emigrated to Springhill. He left the farm at nineteen years of age to learn the trade of sickle-maker. After working a short time, his employer died, when he engaged with his brother to learn the trade of blacksmith. On learning this trade he began farming and blacksmithing, and was thus engaged during his life. He manufactured the old Barshear plow. He owned a farm of 190 acres of good land, was a justice of the peace for many years, writing all the deeds, wills and legal documents of his community. He was an excellent citizen, a devoted member of the Lutheran church, and died January 11, 1853.

Jesse E. Stentz at school became a fair scholar and an excellent mathematician. He was engaged in farming until 1845, when he formed a partnership with Alex. Patton, with whom he operated a tannery until 1863. Since then his attention and time have been given mainly to farming and stock raising. At the death of his mother, he bought the home farm. He now owns three farms in Pennsylvania and two in West Virginia, besides being the owner of Old Valley Furnace in the latter State. Mr. Stentz has a fine residence on the old home farm, where he resides. October 3, 1844, he married Miss Lydia, daughter of John Conn. To this union were born seven children: Sarah E., John D. (dead), Catherine A., William J., Mary Jane (dead), Alvin J. and Maggie O. Alvin J. is a partner with his father in operating a saw-mill.

Mr. Stentz is a republican-prohibitionist, has served as school director, and has been an elder in the Presbyterian church at Springhill Furnace since 1848, and a member since 1836. His family are members of the same church. He began business with a capital of five hundred dollars; by perseverance and industry he has accumulated considerable wealth.

JAMES ESTEP STURGIS is of English-Welsh and Irish descent. He was born August 29, 1841, near Pt. Marion, Springhill township, Fayette county, Pennsylvania, and is a son of Isaac P. and Diana (Ross) Sturgis.

Isaac P. Sturgis was born January 19, 1807, near Smithfield, Fayette county, Pennsylvania. He was reared on a farm, and acquired a good business education. He followed farming, bought and sold one farm, afterward rented, until he purchased a farm of 134¾ acres near Pt. Marion in 1836, on which he resided untill his death, March 21, 1876. He was a whig until the death of that grand old party, when he became a republican, and continued to affiliate with the republican party until his death. He was for many years a member of the Baptist church. He accumulated considerable property by his own energy and individual efforts. He married Miss Diana Ross, who was born June 7, 1808. She is now a well preserved old lady, and possesses a remarkable memory. They had seven children, three sons and four daughters. Two of the sons were soldiers in the Union army and died from cold contracted in the siege of Yorktown. Mrs. Diana (Ross) Sturgis was a daughter of David Ross, who was born and reared in Dunkard township, Greene county, Pennsylvania.

Phineas Sturgis (paternal grandfather) was a Fayette county farmer, and for many years an iron ore contractor at the old Fairchance furnace. His father was one of three brothers, who came from England to America in an early day, and from them are descended all the Sturgises in the United States.

James Estep Sturgis was reared on a farm, educated in the common schools, and attended one five months' term at Georges Creek Academy. In 1860 he taught school in West Virginia, and subsequently taught five successive terms in Greene and Fayette counties.

When his father died he was appointed executor of the estate and took charge of the home farm, where he now resides.

He was married November 19, 1868, to Miss

Lydia Frances, daughter of Ambrose Dilliner, a millwright and farmer of Greene county, Pennsylvania. Their union has been blessed with three children: Carrie Leonard, Ross and Lizzie.

For twenty-five years he has been a member of the Mt. Moriah Baptist church at Smithfield, while his wife is a member of the Methodist Episcopal church at Pt. Marion.

He has been a life-long republican, never asked for an office, and is not an office seeker. He takes considerable interest in agricultural matters and represents a Cleveland fertilizing company. He has pronounced opinions on the agricultural, political and religious topics of the day, and can well express them.

MATTHEW STOREY, the popular proprietor of the well known Storey House, of Brownsville, was born in England, August 29, 1839. He is a son of Matthew and Elizabeth (Palmer) Storey, both natives of the town of Early in Cambridgeshire, England.

His father, Matthew Storey, Sr., came from England to Seneca Falls, N. Y., in 1847, and remained there until 1851, when he removed to Brownsville. Here he worked for several years in Snowdon's machine shops. He was born in 1800, and died in 1870. His wife survived him until 1882, when she died. They were both members of the Methodist Episcopal church.

Matthew Storey learned the trade of a machine blacksmith, under John Snowdon, and continued with him for five years.

In 1859 he learned the trade of a steamboat engineer, and continued in that calling for twenty years on the Mississippi river and its tributaries.

He was at New Orleans when Fort Sumter was fired on, and saw the first Confederate troops from Louisiana leave for Richmond. He was assistant engineer on the "New Falls City," which, with the "Capital," carried the Confederate troops from New Orleans who captured the United States arsenal at Baton Rouge. The guns were taken from the "New Falls City" and placed on the Confederate fortifications at Columbus, Ky. From this place he walked to Bird's Point on the Ohio river, opposite Cairo, Ill., and from there came home via St. Louis.

After a two months' stay he returned to St. Louis and engaged as an engineer on a government transportation boat, continued in this line of work until nearly the close of the war. He was on the Cumberland river and was at Fort Henry, Fort Donelson and Pittsburg Landing, when the transport fleet returned to and passed down the Mississippi river. He was present at the siege of Vicksburg. In October, 1864, he engaged as engineer on the "H. A. Homayer," a boat owned and operated by the cotton firm of Parkman, Brooks & Co., of Menphis, Tenn. This boat plied for seven months on the Washita and Yazoo rivers.

He was chief engineer on different boats for sixteen years after the war closed. In 1881 he returned to Brownsville and engaged in the hotel business. He conducted the Bar House for three years, and afterwards purchased the Storey House.

Mr. Storey was married in 1860 to Miss Julia Baker of Brownsville, a daughter of Charles Baker of St. Clairsville, Ohio. They have six children, four sons and two daughters: Albert, Margaret, Louis, Charles, Blanch and Matthew, Jr.

He is a member of the I. O. R. M., and has been a Mason for twenty-two years. In political affairs he is a democrat.

The Storey House when he purchased it was known as the Snowdon House. He placed an additional story on the building and remodeled it throughout. It is now one of the best hotels in the county.

Mr. Storey is a popular and accommodating landlord, and one of the prominent citizens of Brownsville.

FRANCIS MARION TERNEY is of French and German descent. His father, a Mr. McDonald—a resident of Virginia, and while traveling through the woods at night lost his path, and in his wanderings fell over a precipice and was killed. This occurred before the birth of F. M. Terney. His mother afterwards married James Terney, when he assumed his stepfather's name and has always been known as F. M. Terney.

He was born February 22, 1832, in Fayette county, Pa., and was raised partly in Pennsylvania, Virginia and Maryland. At the age of fourteen years he came to Masontown with his parents and there attended the common schools and secured a fair knowledge of reading, writing and arithmetic. He has traveled over the greater part of the United States and has learned the geography and history of the country in that way. At the age of fourteen years he left home and worked by the month until he was twenty-two years old. He worked at carpenter work, masonry, and was a moulder and burner of brick.

In 1856 he was married to Miss Desdemona Poundstone, a daughter of Jesse Poundstone, the latter a farmer of the county. Of this union were born eight children: James C., Mary Ellen, Waitman T., Willie, Sarah Elizabeth, George Loamia, David Yoe, Carrie Ann and Horace Greeley. Carrie died September 19, 1886; the others are all living. His wife died September 5, 1886.

From his marriage up to 1883 he has devoted the greater part of his time to farming. Since 1883 he has turned his attention more to the nursery business.

He supplies the country for a circuit of twenty-five miles around with the finest fruit grown in the county.

Mr. Terney is a strong democrat, has been judge of the election board, inspector of elections, tax collector and road commissioner. He is a member of the M. P. church at Fallen Timbers. His wife was a member of the same church during her life-time. The mother of Francis M., was born in this county about 1803 and is still living. She was the daughter of Daniel Anvil, who was one of the oldest settlers of Fayette county, where he took up a farm of about five hundred acres of land. He was a gunsmith by trade and an excellent mechanic, and made guns that were used in the War of 1812. He also made hackles, some are still to be found in the county.

BENJAMIN FRANKLIN TITUS was born on Dunkard Creek, Dunkard township, Greene county, Pa., February 19, 1846. He was brought up in his native township on a farm and attended the common schools until seventeen years of age, when he went to the Southwestern Normal College, at California, Washington county, Pa., and took a two years' course. Leaving college, he engaged in the merchentile business at Point Marion for nine months, went to Rosedale, Greene county, and there he engaged in the same business, which he continued for about eighteen months. He then engaged in farming in Greene county for a short time, when he went to San Antonia, Texas, as deputy surveyor of Bexar district, and served as such for two years. He then took a position with the International and Great Northern R. R., as Supervisor of the Loredo Section of that road, where he remained for four years. He returned to Pennsylvania, located near Point Marion engaged in farming on the old homestead of his wife's family, where he is still engaged, and now owns fifty acres of valuable river bottom land. Point Marion now stands upon a part of the old homestead.

On March 17, 1868, he was married to Miss Jennie M. Saddler, a native of Springhill township, and is the daughter of Moses Saddler, also a native of the same township. They have had six children: Moses Franklin, Charles Louis, Montie Lee, Binnie, Garrett and Birdie Cotula; all of whom are living at home with their parents.

In 1870 Mr. Titus was elected on the democratic ticket, by a large majority, to the office of auditor of Greene county, and held it for four years. At present he is tax collector for Spring hill township. He is a prominent member of the Masons, belongs to LaSalle Lodge, No. 572, Texas, and is a prominent member of the Disciple Church, at Point Marion.

B. F. Titus is a son of Levi and Anna (Stewart) Titus. His father was a native of Greene county, Pa., his mother of Monongalia county, W. Va. His father was born in 1821, and died in 1887. His mother was born in 1823 and is still living, at the age of sixty-seven years.

Benjamin Titus—the grandfather of the subject of this sketch—was one of the oldest and earliest settlers of Greene county. He fought in the war for independence, and endured the hardships of Valley Forge. He enlisted at the age of seventeen and served throughout the war.

EWING TODD, of Brownsville, is of Irish descent, and was born December 30, 1831, in Redstone township, Fayette county, Pa., and is the son of Huston and Catherine (Gadd) Todd.

The ancestry of Mr. Todd's family can be traced back to his paternal grandfather, Thomas Todd, who was a native of County Down, Ireland. He came to the United States in 1785, and settled for a short time at Wilmington, Del., where he was married. Leaving Wilmington in 1790 he came to Franklin Township, where he passed the remainder of his days. His death, at ninety years of age, occurred in 1855. He was a noted "sale crier" (then called "vendue crier"), for which he was specially qualified, and in which he was wonderfully successful.

Huston Todd (father) was born in Franklin township in 1807, and died in Menallen township in December, 1849. His life was principally spent in Redstone township as a farmer. He was a Jackson democrat, and was married to Miss Catherine Gadd, of Redstone township, born in 1808, and died in October, 1888.

Ewing Todd was raised on a farm and attended the common school until he was eighteen years of age, when he came to Brownsville to learn the trade of a plasterer.

For nearly forty years, Mr. Todd has worked successfully at his trade, and his services have always been in good demand.

He was married in 1860, to Miss Margaret, daughter of Martin Claybaugh, a blacksmith of Brownsville township.

Their union has been blessed with nine children, six sons and three daughters: William H., Lucy, Harry M., Cora, Samuel C., Thomas, Bessie, Alford and Ewing, Jr.

He is a good workman, a reliable citizen, and is an active member of the I. O. O. F., and is a democrat.

JAMES I. THORNTON. The coal industry of Pennsylvania ranks next in importance to that of agriculture. Among the young, energetic and successful coal operators is James I. Thornton, of the Knob Coal Company. He was born in Ironton, Ohio, January 14, 1857, and is a son of James and Ann (Lewis) Thornton, both natives of Wales.

James Thornton emigrated to the United States in 1854 and located at Pittsburgh, but subsequently removed to Ironton, Ohio, and in a few years returned to Pittsburgh, where he died in 1863. He was a marble-cutter and machinist and a consistent member of the Baptist church.

Three of his daughters are married and live in Pittsburgh. His wife died in 1868 at the age of forty-seven years.

James I. Thornton removed with his parents from Ohio to Pittsburgh. At Pittsburgh he attended the public schools for some years; leaving school he engaged in digging coal along the Monongahela river, and continued in this work up to 1878.

In 1878 he became a member of the Knob Coal Company.[See sketch of D. H. Pearsall.]

This company has been very successful in mining and shipping coal, and do an extensive business.

Mr. Thornton was married in July, 1879, to Miss Jennie, daughter of Benjamin Scease, the latter a farmer of Redstone township. They have four living children: Charlie A., James A., Annie M. and De Wayne Thornton.

Mr. Thornton is now a resident of Bridgeport. He is a member of I. O. of O. F. and Royal Arcanum.

He is one of Bridgeport's most public-spirited young business men. He is self-made, and his rise from a coal digger to a successful coal operator is an illustration of what intelligence, combined with energy and determination, can achieve for a man.

SAMUEL THOMPSON is an extensive land holder, a large coal operator along the Monongahela river, in the Pittsburgh bed of the great Appalachian coal field. He is a son of John and Ruth (Lewis) Thompson, and was born in East Bethlehem township, Washington county, Pa., March 23, 1820.

John Thompson, was born in New Jersey in 1776. He removed in early life to Washington county and located on a farm in East Bethlehem township. He was a farmer and trader and owned four hundred acres of land. He was a member of the M. E. church and died March 31, 1860, in his eighty fourth year. His wife was a native of Pennsylvania, and died September 17, 1876, in her ninenty-third year.

Samuel Thompson was reared on a farm and received a limited education in the old subscription schools. He engaged in farming and purchased a farm in 1850, and in the same year he engaged in the distilling business. He began with a small distillery of eight bushels capacity, enlarged it into an extensive building, and continued for twenty years in the farming and distilling business.

In 1857 Mr. Thompson removed to his present residence in Bridgeport, and in 1879 engaged in the coal business. He now owns the Champion, Caledonian and Wood's Run Coal Works, that have a combined output of ten thousand bushels of coal per day. These three works are situated close together in Washington county, and produce a desirable article of coal, which is in great demand in the Western and Southern markets.

He owns seventeen farms, aggregating three thousand acres of good farming land. Seven of these farms are in Washington county, five in Fayette, two in Iowa and three in Kansas, and are all underlaid with coal.

Mr. Thompson was united in marriage in 1843 to Miss Martha Cooper, who died in 1848. July 12, 1859, he married Miss Esther Wilson, of Washington county, who died May 30, 1864, leaving three children: Robert W., now in Kansas; George D., managing a farm of four hundred acres in Washington county, and Thomas H., in charge of a Washington county farm of five hundred acres. February 25, 1872, Mr. Thompson married for his third wife Miss Elizabeth Crawford, of Fayette county. She died June 20, 1877. In 1882 Mr. Thompson married his fourth wife, Mrs. Bridget Dawson, widow of Elias Dawson.

Samuel Thompson has been a director of the First National Bank of Brownsville for fifteen years, and also a director of the National Deposit Bank of Brownsville since its organization. He owns stock in the Citizens' Bank of Washington, Pa., and is a stockholder of the Bridgeport Natural Gas Company, and he and his nephew have a bank in Eureka, Kansas.

Being one of nine children, he received but a small sum from his father's estate. By energy, care, good management and close attention to business, he has won a competency. He is a prominent business man of Fayette county, and his large business enterprises are conducted energetically and systematically.

LEVI C. WAGGONER was born December 28, 1851, at Brownsville, Fayette county, Pennsylvania, where he was brought up, and attended the common schools. Leaving school he learned the marble trade with M. & T. S. Wright, a firm then engaged in the business at Brownsville. He continued at this business for twelve years. In 1880 he commenced the business of groceries, provisions and feed, and has since successfully carried it on. He has built up a good trade, and is located in "The Neck" or Main street.

He is a member of I. O. O. F. and of the Royal Arcanum, and is part owner and manager of the Brownsville Lyceum, and president of the Brownsville Natural Gas Co.

He was married in 1875 to Miss Ella Aubrey, the daughter of Thomas Aubrey, the proprietor of Aubrey Planing Mills at West Brownsville. They have three children: Thomas A., Leroy C., and Carrie.

He is the son of George and Mary M. (Craft) Waggoner, both natives of Redstone township, Fayette county, Pennsylvania, and are now living at Brownsville, where they removed in 1851.

George Waggoner, the father of Levi C., served for three years in the army during the Civil War. He belonged to Company D, Eighth Pennsylvania Reserves; was mustered out of the service at Harrisburg, Pennsylvania, just after the battle of the Wilderness, and held the position of wagon-master for a part of the time.

Oliver A. Waggoner, a brother of Levi C., was in the same company and regiment with his father in the war. He was only sixteen years of age when he entered the service, remained till the close of the war, and was mustered out of the service at the same time with his father.

Joshua Waggoner, the grandfather of Levi C., was a native of Westmoreland county, Pennsylvania, came to Fayette when quite a young man, and settled upon a farm in Redstone township. He was an elder in the Cumberland Presbyterian church for many years, and died in 1877, at the age of eighty-four years.

George B. Craft, grandfather of Levi C. Waggoner, was a native of Fayette county, Pennsylvania; was a farmer, and was a writer of poetry published in the Brownsville papers. He died in 1877, at the age of ninety-two years.

MORGAN WEST, one of the successful carriage builders of Fayette county, is a native of Redstone township, Fayette county, Pa. He was born June 8, 1842, and is a son of James and Louisiana (Ball) West, the former was born in Redstone township, Fayette county, Pa., June 5, 1805, and died July 6, 1888.

Morgan West's grandfather, Samuel West, lived and died on the farm now owned by Thomas Simpson in same township.

Morgan West was married to Martha H. Hubbs, a daughter of Dr. W. G. Hubbs, of Bridgeport. To their marriage have been born two children: William J., born July 19, 1878, in Bridgeport, Pa., and Allen G., born in Redstone township, Fayette county, Pa., December 9, 1882.

Morgan West, on leaving the common school, attended the Dunlap's Creek Academy, at Merrittstown. Early in life, he learned the trade of carriage builder and is at the present time successfully engaged at his trade at Sandy Hollow, on the National Pike, ½ mile east of Brownsville. He is a democrat. Where he now resides he owns thirteen acres of land, containing valuable deposits of coal and sandstone. He holds at present the collectorship of Brownsville township, the office to which he was elected in the spring of 1889.

THEOPHILUS WILLIAMS, son of Theophilus P. and Rebecca (Thompson) Williams, was born at Smithfield, Fayette county, Pa., April 24, 1836.

His father, Theophilus P. Williams, was born at New Geneva, July 29, 1802, and was the son of Thomas Williams, a tailor by trade. His mother was a daughter of Theophilus Philips. Theophilus P. Williams learned the tailor trade and improved a limited education by studying during all his spare moments from work. He was a good mathematician and a fine penman. He wrote nearly all the legal documents written in his neighborhood, and attended to a large amount of legal business before the justice of the peace. He worked at the tailor trade until 1856, when he went on a farm. He died Februay 12, 1889, aged eighty-seven years.

His paternal grandfather, Thomas Williams, came from Wales to New Orleans and walked from that city to New Geneva, subsisting for several days during his journey on parched corn. He was also a tailor by trade.

His mother, Rebecca Thompson, was born September 3, 1804, and died October 13, 1886. She was the mother of eleven children, six sons and five daughters, of whom four sons and two daughters are living. She was a daughter of James Thompson, who left Maryland, his native State, when Washington city was captured by the British. He came to Fayette county and was killed while mining iron ore by the roof of the mine falling in and crushing him.

Theophilus Williams, the subject of this sketch, removed from Smithfield to Greensboro, Greene county, Pa., when quite young. He attended the common schools until nineteen years of age, then engaged in farming for twenty-four years, and while farming he learned the carpenter trade. In 1882 he and his brother engaged in the mercantile business at New Geneva. They do business under the firm name of J. G. & T. Williams, and are successful merchants, having a large custom. They own a farm of forty-nine acres in the county, and on this farm General Washington stopped over night with Theophilus Phillips, their mother's paternal grandfather.

Theophilus Williams was married July 22, 1884, to Emma Baker, daughter of James and Mary (Eckert) Baker, both natives of West Virginia. They had one child, Rebecca May, born February 20, 1887. His wife, Emma (Baker) Williams, died December 13, 1887, and was a member of the Methodist Episcopal church at Drummond's Chapel.

Mr. Williams is a democrat, and never voted anything but the democratic ticket.

He is a member of the Old Frame Presbyterian church, and is a good business man. He was again married in 1876, to Miss Rachel, daughter of Isaac Blaney. They have four children: Addie, Ashbel F., Blackburn and an infant. Blackburn died when two years old.

Thomas Williams is a member of the G. A. R. post at Smithfield, and he and his wife are members of the Presbyterian church at Springhill.

THOMAS WILLIAMS was born in Springhill township, Fayette county, Pa., of Welsh and Irish parentage, and is the son of John and Margaret (Shay) Williams.

John Williams was born at South Wales and came to the United States when eighteen years old, and landed at Philadelphia. For a number of years he was employed in iron works, near the line of Va. and Pa. He did the work of two men at Springhill furnace, Pa., for five years, and at Wood Grove furnace, Va., for seven years. He was an economical man, and notwithstanding a loss of $1,200 of hard earned money, he was able in 1835 to buy a farm of 105 acres, near Springfield furnace. He was married and moved upon his farm the same year, where he lived the remainder of his life. He was a member of the Presbyterian Church, at Springfield furnace, for many years, and was a devout, earnest Christian. In politics he was a staunch Democrat. He died February, 1868.

Margaret (Shay) Williams was born in eastern Pennsylvania, and came to Fayette county when eleven years old, and was the mother of five children—all living but one. She is a member of the Presbyterian Church.

Thomas Williams was born February 13, 1829, remained on the farm until at the age of twenty-one years, and attended the subscription schools of the county. Leaving school, he continued on the farm till 1851, when he went to Kentucky, and remained there till 1858. While in Kentucky he was employed as an engineer and kept a hotel. In 1858 he returned to Fayette county, and soon after took charge of his father's farm and managed it for some years. In 1862, he volunteered in Company E, Fourteenth Pennsylvania Cavalry, under Col. Schoonmaker, was in the engagements at White Sulphur, Winchester and Cedar Creek, and was with Sheridan in the Shenandoah Valley. In the last campaign he received injuries from which he has never recovered. He was mustered out of the service at Alexandria, Va., in May, 1865, and returned home, after nearly three years of faithful service.

After his father's death he purchased the interest of the other heirs and obtained full possession of the old homestead. He greatly improved the farm and built a large barn. For nine years he was the superintendent of the farms of the Fairchance Iron Co., and at the same time he managed his own farm.

He was married to Miss Harriet Huston, in 1850. Of this union nine children were born: John C., James H., Margaret A., Elizabeth J., Thomas F., Samuel H., Edgar L., Herman R., Effie May and Lydia. Mr. Williams' wife died October, 1875. She was a member of the Presbyterian church and a devoted Christian.

JOSEPH GORDON WILLIAMS, of Springhill township, is of Scotch-Irish and Welsh descent, and was born in Greensboro, Greene county, Pa., September 24, 1842. [See sketch of Theophilus Williams for family history.]

He was educated in the common schools until fourteen years of age, when he entered Monongalia Academy, Morgantown, W.Va., attended eight terms at that institution; leaving there, he engaged in teaching, and taught his first term of school at Morris' X Roads. He continued to teach for four years. In 1865 he began handling cord wood, and continued in the same for eight years.

In 1873 he returned to teaching, and taught for four years in Monongalia county, W. Va.

For the next two years he conducted a farm belonging to J. G., T. and B. K. Williams.

In 1882 he came to New Geneva, Fayette county, Pa., and became a member of the mercantile firm of J. G. & T. Williams. On September 24, 1885, he was a appointed postmaster at New Geneva, and held the office until July 18, 1889. Under his administration two extra daily mail lines were established in his district. On May 21, 1874, he was married to Miss Mary V. Burtnett, daughter of Thomas Burtnett, of Uniontown. Of this union three children were born: Joseph G., James Hysen and Charles Carroll. Mrs. (Burtnett) Williams' maternal grandfather was William Hale, usually called "Old Master Hale," as he was an old-time school-teacher.

Joseph G. Williams is a man of intelligence, has been successful in various kinds of business, and is a descendant of one of the old, useful and time-honored families of southern Fayette county.

REV. WILLIAM ORRIS WILSON, was born May 2, 1837, near West Chester, Chester county, Pa. On the paternal side, he is of Scotch-Irish lineage, and on the maternal side, of English descent. His grandfather was born in Edinburgh, Scotland, and was a descendant of the celebrated Wilson family who took a leading and distinguished part in the struggle for liberty. Rev. William O. Wilson was educated at Academia, in Juniata county, Pa., in the Tuscarora valley. He entered the academic course in his seventeenth year, and continued for four years. His father, a well-to-do farmer, having met with some financial reverses, by generously, but unwisely, indorsing for a friend, rendered him unable to continue his son at the academy, but with commendable pluck and energy, at the same time with the determination not to be a charge upon his parents, during his vacations clerked in a store to obtain the means to continue his studies in the academy. After completing his course, he entered the private study of the Rev. Dr. Thompson, an eminent Presbyterian minister, to commence a theological course. The Rev. Thompson becoming too ill to instruct him, Mr. Wilson made arrangements with the Rev. Dr. D. H. Focht, to continue the course. He was thus engaged for two years, then entered the Theological Institute at Selin's Grove, in Snyder county, Pa., under the tuition of the Rev. D. H. Zeigler, who is still living, at an advanced age, in Chicago, Ill. He remained in this institute one year.

W. O. Wilson and Mary J. Wallis, of Lewistown, Pa., were married in January, 1860, by the Rev. Dr. Wood. In May, 1861, he was ordained by the Synod of Central Pennsylvania, and immediately entered upon his ministerial duties at Millerstown, in Perry county, Pa. At this place, under his immediate supervision, was erected an elegant church edifice, and three other congregations were organized in the vicinity. In September, 1864, Rev. W. O. Wilson, was called to Wheeling, W. Va., to engage in mission work, and continued till the fall of 1865. He was then called by the congregations at Oakland, Md., and at Scenery Hill, in Washington county, Pa., at the same time. He accepted the Washington county call. Here he remained eight years; built a parsonage at a cost of $3,200, also a magnificent church edifice at Zollersville, at a cost of $9,000. Here he established and obtained corporate privileges for the first rural cemetory in western Pennsylvania. During his stay in Washington county he made frequent visits to the Kanawha valley, in West Virginia, and established missions. He was next called to the Fayette county charge, embracing Jacob's and St. John's congregations, in German and Springhill townships. He remained in charge of these congregations for twelve years; rebuilt the church edifice in German township; established, with corporate franchises, cemeteries for both congregations, and added more than two hundred communicants.

While resident in the parsonage, near Jacob's church, the title, doctor of divinity, was conferred upon him by the board of trustees, of Ripon College, Wisconsin.

He was next called, by a unanimous vote of the general council of the Lutheran church, and was elected and commissioned to labor in Bismarck, Dak., for the Scandinavians. After a short stay among these people, much to his regret and also of the citizens of Bismarck, Rev. Wilson had to give up the charge. Having been afflicted for years with heart disease, the attitude of Bismarck, together with the rarified air of that region, increased the malady to such an extent, that there was but the alternative to leave or die. He returned to Fayette county, Pa., in May, 1886, much impaired in health, but soon recovered sufficiently to resume the charge of the St. John's congregation, near Morris Cross Roads, Pa., which position he is at present filling very acceptably. Eleven children have been born to Mr. and Mrs. Wilson, six of whom are living, viz.: Anna E., intermarried with John W. Bowers; Harry L., Charles K., Ella, Ettie and Lena. Mrs. Wilson is of Scotch descent. Rev. W. O. Wilson is a man of fine presence, easy and affable in manner, firm and abiding in his attachments and unswerving in his convictions of the right. While he rightfully abhors the mingling of church and State affairs, he is not afraid, on all proper occasions, to express his political opinions and preferences. Rev. Mr. Wilson is an easy, fluent and pleasant speaker, and never tires his congregation. He is well versed on the general topics of the day, eminently social in disposition, and enjoys the companionship of his friends and neighbors.

FRANKLIN, MENALLEN TYRONE AND WASHINGTON

JOSEPH D. ANTRAM, one of the most substantial farmers of Menallen, was born on the farm he now resides on, in the same house he is now living in, one-eighth of a mile east of New Salem, Menallen township, Fayette county, Pa., October 16, 1840, and is a son of Caleb and Nancy Antram (nee Boyd) (See A. D. Boyd's sketch), the former born 1805, on the same farm of his son, the latter was born near New Salem in 1808.

Caleb Antram was a prosperous farmer in his day, a quiet, unassuming citizen, is now an elder in the Cumberland Presbyterian church at New Salem. He is the father of five children, of whom three are living: Robert, Rebecca and Joseph D.

Caleb Antram (grandfather) was born in New Jersey, and was married in Virginia to Martha Morgan and came to Fayette county soon after marriage; secured the same farm Washington formerly owned, near the present site of Perryopolis, and which he afterwards gave to his daughter Mary, the wife of William Campbell.

On March 2, 1869, Joseph D. Antram was married to Mary F., a daughter of David Hibbs, of Redstone. She was born in 1843. David Hibbs married Hannah Walters, a daughter of Ephraim Walters, of Nicholson township. Mr. Antram has two children: William G., born September 9, 1870, and Jessie, born March 25, 1878.

He was educated in the common schools of New Salem; has always been a farmer, and is now holding the office of justice of the peace; he has also served at different times as school director. As to politics he is a strong democrat and never wavers in the faith. His beautiful and well-improved farm of 170 acres is richly underlaid with coal.

MATTHEW ARISON, one of Fayette county's self-made men and highly-respected citizens, was born in Loudon county, Va., March 4, 1816, and is a son of John and Catherine (Day) Arison.

His grandfather, Andrew Arison, was born in New Jersey, in 1750; he married, in 1782, Ann Davis of Loudon county, Va., and had six children: Lucinda, John, Matthew, Ann, Elizabeth and Ananias, none of whom are now living.

His father, John Arison, was born June 7, 1780, in Loudon county, Va., died in Franklin township, March 1, 1870, and was a cooper by trade, but always followed farming. He was a soldier in a cavalry company during the War of 1812, and was a well-respected citizen both in Virginia and

Pennsylvania. On September 12, 1812, he married Catherine Day; their union was blessed with twelve children: Samuel (dead), Matthew, Jonah, William (dead), John D. (dead), Benjamin S. (dead), Elizabeth J., Ann, Mariah, Levi H. (dead), Celina (dead) and Lydia C.

His mother, Catherine Day, was born April 22, 1796, died June 6, 1887, and was a member of the "Old Side Baptist." Her father, George Day, was born in 1756 at Alexandria, Va., and in 1780 was married to Mary Weaver, of Baltimore, Md. They had five children: Mary, Susan, Sarah, Catherine and George W., all of whom are dead.

Matthew Arison married Eliza Gettys, December 29, 1842. They had six children: Sarah Ellen (dead), John D., Samuel G. (dead), Ann Mariah (dead), William H. and Matthew Hickman. Samuel G. was thrown from a horse and instantly killed August 28, 1878. Mrs. Arison died May 4, 1864. Mr. Arison married again December 29, 1864. His second wife was Miss Margaret Ann, daughter of Henry Foster (deceased). They have six children: Charles T., Enoch A., Eliza Jane, James E., Roxalina M. and Minnie L.

Matthew Arison came with his father to Georges township in 1819, and from thence to Menallen township in 1823, where he received a limited school education.

Being a poor boy, he started in the world without friends or influence, but, industrious and ambitious, he taught school, summer and winter, for about twenty-two years. In 1848 he bought a farm of eighty-seven acres in Franklin township. He now owns 150 acres of good land in the same township.

In 1867-8 he with Henry Galley embarked in the oil business in Fayette county, but every well drilled for oil was a failure. In 1889 he assisted in leasing over six thousand acres of land in Franklin and Tyrone townships for the Virgin Run Gas Company.

He is a republican, and served as justice of the peace in Franklin township from 1855 to 1860 and from 1869 to the present time. From 1859 to 1862 he resided in Menallen township, and was justice of the peace in that township.

He became a member of the Baptist church in 1854 and ordained a deacon in the same church shortly afterwards.

He is one whose profession of Christianity has been nobly illustrated by an honorable and useful life. For thirty-five years he has been known throughout Fayette county as an earnest and zealous Baptist, an honest and consistent Christian gentleman, respected and honored by all who know him.

JOHN ARMEL. Some years before the Revolutionary War, a Mr. Armel came from Hamburg, Germany, and settled in Pennsylvania, Franklin county, somewhere east of the mountains. He was a miller, and is supposed to have operated a mill at the place of his first location. Later he removed to what is now Westmoreland county. A colony of four families came over the mountains together, two Armel families, a family named Smith and one of the name of Stockbarger. They were all Lutherans, and settled near the present location of Pleasant Unity, and took tomahawk claims on large tracts of land.

John and Daniel were soldiers in the Revolution, and were also in the Indian wars that followed. Jacob Armel was born May 11, 1784, and was married to Susan Bonbright, daughter of Daniel Bonbright, who was a native of Franklin county. Jacob Armel's family consisted of ten children: John (subject), the second son, was born in Westmoreland county, October 8, 1816. He worked at carpentry during his younger days. He had a poor education. In 1848 he built a mill at New Haven for Joseph

Strickler and Daniel Kain, and in 1850 bought the mill in Perry township, known as the Washington Run steam mill, and operated it till 1857, when he bought one-half interest in the mill on Little Redstone creek, where he now resides. He built this mill in 1872, and purchased the other half of it in 1889.

He was married in 1852 to Margaret Essington of Fayette county. They have two children: John and Mary C. Mary C. married Humphrey F. Blythe, and John is living at home.

Mr. Armel is a member of I. O. of O. F. He has held several township offices at different times.

THORNTON F. BALDWIN, a stirring business man of Washington township, was born at Fayette City, Fayette county, Pa., September 27, 1840, and is a son of Robert Baldwin.

Thornton F. Baldwin was educated in the early common schools of Fayette county, and took care of a school building in order to secure some additional and higher school learning. At an early age he began to do for himself, was a cabin boy on the river for about five years, when he learned the trade of butcher. He was engaged in boring for oil in West Virginia for several years prior to the breaking out of the late war. He came back to Fayette City in 1862 and engaged in butchering and the livery business. After sixteen years' experience in this work, he removed to Pittsburgh and opened a hotel. Owing to the loss of several members of his family he abandoned hotel-keeping, returned a second time to Fayette City and resumed his former employment of butchering. He continued it for two years, when he secured his present position on the river, of steward on the "Hunter No. 2."

In 1863 he was married to Miss Sarah McClinch, a native of Sheltersville, N. J. They have one son, John W. Baldwin, born in 1880. Mrs. Baldwin is of Irish descent.

Thornton F. Baldwin is a K. of P., U. O. of A. W., Red Men and a member of the N. B. A. He is industrious, energetic, and never idle.

JOHN BALDWIN was born at Fayette City, Fayette county, Pa., April 3, 1832, reared there and was educated in the common schools of the township. He learned the business of tinsmith and coppersmith, which he followed for some years. In 1850 he went to St. Louis, Mo., and soon thereafter began steamboating as an engineer, and continued till the close of the war. After the close of the war he commenced to travel through the Southern States, setting up machinery. He lost an arm while he was engaged in putting up a cotton gin in Tennessee. He returned to his native town, engaged in the hotel business and in contract work.

He was married in 1867 to Susan Stickle, the daughter of Henry and Anna (Stark) Stickle. Both of her parents were of old families in the county, and her father was a soldier in the war of 1812.

Mr. Baldwin and wife have three living children: Thornton H., born August 1, 1868; Tillie, born November 17, 1869, and Georgie, born December 25, 1874. John Baldwin has held the office of burgess of Fayette City, was a member of the school board, and is at present a member of the borough council.

Robert Baldwin (father) was born December 25, 1805; was married January 24, 1824, to Matilda McFee, who was born November 14, 1807; and her father, William McFee, was one of the early settlers of Cookstown. Their family consisted of the following members: William D., born March 26, 1828, died May 12, 1832; John, born April 3, 1832;

Elmira, born March 8, 1834, died April 27, 1839; Eli A., born February 14, 1836, died at about thirty-five years of age, was pilot on the Upper Mississippi river; Thornton F., born September 27, 1840; Clara M., born May 2, 1841, died at nineteen years old; Ford McFee, born February, 1844, died at four years old; Mary F. and Charles C. (twins) born February 20, 1847. Robert Baldwin died in 1870; his wife died in 1876.

William, the paternal grandfather of John Baldwin, was one of the early settlers of the county, and was justice of the peace for many years in the Quakers' settlement, near what is now known as Red Lion. The Baldwins were members principally of the Methodist Episcopal church.

William McFee, the maternal grandfather of Mr. Baldwin, was the first tailor of Cookstown.

JOSEPH BATES, of Lower Tyrone, is a son of William and Eliza (Moore) Bates, and was born at Merrittstown, Luzerne township, Fayette county, Pa., August 12, 1844.

William Bates was born in Baltimore, in 1798, and in 1814 came with his widowed mother to Vance's Mill in North Union township. He was a day laborer during his life. In January, 1864, near Upper Middletown, in falling a tree was struck by it and killed. His wife was a native of Fayette county and died in 1882, aged seventy-seven years.

Joseph Bates was bound at the age of seven years to Joseph Newcomer, of Georges township, and remained with him for fourteen years. He engaged as a day-laborer until 1871, when he began farming on the shares for Ellis Phillips, of North Union township. His farming capital was $50 and one cow. In 1877 he left the farm with $1,700, two blooded cows and one horse. July 3, 1880, he purchased sixty acres of his present farm in Lower Tyrone, situated two miles north of Dawson. He now has seventy acres of productive land.

On April 28, 1864, he was married to Rose Ann, daughter of Elijah Moore. Unto their union have been born eight children: William H., Thomas S., Isaac E., Joseph S., Albert S., Charles S., Mary Ann and Emma May Bates.

Joseph Bates being bound received no schooling, but after his marriage, by night study, acquired a limited but practical education. He is a republican, has served as assessor and school director.

Mr. Bates is a member of the Methodist Episcopal church, and his success in life is a remarkable illustration of what energy, honesty and perseverance will accomplish.

BENJAMIN F. BEAL, one of the substantial farmers of the prosperous township of Menallen, is a son of Joseph and Margaret (Hutton) Beal, and was born on the old Beal homestead, Menallen township, Fayette county, Pennsylvania, January 11, 1837.

His grandfather, Benjamin Beal, was an industrious and well-to-do farmer. By occupation he was a stonecutter. By industry and patient labor he acquired two very good farms.

His great-grandfathers were William Beal and John Hutton. His father, Joseph Beal, was born in Menallen township, and was engaged during his lifetime in farming. His wife was Margaret Hutton. To their union were born eight children, of whom four are living.

Benjamin F. Beal was educated in the common schools of Menallen township, and, on leaving school, engaged in his present business of farming. December 14, 1865, he was married to Elizabeth Hibbs, a daughter of John Hibbs. To their marriage have been born two children: Violet J. and Elizabeth E.

Benjamin F. Beal is a democrat, has served his native township as school director for six years, and has held various other local offices in Menallen township. He owns a valuable farm, well adapted to grain raising and grazing, and is underlaid with a good vein of coal. He is a good farmer, and is well and favorably known throughout the township

DAVID V. BIXLER, the accommodating and efficient freight and passenger agent at Everson, Upper Tyrone, was born at Black Oak Town, within one mile of McClellandtown, Fayette county, Pa., March 9, 1840, and is a son of Jesse and Sarah (Dean) Bixler.

The Bixlers originally came from Switzerland. Jesse Bixler was a distiller of Lancaster county, and in 1830 he removed to Cincinnati, thence to Black Oak Town, where he was engaged for ten years by Perry Grove, from 1840 to 1850. The last year of his services he was engaged in the distilling business at West Overton.

Subsequently he removed to Broad Ford, where he was engaged in the same business until his death, in September, 1880.

His wife was born near McClellandtown in 1816, and died August 1, 1889.

In 1851 David V. Bixler removed with his parents to Broad Ford, where he received his education in the common schools. He learned the trade of cooper, was engaged at that for twelve years, when he entered the employ of the B. & O. R. R. Company. His first appointment in 1872 under that company was station agent at Broad Ford. Eighteen months later he was transferred to Mt. Pleasant in the same capacity, after six months' satisfactory service was sent to his present position at Everson.

In 1867 he was united in marriage to Miss Eliza, daughter of John Shallenberger, the latter a farmer of Connellsville township. Their union has been blessed with eight children: Hiester C., telegraph operator, Union depot, Pittsburgh; George S., car inspector for the B. & O. R. R. Company at Port Perry; John F., Charles S., Lula, Minnie, William and Roy.

JOHN P. BLYTHE, who prospected for gold on the Pacific Slope ere an iron pathway crossed the Rocky Mountains, is now a successful farmer of Washington township, Fayette county, Pa., where he was born January 18, 1817, and is a son of John and Ellen (Fullerton) Blythe.

John Blythe emigrated from Ireland to Washington county, in 1790, at the age of twenty-three years. From Washington county he removed to Washington township, Fayette county, and purchased a farm. He married Ellen, daughter of David Fullerton, a Scotchman and an early settler in Eastern Pennsylvania. John Blythe reared a family of eleven children.

John P. Blythe received his education in the old subscription schools. He was engaged in farming until 1851. In the same year, he went by water to California, where he spent four years in digging and prospecting for gold dust. He passed through the "Starving Time," when flour sold for $500 per barrel. He passed through many perils and after enduring much suffering he left the gold fields in 1855. He returned home via South America, where he remained several weeks and visited several of the principal South American cities.

On December 17, 1857, he married Miss Margaret, daughter of John and Mary (Shearer) Bortner, of Redstone township. The Bortners were of German descent and were early settlers in Maryland. Mr. and

Mrs. John P. Blythe have seven children: Anna V., born December 20, 1858, married Harmer Denny June 30, 1885, and has one child; Humphrey F., born August 23, 1860, married Mary C. Armel July 13, 1886, and has one child; John F., born September 6, 1862; George B. McClellan, born August 19, 1864, married Maggie Wells February 7, 1889; Mary E., born September 19, 1866, married Charles M. Ford and has two children; James B., born August 4, 1868, and Ellen, born June 23, 1871.

After his marriage Mr. Blythe removed in 1863 to Lynn county, Iowa, and from thence to Missouri, where he remained seven years. In 1874 he removed form Missouri to his present farm and began farming, at which he is still engaged.

His farm consists of one hundred and twenty acres of choice and well improved land. He and his family are members of the Presbyterian church. Politically he is a democrat and is one of the leading farmers of Washington township.

HENRY G. BOWMAN of German descent, was born February 18, 1838, on the farm where he now resides in Franklin township, Fayette county, Pa., and was educated in the common schools of the township. In politics he is a republican, and the religion of the family is Baptist and Disciple. He has always been a farmer, and owns 300 acres of land, inherited from his father.

Andrew Bowman, the father, was born at Hagerstown, Maryland, May 16, 1797, and came to the farm now owned by Henry G. with his parents when he was but two years old. He was educated in the subscription schools. In politics he was first a democrat, later a whig and was afterwards a republican. He was a Baptist in religion, but joined the Disciple church in 1844. On May 19, 1825, he was married to Ruth, daughter of Thomas Cook, of Redstone township. They had five children: John, born July 9, 1826, died July 2, 1877; Ann Eliza, born April 11, 1828, now living with her brother Henry; Thomas C., born May 25, 1830, died November 9, 1851; Henry G. and Andrew, who died February 17, 1874.

John Bowman, grandfather, was born in Franklin county, Pa., in 1772, and was a wagonmaker by trade. He married Miss Catherine, daughter of Andrew Snively, in 1796. After his marriage he removed to Hagerstown, Md., and in 1800 removed to Fayette county, Pa., where he died in 1858. He gave to each of his four daughters a quarter section of land.

Henry Bowman, great-grandfather, ran away from his home in Germany at the age of eleven years, came to the United States, and, as was the custom in those days, he was sold upon his arrival here to pay for his passage across the ocean.

Andrew Snively, great-grandfather, took out a patent in 1778 for 307 acres of land, in what is now Franklin township, which adjoined the lands of George Washington and Jacob Snively. He deeded this land to his two daughters, Catherine Bowman and Susan Newman. John Bowman bought Susan Newman's half of the land and deeded the whole tract to his son, Andrew Bowman.

Thomas Cook, maternal grandfather, was born in Nottingham township, Chester county, Pa., July 28, 1756, died February 14, 1842, and was married three times. First, to Susannah Cousins of Washington county, Pa., born September 18, 1783; second time, to Elizabeth Cope, daughter of John and Mary Cope, in 1786. The Cope family, in this country, originated from Oliver Cope and Mary, his wife, who came over to this country with Willian Penn in 1682. Four children where born to them: William, Elizabeth,

Ruth and John. John was the father of Henry G. Bowman's grandmother, Elizabeth Cook.

Henry G. Bowman and his sister Ann, live on his farm. They are both single, but their home is always full of children of their friends and relatives. They are known throughout the whole surrounding country for their acts of philanthropy and charity. They reared four orphans: In 1854 they took Sarah J. Sinclair (a relative orphan), in 1858 Nancy Wadsworth, in 1866 William Rhodaback, in 1870 Sanford Rhodaback, and John Hodge was with them for three years, when he went West with his mother, remained there four years, then returned to the Bowman home and continued to live with them till his death. Only one of all these was related to the Bowmans.

WILLIAM H. BRADMAN was born in Jefferson township, Fayette county, Pa., February 22, 1850, and was educated in the common schools of Franklin township. In politics he is a democrat; in religion he is a Protestant Methodist, and has been a member of the church since 1879. He is a carpenter by trade, and works it in connection with farming.

May 20, 1880, he was married to Martha A. Chalfant, a daughter of James W. Chalfant, who resides near Brownsville. They have the following children: Bessie L. and Margaret O. who are living, and an infant and Ethel V. who are dead.

William Bradman (father) was born in Maryland, October 22, 1811, and is of English descent. His father emigrated from Maryland, and settled near Searight in 1812. His father died when he was about eight years of age, when he was bound to Abraham Vale, a Quaker of Searight, with whom he remained until he was sixteen years old, after which he worked at farming for different persons till he went to learn his trade. He was one of a family of twelve children, whom their widowed mother was unable to provide for, and they were scattered. He learned the trade of carpenter with Robert Graham, of Indiana county, Pa., in 1829-32. He worked at his trade for about forty years in Fayette county.

He is a democrat, and voted for General Jackson in 1832, and for Grover Cleveland in 1888. He has held the offices of constable, school director and auditor of Franklin township. In 1855 he was elected treasurer of Fayette county, and served one term of two years. He has been a member of the Methodist Protestant church since 1840, and has been a steward and trustee of the same for many years.

In 1850 he bought eighty-four acres of land from the heirs of Francis Lewis, of Franklin township, and has resided upon the farm ever since. In 1856 his house and all of the contents were destroyed by fire, and not a change of clothing even was left to him or his family. He rebuilt, and now the buildings of the farm are all in first-class order.

He has been twice married—in 1833, to Jane Dearman, daughter of Alexander and Jane Dearman, of Jefferson township. They had two children: Mary Jane, who died at the age of twelve, and John A., who resides in Lansing, Michigan. His wife died in 1837.

In 1840 he was again married, to Hannah, daughter of Jacob Wolf, of Franklin township. Their children were: Ann, Jacob, Austman, George, William, Kate and Agnes. Agnes is dead. Jacob and Austman died in infancy. The three living sons are carpenters. His second wife died in 1887, aged seventy-five years, seven months and twenty-eight days.

His father, John Bradman, was born east of the mountains, married Mary Winset, of

Maryland, and was a farmer by occupation. His children were: Ellen, Priscilla, Ketura. Tabitha, William, James P., John, Nancy, Rachel and Agnes. Two other children died in infancy. It can be truthfully said that the Bradman family are, and have always been, honest and industrious citizens, and conscientious Christians.

ALEXANDER BROWN was born at Davidson's upper ferry (now East Riverside), Fayette county, Pa., July 21, 1828. He was reared in the village of Merrittstown, and attended school there. He began business with his father as a clerk in a store. He clerked for various firms until he came to Belle Vernon, and engaged as book-keeper for L. M. Speer, boat builder. He remained at Belle Vernon, employed by several different firms, until 1878, when he went to Pittsburgh as book-keeper for Captain J. W. Clark, and there he continued for five or six years. He was next employed with the Speer & White Land Company, and remained with them for two years. Since then he has been engaged with the First National Bank of Pittsburgh, in looking after their coal interests in West Moreland county.

He was married November 8, 1848, to Miss Catherine R. Dunaway, daughter of John and Margaret (Robinson) Dunaway, natives of Fayette county, and of Irish descent. They are the parents of five children, three in the drug business and one a practicing physician. The daughter is the wife of O. R. Springer.

William Brown, the great-grandfather of Alexander Brown, came to this county about 100 years ago, settled on Redstone creek, and was one of the earliest settlers here. He came from Virginia to the county and had been a teacher in a college in New Jersey. He was a soldier in the Revolutionary War, and fought at the battle of Brandywine Creek. He built the first distillery in this county. He owned large landed estates in Virginia, and sold a farm near Winchester, which was paid for in Continental money. The wife of this member of the Brown family was of the Piersol stock. Alexander Brown, son of William, was born in Fayette county, and was the father of George Brown, the latter the father of Alexander Brown.

George Brown married Miss Elizabeth Davidson, the daughter of Jeremiah and Anna (Alexander) Davidson, who were of Scotch origin, and of families who settled very early in Fayette county.

The Davidsons were Presbyterians, and are a prominent family in this section of the State.

AARON BUGHER (deceased) was born in Fayette county, Pa., in March, 1798; was reared on a farm, until at about the age of twelve years, when his parents removed to Freeport — now Fayette City. He learned the trade, and began boat-building, and owned an interest in the Jewess and other steamboats. He built the first steamboat built at Cooktown in 1836, and it was known as the Exchange. From 1836 on for many years he was interested in boat-building. His sons for many years owned a line of steamers that ran between Cincinnati and Memphis. Among the number were the Silver Moon, Glendale, Lady Jackson, Lady Franklin and Lady Pike.

Aaron Bugher was married November 10, 1816, to Lovina McLain, of German descent. They raised seven children: Sarah A., Margaret, James, John, William H. (born September 9, 1838), and Ellen. His wife died October 21, 1833. He was again remarried, to Rachel Farquhar, a daughter of Robert and Esther (Dalson) Farquhar; the former a native of Scotland, and the latter a native of Maryland. The Farquhars were Quakers. To this marriage were born four children: Alling, born February 2, 1839, married M. J. Speer; Steven D., born December 16, 1840; Aaron H., born May 18, 1841; Larretta, born May 23, 1843, and Anna, born June 23, 1846.

Ellen was married to Philip Coons March 18, 1843; Sarah A. married Thomas Todd, Margaret married Griffith Wells; James married Margaret Housemay; A. H. married Mary McClain; Stephen married Sarah Ransom, of North Carolina; Laura married Dr. S. Conklin, of Washington county; Anna married Martin L. Streater, of Washington county, and is now a prominent minister of the Christian church at Helena, Montana.

Mr. Bugher was elected to the Legislature of Pennsylvania in 1841. He was a prominent member of the Christian church. He died in Cincinnati, Ohio, in 1847.

Mrs. Bugher still lives at Fayette City, and is in the eighty-first year of her age.

WILLIAM BUSH is the son of Henry and Elizabeth (Ames) Bush. Henry Bush was born in 1827, in Washington county, Pa., and was a farmer of West Bethlehem township. He served through the War of the Rebellion in the Eighty-fifth Regiment Pennsylvania Infantry, and was wounded at Roanoke, Va., by the bursting of a shell, causing such a fracture of his leg that it had to be amputated. He was killed in June, 1875, while he was cleaning a well at Hillsboro, by a bucket falling on him. His widow is still living and resides at Hillsboro.

William Bush was born June 26, 1850, at Hillsboro, Washington county, Pa.; was reared and educated at that place. At the age of eighteen years he went to Marshall county, Ill., where he remained for two years. Returned to Fayette county and worked at mining till 1880, when he went to Colorado and worked in the silver mines for about eighteen months, when he returned to Fayette county and established himself in the furniture and undertaker business at Dawson. He occupies a large building on Railroad street, near the depot, where he keeps a large stock of furniture, and has built up a good and paying trade.

He was elected burgess of Dawson in 1885, and held the office for two years; was re-elected in 1889, and is the present incumbent. In 1888 he was elected a member of the school board. He is a member of the F. & A. M., the I. O. O. F. and Royal Arcanum.

Mr. Bush was married in 1878, to Miss Katie E. Cox, daughter of Harrison Cox, a farmer of Upper Tyrone township. They have three children: Della, Harry and Bessie, and all are living.

JOSEPH BUTE, of Scotch descent, was born at Upper Middleton, Menallen township, Fayette county, Pa., July 27, 1812, and is a son of John and Mary (Morrison) Bute.

Joseph Bute (great grandfather) was born in Scotland; was a soldier under General Braddock, and was one of the survivors of Braddock's defeat. When his term of enlistment was out, he settled in Virginia and was married there. The result of the marriage was one child: a son.

Joseph Bute (paternal grandfather) was born in Virginia and married a Miss Dick, of Virginia, and when he died left two sons and two daughters.

John Bute (father) was born in Virginia in 1785. When a small boy he removed with his mother and stepfather to near Wheeling, but at sixteen years of age left home on account of his stepfather's idleness. After working three years he removed to Upper Middleton (then known as "Plumsock") and engaged for a time as bar-tender with his uncle, Henry Dick. He soon purchased the Pierce farm in Franklin township, where, in 1829, he built a saw-mill and grist-mill. He died in 1857. In 1808 he married Miss Mary, daughter of Joseph Morrison. They had the following children: Washington, born May 30, 1809; married Hope Rosser and now living in Ford county, Ill.; Madison, born February 20, 1811, died 1885, was married to Mariah Humbert, who died in 1842, then to Lutelia Black, now living in Iowa; Joseph Mephibosheth died in infancy; John, born September 11, 1815, married Nancy crop, lives in Illinois, where his wife died in 1889; Jane Ann, born June 20, 1817, married Benjamin Archibald (dead); Cyrus, born September 26, 1819; married, first to a Miss Winey, then to Margaret Gibson; they live in Warren county, Ill.; Jefferson and Monroe, twins, born January 26, 1822, Jefferson married Rebecca Crop (dead); Monroe married Elizabeth Ball (dead , widow lives in Hastings, Nebraska; Andrew Jackson, born May 15, 1824, married Martha McLaughlin (dead); William M., born July 10, 1826, married Ellen Woods, reside in Page county, Iowa; Franklin, born August 24, 1829, married Mariah Huston, and lives in La Salle county, Ill.

Joseph Bute received a very good education and when twenty five years old removed from the Phillips farm to the farm he now owns in Franklin township.

He was married in April, 1837 to Sarah Ann, daughter of Isaac Sparks, of Perry township. She died March 29, 1838. They had one child: Jackson, born February 4, 1838, and is now living near Grand Ridge, Ill.

Mr. Bute's second wife was Miss Clarissa, daughter of William Black of Perryopolis, and she died February 17, 1875. They were married June 1, 1839. They had the following children: John, who died at two years of age; William Franklin, married Mary Smith, is a merchant of Vanderbilt; Horatio S.; Espey, married Elisabeth, daughter of Jesse Oglevee, now in Page county Ill.; Sarah Jane, married Isaac S. Byers, lives near Aurora, Nebraska; Arabella, married James E. McMullan is at Grand Ridge, Ill.; Susan E., married Robt. McBurney; Joseph Pierce, married Emma, daughter of Samuel S. Strickler, lives near Aurora, Nebraska; Mary Clarissa, married Rev. D. H. McKee, now pastor of Bridgeville M. E. church, Allegheny county, Pa.; George C., married Sarah, daughter of Jacob Strickler; C. L. V., Cora S. and Olive E.

Joseph Bute has always been a democrat, has been a member of the Baptist church for forty-seven years. He has been clerk of the Flatwoods Baptist church since 1862, and deacon since 1863.

He inherited one hundred acres of land, by good management has increased it to five hundred acres, besides owning a tract of 320 acres near Aurora, Neb.

He is engaged largely in stock raising.

CHARLES CALL (deceased) was born in Wood county, Ohio. His educational advantages were limited on account of the scarcity of schools in the section where he was reared.

His father, John Call, a native of Ohio, was a very prominent stock dealer of his day. He bought horses, cattle and sheep in Ohio, and would drive them to Baltimore to market. For many years he followed this business. In about 1832 or 1833 he started from home with a drove of horses, destined for Baltimore, and was never heard of afterward. His family removed to Pennsylvania and settled at Greensboro, Greene county. As soon as Charles Call was old enough he went to work as a tender-boy in the glass factory operated at that place. He afterward learned the glass-blower's trade, and followed that business most of his life.

His mother belonged to the Minor family, who were of the earliest families that settled in Greene county. Her brother, Theophilus Minor, was a well-known river man, and with him Charles Call ran on the river for some time..

Charles Call was married to Miss Hannah R. Lynn. They reared a family of seven children. (For his ancestry see a sketch of Mr. Lynn's family in this book.) Mr. Call was prominent as a Mason; he served several years as justice of the peace of the borough of Belle Vernon; he had a remarkable memory, could retain whatever he read. He was highly respected by all who knew him; he was ever ready to help the needy, and to minister to all who were in distress; he died at Belle Vernon, where he had lived for many years; his wife died eleven years previous to his death.

EMANUEL CAMPBELL, of Menallen, is a son of David Campbell, who came to Fayette county when young, and was married to Nancy Stewart; both died when Emanuel was quite young.

Emanuel Campbell was born May 9, 1824, in Springhill township, Fayette county, Pa. His mother died when he was four years old. He was bound to Colonel A. M. Hill, of Dunbar township, until twenty-one years of age. He learned of him the trade of a tanner and the business of farming. His three brothers were bound at the same time as himself, the two elder to learn the trade of hatter and the younger one that of saddler. He was educated in the Dunbar township schools.

Emanuel Campbell has been married three times; his first wife, Lydia Morgan, was born in Springhill township in 1825, and a daughter of Morris Morgan, a brother of Colonel John Morgan. Her mother was Susan Stertz, of Springhill township. There were two children of this marriage: John Morgan, born June 15, 1850, married Lydia Miller, have four children, and live in Hopwood. The other child died in infancy. His first wife died April 28, 1852. On May 12, 1853, he married Miss Mary Ball, born in 1823, and was the daughter of John H. Ball, of Dunbar township. Of this union three children were born, all living: Mary Elizabeth, born May 26, 1854, married Job Frasher, of Franklin township, and has one child; William Hanna Campbell, born June 22, 1856, married Alice Murphy, they have three children: Lydia Jane, born March 23, 1863, married to Moses B. Porter, of Franklin township, they have three children. Second wife died June 18, 1865.

His third wife was Charity Ann Kindall, of German township, widow of William Kindall, of the same township. She was the daughter of John Sharpnack. (See sketch of William G. Sharpnack.) They had four children: one died in infancy; Martha Estella, born March 4, 1877; Sarah Argosa, born September 23, 1879, and Ann Eliza, born February 10, 1882.

Mr. Campbell was elected poor-house director in 1874, and has held all the offices of his township, except that of justice of the peace. He was one of the first elders of the Cumberland Presbyterian church at Pleasant View, and is at present an elder. He joined the church at East Liberty in 1849. He is a democrat.

His last wife's mother was a daughter of Jesse Antrim, of German township, who was one of the township's earliest settlers.

EDWARD C. CARR, of Dawson, is the son of John and Agnes (Miller) Carr. John Carr, his father, was a native of Ireland, and came to the United States in 1845, at the age of eighteen; first located at Philadelphia, thence to Greensburg, and had horses and carts working on the grade of the P. R. R. From there he removed to Layton, Fayette county, where he lived for thirty-three years, and died there November 9, 1888, at the age of sixty-one years. From the time he came to Layton till his death he was a section foreman on the B. & O. R. R. He was a member of the Catholic church. His wife was Agnes Miller, born in Scotland, and came to the United States with her parents when but two years old. She is still living and resides at Layton.

Edward C. Carr was born February 1, 1855, at West Newton, Westmoreland county, Pa., but was reared at Layton and attended the common schools of that neighborhood.

In September, 1872, at the age of seventeen, he was made a section foreman of the B. & O. R. R., and has held that position ever since. In 1876 he was married to Miss Lila Carson, of Perry township, daughter of James Carson, a farmer of that township. They have two children living: Willy B. and Bertha B.

In October, 1885, he removed to Dawson, and has made that place his home to the present time. Mr. Carr is a member of the Methodist Episcopal church, and is a member of the B. & O. R. R. relief department. He is a democrat, elected by his party to the borough council, and is now a member of that body.

CAPTAIN JOSEPH W. CLARKE was born July 21, 1825, in Clarksville, Pa. He was reared on a farm, attended the subscription schools until sixteen years of age, when he went to Brownsville, and in two years learned engineering sufficiently well to obtain the position of assistant engineer on a steamboat. He was soon promoted to chief engineer, he next became pilot and in a short time thereafter was a captain or master. He owned seven steamboats: Tempest, two Clippers, Leader, Tiger Sam, Charley Clarke, Sampson, Baltic and Petrel.

He was one of the most prominent coal operators on the Monongahela River, at the time he owned the Tremont, Clipper and Rostraver mines.

He operated the sand works at Belle Vernon for two years.

He was united in marriage to Miss Hannah, daughter of Joseph and Mary (Round) Reed, natives of England. Her grandfather, Richard Reed, at the time of his death, left over one hundred descendants behind him. Captain Clarke and wife were the parents of eleven children: Mary A., wife of W. C. Byers, M. D., of Pittsburgh; Sarah N., wife of I. E. Byers; Amy A., wife of Professor W. D. Rowan; Martha J., deceased; Cora A., deceased; Virginia, Charles W. and John F.

Captain Clarke was a correct and successful business man, attentive to the wants of all who traveled with him, was well liked, wherever known, and was a most highly respected gentleman.

He died at his residence near Belle Vernon, July 3, 1889, was followed on the 5th of July to his last resting-place in the Belle Vernon cemetery by a large number of sorrowing friends and relatives.

CLARK G. COCHRAN, the leading and prosperous liveryman of Dawson, Pa., is a son of Isaac and Lydia C. (Merrell) Cochran, and was born in Lower Tyrone township, Fayette county, Pa., February 17, 1852. Isaac Cochran, grandson of Samuel Cochran, was born at what is now Dawson, June 22, 1821. In early life he engaged in flat-boating coke and a few years later engaged in coke manufacturing. As agent for Alfred Howell he laid out the town of Dawson in 1857 and has been agent for the sale of its lots ever since. He is a democrat, Free Mason and large land holder. In 1851 he married Miss Lydia, daughter of Abraham Merrell. They have three children: Lizzie J., wife of M. Keepers, dentist at Latrobe; Sarah J., wife of Dr. McKay, of Fayette City, and Clark G.

Clark G. Cochran received the advantages of a common-school education and at twenty-one years of age he became superintendent of the coal works now known as the Jackson mines. From 1877 to 1884 he was engaged in farming in Dunbar township and then removed to his present beautiful farm near Dawson in Lower Tyrone township. In 1873 he was married to Mary L., daughter of Robt. T. Given, a prominent citizen of Dawson. They have seven children: Maud, Millie, Isaac E., Robert, Clark G., Jr., Lydia and Edward.

Clark G. Cochran has the finest livery, feed and sale stables at Dawson, and are well equipped with all facilities for the accommodation of the traveling public. The stock consists of eighteen head of horses and a large number of fine carriages and buggies. He is a democrat, a member of K. P., and Junior Mechanics. He is one of the enterprising and live business men of Dawson.

JAMES COCHRAN, of Scotch-Irish descent, and one of the prominent and substantial business men of Fayette county, is a son of Isaac and Rosanna (Sample) Cochran, and was born in what is now Lower Tyrone township, Fayette county, Pa., Jan. 15, 1823.

His grandfather, Samuel Cochran, was a Revolutionary soldier, and came from Chester to Fayette county in 1789. He purchased a large tract of land in Lower Tyrone township, of Capt. Joseph Huston. He reared a family of seven children: Samuel, James (died at ninety-four years of age), Thomas, John, Isaac, Mordica and Esther.

His father, Isaac Cochran, was born in Chester county, Pa., was a prominent farmer and a member of the Presbyterian church. In 1822 he helped drill, on Dickerson's Run, the first salt well in Fayette county.

Isaac Cochran died in 1862, at seventy years of age. His wife was Rosanna Sample, whose father, Eziel Sample, was a Westmoreland county farmer of Scotch-Irish descent, and a native of Scotland. (See sketch of M. M. Cochran.)

James Cochran remained on the farm until he became sixteen years of age, when he left home and engaged in boating on the Monongahela river, carrying sand, rock, cinders and such like, to Pittsburgh. In 1842 he, with his brother and uncle, manufactured and boated to Cincinnati 12,000 bushels of twenty-four hour coke, made at what is now the Fayette Works. It was the first Connellsville coke ever sold for money.

Since 1842 Mr. Cochran has continued in the manufacture of coke, has a large interest in the Spring Grove Works and the Fayette Works. He is interested in the Jackson, Franklin and Clinton mines, and is also member of a company owning over 1,200 acres of bituminous coal lands in Dunbar township.

On February 24, 1848, he married Miss Clarissa, daughter of Joseph and Mary A. (Hazen) Huston. They have had eleven children, of whom six sons and one daughter are living.

James Cochran for over twenty-five years safely piloted boats down the dangerous channel of the Youghiogheny river. One writer has said of him that he "is one of the most remarkable of the self-made men of Fayette county, a man of clear understanding, of great energy, indomitable will, but of a generous nature, tender-hearted withal, and, in short, a fine example of hearty, robust manhood."

ABEL COLLEY, a prominent citizen of Menallen township and a prosperous merchant at Haddenville, was born November 27, 1842, on the "Old Colley Homestead" in Redstone township, Fayette county, Pa., and is a son of Levi Colley, born in Redstone township, on the farm now owned by Mr. Sawyer, near Searights, Pa. He was an industrious farmer and a very successful business man, and was married to Lydia C. Colley, daughter of George Colley, who was the sole owner of the "Colley Homestead." To this union were born three children, two of whom are living: George W. and Abel Colley. Levi died February 28, 1884, in Menallen township, was a devout Christian and a member of the Disciple church. His widow still survives and lives with her two sons. His grandfather, Abel Colley, was a hotel-keeper where S. W. Colley now lives. He was industrious and accumulated considerable wealth. He died in Menallen township.

Abel Colley received his education in the common schools of Menallen township, and has been principally engaged in farming up to the spring of 1887, when he engaged in mercantile business at Haddenville. He had the postoffice established there June 16, 1887, and was appointed first postmaster, the office he now holds. He has a profitable and paying business, which is constantly increasing.

On September 25, 1862, he was married to Sarah Miller, daughter of Warwick Miller, the latter now of North Union township, and was the former owner and operator of "State Flouring Mill" in Menallen township. Abel Colley is the father of five children, four of whom are living: William S., born February 7, 1864, and married Jennie E. Courtney of Menallen township; Orlando, born March 12, 1866, is now the owner and proprietor of "Clinton House Livery Stable" at Uniontown, and Brown, born April 14, 1868, has been a teacher and is now in the employ of the publisher of this book, and Sarah Allie, born August 24, 1873.

Abel Colley owns two good farms in Menallen township, and takes great interest in both farming and stock-raising. He is an influential democrat and by that party was elected county auditor in 1877, the duties of which, he filled creditably to himself and the party that elected him. He is a member of the Disciple church, and a very successful business man.

SEARIGHT W. COLLEY, a son of Abel and Nancy (Noland) Colley, was born January 11, 1828, in Redstone township, Fayette county, Pa. His grandfather, Peter Colley, was born on board the ship crossing the ocean from Ireland to America.

Abel Colley, Sr., was born March 11, 1792, in Redstone township, on what is now the Dempsey Woodward farm, was a well-to-do farmer, and owned one thousand acres of land. On January 10, 1811, he married Miss Nancy, daughter of William Noland. They had five children, three sons and two daughters, of whom but one, Searight W. Colley, is living.

Searight W. Colley was reared on a farm, and received his education in the subscription schools. On November 26, 1858, he was married to Miss Catherine Smouse, by the Rev. Samuel Wilson. They have two children: Laura Belle, born February 12, 1860, married Hayden R. Craft, of Redstone. To their marriage were born Elizabeth, and Ellen, at home. They were educated in the common schools and at the Pittsburgh Female College, at which Laura Belle carried away the honors at the musical contest.

Catherine (Smouse) Colley was born in Wills Creek valley, Md., January 31, 1838, and is a daughter of Samuel Smouse, of Brownsville township, who was born February 19, 1810, in West Virginia, and died May 24, 1884. He married Elizabeth Troutman, born in Martinsburg, W. Va., March 23, 1814, and died April 24, 1874. They had six children: Ellen, wife of Colonel E. Bierer, of Hiawatha, Kas. (see Colonel Bierer's sketch); Catherine, Daniel T.; Anna, wife of George W. Seaman; John L., of Texas, and Ada, wife of John Buckley.

Mr. Colley is a farmer, and owns 142 acres of valuable land in Menallen township. He is a member of the Masonic fraternity, and belongs to Fayette lodge, No. 228, of Uniontown. He is a democrat, and has served as jury commissioner for one term. He is one of Menallen's esteemed citizens, and is a member of the Presbyterian church, of New Salem, of which his wife is also a member.

JOHN COLDREN was born January 20, 1822, in Washington township, Fayette county, Pennsylvania; was reared on a farm and educated in the common schools.

At the age of 21 years, he bought one-half of the Red Lion store, on Redstone creek, engaged in merchandising for one year, when he bought half interest in Arnold's Mills, located a short distance from Fayette City, and operated them up to a year ago when he sold the property, and is at present engaged with a mill company at Fayette City.

He was married March 4, 1863, to Lurena Gould, a native of the county, a daughter of John and Jane (Trainor) Gould, the former a native of Maine, and was one of the pioneer school teachers of the county. John Coldren had no children of his own, but has raised two adopted ones: Frank Bean, and Minnie Sample. Minnie married Robert W. Hall.

Mr. Coldren and wife are members of the Disciples church. He is a member of the F. & A. M., and owns a comfortable home, containing ten acres of ground, near Fayette City. He has held several township offices, and is a sober, industrious and upright citizen.

His parents were Jesse and Anna (Stephens) Coldren. His father was born in Maryland and removed from there, with his parents to Virginia, and subsequently, while he was yet a young man, to Pennsylvania. He learned scythe and sickle making with Samuel Cope.

Anna Stephens was the daughter of Levi Stephens. (See his sketch.)

The Coldren family were originally Quakers.

JOHN BELL COOK, a grandson of Colonel Edward Cook, of Revolutionary fame, is a son of James and Mary (Bell) Cook, and was born on the old Cook homestead, in Washington township, August 26, 1808.

Colonel Edward Cook (grandfather) has rightfully been called the pioneer of civilization in Washington township. He came in 1770 from Conococheague, Franklin county. His wife was Miss Martha Crawford, born on Christmas, 1743, died April 20, 1837, and had one child, James Cook.

Colonel Edward Cook was prominent during the Revolution in the frontier history of Fayette county. He died November 27, 1808, in the seventieth year of his age.

From the truthful tribute placed on his tomb by his pastor, Rev. Willliam Wylie, we quote a part: "Few men have deserved and possessed more eminently than Colonel Cook, the consideration and esteem of the people in the western country. In public spirit, disinterestedness, and zeal for the general welfare, he was excelled by none. In private life, his unsullied integrity, his liberality, the amiable benevolence of his temper, endeared him to his friends, and marked him as a sanctuary to which the poor might confidently resort for relief."

James Cook (father) was born in Washington township, August 13, 1772, and engaged in farming as his life pursuit. On May 6, 1806, he was married to Miss Mary Bell, a native of Ireland, and had six children.

John Bell Cook was reared on a farm, and received his early education in the old subscription schools. When he reached his majority he engaged in farming, and has continued in that business ever since.

On October 18, 1837, he was married to Miss Matilda, daughter of William and Nancy (Forsythe) Cunningham; both Presbyterians, and came out with Colonel Cook. The former died in 1816. James, a son, was born May 14, 1840, enlisted in Company F, Eighteenth Pennsylvania Cavalry, was taken prisoner and exchanged, thrown by a horse and instantly killed August 16, 1864, at City Point, and now sleeps in the cemetery at Rehoboth church; Sarah A., a daughter, was born August 23, 1842, was finely educated, married A. M. Fulton, and died December 12, 1874; William J., died in infancy; Joseph A., born December 11, 1846, and Robert Johnson Cook, born March 21, 1849. He was graduated from Yale in 1876 was captain of the Yale boat crew from 1873 to 1876; read law, and was admitted to the Pittsburgh bar in 1878. He married Miss Annie Wells, of Pittsburgh, April 26, 1881, and in 1882 took a special course in a German university.

John Bell Cook is now in his eighty-second year. His wife died December 12, 1887. She was an estimable woman, and a devout Christian.

Mr. Cook is an honored citizen, and a highly esteemed member of the Presbyterian church.

JOHN W. CORWIN is a native of Fayette county, Pa., was born July 6, 1834, and is a son of Barnet and Nellie (Call) Corwin.

Morris Corwin (John W.'s paternal grandfather) came to Fayette county in an early day and engaged as cooper. His wife was Mary, daughter of Barnet Smock, who lived to be ninety-seven years of age, and had an odd collection of bonnets representing all the styles in vogue during a period of one hundred years.

Barnet Corwin was born in Westmoreland county, Pa., in 1814, and was by trade a ship carpenter. He married Nellie, daughter of Daniel Call, who was a weaver by trade.

John W. Corwin was raised at Belle Vernon, and was educated there. When twenty years of age he learned the trade of engineer, and continued in that business for sixteen years. In 1870 he engaged in the grocery and bakery business, in which he has continued successfully ever since.

He was married June 21, 1866, to Miss Margaret J., daughter of William Jacobs. They have one child, a son, Edgar, born May 14, 1867, married to Miss Araminta, daughter of John S. Clegg, and is engaged in the glass business.

John W. Corwin is one of the substantial citizens of Belle Vernon, has never sought office, but has filled several positions of trust and responsibility of his borough, and is a member of the Free-will Baptist church.

ETHELBERT O. COURTNEY was born May 7, 1829, on what is now the Phillips farm in North Union township, Fayette county, Pa., and is a son of Benjamin and Sarah (Wilkey) Courtney.

Benjamin Courtney was born in North Union township, and was a carpenter by trade, but was principally engaged in farming. In 1821 he married Miss Sarah Wilkey, who was born in 1798, near New Haven, and was a daughter of James Wilkey. Mr. and Mrs. Courtney have had six children: Henry, Jackson, John, Ethelbert O., William and Margaret Elizabeth; all are dead except Ethelbert.

Benjamin Courtney's father, John Courtney, was born in the eastern part of the State and came to North Union township, where he married Elizabeth Carter and engaged in farming.

Ethelbert O. Courtney was reared on a farm, was educated in the common schools of North Union and Menallen; and for a time was a pupil of Hugh Espy, a prominent teacher of that day.

Mr. Courtney was married September 15, 1859, to Miss Lucinda N., daughter of John Foster, of North Union, a farmer and stock buyer, and a member of the Presbyterian church. Mr. and Mrs. Courtney are the parents of two children: Emily Jane, born August, 1861, married to William Colley, of Uniontown, and has one child, Ethelbert; James William, born April 9, 1867, and was married to Elizabeth, daughter of William Jeffries, of Menallen township.

Mr. Courtney is a democrat and has voted for every democratic candidate since he became a voter. He has held the offices of school director, township auditor, judge of election and road supervisor. He and his wife are members of the Presbyterian church at Laurel Hill. He has made farming the business of his life, and owns a good farm in Menallen township, where he now resides.

ELIJAH CROSSLAND, a prosperous citizen of Menallen township, is a son of Greenbury and Sarah (Stearns) Crossland, and was born at Uniontown, April 23, 1845.

Greenbury Crossland, one of the worthy and self-made men of Uniontown, was born at Connellsville, June 13, 1813, and is a son of Elijah and Catharine (Smith) Crossland. Greenbury Crossland came to Uniontown at nine years of age, where he received a limited education, but by push and vim won his way to fortune and high standing as a citizen. In 1833 he engaged in butchering with a capital of $23, ten of which were borrowed from his wife. Since 1841 he has been very successful in buying cattle for the Eastern markets. In 1847 he effected his first purchase of real estate, and now owns nearly a thousand acres of choice farming and rich mineral land in the vicinity of Uniontown. He and his wife have been members of the Methodist Episcopal church in Uniontown since January 1, 1845, and he is one of the church's most liberal contributors. A man of high repute has analyzed his character as follows: "Moral characteristics, faithfulness, honor, honesty, benevolence and regard for the rights of others. Business characteristics, good judgment, caution, energy, perseverance, watchfulness, combined with great shrewdness and knowledge of market values. Religious charactertics, enthusiasm, sincerity, simplicity in manners and dress, charity and single-mindedness."

Elijah Crossland was raised in North Union township and educated in the common schools. He engaged in farming and in 1876 removed to his present farm which contrins 154 acres of well improved and highly cultivated land.

On October 31, 1867, he married Miss Nancy J., daughter of Edward and Mary (Martin) Rose of Uniontown. Their union has been blessed with five children: Mary Elizabeth, born August 10, 1868, and married December 30, 1886, to Evan Jeffries, son of Harvey Jeffries; Sarah, born May 25, 1870; Alice, born December 2, 1872; Anna, born December 13, 1874, and William Crossland, born April 10, 1878.

Elijah Crossland devotes his time and attention to his business, and is a prompt, honorable and capable business man. He is a republican and a member of the Methodist Episcopal church at Uniontown.

HIRAM COTTOM, one of Lower Tyrone's leading merchants, is a son of Samuel and Elizabeth (Shallenberger) Cottom, and was born in Franklin township, January 18, 1849. (See sketch of Irving H. Cottom).

William Cottom was a farmer of Lower Tyrone, and was noted for strictly attending to his own business. He was a Methodist, and died at the age of eighty-six years. One of his sons, Samuel Cottom, was born in Rostravor township, Westmoreland county, Pa., and married Elizabeth Shallenberger. He is now a substantial farmer of Lower Tyrone.

He is a democrat, and has served several terms as school director. His wife was born in 1807, and died in 1867.

Hiram Cottom was brought by his parents to Lower Tyrone township, in 1854, was there educated in the common schools, and a commercial school, at Uniontown. At fourteen years of age, he engaged as a clerk in a store with G. W. Anderson, and remained with him thirteen years.

In 1876 he purchased Mr. Anderson's property and stock of goods, and is now engaged in general merchandising.

He improved the property and built two large store-rooms. He carries a large and completely assorted stock of goods, and has a full line of everything needed in a first-class general store.

He was married in 1874 to Miss Cordelia, daughter of G. W. Anderson. To their union have been born four children: George W. A., born November 13, 1875, died March 24, 1887; Bessie K., born May 11, 1880, died March 22, 1887; Lela, born September 10, 1885, died March 25, 1887, and Stewart Cottom, born February 26, 1888.

Mr. Cottom is an active and influential democrat; has served one term as township auditor, and two terms as school director. He is a man of marked business ability, well merits and fully deserves the confidence reposed in him by the business public.

IRVING H. COTTOM, a progressive farmer of Lower Tyrone township, is a son of William and Catherine (Goodge) Cottom, and was born on the farm where he now resides, in Lower Tyrone township, August 12, 1840.

Richard Cottom, grandfather, was a native of England, who emigrated to Maryland, and from thence to Lower Tyrone township, where he died in 1845.

William Cottom (father) was born in Maryland in 1791, and came to the Work farm, in Dunbar township, in 1810. Five years later he moved to the mouth of Jacob's creek, and in 1822 removed to Lower Tyrone township, where he died October 5, 1875 He was a member of the Methodist Episcopal church, and a just man, whose life motto was honesty. His wife was born near the site of the opera house at Uniontown, in 1798, and died April 20, 1884. She was a member of the Methodist Episcopal church. Six of their children are living: Samuel, a farmer; William, a wagon-maker; John, a farmer; Wesley; Elizabeth, wife of Josiah Reed, and Irving H.

Irving H. Cottom was raised on a farm, and received his education in the common schools; at the close of his school days he engaged in farming at home, and in 1861 removed to Westmoreland county, where he remained four years. In 1865 he bought his present farm, containing 115 acres of fine land, situated 2½ miles north of Dawson, on the Connellsville and Perryopolis road. January 30, 1862, he married Miss Annie S., daughter of Joseph L. Walter, the latter a Westmoreland county farmer. Unto this union have been born eight children: Alva W., a butcher of Vanderbilt, married Belle B. Hepplewhite, of England; Frank P., a normal student at California, Pa.; Mary L., Lester M., Joseph H., Harry A., Ethel M. and Clyde Cottom.

Irving H. Cottom is a stanch democrat, and has served as supervisor of roads and assessor. He is a member and class-leader of the Methodist Episcopal church, is a man of decided views upon the leading issues of the day, and is a reliable and prominent citizen of his township.

MATTHEW G. CUNNINGHAM, farmer of Lower Tyrone township, is the son of Joseph and Jane (Gaut) Cunningham, both natives of Tyrone township, Fayette county, Pa.

His father, Joseph Cunningham, was a farmer in what is now Lower Tyrone. He was born March 22, 1801, in Fayette county, Pa., and died April 8, 1877, aged seventy-six years. He was a democrat, and held the offices of county commissioner, from 1851 to 1853, inclusive, school director and justice of the peace of his township. He was a prominent man in his time and well liked by all who knew him. He attended to a great deal of business as administrator and executor of estates in this county. He was a member of the Tyrone Presbyterian church, and a ruling elder of the same, for thirty years. In 1827 he married Miss Jane Gaut, who survived him nearly nine year, and died January 30, 1886, in her eightieth year. She was the daughter of Matthew Gaut, better known as Squire Gaut, a farmer of Tyrone township and for many years a justice of the peace.

Matthew G. Cunningham was born January 3, 1832, in what is now Lower Tyrone township, Fayette county, Pa. He was brought up on the farm, and has continued to follow farming all his life. He got his education in the common schools, and now resides on the farm formerly owned by his father, situated two miles northwest of Dawson, on the Dawson and Tyrone Mills road, and contains one hundred acres of good, well-improved land.

He was married September 25, 1856, to Miss Lydia Newcomer, daughter of Christian Newcomer, a farmer of Tyrone township; the latter died April 25, 1855, at the age of sixty-five. Of this marriage there are now living eight children: Charles B., William D., Joseph B., Herman R., Judson J., David O., Harry G. and Clayton C.; Charles B. is now engaged in the lumber business in Scott Haven, Allegheny county; William D. is the principal of the West Newton school; the rest are all at home.

Matthew G. Cunningham is one of the best citizens of Lower Tyrone, and has always lead a quiet, honorable life.

WILLIAM CUNNINGHAM, grandfather of Matthew G., was born 1767. After spending his earlier years at Old Laurel Furnace near Uniontown he established an inn for the accommodation of coach travelers on the National pike where now stands the enterprising county-seat.

In addition to his inn interests he sent teams over the mountains, frequently made trips himself to Cumberland and Baltimore, carrying over grain and other produce and returning with salt and manufactured articles.

Later in life he removed to Tyrone township and at the breaking out of the second war for independence he left his home and family to maintain the liberty which doubtless his father had struggled to secure. At the close of the war he returned to his home, where he soon after (1817) died, leaving to his two sons, Joseph and William, a farm of several hundred acres, a part of which has been held by the family and is now being tilled by the fourth generation.

He married Mary Huston who died fifteen years after the decease of her husband.

AUGUSTUS CUSTER was born near the village of Carpowen, Germany, September 5, 1856, paternal ancestors of the fifth generation migrated in 1732 to Germany from Switzerland, who were forced to leave the native country on account of the persecution of Protestants by the Roman Catholic church.

Charles Custer, a native of Germany, was the grandfather of Augustus Custer, and he was the grandson of the ancestor above mentioned.

John Custer, the father of Augustus, was born in Germany, September 3, 1820. He learned the tailor's trade, but followed it only a short time.

In 1844 he married a Miss Jackstice of his native village, and they had three children: Wilhelmina, Julius and Charles C. Julius was a corporal in the Franco-Prussian war of 1870, and was killed in an infantry charge at Courcelles, near Metz, in Lorraine. The other two children are married and live in Allegheny City. His first wife died in 1850, and John Custer married again in 1855 to Henrietta Heidemann, of Germany. By this marriage four children were born: Augustus, Augusta, Edward and Anna.

For eighteen years he was the overseer of lands owned by a nobleman, and his income was only sufficient to clothe and feed himself and family.

Auguste Custer was educated in the school of his native village, afterwards took a three years course in the graded schools. Immediately after leaving school he came to America with his father in 1873. Eighty dollars in money, and a scanty outfit of clothing was the entire possessions of the family on their arrival here.

Augustus Custer located in Pittsburgh and engaged as a day laborer for one year, he then came to Franklin township, Fayette county, and rented a farm and in 1880 he bought a farm of 70 acres of land from Josiah King, of Perry township. When he purchased this land it was a perfect wilderness, and the soil exceedingly sterile. In 1881 he bought what is known as the "Robinson tract" from the Robinson heirs of Pittsburgh, containing 102 acres, which was in bad condition and had been without a tenant for over twenty years In 1882 he bought 28 acres of land from David R. Snyder. This land, except 28 acres, was all in quite bad condition. He now has about 186 acres in a good condition and is well stocked. Mr. Custer has some of the finest blooded stock in the county and of which he makes a specialty. Mr. Custer is a good example of what industry will do for a man; in less than twenty years he has grown wealthy, and is one of the representative farmers of Fayette county.

HENRY B. DENNY was born January 22, 1817, at Uniontown, Fayette county, Pa., and was educated in old William Beggs' school. At seventeen years of age he began to work at quarrying rock on the National road for James Snyder, continuing to work for him for three years, when he learned the carpenter trade with John Mustard and Daniel Sharpnack, and worked at that business till the spring of 1888.

On November 29, 1857, he was married to Miss Salina Park, of New Geneva, a daughter of Andrew Park, who served in the War of 1812, was pensioned for services in that war and died in 1859. They have nine living children: Ellen Potter, born January 30, 1859, married William Elliot, of Uniontown; N. Ewing, March 17, 1860, a carpenter; B. Wade, July 6, 1861; Taylor, October 17, 1863, married Margaret Storkey, and has one child living; Lizzie, born September 11, 1864, a school teacher; Davie P., June 9, 1865; George, September 8, 1867; Ettie, February 1, 1872, and Harry, born March 25, 1874.

He is quite strong and in good health at the age of seventy-two and one-half years. He voted for Gen. William H. Harrison in 1840, was a whig and is now a republican.

John Denny, the father of Henry B., was born in 1789, and raised by Judge Minor, of Greene county, Pa. He learned the trade of a miller, and married a daughter of Judge Minor, whose wife died, and he then removed to Fayette county, and ran Boyd's mill. In this county he married Miss Susannah Poundstone, afterwards removed to Uniontown and managed Beeson's mill.

James Denny, the grandfather of Henry B., was born in Ireland, and came to America with two of his brothers, and was sold for his passage money. He enlisted in the army under Captain Cluggage, and served through the entire War of the Revolution. He was at Yorktown and saw Lord Cornwallis give his sword to General Washington, by the hand of General O'Hara. He was also at the battle of Brandywine, and was with Washington in his flight through New Jersey. He was a fine scholar, and taught schools throughout a great part of western Pennsylvania in his day. He removed to Greene county after the war was over, settled near Dunkards Creek and died at an advanced age. He is buried near New Geneva. He drew a pension for his services in the War of the Revolution from 1828,and received it up till the time of his death. His two brothers came to Pittsburgh, and it is likely that the Dennys of that city are their descendants.

Henry B. Denny's mother was the daughter of George Poundstone, whose father, George Poundstone, Sr., was a driver on the "Old Road" before the pike was made and the government took charge of it. He hauled goods from Baltimore to points in the West. Her mother was a sister of Isaac and George Messmore.

ZIMRI FARQUHAR, of Washington township, is the son of William Farquhar, a native of Washington township, whose father, Robert Farquhar (subject's grandfather), came with the Copes and others to the township in an early day.

Zimri Farquhar, born in August, 1834, was reared on a farm, where he worked in summer and attended school in winter. He followed farming from 1854 to 1861.

When the war broke out he enlisted as a private in the Sixty-second Pennsylvania Infantry served on detached duty from the time of his enlistment until he was discharged at the end of his term, dressed nearly all of the time in the garb of a citizen, and served principally as an army detective. His duty was to gather up straggling soldiers, to arrest deserters and return them to their regiments.

After the war he removed to Illoinis, where he remained one year, when he returned to Fayette county, engaged in the mixing department of the Fayette City Glass Works, and was here employed for eighteen years without missing a day.

He was married in 1856 to Miss Mariah Burges, daughter of Charles Burges of Fayette City. Charles Burges' ancestors were early settlers in southwestern Pennsylvania, coming from Old Town, Va. Mr. Farquhar has seven children: Rachael A. B., married; Lizzie B., married; Thornton K., educated at Lock Haven and a teacher; Frank S., educated for a stenographer, and is in a printing office at McKeesport; Duncan, a musician; Flora M. and Viola E.

Mr. Farquhar has quite a valuable collection of Indian relics, also of rare coins, noticeable among which is a five-dollar gold piece of Beechtler's (assayist) make. He has a tooth brush given him by John Morgan (the raider) and a knife given him by an aid of Robert E. Lee. He has been councilman for some years, but has never sought office.

He belongs to the A. O. U. W., and is a prominent member of the G. A. R.

He is a good workman, a man of considerable observation, and is always interested in whatever is best for his town and county.

CHARLES FARQUHAR, of Washington township, was born in Fayette county, Pa., August 28, 1843, and is a son of Robert Farquhar. He was reared on a farm, educated in the common schools, and at the age of twenty-one years he began farming, at which he is at present engaged. His father, Robert Farquhar, was a farmer, was married to Miss Naomi, a daughter of Joshua Tiernan (a native of Fayette county), whose father, John Tiernan, was a prominent citizen of the county, and served two terms as treasurer of Fayette county. To their union were born three children: Laura, Joshua and Robert. Mr. Farquhar has followed farming, and has operated some in coal mining. He is the owner of thirty-two acres of well-improved land in the county, and possesses a comfortable home at Fayette City. He is a member of the A. O. of U. W.

EBENEZER FINLEY, JR., is a prominent citizen of Menallen township, and member of one of the best known and most reliable families of Fayette county. He is a grandson of the scholarly and able Rev. James Finley, who was the first minister to plant the banner of Presbyterianism west of the Alleghanies.

Ebenezer Finler, Jr., was born in Fayette county, Pa., October 24, 1804, and is the son of Ebenezer Finley, Sr. His mother's maiden name was Violet Lowry.

His grandfather, the Rev. James Finley, was a native of Cecil county, Md., came to Fayette county in 1765, on a missionary tour, and to seek out land locations for his sons. He made a second trip in 1767, and a third trip in 1771, when he purchased a large tract of land on Dunlap's creek. He was instrumental in bringing thirty-four Presbyterian families from Maryland into Fayette county, and establishing five churches of his religious faith in Southwestern Pennsylvania. He had charge of Rehoboth church in Westmoreland county, Pa., in 1783, died in 1795, having faithfully spent a long life in the service of his Divine master.

Ebenezer Finley, Sr., when fourteen years of age came from Maryland to Fayette county, labored on the farm, and had a perilous adventure with Indians near Fort Wallace, while serving as a soldier on the frontier. He erected one of the first sawmills and grist-mills in the county, and was a prominent and useful citizen till his death in 1849, aged eighty-eight years. He now sleeps with his four wives in Dunlap's creek graveyard. Four of his sons, Ebenezer, Jr., Robert (deceased), and Eli H. settled on different parts of the Finley estate.

Ebenezer Finley, Jr., was raised on a farm and received but the limited educational privileges of his boyhood days. He was married on February 9, 1826, to Miss Phebe, daughter of Caleb Woodward, a skillful mechanic, who came from Chester county, Pa. They had ten children: Caleb W., born January 15, 1849, died April 13, 1877; Ebenezer L., born October 2, 1828, died September 10,

1849; Robert F., born May 29, 1830; Evans, born August 16, 1832; Elijah V., born July 10, 1834, died November 25, 1859; James G., born April 16, 1836; Phebe J., born July 25, 1840; Albert W., born March 28, 1843; John H., born April 7, 1847, and Violet, born April 18, 1849. The oldest son, the Rev. Caleb Woodward Finley, was pastor of the Presbyterian church at London, Madison county, Ohio, for twenty-one years, where he died in 1877. Robert Finley is living in Colorado. Phebe Jane Finley married John Thomas Porter, and they now reside in Alco, Ala. Dr. John Huston Finley was killed at Streator, Illinois, November 16, 1883, in a railroad collision. Violet Finley married Dr. C. D. Chalfant and resides at Streator, Ill.

Albert W. Finley, the seventh son, was educated in the common schools, Dunlap's Creek Academy and Duff's Business College, Pittsburgh, Pa., taught school for two years and has since been engaged in farming. He married, on July 18, 1872, Emma Mosier, a daughter of William L. Mosier of Georges township and grand-daughter of John De Ford, one of the pioneers of Fayette county. A. W. Finley early in life became a member of the Dunlap's Creek Presbyterian church, and has been for some time a ruling elder in the Presbyterian church at New Salem, where he now resides.

In 1876 Ebenezer Finley, Jr. and wife celebrated the golden anniversary of their marriage and their sixty third anniversary February 9, 1889.

He has been identified with the temperance cause in Fayette county for over half a century, and for forty years has been president of the New Salem Temperance Society.

On August 13, 1834, he was elected a ruling elder in the Dunlap's Creek Presbyterian church, and has since served as such.

He has been a very useful man in Fayette county, settled thirty eight estates, written sixty-four wills, seventy-one deeds, has been executor, administrator, guardian and assignee.

He served three years as poor house director, and in 1841 was elected school director in Menallen township.

Mr. Finley is implicitly trusted by all who know him, his word is as good as his bond. He and his wife are a hale, hearty, well preserved old couple, although past their four score years.

He is well versed in the local and early history of Menallen and adjoining townships, and is highly respected by his neighbors for his many good qualities of head and heart.

REV. DAVID FLANIGAN, an agreeable, energetic and talented minister of the Methodist Episcopal church, at Dawson, is a son of Clark and Martha (Roberts) Flanigan, and was born in Henry Clay township, Fayette county, Pa., November 10, 1850.

His grandfather, Andrew Flanigan, was born in what is now Henry Clay township, and died in 1867. He was a farmer, a soldier of the War of 1812, and kept a hotel for many years at Jockey Valley, on the National Road, where he owned the valuable Jockey Valley farm.

His father, Clark Flanigan, is a native of Henry Clay township, where he owns a good farm. He is a member of the Methodist Episcopal church, has served as school director and filled various other township offices. He is seventy-eight years old, is active for his years, and is well liked by his neighbors. He married Miss Martha Roberts, a niece of the celebrated Richard Roberts.

Rev. David Flanigan was reared on a farm, educated in the common-schools, normal schools of Somerset county, and Smithfield and Terra Alta academies. He taught his home school for four successive years, and was licensed to preach in the spring of 1879, by the Rev. J. H. Miller, of the Methodist Episcopal church.

In the fall of the same year he was given work by the West Virginia Methodist Episcopal Conference, and was sent as a supply to the Grantsville charge in Maryland, where he remained three years. Rev. Flanigan was next sent to the Albrightsville charge, in Preston county, W. Va., and the next year, on account of his wife's ill health, was transferred to Brandonville, where he remained for two years. In 1885 he asked for and received a certificate of location and became a member of the Pittsburgh Conference. His first field of service in Pennsylvania was Addison charge in Somerset county, served two years, and was sent in October, 1877, to his present charge at Dawson.

In 1880 he married Miss Sallie, daughter of Charles and Amy Tissue, of Henry Clay township. To them have been born three children: Gratta Lee, born at Grantsville, Md.; Wilbur Dwight, born at Brandonville, W. Va., and Mary E., born at Dawson, Pa.

Rev. David Flanigan is pleasant and courteous in manner, and in the pulpit he is logical, earnest and forcible.

OLIVER JENKINS GADDIS (deceased), who was a highly esteemed and very charitable citizen of Menallen township was a son of Jacob and Sarah (Combs) Gaddis. He was born on the old Gaddis farm near Upper Middletown, August 1, 1826, and died July 20, 1889. In the tide of emigration from Virginia that crossed the Alleghanies to the "Redstone country" in 1785, was John Gaddis, a son of William Gaddis, of eastern Virginia. John Gaddis was born near Winchester, Va., October 7, 1741 and died in Menallen township, April 12 1827. He bought 295 acres of land, called Gaddistown, near the site of Upper Middletown, and engaged in farming. He was a leading member of the Baptist church at Uniontown and was a industrious farmer. He married May 22, 1768, Sarah Jenkins, born February 9, 1751, and died January 2, 1802. They had five sons and six daughters. One of these sons, Jacob Gaddis, was born September 8, 1778. He married Sarah Combs, born September 3, 1805, and died August 20, 1887. He was an industrious farmer, and traded in furs.

Oliver J. Gaddis was raised on the home farm, educated in the old subscription schools of the day and was a fine penman and good accountant. He was married to Miss Mary E., daughter of Jonathan G. Allen, a merchant of Uniontown. Eight children blessed their union: Jacob E. Gaddis, M. D., of Uniontown; one son who died in infancy; Charles, Lizzie, wife of Ewing Baily; Louisa, wife of Judson Arison, Antoinette, Drusilla A., and Jesse M. Gaddis.

Oliver J. Gaddis was a thrifty and prosperous farmer, was an ardent republican and deeply interested in the education of his children. He was noted for his uprightness and integrity. A prominent feature of his excellent character, was charity, contributing freely to help the church and aid the worthy poor. None were ever turned from his door who sought food or shelter.

HON. HENRY GALLEY was born June 12, 1819. He was the youngest of his father's family, and when he was but two years old his father removed from Tyrone to Franklin township. Being the youngest, he had greater advantages in the way of schooling than his brothers. He attended school more or less each year from the time he was six years old until he became of age. Having acquired a good common-school education and a taste for reading, at an early age he became interested in political affairs, and espoused the principles of the democratic party. At the time

Henry Galley

Ritner was elected governor on the Anti-Mason issue, he remembers well the scenes enacted during the buckshot war. As a boy he hurrahed for Jackson. After having reached the age of twenty-one, he cast his first vote in 1840 for Martin Van Buren; has voted for every nominee of the democratic party from that time up to 1888, and has voted thirteen times for president, his first vote being lost on the present incumbent's grandfather, and his last on the grandson. He has always been ardently attached to the democratic party; and was elected to various township offices: judge and inspector of elections, assessor, supervisor of road, school director, etc.

At the age of twenty-five he married Miss Ruth, daughter of Edmund Freeman, of Franklin township. Their marriage has been blessed with nine children, three sons and six daughters: Elizabeth C., Franklin M., Allen, Emma W., Sabina, J. K. Ewing, Kate, Belle N. and Henrietta, and all lived to be men and women. Franklin M. died in 1874, aged twenty-seven years, and his remains rest in Locust Grove cemetery on the hill; Elizabeth C., married Samuel Luce, of Perry township; Sabina married O. F. Arnold, of Franklin township, and Allen married Miss Belle, daughter of Samuel Gallatin of Tyrone township. Henry Galley being the youngest of his father's family, inherited one-half of the old homestead farm on the banks of the Youghiogheny river, opposite Dawson, where he has since continued to live.

During all of his active life he has followed farming as his principal business; but has dealt in stock, bought and sold real estate and was for a time engaged in the mercantile business at Dawson. He contributed largely to the upbuilding of the town of Dawson. Among other improvements he built the brick hotel near the B. & O. station, known as the "Central." Being a sober and industrious man, he gave his personal attention to his affairs, and has been successful in all his business enterprises. He was noted as a good farmer, raising heavy crops of grain, especially of corn.

It was due to his adherence to the principles of the democratic party, his knowledge of political affairs, that he was prevailed upon to offer himself as a candidate for legislative honors, and permitted his name to be announced in the spring of 1858 for the nomination. He was nominated, and in the fall of the same year was elected. He served during the session of 1859 and was a useful member in that body. He was renominated by his party in the spring of 1859, but was defeated on account of a split in the democratic party that grew out of the passage of the "Kansas-Nebraska Act," or better known as the Lecompton and Anti-Lecompton contest, in which Stephen A. Douglas and James Buchanan were the principal actors. Although defeated, Mr. Galley, remained firmly attached to his party principles opposed to all sectional issues and hate and was in favor of all rights, absolutely conferred on our people by the Constitution. He firmly believed in the views expressed by General Washington, that sectional parties or sectional geographical division of the country would lead to war. Consequently he has always been opposed to the policy of the republican party, as in his opinion its policy and radical leadership were the primary causes that led to the Rebellion. He was opposed to war as a means of preserving the Union. For thus expressing his views he was denounced as disloyal; and several ineffectual attempts were made to arrest him. He is firm in his belief that war could have been averted if reason and patriotism had pervaded the country, instead of sectional hate and party frenzy. In regard to the question of slavery he was willing to leave that with the States themselves; granting other States the same rights that Pennsylvanians exercised on the subject, believing as he did that the advanced civilization of time would correct all wrongs and eradicate all evils. He is a man of strong convictions and marked individuality, not easily carried away by other men's opinions or prompted by their suggestions. He is decidedly a man who thinks for himself. In his social capacity he is kindly disposed towards all men, a good conversationalist, always inclined to pry into causes rather than be blinded by effect.

His father, Philip Galley, was of German descent. His grandfather, Peter Galley, emigrated from Germany to America in about 1770, came to Lancaster county, Pa., and married Sophia Stern. To them were born two children, a son and daughter; the daughter died in infancy, leaving Philip as the only survivor. Peter Galley joined the Army of the Revolution as musician, died soon after enlistment, thus leaving the boy Philip to be cared for by his mother.

After some two years the mother married again, and the boy Philip was taken in charge by his uncle Philip Stern. He was raised to industry; learned the art of weaving and also that of grafting fruit trees.

Subsequently he married Magdalene Newcomer, of Washington county, Maryland. She was the daughter of Peter and Catherine Newcomer. The Newcomers were formerly residents of Lancaster county Pa., and from there removed over into Washington county, Md., where Philip Galley soon after followed and married the mother of the Galley family, consisting of eight sons and three daughters: Peter, Catherine, John, Jacob, David, Elizabeth, Samuel, Jonathan, Barbara, Abraham and Henry. After settling on a piece of land in Washington county, Md., Philip Galley and wife sold their land, and with Peter, the only child at that time, moved to what was then known as "the West," settling in Tyrone township, on a farm now on the line of the Broad Ford & Mount Pleasant railroad, Morgan Station being on a part of the same farm. There they lived until ten more children were born.

Philip Galley was the first man in the county to engage in the nursery business, strong-handed and very energetic, he accumulated wealth rapidly, so that he was not only able to pay for his Tyrone farm, but bought the Riverbottom farm, and removed there in 1821. With the help he then had he soon engaged in the nursery business, and after building the brick mansion-house and barn, became a successful fruit-tree grower, as well as a successful farmer. After assisting each of his eight sons to a farm, he retired from business and gave the home farm over to his two youngest sons: Abraham and Henry. He remained in the old mansion-house until his death, on the 31st of August, 1852, aged seventy-seven years. The wife and mother died the year previous at the same age. Their remains now rest on the hill in Locust Grove cemetery, in the shadow of a beautiful granite monument.

Mr. Galley having passed the seventieth mile-stone in his journey through life, has retired from labor and given his farm over to his two sons: Allen and Ewing.

Great changes have been wrought within the past few years on the old homestead farm, due to the construction of the Pittsburg, McKeesport & Youghiogheny railroad. Where lofty corn, wheat and grass once grew, there now stand railroad buildings: round-house, shops, sidings, weigh-scales, offices, etc. Instead of a well-cultivated farm, can now be seen numerous railroad tracks covered with long trains of loaded coke cars, and a fair start for a town has sprung up, known by the name of "La Belle." Dickerson Run station is on a part of the Galley farm, and the branch railroad called by that name, intersects the main line near the center of the farm. Mr. Galley has advertised lots for sale, and offers to donate to any manufacturing company from five to twenty acres in case such company will erect works that will justify. In addition to his home farm, he now owns the adjoining farm, known as the Strickler fruit farm. Although he has passed his seventieth year, he is as active and walks as erect as many others do at forty-five or fifty. He has, within the past year, erected a new residence for himself and family, some two hundred yards distant from the old brick mansion, where he is spending his time in adding such improvements as he deems either necessary or ornamental.

Religiously, he adheres to the Christian religion, and, as he terms it, is a free man; free from all ecclesiastical combinations; free to read and interpret the Bible according to his own understanding and judgment. In his younger and less experienced days, he submitted to ecclesiastical intolerance by uniting with the Cumberland Presbyterian organization. He threw off that yoke of intolerance, and proclaimed himself free from ecclesiasticism, accountable only to God, and not to "man, or man-made societies," accepting the Bible as a sufficient directory to guide man from earth to heaven.

THOMAS BAIRD GRAHAM. Of Fayette county's citizens who have seen something of the "West" by travel and experience and endangerd their lives on Western fields of battle, one is Thomas Baird Graham. He was born July 5, 1833, on the Graham homestead in Menallen township, Fayette county, Pa., and is a son of Hugh and Margaret (Black) Graham.

His father, Hugh Graham, was an honored citizen of Fayette county, whose life is noticed in full in the sketch of Jacob B. Graham, in this volume.

Thomas Baird Graham was educated in common schools of Fayette county, in the primary schools of Jonesboro, Tenn., in the Fall Branch Academy of the same State, and spent two years in Emory and Henry College, Virginia.

On recommendation of Governor Johnson of Tennessee, he was appointed to a first-class clerkship under Hon. Thomas A. Hendricks, commissioner of the land office, and was a firm friend of that able statesman.

After two years' service as a clerk he went to Jonesboro, Tenn., where he read law with Chancellor Luckey, and graduated June 22, 1859, from the law school of Cumberland University, at Lebanon, Tenn.

He was practicing law at Chillicothe in Livingston county, Mo., when the late Civil War began, and was a third lieutenant and drill master in a regiment of State troops. He believed in "State's Rights," but not in "Secession," and while fighting in the Missouri State Guard, to drive Federal troops out of that State, yet he would not join the Confederate army. He fought at Carthage, was in the thickest of the fight at Wilson's Creek, and in the two battles at Lexington. After these last battles, he was appointed judge advocate of the Fourth Division of the Missouri State Guard, with the rank of lieutenant-colonel, for his bravery in the field. The rebels threatened to hang him for making a speech against uniting the State Guard with the Confederate army. He would not enter the Confederate service, and had only resisted what he considered the abuse of Federal power in his adopted State.

In 1862 he returned home, was admitted to the bar at Uniontown, but soon after went to Pittsburgh, where he practiced law until 1868, when his health becoming impaired he removed to Menallen township.

On October 6, 1887, he married Mary, daughter of Andrew and Elizabeth (Wood) Keys. They have one child: Keys Graham, born August 8, 1888. Mrs. Mary Graham is a California graduate, and was vice-principal of the public schools in Monongahela City. Mr. Graham and wife are persons of literary taste, and are members of Grace (Episcopal) church in Menallen. Mr. Graham, over the *nom de plume* of "Tempo," has many fugitive pieces, both of prose and poetry, published in various magazines and newspapers, which, if gathered together, would make a respectable volume. He thinks, though, that the life of a farmer is necessary to his health, and now resides at his country seat in Menallen, known as Selma.

JOHN B. GRANT, one of the industrious citizens of Everson, Tyrone township, is a son of William and Ann (Bailey) Grant, and was born in England.

William Grant was a native of Lincolnshire, England, born 1795, died 1840. He was a farmer, a good neighbor, and a member of the Church of England. His wife was born in 1800 and died in 1856.

John B. Grant was raised on a farm and received his education in the pay schools of England. In 1873 he emigrated to Pennsylvania, located at East Broad Top, Huntingdon county, and engaged in mining coal until 1876. In 1876 he attended the Centennial at Philadelphia; from thence he went to Europe, returned in 1879 to East Broad Top, and again engaged in mining. After nine months' labor in the mines, he with sixteen other miners were discharged for joining the Knights of Labor. He then removed to Everson, engaged in coal mining and has since continued to mine.

In 1866 he was married to Miss Martha, daughter of Robert Vance, of Glasgow, Scotland, and a member of the Methodist Episcopal church.

John B. Grant was treasurer of the Amalgamated Association during its three years' existence at Everson. He owns two large double houses in Everson, and is otherwise well fixed in life.

JACOB B. GRAHAM is of Scotch-Irish and German extraction, and was born on the Graham homestead in Menallen township, Fayette county, Pa., January 3, 1824. He is a son of Hugh and Margaret (Black) Graham.

Hugh Graham, a sturdy, honest, genial and determined Scotch-Irishman, was born May 2, 1796, near Londonderry, and came to Philadelphia in 1818. He had learned carpentering in all its branches, and here, in the employ of the celebrated Stephen Girard, he built some of the finest houses in that city. He walked from Philadelphia to Pittsburgh in six days, and from thence to Uniontown. In 1822 he married Miss Margaret, daughter of Jacob and Catherine Black. They had eight children: Catherine, dead; William, dead; Jacob B., Albert G., college graduate, editor and lawyer, died in Tennessee; Margaret, wife of L. B. Bowie, now dead; Thomas B. (see his sketch); Hugh, Jr., died at eighteen years of age; Jennie G., married William Thorndell, deceased. Mrs. Graham died in 1873. She was a daughter of Jacob Black, who settled in Fayette county about 1788, and owned large tracts of land in the county. He received a fine education in the universities of Germany, and was one of the best educated men in the county.

Hugh Graham had no superior as a workman in the county. He built the "Friendship Hill" mansion, and erected the fine residences of the late Judges Nathaniel Ewing and A. E. Wilson. He erected fine buildings throughout the county, and died May 19, 1879, aged eighty-three years. He was a great loss to Fayette county as a useful citizen, and to the Cumberland Presbyterian church as an efficient member. He was modest in demeanor, but firm as a rock in his convictions of what he thought to be right, of fine judgment, keen wit, genial disposition and unquestioned honesty, he was possessed of a very retentive memory, a vast store of information, he left behind him a character worthy of study and fit for imitation.

Jacob B. Graham received his education in the subscription schools of Menallen, and engaged in farming for a livelihood. April 3, 1856, he married Caroline, daughter of Jacob and Sallie Gaddis. They have had seven children: Margaret Jane, born March 8, 1857, married Enoch Rossel May 27, 1877, has two children, Grethel and Ottis; Adaline Emmerson, born March 18, 1862, married James P. McGill, M. D., of Chicago, December 29, 1886; Hugh, born January 2, 1865, dead; Harvey Gaddis, born April 19, 1868; Thomas E., born May 11, 1870; William B., born September 16, 1874. Mrs. Caroline Graham was a daughter of Jacob Gaddis, who was born on Redstone Creek in 1776, and married Sarah Coombs, born in 1803. They had ten children.

Jacob B. Graham owns six hundred acres of good farming land in Menallen and North Union townships, and devotes his time largely to the management of his farms.

He is a conservative democrat, and cast his first ballot for Franklin Pierce for president. He has been road supervisor and school director, and is one of the responsible citizens of Menallen.

JOHN HACKNEY, Jr. The Hackneys originally came from England, prior to the Revolutionary War, and were participants in the struggle for independence.

Aaron Hackney, the paternal grandfather of the subject of this sketch, was born in Berkeley county, Va., and came to Fayette county, in early life and settled near Heistersburg, Luzerne township.

John Hackney, Sr., was born in Luzerne township, March 20, 1783, was a farmer and married Lydia Sidwell, in 1812. They had eight children: James, Aaron, Amy, John, Hiram, Samuel, Lydia Jane and Hannah. Lydia (Sidwell) Hackney was born in Virginia in 1787, and was a daughter of James Sidwell, who was married to Amy Long, daughter of Dr. Owen Long, who lived near Winchester, Va.

Jno. Hackney, Jr., was born August 15, 1820, on the old Hackney farm, near New Salem, Menallen township, and on December 5, 1844 was married to Isabella Ebbert.

They had ten children: James, Hiram and Mary Frances, deceased, and Samuel, born July 9, 1851, is a farmer, is married to Anna M. Lickey, and lives in Harvey county, Kan.

Jno. William, born December 17, 1853, at home. Lydia Jane born June 29, 1856, is married to Aaron T. Porter, and lives in Lyon county, Kan., Alvin E., born October 8, 1858, at home. Eliza Ellen, born December 29, 1861, music teacher; Laura Bell, born May 4, 1864, and George Wyly, born June 21, 1867, and is now in the senior class in the Philadelphia College of Pharmacy, Philadelphia.

Mrs. Hackney's grandfather was George Ebbert, and was a merchant and had his store on Main street in the early history of Uniontown. Her father, James Ebbert, was born at Uniontown in 1792, and was a farmer and lived on the farm now owned by Jno. W. Carothers, near the County Home. Her maternal grandfather was a Frenchman by the name of Devieman, and settled near Oakland, Md.

Mr. Hackney was raised on the home farm and is one of the best farmers of the county. He was educated in the subscription schools of the neighborhood, and also at Aaron Hague and Richard Taylor's school. He is an ardent Republican and takes considerable interest in political matters. He was raised a Quaker, but with wife and entire family are members of the Cumberland Presbyterian church. Mr. Hackney is a conscientious, useful and intelligent member of society, and an honest and successful business man.

THOMAS HAGERTY, a successful trader and one of Fayette City's leading citizens, is a native of Fayette county. He is a son of William and Elizabeth (Johnson) Hagerty, and was born July 22, 1829.

His father, William Hagerty, was a native of Ireland, and with his mother emigrated to the United States at fourteen years of age and settled in Fayette county. His wife was Elizabeth Johnson, a descendant of one of the early families of Washington county.

Thomas Hagerty was reared on a farm, and obtained a fair education in the subscription schools of the neighborhood.

At the age of eighteen he was apprenticed to his elder brothers, Robert and Samuel Hagerty, to learn the trade of a stonemason. After three years' service as apprentice he engaged in business for himself, and has continued successfully at his trade up to the present time.

He was married March 18, 1851, to Miss Rizpah Fell, of Westmoreland county. They had ten children: Linda, Omer E., Elizabeth, Mina, Rena, Ollie, Ella and three who died in infancy. Mrs. Hagerty died in July, 1874.

Two years later Mr. Hagerty again married; his second wife was Mrs. Elizabeth Bake, whose maiden name was Jones. They have two children: Bertha and Alva. Mrs. Elizabeth Hagerty is a daughter of Samuel Jones, of Westmoreland county. Her first husband was John M. Bake (deceased). By him she had two children: Edgar J. and Frank L., both married, the former living in Fayette and the latter in Westmoreland county.

Mr. Hagerty owns a comfortable home, and twenty-two acres of well-improved land, on which he has opened a coal mine.

He has held the ordinary offices of the borough, and discharged their duties in a satisfactory manner.

JAMES HAMER, an enterprising citizen and a well-known manufacturer of woolen goods, was born in England February 3, 1804. He is a son of James and Alice (Bingham) Hamer, both natives of England.

James Hamer was an operative for three years in English woolen factories, and fully mastered all the intricacies of manufacturing woolen goods. At twenty-three years of age he emigrated to America, and landed at Philadelphia in 1827. In that city and vicinity he found employment for some time in various woolen factories, but he saw no opportunity for starting in business for himself, and concluded to still better his condition by pushing westward. Starting on foot, he arrived in Fayette county, after a journey of fourteen days. He went to Redstone, where he introduced fabric-weaving; afterward associated himself with James and Ephraim Pilling, and engaged in the manufacture of woolen cloths at Cook's mills. In 1835 he removed to Little Redstone, and five years later became a resident of Fayette City. He here erected, at a cost of $1,600, the Fayette City Woolen Factory, which he has owned and operated until the present time. He manufactures principally woolen goods and yarns for the local trade. The equipments of the factory are three carding machines, one spinning-jack and 150 spindles.

Mr. Hamer was married to Miss Elizabeth daughter of Thomas Cook, a prominent citizen of Redstone township. They are the parents of six children: Mary, Ellen (dead), Alice, Sarah, Elizabeth and Rachel R. (dead). Mrs. Hamer died July 14, 1878.

In 1840 Mr. Hamer purchased a valuable farm, at a cost of $7,000, which he now owns and has greatly improved. He is a consistent and useful member of the Christian church. He is a man who has won respect by a long life of hard and honest labor.

CLARK B. HANEY, a gallant survivor of the late Civil War, was born on the William Moore farm in Menallen township, Fayette county, Pa.

His father, John Haney, was born on the old original Haney farm in German township, October 6, 1806, and died in 1884. The grandfather of C. B. Haney was also born on the same farm.

C. B. Haney's great-grandfather, William Haney, was the founder of the Haney family in Fayette county. C. B. Haney's mother, Ann Moss, daughter of Jacob Moss, was born in German township, July 13, 1807. She was married to John Haney in 1832. Jacob Moss was born in German township, Fayette county, Pa., in 1775.

Joseph, the father of Jacob Moss, settled in Fayette county. C. B. Haney is one of the substantial farmers of Menallen township, and was a Union soldier.

JOHN W. HARMONY was born in Brownsville, Fayette county, Pa., January 26, 1856. When he was four years of age his parents removed to Kent, Franklin county, Ohio, but soon returned to Pennsylvania, locating at Albany; leaving that place in 1864, they came to Fayette City. He was educated in the common schools, and engaged in clerking until 1875. He was with J. L. Cooper, Colvin, Atwell & Co. of Pittsburgh for two years, and G. W. Maxwell & Co., coal dealers of Washington county, Pa. In 1875 he engaged in glass cutting, and has continued in that business to the present time. He is a member of the following orders: Mystic Chain, Royal Arcanum, and J. O. of A. M.

Mr. Harmony was united in marriage December 27, 1882, to Miss Mollie E. Shearer, daughter of Daniel M. Shearer, a native of Jefferson township, and whose people were natives of Ohio. Their union has been blessed with two children: Raymond D. and Stella.

John W. Harmony is one of the enterprising young men of Fayette county. He was a good clerk, is a skillful workman, and is interested in whatever is for the weal of Fayette City.

ELIAS HATFIELD comes of a widely known and highly respected family of Fayette county, and his life is adding additional luster to the many good qualities of his worthy ancestors. He is a son of Samuel and Rebecca (Vance) Hatfield, and was born in South Union township, Fayette county, Pa., February 1, 1831.

Samuel Hatfield was born in Georges township, Fayette county, Pa., December 6, 1797. He married Miss Rebecca Vance, they removed to South Union township, where they lived for many years and raised a family of eleven children, namely: Sarah Jane, born July 25, 1821, died March, 1886; Lydia Ann, born November 7, 1822, died October 25, 1885; Rachel, born April 11, 1824, died March 25, 1861; Lucinda, born February 7, ——, died October 26, 1852; William Vance, born December 31, 1827, died September —, 1856; Elias (subject), born February 1, 1831; Freeman Lindsay, born February 3, 1833, died November 28, 1865; Samuel, Jr., born November 5, 1834, living in Uniontown; Minton, born October 24, 1836, living in Macomb, Ill.; Rebecca, born January 3, 1840, living in Grand Ridge, Ill.; Mary Elizabeth, December 20, 1843, living in Neb. Mrs. Rebecca (Vance) Hatfield was born in 1802 and died in 1862, and was a daughter of William Vance of Georges township, and a member of Great Bethel Regular Baptist church of Uniontown.

Samuel Hatfield was a Baptist, and for many years a deacon in the church to which his wife belonged, with his eleven children, who united at an early age. He removed to McDonough county, Ill., in the spring of 1869, and died there August 25, 1877, in the eightieth year of his age. He was a good neighbor, an exemplary church member, and a highly respected citizen.

Elias Hatfield (grandfather) was born March 11, 1760, and married Ann Lindsay, who was born in 1767. He died in 1839, aged seventy-nine years, one month and seventeen days, and she followed him into the dreamless sleep September 21, 1852. They removed to Georges township over a hundred years ago, and among the early settlers were held in high esteem.

William Hatfield (great-grandfather) was born in New Jersey, December 28, 1736, and married Ann Wright who died in 1762. He married for his second wife Sarah Kindall, who died in 1799. He raised a family of eleven children, of which our subject's grandfather was a son of the first wife.

William Hatfield's father, Abraham Hatfield, Jr., was born in New Jersey in 1695, he and his wife Margaret both died in 1745, leaving nine children. His father was Abraham Hatfield, Sr., who was a son of Matthias Hatfield, and was born at Elizabethtown, N. J. in 1760, and died in 1806, leaving four sons.

Matthias Hatfield was an intelligent Scotchman, who left his native land and settled in Elizabethtown, N. J., in 1665, where he died in December, 1687, leaving three sons. From him are descended the Hatfields of Fayette county.

Elias Hatfield, the subject of this sketch, attended several common schools in the Hatfield school house, and was enrolled for one term in 1844, as a student of Madison college. He taught five terms of school in South Union township, one term was in the Hatfield school house, which was his home district.

On the 15th of March, 1851, he went west by boat, to Allamakee county, Iowa, where he engaged in farming.

On April 15, 1853, he married Miss Mary A. Beeman, who was born in Vermont, November 20, 1836. They had four children: Orton Monroe, Emma Jane, who married William J. Holstine in 1876; Elsie Rebecca and Henry Cullen. The latter two died in infancy, and the mother died on the 1st of August, 1868.

In November, 1868, he brought his children back to Fayette county, and remained on a visit at the old homestead until March 1, 1869, when he bought a half interest in the store of the late James M. Dixon, at Farmington.

On the 25th of July, 1869, he married, a second time, Miss Mary E. Dixon, daughter of his senior partner, and who was born January 20, 1836. To this union one child was born: Clara Addie, now ten years of age.

In 1870 the firm of Dixon & Hatfield dissolved. Mr Dixon purchased the Braddock Grave farm, and Mr. Hatfield removed to Fandon, McDonough county, Ill., and engaged in the mercantile business. In 1870, there being no republican in the village, he was appointed postmaster. In 1876 he exchanged his store and town property, with his brother Minton, for a farm, on which Mr. and Mrs. W. J. Holstine now reside.

After this exchange he returned to Fayette county and remained with his father-in-law, J. M. Dixon, until the latter died, December 31, 1876.

From 1877 to 1883 he was engaged in the mercantile business at Searight. In 1883 he removed to New Salem, purchased some valuable property and began merchandising, being to-day one of the most prosperous and successful merchants in the county.

He is a member of Ft. Necessity lodge, No. 254, I. O. O. F.

He is a democrat, and has never missed an election since 1852, when he cast his first vote. In November, 1887, he was elected commissioner of Fayette county, for three years. He united with the Baptist church over forty years ago.

DANIEL HARMONY, JR., was born in Mapleton, Greene county, Pa., July 13, 1818. At fifteen years of age he began clerking and later engaged in glass-blowing at Fayette City. Since 1865, has been in the mercantile business, and for the last twelve years has been superintendent of the Noroon Glass Works.

His father, Daniel Harmony, Sr., whose father came from Germany, was a native of Berks county, Pa., and married Miss Anna Hathaway.

Daniel Harmony, Jr., was married in 1846, to Miss Rebecca T., daughter of James McClain who settled many years ago near Uniontown. They have had nine children, five of whom are living.

He has always been an advocate of education, and has fairly educated his children, two of whom are teachers.

He belongs to no secret order, has never been an office seeker, and is one of the good and substantial men of Fayette City. He has in his possession the last letter written by President W. H. Harrison.

BENJAMIN W. HAZEN. The Hazen family of this country, on the paternal side, is of New England extraction. Emigrant Edward Hazen, the great ancestor, went to Rawley, Mass., as early as 1649; one tradition says from Scotland, another from England, where children were born, some of whom settled at Lyme, Conn. John Hazen, whose descendants are numerous, was born in Boxford, Mass., February 21, 1710. His brother Thomas, the great grandfather of the present generation of the Hazens in Fayette county, was born at Lyme, Conn., February 12, 1722 or 1723. He removed to New Jersey, where Thomas, Aaron, Ezekiel, Joshua, Moses, Abraham and David were born. The latter (David) was the pioneer of the Hazens of Fayette county, Pa., and was born February 6, 1770. He married December 6, 1795, Elcy Wintermute, born June 17, 1776, of New Jersey. From this union were born: George W., September 2, 1796; Abraham, August 22, 1798; Thomas, October 20, 1800; Elizabeth, November 20, 1802; Mary Ann, February 14, 1805; Clarissa, October 15, 1807; Elcy, July 9, 1810; David, March 5, 1814, and Sarah, February 25, 1818.

With his wife and, at that time (about 1808), six children, David Hazen took up his tedious journey by wagon across the mountains from Sussex county, N. J., to seek a home on Big Redstone, in Fayette county, Pa. He purchased a farm in Franklin township, in 1809, and occupied it until his death, November 11, 1848. His wife, Elcy, died May 3, 1850.

The members of this family are all dead except Sarah, widow of the late Henry Cook, Esq., who resides with her youngest daughter, Clarissa H. Cook, on the old home farm now owned by her son David H., and stepson, John A. Cook.

Of David Hazen's family, George W. married Nancy Bowman, of Franklin township, and moved to a farm in Belmont county, Ohio, where some of his family still reside. The eldest son, David, a lawyer by profession, lives in Iowa. Thomas, third in the family, married Phebe Cope, sister of ex-Sheriff Eli Cope, and Pierson Cope, of Perry township. She survives her husband, and lives in Vanderbilt, Pa. Eli C. is the only one of their children living. A grandson, Thomas H. Hazen, owns and tills a farm in Jefferson township. Elizabeth married Jacob Reicheneker, of Brownsville. Mary Ann married Joseph Huston, of Tyrone township, of whose family Mrs. James Cochran and John Huston, of Dawson, Pa., and Mrs. Phebe Martin, of Perry township, are the only survivors. Clarissa remained single, and died a few years ago in Brownsville. Eley and David died young.

Abraham, the second son of David Hazen, was born in New Jersey, and came with the family to Fayette county when about ten years old. March 24, 1824, he married Dorcas Downs, of Redstone township; she was born November 4, 1802. Abraham was a blacksmith by trade, as was his father, but chose farming as his occupation, and tilled his father's farm until April, 1846, when he purchased the farm, near by, on Crabapple Run, now owned and occupied by his sons, George and Benjamin W., together with subsequent purchases. Abraham Hazen died October 7, 1870, and his wife Dorcas, April 15, 1876. They raised a family of ten children: Moses, the oldest, was a stone-cutter by trade, but subsequently dealt in stock, and for several years was engaged in farming. He married Caroline Smith, of Franklin township, August 24, 1854. In 1856 he was elected county auditor, but served only for one year. He died May 2, 1857, leaving two children: Dorcas, now the wife of William Henshaw, of South Union township, and James W. Hazen, who married a daughter of Levi Crossland of Uniontown, and now lives in Hazelwood Pa.

William, second son, a farmer, married Eliza A. Hill, of Washington county, Pa., November 5, 1860, and now lives in Beallsville, that county. He was elected county auditor of Fayette county in 1857, and served the term; he was also elected and served a term as county commissioner of Washington county, from January, 1876, to January, 1879. His only child, Alpha, married Dr. Frye and lives in the same town.

George, another son, lives in Franklin township, and is a successful farmer and stock-raiser. His first wife, Mary J. Deyarmon, daughter of the late David Deyarmon, Esq., of Jefferson township, died January 2, 1875. Three children are living: Dorcas, Belle and Lizzie, all of whom are married. George married again, this time Caroline C. Carson, of Washington county, Pa., April 17, 1880. Elizabeth, oldest daughter, died in 1833, while young. Mariah, the second daughter, married Jonathan Sharpless, November 17, 1855, grandson of Jonathan Sharpless, Sr., who came from Philadelphia, and was among the early settlers of Fayette county. They have a family and live in Williams county, Ohio.

Thomas, another son, lived on the home farm until 1883, when he sold out to his brothers George and Benjamin, and now makes his home in Uniontown. He was elected county commissioner in 1878, and served the term with credit to himself and the people of the county. He was connected with the *Genius of Liberty* for over four years, retiring March 1, 1889.

Benjamin W., another son, lives on the home farm on Crabapple Run, and is among the thrifty farmers and stock-raisers of the county. He married Edith S. Piersol, daughter of James Piersol, now dead, of Perry township, October 30, 1862; her grandfather, William Piersol, was of Welsh descent, and came from Chester county, Pa., to Perry township, in 1784. They have five children: James P., Annette, Ella, Wilford (Will) and Leora.

David, the youngest son of Abraham Hazen's family, died in 1854, while young.

Harriet married James, only son of Watson Murphy, of Franklin township. They live on a farm near the home place and have a number of children, some of whom are grown.

Phebe, the youngest of the family, married John Arnold in 1881. They have a nice home near Vanderbilt, Pa.

GEORGE W. HESS was born April 22, 1836, in German township, near the town of New Salem. He is a great-grandson of Peter and Susanna Hess, who were among the first settlers west of the Allegheny mountains, having come from Lancaster county, Pa. His grandfather, George Hess, was born in Fayette county, Pa., in 1790. In 1811 he married Mary Fuller, daughter of Daniel Fuller. He died October 21, 1858, leaving six children, of whom John was the oldest.

John Hess, the father of the subject of this sketch, was born February 6, 1812, in Menallen township, Fayette county Pa. In 1834 he married Amanda Offord, daughter of Brooks Offord of Greene county, Pa. He was an extensive farmer, and by his industry and business tact he became one of the wealthiest farmers in the county. He died October 17, 1882, leaving a wife and nine children: George W., Mary A., Eliza J., Clark R., Sarah E., Elvira, John F., Evans W. and Amanda L.

George W. Hess, January 6, 1857, married Mary L. Grove, oldest daughter of Harvey and Elizabeth Grove of German township. He located on a farm in Menallen township near the town of New Salem, where he has since resided. While attending to his farm he has engaged in dealing in cattle, sheep and wool, and has been successful in all his undertakings. His excellent business qualifications, temperate habits and moral principles have recommended him to the confidence of his neighbors, and in consequence he has been in constant demand as executor, administrator, assignee, guardian and all the offices and positions where good management and trustworthiness are essentials. Frequently he has been chosen as arbitrator in settling disputes, and almost universally has met with success in such cases, as he has been in favor of the amicable settlement of disputes of neighbors. Having been so successful in the management of his own affairs, he was made a director of the First National Bank of Uniontown in 1888, which position he yet holds.

In politics he has ever been a stanch republican from principle, being elected auditor of the county in 1874. Owing to his success in business he has amassed considerable wealth, owning valuable real and personal property in Menallen and German townships and Uniontown. He has two children, Laura, who, on September 17, 1885, married Monroe Hopwood, Esq., a prominent young lawyer of Uniontown, and John E. Hess, who obtained a good common school education, and remains at home with his parents. He has been trained in business principles and is following in the footsteps of his father. He takes an active part in literary and school work, and for some years has held the office of school director. Having been raised a republican, he is one of the active workers of his party.

The Hess family is of German origin, but for two centuries have been Americans. It is a family that possesses many sterling qualities of character, and is one of the substantial and influential families of Fayette county.

HARVEY HENDERSON was born March 11, 1819, about thirteen miles south of Erie, Venango township, Erie county, Pa. He is of Scotch-Irish descent. His education—which was a limited one—was obtained principally in the schools of Dunbar township.

He is a republican in his political faith,

but he has never sought or held a public office. In religion he is a Methodist.

He has been twice married. His first wife, Eliza Harris, was a daughter of Jacob Harris, of near Perryopolis, by whom he had twelve children: Rebecca Ann, born February 28, 1842, died May 16, 1842; Jacob, born March 14, 1843, died February 21, 1861; David, born January 16, 1845; Joseph, born May 30, 1847, died July 12, 1847; Steward S., born May 27, 1848; Syntha, born March 23, 1851, died August 21, 1851; Sarah E. (Long), born November 10, 1852, died June 24, 1874; Isaac, born August 29, 1855; Thomas S., born March 26, 1857; Samuel, born May 30, 1859, died May 31, 1859; Charles C., born January 5, 1860, died December 22, 1869, and Lincoln, born January 21, 1864. His first wife died March 12, 1870, aged fifty years.

On February 8, 1872, he married his second wife, Mary Amanda Strickler, a daughter of Jacob Strickler, of Perryopolis.

Harvey Henderson is a farmer, stock and real estate broker, which he has followed since he became of age. He has always been successful in his business undertakings, and has bought and sold a great deal of land in this county.

When he began life for himself he owned but fifty-nine acres of inferior land, which has been willed to him by his father. Some seven or eight years afterward he was married.

With strict attention to business, and a clear conception of how to make money, he has amassed sufficient wealth to purchase nearly 400 acres of good farming land, situated in Franklin and Dunbar townships. He has also purchased for each of his five boys 160 acres of fine farming land in Knox and Warren counties, Ill. For one lot he paid $10,000, for another $9,000, and for the other three $8,700 each. Besides this he owns 240 acres in one tract in Knox county, Ill., crossed by the Rockford, Rock Island & St. Louis Railroad, which cost him $19,325. He also owns forty acres of land in Warren county, Ill., valued at $4,000. All of this western land is underlaid by a seven-foot vein of bituminous coal.

Stewart Henderson, the father of Harvey, was born in County Derry, Ireland, about forty miles from Dublin. He came to this country when about eighteen years old, in 1772, with but one shilling in his pocket. He afterwards owned over five hundred acres of land near East Leisenring.

He married Miss Ann Hunt, the daughter of Jacob Hunt, of Fayette county. They have the following children: Nancy, Thomas, Stewart, Isaac, Alexander, Harvey, David, Jacob, Joseph and Mary Ann. Of these, Thomas, Nancy, Stewart, Jacob and Joseph are dead.

Jacob Hunt, maternal grandfather of Mr. Henderson, married Nancy Delaney, and they had five children: Isaac, the father of William Hunt, silversmith of Uniontown; Olive, Elizabeth, Kate and Ann.

AMOS HIXON, a farmer of Lower Tyrone township, Fayette county, Pa., is the son of Moses and Bridget (Dogan) Hixon.

Moses Hixon, the father of Amos Hixon, was a native of East Huntington township, Westmoreland, Pa., where he lived all of his life on a farm and died in 1877, aged eighty-six years. He was married in that township to Miss Bridget Dogan, born and raised in the same township, and died.

Joseph Hixon, grandfather of Amos, was also a native of East Huntington township, Westmoreland county, Pa., where he lived and died a farmer.

Amos Hixon was born in East Huntington township, Westmoreland county, Pa., June 27, 1835, brought up on a farm, and attended the common schools of the township. On September 1, 1859, he was married to Miss Elizabeth Freed, daughter of Peter Freed. The latter born in Bullskin township and lived many years in Lower Tyrone township, on the farm at present owned and occupied by his son-in-law. He died in 1861, at fifty years of age. From this marriage were born twelve children: Annie E., Mary B., Clark F., Joseph F., Albert S., Flora, Katie, Freed, Willie, May, Odie and Lizzie. Annie E. is married to H. R. Ober and living in Tyrone township; Mary B. is married to James L. Strickler and lives in Dawson borough; the rest are all unmarried. The twelve children are all living except Albert S., who died January 30, 1889.

In 1862 Mr. Hixon removed to Fayette county, and located upon the farm where he now resides; it contains 125 acres of moderate land well improved. His wife was born on this farm in 1837.

Amos Hixon is a democrat, has served several times as school director in his township, and as auditor, tax collector, supervisor, assessor and on the election board.

WILLIAM H. HOPWOOD, M. D., a son of William and Eleanor (Hudson) Hopwood was born in the town of Monroe, Fayette county, Pa., October 20, 1850. Few are the families who can trace their lineal history so far back as the Hopwoods. In 1066, when William the Conqueror invaded England and won the kingdom at the battle of Hastings, the De Hopwoods were with him. The manor of Middleton was held by the De Hopwoods at an early date after the conquest. In the northern portion of the churchyard of the manor of Middleton is a monument erected to the Hopwood family. It is so old that the inscriptions are somewhat indistinct. Robert de Hopwood was rector of the church of Middleton from 1421 to 1457. The Hopwood chapel is enclosed with rails of the period of the Restoration and contains the Kiscina and a mural monument to Robert Gregg Hopwood, of Hopwood Hall. It was built by John Hopwood in the reign of Henry VIII., soon after 1500. About this time the Norman-French prefix de was elided from the name. About 1700, Moses Hopwood, the great-great-grandfather of W. H. Hopwood, M. D., came to America from England and settled in Virginia. He was then a young man and soon after coming he married a most estimable Virginia lady. Of this union were born fourteen children, eleven being sons. The father had received superior literary training in England and was remarkably religious, and a member of the Church of England. He was the head of the family in America. His son John Hopwood was born in 1745, and was the great-grandfather of William H. Hopwood, M. D. He married into the family of Governor Humphreys, of Virginia, and six children were born, five daughters and one son. He removed from Stafford county, Va., to Pennsylvania, soon after the close of the War of 1776. Before moving he liberated his slaves, but some of them followed him to his new home. His son, Moses Hopwood, was educated at old Cannonsburg College, Pennsylvania, and in 1795 was married to Hannah, daughter of Colonel Thomas Gaddis, so prominent in the early history of Western Pennsylvania. John Hopwood, like Colonel Gaddis, had been in the Revolutionary War. John Hopwood had been one of General Washington's aids, and was by him selected to choose a suitable site for winter quarters for the continental army, which duty he performed and then acted as escort in conducting them to their quarters. The son, Moses Hopwood, was born at Dumfries, Va., April 22, 1772, and died in Hopwood, March 21, 1857. Moses and Hannah

(Gaddis) Hopwood had fourteen children, ten sons and four daughters. One of these sons, William Hopwood, who died August 3, 1889, at the age of eighty-two, was the father of William H. Hopwood, M. D. In 1838 he married Eleanor, daughter of George Hudson, of Huntingdon county, Pa. She was a woman of great worth of character and a devoted mother. He was an architect and builder by profession. He possessed excellent business qualifications, and acquired a valuable estate. For many years he was a director of the First National Bank of Uniontown. Intellectually and morally he was of a high standard. To William and Eleanor (Hudson) Hopwood were born seven children, five boys and two girls. Walter died in youth. Thomas Hudson Hopwood served through the Civil War of 1861–65, and received a brevet for bravery. He was a major in the regular army until he died from injuries received in the war. In 1865 he married Sarah, daughter of General James G. Anthony, and niece of United States Senator H. B. Anthony, of Rhode Island. Major Hopwood died December 31, 1867. Dr. William H. Hopwood has a sister, Mrs. Jennie H. Fenner, living in Providence, Rhode Island, and another sister, Miss Julia E. Hopwood, of Uniontown, Pa. George Hopwood, a brother, is a prominent and leading citizen of South Union township, and Monroe Hopwood, another brother, is a rising young attorney-at-law of the Uniontown bar. The Hopwoods have been tall and powerfully muscular men. No greater athletes have ever lived in Western Pennsylvania than some of the members of this family. They have had fair complexions and blue eyes with few exceptions. William H. Hopwood, the subject of this sketch, received his first education at Hatfield's school house, in South Union township. After leaving the common school, he attended Madison College, at Uniontown, Mount Union College, Ohio, and after completing his literary training, he read medicine under that eminent physician, Smith Fuller, M. D., and entered the medical department of the University of Michigan in the class of 1875. Completing the prescribed course there, he attended Jefferson Medical College at Philadelphia, and graduated with honor from that celebrated institution in the class of 1877. He located at Upper Middletown on the P. V. & C. Ry., five miles below Uniontown, and his untiring energy and great skill have placed him among the most eminent physicians and surgeons in Fayette county. His practive is large and remunerative, and he enjoys the highest esteem of all who know him. Through purchase and inheritance, he has acquired valuable possessions, and is ever free to give to charitable and religious objects. He is a member of the Laurel Hill Presbyterian church. He has been connected with the Fayette County Medical Society for a number of years, and is ever willing to contribute his share in advancing the medical, scientific and material interests of his native county. He is a young man who has been the arbiter of his own good fortune, and his labor and talents have wrought out marked success, and assure for him an unusually bright future.

LACY HIBBS was born November 7, 1826, in Redstone township, Fayette county, Pa., on the old Hibbs' farm where he was raised, and attended schools of the township. Educational advantages were quite limited in those days, and the course of study was even more so. The first business he followed was that of farming in North Union township, and has continued at that business all of his life and now owns one hundred and twenty-six acres of land near Scarights in Menallen township.

He is a member of the Presbyterian

church of New Salem, and his wife and family are also members of the same church. He is an exemplary man and a good citizen, and is firm in the democratic faith. He was elected poorhouse director in 1868.

His first wife was Mary Margaret Poundstone, a daughter of Philip Poundstone of German township. They had two children: Eunice Violet, born in 1852, living with her father, and John Newton, born June 9, 1859, married Lizzie Ball and has one child: Earnest. His second wife was Mrs.' Harriet A. Kerr, they were married March 8, 1866. They have one child: Olive, born May 28, 1869, who is a teacher. Mrs. Hibbs was the daughter of Samuel Cochran, born in Fayette county, in 1788, and Elizabeth Porter his wife, a daughter of John Porter who lived near Dunlap's creek. Her maternal grandmother was Margaret Baird.

Lacy Hibbs is the son of John and Jane (Finley) Hibbs, who were married April 12, 1821. John Hibbs was born January 1, 1791, and died January 14, 1881. Jane Finley was born June 7, 1802 (for her family ancestry, see sketch of Ebenezer Finley). Lacy Hibbs, grandfather of subject of sketch, was born in 1768, in Cumberland county, Pa., afterwards Bedford county, then Westmoreland, now Greene. He married Sarah Craft, a member of the Fayette county Crafts.

ANTONY HUGG, one of Belle Vernon's reliable citizens, and by travel has seen something of life in the old and new world, was born March 5, 1841, in the Department of the Loire, France. He is a son of John Baptiste and Victoire (Louvet) Hugg, both natives of France.

John Baptiste Hugg was an excellent glassblower, and had no trouble in finding employment in England and in France. He was a consistent member of the Roman Catholic church. His wife's people were interested in the glass manufacturing.

Antony Hugg was educated in the boarding and high schools of France. He alternately resided in France and England until fourteen years of age, when he entered an English glass works under his father, where he remained three years. At the age of seventeen years he went to Spain, but remained only eight months, on account of the natives of that country refusing to let him finish his trade. He then returned to England and completed his trade of glassblower.

Concluding to seek his fortune in the western hemisphere, he sailed for New York August 11, 1865, where he landed on the 25th of the same month. He pursued his trade at Boston and Berkshire, Mass., Bernard's Bay, N. Y. and at New Albany, Ind. In 1870 he removed from Indiana to Belle Vernon, where he has successfully continued up to the present time at this trade.

When twenty-three years of age he married Miss Elizabeth, daughter of Peter and Margaret Kelly, natives of Ireland. They had five children: John, born in 1864; Margaret E., born in 1865, on shipboard; Victoria, 1867, Massachusetts; Elizabeth, 1868, New York; Matilda, 1869, Indiana (deceased). Margaret, Victoria and Elizabeth are married and reside in Belle Vernon.

His wife died in New Albany. He married, in 1870, for his second wife Miss Elizabeth J. Wilkinson of that place. By his last marriage he has two children: Ida May, born in 1871, and Ernestine B., born in 1873.

Mr. Hugg is a member of the Sons of Temperance, Royal Arcanum and the Independent Order of Odd Fellows. At one time in England he belonged to the Foresters.

He and his family are Protestants in religious belief. He has derived a valuable experience from his extended travels, and is an honest and upright citizen.

JOSEPH HUTCHINSON was born near the Round Hill church, Elizabeth township, Allegheny county, Pa., March 21, 1828. His father, John, was born in New Jersey, and came to Pennsylvania with his father, Joseph Hutchinson. He afterwards, on his return East, died from the effects of the measles. His wife, Ann Bennett, who lived to be 105 years of age, was a daughter of a captain of the War of the Revolution. The Bennetts were a most remarkable people for their longevity and physical endurance, and were noted for their abstemious and temperate habits. John Bennett, a brother of Mrs. Ann Hutchinson, was a soldier under General Markle in the War of 1812-15.

The Hutchinsons are of English stock. John Hutchinson was a leading farmer and speculator of Allegheny and later of Westmoreland county, Pa.

Joseph Hutchinson, whose name heads this sketch, was married March 21, 1849, to Ann E., a daughter of John McDonal, of Sewickly township, Westmoreland county, Pa. (the great-grandfather of the latter was one of the heroes of the Revolution), and has had seven children, of whom two are dead: John M., a well-driller by occupation, was born in 1850; Margaret Jane, now the wife of Amos Shrum, formerly of Westmoreland county; Travilo W. (deceased); Elizabeth, wife of Harvey Knox; Huldah Belle (deceased); H. D. and Minnie B.

Joseph Hutchinson worked on the farm until he learned the blacksmith trade, and has since worked at this and the oil-drilling business. He removed and located in Menallen township in 1882.

HIRAM BENTON JACKSON, an industrious and successful farmer, of Menallen, is a son of Zadock and Lydia (Woodward) Jackson, and was born on the Jackson farm in Menallen township, Fayette county, Pa., October 8, 1855.

Zadock Jackson, of Irish extraction, was born in Menallen township in 1805 and died May 7, 1861. His father, Robt. Jackson, settled in 1790 on the John Dearth farm. Zadock Jackson married Miss Lydia Woodward. They had eight children, three of whom are living: Robert, Hiram B. and Elizabeth, wife of Ewing Searight. Mrs. Jackson was born August 17, 1811, and resides at New Salem. Her father, Caleb Woodward moved from Chester county, at an early day and was a noted and skilled blacksmith whose good work secured him all the custom of the country for nine miles around. He was very pious and well beloved by all who knew him.

Hiram B. Jackson was reared on a farm, was educated in the common schools, Uniontown public schools and Waynesburg College. Leaving school, he engaged successfully in his present business of farming and stock raising. He has been married three times. His first wife was Miss Ellen, daughter of Lorenzo Dow and Margaret (Craft) Burnsworth, the former, a religious man and a farmer, of Stewart township, the latter a daughter of John S. Craft, of Redstone township. Mrs. Jackson died February 16, 1886, and left three children: Lydia, born December 12, 1882; Lyman R., born February 9, 1884, and William Zadock Hopwood Jackson, born January 23, 1885. He was again married November 16, 1887, to Mrs. Nannie (Fouch) Jacobs, widow of William Jacobs and daughter of Charles Fouch, of South Union. The second wife died August 6, 1889. September 10, 1889, Mr. Jackson married for his third wife, Miss Sophronia, daughter of Nelson and Eliza Eagle. Mrs. Eagle resides in Merrittstown.

Hiram B. Jackson owns a well improved farm which is heavily underlaid with coal and limestone. He is a democrat, delights in the success of his party and was elected township auditor but declined to serve. He is a member of Ft. Necessity Lodge No. 254, I. O. O. F. at Uniontown. He is well situated to enjoy life and its substantial comforts. In religious views he is favorable to the doctrines and practices of the Christian or Disciple church.

Mr. Jackson is in the prime of manhood and has the respect and esteem of the community in which he resides.

TAYLOR JEFFRIES, one of Menallen township's reliable farmers, was born on the homestead farm, Menallen township, Fayette county, Pa., December 22, 1843, and is a son of Taylor and Jane (Buchanan) Jeffries.

His grandfather, Elias Jeffries, was born in Chester county, Pa.; came to Menallen about 1800, and settled on the farm now owned by Taylor Jeffries. His wife was Elizabeth Woodward, of Chester county, Pa.

His father, Taylor Jeffries, Sr., was born March 9, 1806, married Miss Jane, daughter of Christopher Buchanan, a native of Ireland. He was a farmer of Menallen, where he died June 2, 1888.

Taylor Jeffries was reared on the farm where he was born, and was educated in the common schools. One of his old teachers was Lewis Hess. Leaving school, he devoted himself to farming, and has continued successfully in that business up to the present time. On February 13, 1873, he married Miss Martha, daughter of Samuel Frederick. Their union has been blessed with four children, of whom two are living: Taylor, Jr., born April 20, 1878, and Elmer W., born February 24, 1881.

Taylor Jeffries is a democrat; has served as central committee-man of his township, and cast his first vote for Seymour and Blair, in 1868. He owns the old homestead farm, is deeply interested in whatever benefits farming, and is a member of the Cumberland Presbyterian church, at New Salem.

CHRISTIAN KECK, a successful merchant of Everson, was born at Lidergengin, Sule county, Wurtemberg, Germany, September 13, 1837 and is a son of Christian and Rosina (Swartz) Keck, the former a farmer and weaver, who came to Westmoreland county in 1867, and died October 10, 1881, aged seventy-five years; the latter died in Germany in 1855, aged forty-six years.

Christian Keck was a farmer's son and enjoyed for eight years the privileges of the fine system of the German primary schools, and at intervals he worked on the farm. He emigrated to the United States in 1865, landing in New York, November 29th, locating at Paintersville in Westmoreland county, December 3d, of the same year. He engaged in salt boiling until April 12, 1870, when he removed to Morgan Station, Fayette county, and worked at the coke-works of the Morgan mines for Col. Sydney Morgan and H. C. Frick until August 12, 1878, and then entered the service of Keister and Cochran, at the Summit mines, remaining with them until February, 1879, when he took sick and was rendered unfit for labor during the remainder of that year. In 1880 he engaged in the grocery business at Scottdale, but in the following year came to Everson and engaged in the general mercantile business at which he has continued successfully up to the present time. He owns his store-room and residence and has built up a splendid trade.

On October 16, 1866, he was married to Miss Annie Hunker, a native of Germany. They have three children: Annie U., Christian M., clerk for his uncle, Leonard Keck at Greensburg, and Fred L.

He has two brothers in the mercantile business; Leonard the proprietor of four stores in Greensburg and J. M. Keck, located at Kecksburg, Westmoreland county, Pa. Christian Keck is an ardent democrat, and is always interested in the success of that party. He is a consistent member of the German Lutheran church, and by his honest, energetic and persistent labor, has made his business life a success.

JOHN W. KENNEDY, the popular proprietor of the leading house at Everson, is a son of John and Julia (Leaky) Kennedy, and was born in Wales, June 29, 1858.

John Kennedy of Limerick, Ireland, married Julia Leaky, of Cork, and removed to Wales. From there he emigrated in 1866 to Huntingdon county, Pa., where he remained for twelve years. In 1878, he removed to Upper Tyrone township, and located at Everson, his present place of residence.

John W. Kennedy came with his parents to Huntingdon county, Pa., where he received a good education in the schools of that county. In May, 1881, he engaged in the hotel business at Everson. In two years his patronage became so large as to necessitate larger buildings than he possessed for the accommodation of the traveling public and in order to meet this want he erected his present fine hotel in 1883. This hotel is located at the corner of Brown and Railroad streets, and is the finest and best equipped house of the kind at Everson. It is a large three-story brick structure containing twenty-five rooms, neatly fitted up and well furnished.

It is perfect and complete in every particular, provided with all modern conveniences, including an ice-house conveniently near, and so arranged and conducted as to fully meet every want of the traveling public. In addition to the erection of his hotel, he has built two large three-story double tenement houses, one of brick and the other a frame. He owns the square upon which his hotel stands, together with sixteen of the finest building lots in the town.

In November, 1882, he was married to Miss Ella O'Conner of Connellsville. They have three children: Robert, Margaret and Mary.

J. W. Kennedy is a democrat. He is a member of the Catholic church and is one of the stirring, enterprising citizens of northern Fayette county. Mr. Kennedy is in the early prime of life and is destined to hold a prominent position for years to come in the business of his adopted town.

FRANK KESSLER, one of Belle Vernon's industrious citizens and a faithful soldier in the late war, was born in Allegheny county, Pa., March 12, 1838. He is a son of John and Lavina (McClain) Kessler.

John Kessler was born in Westmoreland county, and died in about 1848. He married Miss Lovence, daughter of Samuel McClain, of German descent, and was a soldier in the War of 1812. John Kessler was of Swiss extraction, and his father was a native of Lancaster county, Pa.

When Frank Kessler was ten years of age both of his parents died, and he was taken and reared by his grandfather, Samuel McClain. Frank Kessler was educated in the common schools; at nineteen years of age he engaged with George Whiting to learn the carpenter's trade.

After remaining some time at his trade he enlisted in 1861 for three months in Company D, First Virginia (afterwards West Virginia) Cavalry. At the expiration of his three months' term he re-enlisted and entered the Forty-sixth Pennsylvania Infantry Volunteers. He was with his regiment in all its battles, and was with Sherman in his "March to the Sea," and with him in his Atlanta campaign. He was discharged in August, 1865.

He was married in 1862 to Miss Eliza, daughter of Kinney and Rachel (Burgar) Harris, the former a native of Wayne county, Ohio, and a son of Daniel Burgan, a Revolutionary soldier, who was wounded at the battle of Brandywine, the latter was born in Westmoreland county, Pa.

Mr. and Mrs. Kessler are the parents of four children: Mary E., Samuel A. (died in infancy), Florence L. and Harry Lee.

Mr. Kessler located in North Belle Vernon, where he engaged in carpentering and boat-building, and in this business he is at present engaged.

He has held all the offices of the borough, and discharged their duties in a very satisfactory manner.

NATHANIEL KING, one of Upper Tyrone's worthy farmers and good citizens, is a son of David and Eliza (Graft) King, born in Milford township, Somerset county, Pa., May 23, 1838.

Samuel King, grandfather, was born in Schuylkill county, was a wagon-maker by trade, removed in 1844 to Athens, Ohio, where he bought a farm, and died in the ninety-first year of his age.

David King, father, was a native of Somerset county, removed to Upper Tyrone township in 1852, engaged as a day laborer, and died in 1870, at sixty-two years of age. His widow, a very active old lady, is living at seventy-five years of age. She is a member of the United Brethren church. Her father, John Graft, was a tailor by trade, and removed to Westmoreland county, where he died in 1855 at sixty years of age.

Nathan. King came to Tyrone township at nine years of age, where he received a good farm training and a practical common-school education. He was engaged in farming up to 1862, when he enlisted in Company B, (sharpshooters) Seventy-seventh Pennsylvania Volunteers, and was wounded in his left hand at the battle of Liberty Gap. He fought under Sherman in Georgia, marched with Stanley after Hood, and was honorably discharged in June, 1865.

After the war Mr. King engaged in farming on shares until 1881, when he purchased his present farm, one mile south of Scottdale, containing 117 acres of well-improved, good farming land. It is bounded by three public roads, and underlaid with the Connellsville vein of coking coal.

He was first married in 1862, his wife died in 1869, leaving two children: Norman and William. In 1870 he married Miss Rachel, daughter of Jacob Ridenour. Unto this second union twelve children have been born, of whom ten are living: Jefferson, Nelson, Rogers, Mitchel, Blanche, Carrie, Laura, Kate, Allen and Wade.

Nathaniel King is a democrat, has been tax collector, and has served twelve years as a school director. He is a member of the United Brethren church, a good farmer, and stands well as a citizen wherever he is known.

JAMES P. KREPPS was born at Fayette City, Pa., July 23, 1846. His parents were William and Sophia (Bortner) Krepps.

James P. Krepps is able to trace his paternal ancestors back to Joshua Ludwig Krepps, his paternal great-grandfather, born in January, 1718, died in York county, Pa., in 1784.

Jeremiah Krepps, his paternal grandfather was born May 26, 1775.

William Krepps, his father was born at Harper's Ferry, Va., December 27, 1799, and died August 10, 1866. He married Sophia, daughter of Philip Bortner, the latter a son of a Revolutionary soldier. William Krepps' children are named and born respectively: Martha M., December 8, 1833, lives in De

Kalb county, Ind.; Anna C., August 26, 1835, lives in Allegheny county; Mary M., February 23, 1837; Sarah E., born November 27, 1838; William B., July 26, 1841, died January 28, 1842; Sophia C., October 2, 1843, lives in Allegheny county; James P.; Ellen B., January 16, 1849; Aaron B., November 18, 1851; Edna J., March 8, 1854, died January 31, 1855. James P. Krepps was educated in the common schools, at twenty years of age he engaged in operating a saw-mill, and has continued in the same business ever since, excepting one year spent as a carpenter in Indiana. He operates the only saw-mill at Fayette City.

He was united in marriage on his twenty-sixth birthday to Miss Tillie, daughter of William Valentine, a native of Philadelphia and a hatter by trade. Three children were born to this union: William A., Martha S. and Frank. Mrs. Krepps died in 1881.

Mr. Krepps, on December 25, 1888, was married to his second wife, Miss Nancy J. Masten, daughter of Levi and Elizabeth (Snider) Masten, the former a native of Fayette, and the latter of Westmoreland county.

Mr. Krepps is an industrious citizen, and one of the business men of Fayette City.

He is a member of the I. O. O. F., R. A., E. A. U., and Order of Solan.

NICHOLAS KROMER, the popular proprietor of the Kromer House at Everson is a son of Jacob and Catherine (Morth) Kromer, and was born in France in 1839.

Jacob Kromer is a native of Lorrintz, France. He was a farmer, emigrating to America and settled at Baltimore. He is a member of the Lutheran church, and is in the seventy-seventh year of his age. His wife, of the same nativity and religion as himself, died in 1889; aged seventy-two years.

Nicholas Kromer was raised in Lorrintz, educated in the French schools, and emigrated to Connellsville, where he mined coal for seven years. Leaving that business he learned photography, in which he was engaged successfully until 1885, when he removed to Everson and engaged in the hotel business.

In 1865 he was married to Miss Katie Wybell, a native of France. They have six children: Katie, married to Nicholas Kaff a blacksmith of Scottdale; Jacob, Harry, Charlie, Lizzie and Philip.

He belongs to the Uniformed Rank of the K. of P., Red Men and K. M. C. He owns a good house in Connellsville, besides several other buildings and a hotel. He is a democrat, and is a member of the German Lutheran church.

GEORGE LANG was born in Germany, Wurtemburg ober Lanningham, in 1826. He learned the wagon-maker trade, and at the age of sixteen years went to Switzerland, where he remained five years. At twenty-one years of age he returned to his native State to stand his chance of being drafted into the military service. He was not drawn and immediately emigrated to America.

He worked at his trade on Pine creek, near Pittsburgh, for some years, when he removed to Belle Vernon, worked for Christian Amalong, and a year later bought his employer out. He continued wagon-making until 1850, when he engaged in the livery business, and continued in it up to the time of his death, February 1, 1885.

Mr. Lang, in 1849, married Miss Emily, daughter of John McCrory, a descendant of one of the early settled families of Washington county, Pa. Their union was blessed with six children: Henry, born March 8, 1850; Clara, May 19, 1852; Regina, October 16, 1855; Josephine, February 25, 1857;

Wilson, March 22, 1862; Estella, August 15, 1869 (dead). Mrs. Lang, who still resides in Belle Vernon, is a descendant of the well-known Spear family that settled at an early date in Pennsylvania and Kentucky.

Henry Lang, eldest son, is a successful druggist at Belle Vernon and was married in 1872, to Miss Frances, daughter of Jesse and Margaret (Ewing) Billitter. Their union has been blessed with six children: Woods, Bessie, Fannie, George, Edna and Elsie, the latter being dead.

Wilson Lang (youngest son) is in the livery business in his native town at his father's old stand. He is an energetic and enterprising citizen and has built up a successful business.

George Lang, deceased (subject of sketch), was an exemplary citizen, and was a useful and consistent member of the Evangelical Lutheran church, to which he had belonged for many years. He was a man who attended strictly to his own business, and whose hand was always open to the wants of the worthy poor.

EDMUND LEONARD, a farmer of Menallen township, is a son of William and Mary (Van Ort) Leonard, and was born near Bentleyville, Somerset township, Washington county, Pa., June 8, 1825.

Caleb Leonard, great-grandfather, was a native of England and died at 103 years of age He came from New Jersey to Washington county, where his son, Daniel, married Miss Lucretia, daughter of Dr. Jennings. They reared a family of several children. One of their sons, William, father of Edmund Leonard, was born in 1803, and was a farmer and a Methodist. His wife was a daughter of Richard Van Ort. They had nine children.

Edmund Leonard was educated in the limited schools of that day. His first business in was saddle and harness-making, which he followed for fifteen years and then relinquished it for his present occupation of farming.

March 1, 1849, he was married to Miss Sarah, daughter of William Hatfield, an associate judge of Fayette county, from 1861 to 1865. They have nine children: William H., dead; Howard M., born July 13, 1854, carpenter; Hickman W., born January 22, 1857, at Pittsburgh; Ewing A., February 10, 1860, Pittsburgh grocer; Mary E., March 26, 1862; William J., June 4, 1863, oil driller; George McClard, August 13, 1864, carpenter; James T., December 9, 1866, and Jennie G., June 22, 1871.

Edmund Leonard is a pronounced democrat and has held various township offices. He has been a member of the Uniontown Baptist church since 1846, and several years ago was elected deacon. He began life as a poor boy, but by prudence and frugality has become a man of some means. He is an earnest man and engages in any enterprise with a determination to win.

ROBERT JOHN LINTON. The world honors those men who have won respectable and important standing in life by their own unaided efforts, and in this class will be found Robert John Linton, son of Joseph and Mary Linton, who was born July 24, 1834, in County Antrim, Ireland. His father, while not a rich man, was yet in very comfortable circumstances.

Robert J. Linton was raised on a farm, was partly educated in Ireland, where he attended the pay schools of that country, then celebrated for their thorough training and effective work.

Ambitious and energetic, he sought for a wider sphere of action in the business world than could be found in Ireland at that time, and upon attaining his majority, came in September, 1855, to Pittsburgh, Pa., with a determination to do something, but with no definite idea of what that something would be. In a short time he engaged with the Adams Express Company, having charge of the trains, continuing with them but a short time and quitting with a few hundred dollars that he had saved.

He now proposed to secure a better education and attended Twinsburg Academy for two years. On leaving school he engaged with R. C. Schmertz & Co., manufacturers and dealers in glass lamps. He continued in their employ at Pittsburgh until 1865, when the firm bought out George A. Berry & Co.'s window glass works at Belle Vernon and increased their capacity from sixteen pots to forty pots, being four ten-pot furnaces.

From 1862 to 1868 he traveled and sold goods for the firm, and in the latter year located at Belle Vernon as general manager of the R. C. Schmertz & Co.'s window glass works.

In 1872 he became a member of the firm, and by his active exertions and good management, has contributed to build up their business into its present prosperous condition.

These glass works are the largest of their kind in the world. The works cover three acres of ground, with improvements amounting to $125,000, and operated on an invested capital of $200,000 and do a yearly business amounting to $360,000; 312 men are employed, and 136,800 boxes of window glass are made on an average every year. Their goods sell from Boston to San Francisco and from the lakes to the gulf.

Mr. Linton was married in 1864, to Miss Caroline S. Doolittle, a native of Henderson, Ohio. They had three children: Robert, Grace and Clara. Clara married Rev. W. B. Hamilton of Washington, Pa., missionary, and went to China, where she died in six weeks after her arrival.

Mr. Linton is an extensive stockholder in the Belle Vernon Light and Heat Co.

He is a Mason, is a highly respected member of the Belle Vernon Presbyterian church and in which he has been an elder for several years.

Robert J. Linton has been emphatically the architect of his own fortune. He is a most excellent and accomodating manager, an honest man, a consistent Christian, and a worthy, intelligent citizen. He is liberal in his views, but earnest in his convictions. His thought upon any subject is good, and his expression clear. He is naturally and amply qualified for leadership in any great enterprise of the business world.

AARON LEWELLEN, of Belle Vernon, was born on a farm near the Pennsylvania line in West Virginia, January 7, 1844. He grew up on the farm till at the age of eighteen years, when he volunteered as a soldier in the Civil War; he enlisted in Company I, Fourteenth West Virginia Regiment of infantry. He was engaged in all the hard-fought battles in which his regiment took part; among the more noted were that of Cedar Creek, and all the battles fought in the Shenandoah valley. He was in the battle of Cedar Creek when Sheridan arrived, after making his famous ride from Winchester, twenty miles away.

After Mr. Lewellen's return home he was married January 16, 1868, to Leonora, grand-daughter of John Tearnin (deceased), who was once treasurer of the county (see his sketch on another page), and a daughter of Joshua and Catherine Tearnin (Clegg). Her father was a volunteer soldier in the Civil War; returned home after his discharge, and soon sickened and died. Her mother's death occurred February 15, 1889. Her marriage to Mr. Lewellen has been blessed with seven children: Arabella, born January 5, 1869; John, January 29, 1870 (died at the age three years); Katie, December 16, 1873; Harry, August 23, 1876; Thomas, May 27, 1879; Fred, September 6, 1882, and Louis E., July 7, 1889.

Mr. Lewellen has lived since his marriage principally at Fayette City, where he was engaged in the coal business. For the past few years he has lived at Belle Vernon, engaged in the hotel business. He and all his family are Methodists.

His father, Jacob Lewellen, is a native of West Virginia, and removed from that State to Uniontown during the war. He is now a resident of Connellsville. Aaron Lewellen's mother's maiden name was Mary Bell. His grandfather, John Lewellen, settled in West Virginia, many years ago.

EPHRAIM LEWIS was born July 8, 1836, at Albany, Fayette county, Pa., and was educated in the common-schools of the county. He began work in the glass factory as tender boy, when a mere lad. He moved to Fayette City, thence to Belle Vernon, to Pittsburgh in 1845, and again to Belle Vernon in 1846, where he still resides.

He was married in 1861 to Miss Sabina Van Hook, a daughter of Samuel Van Hook, a native of Virginia, and now a resident of Brownsville, Pa., he was at one time a part owner of the Belle Vernon Glass Works. Mr. Lewis has six children: Lizzie, married to John Kittle; Samuel C., resides in Bellaire; O., Margaret, William H., Mary S. and Charles A. V., living at home. Mrs. Lewis died June 17, 1874.

Mr. Lewis is a member of the K. of L., of the I. O. of O. F., and has been a member of the school board for nine years. He owns a comfortable home and has some good property in the town. He began blowing glass in 1861, and is still engaged in that business at the Belle Vernon glass works. He is the preceptor of the K. of G.

Ephraim Lewis is the son of William H. and Margaret (Sutton) Lewis. William H. Lewis was born in Virginia, in 1806, and came to Pennsylvania when a boy with his parents, who settled at Monongahela City. His father, Burton Lewis, the grandfather of Ephraim Lewis, was born in Delaware, and was one of the early settlers of Pennsylvania.

Mr. Lewis' mother, Margaret Sutton, was born in 1804, at Perryopolis. She lives with her son Ephraim in Belle Vernon. His father, Nathaniel Sutton, was a farmer, one of the early settlers of Fayette county, and was one of the leading men in the Methodist Episcopal church. He married Miss Brown. (See Alexander Brown's sketch in this volume.) Ephraim Lewis' mother has in her possession a table set of four pieces of pewterware that has been handed down in the Brown family for over 200 years.

L. V. MARSHALL, an experienced and competent clerk in the Union Supply Company's store at Summit, was born in Wayne township, Lawrence county, Pa., September 6, 1854, and is a son of John H. and Sue S. Marshall, both natives of Washington county, Pa.

The Marshalls are of Scotch-Irish descent and of a long-life race of people. John H. Marshall was born in 1810; at thirteen years of age he was engaged in driving a team across the mountain, and at the age of sixteen owned and drove a six-horse team. He drove between Pittsburgh and Philadelphia; he afterwards engaged in the farming and mercantile business, and died in 1887. His wife, born in 1817, was a Presbyterian, and died in 1886. His father, Thomas Marshall, was a large land owner of Washington county.

L. V. Marshall received his education in the common schools of Lawrence county and North Sewickley Academy. At sixteen years of age he obtained a position as clerk with the Wheatland Coal Company of Mercer county, Pa., and remained in their employ for three years. The next three years of his life were spent in the Western States. In 1877 he was engaged in the "oil region" above Pittsburgh as a tool dresser and pipe-line gauger. He worked for three companies and remained in the oil region until 1880, when he taught a term of school. He became a clerk in the Sharon Iron Works store in Mercer county, Pa., where he continued till 1884, and in the year succeeding he clerked for G. G. Lyon & Co., of Connellsville. In October, 1885, he became a traveling salesman for the tea house of Ramsey Brothers, when in April, 1886, he accepted a position as clerk in the Broad Ford store of the Union Supply Company. His duties were discharged satisfactorily, and July 1, 1887, he was transferred to his present important clerkship in the Summit store.

L. V. Marshall was married in 1877 to Miss Emma, daughter of W. C. Lyon of Pennsville. They have two children: Deomidas W. and Anna M. Two of his brothers, Thomas J. and W. B., are engaged in the mercantile business, while another brother, Ed. H., is a store manager. L. V. Marshall is a Heptasoph, and a member of the United Brethren church. He is a reliable young man and is well qualified by years of experience for the discharge of his responsible duties.

BENJAMIN B. MARTIN was born in Fayette county, Pa., June 18, 1862, and is a son of Edmund and Elizabeth (Brown) Martin.

Benjamin Martin (grandfather) was one of the early settlers in the county, and was a soldier in the war of 1812.

Edmund Martin was in his time one of the leading merchants of Belle Vernon, as well as an extensive dealer in stock in Fayette and Westmoreland counties. He is a native of Pennsylvania, born December 1, 1806, and died February 5, 1876. He was an earnest supporter of the Baptist church, a good citizen, and a useful business man. His wife, Elizabeth (Brown) Martin was a native of Pennsylvania, a daughter of Benjamin Brown, who was an old settler and leading citizen in his day.

Benjamin B. Martin, whose name is the caption of this sketch, received his education in the common schools. At an early age he entered into the mercantile business at Belle Vernon, and successfully continued it until 1889.

He was married September 30, 1886, to Miss Lizzie Springer, daughter of James M. Springer. (See sketch.) Their union has been blessed with one child: Sarah E.

Mr. Martin is a young man qualified by good business training and considerable business experience to successfully prosecute any enterprise in which he may embark.

HENRY MERRITT, farmer in Lower Tyrone township, is the son of Lewis and Nancy Ann (Sechrist) Merritt.

His father was born April 30, 1823, and a native of South Huntington township, Westmoreland county, where he lived till 1853, when he came to Fayette county, and located on the farm he now resides on, in Lower Tyrone township. This farm is situated on the hill, just above Layton Station, and contains sixty-three acres of good and well-improved land, about fifty acres of which is cleared. He was married to Miss Nancy Ann Sechrist, born October 23, 1824, and a native of Perry township, Fayette county. They are both members of the Methodist Episcopal church. He is a republican.

Jonathan Merritt, grandfather of Henry Merritt, was a farmer of South Huntington township, Westmoreland county, settled there in an early day, and was from near Philadelphia. He was of German descent.

David Sechrist, maternal grandfather of Henry Merritt, was a farmer of Perry township, Fayette county.

Henry Merritt was born March 29, 1852, on a farm in Lower Tyrone township, Fayette county, Pa., where he was brought up and attended the common schools of the township. He remained on the farm with his father till the fall of 1876, when he began life for himself. In 1877 he went to mining fire-clay for the Diamond Brick Company at Layton, and worked for them three years, the greater portion of this time as foreman. In 1878 he bought an unimproved farm of 140 acres, at sheriff's sale, which he greatly improved and put in a fine state of cultivation. In 1880 he engaged in mining, where he remained some time, when he engaged as foreman of the mines for ten months at the Cochran brick-yard, near Oakdale, owned by James Cochran & Brother. He then took a contract to furnish the clay by the ton to them, which he did for six months. In 1887 he bought what is known as the Layton farm, containing sixty-eight acres, and has since bought a piece of land as an outlet to the road to the Layton farm. He is a thrifty, energetic man, ready to do anything that is honest for a livelihood, and has accumulated considerable property. He keeps a team going all of the time hauling, and at present has the contract for supplying all of the clay used by the Keystone and Diamond Company's brick-works. In politics he is a republican, and is at present worh about $7,000.

JAMES McCRORY was born October 26, 1820, at Fayette City, Pennsylvania. He remained at home until 1840 when he went to Geneva and learned the trade of glass cutter. He followed this business until 1850, when he went to California, and engagad in gold mining until 1856. In 1856 he came home and purchased a farm of one hundred and forty acres in Washington township, where he still resides.

In 1848 he was married to Rebecca Nutt, the daughter of William B. Nutt, a native of Fayette county. By this marriage there were nine children: Charles H , George, Seneca, Anna, Thomas, Sarah T., Nancy S., James A. and Mary. Thomas, Anna and Sarah Tunissa are dead.

Mr. McCrory is a member of the I. O. of O. F., he is the oldest member of the order now living in the vicinity of Fayette City. He also belongs to the Equitable Aid Union and is in good standing in both organizations.

He is the son of Thomas and Eliza (Brown) McCrory. His father kept hotel in Fayette City for forty years, was one of the early settlers of the town and was a good, substantial man. His children were James, Seneca, Wilson, Achsa, Mary E. and Sarah Jane. The two brothers of James McCrory went to California at the same time as himself, but have never returned.

WILLIAM D. MULLEN. The late William D. Mullen, one of the oldest and most highly respected citizens of northwestern Fayette county, was born in Cumberland county, Pa., January 6, 1787.

He established in 1809 the first hat-making establishment of Fayette City (Cookstown), and was successfully engaged for years in that line of business. He was a Free Mason, a democrat and was a patron of the Genius of Liberty for over half a century. He was for years a justice of the peace and was a consistent member of the Methodist Episcopal church. He was a sober, honest and industrious citizen.

He married Miss Margaret Graham and they had a family of eight children. Mrs. Mullen died March 25, 1871.

The oldest son, Robert Mullen, was born December 19, 1814, and was reared to the hatting business, but engaged in the cabinet making business for several years. In 1850 he engagad in mercantile business and died June 22, 1887. He was a prominet Mason and has filled all the important offices of the "Blue Lodge."

Robert Mullen married Miss Elizabeth Allen. They had one child: Sallie, wife of Roscoe Thirkil. After the death of his wife he married Miss Margaret Bently, and by the second marriage had two daughters: Frances, married Joseph L. Cooper, and Othelia, married October 28, 1867, to William McCune, the latter was born in Cumberland county, Pa., in 1844 and died in 1882. Mrs. McCune has two sons: Robert M. and Edward. Robert Mullen, after the death of his second wife, married a third time. His third wife was Miss Elizabeth Shupe, who, with her two children, Robert and Emma, resides at Fayette City.

Robert Mullen's store is successfully conducted by its present proprietors, his daughter Mrs. Othella McCune and her eldest son, Robert McCune, one of the young business men of Fayette City.

WILLIAM McCRORY is a native of Fayette City, and was born March 11, 1822. He attended school and worked in his father's blacksmith shop until he was nineteen years of age, when he became a steamboat engineer. He ran for many years on the Monongahela and Ohio rivers, and was in the "Lower Trade" on the Mississippi for some years.

He was married in 1850 to Miss Mary Banks, daughter of William Banks, who was a prominent glass-blower. She died in 1853. In 1858 he married again, his second wife being Miss Mary Wilson, daughter of David Wilson, who came from Ireland to Fayette county prior to 1794. During the whiskey insurrection he and three of his neighbors assisted in preventing the burning of Pittsburgh.

Mr. McCrory made a trip to California in 1850, going by water via the Isthmus of Panama. He remained on the Pacific coast for two years and a half.

He has invented a life preserver that is claimed to be superior to any other in existence. It is a gum jacket that can be inflated at will, and is sufficiently strong to float the weight of two ordinary persons. His friends, and many who have examined this preserver, are enthusiastic in its praises, and claim the day is not far distant when it will be in universal use.

WILSON McCRORY, of Washington township, is a son of James and Hester (Sisley) McCrory, and was born at Cookstown, now Fayette City, November 2, 1812.

He is of English descent. His father, James McCrory, was a native of Fayette county, and a son of James McCrory, who came from England and settled near Allenport, Washington county, over one hundred years ago. His mother, Hester Sisley, was a daughter of Lewis Sisley, who settled in the county over one hundred years ago.

Wilson McCrory attended several subscription schools, later learned the blacksmith trade under his father, who was an early settler of "Cookstown," and cut the logs on the ground where he erected his house and shop.

He followed blacksmithing for four years, and then engaged in steamboating, which he continued up to 1885.

He was married November 2, 1870, to Mary, daughter of James Hamer, the latter a native of Manchester, England, who came to Brownsville in 1822, and removed thence to "Cookstown." They have two children: James H. and Nelson. The older son is mechanically inclined, and without any assistance when thirteen years of age built a steam engine. His third and last engine is one of four horse-power. With it he has drilled a well thirty-six feet deep, and found a small flow of gas.

Mr. McCrory has in his possession as relics the Sisley conch shell, bearing date of 1806, and the old indentures—over a century in age—by which his father was bound to work three years for about two pounds sterling, three months schooling and a "freedom suit."

He served as tax collector, was elected school director and has filled several other offices of the borough.

Mr. McCrory was at the siege of Vicksburg, in the Morgan raid from Kentucky to Ohio, and was at Buffington Island.

After a long life of activity and hard labor, he has now retired from business, and is a highly respected citizen of Fayette City, where he at present resides.

WILLIAM McCORMICK, of Menallen township, was born on the McCormick farm in the same township, Fayette county, Pa., September 11, 1819, and is a son of Charles and Margaret McCormick.

James McCormick (paterntal grandfather) was born in the north of Ireland and settled in Redstone township, nearly one hundred years ago.

Charles McCormick (father) was born in 1772, died in 1835, and was an active working member in the Dunlap's Creek Presbyterian church. His wife was Margaret, daughter of James McCormick.

William McCormick was raised on a farm and attended the schools of the neighborhood. On March 6, 1844, he was married by the Rev. Hudson, to Phebe Jones. Her father, Edward Cook Jones, was born March 27, 1799, and married Hannah J., daughter of Caleb Woodward who came from Chester county in an early day. William McCormick has nine children: Caleb Finley, born December 21, 1844, married Margaret Carter, has six children and lives at Uniontown; Charles Jackson, born March 18, 1847, married Rachel, daughter of Ewing Searight, has one child; Hannah Rebecca, born May 30, 1849, married John Moore, has one child; Margaret E., born November 17, 1851, married John A. McCombs, has four children, Lydia Jane, born June 14, 1854, married William Moore, has three children; Ewing S., born September 22, 1859, married Annie French, has three children, lives in Nebraska; Noble, born February 26, 1857, married May De Tar, of Kansas, has four children; William born August 7, 1863, and Anna E., born June 25, 1866.

He owns a fine farm in Menallen township, and for the last twenty years he has extensively engaged in wool-buying, together with his farm interests.

For a man of seventy years of age he is very active and successfully manages his different kinds of business. He has lived an industrious, useful life, and has many friends.

He united in early life with the Presbyterian church at Uniontown, then under the pastoral care of the Rev. Joel Stoneroad, and now he and his wife have their membership in the New Salem Cumberland Presbyterian church.

JOHN McCRAY, of Menallen, was born on the McCray homestead, four miles west of Uniontown, September 18, 1824. He is a son of Adam and Anna (Jackson) McCray.

Adam McCray (father), was born April 12, 1780, and died August 12, 1855. In 1807 he married Miss Anna, daughter of

Isaac Jackson of Menallen township. They had ten children: John, Isaac, Margaret, Sarah Ann, Mary, Rebecca, Eleanor, John, Martha and Emily.

John McCray (paternal grandfather) was of Scotch-Irish descent, born in Ireland, where he learned the trade of weaver. He came to America, and with three of his brothers served under Washington in the Revolutionary War. After that struggle closed, he removed to Menallen township, where he died. His wife's father made the first crown glass in Scotland.

John McCray was reared on the home farm, and educated in the subscription schools of Menallen. He owns one hundred acres of fine land in the township, and is engaged in farming and stock raising. He married Mrs. Catherine Filley, widow of Dr. Horace Filley, and daughter of John Deal of Pittsburgh, March, 1854. Their union has been blessed with four children: Maggie E. (died in infancy), Mary, Ida (died at fifteen years years of age), Anna J., born November 2, 1855, married to Alex. H. Patterson, lives near Martinsburgh, W. Va., and has five children; Sarah Louisa, born July 30, 1862, married to Oliver B. Jeffries, of Uniontown, and has one child.

Mr. McCray is a good business man, a good farmer, a respectable citizen, and has for many years been a follower of "the lowly Nazarene," being a highly respected member of the Presbyterian church at New Salem.

JOHN J. McCLARY, one of the capable and thorough young business men of Fayette county, was born in Springhill township, Fayette county, Pa., August 21, 1865, and is a son of William and Catherine (Kussart) McClary, the latter a native of Greene county, Pa.

William McClary was born in Springhill township, December 6, 1818. For thirty years he was a thorough, stirring and energetic farmer. In 1870 he was engaged in the lumber business at Confluence, Pa., and three years later he retired from active life. He has resided at Connellsville since 1873, is a strong democrat, and was justice of the peace for five years in his native township. He has reared a family of five sons and three daughters.

John J. McClary was reared at Pennsville, received his early education in the schools of Bullskin township, and finished his studies at Grand River Institute, Ohio, where he attended two terms. During the summer months of 1883 and 1884 he labored at the coke works, and in the winters of those years taught in the common schools of Bullskin township. In 1885 he secured a position as clerk with the Union Supply Company, limited, at their Trotter store. His services were of such a character as to favorably commend him to the attention of his employers, and on May 1, 1889, he was given his present responsible position, that of manager of their store at Morgan. Step by step he won his own way from the coke yard to the office desk.

In politics Mr. McClary is a Cleveland democrat. He is a Heptasoph, and a member of the First Presbyterian church, at Connellsville. Although young in years he has been remarkably successfull and stands high as a business man and private citizen, wherever known.

JOHN McKEE, Sr., was born in Ireland, and came to America when a young man. He soon enlisted in the Continental army, and served for four years. He married Mary Seabird of Bucks county, Pa., and they had the following children: Anna, born April 16, 1790; John, born October 17, 1792; Thomas, born January 22, 1796; Henry, born May 11, 1798; Hugh, born April 18, 1800; Catherine, born January 29, 1802; Francis, born September 19, 1806; Mary, born January 17, 1807; Margaret, born January 5, 1810; Jesse, born January 6, 1812; Ephraim, born January 4, 1815. He removed from Bucks county to Northampton county, thence to Williamsport, Lycoming county, and then to Washington township, Fayette county, where he settled in 1809 and lived till his death.

Of his family, John died in Washington township; Francis at present resides in Washington township; Hugh and Henry live in Washington county, Pa.; Thomas removed to Wayne county, Ohio, where he reared a large family.

Francis McKee married Miss Joanna, daughter of Joseph and Anna (Thompson) Allen, and they reared five children; Annette, married to John Harah of Uniontown; Josephine, married to S. S. Jack of Decatur, Ill.; Joseph A., Mary and Celia.

Joseph A. McKee was born December 4, 1839, attended the common schools of the township, and the school at Washington, Pa. He was married December 20, 1877, to Susan Church, daughter of Samuel and Margaret (Kuhns) Church of Greensburgh, Pa. He was a descendant of the Church family, which came over to this country in early colonial days. The ancestor was Captain Church, who was founder of the family in this country. The Kuhns family came from Northumberland county, Pa., to West Moreland county. From this marriage were five children, two of whom are living; infant dead; Fred, nine years old; Anna, died an infant; Bettie, two and a half years old; Sallie, died an infant.

Joseph A. McKee has held numerous township and borough offices, is now burgess of Fayette City, and justice of peace of the township. He is a member of the Royal Arcanum, owns 400 acres of land in Washington township, and an elegant home on the higher grounds at Fayette City. He has lived the principal part of his life in Fayette City. He is a leading democrat of his township.

REV. HENRY J. MOLLESTON, postmaster at Dawson, is the son of Jonathan M. and Sarah (Waggoner) Molleston.

His father was born in Delaware and migrated to Pennsylvania and located at Greenfield, Washington county, Pa., over fifty years ago, where he engaged in the practice of medicine, which he continued successfully to the time of his death. He was a student at Jefferson Medical College, Philadelphia, from where he was graduated, and was a minister of the Cumberland Presbyterian church. His wife was Sarah Waggoner, a native of Jefferson township, Fayette county, Pa., and was born in 1819. She is living at Verona, Allegheny county, an active, strong woman. Her father, Joshua Waggoner, was a native of Westmoreland county, and a devout member of the Cumberland Presbyterian church.

The paternal grandfather of Henry G. was a resident of Delaware, and was elected Governor of Delaware on the whig ticket, but died before he was installed as such. He was a prominent lawyer of Delaware and a successful politician. The Mollestons are of English descent.

Henry G. Molleston was born February 25, 1838, in Greenfield, now Coal Center, Washington county, Pa. After his father's death he was principally reared by his grandfather Waggoner, on a farm in Redstone township, where he attended the common schools and afterwards the normal school at California, Pa.

In 1861 he enlisted in Company I, Eighty-fifth Pennsylvania Volunteer Infantry, was made a sergeant of the company, and served for three years, participating in all the battles of his regiment, and was discharged at Philadelphia in 1864, when he returned to Redstone township, and engaged in farming till 1870. In the same year he located at Dawson, and worked for James Cochran as engineer at his coke works for about seventeen years. July 1, 1889, he took charge of the postoffice at Dawson.

In 1864 he was married to Miss Charlotte Skinner, the daughter of Courtland Skinner, a Baptist preacher of Fayette county. They have four children: William J., Sarah R., Trevyllian and Ella S.

Mr. Molleston is a member of the I. O. O. F., K. of P. and the Redmen, and is a local preacher in the Methodist Episcopal church.

ROBERT F. MOORE, a thorough and trustworthy citizen and miller, of Menallen township was born on the old Moore farm, in Redstone township, January 24, 1854, and is a son of William and Nancy (Frost) Moore.

Rezin Moore, grandfather, was a native of Redstone township, was a farmer and married Miss Mary Landers. They reared a large family and their descendants are now among the most thrifty of the county, and he was a whig in politics.

William R. Moore is a successful farmer and an active republican. His wife was Miss Nancy, daughter of Jesse Frost of Redstone township. They have reared a family of ten children.

Robert F. Moore was raised in Menallen township, educated in the common schools of that township and in the New Salem schools. He learned the trade of a miller with Samuel Frederick, of the "Star Mills" in Menallen, and after completing his trade he had part charge of the Star Mills from 1873 to 1875; owned New Salem Mills from 1875 to 1881; was for a time head miller in Reynold's Mill, at Uniontown, and milled at Coal Center in 1887. He returned to the Star Mills and assumed charge of them in 1888. He is building up a large and constantly increasing patronage. He is a quiet, unassuming man, but withal courteous, genial and obliging.

Mr. Moore was married June 29, 1876, to Miss Irene, daughter of F. A. Lewis, a blacksmith of New Salem. She was born September 12, 1855. Unto their union have been born two children: Della P., born December 6, 1877, and Francis W. Moore, born July 23, 1880.

WILLIAM C. MULLAN, the time clerk and assistant superintendent of Henry Clay, Frick and Rist coke plants of H. C. Frick Coke Company, Broad Ford, Pa., is a son of William and Mary A. (Williams) Mullan, and was born at Ft. Loudon, Franklin county, Pa., February 15, 1859.

William Mullan was of Irish descent, and a native of Franklin county. He learned the blacksmith trade, and was a member of the Catholic church. He was a democrat, and had held the offices of judge of elections and school director of his township. He was born in 1820, died in 1887, and was much missed at Ft. Loudon.

William C. Mullan was reared at Ft. Loudon, and was educated in the common schools. Manifesting an aptitude for commercial business, at fourteen years of age he became a successful clerk in a general mercantile store. After seven years' efficient service in three stores of Ft. Loudon, he removed to Dunbar, and engaged as a clerk with R. J. Carter. In October, 1881, he accepted a position at Broad Ford in the store of the Union Supply Company. In one year he was promoted from a clerkship to store manager, and, after twelve months' service, was made manager of the Summit store and time clerk for Summit coke plant of H. C. Frick Coke Company. After two years of successful management, he was recalled, in 1885, to Broad Ford, and given his present position of timekeeper and assistant superintendent of the works under Thomas Lynch, general superintendent.

He is a democrat, has held the office of township auditor, central committee-man, and was elected delegate to the democratic State convention from Fayette county in 1889. He is a member of the Heptasophs. He has always enjoyed the confidence of his employers and the customers whom he serves. His past experience and success give promise of a prominent and successful business career for the future.

PRESLEY PATTERSON MURPHY was born February 22, 1841, in Perryopolis, Fayette county, Pa., and is the son of John A. and Clarissa J. (Patterson) Murphy.

John A. Murphy was born in Jefferson township, in January, 1817. He learned the cabinet-maker trade in 1834, has since followed it, and now has a furniture store at Perryopolis. He is a Presbyterian; served five years as justice of the peace; was postmaster at Perryopolis for several years, and is now a republican, having changed his original political faith upon the tariff issue of 1842.

He married Clarissa J., daughter of James Patterson of Franklin township, in 1839. They had two children: Presley P. and Seturah, who died August 31, 1844. Mrs. Murphy (subject's mother) died January 12, 1846, aged twenty-six years.

For his second wife Mr. Murphy married in 1851 Mary, daughter of David Freeman, and she died September 27, 1863. This union was blessed with four children: David Freeman, Cecelia, Lizzie (dead) and Ella.

In 1868 Mr. Murphy was united in marriage to his third and present wife Mrs. Araminta McBride, widow of George McBride. They have three children: Irvin, Katie and Ada.

John Murphy (paternal grandfather) came with parents to Jefferson township and took up three hundred acres of land. He married Nancy Jane Allen. Their children were: Thomas, John A. (subject's father), Elizabeth (dead), James, Henry, Mary (dead), Susan (dead), Andrew (is living) and David (dead). Mrs. Murphy's father, William Allen, was one of Franklin's first settlers, taking up what is now known as the Smith, Ridlinghafer and Whetsel farms.

Major James Patterson (maternal grandfather) married Jane, daughter of Robert Smith, Sr., in 1784. Their children were: John A., Robert (dead), William, Andrew (dead), Clarissa J. (subject's mother, dead), Hugh H., Allen (dead), Presley (dead), James, Milton W. and Mary Elizabeth. Major James H. was the son of James Patterson, an early settler of Scotch descent, but who had English ideas and left all his property to the major, who in turn left the bulk of his possessions to Milton W. Major Patterson was a farmer, and a democrat. He served one term as county commissioner, and died March 14, 1854, aged sixty-one years, one month and twenty-seven days.

Presley Patterson Murphy was educated in the common school, and worked with his father at the cabinet-maker's trade until 1865, when he went on his father-in-law's farm one year. Since 1866 he has been a very successful merchant at Flatwoods, where he owns 119 acres of land located in the Anti-clinal Gas Belt, and on this farm a well for gas is being drilled. He also owns ten acres of island land near Burnsford. His wife also owns 114 acres inherited from her father.

On June 15, 1865, he married Roxey L., only child of John and Harriet (Colvin)

Townsend. They have two children: John A. and Harriet C. John A. was graduated from Mt. Pleasant Institute in 1886, afterwards from Ann Arbor (Mich.) law school in 1888, and was admitted to the Pittsburgh bar in December of the same year. Harriet C. graduated in 1887 from the Mt. Pleasant Institute, and is now attending the Cleveland (Ohio) Female Seminary.

Mr. Murphy is a republican and has been postmaster at Flatwood since 1866. He is a deacon and Sabbath-school superintendent in the Baptist church, to which he has belonged since 1872. He has been a successful business man, and is an intelligent and enterprising citizen.

JOSEPH S. NEWCOMER, a prominent merchant of Fayette county, and one of the enterprising citizens of Morgan, was born in Upper Tyrone township, Fayette county, Pa., March 22, 1839, and is a son of Uriah and Frances (Smith) Newcomer.

His grandfather, Abraham Newcomer, was descended from a Newcomer family of eastern Pennsylvania, was a native of what is now Upper Tyrone township, and a farmer by occupation.

His father, Uriah Newcomer, was born in 1799, and died at the age of fifty-two years. He was an extensive farmer, a republican, and a leading member of the Mennonite church. His wife, born in 1803 and died in 1853, was a daughter of Jacob Smith, a farmer.

Joseph S. Newcomer was raised on a farm and obtained his education in the common schools. In 1861 he enlisted in Company B, Eighty-fifth Pennsylvania Infantry Volunteers, and was engaged in the battles of Williamsburg, Fair Oaks, Malvern Hill, the sieges of Morris Island and Petersburg, and many other battles of the war, and was honorably discharged in October, 1864, at Pittsburgh, Pa. Leaving the Union service, he spent a short time in the "oil region" of Pennsylvania, and then returned to Tyrone township. In 1866 he engaged in merchandising at Morgan's Station, on the Mt. Pleasant branch of the Pittsburgh & Connellsville Railroad. Since 1866 Mr. Newcomer has steadily built up a very flattering trade in his business at Morgan. His present commodious storeroom is filled with a large and well-selected stock of fancy and staple dry goods, groceries, hardware and notions. He has large interests in central Kansas real estate, etc., etc.

In 1868 he was married to Miss Mary A., daughter of William Stacy, a farmer of Connellsville township. To their union have been born three children: Bertha S., born 1870, died 1882; Frank S. and Nora F.

J. S. Newcomer is a republican, and has served his township as auditor and treasurer of the school board. He is a member of the K. of P., I. O. O. F. and Heptasophs. Mr. Newcomer stands deservedly high as a business man and as a citizen. He is a member of the Disciple church.

JOHN O'NEIL was born in 1815, in Allegheny county, Pa., and is the son of John O'Neil.

John O'Neil, Sr., was born at Carlisle, Pa. His father was a devout Catholic who came from Ireland to America previous to the War of the Revolution. He died and was buried in a Catholic cemetery. His widow and children embraced the Protestant faith and joined the Methodist Episcopal church.

John O'Neil, Jr., received an elementary education in the subscription school of Allegheny county, and was variously employed until 1848, when he engaged in the coal business. In 1887 he purchased the Fayette City Coal Works, and operated the same until his death, March 12, 1889.

July 22, 1837, he was married to Margaret Craven, daughter of James Craven, of Washington county, who lived three years beyond the age of an nonegenarian. Of their union was born six children: Sarah, dead; Samuel, Elizabeth, dead; Denny, James and John W. Denny is in the coal business in Tennessee. Samuel, in 1866, was married to Miss Martha Lloyd, of Huntingdon county, Pa. They have eight living children. He is a member of the Masonic fraternity, and also belongs to the American Mechanics. He ranks high as a business man, and stands well as a citizen.

Samuel, James and John W., are operating the Fayette City Coal Works, and are doing a splendid business, considering the disadvantages under which they have labored. In July, 1888, their works were swept away by a flood. At present they employ 160 miners, their daily out-put of coal is 15,000 bushels. The neccessary arrangements are now being made by them to largely increase the capacity of these works, and will be among the most important coal mines in Western Pennsylvania.

John O'Neil, Jr., was a man of sterling integrity, and deservedly popular; he began business with but little capital, but acquired a fortune and lost most of it by reverses. He enjoyed the confidence of his associates and the respect of the public generally.

During the strikes, the men in his employ remainded at their work, and always sustained and defended the course he pursued.

During the late war, he sought out and gave unsparingly of his means to the families of Union soldiers and lived to see the country again reuited and prosperous. He was a member of church, and for fifty years his house was a home for the minister of the Gospel.

The *Christian Advocate* said: "But few men of his time were more extensively or more favorably known by the people of Pittsburgh. He was a patriot without boasting, and a Christian without cant. His loyalty and devotion to country and church alike made him popular. With all his public duties and repeated acts of beneficence, his immediate home circle was the center of his influence, and the recipient of his thought and sweetest affection."

JOHN ONG was born at Fayette City in 1834 and attended school till at the age of nine years, when he went into a glass factory as errand boy.

At the age of fourteen he began work as a glass blower, at which he has worked at various places in Pennsylvania ever since.

His father, Alexander Ong, was a native of Pa., and was quite active in advancing the interests of the glass business when that great industry was in its infancy in Pennsylvania.

John Ong's mother was Catherine Abbott, a daughter of Jeremiah Abbot, who was one of the early settlers of the county. Mrs. Catherine Ong is still living and is in the seventy-fourth year of her age.

In 1856 the subject of this sketch was married to Miss Mary, daughter of Denton Lynn of Fayette county. They have had no children but have reared and educated five children, whose names are as follows: William Chess, Harry Safoot, Celia Safoot, Amelia Safoot and May Safoot, who are all the children of Mrs. Ong's sister.

John Ong was a private in Company E, One Hundred and Fifty-five Pennsylvania Volunteers, but was only out about nine months when he was discharged for disability. He was with his regiment at the battle of Fredericksburg. Jeremiah Abbott, maternal grandfather, was one of the earliest settlers in the county. Before coming here he owned a large farm east of the mountains (on the present site of Harrisburg). He was an extensive land owner before he emigrated West; he also followed blacksmithing and was the first man to do blacksmithing at Cookstown (now Fayette City). John Ong is a member of the G. A. R. and K. of L.

WILKINS W. OSBORN, M. D., of Upper Middletown, was born and reared near Fairchance, Fayette county, Pa. He is the seventh child born to the marriage of Andrew G. Osborn and Jane Lynn. His paternal grandfather, Joseph Osborn, was of Scotch-Irish descent, and came to Fayette county in an early day from Orange county, N. J. The maiden name of his wife was Jane Lucky, to whom he was married in about 1790. His father, Rev. Andrew G. Osborn, was the fourth son of his parents, and on April 26, 1826, he was married to Miss Jane, a daughter of Alexander and Margaret Lynn, of Somerset, Pa., both of English descent, and were born near the city of Philadelphia. They were life-long believers in the doctrines of, and strong in the faith on which the Church of England is founded. Dr. Osborn's maternal grandfather, Alexander Lynn, served as a soldier in the War of 1812, and afterwards died at Somerset, Pa.

Rev. Andrew G. Osborn's education was received in the ordinary subscription schools and later at Madison College. He was ordained as minister of the Cumberland Presbyterian church in 1833 and faithfully served and earnestly preached to various congregations for many years. Among some of his charges were at Hopewell, Harmony, New Salem, Masontown and East Liberty. Being loyal to the cause of the Union during the dark days of the rebellion, he tendered his services to the Federal government, and was accordingly appointed chaplain of the Fourteenth Regiment Pennsylvania Volunteer Cavalry. He joined this regiment at Harper's Ferry late in the fall of 1863, and from that time until May, 1865, he was on the field administering alike to the physical as well as the spiritual wants of the soldiers. Possessing some knowledge of medicine and surgery, he dressed the wounds of many soldiers in camp and on the field. He was admired and beloved wherever known, for his many manly qualities, his clear head and generous disposition. After a lingering illness of a disease, contracted from exposure while in the army, on October 19, 1868, he passed peacefully to rest. He was the father of twelve children, eight sons and four daughters, and what is most remarkable, seven of his sons were soldiers in the war and fought bravely for a reunited country and the preservation of the Union.

Dr. Wilkins W. Osborn, whose name heads this sketch, spent his boyhood days on his father's farm and received his education in the ordinary schools of the neighborhood. On September 19, 1862, he joined Company E. Fourteenth Regiment Pennsylvania Cavalry Volunteers as a private soldier and faithfully served throughout the war, and was honorably discharged on May 30, 1865, at Alexandria, Va.

Returning home, he entered the office of Dr. F. C. Robinson at Uniontown, as a student of medicine and concluded his studies with his brother, W. F. Osborn, M. D., at Mount Pleasant, Pa. He attended lectures at the medical department of Ann Arbor University, Mich., and subsequently at the Western Reserve Medical College, Cleveland, Ohio.

On March 3, 1868, he began the practice of medicine at Upper Middletown, where for over twenty years he has been most successfully engaged in the active practice of his profession. By close application to his work and careful study of standard medical literature and periodicals, and having been a hard student and a man of naturally strong mind,

W. W. Osborn, M.D.

he has become one of the prominent and successful physicians of Fayette county. He has for several years been an active and leading member of the Fayette County Medical Society. As Doctor Osborn is as yet unmarried, his youngest sister, Miss Virginia Osborn, presides over his home at Upper Middletown, which is a model of neatness, elegance and comfort. For many years he has been one of the trustees of the Presbyterian church of which he is an honored and useful member. He believes in the old adage: that "character is the key that unlocks the door to success," and has governed his life accordingly. He is well informed in currant literature of the day and is always ready to lend a hand toward the advancement of any cause calculated to elevate the standard of culture, the advancement of civilization and the betterment of the condition of society.

He is a liberal contributor to the current medical literature and science of the times. He possesses fine business ability, is a leading member of the Presbyterian church, and from a social and moral standpoint his reputation both as a gentleman and physician is first-class.

LUKE F. PATTERSON, a successful farmer and proprietor of the Star Flowering Mills of Menallen, is a son of Sidney and Martha (McCoy) Patterson and was born in Franklin township, Fayette county, Penn., March 10, 1843.

Sidney Patterson was a native of New Jersey, and was born December 12, 1803. He came to Fayette county with his father, Safety Patterson, who settled in Franklin township. Sidney Patterson engaged in farming and married Miss Martha McCoy, born in 1803.

Luke F. Patterson is of Irish descent, he was reared on a farm and educated in the common schools. Leaving school, he turned his attention to farming and has continued in that business until the present time.

In 1871 he married Miss Mattie Leighty. She died October 1, 1881, and left one child: Norman Patterson, born April 29, 1879. Mr. Patterson, for his second wife, married Miss Lizzie, daughter of John Snider. (See his sketch.) To them were born one child: Andrew Snider Patterson, born January 1, 1889.

Luke F. Patterson purchased the Star Flouring Mills in Menallen township, and has successfully operated them up to the present time. Their capacity is twenty barrels per day, which barely supplies his large and increasing home and county trade. For twenty-five years, he has been a member of I. O. O. F. and is a K. of P. Mr. Patterson is a democrat of the Jeffersonian type. He believes implicitly in the time-honored principles of the democratic party, and is always found working it its interests. He is an influential and prominent citizen of Menallen township.

JOHN PFLEGHARDT, SR., was born in Bavaria, Germany, August 22, 1823, and is a son of Louis L. and Anna B. (Price) Pfleghardt. The former was a shoemaker, shipwrecked and drowned in coming to America in 1836, on the ill-fated Frederick William; the latter is also deceased.

John Pfleghardt, Sr., until thirteen years of age, received a thorough training in the German schools, he then learned the trade of shoemaker, and continued in it until 1848, when he left his native land for America. He worked for six years at his trade in New York City, and in 1854 removed to Fayette City. Here he began in the boot and shoe business, in which he is still engaged.

In 1850 he was married to Miss Charlotte Bodendorfer, who came from Germany, with her brother, in 1849. Nine children have been born unto them: Julia (dead), John H. (in Nebraska), John N., Louis L. (dead), Mary E., William B., Louisa, Benjamin F., Anna C. (wife of John A. Wilson).

John N. Pfleghardt (son) was born December 26, 1855, and learned the shoe business with his father. He married, in 1878, Miss Anna C., daughter of James McCrory, and she died in September of the same year. In 1880 he was united in marriage to his present wife, Miss Ida M., daughter of William Beatty. They have four living children: Louis H., Charles W. (dead), William E., Elsie and Opal (twins). He is associated with his father in the shoe business, and belongs to the I. O. O. F. and K. M. C., and denominationally he is a Methodist, with his wife. Mr. Pfleghardt, Sr., carries from three to five thousand dollars worth of stock in the boot and shoe business, and is doing the best business of any other of the kind in his section of the county.

Mr. Pfleghardt, Sr., is an F. & A. M., K. of P. and belongs to the Equable Aid Union, and in company with his wife is a Lutheran. He is a successful business man, and is one of the solid and influential citizens of Fayette City.

MOSES E. PORTER, a leading druggist, was born July 14, 1854, and is a son of Samuel S. and Mary A. (Smith) Porter. (See history of Samuel S. Porter, in sketch of Samuel E. Porter.)

Moses Porter (grandfather) was born in Allegany county, Md., near Frostburg, January 10, 1804. April 20, 1826, he married Emly, daughter of Henry and Sarah (McKenzie) Wade. To them were born fifteen children, of whom eight are living: Margaret Rebecca, Gabriel Ellis, Samuel Smith, James Dennis, George Wesley, Elisha, Lydia and Lutellus Lindley.

Moses Porter owned a farm and farmed in Tyrone township, where he died June 10, 1880, and was buried on the farm.

Emly (Wade) Porter, the grandmother, was born in Allegany county, near Creasip Town, Md., August 12, 1810, and is now living with her daughter Lydia on the homestead farm.

Henry E. Smith (maternal grandfather) was born in Westmoreland county, Pa., March 28, 1803; was married to Margaret Barr, June 1, 1826, and had nine children, of whom five are living: Nathan, Mary Ann, Elisabeth Kennedy, Jane and Nancy.

He owned two adjoining farms in South Huntingdon township: the Sample farm and the homestead farm. He died January 17, 1888, at the advanced age of nearly eighty-five, and was buried in the Scottdale Cemetery.

Margaret (Barr) Smith (maternal grandmother) was born in Westmoreland county, Pa., February 19, 1800. She died December 30, 1872, and is buried in the graveyard at Tyrone church.

Gabriel McKenzie Porter (great-grandfather) was born in Baltimore, September 17, 1776, came to Allegany with his parents in 1782, married Rebecca Frost, of Frostburg, by whom he had five children: Jane, Josiah, John, Moses and Margaret. He died April 20, 1842, and is buried in the graveyard on the Porter farm.

Rebecca (Frost) Porter (great-grandmother) was a daughter of Josiah Frost and a native of Allegany county, Md. Her father owned the land where now stands the town of Frostburg, and built the first house in the place. He was a contractor on the "Old Pike."

Nathan Smith (maternal great-grandfather) was born in County Tyrone, Ireland, in 1770; obtained his education in the city of Dublin. He sailed from Movill Bay in 1793, was thirteen weeks on the water, had yellow fever; the ship, commanded by Captain Powell, was quarantined; he was sent to the hospital at Philadelphia, recovered, came to Lancaster county, Pa., and taught school. He came to Fayette county, near Connellsville, where there was a forge owned by a Quaker; clerked at Alliance furnace on Jacob's Creek; married Margery, daughter of Henry Irwin, January 29, 1801, by whom he had six children: Henry E., March 28, 1803; Anna Foster, March 26, 1805; James H., May 25, 1807; Rebecca Morrow, January 8, 1812; Eleanor McCurdy, June 1, 1814; Nathan, Jr., October 15, 1820.

In 1809 he purchased the farm now owned by Henry E. Smith's heirs, and remained on it till 1822, when he exchanged it to his son, Henry E., for a farm now owned by Samuel McCurdy's heir, in East Huntingdon township, Westmoreland county, on which he remained during the latter part of his life. He died March 25, 1850, in his eightieth year, and is buried in Tyrone churchyard.

Margery(Irwin)Smith (great-grandmother) was born August 2, 1776, probably in Lancaster county, Pa. She was a stout woman, a good harvest hand, and would remain at home with her children while her husband would cross the mountains and bring salt for himself and neighbors on pack-horses. She and her husband were members of the Presbyterian church, died May 18, 1867, and is buried in the graveyard at Tyrone church.

John Porter, Jr., (great-great-grandfather) was born in Baltimore. He married a Miss Nancy McKinzie, and was the first of the name who settled (1782) in Allegany county, Md. He first purchased a farm near Mt. Savage, supposed to be in Maryland, but afterward found to be in Pennsylvania; on this account he sold it, and purchased another farm near Mt. Savage. He subsequently sold this farm and settled on one near the Eckhart mine, where he died in 1810. His children were, respectively: Micheal, Samuel, Thomas, Gabriel (the great-grandfather of Moses E.), Henry, Moses, John and Nellie. The first six were born in Baltimore, the latter two on the Pennsylvania farm.

Nancy (McKinzie) Porter (great-great-mother) was born about 1746, and was the daughter of Moses McKinzie, who was murdered and robbed near Cumberland after having sold a farm, on his return home. She had a brother Moses who served through the Revolutionary War as a drummer-boy, enlististing at fourteen years of age.

James Smith (maternal great-great-grandfather) was married to Anna Huston. They lived in county Tyrone, Ireland, on a farm called "Sheep Hill." They had six children: Samuel, James, Robert, William, Nathan and Elisabeth. She never emigrated, was married to a Mr. Ritchie. James Smith emigrated to this country with his son Robert and family in 1796, and settled in South Huntingdon township, Westmoreland county, Pa., on a farm now owned by William Collor's heirs. He was a member of the Presbyterian church, died March 12, 1803, and was buried at Tyrone churchyard. His wife, Anna (Huston) Smith, died in Ireland, in 1776.

John Porter, Sr., (great-great-great-grandfather) was a native of Gloucestershire, near Bristol, England. He made himself obnoxious to the party in power by singing a song of his own composition which was very uncomplimentary to the reigning monarch, George I.; on account of this he was obliged to flee the country. He came to America in about 1715, settled in Baltimore county, Md., and was born about 1690.

Moses E. Porter was brought up on a farm at Porter's Gap, in Upper Tyrone township, attended the common schools of that district until he attained his majority. At the age of twenty-two he went to Moingona, Boone county, Iowa, where he served an apprenticeship of three years in a drug house. In 1880 he returned to Pennsylvania and opened a drug store at Dawson, where he has been engaged in the same ever since. He has succeeded in building up a good trade, and now has the best drug store in the place.

He was married April 11, 1883, to Miss Belle Stacy, daughter of William and Elis abeth (Strickler) Stacy, of Broad Ford, Pa. They have two children: Earle S. and Don S.

He is a member of the Senior Order of American Mechanics, is a good citizen, full of enterprise and pluck.

CURTIS REPPERT was born May 19, 1830, in Greene county, Pa., and is a son of George and Salome Reppert.

George Reppert (father) was born in one week after the arrival of his parents in this country from Germany. He was a son of Louis Reppert, who settled at New Geneva and followed glass blowing.

Curtis Repert received his education in the subscription schools, and then worked for nearly forty years as a glass-blower in the glass-works. In 1843 he removed to Belle Vernon, and in 1878 began the undertaking and furniture business. He has successfully continued in it, and now owns the largest establishment of that kind in the place.

He was married February 26, 1851, to Miss Mary Louisa, daughter of Edward Jordon, of Maine, who had removed to Westmoreland county. Unto this union was born six children: Allen, dead; Louie, Mira, Alfred and Eckley, dead.

He belongs to the Senior Mechanics, Royal Arcanum and Equitable Aid Union.

He is a consistent member of the M. E. church, to which he and his entire family belong.

He is a straightforward business man, and a good and reliable citizen.

JACOB T. ROLEY was born March 14, 1834, in Hempfield township, Westmoreland county, Pa., and was reared in that county till sixteen years old. He attended the common schools, and went one term to Mt. Pleasant College. In 1852 he went to Monongahela City, and followed teaming for two years. He then removed to Belle Vernon, and engaged in merchandising for some twenty years. In 1865, June 18th, he was married to Miss Anna E. Krepps, daughter of Louis Krepps, who is a descendant of one of the earliest families that settled in the county. To this union were born eight children: Anna E., William H., Louis F., Millie, Ellie, Jennie, Jesse and Joseph T.

In 1874 he read law, and has practiced at intervals since that time. At present he is engaged in the livery business. He served as justice of the peace from 1870 to 1875, has been burgess of his borough three times, and was re-elected justice of the peace in 1879.

He is the son of Robert Roley and Eliza Tuman, both of German descent. His father was born on Chestnut Ridge, Westmoreland county, March 14, 1812, and was the son of John Roley, one of the early pioneers of that county. His mother, Eliza Tuman, was a native of Pennsylvania; her father, Jacob Tuman, was amongst the first settlers of this part of the country. Her mother was Sarah Raider, and she was also of one of the earliest families of Southwestern Pennsylvania. The family is of German descent.

MILSON ROSSER, General Superintendent of the Jimtown & Sterling Coke Works, was born in Gloucestershire, England, 12th of January, 1850, and is a son of John and Ann (Jones) Rosser.

John Rosser in 1852 came from Gloucestershire, England, to Temperanceville, Pa., (now a part of the thirty-sixth ward of Pittsburgh) and in the ensuing year was joined by his family. In 1859 he removed to Mason county, Va. (now West Virginia), remained there until 1866, when he returned to Pennsylvania and located in Mansfield Valley, Allegheny county, Pa. He has always been engaged in the coal business, and is now operating a coal bank in Mansfield Valley. Mr. Rosser is a member of the Baptist church. Milson Rosser attended the common schools of Pittsburgh and the pay schools in Mason county, Va. At twelve years of age, he entered the coal mines and went to work at twenty-five cents per day. For twenty years he labored in coal mines and became thoroughly acquainted with all the details of mine management. Where other miners had worked, he had worked, and filled every position to be filled in a coal mine, thought and observed, and in 1875 was selected Huntsman, Miller & Co., as superintendent of their coal works situated twelve miles from Pittsburgh. In 1878 the firm made an assignment, and he accepted the superintendency of the mines of David Steen & Sons' coal works at Camp Hill. From 1880 to 1885 he served as mine superintendent at Jimtown Coke Works of J. M. Schoonmaker. In 1885 he was appointed general superintendent of the Jimtown and Sterling Coke Works, owned and operated by J. M. Schoonmaker, which position he still holds with credit to himself and satisfaction to all concerned.

On December 24, 1871, he was married to Miss Elizabeth, daughter of John W. and Mary Wilcox, one of the first mine inspectors in Western Pennsylvania, and a man now worth considerable money, gained by his own efforts. Mr. and Mrs. Rosser have seven children: George, Mary Ann, Alice, William, Florence, Bertha and Laura Bell.

He is a stanch republican, has been for several years the republican central committee-man of his township, served on the republican county committee, and is now serving as school director of Lower Tyrone township. He is a member of the Masonic Fraternity and belongs to the Odd Fellows. He owns an interest in the stone quarry on the P. McK. Y. R. R., west of Dawson. Mr. Rosser is one of that class of self-made men who only need opportunity to pass the front in most any line of business.

CHARLES W. RUSH is assistant cashier of the Dawson Deposit Bank. The Rush family is of Irish descent and is one of the oldest in Fayette county. Charles W. Rush's grandfather, Charles Rush, was a native of Fayette county and was a tavern-keeper at Farmington "in the Auld Lang Syne," when the National pike was in its glory as the "thoroughfare" of the country, and was considered by many as the tie which bound the nation solidly together.

William H. Rush, the father of Charles W. Rush, was a native of this county, and, following in the footsteps of his father, became the keeper of a hotel and has for the last quarter of a century pursued that business, the last thirteen years of which have been spent in Dawson, where he now lives. He was born in Farmington in 1838, where he was reared and married Miss Anna E. Frost, who was born at Searight. He served in the war as bugler, in Company K, Sixth Pennsylvania Heavy Artillery.

Charles W. Rush was born February 21, 1864, at Farmington, Fayette county, Pa., grew up mainly at Dawson and was educated in the public schools of that town. At the age of nineteen went to the State normal school at California, where he graduated in 1883. Leaving the normal school, he engaged in teaching school in this county, and taught up to 1889; in 1886 he was principal of the Dawson public schools. In the spring of

1889 he resigned his school to take the position he now holds in the Dawson Deposit Bank. Mr. Rush is a democrat and is one of the most promising young men of that section.

JOHN G. SCHNEIDER, burgess of Belle Vernon, was born September 13, 1853, in Wurtemburg, Germany, and is the son of John and Anna (Caturia) Schneider, both natives of Germany. His father was born in 1828 and died in 1842, he was a cabinet-maker and a man of prominence in his native town. The maiden name of the mother of John G. was Messmer. She is still l ving at her old home in Germany.

John G. Schneider was educated in the schools of his native city. From eight to nine years of age he attended the common school. From nine to twelve in the preparatory school and later attended the University at Tubingen. He came to America in 1869, at the age of sixteen, and settled in West Newton, Westmoreland county, Pa., where he learned the trade of painter. He removed to Belle Vernon in 1872 and worked at his trade. In 1875 he was married to Miss Clara Boltz, whose father was a native of Prussia and came to the United States in 1849, married Elsie Spahr, a native of Washington township, whose parents were from Germany, and were early settlers of this county. By this marriage was born one child: Grace D.

Mr. Schneider is a democrat and was elected burgess of Belle Vernon in 1889 by a handsome majority, although the borough is largely republican. He is a very popular man among his fellow-citizens, and is a prominent member of the Royal Arcanum, Improved Order of Red Men, is past officer in both, and has been representative to the Grand Council of each.

SINGLETON SCHROCK, one who has led a life of continual, yet profitable change, was born in Allegany county (now Garret), Maryland, November 11, 1847, and is a son of J. Schrock and Rebecca (Miller) Schrock. His grandfather, John Schrock, was of German extraction and died in Eastern Pennsylvania, in 1803. His father was born near Berlin, Somerset county, Pa., in 1799. He married Miss Rebecca, daughter of John Miller, and they had eleven children: John, Harriet, Lucinda, Malinda, Clarissa, Louisa, Elizabeth, Joseph, Susan, Sarah and Singleton.

Singleton Schrock was educated in the common schools of Markleysburg, served Custer in the late war seven months in the eighteenth Cavalry Regiment, and learned the trade of a blacksmith with George Smith, in Jockey Valley. He worked for one year at his trade in Markleysburg and then removed to Columbus, Ohio. In the latter place he failed to find employment, and being out of money was compelled to beg and tramp his way back to Somerfield. Here he engaged in a blacksmith shop until April 1, 1870, with John Close. His next move was to Confluence where he worked four months as a tool dresser, for D. W. Patton & Co., railway contractors. From Confluence he removed to Brooks Tunnel and labored with Gletzell & Co., contractors, until 1872. From Brooks Tunnel, he removed to Confluence and remained for ten years and twenty three days, in the employ of the P. &. C. R. R. Co., at a salary of $65 per month, making and dressing tools. In 1882 he took charge of a boarding camp for a construction train, and remained fourteen months; when he opened and ran a blacksmith shop in Confluence for six months. His next location was Dickenson Run, where he conducted a boarding house for fourteen months.

In August, 1885, he purchased a fine residence at Dickenson Run. His house is a fine two-story building with mansard roof, 70 feet front, 126 feet depth and contains 15 rooms. He keeps boarders, and is engaged at his trade, working at the P. &. McK. Railway round house; is also a partner of J. F. Black & Co., in the mercantile business.

Singleton Schrock was married August 13, 1874, to Miss Jennie Shaw, of Kingwood, Preston county, W. Va. Two children were born to them: Nellie and Franklin M. Schrock.

Mr. Schrock is a republican, and served one term as councilman of the borough of Confluence, Pa. His life has been one of continual change and many hardships, but by pluck and push, he has secured for himself and family a competency.

WILLIAM A. SHOEMAKER, M. D., is the son of Daniel and Elizabeth (Probst) Shoemaker, both natives of Lock Haven, Clinton county, Pa., and where they at present reside. His father is a farmer of Clinton county, and a stock trader. He is a member of the Methodist Episcopal church.

John Shoemaker, paternal grandfather of Dr. Shoemaker, was a farmer of Clinton county, and died in 1872. The Shoemaker family is an old and respectable family of Clinton county. His maternal grandfather Probst was also a farmer of Clinton county, and respected as an honorable, upright citizen.

Dr. William A. Shoemaker was born November 10, 1859, at Lock Haven, Clinton county, Pa., and grew to manhood in his native town. He received his early education in the public schools, and completed his studies by taking a scientific and classical course at the normal school at Lock Haven. In 1881 he commenced the study of medicine under the tutelage of his cousin, Dr. W. J. Shoemaker, of Lockhaven, with whom he continued for one year, when he went to Baltimore and entered the medical department of the University of Maryland. He took a course of three years' study in medicine, and graduated from there in March, 1885. On March 31, 1885, he located at Dawson in the practice, and has established a large and successful practice at Dawson, and stands high in the community as a successful physician and citizen. He is a general practitioner, and is a member of the Fayette County Medical Association, and the State Medical Association of Pennsylvania. He is a member of the Presbyterian church, and of the Royal Arcanum and Odd Fellows.

He was married, in 1888, to Miss Cora Given, of Dawson, daughter of Robert T. Given. She died soon after her marriage.

In June, 1888, Dr. Shoemaker formed a partnership with Dr. J. C. Smith, of Hampshire, W. Va.

CRAWFORD HARRISON SCOTT, of New Salem, Menallen township, was born August 8, 1840, near Mendenhall's dam. Crawford Scott (his grandfather) came from Ireland, September 30, 1788, and settled in Lancaster county, Pa. Wilson Scott (father of C. H. Scott) was born September 30, 1808, and was a blacksmith by trade, at which he worked nearly all of his life in Menallen township. He married Miss Ann Woodward, who was born October 26, 1813, in Menallen township, the daughter of Joshua Woodward. C. H. Scott was educated in the schools of Menallen township, under George Osborne, a noted teacher of his day. At the age of twenty-one, he enlisted September 19, 1861, under Captain John Weltner, Company I, Eighty-fifth, Regiment Pennsylvania Volunteer Infantry. Colonel Joshua B. Howell's regiment. This regiment was made up in Greene, Fayette and Somerset counties. The following are the principal battles in which he was engaged: Black Water, October, 1862; South

West Creek, N. C., December 13, 1863; Kingston, N. C., December 14, 1863; White Hall, N. C., December 16, 1863; Goldsboro, N. C., December 17, 1863; the siege of Yorktown, 1862; Jones Ford, June 28, 1862; the siege of Charleston, the siege of Richmond at Bermuda Hundreds, Deepbottom, seven days fight. He was wounded at the fight at Strawberry Plain, August 14, 1864, by a shot in the left lung, and still carries the ball. He entered the army as a private, and was promoted to non-commissioned officer in 1862. He served three years and three months, and is now a prominent man in the Grand Army of the Republic. He married Miss Mary Radcliff, daughter of Joseph and Sarah Radcliff, of Upper Middletown. They are both members of the Christian church, and have four children: W. R. Scott, born February 13, 1866, who is now preparing for teaching; Ross Scott, also preparing for teaching, born October 21, 1867, Orrin C., born April 5, 1873, Clarice Gay, born April 29, 1877.

C. H. Scott was a teacher before the war; after leaving the army he went into the mercantile business at New Salem in 1867. He was postmaster at New Salem for nine years, and is a self made man, and has amassed a competence by his own unaided labor. He is a good citizen, and respected by all in his township. He is a republican in politics, and is an effective worker in the party.

THOMAS SCOTT was born in 1833, in County Longford, Ireland, and his parents were James and Catherine Scott. When he was eight years of age, his parents came to Pennsylvania where his father died soon after their arrival, and the boy was thus thrown upon his own resources. He worked three years for Joseph S. Walton, a Quaker of Chester county, receiving as compensation his board, clothing and three months' schooling each winter. His next employment was three and one half years' service in the Doe Run Cotton Mills, thence he went to Lancaster county and labored for a time in a sawmill.

In 1854 he came with his widowed mother to Belle Vernon, where he has since resided.

In the late war he enrolled himself as a volunteer under Lincoln's first call for troops. His enlistment dated from October 16, 1862, in an independent company, but later joined the Ringgold Battalion then consolidated with the Twenty-second Pennsylvania Volunteers. He was in thirty-six engagements, mustered in as a corporal, and came out as a commissary sergeant, October 31, 1865. He has a commission of promotion signed by J. G. Isenberg and A. J. Greenfield. He was married in 1858, to Sarah A. Gamble, daughter of James Gamble, an old and respectable citizen. They had three children: Alice S., married to Samuel McKean and lives in Belle Vernon; John T., is in partnership with Lewis Jobes, in the butcher business, and Anna M. (Mrs. Scott) died May 18, 1883.

Mr. Scott is a prominent member of the Grand Army of the Republic, and belongs to George D. Baird Post, No. 178.

WILLIAM SEARIGHT, of Menallen, the founder of the Fayette county family of Searights, was born near Carlisle, Cumberland county, Pa., December 5, 1791. He was of Scotch-Irish descent on both paternal and maternal sides. His paternal grandfather, William Seawright, came from County Donegal, in the North of Ireland, about the year 1740, settled in Lampiter township, Lancaster county, Pa., and was, at the time of his death, 1771, a prominent citizen and landholder of that county. His paternal grandmother, Ann Hamilton, came from Belfast, Ireland, at the same time, and

Wm. Searight

settled in about the same locality near Lancaster City, Pa. She came to America with her brothers William and Hugh, and a sister Mary. Her brother William was the grandfather of the distinguished Governor of South Carolina in Calhoun's day, who was known as the Nullifier Governor, in consequence of his having advocated the nullification of certain tariff laws passed by Congress, which he considered adverse to the interests of the people of the South. A pretty full though incomplete history of the Hamilton family of Lancaster county, Pa., can be seen in Egles Pennsylvania Genealogies in "Notes and Queries," by Colonel Evans, of Columbia. The ancestors of the Lancaster county Hamilton family, of which, as stated, the grandmother of the subject of this sketch was a member, came from Scotland to Belfast, Ireland, when it became the refuge for persecuted Covenanters. They were a part of the historical Scotch family of Hamiltons, one of whom was chosen as the husband of Queen Mary, and another as the husband of Queen Elizabeth. Family tradition and family history also teach that Alexander Hamilton of revolutionary fame was connected with this same Lancaster county family of Hamiltons. The names of the children of William Seawright and Ann Hamilton were Mary, Esther, Ann, William (the father of the subject of this sketch) and Alexander. (See deed book W. W., page 134, Lancaster county records.) Mary, the eldest of the children, married John Glenn. The Glenns are extinct, and are mostly buried in Pequea churchyard Lancaster county, Pa.; Esther married Gilbert Seawright, and did not change her name. Gilbert Seawright who married Esther was the founder of the large family of Seawrights in and around Carlisle, Cumberland county, Pa.; Ann married William Wood and removed from Lancaster county to Albemarle county, Va., and from there the children of the Wood family moved on to their lands near Lexington, Ky.; Alexander married a Logan, and removed to Augusta county, Va. They had three children: William, Alexander and Margaret, who removed with their families from Augusta county, Va., to Henry county, Tenn., in about the year 1826, where some of their descendants are now living. William (the father of the subject of our sketch) married Jane Ramsey, a daughter of Samuel and Catherine Ramsey (*nee* Seawright).

The maternal great-grandfather of William Searight came from Donegal, Ireland, about 1740, and settled in Leacock township, near Lancaster City, Pa., where he lived and died. His name was also William Seawright. He was for many years a landholder and prominent citizen of Lancaster county, Pa. In the Revolution of 1688, the ancestors of William Seawright threw themselves into the cause of William of Orange. Some of them were driven within the walls of Londonderry when its gates were closed against James the Second, some afterwards died in the besieged city, while others of them survived the siege. The maternal great-grandmother of the subject of this sketch was also a resident of the North of Ireland, whose maiden name was Catherine Jackson. William Seawright and Catherine Jackson had but one child, Catherine. Catherine Seawright married Samuel Ramsey, of Lancaster county, Pa., who afterwards became a wealthy and prominent citizen of Cumberland county, Pa. He owned the famous "Letort Springs" tract near Carlisle, where he lived and died. They were the parents of the mother of the subject of this sketch. The names of the children of Samuel and Catherine (Seawright) Ramsey were: Jane, Catherine, Margaret, Esther, Elizabeth, Samuel, Archibald and Seawright. Jane married William Seawright the father of the subject of this sketch). Catherine, Margaret, Esther and Elizabeth died unmarried. Samuel married a Gettysburg lady and had no children; Archibald married Margaret Dean, some of whose grandchildren are now residents of New Bloomfield, Perry county, Pa. Seawright Ramsey married a Denny, a member of the Pittsburgh family of Dennys, and a sister of the wife of Dr. Murray, of Carlisle, Pa. All of this family, except Jane and Samuel, are buried in the old graveyard at Carlisle, Pa. Samuel is buried in Huntington county, Pa., and Jane in the Legonier Valley. After the death of his wife Catherine, Samuel Ramsey married the widow Macfeely, grandmother of General Robert Macfeely, commissary general, U. S. A., Washington, D. C.

In about 1780 the parents of William Searight removed from Lancaster county, Pa., to Cumberland county, Pa., and from there to Augusta county, Va. They remained in Virginia about eight years, when they returned to Cumberland county. There they remained for a short time, when they started for the western part of the State, stopping a short time in Huntington and Indiana counties, and finally made their permanent settlement in the Legonier Valley, Westmoreland county, Pa., about five miles above Legonier, on the Loyalhanna river.

The names of the brothers and sisters of William Searight were: Samuel, Alexander, Mary, John, Hamilton and Archibald. After 1810 Samuel settled in Tippecanoe county, Indiana. Alexander first settled in Brooke county, Va., and afterwards removed to Morgan county, Ohio, and William, the subject of this sketch, settled in Fayette county, Pa. The other members of the family remained in the Legonier valley, and died without issue. They are buried alongside of their parents in "Pleasant Grove" graveyard about five miles from the town of Legonier. William Searight received only a plain English education, but he was endowed with the precepts of stern integrity, industry and honor, the elements of his future success in business, and of his elevated character. In the neighborhood in which he was reared, he had learned the business of fuller and dyer of cloth, a knowledge of which, with his energy and honor, was his entire stock in hand. He arrived in Fayette county at about the age of twenty one, and commenced business at an old fulling-mill on Dunlap's creek, known as Hammond's mill. He afterwards prosecuted his vocation at Cook's mill, on Redstone creek and also on the old George Washington farm, near Perryapolis. He next purchased a farm and hotel at Searights, the property and village deriving its name from him, and there made his permanent settlement. On March 26, 1826, he married Rachel Brownfield, a daughter of Thomas and Elizabeth Brownfield, of Uniontown, Pa.

Rachel Brownfield (wife of William Searight) was of English Quaker lineage. Her parents were natives of Frederick county, Va. Her grandparents were natives of Bucks county, Pa., and her great-grandparents were natives of Yorkshire and Chester, England. She was born in Gainsboro, Frederick county, Va., February 7, 1805. In 1805, before the National road was built, and when she was only six weeks old, her parents removed from Frederick county, Va., to Uniontown, Pa. She is now living with all her faculties well preserved, within half a square of where she landed in 1805.

At the village of Searights, William Searight laid the foundation of a large fortune. His integrity, united to a generous and benevolent heart, gave him a high place in the esteem and affections of the community in which he lived. His sound judgment soon impressed itself on his own county and he became one of her most influential and useful citizens. He was a prominent and zealous old-time democratic politician, and wielded a large influence. On one occasion he rode on horseback from Searights to Harrisburgh, a distance of over 200 miles, to assist in the preparation to nominate General Jackson for the presidency. He was an intimate friend of the late Simon Cameron, ex-United States senator from Pennsylvania, and had close political relations with the leading politicians of his day.

In the early history of Fayette county, political conventions of both parties were accustomed to meet at Searights and plan campaigns. A memorable meeting, of which Mr. Searight was the chief instigator, was held there in 1828, known as the "Gray Meeting," from the name of the keeper at that time of the local hotel, John Gray. At this meeting the Jackson and Adams men met to test their strength. They turned out in the meadow below the hotel, formed in rank and counted off, the Jackson men outnumbered their opponents decisively, and it was regarded as a great Jackson victory.

In the political campaign of 1836 a large democratic meeting was held at Uniontown, and the delegation from Searights bore a banner with the inscription "Menallen the battle ground of the Gray Meeting." Many politicians of the olden time were there, among them on the Jackson side were General Henry W. Beeson, Colonel Ben Brownfield, Westley Frost, William F. Coplan, Henry J. Rigden, James C. Beckley, Benedict Kimber, Solomon G. Krepps, William Searight, Hugh Keys, William Hatfield, Colonel William L. Miller, John Fuller, Provance McCormick, William Davidson, Alexander Johnson and Thomas Duncan.

On the Adams side were Andrew Stewart, John M. Austin, F. H. Oliphant, John Kennedy, John Dawson, Samuel Evans, James Bowman, William Hogg, Stokely Connell, William P. Wells, Basil Brownfield, George Mason, Kennedy Duncan and John Lyon.

The many similar political meetings with which William Searight was identified, go to show the esteem in which he was held by the citizens of the county by all parties. But Fayette county, although the first, was but little in advance of other communities to learn and admire his worth. He early became known and appreciated throughout the entire State. He was appointed commissioner of the Cumberland road (National road) by Governor Porter in the most palmy days of that great thoroughfare, a position he held for many years. In 1845 he was superseded by Colonel William Hopkins of Washington, Pa. Subsequently an act of the legislature placed the road in the hands of trustees, appointed by the courts, and these trustees restored William Searight to the commissionership, the duties of which office he continued to discharge with great fidelity and industry. He was thoroughly familiar with all the hills and valleys of that grand old thoroughfare, once so stirring and active, but now still and grass-grown. Previous to his appointment as commissioner of the National road, he was a contractor on the same. He was one of the contractors who built the iron bridge over the mouth of Dunlap's creek, between Bridgeport and Brownsville, and was also a contractor on the Erie extension of the Pennsylvania and Ohio canal.

At the time of his death he was the candidate of the democratic party for one of the most important offices in the State, that of canal commissioner. To this office he would have undoubtedly been elected, had not death interposed and called him from the active duties of this life to the realities of another world, as after his death Colonel William Hopkins, of Washington county, was nominated by the democratic party for the same office, and was elected by a large majority. He died at his residence in Menallen township, on the 12th day of August, 1852. He left a widow and six children:

Thomas, Ewing, Jane, William, James, Elizabeth. His widow is living at Uniontown at the advanced age of eighty-four, and has all her faculties as perfect as ever. Of the children, William is dead, the rest are living. Thomas, Jane and James, live in Uniontown. Ewing lives on the old homestead in Menallen township, and Elizabeth is the wife of J. T. Colvin, president of the Pittsburgh National Bank of Commerce, Pittsburgh, Pa., and lives in Pittsburgh.

William Searight was a man of the most generous and humane character, ever ready to lend his counsel, his sympathies, and his purse to the aid of others. Though a strong political party man, yet he always treated his opponents with courtesy. In religion he was like most of the race to which he belonged, imbued with Calvinism. The brightest traits of his character were exemplified in his last hours. So far as human judgment can decide, he died a Christian. His aged widow often quotes an expression he made as he was approaching the sad realities of death, which gave her much comfort then, and still continues to comfort her, as her trembling footsteps near the shores of the same river, over which he passed so many years ago; it was this: "Our prayers have been answered; I feel that if I should die to-night, the Lord will receive me into His Holy Kingdom." Although death plucked him from the very threshold of earthly honors, yet it caused him no regrets. The Kingdom into which he was about to enter presented higher honors, and purer enjoyments. To him they offered:

"No midnight shade, no clouded sun,
But sacred, high, eternal noon."

A more emphatic eulogy than is in the power of language to express was bestowed upon him on the day of his funeral, by the assembling around his coffin, to perform the last sad duty of friendship, of as great if not a greater number of citizens than ever attended the funeral ceremonies of any one who had died within the limits of Fayette county. Among that vast assemblage were both the patriarchs of the county and the rising youth who came to give their testimony to the lofty worth in life of the distinguished dead. A few days after his death a large meeting of the citizens of Fayette county, irrespective of party, convened at the court house for the purpose of bearing suitable testimony to his memory and character. The following gentlemen were chosen officers: Hon. Nathaniel Ewing, president; Hon. Daniel Sturgeon (ex-United States senator), and Z. Ludington, vice-presidents; John B. Krepps and R. P. Flenniken, secretaries. On motion of Hon. James Veech (later author of "Monongahela of Old"), a committee on resolutions, composed of leading citizens, was appointed, which committee presented the following preamble and resolutions, which were unanimously adopted:

"When a valuable citizen dies, it is meet that the community of which he was a member mourn his loss. A public expression of their sorrow at such an event is due as some solace to the grief of the bereaved family and friends, and as an incentive to others to earn for their death the same distinction.

"In the recent death of William Searight, this community has lost such a citizen. Such an event has called this public meeting, into which enter no schemes of political promotion, no partisan purposes of empty eulogy. Against all this, death has shut the door. While yet the tear hangs upon the cheek of his stricken family, and the tidings of death are unread by many of his friends, we, his fellow-citizens, neighbors, friends, of all parties, have assembled to speak to those who knew and loved him best, and to those who knew him not, the words of sorrow and truth, in sincerity and soberness. Therefore as the sense of this meeting,

"*Resolved*, That in the death of William Searight, Fayette county and the commonwealth of Pennsylvania have lost one of their best and most useful citizens. The people at large may not realize their loss, but the community in which he lived, over whose comforts and interests were diffused the influences of his liberality and enterprise, feel it, while his friends, of all classes, parties and professions, to whom he clung, and who clung to him, mourn it.

"*Resolved*, That while we would withhold our steps from the sanctuary of domestic grief, we may be allowed to express to the afflicted widow and children of the deceased our unfeigned sorrow and sympathy in their great bereavement, and to tender them our assurance that while in their hearts the memory of the husband and father will ever be cherished, in our hearts will be kept the liveliest recollections of his virtues as a citizen and a friend.

"*Resolved*, That among the elements which must enter into every truthful estimate of the character of William Searight, are a warm amenity of manner, combined with great dignity of deportment, which were not the less attractive by their plainness and want of ostentation; elevated feelings more pure than passionless; high purposes with untiring energy in their accomplishment; an ennobling sense of honor, and individual independence, which kept him always true to himself and to his engagements; unfaltering fidelity to his friends; a liberality which heeded no restraint but means and merit; great promptness and fearlessness in the discharge of what he believed to be a duty, private or public, guided by a rigid integrity, which stood all tests and withstood all temptations; honesty and truthfulness in word and deed, which no seductions could weaken or assaults overthrow, in all respects the architect of his own fortune and fame. These, with the minor virtues in full proportion, are some of the outlines of character which stamped the man whose death we mourn, as one much above the ordinary level of his race.

"*Resolved*, That while we have here nothing to do or say as to the loss sustained by the political party to which he belonged, and whose candidate he was for an office of great honor and responsibility, we may be allowed to say that had he lived and been successful with a heart so rigidly set as was his, with feelings so high and integrity so firm, and withal an amount of practical intelligence so ample as he possessed, his election could have been regretted by no citizen who knew him, and who placed the public interests beyond selfish ends and party success. As a politician we knew him to hold to his principles and party predilections with a tenacious grasp, yet he was ever courteous and liberal in his deportment and views towards his political opponents.

"*Resolved*, That in the life and character of William Searight we see a most instructive and encouraging example. Starting the struggle of life with an humble business, poor and unbefriended, with an honest mind and a true heart, with high purposes and untiring industry, he by degrees gained friends and means which never forsook him. He thus won for himself and family ample wealth, and attained a position among his fellowmen which those who have had the best advantages our country affords, might well envy. That wealth and that position he used with a just liberality and influence for the benefit of all around and dependent upon him. Though dead, he yet speaketh to every man in humble business—'Go thou and do likewise, and such shall be thy reward in life and in death.'

"*Resolved*, That the proceedings of this meeting be furnished for publication in all the papers of the county, and a copy thereof, signed by the officers, be presented to the family of the deceased."

EWING B. SEARIGHT, of Menallen, was born September 5, 1828, in the "Old Stone Tavern," at what is now the village of Searights. He is the son of William and Rachel (Brownfield) Searight. (For ancestry see sketch of his father, William Searight.) Mr. Searight was raised on a farm and educated in the subscription schools of his day. He was married by the Rev. Page, of Brownsville, on February 3, 1859, to Miss Elizabeth Jackson, daughter of Zadoc and Lydia Jackson. They have two children: Rachel, born August 26, 1860; William J., born August 11, 1863. Rachel married Charles J. McCormick, and died in 1882, leaving one child, Searight Ray McCormick, who was born August 1, 1882. Mrs. Searight was educated in the Brownsville Seminary when it was under the charge of the Rev. Baker. Mr. Searight has served as township auditor for ten years, as school director from 1869 to 1875, and was poorhouse director for three years. He is an ardent Democrat of the old school, and takes an active part in the political affairs of his township and county. Ewing Searight was a man of very humane character. He was generous to a fault, and was always ready to assist or accommodate a neighbor. He is deservedly popular with his friends and all who know him. He and his wife are consistent members of the Episcopal church.

NORVAL P. SMITH, a youthful soldier in the Civil War and a leading merchant of Dawson, was born near Bruceton, Preston county, Va. (now W. Va.), May 10, 1846, and is a son of Squire Henry and Martha (King) Smith. His grandfather, Jacob Smith, was a son of a Revolutionary soldier, and was born in Somerset county, Pa., in 1764. He was a farmer and removed to Preston county, where he died March 30, 1860, at ninety-six years of age. His father, Squire Henry Smith, was born December 7, 1805, in Preston, then Monongalia county; he was a farmer, and served as justice of the peace in Grant district for over twenty years. He owned the present well-known "Smith farm" near Bruceton. On this tract is the celebrated "sulphur spring," whose waters are said to possess remarkable curative properties

Norval P. Smith's maternal grandfather, James King, was raised in Old Town, Va., and was a color-bearer in the war of 1812. He died in Preston county, W. Va., at the age of eighty-seven years; Emma Short King, his wife, died at the age of sixty-four years.

Mr. Smith owned over one thousand acres of land, engaged largely in stock dealing, and was a ruling elder in the Presbyterian church. His death occurred July 29, 1862, occasioned by the running away of his team. His wife was born April 30, 1807, was a member of the Presbyterian church, and died September 20, 1882. Four of his sons served in the late war: Lucian, Ashabel G., N. P. and Henry C., the latter dying in the service.

Norval P. Smith was raised on a farm until fifteen years of age, when the war began. He was too young to enlist, so he became a wagoner in the Federal army in February, 1862, but was soon promoted to wagon master, and was engaged in hauling between Harper's Ferry and Winchester. Having attained to the proper age for enlistment, he joined Company K, Third Regiment Maryland Infantry Volunteers, served until the close of the war, and was honorably discharged at Camp Carroll, Baltimore, in May, 1865.

After the close of the war he completed his education at the Upper Iowa University, in Fayette county, Iowa, and subsequently turned his attention to mercantile pursuits. Mr. Smith was engaged for several years as a clerk with Rush & Smith, of Uniontown, dealers in dry goods and notions; afterward held a position with Brown & Hancock of Osceola, Mo.; next was in the employ of Morehouse & Carson, of Pittsburgh, for a short time, when he became a successful traveling salesman for John A. Horner & Co., of Baltimore. He left their service to accept a clerkship with P. G. Cochran & Co., at Spring Grove, Pa. From 1876 to 1881 he engaged in the general mercantile business as a partner of the firm of Chidester & Smith, at Bruceton W. Va. In May, 1881, he engaged with John T. Cochran at Dawson in the general mercantile business under the firm name of Smith & Cochran, and have successfully continued since in that line of business.

On August 4, 1880, he was married to Miss Annie H., only daughter of James Cochran (see sketch). To this union have been born three children: James H., Lucian P. and Martha C.

Mr. Smith is a stanch republican, and is a good business man. Special adaptability and many years of valuable experience well qualifies him for most any business pursuit.

PHILLIP G. SMITH was born March 26, 1838, in Connellsville township, Fayette county, Pa., and is of German descent. He was educated in the common schools of his native township, and, arriving at the age of maturity, he entered Waynesburg College. Here he remained for two terms. He then entered Pleasant Valley Academy, of Washington county, as an assistant teacher and a pupil, and remained as such for seven months. After this he taught in the common schools in Washington and Fayette counties for twelve terms, farming in the summer time. In 1862 he attended the normal school of Millsboro, Pa.

January 1, 1863, he was married to Miss Hannah L. Snyder, daughter of Jacob Snyder, of near Perryopolis. Six children was the result of this union: Willie E., Laurilla, May, Hattie, Deborah Anna, Hannah Catherine and Emma Dora. Willie E. died in 1878, at the age of fourteen years.

Mr. Smith is a member of the Harmony church, Cumberland Presbyterian. He is a democrat, and has held the position of school director for one term and tax collector of Perry township for two terms.

He engaged in merchandising in 1866 at California, Pa., and at Dawson's Station—now Dawson borough—in 1867-9. Afterwards, for four or five years, he was engaged in farming. In January, 1888, he began the manufacture of red brick near Dickenson, Pa., and still continues in this business, and has been quite successful. His works have a capacity of 700,000 bricks per annum.

The father of the subject of this sketch, Mr. Jacob Smith, was born in the same township where his son was born—Connellsville—in 1799, and was a successful farmer up to his death, in 1868. In 1820 he married Miss Catherine Galley. They had twelve children: Abraham, Henry, Martha, Eliza, Joseph, Samuel, John, Jonathan, Jesse, Philip G., Mary and an infant. Samuel, John, Jonathan, Martha, Abraham and the infant are dead.

Mr. Smith's mother was born in this county in 1801. For her ancestry see the sketch of Hon. H. B. Galley—at another place in this volume.

Henry Smith, the grandfather of Peter G. Smith, was born within the present limits of Fayette county in 1760; he was a farmer, and one of the best in western Pennsylvania. He married a Miss Stauffer, of Westmoreland county.

The great-great-grandfather of Philip G. Smith came from Germany to America in 1700.

SAMUEL SMOCK is of German descent, and was born in Rostraver township, Westmoreland county, Pa., June 19, 1820, and is a son of Henry Smock.

Barnet Smock (paternal grandfather) was a Revolutionary soldier. In 1793 he and his wife came on foot from New Jersey to Westmoreland county. He was a common laborer and his children were Elizabeth, Abraham, Henry and Mary.

Henry Smock (father) was a son of Barnet and Elizabeth Smock, and was born in New Jersey in 1790. He was three years old when his parents came to Westmoreland county. He was a common laborer, and married a Miss Shepler. They had eleven children: Ruhama, Mary, Philip, Jane, Lucinda, Samuel, Barney, Isabella (dead), Sarah, Margaret and Caroline.

Mrs. Smock was a daughter of Philip Shepler, who married Mary Baxter, and whose father was Mott Shepler.

Samuel Smock was a very poor boy, and on April 14, 1839, he went to learn the black smith trade with James Beazel of Belle Vernon; was possessed of scant clothing, and worked bare-footed in the shop until he earned enough money to buy a pair of shoes. In three years he acquired his trade, owned a good suit of clothes worth $31 and had $79.42 in money. He now helped his parents to secure a home, and then sought to make a home for himself. In 1844 he went to Perry township and worked until 1846, saving $500. He next worked in Westmoreland county, when he went to Ohio, and after a short stay removed to Belle Vernon, where he first worked at $25 per month, but soon bought a lot, and built him a house and shop. He pursued his trade for twenty-one years at that place.

At the end of that time, he had accumulated $14,000. Selling his property, he bought in 1868, the farm he now owns at Smock's Station (named for him). His farm contains 190 acres of excellent land, costing $12,000, and for which he lately refused to take $28,000. A town is growing up on his land, around the railroad station which is situated between Uniontown and Brownsville on the Monongahela division of the S. W. P. R. W.

Mr. Smock, in the spring of 1847, married Miss Mary Ann, daughter of Margaret Fields, of Perry township. Unto this union were born the following children: William, dead; Celia; Elzanna, dead; Roley, dead; Odessa, Noah and Alva.

Mrs. Smock died in 1867, and on March 15, 1869, he married his second wife, Miss Susan Hess, a daughter of Martin and Elizabeth Hess of Redstone township. She was born April 1, 1832. In politics he is a democrat, and is emphatically a self-made made, who in middle age, by hard work and good management, attained to a position of ease and affluence.

He started in early life in absolute want, but by industry and a strict application to business overcame every difficulty in carving out for himself a successful business career, and now in advancing years is worthily enjoying the well-earned fruits of his labor.

STOCKDALE SNYDER, a prudent and industrious farmer of Rostraver township, Westmoreland, is a son of Jacob and Hannah (Stockdale) Snyner, and was born in Westmoreland county, Pa., May 10, 1829.

Jacob Snyder was a son of Nicholas Snyder, who came from Germany, and settled at an early day in Westmoreland county. Jacob Snyder married Hannah Stockdale, a Quakeress of Washington county, and soon removed to Fayette county, where he lived and died.

Stockdale Snyder, like all boys of that time, received his education in the subscription schools. His paternal ancestors were members of the Reformed German church, but he is a consistent member of the Cumberland Presbyterian church, and a highly respected citizen. On June 6, 1849, he married Miss Sarah, daughter of William and Mary (Conkle) Browneller. The Browneller family came from Messersburg, Lancaster county, to western Pennsylvania in 1816, and the Conkle family came with them. Stockdale Snyder has ten children: Allen, April 30, 1850; Francis, September 6, 1851; Robert, November 26, 1852; Joseph W., August 1, 1854; Benton, August 7, 1857, died September 8, 1863; Laura B., October 18, 1855; Andrew, March 5, 1859; Mary C., February 7, 1862; Jesse O., January 7, 1864, and Lee S., February 14, 1867, of whom all living and married except Lee S.

Jesse O. Snyder (son) was brought up on a farm and attended the common schools. At seventeen years of age he became an apprentice to learn the trade of a stonemason and bricklayer. In two years he completed his trade, worked one year at journey work, then became a contractor on brick and stone work, and is still profitably engaged in that line of business. About his marriage clusters considerable romance. In the great Belle Vernon flood of July 11, 1888, he was compelled to row a skiff through the streets of the borough after his bride, and encountered sundry mishaps. He was married, July 11, 1888, to Miss Jennie B., daughter of William H. and Cadara (Springer) Noble, the former a native of Oil City, the latter of Belle Vernon.

Mr. Noble was a carpenter by trade, an earnest Presbyterian, and served three years as a soldier in the late war. Mrs. Snyder's maternal grandmother, Rachel Jordon, is a native of Maine. Her father, Thomas Jordan, was a captain in the War of 1812.

Mr. and Mrs. Snyder began housekeeping in Homestead, September 10, 1888, where they have a comfortable home.

Jesse O. Snyder is a young man of ability, energy and enterprise. He is a member of the Junior Order of American Mechanics, and belongs to the Methodist Episcopal church.

PETER SNYDER, one of Lower Tyrone's leading farmers, is a son of Peter and Catherine (Bauthers) Snyder, and was born in Washington township, Westmoreland county, Pa., March 10, 1821.

Peter Snyder's grandfathers, John Snyder and Jacob Bauthers, were companion emigrants from New Jersey to Westmoreland county. John Snyder purchased a large tract of land where the town of Scottdale now stands, and erected thereon a grist-mill. His son, Peter Snyder, Sr., was born in New Jersey about 1796, and after thirty years residence in Westmoreland county, removed with his family to Franklin township, and was there engaged in farming until his death in 1861. His wife was born in 1800, and died in 1865.

Peter Snyder was raised on a farm and attended the subscription schools until eighteen years of age. He learned the trade of a carpenter with Thomas Tiggart of Belle Vernon. After completing his trade, he worked for Thomas Tiggart two years as journeyman and eight years as foreman of the shop. In 1851 he engaged in the carpentering and contracting business and successfully continued in this until 1862. In 1862 he purchased his present farm containing 130 acres of well improved land, and situated two miles north of Dawson, on the Vanmeter and Broad Ford road

On June 12, 1848, he was married to Miss Nancy, daughter of Joseph Kitchel, a Westmoreland county farmer. They have six living children: Rebecca, Mary, in Kansas with an uncle, Levi Norcross; Joan, Charles, Carrie and Oliver, clerking for Cochran & Co. at Vanderbilt.

Peter Snyder is an active democrat, but is not an extremist in political matters. He has served as road supervisor and school director, and deservedly stands well with the public as a good mechanic and an honest man.

JAMES M. SPRINGER is one of the old families of the county. His great-grandfather, Michael Springer, was a native of Switzerland, but came to the county during its earliest settlement. He took a tomahawk claim upon four hundred acres of land in the western part of what is now known as Washington township. His son, Daniel Springer, the grandfather of James M., inherited a part of this land where he lived all of his life as a farmer. He was a soldier in the war with England, in 1812–15. After he came out of the war he settled down to the quiet life of a farmer and continued in that occupation till his death in March, 1845.

Joseph Springer, his son, and the father of the subject of this sketch, was born in Fayette county in 1795, where he died in 1872. He was a farmer and reared a large family of children.

He married Margaret Driver, who was born and reared in York county, near the town of York, Pa. She was born in 1794 and died in 1865, and was the mother of twelve children, ten of whom reached man and womanhood.

James M. Springer was born May 22, 1826, in Washington township, Fayette county, near the borough of Belle Vernon. He was reared on the farm till nineteen years of age, when he learned the cabinetmaker's business with John B. Springer, a cousin of his, and served two years apprenticeship.

He married Miss Sarah A. Reeves, daughter of Samuel and Nancy (Palmer) Reeves, both natives of Westmoreland county, Pa. To this union was born nine children: Laura A., Orville R., Amanda C., Nancy M., Robert D. and Joseph O. twins, Anna, Lizzie M. and Frank A., all of whom are still living. The eldest lives in this county, the second in Pittsburgh, Nancy M. in Westmoreland and the others at Belle Vernon.

Mr. James M. Springer has been successfully engaged in the cabinet and undertaker business at Belle Vernon, for twenty-five years. In 1855 he was elected justice of the peace and has served as such ever since. He was appointed a notary public in 1875, still holds a commission for that office and has also been burgess of the borough for three years. In 1860 he was ordained as minister in the Free Will Baptist church. In 1863 he he attached himself the Church of the Disciples and has been a member and an elder of that denomination ever since.

CHARLES A. SPRINGER, of Fayette City, is a son of Marshall and Susanna (Shroyer) Springer, and was born at Greensboro, Greene county, Pa., November 20, 1839.

Marshal (father) was born near Uniontown, was a shoemaker, and a son of David Springer, a native of this county, who traced his ancestry back to the Springers who came from Wilmington, Delaware. Marshall Springer married Susan, daughter of John Shroyer, of German descent.

Charles A. Springer received his education in the common schools. From eleven to thirteen years of age he attended to the ferry between Greensboro and New Geneva. He learned the trade of a glass blower at Greensboro and Pittsburgh, which he followed for twenty-seven years at different places.

He was married June 25, 1863, to Miss Elizabeth, daughter of Martin Kirkenbower, a millwright, who came from Germany in 1828 and located in Waterford, New Jersey. Mr. and Mrs. Springer have five children: Katie, Susanna, Mary, John and Sadie. Katie married E. G. Hall and lives at Connellsville.

In December, 1888, Mr. Springer became superintendent of the Fayette City Glass Works, the position he continues to hold. These works employ sixty men, and turn out some of the best window glass made in the county. He is a skilled workmen of many years experience, and thoroughly understands the duties of the position which he occupies. He belongs to no secret order, but is an active member of the Baptist church.

CAPT. JOSEPH CLEMENS STACY, of Menallen, comes of an English family on the paternal, and a Scotch family on the maternal side. John Stacy, his paternal grandfather, was born in England and fled for his life to America upon the restoration of King Charles II. to the throne, after the rebellion under Oliver Cromwell. He had been one of the soldiers under Cromwell, and was proscribed by the "Royalist Party," and was subject to the death penalty. A brother of John Stacy, who was a preacher, was burned at the stake, suffering for his religious belief, at the hands of the Papists, about the same time that John made his escape to this country. George Washington Stacy, the father of the subject of this sketch, was born in Philadelphia in 1790, and died in Springfield township in 1862. He served in the war with England of 1812-15. He married Miss Julia Macaulay, who was born in Scotland in 1800, and is still living and in good health.

Joseph Clemens Stacy was born June 26, 1832, educated at Princeton College, New Jersey, and began teaching in Fayette county thirty years ago, and is now teaching in McClellandtown. From 1870 to 1876, he was the county steward. On September 27, 1853, he was married to Miss Mary Ann Jeffries, a daughter of William Jeffries, of German township. They have the following children: Sarah, born August 25, 1854; Julia, born October 21, 1856: George William, born May 21, 1860; Hattie Jeffries, born May 4, 1872, and Joseph Jeffries, born March 21, 1876.

Captain Stacy was in the war; first as captain of a company of volunteers in West Virginia. Afterwards he was made Captain of Company E, One Hundred and Sixty-eighth Regiment Pennsylvania Volunteer Infantry under Col. Joseph Jack. He was mustered out with his regiment at Harrisburg, July 27, 1863. He is a good citizen and is highly respected.

JOHNSON R. STEPHENS, a farmer of Washington township, and descendant of an old Fayette county family, is a son of Levi and Mary (Farquhar) Stephens, and was born in Washington township, May 8, 1824.

John Stephens, great-grandfather of Johnson R. Stevens, emigrated from Wales to Eastern Pennsylvania prior to 1762, and finally removed to Washington township, where he died.

His son, Levi Stephens, was born in Bucks county. At eighteen years of age he came as a land-surveyor to what is now Fayette county, taking land in pay for his services, and became the owner of a large estate. He married Elizabeth Brown, of Westmoreland county. They had nine children, of whom the following seven lived beyond infancy: Nathaniel, Levi, Jr., John, Thomas, Sarah, Nancey and Elizabeth. Six of these children married and reared large families.

Levi Stephens, Jr., was born September 10, 1790, and died January 13, 1878. He married Mary, daughter of Robert Farquhar. (See his sketch.) They were the parents of nine children: Robert (dead), Esther (dead), Johnson R., James, Mary, Jehu, Rachel, Aaron (died 1870), James R., Robert, who was a steamboat engineer, and died at New Orleans in 1837, of yellow fever. James resides in West Virginia. Mrs. Stephens was born in 1796. Levi Stephens, Jr., was an industrious farmer, and highly esteemed in the community where he lived.

Johnson R. Stephens grew up on his father's farm and attended the winter sessions of the old subscription schools. In 1848 he married Miss Sarah, daughter of Nathaniel Stephens. To their union was born seven children: Cassius, Curtis, Mary, Horace, James, William and an infant unnamed, all of whom are dead except Cassius and James, of Dunbar township.

Mr. Stephens owns eighty-five acres of land, well-improved, and makes a very desirable home. This land is a part of the original two thousand acres belonging to Levi Stephens. He is honest in his business relations, enjoys life in his comfortable home, and is an honorable citizen.

The Stephens family have been, and are, largely of the Methodist persuasion. The old stone house, standing on Mr. Stephens' farm, was built in 1801. This house was a favorite stopping-place of Bishops Asbury, George and Mckendrick, of the Methodist Episcopal church.

JOSHUA STRICKLER, an old and highly esteemed citizen of Fayette county, was born on Jacob's creek, Tyrone township, Fayette county, Pa., January 28, 1821, and is a son of Jacob B. and Mary (Fiscus) Strickler.

His grandfather, Jacob Strickler, was a native of Bucks county, Pa., and married Miss Elizabeth Stewart, a relative of Hon. Andrew Stewart. Jacob Strickler owned a large tract of land in what is now Upper Tyrone township. He was a republican and member of the Mennonite church. His father, Jacob B. Strickler, was born in Upper Tyrone township, October 30, 1791, died August 31, 1874, was a republican, a local preacher in the Methodist Episcopal church, and the first farmer of his township that drove whiskey from the harvest field by an increase of wages. He married Miss Mary, daughter of Charles Fiscus, of Westmoreland county, and she, the mother of nine children, was born October 14, 1790, and died September 12, 1868.

Joshua Strickler attended the subscription schools until eighteen years of age, when he went on the National road as a wagoner; but at twenty-eight years of age, he left the "Old Pike" and engaged in common labor. A few hundred dollars received from home gave him a fair start in life and in 1850 he moved on his wife's small farm. In 1860 he purchased a farm and paid for it with his own earnings. In 1880, after the sale of his father's farm, he became the beneficiary of his interest in his father's estate. By careful management and judicious investments, accumulated many thousand dollars' worth of real and personal property.

On January 31, 1850, he was united in marriage to Miss Elizabeth Covert, an excellent lady, and a daughter of Benjamin Covert. They have had six children: Mary A., born December 4, 1852, married Albert Conwell, merchant of Uniontown; Benjamin C., born October 3, 1855, married Velma Nelson; Jacob A., born November 10, 1858, of the firm of Conwell & Strickler, of Uniontown, married Mary Bowlby; Everett, born

December 4, 1860, married Mary Dawson; J. Randolph, born April 20, 1869, and Frank A., born November 3, 1872, and died January 8, 1875.

Mr. Strickler is a republican and useful member of the Methodist Episcopal church. He was exempted from the draft but gave $1,000 to secure volunteers for the Union service. He is hospitable, generous and maintains an excellent reputation in private life.

WILLIAM M. THOMPSON, son of Jasper M. and Eliza C. (Carothers) Thompson, was born two and one half miles from Uniontown, in Menallen township, Fayette county, Pa., November 27, 1851.

His mother, Eliza C. Carothers, was born January 6, 1821, near West Newton, Westmoreland county, Pa., and in 1846, was married to Jasper M. Thompson. She is a daughter of Samuel and Ruth (Elliott) Carothers, whose father, Johnson Elliott lived where Robert Elliott now resides in Jefferson township, Fayette county.

William M. Thompson attended the common schools, prosecuted his academic and began his collegiate studies at Madison College, and was graduated from Washington Jefferson College in 1871.

On January 12, 1887, he married Miss Katherine M. Ruple, of Washington, Pa. Their union has been blessed with two children: Helen Ruple, born November 9, 1887, and Jasper Markle, born January 5, 1889. Mrs. Thompson is a daughter of James Ruple, born in Washington county, in 1812, and married Sarah A. Mayes, of the same county, who was born in 1821.

Since he graduated from college, Mr. Thompson has largely devoted his time and attention to farming and stock dealing. His flocks and herds of blooded sheep and cattle are the largest and finest in Fayette county, and are known throughout the State.

He is a member of the Presbyterian church to which his wife also belongs. He is an honorable business man, and a highly respected citizen of the county.

LYMAN S. STRICKLER, of Lower Tyrone, a reliable business man and one of the progressive farmers of Fayette county, is a son of Stewart and Mary (Newcomer) Strickler, and was born in what is now Lower Tyrone township, January 23, 1843.

Jacob Strickler (grandfather) was one of six brothers who emigrated from Germany to the United States. Jacob Strickler settled in Restone township, was a successful farmer and died in 1855.

Stewart Strickler (father) was the only son of Jacob Strickler and was born in Restone township, February 17, 1812. At three years of age he was taken to Lower Tyrone and received a limited education in the subscription schools. For fifteen years his life was an eventful one of alternate successes and failures. In 1842 he bought ten acres of coal land, and in 1843 shipped the first load of coke to Cincinnati that was ever sold for cash in that city. He built the Fayette and Sterling Coke Works and was a successful coke manufacturer. After several important and successful transactions in coal lands, Mr. Strickler removed in 1876 to Middle Tennessee where he purchased two thousand acres of land, and died there in 1884. He was a fine business man, and his life illustrates how nobly the greatest difficulties of early life can be overcome. He belonged to the Disciple church, was closely read in the Scriptures and very accurate in quoting them. His remains were brought from Tennessee and interred in the Bethel church cemetery. His widow was born in 1816, and resides in her Tennessee home. Her father, Jacob Newcomer, was born in 1782, and died in Lower Tyrone in 1864.

Lyman S. Strickler was reared on a farm until fifteen years of age, when he engaged as a clerk in the store of the Fayette Coke Works, and remained three years. He responded to the call of the Federal government for volunteers, in 1862, and enlisted in a Pennsylvania volunteer regiment. He was engaged in the battles of Antietam, Chickamauga and Stone River; participated in the capture of Jefferson Davis, and was honorably discharged at Nashville, Tenn., in 1865.

In 1866 he married Miss Maggie C., daughter of Pearson and Mary Cope, of Perryopolis, who died in 1882, leaving seven children: Dempsey, Pearson, Emma, Katie, Frank, Cora and Clara. He married, in 1886, for his second wife, Miss Mary, daughter of Conrad and Mary Hoop, of Connellsville. Unto this last union two children have been born: Edna and Ola.

After the late Civil War, Mr. Strickler was engaged for eight years in farming and milling in Franklin county, Tennessee. In 1873 he returned to Lower Tyrone township, and engaged in farming. He now owns the old "Smiley" farm, containing 150 acres of good land, situated one-fourth of a mile north of Dawson, where he deals in Holstein cattle and Chester hogs. He is an active republican, and a prominent member of the Disciple church. Mr. Strickler is a practical business man, and is ever alive to any enterprise calculated to develop the material resources of his township.

JOHN TIERNIN, an old and prominent citizen of Fayette county, was born in Pennsylvania in 1798 and was a son of Michael and Alsie Tiernin, the former a native of Ireland, the latter of Pennsylvania.

John Tiernin was educated in the subscription schools and was a blacksmith by trade. At 25 years of age he engaged in boating from Pittsburgh to New Orleans, going down in the spring on a flat boat (then called a "Broadhorn") to the Crescent City with a cargo of bacon, flour, apples, cider and other productions of this country, returning on foot overland to his home. After several years, he left the river and purchased a farm within the present borough limits of Fayette City, of Hugh C. Ford. This farm was underlaid with a fine vein of coal which Mr. Tiernin opened and furnished three glass factories with their fuel, besides supplying the town and other places for many years, with coal. He was elected treasurer of Fayette county, October 8, 1861, and re-elected October 13, 1863. His services as treasurer were entirely satisfactory to the people and highly creditable to himself.

November 7, 1820 he was married to Miss Eliza J., daughter of Bazilla M. and Elizabeth (Goskill) Newbold, the former a Quaker from New Jersey and an early settler in this county. The family of Mr. Tiernin consisted of ten children: Joshua, born August 16, 1821, married Catherine Clegg; Mary A., born December 15, 1823, married Wm. Mullen; Elizabeth, born February 14, 1826, married Wm. Worf, of Brownsville; Beulah, born March 20, 1828, married J. W. Wright, of Virginia; Sarah, born September 9, 1830; Michael J., born December 2, 1832; Bazilla M., born May 10, 1835, married Rebecca Evans; Catherine, born October 11, 1837, wife of N. B. Brightwell; Eliza J., born May 5, 1840, married Samuel Drumm; John, Jr., born May 28, 1844, lost during the war at twenty-one years of age. These are all dead excepting Mrs. Brightwell.

Nathan B. Brightwell was born at Arnold's Mills, Washington township, Fayette county, Pa., May 18, 1831. His grandfather, Thomas Brightwell, was a native of Maryland, a

Sarah A. Todd

soldier of the War of 1812, and married Mrs. Elizabeth (Madden) Hart. His father was a miller by trade, came from Maryland in 1824 to Brownsville in search of his uncle, Joshua Brightwell, whom he found in Washington township, on the Johnson R. Stephens' farm. November 9, 1826, he was married by Rev. James Sanson to Miss Zeruiah, daughter of Nathan and Althea (Pitcher) Briggs, the former a blacksmith, and both natives of New England. Mr. and Mrs. Brightwell had twelve children, of whom six are living: John B., December 8, 1827; James S., December 7, 1829; Nathan B., May 18, 1831; Elizabeth, August 29, 1833; Margaret P., September, 23, 1835; Nancy J., October 8, 1837; Alathea, March 30, 1840; Wm. F., January 23, 1842; Zeruiah, February 12, 1844; Jemima L., December 2, 1845; Sarah E., December 6, 1846, and Rufus P., September 14, 1848. The father was a Baptist and the mother a Methodist.

Nathan Brightwell was educated in the common schools; was brought up to milling, and followed that business until his mill was burned in 1876, when he removed to his present farm, the John Tiernin farm.

In 1856 he was married to Miss Catherine Tiernin. They have five children: John T., married Margaret Alter; Charles E., married Minnie M. Wilson; Michael W., died at 4½ years of age; William D., a school teacher and United States storekeeper at Gibsonton's Mills, and Eliza K., wife of Wm. M. Finch.

Nathan B. Brightwell has been for over thirty years a prominent member of the Masonic fraternity, and has filled many important positions of the order and in his lodge. He is a charter member of Fayette City Lodge, No. 511, I. O. O. F. He has filled nearly all the offices of his township and borough. He is one of the reputable men of the borough, owns a comfortable home, is well and favorably known throughout the county, and is a stanch democrat.

THOMAS TODD, JR., who so nobly gave his life in the performance of his duty, was the youngest child of Thomas and Elizabeth (Huston) Todd, and was born near Uniontown, September 26, 1811.

Thomas Todd, Sr., was born November 9, 1762, in County Down, Ireland, and came to America in 1783. He married Elizabeth Huston, and removed to the vicinity of Uniontown, in 1795. Their children were as follows: Hannah, wife of Jesse Ross, born July 3, 1790, died November 1, 1849; Nancy, wife of Richard Barnes, born February 4, 1792; John, in War of 1812, born March 11, 1794; Martha, wife of Isaac Beal, born January 13, 1797; Phebe, wife of Richard Mills, born December 3, 1799; Eliza, wife of Walter Brown, born April 4, 1802, died March, 1872; Mary, wife of Thomas Van Hook, born July 8, 1804, died December 25, 1849; Huston married Catherine Gadd, born May 16, 1807, died December 26, 1849, Sarah, wife of Joseph Saliday, born August 13, 1809, and Thomas, Jr.

Thomas Todd, Jr., became a steamboat engineer, and plied his vocation on the Monongahela and Ohio rivers.

April 15, 1835, he married Miss Sarah A. Bugher. Unto this union were born seven children: Huston, born February 27, 1836; Ellen L., born September 4, 1837; William, born July 9, 1840; Elizabeth, born December 21, 1842 (dead); Margaret A., born June 21, 1845, and was married to Edward W. White in 1868; Melissa Jane, born May 15, 1848, dead, and Rachel Emma, born December 23, 1850, dead. The mother died April 1, 1888. She was a noble woman, and the needy never asked in vain for her help. She and her whole family belonged to the Christian church.

Huston (son) married Elma V. Baldwin.

Ellen, (daughter) was married November 12, 1872, to Dr. David H. Hough, the latter born in Washington township, Fayette county, Pa., August 1, 1833. He was educated in the common schools, read medicine, attended lectures at Philadelphia, and at twenty-one years of age was practicing his profession very successfully at Pennsville.

Mrs. Ellen Hough, of Fayette City, inserts the portrait of her mother in this volume as there is no photograph extant of any of the older male members of the family. Mrs. Sarah A. (Bugher) Todd was a daughter of Aaron Bugher, a native of Fayette county, Pennsylvania. She was a noble woman of many Christian graces, and died after a lingering illness in April, 1888. A younger brother married a daughter of Hon. Washington McLain of Cincinnati, the father of John McLain, of the *Enquirer*.

Mrs. Ellen Hough has been a widow since the death of her husband, Dr. Hough, and has no children. She owns a splendid farm in Menallen township besides considerable other property. She is a lady of fine address, and possessed of many accomplishments.

Thomas Todd, Jr., was the carpenter and assistant engineer on the ill-fated steamboat Chickasaw which collided with the William B. Clifton, on April 27, 1852, on the Ohio river. There was a mistake in signal bells, and the Clifton ran into and sank the Chickasaw. Todd remained at his post until the cabin parted from the hull; was standing in four feet of water, when he generously urged his fellow engineer to climb a near post, and sought a distant one by which to make his own escape. He was drowned, but his heroic conduct will not soon be forgotten; and flame-enveloped John Maynard of Lake Erie has his equal in flood-enshrouded Thomas Todd of the Ohio river.

JOHN OSMAN TODD, of Menallen, is a son of John and Catherine (Condon) Todd, and was born on the old Sharpless farm, on the banks of Redstone creek in Redstone township, Fayette county, Pa., January 28, 1823.

His grandfather, Thomas Todd, came from County Down, Ireland, and married Elizabeth Huston, a Quakeress of Chester county, Pa.

His father, John Todd, was born in Chester county; he served in the War of 1812, and was at the siege of Baltimore, and was a soldier in Capt. Giesey's Company, of Brownsville. John Todd married Miss Catherine, daughter of William Condon, who was the first steward of the old poorhouse, and died when his son, John O. Todd, was eighteen months old.

John O. Todd was educated in the schools of William Beggs and Samuel Wilson and later attended one term at Madison College. After his school days, he engaged in farming and still continues in that business. Since the age of eight years he has resided at the same place, and has always been a farmer.

May 10, 1855, he married Miss Elizabeth Springer. To them were born seven children: Ross M., born 1856, machinist in Chicago; John H. married Harriet, daughter of D. B. Craft and in livery business at Uniontown; Thomas S., born 1868, Kate, wife of Calvin Shoaf and dead; Laura, wife of William Barton; Eliza E., wife of George Craft, and Sallie at home. Mrs. Todd died October 31, 1871. Her father was Shepherd Springer.

John O. Todd was an "old line whig." When that great political organization went down he enrolled himself in the ranks of its successor, the republican party. He is an industrious citizen and a careful and prudent farmer.

WILLIAM R. TROY, of Washington township, was born at Greenfield, Washington county, Pa., September 4, 1831, and was educated in the subscription schools of that day. Being left an orphan, at the age of ten years, he began life for himself on the river as a hand on the coal boats used to transport coal before the days of barges and steam tow-boats, and followed that business till quite recently. In 1883 he built a repair dock, and has been since engaged in repairing boats. His dock is near Fayette City, at the mouth of Little Redstone Creek.

He was married in 1862 to Sarah Buxton, daughter of Samuel and Ruth (Floyd) Buxton, the former a native of England, and the latter of Pennsylvania. They have reared five children: Albert W., Harry A., Gemva D., Enola and Walter. They are all living at home.

Mr. Troy is a member of the Masonic fraternity.

His father, David Troy, was a native of Virginia, came to Pennsylvania when a young man and settled in Washington county. He married Elizabeth Fenton, whose parents were early settlers of Fayette county. He and his wife died when their son William R. was quite young.

LLEWELLYN VAUGHAN was born in Brownsville, Fayette county, Pa., December 6, 1841. He is a son of William and Anna (Llewellyn) Vaughan, both natives of Wales, England.

William Vaughan emigrated from Wales to the United States in 1839. He was a puddler in rolling mills, and was a member of the Episcopalian church. His death occurred in 1848.

Llewellyn Vaughan received his education in the common schools. By the death of his father he was thrown upon his own resources at the early age of ten years. He worked in a rolling-mill at Pittsburgh until he was fourteen years of age, when he went to learn the trade of a machinist at Brownsville, Pa. Serving four and a half of his five years' time as an apprentice, when he enlisted as a private in Company G, Eighth Pennsylvania Reserves, May 24, 1861; he re-enlisted in 1863, and was transferred to the One Hundred and Ninety-first Pennsylvania Veterans, in which he served until June, 1865. He was in all the engagements of his regiment, was wounded at Charles City Cross Roads, and was a second time wounded at the second day's fight in the Wilderness, on May 6, 1864.

His experience of army life was completed by being a prisoner of war from August 19, 1864, until March 17, 1865. His capture took place at the Yellow House Tavern, he spent his captivity in Pemberton, Libby prisons, on Belle Island and at Saulsbury, North Carolina.

He married, January 17, 1866, Miss Sarah daughter of John Sheets, an operator in the glass works. They have eight children: Jennie, Mary, Elizabeth, John, Emma, William, Edmund and Irene. After returning from the army, Mr. Vaughan worked for a short time in a Pittsburgh rolling-mill. and subsequently engaged on a steamboat as fireman; from this position he passed to that of assistant engineer, and in 1886 became high-presure chief engineer of steam vessels.

He is a resident of Fayette City, where he belongs to Post 396, G. A. R. and to Lodge 396, K. of P. To his honorable war record he has added the reputation of an efficient engineer.

REV. JACOB M. WERTZ, a scholar, a polished gentleman and a pastor of the Catholic church, was born at Caledonia, Racine county, Wisconsin, November 10, 1857, and is a son of Reinhard and Johanna (Nunnink) Wertz.

Reinhard Wertz is a native of Rhine Province, Prussia, born June 24, 1826, he served in the Prussian army from 1847 to 1851, and then came and settled in Wisconsin in 1853. He immigrated to near Kansas City, Mo., in 1857; served in the Union army from 1862 to 1864, and in 1854 at New Cologne, Wis., he married Miss Johanna Nunnink. To their union were born eight children: Alydia Mary, died in 1859; Rev. Jacob M., Alydia Gertrude, wife of Alex. Hagg, of Tyrone, Pa., John A., married Miss Gertie Kittell and is publisher of the Dawson *News*; Charles R., Mary H.; Anna Gertrude, died in 1867, and Christina Johanna, died in 1882.

Mrs. Wertz's father, Jacob Nunnink, was born in Holland, December 1, 1804, served three years in Company Five, Second Battalion Second Department, and was in the Holland-Belgium war. He was a carpenter and wagonmaker, and married Alydia Hofste, born March 8, 1806. They came to America in 1853. Mrs. Wertz was born at Zwolle, Province Gelderland, Holland, September 17, 1836.

Rev. J. M. Wertz lived until seventeen years of age near Kansas City, Mo., and spent one year of his school life at St Mary's College. He taught school at Glencoe, Minn., where he learned the trade of printer; at nineteen years of age he entered Mt. Calvary College, Wisconsin, and finished his classical education.

Five years later Rev. Wertz came to Tyrone, Pa., where he conceived the idea of entering the Catholic priesthood, and was affiliated into the Pittsburgh Diocese by Rt. Rev. J. Tuigg; afterward he went to St. Vincent's Seminary, Latrobe, Pa., and in five years finished his philosophical and theological course. He was ordained to the priesthood in St. Peter's Pro-Cathedral, Allegheny City, Pa., on April 17, 1886, by Rt. Rev. R. Phelan. He was then sent as assistant to Rev. C. A. McDermott at Connellsville. January 16, 1888, he was appointed pastor of St. Joseph's church (German) at Braddock, Pa., and on the 16th of December, 1888, took charge of Dawson and West Newton missions, which aggregate a membership of 160 families. Rev. Wertz has built two fine churches; one at West Newton, costing $3,000, and the other at Dawson at a cost of $5,000. He has a large number of friends, and is very popular with all who know him.

CHARLES J. WARNOCK, bookkeeper and superintendent of the Union Supply Company's store at Summit, is a son of David and Elizabeth J. (Evans) Warnock, and was born in the edge of Wayne township, Lawrence county, Pa., January 2, 1866. David Warnock, father, was a son of Maj. David Warnock, a pioneer of Western Pennsylvania, an early settler of Beaver county, and a militia officer in the War of 1812. David Warnock is a farmer Beaver county. He is a republican, an industrious citizen, and has been for many years a ruling elder in the United Presbyterian church. Mrs. Warnock's father, Jonathan Evans, was also an early settler of Beaver county. He located at Beaver Falls, but was once chased away by the Indians before he made a permanent settlement at that place.

Charles J. Warnock was raised principally on a farm, educated in the common schools, and attended two terms at North Sewickley Academy. Leaving the school room, he entered the printing office of the Greensburg *Press*, remained six months, and then (1881) accepted a position as timekeeper with Carnegie Bros. & Co., limited, at the Scotia mines, Centre county, Pa. After two years' satisfactory work he left Centre county and came to Broad Ford, where he accepted the position of clerk in the Union Supply Company's store, and remained for two years.

In 1885 Mr. Warnock came to Summit store and clerked so acceptably that in 1887 he was promoted to his present position of bookkeeper and superintendent.

He is a member of the Heptasophs, a republican and a member of the United Brethren church.

His brothers, L. D., John J. and Robert T. are commercial travelers for Pittsburgh houses, and Horace G. and David A. are attorneys-at-law in Dakota and Nebraska, respectively.

C. J. Warnock has faithfully earned, and justly deserves, the confidence and esteem of all with whom he has had business relations.

JOHN D. WOOD, one of Menallen's representative farmers, is a son of Amos Wood, and was born on the Woods farm in Menallen township, April 3, 1857.

Amos Wood was born October 12, 1812; was brought up in the Quaker faith, but he now holds to the doctrines of the Dunkard church. His father, John Wood, was born March 17, 1765, in Winchester, Virginia, where he married Miss Catherine Littler. John Wood was a son of Cornelius and Mary (Sharpless) Wood, the latter a daughter of Samuel Sharpless. She was born March 20, 1737, at Middletown, Va., and died in Winchester, November 11, 1762.

John D. Wood was educated in the common schools of Menallen. Among his early teachers were Dr. Hill and Edward Hackney.

In politics he is a republican; in his religious views he adheres to the doctrines of the Cumberland Presbyterian church.

He was married April 11, 1876, to Miss Retta, daughter of Lewis Stewart. Three children have been born to them: Jemima Bell, born November 21, 1878; Anna Maud, born September 25, 1880; Jennie Pearl, born April 17, 1883.

He owns a valuable farm of 125 acres of land, which is underlaid with coal and limestone. Mr. Wood is descended from the celbrated Sharpless family, and through his paternal great-grandmother, his family traces its ancestry back to 1591. In 1682 John Sharpless of Hatherton, England, came with William Penn to Philadelphia; his descendants scattered over the Eastern States and in Pennsylvania. In 1882 there was a Sharpless reunion at "Sharpless Rock," England, where several hundred descendants of this ancient and honorable family assembled. They were from various parts of the United States and Europe. The Sharpless coat of arms bears the Latin motto, *Pro veritate suffer fortitur.*

SAMUEL WORK WOODWARD is a son of Davis and Mary (Boyd) Woodward, and was born April 24, 1833, in Menallen township, Fayette county, Pa. His paternal grandfather, Caleb Woodward, was born in Chester county, married Phebe McCarty, and removed to Fayette county, where he died October 18, 1856. His father, Davis Woodward, was born June 11, 1805, in Menallen township, on the farm where Frank Elliott now resides. On November 2, 1828, he married Miss Mary Boyd, who was born in 1810, and is a daughter of Robert Boyd, whose father-in-law, Samuel Work, came from Ireland, and purchased a large tract of land near the site of Dunbar Furnace. Davis Woodward had thirteen children: Robert B. Caleb, Samuel W., Davis, Joseph, Rebecca, Ebenezer, Finley, Jno. W., Phebe, Mary E., Eliza Jane, Dempsey and Harriet.

Samuel W. Woodward was raised on a farm and received his education in the common schools of Dunbar township. Among his teachers were James Darby and James Curry. He was married December 29, 1859, by the Rev. Joel Stoneroad, to Mary Curry, who was born April 19, 1842. Her father, James Curry, was born July 11, 1805, and married, in 1840, Elizabeth Parkill. James Curry was a son of Solomon Curry, a native of Ireland, who married Mary A. Hatfield, he lived to be one hundred and one years of age.

Mr. and Mrs. S. W. Woodward have had five children born to them: Elizabeth J., born September 5, 1860, married Edward Gilchrist and has five children; Ida Belle, born October 13, 1862, married Rufus Phillips, has two children, and is living in Harvey county, Kan.; Anna Laura, born February 8, 1865, married to John Frasher of Franklin township; James Curry, born November 8, 1867, and Ewing Finley, born August 26, 1873. Mr. Woodward owns 280 acres of good land in Menallen township, and gives the most of his time to its cultivation and improvement. He and his wife are members of Laurel Hill Presbyterian church.

JAMES W. WILEY, a good business man, a successful coke operator of Fayette county, is a son of Sampson and Sarah (Todd) Wiley, and was born in Sewickley township, Westmoreland county, Pa., October 17, 1845.

Sampson Wiley, Sr. (grandfather), was a native of county Tyrone, Ireland, where he owned a farm of forty-five acres, whose title made it his while "grass grew and water ran." He emigrated to Westmoreland county in 1790, where he died in 1825, at fifty-six years of age. He married Miss Jane McGrew, a member of the old and well-respected McGrew family, of Westmoreland county.

Sampson Wiley (father) was born in Westmoreland county, in 1805, died January 3, 1888, was a farmer until 1840, when he engaged in merchandising, and continued successfully in the mercantile business till 1870, when he retired from active life. He was a democrat, was several times elected to local offices in a strong republican township, but always declined to accept them. He married Miss Jane, daughter of Henry Todd, a native of Ireland, and a farmer in Westmoreland county early as 1812. They had ten children. One of their sons, Sampson M., enlisted in Company A, One Hundred and Fifty-fifth Pennsylvania Volunteers, was in the battle of Gettysburg, and died soon afterward with typhoid fever. Mrs. Wiley was born in 1809, and lives at Everson.

James W. Wiley was reared in Westmoreland county, attended the common schools until twenty years of age, when he engaged as book-keeper for the Youghiogheny Coal Company and remained with them till 1873. Three years of this time, he served as United States gauger at their distillery. From 1873 to 1877 he was engaged in the general mercantile business in the firm of S. Wiley & Son. In 1877 he became member of the mercantile firm of Wiley & Sherrick, and was also engaged in the coke business. In 1881 Mr. Wiley withdrew from the mercantile firm, buying out Mr. Sherrick's interest in the coke works, and forming a partnership with J. R. Staufer in the same business. The firm Staufer & Wiley are successfully engaged in the coke business.

In 1868, he was married to Miss Jennie, daughter of William Gallagher, of Latrobe, Pa. They have seven children: Sadie T., Carrie M., Margaret O., Minnie, Charles S., Sampson M., and James W., Jr.

J. W. Wiley is a democrat, and has served continuously as justice of the peace for ten years. He is a member of the Masonic Order, a stockholder in several banks and is a prominent member of the Methodist Episcopal church. He is a well known and intelligent citizen of Upper Tyrone and has been remarkably successful in all his business ventures.

ELLIS BAILEY WOODWARD, of Menallen, was born July 25, 1816, near Jennings run, South Union township, Fayette county, Pa.; was brought up on a farm, and educated at the winter schools of Menallen and South Union townships. He commenced life as a farmer, but was afterwards a wagoner on the "Old Pike" for about seven years. He commenced wagoning in 1847 on the road from Wheeling to Cumberland. The principal freights were corn, provisions and merchandise. The corn was hauled to the road for the purpose of feeding hogs on the way to market. At that time the hogs were driven on foot, from the States of Ohio, Indiana and Illinois, to market in the cities of Baltimore, Philadelphia and New York. It took thousands of barrels of corn yearly, during the season of driving, which was usually in the fall and early winter, and the wagoner always had a busy time in the hog season. It was the same when cattle were driven to market along the Pike, a great amount of feed had to be hauled to the road, and the merchandise was back freight, from Cumberland to Wheeling.

The old wagon which Mr. Woodward used on the pike is still in use. He stopped over night at fifty-seven different houses on the Pike, between Uniontown and Cumberland, while he was engaged in wagoning. He never drank any whiskey in his life, although it was as plenty as water on the road, while he was teaming. When he quit the road he settled down on a farm and made farming his vocation in life. He owns 106 acres of land in Menallen township, where he nows lives. He was married March 12, 1840, to Miss Mary Jane Lynn, who died in 1856. She was the daughter of Samuel Lynn, of Redstone township. He married for his second wife, Miss Mary Ann Schaeffer, born July 14, 1839, in Wharton township. She was the daughter of Charles Schaeffer, of Stewart township, who died March 15, 1869, aged seventy-nine years, one month and nineteen days. They have seven living children and one dead: Mary Jane, born April 3, 1858 (married Abraham F. Vance); Elizabeth, born April 23, 1859; Sarah, born April 20, 1861 (married to George W. Holland); Prudy, born December 1, 1862 (married to William Schwartz); Felix H., born May 5, 1866 (a farmer); Eliza, born December 21, 1867, and Charles Andrew, born December 4, 1869.

Mr. Woodward is an ardent democrat. In the campaign of 1844 he drove a team of seventeen horses to one of his party's political conventions. His parents were Joshua and Sarah (Dannels) Woodward. His father was born in Chester county, Pa., in 1783, came to Fayette county when he was six years old, and was a blacksmith. His mother was born in Chester county, Pa., in Kennet Square. They had eight children, of whom the subject of this sketch was the fourth. Mr. Richard Woodward, the grandfather of Woodward, was probably a native of Chester county, as he came from there to Fayette county, in 1789, and settled on a farm in Menallen township, where he afterwards lived till his death.

Jesse Dannels, the grandfather of E. B., came from Chester county to Fayette at a very early day.

JOHN H. WURTZ, general manager of the Sterling Supply Company's, Redstone Coke Company's and Youngstown Coke Company's stores, was born near Confluence, Somerset county, Pa., October 10, 1852, and is a son of Christian and Susan (Hyatt) Wurtz.

Among the early settlers of Westmoreland county, from Eastern Pennsylvania, was John Wurtz, Sr. He was an active and honored member of the Mennonite church, in East Huntingdon township. One of his sons, John Wurtz, born in 1789, was a staid and industrious farmer of Westmoreland county, where he died in 1854. Christian Wurtz, son of John Wurtz, was born on the home farm in 1824. He removed to Franklin township, Fayette county; engaged in farming, and died in 1888. He was a life-long democrat, but was very liberal in his views, political or otherwise—an upright, honest and obliging man. He married Miss Susan Hyatt, born in 1832, and now residing with her son, Andrew J., at Abilene, Kas. Her father, Andrew Hyatt, was a farmer near Confluence, Pa., where in early life he was a fine marksman and successful deer-hunter. His death occurred in 1869.

John H. Wurtz came to Fayette county at six years of age. He attended the common schools for ten years, and then took the full course at the Iron City Business College, in Pittsburgh, from which he was graduated in 1872. His first employment was teaching in the common schools, at which he continued from 1869 to 1872, when he accepted the position of book-keeper with Brown & Cochran, at Jimtown Coke Works; he discharged the duties of his position so satisfactorily to his employers that he was retained as long as they operated these works. When Colonel Schoonmaker became proprietor, in 1879, of the Jimtown Coke Works, Mr. Wurtz was continued as book-keeper until the death of Mr. B. F. Oglevee, in January, 1889, when he was promoted to succeed him as general manager of Colonel Schoonmaker's stores at Redstone, Alice, Sterling and Youngstown.

On November 21, 1877, at the Catholic church in Connellsville, he married Miss Ellen Quinn, a native of County Roscommon, Ireland. They have three children: Andrew Jackson, Annie Belle and Nellie. Mrs. Wurtz's father, James Quinn, came to the United States about 1863, and died from injuries received at Alice Mines, in 1886. Mr. Wurtz is a democrat, and while having but little time to spare from his many and pressing business duties, yet he has filled several township offices. He owns the old Wurtz homestead farm of seventy-five acres of good land, in Franklin township, and two fine farms near Abilene, Kas. By industry and economy he has acquired a competency, and has always been true to the many and varied business trusts that have been confided to his care. He has shown, by his energy, skill and judgment, in his past business transactions, that he is capable of managing and controlling large and extensive business enterprises.

WILLIAM R. MOORE, a descendant of Captain John Moore of Revolutionary fame, and an industrious farmer of Menallen township, was born on property now owned by Evans Hess in Redstone township, Fayette county, Pa., February 21, 1824. He is a son of Rezin and Mary (Landers) Moore, the former a native, and a well situated farmer of Redstone township, and the latter a daughter of Abraham Landers, an early settler (1790) of the same township. They have three children living: John M., Mrs. Samuel Herron and William R.

Captain John Moore (W. R. Moore's grandfather) was a prominent character in the early history of Redstone township. He was born east of the Alleghenies, emigrated to the present Evans Hess farm in 1769, made an enviable record in the Revolutionary War, was married to Miss Margaret Colvin and died in his adopted township. His sons were George, John, Aaron, Rezin, Ezekiel and William.

William R. Moore was reared on a farm,

received a practical education for ordinary business pursuits, and has been successfully engaged in farming until the present time.

On March 5, 1846, he was married to Miss Nancy Eliza, daughter of Jesse L. Frost. Mrs. Moore died March 22, 1882, aged sixty years. They had ten children, of whom nine are living, born and named as follows: Rezin, February 1, 1847, married Miss Ann Gribble; Rachel J., May 7, 1848; Hulda A., July 12, 1849, wife of Elijah Holliday; Mary M., February 25, 1852, married G. S. Frederick, May 16, 1871; Robert F. (see his sketch in this volume); Lucy C., April 15, 1856, married Barton Keener; Jesse E., May 24, 1858, married Miss Ellen Brown; Euphemie, July 21, 1866, wife of James Frost; Samuel N., July 10, 1863, married Miss Louisa Harvey. After his wife's death, Mr. Moore was re-married November 15, 1883, by Elder S. M. Cooper, to Mrs. Melissa, widow of Thomas Henderson.

In politics Mr. Moore is a republican and adheres closely to the principles of his party. He owns 108 acres of fine farming land, which is heavily underlaid with limestone and iron ore. He also owns ten acres of valuable timber land. He is a successful farmer, and is highly respected both as a business man and as a citizen.

CONNELLSVILLE AND DUNBAR

ROBINSON ADDIS, one of Vanderbilt's reliable citizens, is a son of Eber and Betsey (Crosier) Addis, and was born in Franklin township, Fayette county, Pa., June 20, 1817.

His grandfather, Jonathan Addis, was of French and English extraction; came from Lancaster county, Pa., and purchased a farm in Franklin township, near Redstone Creek, on which he resided until his death. He married a Miss Laughead, and reared a family of six sons and three daughters.

Eben Addis, father, was born and raised in Franklin township, where he married Miss Betsey Crosier. They had three sons and two daughters. Mrs. Addis' father, Matthew Crosier, came from Ireland and settled in Franklin township, prior to the War of 1812, in which he served as a soldier. Mr. Addis was a prosperous farmer of his native township, where he died.

Robinson Addis was raised on a farm, received his education in the limited subscription schools, and engaged in farming and huckstering. He ran a huckster team from Franklin township to Pittsburgh, and continued successfully in that business until 1870.

He was married to Miss Sarah, daughter of Thomas Gore. To their union were born eight children, of whom four sons and two daughters are living: Thomas, Joseph, Walter, Elizabeth, Caroline and Samuel. Mrs. Addis died August 7, 1881. After her death Mr. Addis sold his property in Franklin township, came to Vanderbilt and purchased the desirable property upon which he lives. He was school director of Franklin township for several terms, and served three terms as constable in Dunbar township. After many years of constant activity Mr. Addis has retired from business, and is enjoying life in his comfortable home.

JAMES ALLEN, of New Haven, comes of a family founded in the United States in about 1740, by David Allen, of Ireland, and Susan White, of Scotland. They were the great-grandparents of James Allen, the subject of this sketch who came to this country on the same vessel and were married after their arrival here. After marriage they settled in Chester county, Pa., where they lived for some years, and removed thence to Franklin township, Fayette county Pa. They had eleven children: Agnes, Nancy, Jane, Margaret, Susanna, David, Anne, James (from whom sprang the immediate family of James Allen), Josiah and George.

James Allen (grandfather) was born August 22, 1758, died February 16, 1840 and was married to Nancy Peairs. She died February 4, 1859, and they both sleep in Laurel

James Allen

Hill Cemetery, in Franklin township. They had two children: Elisha and David.

David Allen, the father of James Allen, was born in 1787, in Franklin township, Fayette county, Pa.; died May 7, 1828, and was by occupation a farmer. He served for a time as a watchman down the Ohio river, against the Indians in the early settlement of the country. He married Rebecca Smith, a daughter of William Smith, native of Scotland. They had the following children: Martha S., born 1817; James, 1818; William, 1819; Mary Peirce, 1820; John White, 1821; David Hunter, 1822; Susan, 1823; Josiah, 1824, and Robert Rush, born 1825.

The maternal grandfather was William Smith, born in Scotland, and came from Edinburgh to Philadelphia. He afterwards started to join Daniel Boone in Kentucky, going as far as Mt. Pleasant, Westmoreland county, Pa., where he spent the winter in a pen that had been built to protect sheep from the wolves. Failing to receive any word from Boone, he settled in what is now the "loop" of Jacobs creek, in Westmoreland county.

James Allen was born in Franklin township, Fayette county, Pa., October 18, 1818, and was the second of nine children born to his parents. Born and reared on a farm, his business through life has been farming in his native township. He continued to farm successfully to 1882, when he retired, and at present resides at New Haven.

James Allen has been three times married. His first wife was Sarah J. Guthrie, a daughter of Rev. James Guthrie, who for forty-five years was pastor of Laurel Hill church. They had the following children: James, Rebecca Ann, Walter L. and Wm. S., all of whom are dead except Walter L., a farmer, and living in Harrison county, Ohio. His second wife was Sarah Louisa Allen, a daughter of Jonathan G. Allen, of Uniontown, to whom he was married March 26, 1856. They have one child: Sarah E. His third wife was Mary Miller, of Connellsville, to whom he was married September 8, 1864.

Mr. Allen has served as director of the county home for three years; was one of the directors of the Youghiogheny Bank, at Connellsville, at the time of its organization and has held the directorship continuously from that time to the present. He has been a director in the Youghiogheny Bridge Company, and is at present school director of New Haven.

He is a member of the Presbyterian church at Connellsville. Prior to 1882 he was a member at Laurel Hill, having joined the church there in 1841; was elected an elder in 1851, and has held the office ever since. He is one of the present trustees of the church at Connellsville. James Allen has always been an earnest worker in the church in all matters of a moral and religious character, and has always supported them with his means as well as with his might. He has represented the Redstone presbytery at different sessions of synod at Pittsburgh, Indiana, Indiana county, Pa.; Parkersburg, W. Va., McKeesport, Kittanning and Bellefonte, Pa.; and was a delegate from the Redstone presbytery to the general assembly of the Presbyterian church at its session in 1862, at Columbus, Ohio.

DAVID ROSS ANDERSON, a member of an old family in the county, was born in Georges township, November 16, 1856. His grandfather, Samuel Anderson, was born in Georges township in 1805, whose death occurred in 1887, at Smithfield, and many years he was engaged in the manufacture of scythes at Haydentown. He was married to Elizabeth Ross. To their union were born eight children: Margaret, Jehu, Ross, Hannah, Sarah, Miranda, Miles and Lovina, all living; Elizabeth and Mary J. are dead. Jehu (father) was born in Georges township in 1832, was a farmer and resident of Nicholson township, and was married to Miss Lydia M., daughter of Daniel Smith of Georges township. They had four children: David R., Samuel, Alvin and Ira. David R. Anderson was educated in the schools of his native township, Georges Creek Academy and at Monongahela College, Greene county, Pa. In 1878 he was married to Sadie J., daughter of Justus Dunn, an old resident of Georges township, but born in Erie, Pa. Ray, Edgar and Mabel are the children born to them. In 1878 Mr. Anderson engaged in the mercantile business, in Nicholson township, as partner of his uncle, Miles Anderson. This partnership was dissolved; in 1881 he removed to Dunbar and took a position with J. M. Heustead, as clerk in the store at Dunbar Furnace, where he won the confidence and respect of his employer in a service of five years. He was appointed postmaster at Dunbar by President Cleveland, on August 14, 1886, and is the present incumbent of that office. He is also extensively engaged in mercantile pursuits at Dunbar, and in 1887 I. N. Blosser became his partner. Mr. Anderson is a charter member of Dunbar Council, No. 754, Royal Arcanum (the council was instituted April 4, 1883), is also a member of Junior Order of American Mechanics and holds the office of deacon of the Baptist church.

JOHN N. ANDERSON is one of Fayette county's successful teachers, earnest institute worker and is a veteran of twenty-nine years experience in the school room. His grandfather Anderson was a native of Wales, and married a lady of German descent. They had a son, George S. Anderson, born September 15, 1810, in Frederick county, Md., who married Miss Mary Ann Nelson, born near Rainesburg, Bedford county, Pa., October 19, 1808. To this union were born six children: the eldest, Sarah Jane, died before her third birthday. Two sons and one daughter are living in Fayette county, and one daughter, Nancy Ellen, resides in West Virginia. John N. Anderson, the second child, and eldest of these children living, was born in Menallen township, Fayette county, Pa., October 18, 1835.

In childhood John N. Anderson was delicate in health, and his opportunities for schooling were limited. His school attendance was under the crude system of public schools when the branch in which the "master" was most proficient was the birch branch. January 1, 1854, he entered the printing office of the Pennsylvania *Democrat*, now Republican *Standard*, and remained two years. During this time he applied himself so assiduously to his studies during his spare moments that he passed an examination in 1856 under County Superintendent Joshua V. Gibbons and entered the profession of teaching. Since 1856 Mr. Anderson has been thus engaged, except four years devoted to other pursuits, and is now engaged in his twenty-ninth year of teaching. He served one year in the Civil War as sergeant in Battery K, Sixth Pennsylvania Heavy Artillery, and was honorably discharged at Fort Ethan Allen, Va., June 13, 1865. His regiment successfully watched John S. Mosby, and helped guard the National capital. March 25, 1862, he was married to Miss Maggie, daughter of John and Eliza Turner; the former was born in Virginia, and the latter a native of Baltimore. Mr. Anderson has one child: Ella Lorena, wife of Charles R. Trew, a mining engineer, who is now in charge of Uniondale mines. In politics Mr. Anderson is a republican, but not radical in his views. A Protestent in religion, he favors the Methodist church, and is a prominent member of several orders: P. W. C. T. of the G. T., a Scarlet Degree member of Fort Necessity Lodge, I. O. O. F., a P. P. Commander of Dunbar Post, Grand Army of the Republic, a Past Chancellor of Dunbar Lodge, K. of P., and a Past District Deputy Grand Chancellor of the First K. of P., District of Fayette County. He is a frequent contributor to Pythian literature, and several very able and eloquent articles of his have appeared in the most prominent Pythian periodicals. The following is from one of his articles: "Sentiment is one thing, opinion is another. Sentiment is a link that joins man to man. Opinions are the separating wedges that divide man from man in an intellectual point of view. Sentiments in their primitive state are elementary, synthetic and concrete, and serve to bind together in harmony the human family. Opinions, rationally viewed, may be said to be composite, serve to divide, to separate, and to scatter."

CHARLES SHEARER BEATTY is a native of Dunbar township Fayette county, Pa., and was born July 27, 1843. He is descended from an Irish family on the paternal, and a German family on the maternal side. His paternal great-grandfather, of New Jersey, served as a soldier in the War of 1812. After the war he removed to Centre county, Pa. He had three sons: Samuel, James and John, who were in the war with him. Samuel engaged in the manufacture of woolen goods at New Haven, soon removed to Belleville, Washington county, Pa., and there engaged in the mercantile business, which he followed till 1840, when he moved to "Little" Washington, Washington county, Pa., and engaged in the woolen business. For twenty-five years he was considered one of the largest wool dealers in the county. He is still living at Washington. His brother James died at Cool Spring Furnace (this county) in about 1849.

John Beatty (paternal grandfather) was born in New Jersey; removed to Centre county, Pa., and settled at Cool Spring Furnace, this county, in about 1820. He was a common laborer, and married Isabella Hyndman. Her father, Charles Shearer, was a native of Germany, born in about 1768, and came to Baltimore in about 1790. He engaged in the fish trade and married Elizabeth Gamble.

Colonel James Beatty (father) was a son of John and Isabella (Hyndman) Beatty, and was born August 21, 1822, in Fayette county, Pa. He was a farmer, colonel of a regiment of state militia that offered its services in the Mexican war, but was never called out. Colonel Beatty was married to Sarah J. Shearer on July 25, 1842. They had nine children, five sons and four daughters: Charles S., Mary, Isabella, William, John, Alice, Emma, Louisa, and Robert.

Charles S. Beatty was educated in the common schools, and is now engaged in farming in Dunbar township. He has lived for twenty years in that township, has taught school for sixteen years and has never taught out of Dunbar except one year. He has served continuously from 1876 to 1879 as a school director of Dunbar township, and was secretary of the board. He was secretary of the democratic county committee in 1873-74. In the fall of 1888 Mr. Beatty was elected from Fayette county to the house of representatives of Pennsylvania, and was the only candidate on the democratic ticket at that time elected. In the Pennsylvania legislature he has been very earnest in advocating measures in the interest of education. His bill providing for a county uniformity of text books to be determined by a majority vote of the citizens of each county of the State is one that commends itself to the careful consideration of everyone.

He is a prominent member in several of the secret societies: Independent Order of Odd Fellows; withdrew in 1873, and became one of the charter members of King David Lodge, No. 826, at Dunbar, of which he was the first Noble Grand; has filled all the offices of the subordinate lodge; was Grand Lodge Representative several times from King David, and has been since 1874 a member of the Grand Lodge of Pennsylvania, of I. O. O. F. He was a charter member of Dunbar Lodge, No. 410, K. of P., organized in October, 1873; withdrew March 23, 1889, and organized a lodge at Leisenring, and at present is its Grand Lodge Representative; has filled all the offices of the subordinate lodge, and has been a member of the Grand Lodge of Pennsylvania since 1874. He is a member of the junior O. U. A. M., and has passed the chairs; was Representative to the State Council at Wilkesbarre, July, 1888, and Harrisburg, July, 1889.

He was married on August 25, 1865, to Rebekah, daughter of Davis and Mary Woodward, natives of Dunbar township. Mr. Beatty has seven children: Louella B., Mary F., Davis W., Sarah J., Charles F., James L. and Robert E.

Mr. Beatty is a Presbyterian, and for four years past, has been elder in the Leisenring church. He is clerk of the session, and has been a delegate three years to the Presbytery. He was elected in 1888 by the Redstone Presbytery to the Synod at Erie City, Pa.

JOHN CLARK BEESON, a prosperous farmer of Dunbar township, and a descendant of two of the old and highly respected families of Fayette county, was born at Uniontown, Fayette county, Pa., January 29, 1828, and is a son of Henry and Annie (Downer) Beeson.

His grandfather, Jacob Beeson, was a native of Martinsburg, Va., (now W. Va.,) and came to Uniontown in 1788. He purchased a tract of land of Henry Beeson, the founder of Uniontown and a relative. Jacob Beeson reared a family of seven children: Henry, Jonas and five daughters. Henry Beeson was a sergeant in the War of 1812, served from August 27, 1812, to August 26, 1813. He married Miss Annie, daughter of Jonathan Downer. (For Downer ancestry see sketch of Daniel Downer.) They had eight children: Jacob S. (dead), Jonathan D. (dead); Monroe, a sergeant who fought bravely through the late war; John C.; Henry H., killed before Richmond, in the Civil War; Augusta, wife of J. O. Allen, a merchant of Uniontown; Elizabeth J. (dead), and Drusilla A.

J. Clark Beeson was educated in Madison College and learned the trade of cabinet-maker, which he pursued at Uniontown until 1870. In 1870 he purchased his present farm in Dunbar township, and has since been successfully engaged in farming and stock-raising. On June 10, 1851, he was married to Miss Affinity Page, of Connellsville. To their union were born eleven children: Mary Virginia, wife of Charles T. Cramer, a merchant of Uniontown; Annie, married John Gilchrist, of North Union township; Samuel P., died in Illinois; William T., engineer on Lake Erie Railroad; Frances A., wife of William French, a conductor on the P. & W. R. R.; Henry M. (dead); Sidney C., foreman on Lake Erie R. R.; Walter F., employed at the Columbia Iron and Steel works, Uniontown; Joseph L., Jessie and Wallace E.

J. Clark Beeson has a set of silver spurs brought from Virginia by Jacob Beeson and worn by him at Gen. La Fayette's reception at Uniontown in 1824. Mr. Beeson is a careful and successful business man and a commendable citizen. In politics he is a republican, and in business matters is always prompt and honest.

DAVID BEVAN, of Dunbar, was born April 1, 1858, in Middlesboro, England. His grandfather, David Bevan, also a native of England, was born about 1761 and died in 1860. His father, Walter Bevan, was born July 10, 1825, in England, and married Susan Davis, a native of England; Susan Davis, her mother, came to America when eighty-seven years of age and died in Beech City, Ohio. To this union were born: William, Joshua and David. He was a roller by trade; was the manager for nineteen years of Balcour, Vaughn & Co.'s rolling mill, which was at that time the largest in the world.

David Bevan was educated at the academy of Stockton, England; served his apprenticeship as tinner and gas fitter seven years, and holds a regular diploma, which is perhaps the only one in the county. He came to America in 1879 and worked at his trade for Terry Brothers, New Castle, Pa., for seven years, afterwards returned to England, and in 1886 came to Dunbar and bought out the firm of O. P. Fulton, went into business and now has a very profitable trade. In 1883 he married Miss Emma L. Mann, daughter of Mr. Samuel Mann of New Lisbon, Ohio. She was a teacher of New Lisbon, Ohio, and graduated from the high school at the age of seventeen.

Mr. Bevan is a member of the Methodist Episcopal church at Dunbar; is a member of the K. of P. and I. O. O. F. Joshua, a brother, is practicing law at Stockton on Tees, England. William, another brother, is proprietor of one of the largest hotels of the same place. Mr. Bevan does a large business in tin roofing and gas fitting. He is a splendid workman in all the various departments of his trade.

MARSHALL D. L. BROOKS, grandfather and father were born in Pennsylvania. Joseph Brooks, the grandfather, was born in about 1789, and married Dollie Bassinger. Their children were John, Henry, Jacob, William, George, Joseph, Samuel and Irwin.

His father, Irwin Brooks, was born in 1837, in Springfield township, Fayette county, Pa., and was married to Hannah Lyons, a native of Somerset county, Pa. She was a daughter of Jonathan Lyons. They had the following children: Dollie, Sparks, Norman and Marshall D. L.

Marshall D. L. Brooks was born May 4, 1865, in Fayette county, Pa., was educated in the public schools and at Mt. Pleasant Institute, Westmoreland county, Pa. On leaving college he taught school three times in Salt Lick township, and two terms in Dunbar borough.

In 1888 he embarked in the mercantile business at Dunbar, under the firm name of Brooks & Herrington. They continued in business, for about two months, when the name of the firm was changed to Brooks & Co. In connection with the general mercantile business, he is agent for Enger & Co., of Cincinnati, extensive manufacturers of carriages and buggies, etc.

In the spring of 1889 he was elected member of the council of Dunbar. He is a member of the Royal Arcanum 754, and is a member of the Junior O. U. A. M. He is an enterprising and successful young merchant, and is fast winning success as a business man.

WINFIELD SCOTT BLANEY, of Dunbar, is a son of Isaac and Sarah (Victor) Blaney, and was born in Monongalia county, W. Va. (then Va.), April 22, 1848. William Blaney (grandfather) was a native of Virginia, where he died. Isaac Blaney (father) was born and reared in Western Virginia, was a farmer, a republican, and a member of the Methodist Protestant church. He married Sarah Victor, Four of their sons served in the Union army, John enlisted in 1861, and was killed at the battle of Fredericksburg; Lawrence served in the Seventh West Virginia; was in all the principal battles of the Army of the Potomac; Henry and William (twins) enlisted, in 1863, in the Fourteenth Pennsylvania Cavalry, the former was killed at Piedmont, the latter was captured and passed six months in Andersonville prison. The father of Mrs. Blaney, Frank Victor, was a native of Virginia. Two of his sons served in the Civil War, one, Lawrence, of the Seventh West Virginia Infantry, lost a leg in the Seven Days' Fight, the other, Jacob, left an arm at Antietam.

W. S. Blaney was educated in the subscription and free schools of Western Virginia. Mr. Blaney removed to Fayette county in 1870, where he engaged in mining for ten years. His next business was farming, and in 1880 he purchased his present farm. In 1869 he married Miss Mary C., daughter of Samuel and Margaret Darnell, both of Morgantown, W. Va. They have seven children: Jennie, a teacher in Dunbar township; Hattie, Walter Scott, Linda, Frank, Fred and Mary Mason. During the war he was engaged for eighteen months in teaming for the Union army. He is a hard-working, energetic farmer; is a republican and takes an active part in politics.

McCLELLAN BRECHBILL was born in Unity township, Westmoreland county, Pa., June 21, 1862.

His grandfather, Christopher Brechbill, was born in Mt. Pleasant township, about 1795 and died at the age of seventy-eight. He married a Miss George, a lady of Irish origin, who died at the age of seventy-two. The children born to their union were: Lucy, Elizabeth, Matilda, Samuel and Bertha. McClellan Brechbill's father, Samuel G. Brechbill, was born in about 1825, in Mt. Pleasant township, Westmoreland county, Pa., and was married to Mary Ann Moser, a native of the same township. They had the following children: George S., Emma B., Charles, Scott, McClellan, John T., Laura A. and Harvey S. Samuel Brechbill served as county commissioner of Westmoreland county, in 1882–3–4. McClellan Brechbill was born and raised on a farm, educated in the common schools of the county, Sewickley Academy and Pleasant Unity Normal School. He studied pharmacy ten months with Dr. T. L. Smith, of Pleasant, Unity, and took the position of pharmacist with Drs. Goodman and Heath, at Mt. Pleasant, in 1880. He remained with them four months, when he engaged with Mr. John V. Stephenson, druggist at Greensburg; remained only a short time, going thence to Pittsburgh, and was there engaged with John T. Kinney for over two years, and attended Pittsburgh College of Pharmacy while in his employ. He came to Dunbar in August, 1883, and engaged with Shepler, Clark & Co. Upon the dissolution of that firm, in 1886, it was merged into the firm of R. W. Clark & Co. Mr. Brechbill still holds in his position. Besides owning property at Percy, where he is interested in a drug store, the firm being Brechbill & Co., of which he is manager. He is a member of the Royal Arcanum, is a popular young druggist and is one of the business young men of Dunbar.

JOHN K. BROWN'S paternal grandfather was of German extraction, and his maternal grandfather, Alexander Kelly, was born in about 1771 in Ireland. The latter came to America and, in all probability, settled in Westmoreland county. He married and had the following children by his first wife: Jane and Elizabeth. He married the second time Catherine Campbell, who was born December 2, 1783, and had the following children: Samuel, George, John, Rebecca, James Paull, Washington, Campbell, Catherine and Susannah.

John K. Brown's parents were Adam Brown and Mary (Kelly) Brown. Adam Brown was born in Westmoreland county, Pa., and was a shoemaker. They had the following children: John K., James (dead), Mary (married David Hepler), Elizabeth, Jane (married David Sherril, of McKeesport), Alexander (dead) and William (dead).

John Kelly Brown was born in Westmoreland county, Pa., September 4, 1811, brought up in that county, and was educated in the subscription schools of that day. He learned the trade of a shoemaker, at which he has worked since he became of age. He has been living in Connellsville for fifty-five years.

July, 1836, he was married to Elizabeth Sheppard (the daughter of Theophilus Sheppard, a native of Westmoreland, who married Elizabeth Stafford, and had the following children: Mary, James, Phœbe Ann, Henry L., Elizabeth, Sarah A., Catherine, Theophilus, Robert W., John, Joseph, Paoli, Athanasia and George). Of this union were born: Theodore M. (deceased), Artemisia S. (married Albert S. Cameron, of Connellsville), Joseph K. (married and lives in Canton, Ohio, and there engaged in glass manufacturing), Fielding D. (dead), Florence Henrietta (married E. Y. White—see his sketch), Mary Alice (dead), George B. (married, lives in Connellsville), Sarah Ann (married to David Baer, and lives in Ohio), William (dead), Eliza Eva (dead), John Charles (a druggist in the West), Ida May (married to Flavius O. Goodwin, a resident of Connellsville, and runs a steam laundry there), Cora Adella (dead), Albert (a traveling salesman for his brother).

Mr. Brown had two sons who served in the Civil War. Theodore volunteered at the beginning, and served during the entire war. Joseph K. enlisted in the One Hundred and Forty-second Pennsylvania Infantry, under Captain Du Shane, in 1862, and served to the close of the war.

Mr. Brown and wife are members of the M. P. church, and have been for the last fifty-three years. He is the president of the board of trustees and a steward of the church. He has served as a delegate to the following conferences: at Pittsburgh, Washington and Beaver Falls. He is a member of the following orders: I. O. O. F., K. of P. and Redmen. He is the only charter member of Gen. Worth's Lodge, at Connellsville, now living. He has never drawn any money from any of the above orders. He has always been a strong advocate of the cause of temperance, and has belonged to various organizations whose objects were for the furtherance of that cause.

He was the originator of the Connellsville Hill Grove Cemetery Company in 1868, is at present the president of the company, and the chief stockholder of the same.

ADAM BRYSON is of Irish descent. His great-grandfather, Andrew Bryson, was a native of Ireland, came to America and settled in Fayette county, Pa. His grandfather, David Bryson, was also a native of Ireland, came with his father in 1700, and settled in Fayette county. He married ancy Wilson, daughter of Alexander Wilson, of Fayette county. They had the following children: Elizabeth and Andrew.

William Laughery, who was born in Fayette county, was the maternal grandfather. He married Susan Kemp of the county, and to them was born, Charlotte, the mother of the subject of this sketch.

Andrew Bryson (father) was born August 4, 1819, and came to Union Furnace at Dunbar when the yield of iron was but three tons per twenty-four hours. Now the yield is 125 tons in the same time. They had the following children: *Surue*, Nancy, Mary, William, Rebecca, John, Adam, Emma and Bella.

Adam Bryson was born February 15, 1860, in Dunbar township, Fayette county, Pa., and was educated in the common schools of the township. He has followed laboring during all of his life, working chiefly for the Dunbar Furnace Company. He is a member of the Good Templar, Odd Fellows, Jr. O. U. A. Mechanics, Orangemen, Knights of the Camp of Israel. He was the first Arch Purple Marks man in Balyer, Sons of Liberty, S. O. L. No. 36 at Dunbar. Presided as W. M. for the first two years, has represented King David Lodge, I. O. O. F., No. 826, and was twice in the Grand Lodge of Pennsylvania. His father is a charter member of King Solomon Lodge of Masons at Connellsville, and King David Lodge of Odd Fellows at Dunbar.

WILLIAM F. BUTE, a successful merchant at Vanderbilt, was born in Franklin township, Fayette county, Pa., July 26, 1843, and is a son of Joseph and Clarissa (Black) Bute.

He erected a distillery, saw-mill and grist-mill and was actively engaged in conducting his various branches of business for many years. He died in 1857. His wife was Miss Mary Morrison. They had ten sons and one daughter. But two of these sons remain in Franklin township; one is dead, and the other, Joseph Bute (father of W. F. Bute), has resided since 1837 on the old Andrew Arnold farm. He was born July 24, 1812, at Upper Middletown.

John Bute (grandfather), although not a pioneer settler of Franklin township, yet was very active in its early history. He was born at Winchester, Va., at about the close of the Revolutionary War; came to what is now Upper Middletown in 1813, where he engaged in butchering and hotel keeping, but soon purchased and removed to the "Pears" farm, on what is now Butes Run in Franklin township. Received his early education under James Adair, a celebrated "master" at Thornbottom school house, and engaged successfully in farming until his death.

Joseph Bute was twice married. His first wife was Miss Sarah Ann Sparks, after her death he married Miss Clarissa, daughter of William and Mary (Sayers) Black, the former a native of Greene county and a glass blower. Joseph Bute had six sons and six daughters by his second marriage.

William F. Bute was reared on a farm and educated in the common schools. Leaving school he devoted most of his time and attention to farming until 1881. In that year he removed to Vanderbilt, and began merchandising, in which he has since continued, with great success. His store-room is eligibly located, well-arranged, and contains a large and well-selected stock of dry goods, groceries and notions.

In 1864 he was united in marriage to Miss Mary, daughter of Jacob Smith, of Connellsville. To their union have been born two children: Evalina C. (dead) and Katie E.

W. F. Bute is a prominent democrat, has served two terms as school director—one in Franklin and one in Dubar township; was elected and re-elected justice of the peace for Franklin township, but only served one year of his second term, before his removal to Dunbar township.

DAVID ANDREW BYERS was born July 22, 1843, in Fayette county, Pa. His father, Andrew Byers, was born in Fayette county, and married Jane Hamilton, daughter of John Hamilton. Their children are Isaac W., Susan B., Sarah J., Margaret, John H., David and Mary.

D. A. Byers was educated in the common schools of the county, and followed farming till 1861.

In 1861 he enlisted in Company H, First Pennsylvania Cavalry, under Captain Davidson, and served three years and three months. He was in the battles of the Army of the Potomac.

In 1868 he engaged in the coke business, at which he was employed till 1873, when he engaged in the mercantile business in Dunbar for five years.

In 1878 he retired from active business and is living at the present time at Dunbar. He is a member of the K. of P., Jr. O. A. M., the Royal Arcanum, and G. A. R. He is a member of the Presbyterian church at Dunbar, and is a leading member of the G. A. R.

He was married March 22, 1871, to Lucretia Spears, a native of Dunbar, and is a daughter of John Spears. They have the following children: Ann, Mary Eva, James A. and Ella S.

ALBERT S. CAMERON, a faithful soldier and a veteran teacher, was born in North Union township, Fayette county, Pa., June 5, 1834, and is a son of Hugh and Jane (White) Cameron.

His grandfather, Alexander Cameron, emigrated from Scotland to near Berryville, Mercer, now Clark county, Va., shortly after the Revolutionary War. He had four children: Hugh, Moses, James and Mary.

His father, Hugh Cameron, was born at Martinsburg, Va., in 1792, was a farmer and shoemaker, and served as a soldier in the War of 1812. Took part in the battle of Baltimore. He was at Fort McHenry when it was attacked by the British, and it was in this fight the Star-Spangled Banner was written by Francis S. Key; he was in several other engagements. His wife was Jane White; they had born unto them fourteen children: George W., soldier in late war; Alexander B., Sophia, widow of George Devan; William L. (deceased); Hugh, second-lieutenant in the One Hundred and Forty-second Pennsylvania Infantry; James, Albert S., Daniel K. (soldier in the late war), Charles (deceased), Nancy A., wife of John H. Martin, county superintendent, Johnson county, Ind.; Mary, wife of Martin B. Pope; Eliza, wife of Miller Dunaway; Margaret A., wife of T. J. Dobson, and Phebe. Mrs. Cameron's father, George White, was a native of Ireland, emigrated to Connellsville he enlisted in the American army in the War of 1812 and died during the war. He left four children: Phebe Jane, Margaret J., George and Mary.

Albert S. Cameron was educated in the common and normal schools of Fayette county. Leaving school, he engaged in teaching, and taught one term in Dunbar, two terms in Franklin, and afterwards taught several terms in Connellsville. In 1862 he went to Indiana and served two years as principal of the Edinburg school. After the war he served as principal of the Fairmont schools West Virginia. On the solicitation of the Connellsville school board in 1870 he accepted the vice-principalship of the Connellsville schools, and served in that capacity till 1875. He was principal of the same schools in 1876, and since 1876 he has taught four years at New Haven. He enlisted in the war as sergeant in Company E, Two Hundred and Eleventh Regiment Pennsylvania Infantry, was in the battles in front of Petersburg, Hatcher's Run and Fort Steadman, and was seriously wounded at

Petersburg. He was married June 27, 1861, to Miss Artemisia, daughter of John K. Brown. Unto their union have been born three children: Lizzie Alice, born April 13, 1862, deceased; Edgar Brown, born May 17, 1867, and Karl Lott, born December 15, 1868.

Leaving the teacher's profession he engaged as a book-keeper with James Calhoun & Co., in the office of chief accountant of B. & O. R. R., then with John W. Miner & Co., and is at present with the Connellsville Fire Brick Company. He is a member of General Worth Lodge, No. 386, of I. O. O. F., G. A. R., E. A. U. of I. O. of H., besides being a member of several temperance organizations.

He has been a member of the Methodist Protestant church since 1851. He is a scholarly gentleman, and a live and highly-respected citizen.

ROBERT W. CLARK, M. D., of Dunbar, whose great grandfather, Robert Clark, emigrated from Londonderry, Ireland, to the United States in 1775, and settled in Lancaster county, Pa. He was a farmer, and died in that county in 1850, upon the same property taken up by his father. His wife's name was Miss Scott, daughter of a Scotch-Irishman. They had eight children: William, Thomas, Robert, James, Mary, Jane' Nancy and Margaret Eliza. His father' Alexander Scott Clark, was born in 1815, and was a member of the Silver Grays Home Guards during the War of the Rebellion. He married Isabella Jane Neeper. daughter of James Neeper, a native of Lancaster county. He engaged in faming until he retired from active business. They had twelve children: Letitia, Robert W., James, Lindley (who is an engineer, now in the interior of Africa, foreman of a diamond mine for a New York company), Laura J., Harry S. and Anna B. Dr. Clark was born in Lancaster county, Pa., August 2, 1848, educated in the schools of the same county and Chestnut Level Academy. He prepared himself to enter La Fayette College, but was prevented on account of failing health. He read medicine with Dr. A. M. McMillen at Lebanon, Ohio, graduated in medical department at Ann Arbor, Mich., and at the University of Pennsylvania in 1872. He went to Winfield and practiced about two years, when he came to Dunbar in 1873, where he has since resided. In 1886 he married Ellen N. Schell, of Somerset, Somerset county, daughter of J. J. Schell, a retired banker of Somerset. They have one child, Robert W.

Dr. Clark is a member of the Fayette County Medical Association, of the Pennsylvania State Medical Association, and has twice served as a delegate to the State Medical Association. He is a member of the Knights Templar, of the Masonic order, of the Royal Arcanum, and Jr. O. of A. M.

Dr. Clark is the nominee of his party—the republicans—for corner of the county; for the office he is eminently qualified. He is esteemed very highly as a gentleman, physician and surgeon by the people who know him.

JOSEPH COLESTOCK, a highly respected citizen of Dunbar township, is a son of Jonas and Margaret (Sese) Colestock, and was born at Connellsville, Fayette county, Pa., June 13, 1808. His grandfather, John Colestock, was born in Saxony, Germany, and in 1740 came to York county, Pa., where he afterwards married Miss Julia Foist. They had two sons: John and Jonas and two daughters.

Jonas Colestock was born in York county, Pa., in 1765, and was a captain in the militia for fourteen years. In 1787 married Margaret Seese, and had the following children: Elizabeth, Margaret, Charlotte, Susan, widow of Wm. McCormick, and living at Uniontown in the eighty-sixth year of her age. Mrs. Colestock's father, Jacob C. Seese, was a native of Lorraine province, France (now a province of Germany). He was of noble birth and well educated, especially in the languages, but being of a military turn of mind became an officer in the French army. He came to America during the Revolution and held a command under General Sullivan in the latter's expedition to avenge the Wyoming massacre. About 1783 he settled in Westmoreland county, where he encountered many hardships of Indian warfare. His wife was Mary Foible of Bavaria, Germany, who was the mother of four sons: Michael, Martin, Christopher and Rudolph.

Joseph Colestock was reared and educated at Connellsville, learned the hatting trade but never followed it. He clerked at Donegal and then for John Gray; taught school at Uniontown for several years, was a merchant in Springfield township for some years, came to Dunbar township in 1867 and engaged successfully in his present business of farming. In 1837 he was married to Isabella, daughter of William and Margaret Spears, of Uniontown. They have the following children: Margaret, wife of James F. Imel, a lumber merchant of Crawford county; Lieutenant John, married Miss Jane King, served in the Eighty-fifth Pennsylvania Volunteers, was distinguished for bravery, never flinched in battle, was promoted from corporal and was in line for a captaincy when the war closed; Minerva, wife of Matthew Patterson of New Haven; Mary, wife of Thomas Pyles of Hagerstown, Md.; Louisa, Joseph, married Miss Zanie White, and lives in Butler county; Samuel, dead; David H. and Anna B.

Joseph Colestock is a member of the Methodist Episcopal church, and gives his time chiefly in the superintendence of his farm.

JOHN COOLEY is a son of Jonathan and Jane (Passmore) Cooley, and was born in Tyrone township, Fayette county, Pa., August 22, 1816. William Cooley (paternal grandfather) was of Irish extraction, and at the time of the Revolutionary War was a resident of Maryland, and followed wagoning. He was married to Elizabeth Firmin. Their children were: John, Jonathan (father), Matthew, Isaac and Frederick.

Jonathan Cooley (father) was born in 1777, and died in 1817. He was a "forgeman," and came from Maryland to Fayette county in 1803. He was married October 31, 1805, to Miss Jane Passmore. Their children were: Matthew, born August 11, 1806; Nancy, born April 22, 1811; Mary P., born March 1, 1808; William, born January 9, 1814; Elizabeth F., born July 6, 1809; John, born August 22, 1816.

John Cooley was educated in the subscription schools, and learned the trade of a carpenter and later that of cabinet-maker. He was married March 20, 1839, to Miss Maria Louisa Bryant of Connellsville. Their children were: Eliza J., born January 17, 1840; Isabella, born September 18, 1841; Wallace H., born May 1, 1843; Amanda, born January 30, 1845; Henry L., born July 16, 1847. Wallace Cooley (son) enlisted in 1861, in Company I, Twenty-fifth Ohio Volunteers; was in the battles of Cheat Mountain, Second Bull Run and Chancellorsville. He was badly wounded in the battle at the latter place. John Cooley married for his second wife, August 12, 1852, Mary Ann Baker of Butler county. Unto their union was born seven children: Samuel, born May 2, 1853; Matthew, born January 22, 1855; Maria L., born December 19, 1856; Frances D., born

November 12, 1858; John B., born October 30, 1860; Harriet D., born March 9, 1863, and Rachel, born May 11, 1865.

Mr. Cooley after his first marriage located at Connellsville and engaged in the cabinet-making business, which he continues at the present time. He is a good workman, a peaceable and respected citizen, and a regular attendant at the services of the Methodist Episcopal church.

WILLIAM H. COOPER, A. M., born September 6, 1821, in Lawrence county, Pa., and is a son of Thomas and Phebe (Dean) Cooper. His grandfather, William Cooper, was born in County Tyrone, Ireland, who came to America; served creditably in the French and Indian War (1754–63). His children were: John, Thomas (father), James, Nancy, Sarah and Jane, who all lived in Lawrence, Mercer and Butler counties. His father Thomas Cooper, was raised in Lancaster county, Pa., and came to Lawrence (formerly Mercer) county, where he married Phebe Dean. They had the following children: Jonathan, William H., John, Robert, James H., Jesse, Marshall, Jacob, Mary and Ellen. Thomas Cooper was a farmer and stock raiser, and amassed quite a sum of money. His wife Phœbe (Dean) Cooper was a daughter of Jonathan Dean, of Scotch descent, was a surveyor. Jonathan Dean came from Huntingdon county to Lawrence, and afterward to Butler county, Pa. In these counties, many of his descendants are now living. He married Eleanor Thompson, and to them were born Aaron, Polly, William, Phœbe and Nancy.

William H. Cooper was educated in the subscription schools of that day. He attended the Butler Academy at Butler, in Butler county, entered Dennison College, Ohio, in 1842, and was graduated from there in 1847. In September of 1847 he and his young wife were elected principals of the London Academy, Ohio. From 1848 to 1870 he taught in several colleges in the South; in 1850 was president of Muscle Shoals College, Alabama, taught mathematics in Enon College, Tenn., and also in Union College, Tenn. From 1855 to 1859 he was president of Mountain Home Female College, Alabama, and taught two years at Christian County College, Christian county, Ky. He left the South in 1870 came to Oil City, Pa., where he was elected principal of the Rouseville High School, and there, in connection with Rev. S. Williams, D.D., established the Baptist church in Rouseville. The next year he served as principal of the New Castle Academic School and also of the Harlansburg Academy one year.

He came to Connellsville, and preached for the Baptist church from 1873 till 1876. He was licensed to preach at the age of nineteen, and has preached more or less ever since. Has spent in the space of thirty-two years about $6,000 in educating poor but talented young gentlemen and ladies.

He is a member of the Sons of Temperance and has always advocated the cause of temperance, as did his father and grandfather.

In 1847 he married Mary E., daughter of Eli Butler, of Granville, Ohio. After her death in 1850 he was re-married in 1852, to Margaret Jones, of Nashville, Tenn. They have five children: John, Charles, Mary, Annie and Agnes.

Prof. Cooper's sentiments and sympathies in the last war were with the North, although he was in the South and surrounded by Southern influences. He was arrested several times by Union soldiers, but was always released. Having lost all his earthly possessions to the amount of several thousand dollars by the issues of war, he returned to his native State, that his dust may mingle in a few years with the dust of a numerous ancestry.

In the spring of 1889 Prof. Cooper was elected justice of the peace for the borough of New Haven, where he is known as a scholar, fine theologian, and a man who possesses considerable information.

LUTELUS LINDLEY COLLINS, a progressive farmer of Dunbar township, is a son of William and Eliza (Cox) Collins, and was born near East Liberty, in Dunbar township, Fayette county, Pa., April 7, 1838. His great-grandfather, William Collins, was born in England in 1762, and came to Kent county, Md., where he married a Miss Gail, and had four sons: William, John, George and James, from whom are descended the large Collins posterity of to-day.

James Collins, the grandfather, married Sarah Dudley; removed from Maryland to Fayette county, Pa., in 1822, and settled in Dunbar township on a farm known as Fort Hill.

William Collins, father of L. L. Collins, was born December 5, 1807; married Miss Eliza, daughter of Joseph Cox, August 28, 1833. The following children were born to them: George W., June 25, 1834; died in 1837. Joseph R., April 9, 1836; died quite young. James C., August 20, 1840; served three years in the Civil War, Fifteenth Pennsylvania Cavalry. William H., February 13, 1843; served nearly four years in Seventh Pennsylvania Cavalry; promoted to captain of his company with the Army of the Cumberland; in a number of battles and raids, and was at the capture of Jefferson Davis. Susan E., October 21, 1845; married William Parkhill, of Franklin township; Sarah L., April 24, 1848; died young. Eliza Alice, October 24, 1849; married Clark Shaw, of Connellsville. They are the children of Eliza (Cox) Collins, who died July 22, 1851. William Collins again married, Mary B. Stone, of Knox county, Ohio, October 1, 1851, and to them were born the following children: Mary A., July 20, 1852; married Henry Ackley, of Kansas. John E., May 26, 1854. Alonzo D., May 18, 1857. Ida M., July 20, 1858; married John Smith, of Kansas. Margaret O., August 17, 1862; died young. Charles E., December 4, 1864.

William Collins was always found on the side of morality and right. He was a public-spirited and highly-respected citizen. He was a member of the Cumberland Presbyterian church at East Liberty. He moved to Kansas in December, 1882, where he lived, pleasantly surrounded by seven of his ten children, and died October 24, 1888, reaching the ripe age of over four-score years. His six sons were, by request, his pall-bearers to the grave.

Lutelus L. Collins was educated in the common schools and at Chesterville Seminary, Ohio. In 1857 he went from Fayette county, Pa., to Kansas, where he helped seat the first free State Legislature at Lecompton, in 1858. He afterwards went overland to California, where he worked in the gold mines of Nevada county. On December 5, 1862, he went from San Francisco to Panama on a Pacific mail steamship; crossed the isthmus from Panama to Aspinwall by railroad; from there to New York on the steamship Aerial, which was chased on the route by the celebrated Confederate cruiser, the Alabama. In August, 1864, he enlisted in the Sixth Regiment of Pennsylvania Heavy Artillery for the defense of Washington City; was soon detailed as clerk at headquarters, De Russey's division, and served in that capacity until mustered out of the service June 13, 1865, at Washington. He returned to Fayette county, and has been engaged in farming and stock business ever since.

On November 5, 1863, he married Miss Anna, daughter of Christian and Mary H. (Shallenberger) Stoner. Their union has been blessed with nine children (two died in infancy), born and named as follows: Mary E., September 21, 1864; died May 18, 1882. George A., November 10, 1866; married Lizzie Leighty, daughter of William Leighty, of Ohio. John W., August 18, 1868; Blanche, April 20, 1871; Curte C., October 26, 1876; Ken H., February 19, 1881, and Florence, March 22, 1886.

L. L. Collins bought the farm where he now lives from his father. He is a good farmer, raises good stock, and everything about the farm is kept in good condition; has served as school director, is an elder in the C. P. church at East Liberty, and a member of the William Kurtz Post 104, G. A. R., at Connellsville.

JOHN DUDLEY COLLINS was born in Kent county, Md., April 29, 1813, and is a son of James and Sarah (Dudley) Collins.

James Collins (father) was born in Maryland, October 17, 1777; served in the War of 1812, in the commissary department; was married to Sarah Dudley February, 17, 1807, and the following children were born to them: William, born December 5, 1807 (died in Kansas, October 24, 1888); James, born April 20, 1810, still living; Louisa, born May 19, 1816, married William Patterson in October, 1834, who died March 8, 1838. There were two children born to them, James C., who died in the forty-ninth year of his age, and Emeline, died young; her second husband was James Parkhill. From this marriage three sons are living: William, David and John D. Louisa died in October, 1886. Edwin born in 1819, died in 1854, and Emeline born in March, 1822, died when quite young. William Collins, the paternal grandfather of John D., was born in 1762 in England; came to America; settled in Kent county, Md.; married a Miss Gail and they had four sons: William, John, George and James.

Nicholas Dudley, maternal grandfather, was born in England and came to America; settled in Maryland; married and had the following children: Benjamin, Nicholas, Francis, Elizabeth, Mary, Sarah (the mother), and Samuel, who came to Pennsylvania and lived the last thirty years of his life with J. D. and James Collins. He died the 25th of May, 1889, in the eighty-seventh year of his age. John D. Collins was educated in the early subscription school; born on a farm and came to Fayette county, Pa., in 1822, with his father and settled near East Liberty on the farm known as Fort Hill, where he and his brother James now lives. He is a member of the Cumberland Presbyterian church; has been trustee and held other offices in the church. He was married on May 24, 1850, to Agnes Stoner, daughter of Christian Stoner (born in Bedford county, Pa., and moved to Westmoreland county, where he was married to Anna Stauffer; afterwards moved to Fayette county, where they raised a family of twelve children, six boys and six girls). There was but one child born to them, a daughter, who died when young.

They are widely known for their charity; no one is ever turned away empty handed.

ROBERT BRUCE COX was born at Brownsville, Fayette county, Pa., March 24, 1840; was reared and attended the common schools there. He began life as a clerk for Jesse H. Duncan, of Brownsville, iron, nails and commission house. From 1857 to 1861 he served an apprenticeship at millwright business, under William H. Barnes, of Uniontown. In 1861 he went into the army, and served till 1864. About three years before the war, however, he joined a company of cavalry, which was organized by Captain Davidson at Merrittstown. This company offered its services to the governor of Virginia at the time of the John Brown raid. On the breaking out of the war they again offered their services, but General Scott thought there was no need for cavalry to quiet the rebellious feeling at the South, and they were not called into action. It was afterward attached to the Sixth Regiment Pennsylvania Cavalry at Camp Wilkins, Pittsburgh; was taken thence to Washington City, where it was disbanded, and the First Pennsylvania Reserve Cavalry was organized under George D. Bayard as colonel. He was killed at the battle of Fredericksburg. Mr. Cox was at the following battles: Drainsville, Va., Harrisonburg, Cross Keys, Cedar Mountain, Gainesville, Bull Run, Fredericksburg, Chancellorsville, Gettysburg, Culpeper, Auburn, Bristow Station, New Home Church, Wilderness, Cold Harbor, and all the battles under General Grant in his attempts to capture Richmond. The regiment was with Sheridan in all of his raids. Mr. Cox was never out of the service one hour from the time he entered till he was discharged; he never had a furlough, and received no wound. He was mustered out September 15, 1864, at Philadelphia. Since then he has been very active in the organization of martial clubs for political parties, and assisted in organizing the William Kurtz Post, G. A. R., at Connellsville. After the war he returned home and engaged in the carpenter trade, and was for several years in the employment of Baltimore & Ohio Railroad Company at Connellsville. In 1877 he commenced as contractor and builder, and has continued as such ever since.

He is a member of "King Solomon's" Lodge, Free and Accepted Masons, No. 346, at Connellsville, of the Knights of Pythias, Independent Order of Odd Fellows, Chosen Friends, Penn Council, No. 30. He has served as secretary in each.

In politics Mr. Cox has been an independent republican. He has always been a strictly temperate man, is a member of the Baptist church, and has served as a member of council for his borough, and as assessor. Mr. Cox has been twice married; first on April 13, 1864, to Mary J. Shallenburger, a daughter of Abraham Shallenburger, an old settler at Connellsville. Four children were born to them: Abraham Shallenburger, Samuel J., Anna and Nannie. His second wife was Jennie Dawson, a native of Connellsville, to whom he married in March, 1889. His parents were Samuel J. and Nancy Cox. Their family consisted of six children: James (dead), Mary A., Robert B., R. B., John C., Samuel J. and Ellen. The latter was burned to death when thirteen years of age. Samuel J. Cox (father) was born at Brownsville, lived there till 1863, when he removed to Connellsville, and has always been engaged in the merchant tailoring business. He married three times. His second wife was Mary Murphy, a native of Redstone township, and had four children: William, Dorcas, Thomas and James. She was killed at Connellsville. For his third wife he married Ella Lingham, a native of Pittsburgh.

The paternal grandfather of R. B. Cox was of German descent, born in Fayette county, and was a farmer. He served in the war of 1812-15, and was killed in battle.

Nancy Works, the mother of R. B. Cox, was a native of Dunbar township, a daughter of James Works, who was also born in Dunbar township.

SAMUEL J. COX was born January 25, 1813, in Luzerne township, Fayette county, Pa. Michael Cox (grandfather) was born in Germany, came to America and settled in the eastern part of Pennsylvania. He was one of five who came to this part of the State and settled on what is known as

Cox's Run, in Luzerne township, taking what was termed "tomahawk possession" of a tract of land. The names of three of this five were, Cox, Sturgeon and Porter. Isaac Doney (maternal grandfather) was of Irish extraction, and came from New Jersey to western Pennsylvania.

Joseph Cox (father) was born in Luzerne township, Fayette county, Pa.; was a farmer and married Mary Doney in about 1805, and died in 1816. They had three children: Eliza, (deceased), William (died in the Civil War after serving about two years) and Samuel J. Samuel J. Cox was educated in the schools at Brownsville, later he learned the trade of tailor under James McSherry, and carried on the merchant tailoring business at Brownsville about thirty years, when he removed to Connellsville in 1863, and has since remained there, engaged in the merchant tailor business.

In 1835 he was married to Miss Nancy Work, a daughter of James Work, native of Dunbar township, Fayette county. They had the following children: James Cox (died in infancy), Mary A. (deceased), who married Jackson Stahl, and went to Kansas City and died there in July, 1888; Robert Bruce, a carpenter and contractor, lives at Connellsville; John, a painter; Joseph, a carpenter, is married and lives in Pittsburg; Thomas Cox, a rail-roader, is married, lives in Connellsville; William is married, lives in Connellsville; James B. Cox lives in Connellsville, is married and is an upholsterer by trade. Dorcas Cox lives in Connellsville with S. J. Cox.

Mr. Cox had three sons in the Civil War. John, who went out in Sickle's Brigade, at the commencement of the war, fought to the close, and took part in the battle of Williamsburg and quite a number of others in the Army of the Potomac. Robert Bruce volunteered in the First Pennsylvania Reserve Cavalry and served about three years, and took part in a number of battles. Joseph served three months, and took part in the capture of Morgan in the Ohio raid.

Mr. Cox has held the office of burgess of Connellsville for two terms, has been school director for two terms, and a member of the council several terms. He is a member of the Protestant Methodist church, was one among its first members, and has held all of the offices of the church. He was sent as a delegate from the Pittsburgh conference to Baltimore, to the convention for the re-uniting of the two branches of the church after the war. He is also a member of the Masonic order at Connellsville.

SAMUEL CROSSLAND, an industrious tradesman, for over fifty years, of Connellsville and New Haven, was born at Poplar Springs, Md., March 17, 1817, and is a son of Richard and Bebecca (Strawbridge) Crossland.

Samuel Crossland traces an English lineage through his paternal grandfather, George Crossland, a Quaker, born in England, and an early settler at Connellsville.

Richard Crossland, a son of George Crossland, was born and reared in Maryland, removed to Connellsville, where he learned the trade of wagonmaking, which he pursued as his life vocation. He married Rebecca Strawbridge, born June 19, 1799, and a daughter of Abram Strawbridge, a native of Baltimore, and was later a settler at Connellsville. They had ten children, five sons and five daughters.

Samuel Crossland received the limited education afforded by the subscription schools of Connellsville, and well remembers his first attendance at school in a small log house near the site of the present main school building of Connellsville. He learned the trade of wagonmaker and at twenty-one years of age bought out his father's wagon-making shop, and continued to operate it successfully for twenty-one years, when he removed to near New Haven, where he erected a commodious wagonmaking factory in 1859, enjoyed a good trade for thirty years, sold out in March, 1889, to his sons, and removed to a previously purchased farm near New Haven.

In 1840 he was married to Miss Nancy McLaine. They had seven children: Albert J., born October 24, 1841, died August 1, 1881. He had a collegiate education, was a successful and well liked business man; Florence, born August 13, 1843, wife of Samuel Smutz and lives in Missouri; Emily (dead); Harriet F., wife of Phillip Wofenberger of Westmoreland county; Irvin, born October 4, 1848, lives in Missouri; Fuller W., born November 11, 1850, lives in Missouri, and McLaine, born June 28, 1852. Mrs. Crossland died in 1852. Mr. Crossland was married in 1853 to Mrs. Eliza Long, widow of William Long, and to his second marriage were born eight children, born and named as follows: Newcomer, August 25, 1854: Frank, born January 28, 1856; Nancy, December 21, 1857; Elmore, June 27, 1860, (dead); Maria, August 20, 1862; Eliza Jane, March 10, 1865; Harry, March 5, 1868, and Bird, July 26, 1872.

Samuel Crossland has retired from the active duties of life and resides on his well improved farm near New Haven. He is a good workman, a peaceable citizen and a well respected member of the Methodist Episcopal church at Connellsville.

JAMES R. CRAY, one of the stirring young business men of Dunbar, was born at Darlington, Beaver county, Pa., March 8, 1860, and is a son of James and Margaret (Meehan) Cray, both born in Ireland.

The name Cray or Creagh, as it was originally spelled, is a common and well known one in the counties of Cork and Limerick, southern Ireland. In the early part of the present century, the male members of the Cray family were among the largest and finest physically developed and most muscular men in that region. The trans-Atlantic Crays have held many positions of trust and profit in their native country. One of this family, Capt. Cray, recently filled the office of Mayor of the City of Cork. Peter Cray, the grandfather of James R. Cray, was born in the county of Cork, was the youngest of six sons and married Bridget Brown, in 1817. They had seven sons and three daughters, of whom four are living: James Cray, the father of James R. Cray, emigrated from Ireland in 1852, to Brady's Bend, Armstrong county, Pa., where four years later he married Margaret Meehan, a daughter of Patrick and Ellen (Noonan) Meehan. Her parents were married about 1820, in Fenah Parish, County Limerick, Ireland. Born to them were one son and three daughters: James, Margaret, Honora and Ellen. James and Margaret (Meehan) Cray had born to them five children: James R., Peter P. M. (now a book-keeper in Pittsburgh); Bridget and Ellen. All living except Peter.

James R. Cray, was principally educated in the thirty-sixth ward and the Central High School, at Pittsburgh. After learning the harnessmaking trade at Pittsburgh, he located in the oil regions of Pennsylvania but soon removed to Dunbar, where in 1878 he opened in business and by his skill and industry soon became one of the foremost business men of the place. He secured an appointment as postal clerk in the railway mail service, on the recommendation of the Hon. C. E. Boyle. This position he did not like, which he soon resigned in order to devote all his attention to his rapidly increasing business at Dunbar.

In 1888 he passed a very creditable preliminary examination for the law, and was registered as a law student under the preceptorship of the firm of Boyle, Mestrezat & Boyle. He has done as much and probably more to promote the interests and develop the resources of the progressive little borough of Dunbar, than any other young man.

PETER R. DEMUTH, farmer, gardener and florist, of Connellsville, is a son of Joseph A. and Jane (Riste) De Muth, and was born on the farm he resides on, near Connellsville, Fayette county, Pa., September 23, 1833.

Joseph A. De Muth was born in Lancaster county, Pa., in 1800, came to Fayette county in 1825, and was principally engaged in farming for a livelihood. He was a member of the Methodist Episcopal church, and died in 1878. His wife was Miss Jane Riste, born in 1795, and died May 5, 1886. She was one of the early members of the Methodist Episcopal church. Her father, John Riste, was born in Lancaster county, came to Fayette county, and was engaged for many years in manufacturing linseed oil and operating a hemp mill.

Peter De Muth was raised on a farm in the manner that farmers' boys are reared, and received his education in the common schools. Leaving school he engaged in his present business of farming and gardening. A few years ago, he embarked in the greenhouse business and has been very successful.

In 1868 he was married to Miss Annie Beidler, daughter of Joseph Beidler, a farmer of Bullskin township. They have five children: Charles E., Albert N., Lizzie B., Joseph A. and Ida May.

Peter R. De Muth owns the old homestead of fifty-five acres, which is one mile north of Connellsville. He is a strong republican, and has served as school director. He is a member of the Methodist Episcopal church, and is a member of the board of stewards of his church. Mr. De Muth is always prompt in his business, and has now completed his preparations to enlarge and extensively stock his greenhouses with everything desirable in that line of business. He will locate his florist office at Connellsville and keep constantly on hand at that place the finest and most beautiful of cut flowers, to accommodate the flattering and substantial patronage that he is receiving. He is highly deserving of credit for the manner in which he has made his life a success, and for the hard labor and close attention that he gives to every detail of business entrusted to his care.

GEORGE CUNNINGHAM, one of Dunbar township's prosperous farmers, is a son of William and Sidney (Marietta) Cunningham, born at Connellsville, Fayette county, Pa., July 1, 1828.

John Cunningham (grandfather) was a native of Somerset county; was a farmer, a member of the Methodist church, and married Miss McClintock, who afterwards died in Fayette county.

William Cunningham (father) was born and raised in Somerset county, where he learned the trade of a potter, and removed to Connellsville, where he was married to Miss Sidney, daughter of George Marietta, a carpenter of that place. His principal employment was teaming, but engaging in a coal mine, he was badly injured by a fall of slate from the roof of the mine, the injuries from which he never recovered, and died four years later.

George Cunningham was educated in public schools of Connellsville, engaged in teaming until 1873, when he purchased a farm in Dunbar township, and since then has given his whole attention to farming. He was married to Harriet, daughter of Joseph Duncan, a soldier in the Mexican War, who was killed in battle. They have two children: William, married Miss Moats, and Isaac, is married to Drusilla Hopwood, of near Uniontown. Mr. Cunningham is a good farmer and an exemplary citizen.

JAMES DOLAN, the accommodating proprietor of the "Central Hotel" at Vanderbilt, was born at Brandy Gap Tunnel near Clarksburg, W. Va., November 9, 1853, and is a son of Michael and Mary (Burk) Dolan.

Michael Dolan, Sr. (grandfather), came from Ireland to Clarksburg, W. Va., about 1846 and died at Grafton aged seventy-six years. His wife was Mary Cummings, who died before he left Ireland.

Michael Dolan (father) was a native of Ireland, he came with his father in 1846, to Virginia (now West Virginia), where he married Miss Mary, daughter of Patrick and Mary (Barry) Burk, natives of Ireland, who are now living at Buckhannon, W. Va., he in the ninety-six year of his age, and she in the ninety-third year of her age.

James Dolan was educated in the primary schools of Virginia, and the academy at Clarksburg; in 1870 was crippled in an explosion at Brooks Tunnel, in Somerset county, Pa. The first regular business that he engaged in, was keeping a grocery at Clarksburg in 1871. In 1874, when able to resume work, he removed to Hill Farm Coke Works in Fayette county, and engaged as a contractor at the mines. He next became proprietor, for two years, of a grocery at Dunbar, and then removed in 1883, to Braddock's Fields, where he opened and conducted for eighteen months, the Central Hotel. Disposing of his Braddock's Fields property, in 1885, he returned to Fayette county, opened the "Central Hotel" at Vanderbilt and has continued to run it successfully up to the present time.

In 1879 he married Miss Mary Elizabeth (Thornton) Rogan, a native of Ireland. The father died at Clarksburg, W. Va., in 1887. To their union were born four children: William Francis, James Edward, Arthur Augustus and Mary Ellen. Mrs. Dolan died August 5, 1888.

FRANCIS P. DOONAN, is of Irish descent and was born January, 13, 1854, near Kingwood, Preston county, West Virginia (then Virginia). He is a son of John and Bridget (Kenney) Doonan, both natives of County Longford, Ireland.

John Doonan (father) emigrated to America in 1837, and resided at Mt. Savage, Allegany county, Maryland, for a time, when he removed to Preston county, Virginia, and died at Wheeling in June, 1860. He had six children: James; Francis P.; John, dead; Mary E., now Mrs. Laffey, of Mineral county, West Virginia; Anna D.; Elizabeth, now Mrs. Locke, of Uniontown.

Francis P. Doonan was educated in the free schools, and Catholic schools of Clarksburgh, West Virginia, and the Normal schools of Somerset, Pennsylvania. He taught six terms of school—two in Mineral county, West Virginia, two in Somerset county, Pennsylvania, and two in this county.

Intelligent, quick and energetic, as a boy he naturally attracted observation, and was in governmental employ at Clarksburgh, West Virginia, when only fourteen years of age.

Being of good business tact and talent, his services have often been in demand in that line, he has successfully clerked at Clarksburgh, kept time on the Baltimore & Ohio Railroad, and been an efficient book-keeper at Lemont Furnace. Specially qualified by this varied commercial experience, he embarked in the general mercantile and drug business at Dunbar in 1882; has built up, and is energetically conducting a very successful business.

Mr. Doonan was married in September, 1887, to Miss Ellen Cray, daughter of James Cray, a successful business man of Dunbar.

In 1886 and in 1888 he was the regular nominee of the democratic party of Fayette county, as one of their candidates for the legislature, but at both elections republicans were elected.

Having determined upon the law as a profession, he pursued the study for one year (1885–86) in the law department of the Georgetown University. Having successfully passed the preliminary examination in Fayette county, is now a registered student at law at Uniontown.

He is intelligent, active and reliable, and gives promise of making his mark in the future.

ALEXANDER C. DUNCAN was born in Butler county, Pa., January 25, 1846. His maternal grandfather, Enos Graham, was a native of Scotland, came to America at the beginning of the eighteenth century and settled in Butler county, Pa. His paternal grandfather, Samuel Duncan, was of Scotch descent, born in Allegheny county, near Pittsburgh, and was married to Nancy Smith, a native also of Allegheny county, Pa. A.C. Duncan's father, Robert Duncan, was born in Butler county, Pa., in 1813, and was a farmer. He married Miss Julia A. Graham, and had nine children: William; Enos G., a resident of Greenfield Iowa; Isaiah M., a farmer of Butler county; Beriah M., president of the board of county commissioners, of Butler county; Alexander C.; Pressly, a plasterer, and a resident of Mars, Butler county; Robert, a farmer of Butler county; Nancy, married to John W. McCaw, of Allegheny county, and Julia A., married to John A. Wilson, a coal merchant of Allegheny City. Alexander C., is the fifth son of his parents; he was educated in the common schools of Butler county, and with four of his brothers he served in the army during the Civil War. Enos G., Isaiah N. and Beriah, were volunteers in Company G, One Hundred and Thirty-fourth Regiment, Pennsylvania Volunteers, enlisting in 1862 and serving for nine months. At the end of that time they enlisted as veterans in Company G, Fourth Pennsylvania Cavalry and served till the close of the war. William volunteered in the spring of 1864 in the Seventy-eighth Regiment, Pennsylvania Volunteers. Alexander C. volunteered in the summer of 1864 in Company B, One and Ninety-third Regiment, Pennsylvania Volunteers. He took part in a skirmish in York county, Pa., and was in some others. After the war, returned home and lived with his parents till 1871. In 1871 he was married to Miss Mary C. Graham, daughter of William J. Graham, a native of Butler county, Pa. They had the following children: Clara E., a telegraph operator in the employ of the B. & O. R. R. Co., at Uniontown; Nancy E. and Allen Ward. His wife died October 31, 1879. He was the second time married, in June, 1881, to Emma Stroud, daughter of William Stroud, of Dunbar. Two children were born by this wife: Alexander R. and Edna W.

Alexander C. Duncan left the farm and engaged in the mercantile business at Ogle, Butler county, in 1875, and continued till 1879. Shortly after this time he came to Dunbar and entered into the general merchandise business, under the firm name of Duncan & Beers, and continued for about one year. After this he engaged as business manager with various coke firms, working for the Pittsburgh Manufacturing, Mining & Supply Company and others.

A. C. Duncan was elected burgess and justice of the peace for the borough of Dunbar, in the spring of 1889.

J. McDushane

He is a member of the Royal Arcanum, Jr. O. U. A. M., and of the Grand Army of the Republic. He is vice regent in the lodge of Royal Arcanum.

CAPTAIN JOSHUA MILTON DU SHANE, who nobly fought in defense of the Union during the darkest days of the Nation's history, and whose life has been one of activity and energy, was born Christmas day, 1827, in Westmoreland county, Pa., and is a son of Joshua and Mary (McCormick) Du Shane. Joshua Du Shane was born near Gettysburg, Adams county, Pa., in 1797. He was a fine teacher in his day, proficient in the languages and was a good surveyor. He married Mary McCormick, daughter of James McCormick; the latter came from Ireland to Broad Ford in about 1790. He and his eldest son, James, served in the War of 1812. James McCormick, Sr. had the following children: James, Jr., John, William and Mary.

Captain Du Shane's paternal grandfather, Andrew, was a French Huguenot who fled from his native land on account of religious persecution, brought with him his father, two sisters, Rachel and Sarah, and located in New Castle county, Del. When the war of the Revolution broke out, Andrew and his father joined the patriot band, fought in many battles, and the father died while in the service. They both belonged th the "Delaware Blues." Andrew Du Shane married Elizabeth Davis of near the battle field of Brandywine, Delaware. They had born to them four children: Isaac, Joshua, Elizabeth and Rachel. Joshua Du Shane died in April, 1878. Captain J. M. Du Shane was one of ten children born to his parents: Francis, Elizabeth, Samuel, Nancy, Margaret, Joshua M., Robert, Jane, Newton and Martha. He was married December, 1850, to Jane, daughter of James Collins and sister to Colonel John Collins. To them have been born five children: James D., Mary, Eliza, Samuel H. and Anna. He received his education in the common schools of New Alexandria, Westmoreland county, Pa., and there learned the tinner's trade. In 1850 he removed to Connellsville and opened a hardware and tinning establishment, conducted the same for eight years when he removed to Somerset county, Pa., where he remained until 1862. In that year he returned to Connellsville and recruited Company H, the only Fayette county company in the One Hundred and Forty-second Regiment Pennsylvania Volunteers, and was commissioned its captain. The regiment became part of the First Brigade, Third Division, First Corps, which was terribly slaughtered at the battle of Fredericksburg and again at Gettysburg. At the battle of Gettysburg, in the evening of the first day's fight, Captain Du Shane was twice wounded, and with most of his company taken prisoner by the Confederates; was confined in Libby prison from July, 1863, to July, 1864, when he was removed and kept in a stockade, Macon, Georgia, until July 28; was then taken to Charleston and placed under the fire of the Union guns that were playing around South Carolina's metropolis. This ordeal he passed in safety, and was next taken to Columbus, S. C., thence to Wilmington, and with several hundred other officers exchanged, arrived at Annapolis March 1, 1865. While at Richmond he was captured and searched by the Confederates, but they failed to find $500 he had secreted. With this money, from time to time, he purchased small quantities of provisions for himself and comrades, and thus survived through a long and terrible captivity and escaped death from starvation. On his return home he entered the revenue service and served six years as gauger in the twenty-first district. In 1872 he assisted in organizing the Youghiogheny Bank at Connellsville, and in 1873 was elected its president, holding the position for eight years. He is now a stockholder in the same bank. In 1878 he became a member of the firm of Boyts, Porter & Company, founders and machinists of Connellsville. He owns a beautiful farm near Connellsville, is also engaged in farming and stock raising, speculates in real estate, and is now the president of the Building and Loan Association at Connellsville. For two terms he served as burgess of Connellsville; has been member of the council, and school director. He is a P. G. in the Odd Fellows, a member of W. F. Kurtz Post, No. 104, G. A. R., and has been twice commissioned major of the National Guards of Pennsylvania. The J. M. Du Shane Camp, No. 77, is named for him. He has attended many republican State conventions. He was at La Fayette Hall, Pittsburgh, at the convention of 1856, and witnessed the birth of the republican party. Reared a Covenanter, but being a Presbyterian in belief, he united with that church in 1874. Captain Du Shane has lead a busy life, and has been of great benefit to the community in which he lives. He was a gallant soldier, and as a gentleman, is held in the highest esteem by all who know him.

ANDREW FAIRCHILD, a successful business man and a popular justice of the peace, is a son of Stephen and Elizabeth (Gillott) Fairchild, and was born in New Haven, Fayette county, Pa., December 10, 1823.

Stephen Fairchild, at fifteen years of age, enlisted and served in the Revolutionary War. His father and six elder brothers having preceded him in joining the American army.

Andrew Fairchild received a practical education, and afterwards learned the trade of cabinet-making, pursuing that line of business for twenty-five years, and is now in the undertaking business at East Liberty. He also purchased the East Liberty mill, and ran it for about eight or nine years. In 1844 he married Miss Eliza Jane Evan, who died and left one child, Susan, wife of Stewart Worthington of Dunbar. Mr. Fairchild was re-married in 1849, to Miss Martha, daughter of Aaron Brewer of Franklin township. To this second union were born three children: Elizabeth, wife of Rodolph Wanaka of California; Aaron J., married Susan Strickler; Joel E., married a Miss Hutchinson, and lives in California. After the death of his second wife he was re-married in 1858, to Miss Sarah Brewer (a sister of his previous wife). To this last union have been born five children, three of whom are still living: Harriet, Annie (wife of Jacob Strawn of Dawson) and John A.

Andrew Fairchild, in political views, is a democrat, and served as auditor in 1857, 1858 and 1859. In 1878 he was elected justice of the peace for Dunbar township, and was re-elected in 1883 and 1888.

DR. J. BRANDT ENOS, a physician in successful practice, and a native of Connellsville, is a son of Jonathan and Mary (Keepers) Enos, and was born at Connellsville, Fayette county, Pa., July 17, 1852. His grandfather, George Enos, was a native of Somerset county, where he died in 1863. His father, Jonathan Enos, came from Somerset county, in 1835, and located at Connellsville, in the foundry and blacksmithing business until his death in 1878. He was a democrat, a member of the Disciple church, and a good citizen. His wife was a second cousin of James K. Polk, and a daughter of Major Joseph Keepers, once proprietor of the Dunbar House, who was born in 1794, and died in 1830. The major's father, John

Keepers, of Carlisle, Pa., was among the first settlers at Connellsville.

Dr. Enos received his education in the common schools, and at seventeen years of age he began life on his own account, as an employe in a railroad office, where he remained for some time. He read medicine with Dr. John R. Nickel, of Connellsville, widely known as a physician and surgeon, attended lectures at Cincinnati, and was graduated in the class of 1874. In the same year he entered into partnership with Dr. Nickel, which was terminated by the death of the latter, when he succeeded to his practice removing to Belle Vernon a few years later. In 1878 he was elected to the chair of anatomy and physiology in the Physio-Medical Institute, Cincinnati, Ohio, and served acceptably in that position for eight years. In 1886, after an extended trip in the Southern States and among the West Indies, Professor Enos located in Pittsburgh, where he secured an extensive practice. In 1889 he came to Connellsville, and has since devoted himself to treating diseases of the throat and lungs.

In 1877 he married Miss Teresa, only daughter of Dr. Nickel. They have two children: Fred W. and J. Clive.

Dr. Enos is first vice-president of the American P. M. Association, and is a valuable and extensive contributor to current medical literature of the day. He left Pittsburgh on account of his health, and expects to make Connellsville his future home. He has a good practice, and is achieving great success as a specialist.

CAPTAIN THOMAS M. FEE is a native of Brownsville, Pa., and was born September 23, 1831. His grandfather, Michael Fee, came from Germany and settled in New Jersey. He enlisted in the War of the Revolution, and served till its close, was at Long Island, Georgetown, Princeton and quite a number of the principal battles of that war. After the war he came to Brownsville, where he died, at the age of ninety-one years, and now lies buried in the old Catholic graveyard at that place. John, Frederick, Rebecca and Thomas were the names of his children.

His maternal grandparents were born in Delaware.

Thomas Fee, the father of Captain Fee, was born at Brownsville, and was a stage-driver on the "Old Pike," from Brownsville to Cumberland, for many years. He died at Mount Pleasant, in 1834, of cholera. Captain Fee's mother, Lydia Ann Reason, came to Uniontown when quite young, and was raised by Judge Dawson. She had one brother, John Reason, who was a farmer in Warren county, Ohio.

Thomas Fee and Lydia Ann Reason were married and had the following children: James A. (dead), Mary Ann (dead) and Thomas.

Captain Thomas M. Fee was educated at the common schools of the county. Leaving school, he learned the trade of shoemaker, afterwards clerked in a shoe store for John D. Boyle, of Uniontown. When Boyle established a branch at Connellsville, in 1861, Captain Fee took charge of it, and ran the business until he enlisted, at Uniontown, in April, 1861, for the Union service. As soon as President Lincoln issued his proclamation, Captain S. D. Oliphant commenced to recruit a company for the service. Captain Fee enlisted as a member of the same in April, and was one of the first men to sign the roll. The company was made up, and started to the rendezvous at Pittsburgh by the 15th of April. The company went into Camp Wilkes under the name of the "Fayette Guards." They were ninety-day men, and were mustered out of service in July, when Captain Fee returned to Connellsville, again assumed charge of the store for a short time, when he purchased it and opened out for himself, and continued in that business until August, 1864. On the 28th day of August, 1864, he re-entered the army as second lieutenant of Company E, Sixth Pennsylvania Artillery. He was soon promoted to first lieutenant, and was mustered out of service June 13, 1865. He returned home and reopened the store, and kept it till 1870. From 1870 till 1882 he was engaged in business as a detective in a force known as "The Central Detective Agency," of which he is the general superintendent and manager.

In 1881 he was appointed as deputy United States marshal, and served during the last three years of President Arthur's administration, and since that time he has been acting as a detective.

He was the last captain of the old military company known as the "Cameron Union Volunteers," which in 1823 were known as the "Union Volunteers." He received his commission from Governor William F. Parker, June 9, 1859, and held it until the company was disbanded in 1860.

He was appointed a railroad policeman in March, 1876, and acted in this capacity for seven years. In politics he was a whig, afterwards became a republican, and has been an active worker in that party ever since. He removed to Connellsville in 1863, was elected burgess of Connellsville in 1866, and was the first republican elected to that office.

He was married on the 24th of August, 1854, in Steubenville, Ohio, to Rachel A. Manly, a daughter of Abel Manly. She was a graduate of the Steubenville Female Seminary. They had nine children: Louisa S., Charles M., James A., Smith F., Minnie E., Thomas M., M. Amelia, George M. and Frank R.

He is a past grand in General Worth's Lodge, No. 386, I. O. O. F., at Connellsville; is past chancellor of K. of P., No. 239, at the same place; past post commander of William Kurtz Post, No. 104, G. A. R., and is at present adjutant of that post. He is one of the most active members of this post, and is frequently sent as delegate to the department and national encampment of the G. A. R.

DR. ROBERT G. FINLAY, an able young physician of East Liberty, was born May 18, 1858, near Perryopolis, Perry township, Fayette County, Pa., and is a son of George and Ruth Ann (Haney) Finlay.

His father, George Finlay, was born in Ireland, came to the United States when about twenty-five years of age, located in Elizabeth, Allegheny county, Pa., where he worked at shoemaking for a number of years and afterwards farmed for about thirty years. He was married twice; the first time to Mary Gailey, the daughter of Archibald Gailey, a native of Fayette county; the second time to Ruth Ann Haney, in 1857. To this last union were born five children. He died in Pittsburgh, January 29, 1886. His father died in Ireland, and his mother came to America in 1840, to Quebec, Canada, thence to Elizabeth, Pa.

Robert G. Finlay was educated in the common schools and in the academy at Uniontown. He read medicine in the office of Dr. A. P. Bowie, of the same place, began his medical studies in the winter of 1878–9, and began his first course of lectures in the fall of 1879, at the Homeopathic Hospital College, at Cleveland, Ohio, where he graduated March 9, 1881. In August, 1881, he located in McKeesport, Allegheny county, remained about one year; from there he located at New Wilmington, Lawrence county, where he remained till September, 1883. In 1883 he removed to Scottdale, Westmoreland county, there practiced successfully until the spring of 1884; thence to Minneapolis, Minn.; was there till May 1, 1889, when he came to East Liberty, where he is at present engaged in his practice. Mrs. Dr. R. G. Finlay, died in Minneapolis, Minn., in February, 1888. He was again married October 25, 1883, at Pittsburgh, to Miss Maggie M. Hoffman, of Eau Claire, Wis., daughter of J. H. and Sarah Hoffman, of that place.

JAMES A. FLENNIKEN, dealer in dry goods, notions, groceries, boots, shoes, tobacco and confections at Broad Ford, Fayette county, Pa., is a son of Elias A. and Mary Ann (Karr) Flenniken, and was born in Cumberland township, Greene county, Pa., February 11, 1860.

His grandfather, John C. Flenniken, was a native of Ireland, and settled in an early day in Greene county, Pa., where he died in 1859.

His father, Elias A. Flenniken, was born near Carmichael's in about 1827, and is a well-situated farmer of Greene county. He is a republican and member of the Presbyterian church. He married Miss Mary Ann Karr, a member of the same church. Her father, William Karr, is one of the oldest men in Greene county. He is a member of the Methodist church.

James A. Flenniken was reared principally on a farm and received his education in the common schools and Greene Academy, was graduated from the later in 1878. In 1879 he accepted a position in the general mercantile store of Ewing, Hanna & Co. at Lemont Furnace, and remained in their employ for seven years. He was engaged as a clerk in the store of H. C. Frick & Co. at Broad Ford for six years. In 1881 he engaged in his present general mercantile business at Broad Ford, and was so successful that in four years he established a general mercantile store in connection with Laughlin & Co., limited, and ran it till 1887.

In November, 1882, he was married to Miss Sallie, daughter of George and Kate Washabaugh. They have three children: George, James H. and Clifton W.

J. A. Flenniken is a republican, and was postmaster at Broad Ford during Garfield and Arthur's administrations.

His store-room is conveniently located and is filled with a complete and well-selected stock of dry goods, notions and all articles to be found in a first-class store. His selections have been made especially to meet the many wants of his numerous and substantial patrons. He is a member of the Connellsville Presbyterian church, and is well and favorably known.

WILLIAM S. GADDIS, one of the most successful young merchants of Dunbar, was born in Fayette county, Pa., February 22, 1853, and is a son of Perry Gaddis, who was born in Fayette county about 1824, and Eliza J. Shaw, daughter of Robert Shaw, of near Uniontown. They were the parents of the following children: Ruth A., William S., Robert, Emma, Thomas, Downie (the latter is engaged in Montana as superintendent of the Montana Coal and Coke Company), Charles E. and Ralph.

William S. Gaddis was educated at Waynesburgh College, Greene county, Pa. Leaving college, he became a clerk in the store of R. J. Carter, of Dunbar, in 1873, and remained one year. He was next engaged with S. Colvin & Co., of Mt. Braddock, as a clerk, and remained with them for about one year, when he took charge of a store as manager for the Mahoning Coke Company for five years. In 1882 he went to Youngstown as manager of the store of the Youngstown Coke Company for four years. In 1886 he engaged in the general merchandise business at Dunbar for himself. On November 25, 1888, he was married to Annie Nennon, daughter of Bernard Nennon, of Dunbar.

JOSEPH FLYDELL, of Dunbar, is a native of Germany, and was born on the 15th day of March, 1835. He was educated in the common schools of Germany and is a member of the Catholic church. He came to the United States in 1871, first engaged in work at a zinc mine in Arkansas for about one year; from there he went to Illinois, and worked in the lead mines. He subsequently removed to Clinton county, Pa., and later to Clearfield county, where he worked in the ore mines. In 1874 he came to Fayette county where he has since resided, engaged as a coke drawer and coal digger.

He was married in Germany in 1868 to Miss Elizabeth Gisler, who came to America about three years after his own arrival. They have had born to their marriage six children: Julias, Mary, John, Joseph, Christina and Frederick; the last two are twins.

GEORGE T. GRIFFIN, time-keeper for the Cambria Iron Co., Dunbar, was born November 18, 1858, in Kent county, Delaware. His father, Jacob Griffin, was a native of Newcastle county, Del., removed to Kent county in 1855, where he engaged in farming and stock raising. His wife, Rachel J. Bennett, was from the eastern shore of Maryland. The children are, Anna E., wife of John Dougherty, of Altoona; Sallie, wife of Rufus Nourse, Boston; Edgar B. and George T., the latter educated in the common schools of his native county, and was engaged in farming pursuits till 1871, when he came to Cambria county and engaged as a common laborer. In 1875 he began the study of telegraphy, soon after took a position as operator with the Penn. R. R. Co., and was stationed at Scottdale, Westmoreland county. In 1879 the company located him at Dunbar. In 1883 he went to Ohio as an operator for the Pittsburgh, Ft. W. & Chi. R. R. Co., and returned to Dunbar in 1886, when he was appointed to his present responsible position, by the Cambria Iron Co. Mr. Griffin was married to Miss Martha L. Taylor, daughter of John Taylor, a coke operator of Fayette county, March 24, 1881. Their children are John C. and Martha E. Mr. Griffin is a member of the I. O. O. F., K. of P., and a member of the Presbyterian church.

DANIEL HARE was born in Franklin township, Fayette county, Pa., December 31, 1826. The family on the father's side is of Scotch extraction. Joseph Hare (grandfather) was a native of Scotland, came to America and settled in Dunbar township, Fayette county, Pa., in 1811. He was the father of Daniel, James, Matthew, John, and three others whose names have been forgotten. Daniel and James served in the war of 1812; James died in the war and Daniel was severely wounded and died in about six months after he returned home.

Joseph Hare (father) was born in Scotland, came to America with his father in 1811, and followed farming. He married Susan Lancaster. They had the following children: Daniel, David, James, John (who served as county commissioner of Fayette county, from 1885 to 1888), Sarah, Mary, Eliza and Susan. Daniel Foster (the maternal grandfather) was born in Lancaster county, Pa., married and had the following children: William, John, Henry, James, Tillie, Catherine, Sarah and Martha.

Daniel Hare, the oldest child of his father, was brought up in Franklin township and attended the common schools. He came to

Dunbar township in about 1835, settled near the town of Dunbar and has since been a farmer and extensive stock raiser. He owns a good farm of 162½ acres and is very pleasantly situated. He has been a member of the Baptist church for about four years.

WILLIAM J. HAMILTON, M. D. Both the grandfather and father of Dr. Hamilton were natives of County Down, Ireland. William Hamilton (father) was born February 13, 1797, emigrated to the United States and married, in Pittsburgh, Miss Frances Staples. They had six children: Elizabeth, Susan, Mary, William, Maria and Alexander. He lived in Pittsburgh till a few years before he died, when he removed to Butler county, where he died in 1855. Dr. William J. Hamilton was born in Butler county, Pa., June, 1847, and was educated in the public schools of his native county. He entered the medical college at Cleveland, Ohio, in 1869, and was graduated in 1873. He came to Dunbar the same year, commenced the practice of his profession and has lived at Dunbar ever since. He is of the homeopathic school. He was married July 2, 1874, to Miss Ella Herron, daughter of Francis Herron, of Fayette county. Dr. Hamilton is a member of the Knights of Pythias.

DANIEL HARPER, the first postmaster of Dunbar, was born January 12, 1818, in the township of Dunbar, Fayette county, Pa. His father, Daniel Harper, was a Pennsylvanian by birth, and was married to Margery Huston, a native of Fayette county. They had nine children: Margaret, William James, Joseph, Daniel, Mary J., Margery, Sarah, Samuel and Eliza. Daniel received only a common-school education. On leaving school he learned the trade of carpenter and continued as such for eight years. On April 4, 1843, he took to wife Miss Sarah, a daughter of James and Mary Hankins. John Hankins, the father of James, came with his father John, to Fayette county in 1784, from North Carolina. Their first settlement was on a farm in North Union and for many years James Hankins operated a wollen mill. After his death Daniel Harper fell heir to the mill property, which he continued to run for twenty-four years. The children born to Daniel and Sarah (Hankins) Harper are: Mary M., Margery H., James, Daniel, William and John M. Mr. Harper was appointed first postmaster of Dunbar under the administration of James Buchanan and continued to serve in that capacity for eight or ten years. He was a member of the Presbyterian church. His death occurred May 31, 1884.

DR. JOSHUA D. HAZLETT, a leading physician of Vanderbilt, is a son of William and Margaret (Dickerson) Hazlett, and was born near Washington, Washington county, Pa., July 15, 1845.

He comes of Irish lineage on his paternal side. His great-grandfather, Samuel Hazlett, Sr., emigrated from Maryland to Washington county, Pa., during the Revolutionary War, where he took up a large tract of land, by "Tomahawk Right," in what is now Franklin township. His son, Samuel, born in 1791, was a farmer and highly respected citizen. Samuel Hazlett was twice married; first to Mrs. Rebecca Loafman, by whom he had four daughters and two sons: Elza, a physician, and William, father of Dr. J. D. Hazlett. After her death, he married a Mrs. Forsythe, and one of his sons by the second marriage is Dr. Isaac C. Hazlett, of Uniontown, Pa.

William Hazlett (father) was born near Washington, Washington county, Pa., March

6, 1819. He is a successful farmer and married Miss Margaret, daughter of Joshua Dickerson. They had eight children, five sons and three daughters.

Joshua Dickerson, maternal grandfather, was a son of Henry Dickerson, a Revolutionary soldier, came from New Jersey, and was an early settler in Washington county. Joshua Dickerson was an active politician in his day, represented Washington county in the Pennsylvania legislature, from 1812 to 1817, was afterwards elected for two terms to the State senate from the district composed of Washington and Greene counties; during his second term of service as senator, he accepted the secretaryship of the land office, which position he held from 1821 to 1828. His last public service was rendered as a member of the State Constitutional Convention of 1837. He was an anti-Jacksonian democrat and opposed the war of 1812.

Dr. Joshua D. Hazlett was educated in the common schools, under private tutors and in Waynesburg College. He entered the Federal army in 1864, enlisted in One Hundred and Fifty-fifth Regiment Pennsylvania Infantry Volunteers, and served until the close of the war. He participated in the battles of Chapin's Farm, Poplar Grove Church, Dabney's Saw-mill, Boydtown, Plank Road, Gravelly Run and Five Forks, and was on the skirmish line at Appomattox Court House, when Lee surrendered the Army of Northern Virginia.

He read medicine with Dr. John R. Wilson, of Washington, Pa., and was graduated from Jefferson Medical College in the class of 1882. In 1873 Dr. Hazlett came to Vanderbilt, and entered upon the general practice of medicine. He has built up quite an extensive practice, is a member of the Fayette County Medical Society and the State Medical Association.

In 1872 he married Miss Mary E., daughter of Jesse Hunnel, a retired merchant of Waynesburg, Pa. They have one child: Jesse, born July 29, 1873.

Dr. Hazlett is a member of Howell Post, No. 410, G. A. R., at Dawson, is a member of the Cumberland Presbyterian church at Vanderbilt, is a good citizen and popular as a physician.

DR. ROBERT M. HILL, a soldier, useful citizen, and a successful physician, is a son of David and Elizabeth Hill, and was born near "Little Washington," Washington county, Pa., November 14, 1842.

His grandfather, —— Hill, came from Scotland and settled in Washington county. One of his sons, Alexander, was an extensive South American traveler, who finally settled in Iowa, where he became wealthy.

His father, David Hill, was born in Washington county, in 1800. He learned the trade of a saddler, but employed the most of his time in wagoning; was a "Pike Boy" when that grand old thoroughfare of a nation was in the meridian of its glory. He was killed in 1854 by a horse falling on him. He married Miss Elizabeth McComb. One of their daughters, Isabella, married J. K. Melhorn, D.D., of Pittsburg, an able minister of the Evangelical Lutheran church. Mrs. Hill's father, Robert McComb, was of Scotch-Irish extraction, and a native of Cross Creek, Washington county. He was a Presbyterian and removed to Iowa.

Dr. R. M. Hill attended the common schools; studied at Hogue's and Georges Creek academies, and after the close of the Civil War completed his education in Conequessing and Millsboro academies. He taught twice in the common school before entering the army, and several terms after the war.

On August 1, 1862, he entered the Union service, enlisting in Company C, of the One Hundred and Thirty-fourth Pennsylvania

Volunteers, commanded by Colonel Matthew Stanley Quay (now U. S. senator from Pennsylvania.) He participated in the battles of South Mountain, Antietam, Sheppardstown, and Fredericksburg; was slightly wounded in the right side and left arm at Chancellorsville.

In 1866 he began the study of medicine under the tutelage of Dr. C. D. Chalfant. After the latter's removal to Illinois in 1868 he completed his reading with Dr. S. Chalfant. In 1869 - 70 he attended lectures at the Western Reserve Medical College, and in 1875 took a special course at Jefferson Medical College.

On February 15, 1870, he located at Farmington, Wharton township, where he practiced his profession successfully for twelve years. In 1882 he removed to Layton, and from thence to Vanderbilt in 1886, where he is now successfully engaged in the practice.

Dr. Hill has been twice married; his first wife was Miss Eliza Jane, daughter of Sebastian Rush, deceased, a prominent business man of the county in his time. To this union were born three children: Robert W. L., Flora Adella, deceased, and Lidie Gertrude. Mrs. Hill died October 8, 1877. For his second wife, he married, June 17, 1880, Miss Lilly, a well-educated and highly-accomplished daughter of Joel Strawn, of Perry township. Unto this second union have been born two children: Annie, dead, and Jesse Cleveland.

Dr. Hill has always been an active democrat. He is a skilled parliamentarian, and has been called to preside at democratic conventions. In 1876 he was elected to the legislature by a large majority; ran ahead of the ticket and served very creditably in the legislative sessions of 1877 and 1878.

He is a member of the Odd Fellows, K. of M. C., and is Crown Head of Youghio Castle-metic Sporting Club, of Vanderbilt. He is genial, courteous and gentlemanly, is public-spirited and a careful and skilled physician.

WINFIELD S. HOOD, one of the successful men and leading hardware and grocery merchants of Connellsville, was born at Connellsville, Fayette county, Pa., September 22, 1841. His father, Daniel Hood, of Scotch origin and was a native of Franklin county, Pa. In 1785 he was married to Mary Shelto, whose father was born in Ireland. Daniel Hood was a soldier in the War of 1812, was wounded in battle, returned home, but soon re-enlisted in the same war. He removed to Fayette county in about 1833, where he lived till his death in 1861. His wife died November 14, 1886, in the 91st year of her age.

W. S. Hood was a soldier in the War of the Rebellion, as were also three of his brothers; David, now deceased, a member of the One Hundred and Forty-second Pennsylvania Volunteers, Company H; Walter S., was in an Indiana regiment of infantry; and Albert W., served in the Fifteenth Pennsylvania Cavalry. Alexander, an older brother, was in the Mexican army and remained out during the entire war, he died just after the city of Mexico was taken, of yellow fever. He was a member of Capt. Quail's company, of Connellsville.

W. S. Hood joined the One Hundred and Forty-second, Company H., as a private soldier and was in active service for three years. In the battle of the wilderness he was twice wounded, received a ball in the right knee-joint and a finger of his left hand was shot off. At the close of the war he returned home, and in 1874 was married to Miss Mary C. Hensel, of Martinsville, W. Va. They have two children: J. Frederick and Anna Eliza, aged seven and five years respectively. Soon after the close of the war Mr. Hood engaged in the mercantile business at Connellsville with J. D. Frisbee as partner and continued with him until 1881. In 1881 he and Mr. Frisbee dissolved, when he engaged in his present business. The style of the firm is W. S. Hood & Co. Mr. Hood is a member of the board of trustees of the Presbyterian church at Connellsville and is one of the representative business men of the county.

MICHAEL HURLEY was born in Ireland, June 9, 1842, and is a son of Peter and Nora (Hennessey) Hurley.

Michael Hurley (paternal grandfather) was a native of County Curry, Ireland, followed farming, married Miss Nora McGraw, and had the following children: John, Nellie (married to Jeremiah Shaughnessy, lives in Columbus, O.), Bessie, Mary (married to Timothy Kelley, lives in Indianapolis, Ind.), Nora (married to James Connor, lives in Indianapolis, Ind.), and Peter.

Peter Hurley (father) was born in 1813, and is still living in Ireland. He was well educated, and, being very apt, was a very successful business man in his day. During the "panic of '49" he was steward and general manager for Stephen Samus, a large landholder. He is now a butcher and jobber. He married Nora, daughter of Edward Horrigan, and of several children born unto them, Michael is the only one living.

Michael Hurley was educated in Ireland and came to the United States, May 11, 1864. He engaged in the oil region of Pennsylvania as a common laborer. He moved to Ursina, and kept a hotel for three years. In 1874 he came to Connellsville and engaged in the hotel business, and is now the proprietor of the Trans-Allegheny Hotel.

He was married to Nora Hennessey, a native of Ireland, and a daughter of Thomas Hennessey. They have eight children: Nora, Birdie, Ellen, Catherine, Bessie, Sarah, Pearl and Michael.

A fact worthy of mention in the hotel experience of Mr. Hurley, is that he has never been refused a hotel license since he began the business—a period of twenty-two years. In all this time, he has never taken a drink of liquor although he sells it every day.

He is a member of the holy Roman Catholic church.

SNYDER S. KELLY was born April 25, 1842, in South Huntingdon township, Westmoreland county, Pa.

His grandfather, Charles Kelly, was a native of Ireland, and came to this county at the beginning of the present century. His paternal grandmother came from Scotland in about 1802 at the age of seven years. They had the following children: Samuel, (contractor on the National pike during its construction), James B., William, John, Jane Dorcas and Louisa.

James B. Kelly (father) was born in 1812, in Westmoreland county, Pa. He married Christina Lowe, daughter of George and Mary Lowe, both born in Pennsylvania, and were of German descent. His first work was on the Kiskimmeta canal of Pennsylvania, afterward he went to Somerset county, and learned the trade of blacksmith, returned to Westmoreland county and was in business there till quite recently, when he retired from labor and lives in South Huntingdon township. The children of this union were: George L., Charles C., Snyder S., John W., Emmeline (deceased), Mary J., Franklin P. and Melissa E.

Snyder S. Kelly was educated in the public schools, and at the Mount Pleasant Institute. He taught school in South Huntingdon township three terms, two terms in Beaver county and three terms in West Virginia. He went to the oil fields of Kenawha Valley in West Virginia in 1863 and remained there until 1868. In 1878 he came to Dunbar and engaged in the jewelry business in which he is at present engaged.

Mr. Kelly was married to Chelsie Frantz, daughter of Thomas Frantz of Selbysport, Garret county, Md. He married a second time, Maria W. Mather of Trenton, New Jersey.

He has five children: William E., James E., Cora V., Lucy E. and Buma C. Charles C., brother of Mr. Kelly, served in the Civil War for three years, in the One Hundred and Forty-second Regiment Pennsylvania Volunteers.

Mr. Kelly is a member of the Knights of Pythias, was elected justice of the peace of Dunbar, in 1886, and is the present incumbent of that office.

CHARLES A. LAING, a coke operator of Dunbar, is a native of Ireland, born August 20, 1837. He came to America in 1851. After his arrival in this country he located in Philadelphia, where he attended school for a time. He soon went to Livingston county, New York, where he attended school and worked in a flouring mill.

In 1854 he removed to Pittsburgh, where he was employed as a clerk in a hardware store for two years. In 1856 he went to the Pacific Slope in search of gold, and for ten years he successfully operated in gold mines, both in California and Idaho. While on the slope, he made two trips abroad, one to China and one to Central America. He was a pioneer in the Idaho discovery of gold in 1862. In 1866 he returned to Pittsburgh, and engaged in the flour and feed business with his brother, George Laing, with him carried on business for one year, when Mr. Laing returned to New York, located in Steuben county, where he was engaged successfully in farming for sixteen years. He sold his farm to the State of New York, for a location of a Soldiers' Home, came to Dunbar in 1883 and engaged in his present business. He was married October 29, 1867, to Anna M. Gardner, daughter of Andrew Gardner, the latter a native of Ireland. To their union have been born four children: John H., Mary A., Maud and George M.

Charles A. Laing is a son of John Laing, born in the County Mayo, Ireland; his wife was Sarah Robinson, daughter of Charles Robinson. They had born to their marriage five children besides Charles A.: John, George, Mariah, Catherine and Sarah. Mr. Laing is a member of the Pennsylvania Manufacturing Mining and Supply Company. The headquarters of which is No. 1004 Penn avenue, Pittsburgh. His brother, George Laing, is president of the company.

ZACHARIAH TAYLOR LEIGHTY is the son of Stephen S. and Eliza (Hutson) Leighty, and was born in Dunbar township, Fayette county, Pa., January 2, 1847.

Stephen S. Leighty, father of Z. T. Leighty, was born in Dunbar township, Fayette county, Pa., and now lives on a farm in that township on the road from Vanderbilt to New Haven. He was married twice, the first time to Miss Eliza Hutson, by whom he has nine living children: William, a physician in Kansas; Henry S., engineer in Illinois; Z. T.; Stephen S.; Margaret, wife of Milton Blair; Rebecca, wife of Joseph Piersol; Anna, wife of Robert Rankin; Eliza J., wife of Davis Woodward, and Agnes C., wife of George W. Cox. The second time to Miss Mary Hare of West Virginia. By the second union he has three living children: Emma, wife of C. A. Guinn, clerk at Vanderbilt; Ulysess G. and John.

Henry Leighty, the paternal grandfather of Zachariah T. Leighty, was born in Dunbar township, and was a very large land owner and farmer, having owned several of the farms in the vicinity of Vanderbilt. He married first time Miss Sarah Smith and had eight children: Henry S., Jacob S., John, William, Frances, Elizabeth, Daniel and Stephen S. Henry Leighty's second wife was Widow Secrease—maiden name Varnes—of Dunbar township, and by her he had five children: Joseph, Christopher, Peter, Sarah and Clarissa.

Jesse Hutson, maternal grandfather, was also a native of Dunbar township and was a farmer; was married to Catherine Oldshoe and had nine children: Eliza, Nathan, Sophia, William and John (twins), Jemima, Jesse, David, Wesley and George.

Zachariah T. Leighty was reared on a farm in Dunbar township, Fayette county, Pa. He was raised and has always lived upon a farm. He was educated in the common schools.

He was married twice; the first time to Miss Martha Murphy, daughter of William Robinson Murphy, from near Perryopolis; their children were: Frederick Cooper, born December 17, 1872, and Melvinia Belle, born August 31, 1874. The second wife was Miss Anna Duff, daughter of Hugh Thompson Duff, near Upper Middletown in Menallen township. Mr. Leighty has always followed farming and stock raising. He is an enterprising, straightforward business man and is a republican.

KELL LONG was born August 16, 1847, in Franklin township, Fayette county, Pa. Robert Long, paternal grandfather, was born in Lancaster county, moved to Connellsville, and was a blacksmith by trade. He served as county commissioner of Fayette county for two terms. He was a member of the United Presbyterian church at Laurel Hill. He was always a very active worker in the church, and was a ruling elder for many years. He married Catherine Foster, a native of Lancaster county. They had the following children: Mary, Sarah, William, John, Samuel and James. John is a farmer and lives in Belmont county, Ohio. Samuel is a farmer of Connellsville township.

Gustavus Kell, the maternal grandfather, was born in Ireland. He came to America and settled in Westmoreland county. He fought at the battle of Cowpens in the Revolutionary War, and married Abigail Smith, of Westmoreland and had the following children: Sarah, born September 16, 1821; Selinda, March 18, 1823; Caroline, October 10, 1825, and Harriet, September 6, 1827.

Kell Long is a son of James M. and Sarah Kell) Long. James M. Long was born in Connellsville in 1819, and followed farming. Kell Long was born and reared on a farm, and was educated in the common schools. In 1872 he married Miss Leonora Patterson, daughter of Hugh Patterson, of Perry township. In 1873 he went west and engaged as a clerk with S. P. Pond & Company, wholesale produce dealers, in Burlington, Ia., where he remained till 1874. He then returned to New Haven, Pa., and engaged in the milling, grain and agricultural implement business. He was married the second time to Miss Elizabeth Curry, daughter of James Curry, of Dunbar township. They have four children: James C., born December 13, 1877; Mabel, July 23, 1879; Sallie, March 25, 1881, and Ralph Kell, September 7, 1882.

He and his wife are members of the United Presbyterian church at Connellsville, and he is one of the trustees of the church. He has served as a member of the school board and of the council several times. His maternal ancestors were noted for their longevity. His great grandfather was one hundred and four years old. His great-grandfather lived to be ninety years old and his grandfather lived to be seventy-two years of age.

DAVID MAHANEY, of New Haven, was born in Washington county, Md., December 15, 1807, and is a son of William and Susanna (Shrader) Mahaney, who were married in 1798. William Mahaney was born in Culpepper county, Va., about 1767, and was drowned in the Potomac river in 1856. Susanna Shrader Mahaney, was the daughter of Henry Shrader, a German who came to America and settled near Boonsboro, Ky.

David Mahaney is one of a remaining few of a once prominent class, the hotel keepers of "The Old Pike" or National road. When the road was in the zenith of its glory, Mr. Mahaney was one of the genial and accommodating Maryland landlords that looked after the comfort of the traveling public. It was no small job to accommodate the throng of people who came on foot, on horseback, in wagons and coaches and to feed and shelter the droves of horses, cattle, sheep, etc.

From 1836 to 1862 Mr. Mahaney kept a hotel at various points along the "National Road" in Maryland, and for some years managed the American House at Cumberland. From 1862 to 1864 he kept the Mountain City Hotel. When the railroads had secured the travel and business of "The Old Road," he left Maryland, and in 1865 came to Fayette county. He ran the Yough House in Connellsville for nine years, when he bought what is now know as the Fulton House, removed to Uniontown, and ran this hotel for three years. He subsequently went to Broad Ford and took charge of the Phillips House for two years; leaving there he removed in 1882 to his present home at New Haven. He has been a member of the town council of Connellsville for number of years, and served for several years as a school director of Connellsville. He was educated in Friends Cove township, Bedford county, Pa., and in Allegany county, Md., and was a classmate of Judge John Cessna. He was married in 1836 to Caroline Smouse, a daughter of Daniel Smouse. She was born in Allegany county, Md. They have the following-named children: Alcinda, George, Lloyd, Mary L., John, David, Jr., Denton and Carrie.

Two of his sons served in the late Civil War. Lloyd, as second lieutenant of Company G, Second Maryland Regiment of the Potomac Home Brigade, was promoted to first lieutenant and served for four years. He was in several battles and was in Hunter's raid to Lynchburg. He is now the proprietor of the Spottsylvania House, at Uniontown. George Mahaney volunteered on August 12, 1862, in Company G, Second Maryland Volunteers, Potomac Home Brigade, and served until the 27th of June, 1864, when he was honorably discharged on account of physical disability.

David Mahaney, now an octogenarian, can look back over a long, busy and useful life spent in serving and accommodating the public; and within that time he has witnessed the birth and growth of nearly all the great American industries of the age, and all of the wonderful modes of modern travel.

WILLIAM J. MARTIN comes of Anglo-Irish stock; his grandfather, Samuel Martin, came from Ireland in 1776, to what was then known as Union Furnace, the present site of Dunbar Furnace, in this county. He was a furnace-man by occupation. He married Mary Brown, a native of Fayette county, and they had the following named children: William, Alexander, John, Samuel and James. His maternal grandfather was a native of England, came to America and served in the Revolution, and afterwards drew a pension for his services. He married a Scotch-Irish lady after his arrival here, and followed farming in Fayette county. They had the following children: Ellen, Mary, Elizabeth, William and Sarah. His parents were John and Elizabeth (Cottom) Martin. John Martin was born at Trumbull Furnace, Westmoreland county, Pa., in 1790. Elizabeth Cottom was born in Fayette county, in 1791. They were married in 1808, and had seven children: Nancy, Alexander, William J., Samuel, James O., Ellen and Henry.

William J. Martin was born at Center Furnace, Dunbar township, Fayette county, Pa., December 9, 1814, and was educated in the pay schools of the county. His business has been chiefly in blowing furnaces, and he has been employed in that capacity in the following furnaces: Fairchance, Laurel Hill furnace, Redstone, Cool Spring and Union, in Fayette county; Hecla, Vesuvius and La Grange, in Ohio; Amanda furnace and Bellefonte, in Kentucky; also Springhill furnace, which was the last charcoal furnace used in Fayette county, and for three or four years past has been in the employ of the Dunbar Furnace Company.

He married his first wife, Miss Minerva Beeson, a daughter of John Beeson, who fought under Commodore Perry in the War of 1812, and received a medal for his bravery. They had the following children: Elizabeth, Calvin, Henrietta, Mahala, Aneliza, James O., Alice, Amanda, Charity and Jane. His eldest son, Calvin, was a soldier in the Sixteenth Pennsylvania Cavalry, and served till his death, March 26, 1863.

Mr. Martin married a second time to Mary Schaeffer, a daughter of Robert McDowell, and the widow of Samuel Schaeffer. They had three children: Robert, who is a school teacher of the county, Bertha and Emma.

Mr. Martin has been a member of the Methodist Protestant church for over forty years, and has been one of the trustees of the church for several years. He has served as school director of his township.

REV. JOHN G. MARTIN is a native of Dunbar township, Fayette county, Pa., and was born December 21, 1837. His grandfather, John Martin, was born in Fayette county about 1790, and was of Irish origin. His wife was Elizabeth Cottom. The children born to their union were: Alexander, Nancy, William, Samuel, Henry, Ellen and James O.

The maternal grandfather was Abraham Lincoln. He was married to Patti Cole, and both were born in Fayette county, Pa. Mr. Martin's father, Samuel J., was born in Fayette county, in 1817, and was married to Sarah, daughter of Abraham Lincoln, in 1836.

Samuel J. Martin for many years has followed mining, but he is now a farmer and resides at Dunbar.

John G. Martin was educated in the common schools of the neighborhood, and the normal schools of Upper Middletown. Leaving school he went to Uniontown, where he spent one year learning the millwright business under the tutelage of William Barnes. At the end of the year he abandoned his trade and took up the carpenter's trade which he has followed ever since. From 1865 to 1868 he resided at Broad Ford, from 1868 to '80 at Dawson, and was at both places extensively engaged in contracting and building.

He located at Dunbar in 1880. He has been a member of the church for twenty-five years, for eighteen years of the time a member of the Methodist Protestant church, and for the last seventeen years he has affiliated with the Methodist Episcopal denomination. He has held the office of class-leader, steward and superintendent of Sabbath-school. In 1875 he was licensed as an exhorter in the Methodist Episcopal church,

Provance McCormick

and is an honored member of the Knights of Pythias.

Rev. Martin was married to Miss Surna, daughter of Andrew Bryson, of Dunbar, in 1864. Their union has been blessed with the following children: Andrew L., operator for B. & O. R. R., born August, 1864, at Dunbar; Fannie D., May 10, 1866; Charles, May 3, 1868; Samuel, March 27, 1870; Franklin, July 9, 1872; Lulu, September 10, 1874, and Walter, born February 8, 1877; Nannie, born May 12, 1880, died October 4, 1881; Effie, who died November 18, 1888. Four of the family are members of the Methodist Episcopal church at Dunbar.

JOSEPH A. MASON is one of the popular merchants and prominent citizens of Gibson, near Connellsville, and is a son of Benjamin and Margaret (Evans) Mason. He was born in Harford county, Md., October 17, 1845.

Benjamin Mason is a native of Yorkshire, England, and when ten years of age came with his parents to Baltimore. He afterwards removed to Harford county, Md., where he has been engaged in merchant tailoring, and is a consistent member of the Methodist Episcopal church. He married Miss Margaret Evans, of Baltimore, who was a member of the Methodist Episcopal church, and died in 1866, age fifty-four years. Her father, George Evans, was a native of Baltimore, served in the War of 1812, was a whig, held some important offices under the State government of Maryland, and died in 1850. His sons, William and Joseph, were in the Mexican War.

Joseph A. Mason was educated in the schools of Harford county and Baltimore. In February, 1862, he left school, enlisted in Company G, Third Maryland Volunteers, and was mustered out as orderly sergeant at Baltimore, in May, 1865. He was with his regiment in all its battles, in Miles' surrender and was paroled on the field. His brother, Charles, was mortally wounded at Frederick City, Md., July 1, 1864. Another brother, Rev. William, of the Southern Methodist Episcopal church, served in Battery B, Fourth Chesapeake Light Artillery of the late C. S. A., and died in 1879.

After the war Joseph A. Mason engaged in the mercantile business at Ridgeville, Carroll county, Md., removed to Sams Creek in 1867, and was appointed postmaster, but sold his property and store in 1870, and removed to Baltimore, where he worked at the trade of carpenter. In 1872 he located in Cumberland, Md., and was engaged for eight years in the stationery and picture business. In 1880 he removed to Gibson, near Connellsville, where he purchased land and erected his present residence. Six years later he became a member of the firm of Gibson & Mason, who are engaged in general mercantile, feed and coal business. In 1889 Mr. Mason purchased his partner's (J. G. Gibson) interest, and continues successfully in his present prosperous business. In 1864 he was married to Miss Sidney A., daughter of William and Sarah Fisher, of Frederick county, Md. Mr. and Mrs. Mason have eight children living: William B., Harvey F., Minnie D., Joseph A., Estelle D., James S., Lillie E. and George H.

Joseph A. Mason is a straight-out republican, and is justice of the peace. He is a member of King Solomon Lodge, No. 386, A. Y. M., a popular merchant and a member of the Connellsville Methodist Episcopal church.

PROVANCE McCORMICK was born near Connellsville, Pa. on the 29th day of July, 1799, and died within sight of his birth-place, June 16, 1887, at the ripe age of eighty-eight years. His ancestors came from

England with the cavaliers who left their native land and fled to Virginia, soon after the execution of Charles I. by Cromwell, about the year 1649.

William Crawford, the great-grandfather of Provance McCormick, was born in Orange county, Va., in the year of 1732. The family afterward emigrated to Winchester, near the foot of the Shenandoah mountains, then the western confines of civilization. His father dying when he was four years of age, he was reared by his mother, Onora, a woman of great energy of character. At the age of seventeen he became acquainted with the youthful Washington, which acquaintance ripened into the warmest friendship, never broken until the death of Crawford. In 1755, as ensign, he accompanied Braddock in the ill-fated campaign against Fort Duquesne, and for gallantry displayed on that occasion was advanced to a lieutenancy. In 1758, appointed to a captaincy by Washington, who was then commander-in-chief of the Virginia troops, he went with Forbes' Expedition against Duquesne. In the spring of 1767 he located a claim at Stewart's Crossing, where the town of New Haven now stands, and in 1769 moved his family there, becoming the first settler west of the Allegheny mountains.

In 1773 Crawford was appointed by Gov. Penn, presiding justice of Westmoreland county, a district which then embraced a great portion of western Pennsylvania.

Upon the news of the battle of Lexington, he at once raised and equipped a regiment for the defense of the colonies; this not being at the time accepted, he was on the 14th of August, 1776, commissioned as colonel of the Seventh Regiment Virginia Battalions. His regiment was sent to Long Island, and participated in all the principal battles in New Jersey, and was with Washington on that memorable Christmas day when the army crossed the icy Delaware; also at the victorious battle of Trenton, on the day succeeding, and at Princeton, soon thereafter. In May, 1778, by order of Congress, he was transferred to the western frontier, to take command of the forces sent against the Indians.

Upon the surrender of Cornwallis, it became evident that the contest with Great Britain was drawing to a close, and Crawford gladly accepted the opportunity of retiring to his home on the banks of the Youghiogheny. Having, as he believed, done his whole duty to his country, he now thought only of spending the remainder of his days in quietude and peace, but the atrocious outrages of the Indians, becoming day by day more numerous, he, with reluctance and gloomy forebodings, took command of an expedition against them in the spring of 1782, an expedition which culminated in his execution by the Indians, with cruel tortures at the stake, near the present town of Little Sandusky, Ohio, on the 11th day of June, the same year.

Effie, the second daughter of Colonel Crawford, born in Virginia, September 2, 1751, was a hardy young girl of seventeen, when the family crossed the mountains into the unbroken wilderness of the Youghiogheny Valley. There, on the 10th of February, 1773, she married William McCormick, a backwoodsman from the hills of Virginia, and a companion of her father's in his frequent adventures with the savages, who, at that time, infested the Shenadoah mountains. William McCormick was born February 22, 1738.

They built their cabin on the east bank of the Yough, near Stewart's Crossing, where it yet stands (1889), the oldest house in the town of Connellsville. They both lived to a good old age, the husband dying in Connellsville in 1816, and the wife in Ohio, in 1825.

William and Effie McCormick were the parents of eleven children, the second of whom, Sarah, born January 8, 1776, and deceased in 1854, was the mother of Provance McCormick.

The early years of the latter were passed amid the hardships of a frontier life, where schools were almost unknown; his inherited energy of mind, however, enabled him without the aid of a teacher to acquire an education sufficient for the time.

On the 2d day of December, 1819, he married Susan Bowers, who was born of Novia Scotian parents, December 16, 1800. Four children were the result of this marriage, viz.: Elizabeth, Jane (wife of Christian Snyder), George B. and Joseph T., all of whom are living, except Jane, who died October 24, 1886. Until about the year 1830, he followed the occupation of a teamster in the transportation of merchandise between Pittsburgh and Philadelphia, and during the next ten years was engaged in various occupations, among others the manufacture of gun barrels for the United States government. About this time he conceived the idea of making "Coke," which he surmised might be made to supersede the use of charcoal in the smelting of iron ores. In pursuance of this idea, in the year of 1842, he had erected on the bank of the Youghiogheny river, about three miles below Connellsville, two coke ovens, (which were exactly similar to those in present use), and proceeded with the experiment. The at tempt seemed to be as successful as could be desired, and with buoyant hope and visions of wealth and honors, a large flat-boat was built, and loaded with the coke, was floated down the Ohio river to Cincinnatti. Vain hope! No one could be found to risk a trial of this strange fuel, and with sad heart the scheme was abandoned. Ten years later the attempt was revived by other hands, and the originator lived to see more than ten thousand ovens in active operation in his immediate neighborhood, with other thousands all over the country, producing millions of tons of coke, finding eager purchasers, and enriching hundreds of more fortunate operators.

After occupying numerous positions of trust, postmaster, justice of the peace, associate judge of Fayette county, etc. He, in his old age, became reduced to poverty through his generous aid to unfortunate friends.

He was a man of unbending integrity, and while courageous in the maintenance of his prerogatives, against those maliciously invading them, he was full of charity for the errors and misfortunes of his fellow-men. This kindly disposition often blinded his better judgment and finally led to his financial ruin. His faith and trust in a Divine Providence was complete and almost childlike, and never for an instant deserted him. Though often sorely afflicted both in body and mind, he bore all with unflinching fortitude and courage. His counsel and advice were largely solicited, and no one, however humble his station, ever failed to receive his kindest sympathy, and, if needed, such material aid as his limited means could afford. This humane disposition was inherent in his nature, and was strikingly shown in almost his last hour on earth. While suffering most intensely, and unable to rise without aid, he insisted upon being supported in the arms of his attendants while he made a last attempt to do an act of kindness.

His ancestors were faithful adherents to the Church of England, but he chose the Baptist denomination as the exponent of his belief, and for nearly sixty years held fast to that faith. His orthodoxy was somewhat of the sterner sort, but with the mellowing influence of age came a more liberal feeling as to the Divine judgments. The unity of Christian churches he greatly desired, but had no hope of such a result. His whole life was an illustration of his belief in the universal brotherhood of mankind, and his memory will be fragrant in the hearts of many that he has comforted.

JOSEPH T. McCORMICK, youngest son of Provance McCormick, was born near Connellsville, Pa., November 23, 1830. The common schools of those days were not of the best, but by faithful application and private study, he managed to obtain an education sufficient for the ordinary affairs of life. At the age of nineteen he began to teach, but at the end of three years abandoned teaching and went into the drug business in Connellsville, retaining an interest therein until 1876. In 1859, and again in 1863, he was engaged in the surveyor-general's office at Harrisburg, and during the latter term superintended the removal of all the records to Philadelphia, to prevent their falling into the hands of the Rebels, who were then at Chambersburgh; after which, in a burst of patriotism, he joined a company of department clerks, who offered their services to Governor Curtin to assist in driving the Rebels out of Pennsylvania, but instead of sending them to the front, he ordered them to pack their knapsacks and march for home, which they did without much loss of time. After this event, patriotism assumed a milder form. At the expiration of his term of office, in 1866, he returned to Connellsville and engaged in the manufacture of cars and machinery, in which business he has since remained.

October 2, 1855, he married Susan Newmyer, a daughter of Jonathan Newmyer. Three children resulted from this union: Mary M., wife of Rev. J. M. Scott; Karl C., now in the hardware trade in Connellsville, and Louis P., student of medicine at the University of Pennsylvania.

The subject of this sketch has always been of a retiring disposition, and has participated as little as possible in the stirring events of the community. The partiality of friends has sometimes drawn him into positions of trust, which he has filled conscientiously and to the best of his ability, but he prefers the tranquility of home and the companionship of his books, and out of business hours is rarely drawn away from them. He inherits a pacific disposition, and is rather inclined to suffer a wrong than to resent it.

JAMES McCUNE, the founder of the McCune family in Fayette county, was born in Scotland, and was a farmer of Cumberland county, Pa. He had the following children: Thomas, George W., Samuel, William, Elizabeth, John B. and Jane.

John B. McCune was born in Cumberland county, Pa., in 1805, and was a farmer, married Mary Wilson, the daughter of John Wilson, a native of Pennsylvania and of Scotch descent. They had the following children: Thomas W., William G., James H., David P., Catherine B., Jane W. and Isabella B. He was married a second time in 1848 to Miss Mary Weddell, and their children were: Robert, John N., Peter W. and Nancy Jane.

David P. McCune was born in Allegheny county, Pa., August 7, 1846, brought up on the farm, and was educated in common schools of the county, and at Curry Institute, at Pittsburgh. He worked as a carpenter for eight years, and in 1874 engaged in the furnace business at which he has since been engaged. He assisted in superintending the erection of Lemont Furnace in Fayette county in 1875. He took the position of labor boss at Scottdale Furnace, Fayette county, in 1877, and went to Powlton Furnace in Bedford county to supervise its erection in 1877. He came to Dunbar in 1882, as a furnace manager, and has remained there ever since. In 1873 he was married to Miss Eliza A. Culbert, daughter of Samuel Culbert, a native of Ireland, and has five children: William H., Arthur C., Emma B., David P. and Jesse W. Mr. McCune is a member of the Masonic order. He is also a

J. C. McClenathan M.A.' M.D.

member of the Presbyterian church. Three of Mr. McCune's brothers served in the Civil War. James H. during the whole war, William served during the whole war, except six months at the beginning. Thomas W. was major of his regiment for two years.

DR. JOHN C. McCLENATHAN, a classical scholar and a prominent physician of Connellsville, was born in Bamwell township, Washington county, Pa., July 9, 1852, and is a son of John and Rachel (Carter) McClenathan, both natives of Washington county, Pa.

Dr. McClenathan is of Irish descent on the paternal, and on the maternal side, of Scotch extraction. His grandfather, William McClenathan was born in Dauphin county, Pa., August 10, 1765, removed to Washington county, Pa., in 1790, where he was engaged extensively in farming, and died June 26, 1850.

John McClenathan, son of William McClenathan, a native of Washington county, was a prominent farmer, a member of the Presbyterian church, a life-long democrat and died November 10, 1878, at the age of seventy-three years. During his life he was a useful and honored citizen. His wife was a daughter of John Carter, a Washington county farmer and a prominent Presbyterian. She was a consistent member of the same church of her husband and died August 22, 1885, at the age of seventy-five years.

Dr. John C. McClenathan grew to man's estate on his father's Washington county farm, and received his early education in the common schools. In the fall of 1872 he entered Washington and Jefferson College, remained two years, after teaching two years returned to the same college and graduated with high honors, in the class of 1878, and received the degree of B. A. He took a classical course and stood near the head of the class of which he was a member at the time of his graduation. The degree of A.M. was conferred on him in 1882. Having acquired a thorough education, he turned his attention to medicine, as his chosen vocation of life. He had on purpose delayed his medical studies in order to get a thorough collegiate education, aware of the fact that such was highly essential, an invaluable aid in the successful practice of his profession; and his experience as a physician has attested the wisdom of his course. He read medicine with Dr. Thomas McKennan, one of the ablest physicians in Washington county, and afterward attended lectures at Jefferson Medical College, where he graduated in the class of 1881. In the same year, he completed a course in operative surgery for "bandaging and fracture dressing." In 1886 he went to New York City and took a post graduate course in the New York Post Graduate Medical College. After his graduation at Philadelphia, he came to Connellsville and engaged as a general practitioner, and has continued successfully in the practice ever since. He has built up and enjoys a very large and lucrative practice.

On January 12, 1882, he was married to Miss Flora, a daughter of Thomas Hanna, a prominent and influential citizen of Washington county.

Dr. McClenathan is a member of the Fayette County Medical Society and of the State Medical Society; was president, for four years, of the Chatauqua Literary Class at Connellsville, of which he is a graduate. His attention has been given to the material interests of his adopted town as well as to his duties as a physician. He is secretary of the Connellsville Improvement Association, and an able promoter of any enterprise calculated to improve the town. He is a member of the Presbyterian church, and is a genial and affable gentleman. A well-read and skilled physician, and has an extensive and well selected library. He is justly and deservedly popular.

JAMES REED McDOWELL (deceased), who was a prominent citizen of Dunbar borough, was born in Mifflin county, Pa., January 7, 1803. His father, Robert McDowell, settled in Mifflin county, Pa., and was born January 18, 1771. Sarah McConkey, the mother of the subject of this sketch, was born in Ireland, and the mother of four children: John, Robert, James Reed and William. James Reed McDowell received only the advantages of a common-school education in his native county; came to Fayette county in 1845, and purchased a farm near the borough of Dunbar, where he continued to farm until his death in September, 1881. He held the office of school director of Dunbar township, and served one term as poorhouse director. He was a successful farmer and a good citizen, filling various stations in life with honor. He was a consistent member of the Presbyterian church at Dunbar, and was a strong advocate of temperance. While he was not a public speaker, and only a plain, practical m , nevertheless, he had strong views on the subject of temperance which he expressed in simple and forcible words, as he felt it to be his duty as a man and a Christian to do. James Reed McDowell was married to Margaret Hazlett, daughter of William Hazlett, who was of Scotch origin. Their union was blessed with five children: Robert W., William A., Sarah Ann, Mary J. and Margaret Emily. Robert W. was a member of the class of 1862, that graduated from Washington and Jefferson College. After graduation he immediately entered the army as first lieutenant of a company in the Sixteenth Pennsylvania Cavalry, but in a short time was made captain, and for his gallantry in the field was promoted to the office of major. A comrade of his writes: "In the closing campaigns of '65 he was actively engaged each day, and distinguished himself by promptness, courage and cool judgment, winning praise from his men and fellow-officers, and being publicly complimented by his general. He was promoted major, and afterward promoted to assistant adjutant-general on the staff of Major-General Irvin Gregg." William A., the other son, leaving school, he entered the law office of C. E. Boyle, and was admitted to the bar at Uniontown, and is at present engaged in the real estate business in Colorado, where he removed in 1882.

JOHN P. McCUSKER, of Dunbar, is of Irish descent. His grandfather, John McCusker, was born in Ireland in 1756, where he lived and died. His father, John McCusker, was born in Ireland in about 1800, and came to America in 1826. He settled in New York City, where he was engaged as a contractor. From New York he went to Frederick City, Md. He was married in Ireland to Miss Margaret Gillogly, daughter of Terrence Gillogly. They had the following children—Ellen Catherine, Mary A., James, Sarah, John P. and Francis. Francis enlisted in Company M, Twelfth Pennsylvania Cavalry, in 1862, and took part in the fight at Bull Run and in other battles.

John P. McCusker was born in March, 1840, in Allegany county, Md. He was educated in the common schools of his native county. In 1852 he engaged in the fire-brick business at Mount Savage, Md., and continued in this business for twenty years. In 1872 he came to Dunbar and engaged in the same business, at which he is now engaged.

He was married in 1861 to Miss Mary A. Kelly, a daughter of John Kelly. The latter was born in Ireland and came to the United States and settled in Mt. Savage, Md. They had the following children: Nora E., Mary C., John F., Margaret Morgan, Elyria, Sarah, Anna, William, Bernadotte, James, Arthur, Maggie and Monicham. His family are all members of the Catholic church. He was elected road supervisor in 1883, and has been re-elected successively ever since.

ROBERT McKEE was born in Ireland, September 18, 1848, where he was educated. He came to Canada in 1869 and followed farming. In June, 1872, he came to Fayette county, and is now engaged as a laborer with the Dunbar Furnace Company at Dunbar. He was married October 1, 1874, to Miss Margaret J. Beers, a daughter of James Beers, a native of Butler county, Pa. They have the following children: George E., Thomas W., Robert C., Jane F. and James B.

Mr. McKee is a member of the Presbyterian church, of I. O. O. F. and K. of P. His father, George McKee, was a native of Ireland, and resided there all of his life. He died at the age of one hundred and two years. He was a farmer and married Jane McKee, and they had eleven children: Ann, Lettie, Mary, Thomas, Jane, Elizabeth, George, Richard, Catherine, Robert, the subject of this sketch, and Andrew.

Thomas McKee, grandfather of Robert McKee, was a native of Ireland. Mr. McKee is intelligent, well informed, and of industrious habits and frugal disposition.

REUBEN MILLER, merchant tailor and dealer in gentlemen's furnishings, of Connellsville, was born in Lebanon county, Pa., February 21, 1833, and is a son of Samuel and Mary (Poorman) Miller.

His great-grandfather, Johan Miller, came from Switzerland to Lebanon county, Pa., where he afterwards owned 500 acres of the finest land in the Lebanon Valley. On this tract of land, the present town of Anville (formerly Millerstown), was founded. One of his sons, David Miller, a farmer and member of the German Reformed church, was the father of Samuel Miller, born in 1805 and died in 1876; he was a linen-weaver and farmer of Lebanon county. Samuel Miller was was a whig, a member of the Union Baptist church. He was married to Mary Poorman, who was born in 1809 and died in 1885, at Anville. Her father, Henry Poorman, was a blacksmith, a Lutheran, and the owner of a large farm.

Reuben Miller attended the free schools in winter and worked on a farm in summer, until fourteen years of age, when he entered on a five years' apprenticeship in learning the trade of tailor with Samuel Seaguer. His compensation was washing, board and two weeks' leave of absence during harvest time. Leaving Seaguer he worked on a saw-mill for three years and was then employed for eighteen years as a journeyman and cutter. During this time he worked in Williamsport, Pittsburgh and Lansing, Michigan. In 1880 Mr. Miller came to Connellsville and engaged as a cutter with Charles Norcross. In September, 1882, he engaged for himself in merchant tailoring business, and has acquired a very liberal share of the best trade of Connellsville and vicinity. He carries a large and complete assortment of choice cloths, cassimeres, suitings and vestings for gentlemen's wear, of both foreign and domestic manufacture. Mr. Miller also has a full stock of hats, caps and all articles to be found in a first-class furnishing store.

In 1858 he married Miss Sarah Foreman, of Middletown, Pa., who died in 1863, leaving one child, Robert N., who soon followed her, Elmer E., another son, who died at the age of fourteen years. He was re-married in 1865 to Miss Emma, daughter of William Clepper, of Shippensburg, Pa. They have one child, Alice May.

Reuben Miller is a Heptasoph and Red Man. He is a democrat and a faithful member of the Methodist Episcopal church. "Both as a business man and a citizen he is highly respected by the many who know him, and enjoys the full confidence of the entire community."

DAVID E. MINERD was born in Fayette county, Pa., July 29, 1855. His paternal grandfather, Henry Minerd, was born in Somerset county, Pa., about 1790, and married Hester Sisler, a native of the same county. They had the following children: Daniel, James, William, Samuel Mary, Mahala, Isaac, Andrew, John, Sarah A., George H., Barbara, Arthur (deceased), Maria and Jesse.

David E. Minerd's father, Andrew Minerd, was born in Dunbar township, Fayette county, Pa., in 1823, and was married to Sarah Devan, daughter of Patrick Devan, a native of Ireland, but a resident of Monroe at the time of the marriage. Andrew Minerd served in the Civil War, volunteered in 1862 in the Fourteenth Pennsylvania Cavalry, and served twenty-eight months. He has the following children: Marshall, Alice, Hester A., David E., Huston, Mary B. and Margaret. He has been a member of the Methodist Protestant church for forty-two years, and has held at various times the offices of trustee and steward, and has always been an active member in church.

David E. Minerd received his education in the common schools of the county, and afterwards learned the trade of blacksmith. He is a leading member of the Methodist Protestant church, and has been for twenty-one years. During the time he has held the office of class-leader, trustee, steward, and in fact all of the offices of the church. Having been an officer most all the time since he first became a member. When the church at Dunbar was first built it was very weak. It has now a membership roll of 250 members. In January, 1884, he was married to Sadie Williams, daughter of Abram Williams, a resident of this county. They have three children: Edna May, Mary Belle, and Bessie R.

JAMES C. MOORE, of Vanderbilt, is a son of James and Sarah (Herbert) Moore, and was born October 30, 1849, in Dunbar township, Fayette county, Pa.

His paternal grandfather, James Moore, was a native of Massachusetts, emigrated at an early age to Fayette county, Pa., where he died. He was a farmer and married Susanna Swink, to whom were born seven children.

James F. Moore, the father of James C. Moore, was the oldest of the children and was born January 15, 1811, in Fayette county, Pa. He married Sarah B. Herbert. To them were born the following children: Martin Luther, Margaret A., James C., Susanna, Agnes, William, Sarah, Lydia and Herbert.

Sarah B. Herbert, was the daughter of Richard Herbert, native of New Jersey, migrated to Fayette county, Pa., when a young man, and married Margaret Shupe, a native of Fayette county. They had five children: Sarah B. being the youngest.

James C. Moore was born and raised on a farm and educated in the common schools of Dunbar township. At the age of twenty-one years he commenced work on his own account, in the coal mines, for some years as a common laborer; and for the last twelve years he has been a mining-boss. He holds a certificate of service, granted November, 1885, which constituted him mining-boss for

James Cochran, Sons & Company, at Vanderbilt; he also holds a certificate of competency as a mining-boss, for any drift bituminous coal mine in the State of Pennsylvania, granted him a short time afterwards.

He was married December 26, 1872, to Sarah A. Strickler. To them were born the following children: Ada, Gracie C., Philip C., Harry S., Nelson R. and Robert E. Sarah A. Strickler is the daughter of Henry Strickler, of Tyrone township.

Mr. Moore and wife are members of the Disciple church at Vanderbilt. He is deacon in the church, is a member of the Royal Arcanum, Knights of Pythias and the Junior Order of American Mechanics, and has passed through all of the chairs of the "Mystic Chain," and Knights of Pythias.

Thomas Herbert, an uncle of James C. Moore, was in the Civil War for about eight months, was taken sick, returned home and died.

JACOB MILLER was born in Fayette county, Pa., in 1832. His father, Andrew Miller, was born in the same county, and was married to Catherine Hiles. They had the following-named children: John, Jacob, Susan, Joseph, William, James, Polly, George, Andrew and Samuel. Jacob Miller was educated in the common schools of the county. On leaving school he learned the blacksmith's trade, a business he has followed all his life. He served in the War of the Rebellion three years and eight months, volunteering August 7, 1861, in the First Virginia Cavalry, and took part in the following-named battles: Mt. Slaughter, Westville, Winchester, Romney, Ft. Republic, and various other battles. He was orderly to Colonel Deponey, and at one time was bearer of important dispatches to General Banks. On his way he ran into the pickets of the rebel army and was immediately taken prisoner. By skillful maneuvering he succeeded in disposing of his dispatches so they failed to get into the hands of the enemy. He returned home and was married to Miss Mary Smiley, daughter of William Smiley, of Frostburg, Maryland. Their union has been blessed with the following-named children: William, Annie, Belle, Andrew, Jacob C., Franklin P. and Elvietta.

He is a member of Post 155, G. A. R., at Dunbar.

GEORGE A. MUNSON, one of the energetic and live business men of Connellsville, is a son of Isaac and Eliza (Collins) Munson, and was born in Connellsville, Fayette county, Pa., November 21, 1856.

Isaac Munson was a son of William Munson, a miller by occupation. Isaac Munson was born in 1824, near Alexandria, Westmoreland county, Pa. He came to Connellsville and engaged in the iron business, afterwards in the mercantile business at New Haven, when he, in 1852, became manager of the Markle Paper Mill Company's store at West Newton. In a short time he was stationed at Pittsburgh as purchasing and sales agent of the company, and occupied that position until his death in 1866. He was married to Eliza, daughter of James Collins, a prominent Baptist and an "old line whig." (For James Collins' history see sketch of Colonel John Collins.) Mrs. Munson resides at Connellsville.

George A. Munson was reared at Connellsville, and at the age of twenty-two he was employed by the Connellsville Gas and Coke Company, and took charge of their yards. He remained with them until they were sold to H. C. Frick & Co. in 1883, when he accepted a clerkship with the Union Supply Company, with whom he continued four years. In 1887 he formed the present partnership with his brothers, James C. and John J. Munson, the firm name being Munson Bros., plumbers, gas and steam fitters, Greenland's block, No. 732, corner Pittsburgh and Apple street, Connellsville.

In 1881 he was married to Miss Ella Jones, of near Uniontown, and daughter of John and Eliza Jones.

Munson Bros. carry a finely selected stock of natural gas supplies, stoves, tin, copper and sheet-iron ware; also a full and complete line of plumbers', gas and steam fitters' supplies of all kinds. They are practical and experienced mechanics, and devote their attention to every department of their business. They are the successors of R. C. Greenland.

George A. Munson is a republican, is a Heptasoph and Junior Mechanic. He is one who has won his own way in life, and has achieved permanent success by continued and persistent effort.

JOHN F. NORCROSS, the leading merchant tailor of Connellsville, as well as of Fayette county, was born at California, Washington county, Pa., December 17, 1856, and is a son of Joshua and Nancy (Mason) Norcross.

The name of Norcross is abbreviated from Northcross, a locality in the Highlands of Scotland. About 300 years ago the Northcross family removed to Glassgow and changed their name to Norcross. A century later some of them came to America and founded the American branch of the Norcross family. William Norcross, grandfather of J. F. Norcross, was born July 17, 1768, and came from Mt. Holly, N. J., to Fayette county, about 1790. One of his sons was Joshua Norcross, born November 29, 1810, and died at Brownsville, May 11, 1887. He was a member of the C. B. church and by occupation a bridge builder. His wife was Miss Nancy, daughter of Robert Mason, who died July 8, 1887, in the seventy-second year of her age.

John F. Norcross was reared principally at Brownsville, where he attended the common schools and learned the trade of merchant tailor with his brother, Charles D. Norcross. In 1884 he succeeded his brother, Charles D. (who died in that year), at No. 730 Pittsburgh St., Connellsville, in the merchant tailoring business. His patronage has rapidly increased until at present, and is now the biggest tailoring establishment in the county. The large assortment of broadcloths, suitings, vestings and piece goods are from English, German, French and domestic looms. He carries as full lines of styles in suitings and pantaloons as any house, in Philadelphia or New York, having 1,000 styles in cloths and more than 400 styles in pantaloon patterns.

He is a reliable citizen and a member of the Masonic fraternity. He is said to be doing a business of $20,000 per year. The following has been written of him and his business:

"Mr. Norcross is a native of Fayette county, a born genius in the art of cutting, a man of push, energy, sound judgment and unquestionable skill, and highly deserves the full measure of success that invariably follows energy and ability well applied."

WORTH KILPATRICK, one of the leading operators in the manufacture of fire-brick, in Fayette county, is a son of John P. and Mary (Marietta) Kilpatrick, and was born in Connellsville, March 31, 1847.

Thomas Kilpatrick, the grandfather of the subject of this sketch came from New Jersey to Connellsville, in about 1795. He married Elizabeth Barnhart, a native of Lancaster, Pa. At about fourteen years old she left her home in Lancaster and walked across the mountains to Connellsville where one of her brothers, John Barnhart, resided.

John P. Kilpatrick (father) is a son of Thomas and Elizabeth Kilpatrick, and was born at Connellsville, October 5, 1821. He enlisted, in January, 1847, in Company H, Second Regiment Pennsylvania Volunteers, and served till the close of the Mexican War, received no wound, and for his bravery in the field was elected lieutenant of his company. He was with Gen. Scott at the battles of Vera Cruz, Cerro Gordo, Contreras, Chapultepec, Belen Gate, City of Mexico, and at other important engagements. He returned home and engaged in the manufacture of fire-brick, at which he continued successfully, up to 1873. The panic of that year caused him to fail in business and has since acted as manager of the same works.

In 1846 he was married to Mary Marietta, daughter of George Marietta, of Connellsville. To them were born eleven children, of whom eight are living. Samuel, one of the sons, was born at Connellsville, is an artist and paints portraits from life. His education was received at the New York schools of art and later at Paris, where he prosecuted his art studies under the great artists of France. He is now engaged in his profession at Pittsburgh.

John P. Kilpatrick was elected county commissioner of Fayette county, in about 1876, and elected to the office of justice of the peace, in 1886 for the borough of Connellsville, but he did not serve. He has served several terms as a member of the Connellsville council.

Worth Kilpatrick attended the public schools of his native town till at the age of fifteen years when he went to the carpenter's trade, and is now an extensive contractor and builder. In 1879 he with Joseph Soisson, as partner, began the manufacture of fire-brick, under firm name of Siosson & Kilpatrick, and the name has since been changed to Siosson, Kilpatrick & Co. They run four plants in making fire-brick, one at Connellsville, one at Moyer, one at White Rock, and one at Braddock, employ about two hundred hands and make from ten to twelve million brick per year.

Mr. Kilpatrick also owns a half interest in the New Haven Red Brick Works, which is operated under the firm name of James Stafford & Co.

He is a director in the Connellsville Flint Glass Co., which runs a ten-pot furnace. He has served one term in council of Connellsville. He has passed through all the chairs of K. of P., I. O. O. F. and was district deputy of the former order for one year.

As deputy he organized lodges at Belle Vernon and Brownsville.

On June 11, 1884, he was married to Miss Christie, daughter of Josiah Kurtz, an old and well-known citizen of Connellsville. They have three children: George, Nell and Paul.

Mr. Kilpatrick is one of the live, and successful young business men of the county.

JOHN KURTZ at a very early date settled in Somerset county, Pa., where for many years, he was an honored and highly respected citizen. He served as associate judge of that county and was a member of the legislature from that district. He was a strong admirer of President Jackson, but his veto of the United States Bank measure changed him to a whig. At one time of his life he was a strong anti-Mason.

He was married to Christina Dively, of Somerset county, who, as well as her husband, lived to a ripe old age. Of twelve children born to them but two now survive: Josiah, of Connellsville, and Mrs. Kate Walter, of Somerset county. Josiah Kurtz was born in the borough of Somerset, Pennsylvania, in October, 1801. He attended the ordinary pay schools of that day and received a very good education, excelling in arithmetic and writing. He learned the hatting business with his father and worked with him at home until he was about twenty-four years of age, when he located at Connellsville. In about one year he returned to Somerset county, married Elizabeth Reisinger, of Somerset, and with his young wife, he returned to Connellsville, where he has since resided. For fifty years he annually visited Somerset, with his wife and children, making the trips overland across the mountains. He made hats at Connellsville until about 1860, setting his own kettles, making his own hat blocks and everything needed in his business. He also made silk hats without teacher or instructions from any one, and for years sold nearly all the hats within five miles of Connellsville, as well as to many of the surrounding counties. He frequently took a boat load of hats, paper, plows, hat bodies, etc., down the river as far as Cincinnati and Louisville. He made large quantities of woolen hats in the winter season and sold them at wholesale to Pittsburgh merchants, who sent them south for use of slaves. He dealt extensively in furs, both foreign and domestic. In about 1860 he gave his hat business over to his son John and engaged in the mercantile business with Henry Shaw, the firm was Shaw & Kurtz. In a few years their safe, containing several thousand dollars, was blown open and robbed. This so crippled the firm, it shortly afterwards dissolved. The firm of J. Kurtz & Sons was then formed, and began a general mercantile business. Mr. Kurtz was burgess of Connellsville and served two terms more than fifty years ago. He was frequently made executor, administrator, assignee, and settled many estates. He served as justice of the peace for two terms, 1856 to 1866. He was appointed notary public by Gov. Pollock, but refused to accept his commission. For many years, he was a school director and a member of the town council. He voted for Jackson but later became a whig, for reasons above mentioned. He was all his life a leading temperance man and belonged to the "Total Abstinence Society" formed at Connellsville, but he was never a member of any secret order. In religion he was originally a Lutheran, but there being no Lutheran church at Connellsville, he united with the Protestant Methodist church.

Four of his sons were volunteer soldiers in the Civil War and a fifth son was drafted, but he paid the required amount and did not go into the army. One of his sons was supposed to have been killed at the battle of Fredericksburg, as he was never seen or heard of afterwards and in his honor, the William Kurtz Post, G. A. R., of Connellsville, was named. Of the immediate Kurtz family there have been no natural deaths, and of the surviving five sons and four daughters, except William lost in battle, all live at Connellsville, except Mary who resides at Pruntytown, Va. Joseph M. Kurtz is the cashier of the First National Bank at Connellsville, Henry Kurtz is a member of the firm of Kurtz & Freed, engaged in the mercantile business; Samuel is engaged in the tinning business; Ellen in the millinery business, member of the firm of Porter & Kurtz; Christie is married to Worth Kilpatrick (see his sketch); Caroline is the wife of J. D. Stillwagon. Josiah Kurtz has eighteen grandchildren and one great-grandchild living. John Kurtz, the eldest son, was born at Connellsville, October, 1826. He attended the public schools of his native town, and later learned the hatting business, but never followed it to any great extent. He afterwards engaged in the general sale of hats, a business he has followed ever since. For sixteen years past, he has been notary public and was burgess of Connellsville, just fifty years after his father filled the same office.

He has belonged to the Odd Fellows for forty years, and is a member of the Methodist Episcopal church of which he has been a trustee for seven years and is now treasurer of the board of trustees. He enlisted for one year in Company C, Sixth Heavy Artillery, Two Hundred and Twelfth Regiment, but the war closed nine months after his enlistment. As his company was not called into active service, he principally did guard duty. In 1850 he was married to Kate, a daughter of Joseph Keepers, of New Haven. To their union have been born five children: the eldest son, J. B., is a member of the firm of Kurtz & Freed; the second son, Isaac W., is a locomotive engineer and master mechanic on Lake Erie & Western railroad and resides at Peru, Indiana; the third son, J. C., is the cashier of the Yough. Bank; the fourth son, Harry L., is assistant book keeper at Leisenring Coal and Coke Works, and the daughter, Elizabeth B., is the wife of George B. Freed, the latter of the firm of Kurtz & Freed.

SAMUEL N. LONG, a prosperous farmer of Connellsville township and a well known citizen of Fayette county, was born at Connellsville, Fayette county, Pa., July 14, 1821, and is a son of Robert and Catherine (Foster) Long.

Robert Long was a blacksmith, and pursued his trade at Connellsville for twenty years, when he removed to the present farm of his son Samuel N., and was engaged in farming from the time of his removal from Connellsville until his death in 1849, at the age of sixty-two years. He was well and favorably known; a democrat, had served as county commissioner and was a strong and active member of the United Presbyterian church, of which his wife was also a member. She died in 1868, aged eighty-one years.

Samuel N. Long is of Welsh-German descent, reared at Connellsville until eleven years of age, when he accompanied his parents to their farm in Connellsville township. His education was received at Connellsville and under the old subscription school masters and while not full in many things, yet was practical and sufficient for all business purposes. Mr. Long has made farming his life vocation, and by good management and intelligent supervision, has achieved great success.

On December 24, 1846, he was married to Miss Jemima Humbert of Dunbar township. She died in 1854, leaving three children: Humber, Catherine and Hannah. He was married in 1855, to Mrs. Elizabeth Cramer, of Dunbar township. She died in 1880 and left three sons: Robert, George and James. In 1881 Mr. Long was married to Mrs. Martha (Smith) Wilson, of near Uniontown.

Samuel N. Long owns his father's farm of 103 acres of choice farming land and has added to it thirty-one acres of adjoining land. His farm is one and a half miles north of Connellsville, and is well improved and in a good state of cultivation. He is a democrat, served from 1881 to 1884 as director of the poor, was school director for twenty-one years and has held nearly all the township offices. He is a member of the First Presbyterian church of Connellsville and is a large and liberal contributor to his church. He is a prosperous farmer, a successful business man and is well known throughout the county.

THOMAS L. NEWILL, a prominent teacher and a valiant soldier of the Civil War, is a son of Joshua S. and Catherine (Latta) Newill, and was born in Mt. Pleasant township, Westmoreland county, Pa., July 20, 1847.

His grandfather, Stephen Newill, was a native of Scotland, where he married Annie

Thompson, came to Maryland in 1771, and subsequently removed to Westmoreland county, where he reared a family of four children and afterwards died there.

His father, Joshua S. Newill, was born in Westmoreland county, Pa., October 16, 1814. He was a school teacher and subsequently engaged in farming. He is an ardent republican and a member of the Presbyterian church. His first wife was Catherine, daughter of Samuel Latta, of near Stauffer Station, who was born in England. After her death he married Christina, daughter of John Hoffman. By his first wife he had two sons and two daughters, and by his second wife four sons and two daughters. A son by his second wife, Frank Newill, was a soldier in the regular army, and while in the service in Washington territory, in 1887, at the risk of his life saved an Indian chief's daughter from drowning and received a full beaded suit from the old chief as a reward for his bravery.

Thomas L. Newill attended the common schools until fourteen years of age, when he ran away from home and entered the Union army. He enlisted in Company F, Eleventh Pennsylvania Volunteers, and was mustered out as an orderly sergeant, July 20, 1865. He was in the battles of Yorktown, Williamsburg, Deep Bottom, Malvern Hill, Second Bull Run, South Mountain, Fredericksburg, Chancellorsville, Gettysburg, the Wilderness, Mine Run and Spottsylvania Court House. At the last-named battle he was wounded, on Sunday, May 8, 1864, in the leg, which was amputated on the Tuesday following, while on the battlefield. The remainder of his time he spent at Staunton and Chester hospitals in Washington City. He was previously wounded in the hand by a ball at Gettysburg.

In 1865 Mr. Newill attended the Sewickly Academy and subsequently attended several normal schools. He taught in 1865 the Franklin school in Bullskin township, and since then has taught continuously, excepting three years.

September 19, 1870, he married Miss Mary A., daughter of Samuel Smith, of Perry township. They have one child: Cora, born May 19, 1872. He is a republican, served as county commissioner from 1882 to 1885, and served five years as justice of the peace in Perry township. He has lived in Dunbar township since 1878 and is called the "champion fox-hunter" of his locality. He is a member of William Kurtz Post, No. 104, G. A. R., at Connellsville, and is recognized as a first-class teacher and a useful citizen.

DR. JAMES J. MULLEN is a native of Ireland, and is a good representative of the people from whom he sprung. Possessing in a full degree the native vivacity and wit of his nation. For many generations his family have resided in the same county. His grandfather, Miles Mullen, was born in County Tyrone about 1789. His sons were: Bernard, Michael and John. Michael, the father of Dr. Mullen, was born in the County Tyrone in about 1821, where he still lives and is a farmer. He married Belle Quinn, a daughter of Henry Quinn, of the same county. Dr. James J. Mullen was born in County Tyrone, Ireland, June 11, 1848, and at the age of twenty, he was married to Catherine, a daughter of John McGarritty, of County Tyrone, Ireland. They have one child, John, a student at the Western Pennsylvania Medical College, at Pittsburgh. In 1871 Dr. Mullen came to the United States and secured employment in the Bethlehem Rolling Mill, thence to Pittsburgh, and worked as puddler. In 1880 by hard work and close economy he had acquired sufficient means to engage in the drug business, and followed that business till after his graduation as M. D. He attended the Medical department of Wooster University, Cleveland, Ohio, where he graduated in 1883, taking first honors of his class of thirty members. He began the practice at Pittsburgh, afterwards removed to Dunbar, where he has since remained in the active practice of medicine. He has achieved great success in his profession and is held in high esteem as an able physician. He is the surgeon for the B. & O. R. R., and for the Cambria Iron Company. Dr. Mullen has prospered at Dunbar, having accumulated considerable wealth during his five years' practice there. He is entirely a self-made man, he has forced his own way up the ladder of social position and professional distinction, and is a practical verification of Daniel Webster's aphorism: "There is always room at the top."

JAMES W. NICHOLSON, farmer, dairyman and florist, of Connellsville, is a son of Christopher and Louisa (Funk) Nicholson, and was born in Monongalia county, Va. (now W. Va.), in 1841.

His father, Christopher Nicholson, was a native of England, but in early life came to Monongalia county, Va., and was engaged in school teaching and milling until his death, in 1862, at seventy-five years of age.

His mother, Louisa (Funk) Nicholson, was a native of Monongalia county, Va., where she died in 1871, at the age of seventy-five years.

James W. Nicholson was trained to farm work and attended the primary schools of Virginia. At an early age he engaged in farming, and continued in that business until 1860, when he removed to Uniontown, this county, where he remained for sixteen years. In 1876 he came to Connellsville, but soon moved to his present farm.

For the last six years Mr. Nicholson has been engaged in dairying with very satisfactory results.

In 1871 he was united in marriage to Miss Martha Rutter, an estimable woman, of Upper Middletown. Her father, Benjamin Rutter, was a farmer.

J. W. Nicholson has a very good farm, containing seventy-nine acres of land well adapted to farming and dairying purposes, and has established a dairy upon this land, complete in all its equipments.

In political belief he is a democrat, and has served as school director of Connellsville township. In religious matters he is a member of the Methodist Episcopal church. Mr. Nicholson has turned his attention of late years to the art of the florist, and his efforts in that direction have been entirely successful. He keeps constantly on hand at Connellsville, a large and well assorted stock of plants, as well as an abundant supply of fresh and choice cut-flowers. He is an industrious citizen and deserving of the success he is achieving.

PATRICK O'CONNOR, a native of Ireland and a citizen of Dunbar township, is a son of Peter and Mary (Murtha) O'Connor, and was born in County Cavan.

Peter O'Connor was born in Monahan county, Ireland, he was a farmer by occupation, and married Miss Mary, daughter of Thomas and Alice (Carroll) Murtha, both natives of County Cavan. Peter O'Connor was a highly respected farmer and citizen. His father, John O'Connor, married a Miss McCluskey, of County Cavan, where they both lived and died.

Patrick O'Connor was educated in the excellent schools of his native county, and in 1871 embarked as a seaman on board the ship Sapphire at Liverpool, bound for Calcutta, along the eastern coast of Hindostan. On this trip he was sixteen months at sea.

He made a second voyage to Hindostan in the capacity of a seaman, and was a sailor on board a vessel that visited Hong Kong, China, and Baker's Island in the South Pacific. His next employment was a year's clerkship in Liverpool. From there he went to County Durham, in the "North of England," and was engaged in the coke business for six years. He emigrated from County Durham to Broad Ford, where he was employed for some time in the coke business, when he engaged with the Cambria Iron Company of Dunbar township, and was in their employ for four years. Leaving the iron business he rented the Rogers farm, and after three years of successful farming he concluded to engage permanently in that business, and accordingly purchased his present farm.

In 1876 he was married to Miss Mary Catherine Hart, of County Durham, England. Unto their union have been born seven children: Thomas, Mary, Arthur, Patrick (deceased), Elesia, Bernard and John H.

With his farming interests he is engaged in the dairy business. Mr. O'Connor is a successful farmer, a well-respected citizen, a good business man, and thoroughly energetic in any enterprise in which he engages.

ELLIS PHILLIPS, M. D., a prominent physician of New Haven, was born in North Union township, Fayette county, Pa., August 31, 1843, and is a son of Ellis Phillips who was born November 12, 1798, near West Brownsville, Washington county, Pa. In 1824 Ellis Phillips married Phebe, daughter of Thomas Lilley, and afterward removed to a farm in North Union township, Fayette county. Their children were eight in number, five sons and three daughters, of whom Dr. Phillips is the youngest son.

Solomon Phillips (paternal grandfather) was born in Delaware, and married Martha Nichols, of Wilmington. He came to Washington county, Pa., in about 1786.

Dr. Ellis Phillips at the age of sixteen went to Madison Academy at Uniontown, remained for two years, when he entered Washington College, and was graduated in the class of 1864. He entered the office of Drs. Smith and J. M. Fuller, of Uniontown, in the study of medicine, attended lectures at Jefferson Medical College, Philadelphia, and from there he was graduated in 1867. Between courses of lectures he practiced at Upper Middletown, but after his graduation he located at New Haven, where Dr. J. K. Rogers became his partner, the partnership lasting till Dr. Rogers' death in 1870. He then associated himself with Dr. J. J. Singer; the partnership after several years dissolved. Since that Dr. Phillips has practiced alone. He has never aspired to political honors, although he has held the offices of school director, town councilman, and president of the board of pension examiners. May 16, 1872, he was married to Ada A. McIlvaine, of New Haven, a daughter of Robert McIlvaine, who was born in Washington county, Pa., and early in life removed to New Haven. Dr. Phillips has two sons and one daughter living: Ada Josephine, James McIlvaine and Arthur Morton. At the close of his partnership with Dr. Rogers he returned to Philadelphia, and took several special courses of study: one on diseases of the eye and ear under Dr. George C. Harland, the celebrated specialist. Immediately after his marriage he made a trip to Europe accompanied by his wife. He remained in Europe some time, and was instructed in the celebrated Rotunda Hospital, Dublin, Ireland, thence to London, where he studied diseases of the eye at the Royal Eye Infirmary; but owing to a severe attack of illness he was obliged to return home in about four months. He resumed his general practice at New Haven until 1883, when he went to New York City and entered

E. Phillips

the office of Dr. Mittendorf as a student of diseases of the eye, taking also a special course of instruction on diseases of the throat.

He began his special studies of throat diseases under the instructions of Sir Morrell Mackenzie, of London, and was among the first physicians to introduce the use of the ophthalmoscope and the laryngscope successfully in this section of the State. Of his specialties Dr. Phillips is the pioneer of Fayette county.

Dr. Phillips is an eye and throat specialist of note and reputation, but he does not, however, confine his practice to those specialties alone. In addition to a large and lucrative general practice, he is building up a fine practice in his specialties, and his patients are from all parts of the country.

GEORGE RANSOM, of Irish extraction and a veteran soldier of the late Civil War, was born in Dunbar township, Fayette county, Pa., July 31, 1833.

He was educated in the subscription schools; at an early age he emigrated to Illinois, where he was engaged in farming for four years, and then spent the succeeding year in traveling through Kansas and Colorado. In 1860 he returned to Illinois and resumed farming. After the defeat of the Union army at Bull Run he was among the first that responded to President Lincoln's call for troops to suppress the "Great Rebellion." He enlisted in Company B, Thirty-seventh Regiment Illinois Infantry or "Fremont Rifles," commanded for a time by General Black, ex-commissioner of pensions. Mr. Ransom, after two years' service, was made drum-major, and was in the battles of Pea Ridge, Prairie Grove, at the siege of Vicksburg, served in Louisiana under Banks and was stationed for some time in Texas on the Rio Grande river. After the war closed he returned to Dunbar township and engaged in various kinds of business, until 1872, when he took charge of the ferry on the Youghiogheny river between Dawson and East Liberty. In 1882 he retired from the ferry and engaged for five or six years in several different pursuits. He is now living a retired life at East Liberty.

In 1865 he married Margaret, daughter of John and Nancy Hannan, both natives of Fayette county and living near the borough of Dunbar. Mr. and Mrs. Ransom have one child, a daughter, Maude, who married William Gillespie, and has one child, a son, George W. Gillespie, born March 2, 1889.

George Ransom is a member of the Cumberland Presbyterian church at Vanderbilt, and is a peace-loving and law-abiding citizen.

DR. ROBERT S. REAGAN, a rising and progressive physician and coroner of Fayette county, is a son of Philip and Rose Ann (Martin) Reagan, and was born in Bullskin township, Fayette county, Pa., March 26, 1852. His great-grandfather, Philip Reagan, was a Scotch-Irishman, an early settler of Westmoreland county, where he laid out the town of Reagantown, which was named in honor of him. He lived to the remarkable age of 109 years. One of his sons, Alexander Reagan (doctor's grandfather), was a potter by trade, a whig in politics, a popular man, and for half a century served in some one of the township offices. His son, Philip Reagan, married Rose, daughter of Frederick Martin, and a native of Maryland. She died in 1883 at eighty years of age. Her father was a farmer and came to Fayette county, where he died in 1867.

Dr. Robert S. Reagan was reared principally on a farm, educated in the common schools, Mt. Pleasant Institute, and Waynesburg College, and was graduated from the latter in the class of 1876. He read medicine with Dr. J. J. Singer, of Connellsville, attended lectures at Jefferson Medical College, at Philadelphia, and was graduated from that school in the spring of 1880. In May, 1880, he began the practice of medicine at Broad Ford, and has successfully continued there in the practice of his profession up to the present time. He enjoys a good and paying practice. He was married in 1881 to Miss Hattie, daughter of William Stacy, who is a well-to-do farmer. They have three children: Roy S,, Edna S., and Frank S. In politics he is a democrat and takes an active part in the interests of his party. In 1886 he was appointed to fill the unexpired term of Dr. John Batton, as coroner of Fayette county. In the fall of the same year he was elected coroner, and is now serving very satisfactorily in that office. In 1881 he established his present successful drug and grocery store at Broad Ford. Dr. Reagan is a member of the Masonic fraternity and the Improved Order of Heptasophs. He is pleasant and gentlemanly, and a well-read and skillful physician.

SAMUEL E. PORTER, a well and favorably known druggist of Vanderbilt, is a son of Samuel S. and Mary Ann (Smith) Porter, and was born in Tyrone township, Fayette county, Pa., April 25, 1863.

His father, Samuel S. Porter, came from Maryland when quite young. He received a good education and engaged in teaching tor sixteen years. After the breaking out of the "Great Rebellion," he enlisted as a private in Company B, Sixteenth Regiment Volunteer Cavalry, and by successive promotions attained to the rank of second lieutenant under General Sheridan, in Second Maryland Volunteers. He participated at Gettysburg, was in several other battles and was honorably discharged in September 30, ——.

Samuel S. Porter and Mary A. Smith were married February 19, 1852, at Wesley Chapel near Scottdale, Westmoreland county, Pa., Rev. John Covert officiating clergyman.

Their family consists of six children living and three dead; all born in Fayette county, Pa.: Margaret E., April 17, 1853; Moses E., July 14, 1854; Mary Alice, October 16, 1855, died September 29, 1856; Rachel Jane, December 28, 1856, died February 8, 1858. Ella, born August 24, 1858; Nathan S., December 31, 1859, died June 13, 1870; Alcinda E., February 1, 1862; Samuel E., April 25, 1863, and Hettie, September 7, 1866.

Samuel E. Porter was raised on a farm in Upper Tyrone township, Fayette county, Pa., and was educated in the common schools of that district, with the exception of two or three winters that he attended a common school in South Huntingdon township, Westmoreland county. At the age of nineteen years he engaged as a clerk with his brother, Moses E., a druggist of Dawson. Learning the business he opened a drug store at Dawson with Dr. George (George being a silent partner). In the spring of 1885 he closed his business at Dawson, removed to Vanderbilt and established his present drug store. Within the last year he has erected a good store building, which is one among the finest drug rooms in the county. He keeps a full stock of drugs, medicines and proprietary remedies, together with a good assortment of everything generally called for in an establishment of this kind. In less than five years he has built up a large and remunerative business.

In October, 1886, he married Miss Della, daughter of Milo and Anna (Smith) Jenkins of Preston county, W. Va. They have two children, both sons: Van Dale and Milo Smith.

S. E. Porter is a member of Boone Castle,

No. 125, Knights of the Mystic Chain, and Vanderbilt Counsel, No. 104, J. O. of U. A. M. He is a young, active and energetic business man.

JAMES MADISON REID. There are men who, by marked ability, ceaseless energy and great success, commend themselves to public attention. To this class Mr. Reid justly belongs. He is a resident of Connellsville, and was born in West Newton, Westmoreland county, Pa., April 10, 1849. He is the third child of James Dunlap and Mary (Henry) Reid. The former came from Belfast, Ireland, in about 1840, the latter (whose mother was a McAuley) was a daughter of Edward Henry.

His blood relations have given prominent characters to American history. Several of the Reids attained distinction in battles of war and victories of peace. One of them was the celebrated Captain Samuel C. Reid, a distinguished naval officer, who, in command of the privateer General Armstrong, in 1814, engaged a British fleet and fought the most brilliant naval battle of which we have any record. The Washington *Union* of April 30, 1858, says: "It was Captain Reid who, in 1818, at the complimentary request of a committee of congress, designed our present national flag." The first brigadier-general in the Revolutionary War was a Reid. On the maternal side J. M. Reid comes of the notable Henry family, of which Patrick Henry, the great orator, was a member, and the late Professor Henry, of the Smithsonian Institution, whose fame is world-wide. John McAuley, a very brave officer, who served on General Washington's staff, was a great-uncle to the mother of J. M. Reid. The Reids and Henrys trace their ancestry to the old world, where, in past ages, members of each family have held important political positions, and were conspicuous in deeds of daring.

James M. Reid, while a mere child, went to Allegheny county, Pa., was educated in the common schools till in his fourteenth year, when he attended the Allegheny Institute for a short time.

At about the age of fourteen he began to do for himself, with no resources but strong will and determination. He weighed coal, later he clerked in a store for about a year, when he went to Broadford, and was engaged for about four years as a clerk with his brother, E. H. Reid. From Broadford he went to Dunbar, and, with others, engaged in the mercantile business, which he continued most successfully for six years.

Having clearly shown his adaptability for business by his success in mercantile pursuits, he proceeded to enlarge his sphere of operations by engaging in coal mining and the manufacture of coke; and by a successful prosecution of these industries, fully demonstrated his capability to manage an extensive business, or control and direct a combination of several great enterprises. In 1882 he had bought out all of his partners in the coke and coal business. He owns a controling interest in several coal-fields whose combined area is more than seven thousand acres. In February, 1882, he organized the Connellsville and Ursina Coal and Coke Company, with a capital of $400,000. He was elected its president in 1882 and has continued to act as such ever since. This company owns over seven thousand acres of land. The Ursina & North Fork R. R., starts at Ursina Station, on the B. & O. R. R., and extends for several miles up the north fork of the Youghiogheny river, through the property of this company which own their own cars and engines. Their object is to develop the limestone, iron ore and coal of their lands.

He is a member of the firm of Boyts, Porter & Co., of Connellsville, manufacturers of steam pumps, supplies for furnaces and coke works and dealers in steam and water pipe, brass and iron fittings, etc.

Mr. Reid was unanimously elected chairman of the republican county committee of Fayette county in 1884, 1885, 1886 and 1887. In 1888 he was unanimously nominated by the republicans of Fayette county for congress, the district of Fayette, Greene and Washington counties. The Fayette county conferees met with those of Greene, Washington and part of Allegheny counties, and held five meetings of several several days each. At the last meeting at Pittsburgh, on the 206th ballot, Mr. Reid moved to nominate Ray, of Greene county, who easily secured the nomination, principally through the support of Mr. Reid, and was elected.

Mr. Reid was a member of the republican State central committee for several years, and received the congratulations of his party in Pennsylvania for the work he did in his district while a committeeman. He is a man of great determination, fine intelligence, and business energy, and has a large personal and political following in Fayette and adjoining counties.

JAMES F. RIDGEWAY, one of the enterprising young business men of Dunbar, was born in Monongalia county, W. Va., March 10, 1854. His father, at the breaking out of the war, joined the Union army and fought at the second battle of Bull Run and was in various other engagements; afterwards was taken prisoner, and for eighteen months he was confined in Southern prisons; five months in Libby and thirteen months at Andersonville. His death occurred from disease contracted while in the war on April 27, 1881. James F. Ridgeway's mother's maiden name was Martha Goodwin.

His great-grandfather, Whorton Ridgeway, was a native Scotchman. His grandfather, Joel Ridgeway, was born near Morgantown, in 1798, and was married to Jerushia Dawson.

For many years Sylvester Ridgeway resided at Dunbar, and was engaged as brick-molder and mining boss.

J. F. Ridgeway received his education in the West Virginia State Normal School, at Fairmont. On leaving school he taught for about seven years in the public schools of that State. He went to Scottdale, Westmoreland county, and for five years was engaged in the mining business. In 1884 he located at Dunbar and began the manufacture of cigars; he continued at this business a few years, when he engaged in his present business, grocery and restaurant. His wife Sophia is a daughter of Samuel A. Hall, who was born in Fayette county, and served three years in the war. Samuel A. Hall's wife was Mary A. Morrison, a native of Fayette county, and a daughter of Francis Morrison, who was born in Ireland.

Mr. Ridgeway is a member and treasurer of the Baptist church at Dunbar, and is a member of K. of P. and I. O. O. F.

ALBERT ROBINSON, a prosperous farmer near Leisenring, is a son of James and Nancy (Tintsman) Robinson, and was born near Connellsville, in Dunbar township, Fayette county, Pa., October 11, 1837.

His grandfather, Duncan Robinson, came from Scotland to Lancaster county, Pa., in 1720, where he married Miss Jennie Doulan, a native of Ireland. His children were: James, Alexander, John, William, Susan and Sarah.

His father, James Robinson, was born in Lancaster county, Pa., in 1787, and died March 21, 1874. He came to Westmoreland county and subsequently removed to Dunbar township, about 1820. He was an "old line whig" and married Miss Nancy Tintsman, daughter of Abraham Tintsman of

Westmoreland county, Pa. Mr. Tintsman was a native of Germany and came from Berks county. His children were: Abraham, Judah, Fanny, Betsey, Nancy and Barbara.

Mr. and Mrs. Robison's children were: Cyrus, born 1816, killed by a tree, married Fannie Galley; Eliza, born 1817, married N. H. White; Frances, born 1818, married John Freed; Susan, born 1821, married David Garlits; Margaret, born 1822, married O. J. McCormick; Nancy, born 1824, married A. H. Patterson, and Adaline, born 1827, married I. A. Hugus. Mrs. Robinson was born 1795, died 1813. He was reared on a farm and well trained in the farming business. He was educated in the common schools of his native township. After leaving school he engaged in farming and stock-raising and has successfully continued in that line of business until this time.

Albert Robinson married in March, 1872, Miss Lydia, daughter of Philip and Lydia (Watson) Morgan. Mr. Robinson has two children: Maud, born April 14, 1873, and Ira, born July 5, 1875. Mrs. Robinson's sisters and brothers were: Margaret, Nancy, dead; Eliza; Lydia A., dead; Maria, dead; Lydia; Julia, dead; James, Judson and Thomas, dead. He owns a valuable and productive farm of seventy-five acres near Leisenring. He is a successful farmer of Dunbar township and is a stanch republican.

JACOB D. SIMERAL, the accurate and accommodation agent at Dickerson Run station, on the P. McK. & A. railroad, is a son of James and Margaret (De Walt) Simeral, and was born near Shaner station, Westmoreland county, Pa., September 30, 1859.

His father, James Simeral, is a native of Westmoreland county, and resides at Buena Vista, this county. He married Miss Margaret, daughter of Jacob De Walt. (One of her brothers, William, lost an arm in the late war; another, James, was a corporal and served in Sherman's army.)

Jacob D. Simeral received his education in the common schools of Allegheny county, was engaged for some time in digging coal, and for several years later, as a track layer on a railroad. While thus engaged as a day laborer, he assiduously employed every spare moment in fitting himself for a position in the business world. He learned telegraphy and other work pertaining to a station agent's work, and was successful in July 1886, in securing the position of night agent at Dickerson's Run station, opposite Dawson. He was accurate in all his business and gave strict attention to the most minute details of his work. This thoroughness in work soon secured his promotion to the position of general agent, which he has held ever since, with satisfaction to his employers and the public.

He was married to Miss Isaphine M., daughter of George M. Collins. They have three children: Clara E., Alice P. and Maggie L.

Jacob D. Simeral is a member of the Baptist church, and his wife is a member of the Methodist Episcopal church. His success in life is but another illustration of what intelligence, energy and perseverance will accomplish for a man, who has a definite aim or object in life, and works earnestly to reach it.

WILLIAM M. SISLEY, an enterprising and successful merchant of Gibson, near Connellsville, is a native of Pennsylvania, and was born in Fayette county, June 14, 1858. He is a son of John L. and Hannah J. (Wilgus) Sisley, both natives of Fayette county, and living.

The paternal grandfather, Morgan Sisley, was born in Fayette county, and engaged in farming for many years, but the latter part of his life was spent in keeping the Perry Hotel at Perryopolis. The maternal grandfather, Edward Wilgus, was by trade a shoemaker.

John L. Sisley (father) is a carpenter, and has been a resident of Gibson for over twenty years, and in politics he is a democrat. William M. Sisley was reared on a farm until he was eleven years of age, when he came with his parents to Gibson; received his education in the common schools, and was engaged for ten years in carpentering. Leaving his trade in April, 1888, he commenced his present business of general merchandising.

In 1878 he was united in marriage to Alice Kincell, daughter of Alfred and Evaline Kincell, both natives of Wheeler, Fayette county. They have three children living—two sons and one daughter: Joseph, Ella and John A.

At Gibson Mr. Sisley has a good store, well filled with dry goods, notions, groceries, hardware and everything needed to supply the wants of his large custom. In political matters he is a republican, a member of the J. O. of A. M., and is one of the foremost and leading citizen of Gibson.

DR. JAMES J. SINGER, a leading physician of Fayette county, is a native of Pennsylvania. He was born in Donegal township, Westmoreland county, November 25, 1850, educated in the public schools of Greensburg, and was graduated from the high school in 1868, when he began the study of medicine with Dr. Robert Brown. He afterwards took a full course of lectures at the Jefferson Medical College, and was graduated in March, 1871, before he was twenty-one years of age. He came to Connellsville, in June of the same year, where he has resided and practiced medicine most successfully ever since. He was for several years in partnership with Dr. Phillips, and has been surgeon for the B. & O. R. R. Co., at Connellsville, for the past seventeen years. After four years' practice Dr. Singer took a course in King's College Hospital, London, and a clinical course in the various hospitals throughout that city. He makes surgery a specialty, and has been signally successful.

He is a son of Robert W. and Eleanor (Warren) Singer, both born in Westmoreland county. Robert W. Singer removed from Donegal township to Greensburgh, to take charge of the office of clerk of courts to which he had previously been elected. Dr. Singer was married to Miss Jennie Johnston, of Fayette county, and have five children, three boys and two girls. He has a very beautiful home.

Dr. Singer is one of the most talented of the young physicians of the county, and his success is of that kind which only comes to men of brains and energy.

ROBERT L. SMITH, of Connellsville, is a son of James and Sarah (Young) Smith, both natives of Carlisle, Cumberland Co., Pa., who crossed the mountains and settled in Pittsburgh in 1826. Remaining at Pittsburgh but a short time, they came to Fayette county, and located in Redstone township. James Smith was a paper-maker, and in 1832 he located at Connellsville and worked at his trade. In 1833 he removed to Brownsville, where he continued for two years at the same business. In 1835 he returned to Connellsville, and continued to reside there till his death, in 1856, at the age of fifty-nine years. His wife died at Brownsville, in 1844, at the age of forty-eight years.

Robert L. Smith was born at Carlisle, Cumberland county, Pa., March 28, 1819. At the age of fourteen years he went as second cook on the "Lady Washington," which ran from Pittsburgh to Cincinnati. In a short time he was promoted to steward, in which capacity he continued to serve till the breaking out of the War of the Rebellion. During this time, however, he worked on different boats, and for several years he was with Captain Cox, of Brownsville. Subsequently he was engaged in the Pittsburgh and St. Louis trade; relinquished that, he went South, where he was at the breaking out of the war, engaged on one of the finest boats that plied the Mississippi river. He left New Orleans the day Colonel Ellsworth fell, on May 24, 1861. Returned to Connellsville, engaged in the hotel business, at which he was employed up to 1882. He first ran the Yough House. In 1869 he bought and opened as a hotel, the house which is now known as the Smith House. In 1882 he rented this hotel and retired from active life. In 1832 the fine stone residence in which he now resides was the leading hotel of Connellsville, and was known as the Page House. He was married in 1855 to Miss Bettanna R. Heobdinger, a daughter of John Heobdinger, the latter a farmer of Westmoreland county. Mr. Smith and wife are both highly respected members of the Lutheran church. He is one of the oldest, if not the oldest, steamboat-men now living in the county. He is a remarkably well preserved man for his age, and is now spending the declining years of his life in peace and plenty.

HENRY B. SNYDER, the well known proprietor of East Liberty foundry and repair shops, is a son of Peter and Catherine (Bothers) Snyder, of German extraction, and was born in Rostravor township, Westmoreland county, Pa., November 3, 1831.

His grandfather was a native of Germany. He came to America, first settling in New Jersey, was a soldier in the Revolutionary War, but subsequently removed to Westmoreland county, Pa., where he owned a grist-mill that stood on the site of the present Scottdale Furnace. His children were: John, Nicholas, Peter, Gasper and Elizabeth. Peter Snyder was born in 1792 and removed in 1842 to Franklin township, where he purchased a small farm and resided until his death, December 25, 1857. He married Miss Catherine Bothers, and unto them were born ten children: John, Jacob, Peter, William, Daniel (father of Prof. Z. X. Snyder), Francis, a soldier in the late war, was wounded in the Battle of the Wilderness; Margaret, Mary, Eli and Henry B. Mrs. Snyder died in 1863, in the sixty-ninth year of her age.

Henry B. Snyder was reared on a farm in Westmoreland county, attending the common schools; leaving school he learned the trade of carpenter, which he pursued for fourteen years in Fayette county and in Pittsburgh. He afterwards learned the trade of molder, and erected a foundry at East Liberty, and has successfully prosecuted the molding and foundry business up to the present time.

In 1857 he married Miss Mary Ann, daughter of John Knight. They have eleven children: George, an engineer, married Miss Etta Eneix; Emma and Belle are successful teachers; Maggie, an experienced teacher of the graded schools of Greensburg; Minnie, Frank, Florence, Frances, Alva, Myrtle and Maude. The sons are all fine mechanics and the daughters excel in drawing and painting.

Henry B. Snyder has added successive additions to his foundry and has established in connection with it a wagon-making and machine shop. He has machinery for doing almost any kind of work in wood, iron, steel, brass or copper, and is fully prepared to repair anything, from a pin to a locomotive. He is the inventor and manufacturer of a valuable plow. In politics he is a democrat. He started in life with nothing, and every obstacle he met only nerved him to more determined efforts to succeed. After many years of hard but honest battling with adverse fortune, he achieved success and won respect by his manly, determined course. To a limited education he has added large stores of information by reading, observation and reflection. Plain and unassuming, he is true to his friends and abhors dishonesty. He is perhaps one of the most remarkable men in the community in which he lives, in winning honorable success from discouraging adversity. He has been pre-eminently the architect of his own fortune.

GEORGE W. STILLWAGON was born at Connellsville, Fayette county, Pa., November 15, 1826, and is the son of Peter and Margaret Stillwagon (nee White). His great-grandfather, Peter Stillwagon, was born on the site of Connellsville, and was enrolled as one of the "minute-men" in the Revolution. He was taken prisoner in one of the battles by the British, and was held for some time. His wife was accidentally burned to death at the advanced age of one hundred and fifteen years. His grandfather, William Stillwagon, was born at Connellsville, where he lived and died. He married Margaret Wilson; eight children were born unto them: Josiah, Joseph, Wilson, Sarah, Henry, John, Eliza and Mary. His father, Peter Stillwagon, was born at Connellsville, where he lived and died. He married Margaret White. To their union were born seven children: George W., Hugh C., Joseph L., William, Barton, Charles K. and Crawford. Mrs. Stillwagon was a daughter of George and Nancy (Crawford) White. They had six children: William, Phebe A., Margaret, George, Jennie and Mary.

George W. Stillwagon was reared in Connellsville and attended the schools of that town. He began to do for himself at an early age, worked by the day for several years, and then engaged in farming. In 1865 he purchased the comfortable home where he now resides. On September 28, 1848, he was married to Elizabeth French, and had nine children: Hugh C., William O., Barton, Peter C., Mary, Jennie R., Margaret, Ida and Mattie. George W. Stillwagon has served as member of the town council at different times, and as school director. He has been a member of the United Brethren church for forty-two years, and a local preacher of the same denomination for 20 years. He is one of the steady and useful citizens of Connellsville.

JOHN B. STROUD was born in 1856, at Uniontown, Fayette county, Pa. His grandfather, Quiller Stroud, was also born in Fayette county. His wife, Susan Dixon, was a daughter of George Dixon; the latter was born in England, came to this country and served in the War of the Revolution. Their children were as follows: Rachel, Mary, William, George, Thomas, Lindsey, Acteus, Keziah, Harland, Joshua and Joseph.

William Stroud (father) was a native of Washington county, Pa., and was born December 25, 1814. He is a weaver by trade. He was married, in March, 1836, to Warnetta Houser, daughter of Henry Houser, a native of Maryland. Their children are as follows: Isabella, Rachel, Mary, Eliza, John B. and Emma. William Stroud was a volunteer soldier in the Civil War for three years. He was mustered into service in 1862, in the One Hundred and Twelfth Pennsylvania Artillery, in Captain Fuller's company, and participated in the battles around Petersburg and Richmond. His son, Henry, also served a short time in service, till his death, at Clarksburg, W. Va.

John B. Stroud's education embraced only

a knowledge of the text books taught in the common schools of the county. He is a painter by trade. His wife, Alwilda McCormick, to whom he was married April 2, 1878, was a daughter of Rev. Jacob McCormick, of Connellsville. They have four children: Walter, Warnette, Lizza and William. For a time after his marriage Mr. Stroud lived in Grafton, W. Va., where his wife died March 14, 1886. He subsequently returned to Dunbar, where he at present resides, and is a member of the Methodist Episcopal church at Dunbar.

SAMUEL STRAESSER was born in Martinsburg, Blair county, Pa. His father, John Straesser, was born December 6, 1809, a native of Germany and came to this country in about 1829. He settled in Blair county, Pa., and married Margaret Smaltz who was also born in Germany, and came to America in 1837. The children born to them are as follows: David, Mary E., Louisa, Christian, John, Samuel, Catherine, Charles A., Margaret, Minnie and Edward. Samuel Straesser was educated in the common schools of Martinsburg, and at the Juniata Collegiate Institute. He engaged in a drug store, where he remained for about seven years. He embarked in the drug business on his own account at Williamsburg, Pa., from 1872 to 1882. On May 1, 1888, he came to Dunbar, and engaged with Lang & Doonan as druggist and business manager.

He married Miss C. B. Fry, daughter of Mrs. Susan Fry, and has two children: J. Edward and Franklin.

SAMUEL TARR. Gasper Tarr, the paternal grandfather of Samuel Tarr, was a native of Westmoreland county, Pa., and married Annie Taylor, who was born in Ligonier Valley of the same county. They had the following children: Annie, Nancy, Gasper C., Martha, John T., Mary M. and Ellen.

Gasper C., father of Samuel Tarr, is at present living on a farm with his son Philip, in East Huntingdon township, Westmoreland county. He married Jane Butterworth, daughter of John Butterworth, a native of Fayette county, Pa. The children born to their union were: Samuel, Mary A., Philip, Martha, John, Buell, Gasper, Emma, George, Maggie, Irwin and James—all living. He was a soldier in the Civil War; served in the Sixty-second Regiment of Pennsylvania Volunteers for two years and four months. He took part in the battles of Cold Harbor, Spottsylvania, Fair Oaks and quite a number of other battles around Richmond.

Samuel Tarr was born in Westmoreland county, Pa., May 16, 1853; was educated in the common schools of that county and at Mt. Pleasant Classical and Scientific Institute. On leaving college he taught school for six years in Westmoreland county. In 1880 he accepted the position of assistant agent of P. R. R. Co. at Dunbar, under W. N. Roddy; was made principal agent of P. R. R. Co., in 1883, at the same place, and still holds the position. In 1878 he was married to Miss Ella McKean, a daughter of James McKean, of Westmoreland county. They have three children: Homer, Scott and Nannie.

Mr. Tarr is a member of the Methodist Episcopal church at Dunbar, and has been a member of the church for sixteen years, and has been trustee and steward of the same.

BUELL TARR was born March 4, 1862, near Tarr's Station, in Westmoreland county, Pa. His father, Gasper C. Tarr, was born in Westmoreland county, Pa., in about 1835, married Jane Buttermore, a native of Fayette county and of German descent.

Gasper O. Tarr was a miner, but later in life was a farmer. Ten children were born to this marriage: Samuel, Mary A., Philip, Martha E., John, Buell, Gasper, Emma, George, Maggie, Irwin and James. Buell Tarr was educated in the common schools of Westmoreland county and at Mt. Pleasant Institute. He taught school two terms in Westmoreland county, came to Dunbar as assistant agent for the P. R. R. Co., and in capacity he served for over three years. In October, 1887, he became clerk for the Dunbar Furnace Company, the position he still retains.

He was married in 1885 to Nancy J. Ellenberger, a daughter of Elijah Ellenberger, and a resident of Westmoreland county. They have the following named children: Walter Lewis and Cora Belle.

Mr. Tarr is a member of the Methodist Episcopal church, and has been for about ten years past. He is one of the trustees of the church at Dunbar, and is secretary of the board, and has been the superintendent of the Sabbath school for two years.

His father served for three years in the Civil War.

JAMES W. STOUFFER, one of Connellsville's leading liverymen and an energetic and clear-headed business man, is a son of John D., and Betsey (Cunningham) Stouffer, and was born in Dunbar township, Fayette county, Pa., March 25, 1845.

John D. Stouffer was born in Lancaster county, Pa., in 1803, and at three years of age accompanied his parents to Fayette county. He was a miller by trade, but gave most of his time and attention to farming. He was a republican, a member of the Presbyterian church and died in 1879. His wife was a daughter of Joseph H. Cunningham, a farmer and strong Presbyterian of Tyrone township. She died in 1856, aged fifty-three years.

James W. Stouffer was raised on a farm, attended the common-schools and was engaged in farming until 1871, when he came to Connellsville and accepted a clerkship with John Coulson. At the expiration of one year, he engaged as a clerk with Speers & Co., at Dunbar and remained with them for one year. In 1875 he removed to Connellsville and engaged in his present livery business.

In 1875 he was married to Miss Elizabeth Pritchard, daughter of Benjamin Pritchard. They have two children: Charles H., and Harriet F.

J. W. Stouffer's livery, feed and sale stables have always received a liberal patronage. His premises are commodious, stables well ventilated and a large stock of fine carriages, excellent buggies and carefully selected horses, are constantly kept on hand for the accommodation of his numerous patrons. Prompt attention and careful consideration are given to every want of the traveling public in his line of business. J. W. Stouffer is a republican and a member of the Methodist Episcopal church. He is a Mason, Odd Fellow, K. of P., Heptasoph, and a member of the Royal Arcanum. His business ability is amply attested by the permanent success he has attained.

JOHN M. TAYLOR was born in Bullskin township, Fayette county, Pa., January 26, 1857. His grandfather, Isaac Taylor, was born in 1792, and was the father of John, Mary, Robert, Margaret and Lizzie. J. M. Taylor's father, John Taylor, was born at Connellsville, in about 1810; was a farmer, but in 1867 he engaged in the coke business, at which he continued till 1873. He married Matilda McCrea in about 1836, a daughter of

John McCrea, who was a native of Indiana county, Pa.

John M. Taylor was educated in the common schools of the county, and at Elder Ridge Academy in Indiana county. He engaged in the mercantile business at Dunbar in 1878.

In June, 1886, he was married to Miss M. Agnes Nennon, daughter of Bernard Nennon of German birth, a resident of Dunbar. They have the following named children: Wilson and Bernard. Mr. Taylor is a member of the Presbyterian church, and is one of the trustees of the church at Dunbar.

The family of his father consisted of the following named children: Mary E., Rachel, Margaret S., Isaac, Jane L., John M. and Leslie L. His father died in 1875.

GEORGE W. WAGNER'S maternal grandfather, William Holland, was a native of Fayette county, Pa., and resided at Uniontown up to the time of his death in 1858. He married Miss Mary Ellis, by whom he had the following children: Ellis, Sarah, Jane, Ann (deceased) and Rebecca, the latter the mother of the subject of this sketch.

Joseph Wagner (father) was born in about 1829 in Fayette county. He was a blacksmith by trade, and worked at that business on the national pike at Uniontown and Searights. He was one of the old pike boys and drove a team from Uniontown to Cumberland for about four years before the B. & O. R. R. was built to Uniontown. He married Miss Rebecca Holland in 1849, and they had the following children: Watson, George W., Martha, Rachel and Ellis. His wife died, and he married for his second wife Martha Holland, a sister of his first wife. They had the following children: Paris, Mary, Tillie and Samuel. Joseph Wagner removed to Mahoning county, Ohio, in about 1886, and is a farmer.

George W. Wagner was born May 29, 1851, in Menallen township, Fayette county, Pa., and was educated in the common schools, principally at Uniontown. He is a brickmaker by trade, having worked at his trade from the age of sixteen years, up to 1888, since that he has been engaged with the Dunbar Furnace Company, with the exception of three years he spent in Illinois making brick.

George W. Wagner came to Dunbar in 1869, where he remained until 1874, when he went to Tazewell county, Illinois, remained for three years, and returned to Dunbar, where he now resides. In 1879 he was married to Hattie Artis, and has one child, Christy, born in 1880. Mr. Wagner is a member of the Jr. O. U. A. M.

Christy Artis (father of Mrs. Wagner) was born July 11, 1822, and married Mary A. McDowal in 1841. They had the following children: Bertha, Irwin, John A., Mary Ellen and Hattie. He was a farmer by occupation. Christy Artis served three years as county treasurer of Fayette county from 1876 including 1878.

THOMAS W. WATT was born in Donegal county, Ireland. His great-grandparents on both sides of the family were of Scotch origin.

His grandfather, John Watt, a native of Ireland, was married to Mary Ann Breading, and had the following children: John, Sarah, George, Mary, Martha and Elizabeth.

George Watt (father) was born in Ireland, was a farmer and was married to Jane Wilson, a daughter of Thomas Williams, also a native of Ireland. They had the following children: Martha, John, Mary Ann, Sarah, Margaret, Eliza, Thomas W. William and Jane. Thomas W. Watt was born in the county of Donegal, Ireland, August 12, 1828, and came to America in June,

1853, in the ship "Helen Thompson." He settled near Dunbar, and was in the employ of his brother, in the Union Furnace owned by John Watt & Co. . He took charge of the mill and store at the furnace for his brother; in 1856 his brother sold out, and the furnace was purchased by Baldwin and Cheeney, and T. W. Watt became their general superintendent for one year, when he resigned that position and went to manufacturing coke for same firm for one year. In 1858 he purchased a farm near Dunbar, where he now lives. The following year he built one section of the Fayette county railroad, known as the Baltimore and Ohio branch, from Connellsville to Uniontown, and carried on farming at the same time. In 1860 he started in the manufacture of oil barrels, at which he continued for three years. In 1864 he engaged in the lumber business, in this he remained for about two years. As superintendent of "The New York and New England Petroleum Oil Co." he commenced boring for oil in Dunbar township, and worked at it until 1868. He assisted to organize the coal and coke company, known as "The Taylor, Watt & Co. Uniondale Coke Works." In 1872 he aided in organizing another company, known as the "Hogsett, Watt & Co. Coke Co.," at Mt. Braddock. In 1873 he organized the Henderson, Watt & Co. Coke works, known as the Anchor Coke works. He was the superintendent of the works at Mt. Braddock and one for Taylor, Watt & Co. He continued in the coke business until 1878. Since 1878 he has resided on his farm, at intervals furnishing the Connellsville Coke and Iron Co., at Leisenring, with supplies for their pits. He was married in 1856 to Sarah Stevenson, a native of Ireland. They have the following children: Jennie, Lavinia, William, Margaret A., Martha S., John, James S. and George. Mr. Watt and wife are members of the Presbyterian church. He has been a member since seventeen years of age, and his wife since 1846. Their children are also members of the same church, except William, who died when an infant. Mr. Watt has been a ruling elder in the church for eighteen years. He was mainly instrumental in establishing a Presbyterian church at Dunbar. In the early beginning of railroads, only a few Presbyterians lived at Dunbar. At Connellsville was the nearest church, and in order that they might be able to attend Mr. Watt and Joseph Paull had a hand car built which carried them to Connellsville to church. After a time the hand car was too small to accommodate the people, and Mr. Watt chartered a special car for their use, at a monthly cost of thirty dollars. Members of other churches using this train were charged half fare. This continued till a Presbyterian church was organized at Dunbar, with a membership of eighty-four members. He gave the ground for the church building and the parsonage and contributed largely towards erecting the building. The church at present numbers 157 members. He also gave the ground for the Methodist Protestant church.

CHARLES H. WAYS, dealer in fine watches, clocks and jewelry at Connellsville, was born at Cumberland, Maryland, May 24, 1850, and is a son of Joseph H. and Elizabeth (Miller) Ways.

Joseph H. Ways was born in Maryland in 1827. He is a member of the Catholic church, a democrat, and was engaged for several years in the confectionery business at Cumberland, where he now resides. He was a member of the city council for several years. His wife was born in 1829. She is a daughter of Conrad Miller, a native of Germany,

Charles H. Ways was educated in the select schools and academy in Cumberland. Leaving school, he learned the trade of jeweler with P. J. Smith and S. T. Little of the same place. In January, 1875, he came to Connellsville and engaged in the jewelry business, in which he is successfully engaged at the present time. June 27, 1887, he married Miss Josephine, daughter of Frank T. Browning, a lumber dealer at Ohio Pyle Falls, and a native of Garrett county, Md. They have one child: Arthur Ways.

Charles H. Ways is a member of the Catholic church and is a democrat. Mr. Ways' jewelry establishment is at No. 32, Main street, Connellsville, and contains a large stock of valuable goods, embracing fine gold and silver watches, the latest fashionable jewelry, rich designs in silver ware, and a complete assortment of novelties in crockery and art goods. The repairing department is fully equipped for repairing all kinds of work in his line. Mr. Ways personally superintends all his work, and enjoys an ample patronage and a well-merited popularity.

REV. NATHAN GRIER WHITE was born at Fagg's Manor, Chester county, Pennsylvania, April 11, 1810.

Nathan Grier (maternal grandfather) was born near Easton, Lehigh county, Pennsylvania. He was a Prebyterian minister, and pastor of the Presbyterian church of the "Forks of Brandywine," Chester county, Pennsylvania. He married Susanna Smith and they had the following children: Nancy S., Robert S. (a Presbyterian preacher, pastor for fifty-four years of the church at Tom's Creek, Adams county, Pennsylvania), Martha, who married Samuel Park, a Presbyterian preacher, of Chester county, Pennsylvania, pastor of Slate Ridge church, York county, Pennsylvania; John N. C., who succeeded his father as pastor of the church of Brandywine Manor for fifty-two years, and Sarah, who married a physician, Robert Thompson.

Abner White (paternal grandfather) was born near Norristown; Montgomery county, Pennsylvania, and was married to Jane McCrea, who was born and raised in Montgomery county, Pennsylvania. They had children named: Joseph, Robert, William, James, and two daughters, Martha and Hannah.

Rev. Robert White (father of Rev. N. G. White) was born July 26, 1784, near Norristown, Montgomery county, Pennsylvania. He was a Presbyterian preacher, pastor of the church of Fagg's Manor for twenty-six years, and preached till his death in September 20, 1835.

On June 1, 1809, he was married to Miss Nancy S. Grier, who died September 27, 1870. They had six children: Nathan G., Robert M., Sarah J., Anna E., Martha and Mary E.

Rev. Nathan G. White spent three and one-half years at West Nottingham Academy, Cecil county, Maryland, preparatory to entering Dickinson College, Carlisle, Pa.; entered that college in 1826 and was graduated in 1828. He spent two years in teaching in classical schools—one year in Reading, Pa., and one year in Harford county, Md. He entered the Theological Seminary at Princeton, N. J., in 1830, and took the full course of three years' study and was graduated in theology in October. 1833.

He was licensed to preach in October, 1833, by the Presbytery of New Castle. He received calls from McConnellsburg, Greenhill and Wells Valley churches, was ordained and installed as pastor of these churches, on June 11, 1834, by the Presbytery of Carlisle, and served them till 1864. Having received a unanimous call from the church he went to Williamsburg, Blair county, Pa., in the Presbytery of Huntingdon, where he remained as pastor till the spring of 1883, when he resigned his charge on account of age, and came to New Haven, where he still resides and preaches occasionally, as age and its attendant infirmities permit.

He was married to Susan Mayers on January 31, 1837. They had one child: Robert G., who died while in the army during the late Civil War.

He was married a second time, on November 1, 1842, to Catherine McDowell, of Franklin county, Pa. They had the following children: Thomas H., Anna M. and Edwin M.

Thomas Henry, the only living son of Rev. N. G. White, is a practicing physician of Connellsville, and is a man of recognized ability in his profession. He is a young man of thorough education, both literary and professional. (See his sketch.)

Rev. White has been a power in the Presbyterian church in Pennsylvania. His counsel is sought by the clergy and laity in his neighborhood and throughout the Presbytery. He is esteemed as an "Elder of Israel," a "Holy man of God."

DR. THOMAS H. WHITE, a prominent physician and surgeon of Connellsville, was born at McConnellsburgh, Fulton county, Pa., October 26, 1845. His father, Rev. N. G. White, married Catherine McDowell, of Franklin county, Pa. He was born at Fagg's Manor, an old place of Revolutionary note in Pennsylvania. (See his sketch.)

Of Rev. N. G. White's four children two are now living: Mrs. Captain W. L. Neff, of New Haven, and Dr. Thomas H. White, the subject of this sketch, who was educated in the common schools of Fulton county, and afterwards attended Tuscarora Academy, which at that time was under the control of J. H. Shoemaker. Subsequently he entered Princeton College, and was graduated in 1867, ninth in a class of ninety. Leaving college he soon began the study of medicine, and in 1870 was graduated from Jefferson Medical College, Philadelphia. The first twelve years of his practice was done at Williamsburg, Pa., when he came to Connellsville. At Connellsville he has built up a large and paying practice, and has the reputation of being an excellent physician. In 1873 he was married to Miss Clara V. Ake, a granddaughter of the founder of Williamsburg. They have three children. He is medical examiner for the Royal Arcanum of Connellsville, is also the efficient secretary of the board of pension examiners, Connellsville district, and has been for seven years or since the organization of the board. He is a member of the Presbyterian church.

EDWARD Y. WHITE, of Connellsville, was born April 21, 1842, in Bullskin township, Fayette county, Pa., and is the son of Henry and Elizabeth (Giles) White.

Stouffel White (grandfather) came from Germany in 1750, and was among the first settlers in Bullskin township. He came to the site of Gillmore's Mill and built a grist-mill and distillery. He owned two mills, eight farms and eight hundred acres of land in Ohio. He married Peggy Poe, a niece of Andrew Poe, the celebrated Indian fighter. To their union were born seven children: Henry, David, Peter, George, Sarah, Peggy and Mary.

Henry White born January 2, 1799, was a miller by trade, and married Elizabeth Giles, on August 14, 1826. Their children were as follows: Christopher C., born May 27, 1827; engaged in work on a boat that plied the Mississippi river and was never heard of after leaving home; Samuel B., born November 23, 1828, died May 2, 1880; he was a contractor at Connellsville; George W., born October 27, 1830, a patternmaker, resides at McKeesport; Elizabeth A., born November 3, 1832, wife of John McCormick and lives in Illinois; David S., born December 9, 1834, was a carpenter by trade; Eliza C., born April 30, 1836, wife of John Kerr of New Haven; Henry B., born February 24, 1838, tank and rig builder at Findlay, Ohio; Mary E., born July 29, 1840, wife of John Trader, lives at Pennsville; Edward; Sarah J., born July 21, 1844, wife of James English, resides in Pittsburgh; Minerva E., born August 20, 1846, the widow of H. J. English, and lives in Birmingham, Ala.

Samuel Giles (grandfather) whose father was killed at Braddock's defeat at Braddock's Fields, was born in 1766; came to Fayette county in 1814, and married Dorotha Day. Their children were eight in number: Anna, Dolly, Mary, Sallie, dead; John, Thomas, Elizabeth (mother) and Samuel.

Edward Y. White was educated in the subscription schools of the county. He enlisted August 12, 1862, in Company H, One Hundred and Forty-second Pennsylvania Volunteers, commanded by Captain J. M. Du Shane, and was mustered out May 15, 1865. He fought in the battles of Fredericksburg, Wilderness and Gettysburg; at the latter place he was wounded in the leg and taken prisoner; when exchanged he went back to his regiment then before Richmond; on June 18, 1864, in a charge on Fort Hell, he was again wounded in the leg and entirely disabled for active service.

He married on April 27, 1868, Florence Henrietta, daughter of John K. and Elizabeth Brown of Connellsville, a lineal descendant of General Warren of Revolutionary fame. Three children have been born to them: Alice Kate, born April 29, 1869; John Henry, born August 13, 1871, and Samuel Basil, born March 15, 1884.

Edward Y. White was engaged in the confectionery business in Connellsville for seven years; he is now a traveling salesman for the firm of Boyts, Porter & Co., of Connellsville. He has been a supervisor of the construction and operation of coke works for Hutchinson & Bro., McClure & Co., Colonel J. M. Schoonmaker, and A. O. Tintsman. He served in the N. G. P. for five years and was first lieutenant at the expiration of his term of service.

He has passed the chairs in General Worth Lodge, No. 386, I. O. O. F., and in Council, No. 346, of R. A.; he also belongs to Lodge No. 239, K. P., and is a Master Mason. He is a man of extended business experience, and his services are always in demand.

SAMUEL D. WOODS, a leading dentist of Connellsville and a soldier of the late Civil War, was born at Rogersville, near Waynesburg, Greene county, Pa., January 20, 1848. He is a son of Samuel and Leah (Divers) Woods.

His grandfather, Samuel Woods, Sr., was a native of New Jersey and was twice married. His second wife was Miss Mary Ann McCoy, by whom he had seven children. He removed to Washington county, was elected constable and meeting with reverses of fortune he died soon afterwards. One of his sons, Samuel, was apprenticed to A. Shannon to learn the trade of shoemaker. After completing his trade he married Miss Leah Divers. They had eleven children. Samuel Woods was born March 16, 1803, and died June 21, 1887. His wife was born December 4, 1805, and died June 6, 1885. She was a daughter of John and Anna (Ford) Divers, the latter afterwards married John Scott.

Samuel D. Woods was educated in the common schools and Waynesburg College. In 1868 he studied dentistry with Dr. Kramer, of Greensboro, Greene county, Pa., and after six years' practice he went to Chicago and learned the finer and more difficult parts of dentistry. After three years' practice in the city of Chicago and vacinity he returned to Pennsylvania and located at Connellsville, where he has built up a large and lucrative practice. In 1869 he married Miss Alice, daughter of Daniel Coughenour, of Greensboro, Pa. They have five children: Margaret L., James B., Alfred H., John Y. and Flora A. At the age of seventeen years he entered the Union service, enlisted in Company K, Sixteenth Pennsylvania Cavalry, and served till the end of the war.

He belongs to the Royal Arcanum; is a member of the Presbyterian church, and a prohibitionist. He has an interest in a large tract of valuable mineral land in Eastern Virginia, and is a skillful dentist and one of the enterprising citizens of Connellsville.

EBENEZER FINLEY WOODWARD, a prosperous farmer and stock raiser, was born in Dunbar township, Fayette county, Pa., September 11, 1840, and is a son of Davis and Mary (Boyd) Woodward.

His grandfather, Caleb Woodward, came from Chester county, Pa., to near New Salem, early in the present century. He was born in 1799 and died October 18, 1856, and was married to Phebe McCarty, and had six children, five daughters and one son. Mrs. Woodward was born 1780 and died December 4, 1856. His father, Davis Woodward, was born in Menallen township, June 11, 1806 and died April 6, 1882. He was a farmer and stock dealer, a truthful man and consistent member of the Presbyterian church. On November 2, 1828, he was married to Phebe, a daughter of Judge Robert and Rebecca (Work) Boyd. They had thirteen children. One of their daughters, Rebecca, married Hon. Charles S. Beatty, member of the Pennsylvania legislature. Mrs. Woodward was born April 13, 1810. Her grandfather, William Boyd, was a native of Ireland and settled in Tyrone township. His father was killed by the Indians on the Potomac river, April 13, 1757.

Ebenezer F. Woodward was reared on a farm and received his education in the common schools, and has since been engaged in farming and stock raising.

On March 25, 1869, he was married to Elma, daughter of George Cox. They have had ten children born and named as follows: Elizabeth, January 15, 1870; Dempsey, March 5, 1871; George, June 28, 1873, Mary, March 2, 1875; Jessie, November 12, 1876; Jennie, November 1, 1878; Finley, November 8, 1880: Belle (dead); Joseph, July 29, 1884, and Elma, May 10, 1887.

Mr. Woodward is road commissioner of Dunbar township and is a member of the K. of P. and the J. O. of U. A. M. at Leisenring. He is a member of the Presbyterian church and is a prudent, careful and reliable business man.

JAMES A. ZIMMERMAN, a leading grocer of Connellsville, is a son of Jacob E. and Anna (Houck) Zimmerman, natives of Fulton and Franklin counties, Pa., respectively. His father is one of the leading farmers of Fulton county, where he owns a fine farm of four hundred acres of land.

The grandfather of James A., George Zimmerman, born in Pennsylvania, and was in his day one of the leading farmers and merchants of Fulton till his death in 1867.

Jacob Zimmerman, the great-grandfather of the subject of this sketch, was born in Pennsylvania, making the Zimmerman family one of the earliest that settled in Pennsylvania. He was of German origin, and a farmer and miller of Franklin county. J. A. Zimmerman's maternal grandfather, Michael Houck, was also of German extraction, and followed farming in Franklin county. James A. Zimmerman was born in Fulton county, Pa., February 27, 1851.

Reared on the farm, educated in the common schools of his native county, and at the Normal school at Shippensburg, Pa. He afterwards graduated from the commercial college at Williamsport, Pa., in 1876. At the age of twenty years he began teaching district school in Fulton and Lycoming counties. In 1881 he went to Altoona, where he was engaged as a teacher in the commercial college. He continued to teach therein till 1883, when he located at Connellsville and started in the grocery business, and has been very successful in building up one of the most paying mercantile businesses at Connellsville. He is a member of the Methodist Episcopal church; of the Masonic fraternity; of Knights of Pythias; of the Knights of the Golden Eagle; of the Senior Order of American Mechanics; of the Heptasophs, and is a republican. He was married in 1884 to Miss Carrie Fields, of Hancock, Md. They have one child: Etta. Mr. Zimmerman is a stockholder in the Connellsville Flint and Glass Works, and is also interested in a loan association at Minneapolis, Minn. He owns considerable property at Garden City, Kansas, and is one of the most enterprising and progressive young business men of the county.

HON. WILLIAM DAVIDSON (deceased). The late Hon. William Davidson was a distinguished citizen of Fayette county. A man of fine intellect, he was born in Carlisle, Cumberland county, Pa., February 14, 1783, and died at Connellsville, March 2, 1867, aged eighty-four years. He was descended from a Davidson who was a native of the north of Ireland, and was a resident of Londonderry during its celebrated siege.

William Davidson was a surveyor in Cumberland county, came to Connellsville in 1808, where he remained during his long and useful life; was engaged in farming, merchandising and in the iron business. Mr. Davidson was manager of Laurel Iron Works, and afterwards proprietor of Break-neck Furnace. In the War of 1812 he was taken prisoner at the disgraceful surrender of Detroit.

He served several years in the legislature of Pennsylvania, was speaker of the house in 1818, and afterwards served acceptably in the State senate. On December 19, 1813, he was married to Mrs. Sarah (Rogers) Blackstone, a woman of great talent and wonderful energy. They had five children: Thomas R., a prominent lawyer of western Pennsylvania, married Isabella Austin, and died November 3, 1875; William H.; John R., dead; Col. Daniel R., dead, and Sarah, wife of Baldwin Norton, of Ohio, and dead. Mrs. Sarah Davidson died November 21, 1856, aged seventy-two years.

William Davidson read the Bible through twice before he was nine years of age, and mastered the Latin, Greek and Hebrew languages without a teacher. He was over six feet in height, and of fine personal address. He was an "Old Line Whig," a member of the Disciple church, a fluent talker and a perfect gentleman.

The late Col. Daniel Rogers Davidson, fourth son of Hon. William Davidson, was born at Connellsville, January 12, 1820. He attended school; gave no heed to his lessons, but seemed to acquire knowledge by intuition. At sixteen he was placed in charge of a farmer, and his wonderful management of the land and stock gave promise of a future successful career.

In 1846 he was married to Miss M. C. Johnston. Col. Davidson was the master-spirit—acting quietly but all-powerfully—in the successful development of Fayette county's wonderful mineral resources. To him Fayette county principally owes her connection with the outside world by railways. Against great opposition he was largely instrumental in securing a railroad from Pittsburgh to Connellsville (the present Pittsburgh division of the B. & O. R. R.) He was the principal promoter of the Fayette County Railroad, and was the originator of the project for building the Southwest Pennsylvania Railroad. In 1884 Col. Davidson repaired to Hot Springs, Ark., on account of his health, and where he died on March 18th of the same year. His remains were brought home and interred in the Connellsville cemetery. He always took great interest in the history of Fayette county. "He liked politics intensely for the field it opened for the play of his forces, but he did not care for office. Sensible persons never questioned Col. Daniel Davidson's judgment, his prognostic powers, his great capacity and energy. The history of Fayette county will be searched in vain for one native born the superior of Col. Davidson in all that goes to make great manhood."

GEORGES, GERMAN, NICHOLSON AND REDSTONE

MAJOR ISAAC M. ABRAHAM was born in Georges (now Nicholson) township November 13, 1817, and is a son of James Abraham, a soldier in the War of 1812, and served in a company from Fayette county, under Gerneral Harrison. In the siege of Fort Meigs his horse was shot from under him.

His grandfather, Enoch Abraham, came from Chester county, Pa., and settled on York's Run (a branch of George's Creek) in about 1780. Isaac Morgan Abraham, brother of James Abraham, was murdered by the Indians at the mouth of the Cumberland river in 1790. Enoch Abraham, the grandfather of the subject of this sketch, married Jane Hamilton, a sister of Judge Hamilton, of Washington county, Pa., who figured so conspicuously in the whisky insurrection, and was elected to congress while imprisoned in Philadelphia in 1794. He was afterwards pardoned by the president of the United States.

Major I. M. Abraham was married to Sarah Ann Showalter on March 16, 1843. Mrs. Abraham was a daughter of John Showalter, who came from Rockingham county, Va., and settled on York's Run in 1806. She died April 6, 1887, in her sixty-seventh year. She an amiable Christian woman, held to the Presbyterian faith, and was the mother of eight children, five of whom survived her.

Major Abraham was born and raised on a farm, and followed the occupation of farmer until the breaking out of the Rebellion in 1861, when he joined the Union army as captain of Company G, Eighty-fifth Regiment Pennsylvania Infantry Volunteers, the history of which is his history, and want of space will not admit of our giving more than a glance at the record of one who served at the front for over three years. We take the following from an article by Captain McHenry, formerly captain of Company K and adjutant of Eighty-fifth Regiment, in *Philadelphia Weekly Press*, of July 3, 1886:

"Major I. M. Abraham was a native of Fayette county. He had recruited Company G, which he brought into the regiment, and had served continuously with it since its organization. A man of quiet, modest demeanor, but who did possess a large stock of good common sense, which, with his unquestioned courage and determination, enabled him to act with good judgment." The Eighty-fifth Regiment left Uniontown in November, 1861, with ten full companies of over one thousand men, encamped around Washington City, D. C., through the winter of '61 and '62, and landed at Fort Monroe April 1, 1862, and at once joined the Army of the Potomac, under McClellan, in front of Yorktown, participating in all the principal battles of the Peninsula, losing eighty-four men, killed and wounded. At the close of that campaign, in August, 1862, Captain Abraham was the only original captain with the regiment, all the others having resigned and gone home, except Captain Purviance, who had been promoted to lieutenant-colonel. When the Army of the Potomac came North from Harrison's Landing the Eighty-fifth Regiment was sent to Suffolk, Va., from where it made frequent raids to the Black Water, making skirmishes with and annoying the enemy in that quarter. On December 6th, with Wessel's brigade, the Eighty-fifth went to New Berne, N. C., and joined General Foster, who commanded the Eighteenth Army Corps, and immediately started to destroy a Rebel gunboat at Whitehall, on the Nuce river, and burn a bridge at Goldsboro. They defeated the Rebel army under Petigrew, at West Creek, Kingston, Whitehall and Goldsboro; succeeded in destroying the gunboat and burning the bridge. In January, 1863, the Eighty-fifth left its old brigade and sailed for South Carolina, arriving at Port Royal February 1st following. The Eighty-fifth took a conspicuous part in the siege of Morris Island and Fort Wagner. At the latter place Lieutenant-Colonel Purviance was killed, August 30th. No other field officer being with the regiment, Captain Abraham, being the senior line officer, assumed command of the same until the following May, with the exception of three weeks commanded by Lieutenant-Colonel Edward Campbell, of Uniontown.

After the close of the siege of Morris Island the enlisted men of the regiment gave evidence of their appreciation by presenting Captain Abrahan with a sword, sash and belt costing $350. He knew nothing of the matter until its presentation, while the regiment was on dress parade. "Captain I. M. Abraham, from the enlisted men of the Eighty-fifth Pennsylvania Infantry Volunteers," is the inscription on the sword. About this time Governor Curtin surprised Captain Abraham by sending him (unsolicited) a major's commission, dated September 8, 1863. Although in command of the regiment, Captain Abraham declined being mustered, as he was the senior captain of the Tenth Corps, with which his regiment was then serving. In April, 1864, after bringing his regiment back to Virginia, he was, at the request of General Terry, commanding the division, mustered as major, April 28, 1864, and, with one single exception, the Eighty-fifth was never under fire without Major Abraham with them, that was on Augus 16, 1864, when he was unable for duty because of a wound received near Deep Bottom the day before. On expiration of term of service, November 22, 1864, his regiment was mustered out at Pittsburgh, Pa., Major Abraham, at the time, being detailed to assist Colonel Mulford in the exchange of prisoners at Savannah, Ga. When they arrived off that city, they found Sherman thundering at its gates, and they sailed for Charleston, S. C., where they received 15,000 exchanged and starving prisoners, among whom was Colonel "Andy" Stewart, of this county, returning with the exchanged men in a fleet of thirty-two vessels to Annapolis, Md., and from there Major Abraham returned home, December 25, 1864. Major Abraham is a member of "Jerry Jones" Post, No. 541, G. A. R., at Smithfield, Pa.

CAPTAIN JAMES ABRAHAM, of Scotch-Irish lineage and a brave soldier in the war of the great Rebellion, is a son of James and Mary (Jones) Abraham, and was born in Georges (now Nicholson) township, November 14, 1830.

James Abraham was a soldier of the War of 1812, was in Captain James McClelland's company of cavalry and fought at Tippecanoe and Fort Meigs, where he had a horse shot from under him. He was a whig and afterwards a republican. A member of no church, yet a liberal contributor to all. His wife was a member of the Mt. Moriah Baptist church. He owned a fine farm of 280 acres and was a moral, upright man. He was born in Fayette county, December, 19, 1786, and died January, 1862. He married Miss Mary Jones, and unto them were born eleven children: Sarah (dead), Isaac, Aaron Jones (dead), Jane, Elizabeth (dead), Mary, Enoch H. and A. Jones (twins), James, Caroline (dead), and William. Enoch was one of the fifteen hundred passengers lost on the steamer Independence, that went down off the coast of California, February 16, 1853. William was a sergeant in the Fourteenth Pennsylvania Cavalry and died in Jarvis hospital, at Baltimore, of disease contracted in the Shenandoah Valley, under Sheridan in 1864, and sleeps in the Baptist cemetery at Smithfield.

Captain Abraham was reared on a farm and educated in the common schools. He went to Virginia in 1854, was engaged in business there until the spring of 1861, when he returned home and, in connection with Captain George W. Gilmore, recruited a company of cavalry under a special order from General McClellan; was elected and commissioned first lieutenant of the same, and with the company was mustered into the service at Clarksburg, Va., July 24, 1861, as "Pennsylvania Dragoons," and immediately sent to the front.

His company scouted over most of the counties of West Virginia, from the Pennsylvania to the Kentucky line and encountered in their line of duty every conceivable hardship of military life. Captain Abraham was in the battles of Carnifex Ferry and Cotton Mountain, and in six months thirty-five per cent. of the company were killed or wounded. In 1862 he served under General Pope and took part in the second Bull Run battle. After Pope's retreat, his company led McClellan's advance into Maryland and fought gallantly at South Mountain and on the blody field of Antietam. After the last battle the company helped drive J. E. B. Stuart across the Potomac, when Captain Abraham was ordered back to Clarksburg.

In 1863 he was with Colonel Tolland in an ill-starred raid to Wytheville, where twenty-two out of thirty men of the company engaged were killed and wounded. In 1864 he was with Generel Averill in his celebrated cavalry raids. He was next with General Hunter in his disastrous Lynchburg expedition, later served in the Shenandoah Valley under Generals Crook and Averill, and participated in the fights at Stephenson's Depot and Winchester. Afterwards his company was engaged in the pursuit of the Confederate force that burned Chambersburg, July 30, 1864, and helped to drive it into the mountains of West Virginia. At Wheeling, W. Va., August 24, 1864, he was mustered out of the Federal service, after thirty-seven months of continuous hard fighting and marching.

Capt. Abraham wrote a very accurate and interesting account of his company and its campaigns, which has been published in the *Republican Standard*. Returning home from the army, he engaged in farming for two years, when he removed to Springhill Furnace, and engaged in stock raising until 1873. From 1873 to 1876 he was a resident of Smithfield, removed thence to his present comfortable residence in Nicholson township.

On May 16, 1868 he was married to Miss Jennie, daughter of Capt. James O'Donovan. Of this union nine children have been born:

William R., Mary, Roy, Hayes, Lucy Gertrude, Donald, Perie, Jones Rudolph and Birdie Abrahams. He owns 50 acres of the home farm, and his sister Mary, resides with him, and owns an additional twenty-five acres of the same farm. He was engaged in carrying the mail and operated a hack line from Morgantown, W. Va., to Uniontown for several years. He is an Odd Fellow and is a prominent and influential republican of Fayette county. He is a member and was the first commander of Jerry Jones Post, No. 541, of the Grand Army of the Republic.

ROBERT JUNK ALLEN, a very pleasant gentleman and an industrious farmer of Georges township, is a son of Capt. Matthew and Elizabeth (Junk) Allen, and was born in North Union township, Fayette county, Pa., January 29, 1835.

His paternal great-grandfather, David Allen, married Susan White and came from Scotland to America in 1740, settled at Fagg's Manor, Chester county, and subsequently removed in 1772 to the Robert Smith farm. near Laurel Hill church, in Fayette county. One of his sons, George Allen, married Miss Jane, a sister of Col. James Paul. Their children were: Susan Hibben, Martha Miller, Mary Junk, Josiah (died unmarried in Ohio), and Matthew.

Matthew Allen married Elizabeth Catlin on June 2, 1822. Their children were: Matthew, Jr., a soldier in the Mexican War, died at Perote, November 15, 1847; Susan, wife of William B. McCormick, and Mary Ann, wife of John R. Crawford. Mrs. Allen died December 6, 1826: Mr. Allen was re-married December 15, 1831, to Miss Elizabeth Junk. To this union were born four children: George, born November 27, 1832, died March 18, 1860; Robert J.;' Josiah, born March 4, 1837, married Sarah M. Clark—children are: Mary Ann, Matthew, Nancy and George (deceased). Matthew Allen was a militia captain about 1830. He was elected sheriff of Fayette county, November 11, 1835, and was elected for a second term, October 8, 1850. He was very popular as a sheriff, well liked as a citizen, and died at Uniontown, August 17, 1875, and Mrs. Elizabeth Junk Allen died in Dunbar township March 29, 1872.

Robert Junk Allen was reared on a farm, received his education in the common schools, and taught successfully for a number of years, after which he engaged in his present business of farming. On December 29, 1870, he was married to Miss Bertha, daughter of Col. Jesse Bunker. They have three children: Lizzie, born October 19, 1871; Cora M. G., born August 3, 1875, and Rachel L., born February 26, 1880.

Robert Junk Allen owns a small but well-improved and very valuable farm in Georges township, and is a member of the Presbyterian church, a good neighbor and a respected citizen.

MILES S. ANDERSON, a steady-going and reliable merchant of Nicholson township, was born in Georges township, Fayette county, Pa., September 6, 1846, and is a son of Samuel and Nancy (Ross) Anderson. His father, Samuel Anderson, was born in Mt. Pleasant, Westmoreland county, Pa., in January, 1804. He came to Fayette county when a mere child. Learning the trade of a scythe-maker, he engaged in that business from 1820 to 1854, when he purchased a farm of 110 acres and passed the remainder of his days as a farmer. He was married to Nancy Ross, and they were the parents of eleven children: Margaret, John K., W. R., Sallie, Hannah, Miranda, Miles S. and Lou (twins), Elizabeth (dead), Mary Jane (dead), Ann (dead). Mrs. Anderson died March 10, 1866. Samuel

Anderson was a whig, afterwards became a republican, and was an honored deacon in the Mt. Moriah Baptist church. After a long, useful and honorable life, he passed from time to eternity September 19, 1886.

M. S. Anderson was educated in the common schools, and in Georges Creek Academy. He was engaged in farming in Georges township until 1870, when he purchased his present farm of seventy-nine acres in Nicholson township, where he has erected two fine residences, one of them containing a commodious store-room. His location was named Anderson's Cross Roads. In 1876 he engaged in the mercantile business, and has continued successfully up to the present time. He was appointed postmaster in 1876 and is at present holding that office. He was married in 1871 to Mary, daughter of Rev. B. F. Brown, and has two children: Laura and Lloyd. Mr. Anderson, with his wife and daughter, are members of the Baptist church. He is doing a good mercantile business, and is an upright and respected citizen.

JONAH ARISON, a well-informed gentleman and well-situated farmer, of German township, is a son of John and Catherine (Day) Arison, and was born in Loudoun county, Va., August 4, 1818.

His grandfather, Andrew Arison, was born and reared in New Jersey, but emigrated in early life to Virginia, where he was engaged in farming.

His father, John Arison, was a native of Virginia, a soldier of the War of 1812, emigrated in about 1820 to Uniontown, and in a short time removed to Georges township, and afterwards to Franklin township, where he died. He was a democrat and a member of the Baptist church. He married Miss Catherine, daughter of George Day, of Virginia, and reared a family of twelve children.

Jonah Arison was reared on a farm in Fayette county, and received his education in the subscription schools of his day. He chose farming as his life pursuit, was in Indiana for a time, but returned to Fayette county, he farmed for some time when he purchased his present highly productive farm in German township, and has been successfully engaged ever since in farming and stock raising.

In 1840 he married Miss Lydia A., daughter of Michael Franks, of German township. To their union were born six children: Elizabeth A., married Aaron Hostetler, killed in one of the Wilderness battles, and after his death she became the wife of W. A. Cofman; Simon F., married Susannah, daughter of Michael Franks, of German township; Emanuel (dead), William, Amanda E., wife of George N. Crable, and Mary C., wife of William Honsaker.

Jonah Arison is an extensive reader, and is conversant with the history of his country and the current events of the day. In political opinions he is a democrat, and has served his township as inspector, assessor and school director. He is a member of the Lutheran church at High House, and is widely known as a meritorious citizen and successful farmer.

REV. MALACHI CURTIS BAILEY, Ph. D., an earnest, able and efficient minister of the Presbyterian church, is a son of William S. and Elizabeth (Barker) Bailey. He was born at Sandy Lake, Mercer county, Pa., July 31, 1848, and is a descendant of a Yankee family on both his paternal and maternal side.

His father, William S. Bailey, was born in New York, in 1818, removed to Mercer county, Pa., when a young man, and settled on a farm. He is a democrat and a ruling elder in the Presbyterian church. He now resides at Leesburg, and near there he owns a farm of sixty-five acres. W. S. Bailey married Miss Elizabeth, daughter of Jason Barker, a farmer. They have had five children born to them: Rev. M. C., William Newil, a physician at East Liverpool, Ohio; Ada Belle, wife of T. J. Armstrong, of Leesburg; Jason (dead) and Everett (dead). Mrs. Bailey was born April 22, 1823, and has been a lifelong member of the Presbyterian church.

Rev. M. C. Bailey remained on the farm until at the age of fifteen years, when he engaged as a clerk in a store at Sandy Lake, and continued as such for four years. At nineteen years of age he engaged in a dry goods store at Meadville, where he clerked, at intervals, till 1875. In 1869 and 1870 he attended Westminster College, at Wilmington, Pa. From 1870 to 1875 he was a student in Allegheny College, at Meadville. During that time he was the author of the Kalamathean prize essay, and was also the successful one of ten competitors for a declamation prize, besides being elected, in the last year, valedictorian of the Franklin Literary Society. In 1875 he attended the Western Theological Seminary, at Allegheny City, and studied theology three years. In 1878 he was called as pastor to the Presbyterian church at Middletown, near Harrisburg, Pa., and served acceptably until 1881, when he came to Fairchance, where he has since labored zealously and efficiently for the best interests of his church.

October 10, 1878, he was married to Miss Brightie, daughter of Matthew Murdock, a skilled mechanic at Natrona, Pa. To their union have been born three children: Charles Hodge, Rose and Lily (twins), Rose being dead.

In 1886 Rev. M. C. Bailey completed the two years post graduate course of Wooster University, Ohio, and received the degree of doctor of philosophy. In 1885 he was elected stated clerk of the Redstone Presbytery, and in 1887 was a delegate from the same body to the general assembly of the Presbyterian church, at Omaha, Neb.

His charge embraces the Fairchance, Tent and McClellandtown churches, and includes one hundred square miles of territory. He has conducted over one hundred funerals in the last seven years, besides preaching three times every Sabbath. He reaches about four thousand people in his regular work, and through his able and practical sermons, published in the press of the county, addresses over 25,000 people.

DAVID DOWNS, one of the old and highly respected citizens of New Geneva, was born in Redstone township, Fayette county, Pa., September 9, 1812, and is a son of Jonathan and Mary (Miller) Downs.

Jonathan Downs was a son of Jeremiah Downs, an early settler and well-to-do farmer of Redstone township. Jonathan Downs was reared and educated in his native township, where he purchased a farm of 150 acres of desirable land and worked at his trade of a carpenter.

He married Miss Mary, daughter of Peter Miller, a farmer and early settler in Redstone township. They had ten children: Lucinda, David, Margaret (dead), Joseph M., Alexander C., William B., Jonathan, Caleb B., Isaac N. and Mary. Mr. Downs was a whig, an exemplary citizen and a worthy member of the Baptist church. He died September 9, 1844, and was buried at Uniontown.

David Downs was reared on a farm, educated in the subscription schools and learned the trade of carpenter. In 1836, he located at Brownsville in the manufacture of threshing machines. Two years later, he removed to New Geneva, purchased a lot, erected a dwelling-house, and continued in the threshing-machine business until 1863, when he, in company with Mr. James Davenport, a very respectable merchant of New Geneva, bought the Mellier Flouring Mill in that year, and operated it with his other business until 1885, when the partnership was dissolved.

On December 21, 1836, he married Miss Anna Harford, who died August 15, 1844. His second wife was Miss Sarah Campbell, to whom he was married November 2, 1845. She died September 9, 1850, leaving two children: Anna, wife of Mathias Hartley now living in Illinois, Caroline (now dead). He was married March 18, 1852, to Miss Ellen Thompson, and to this third union were born two children: Mary, wife of John A. Simpson, D.D., of Washington, Pa., and Ashabel F., an attorney-at-law and treasurer of Fayette county (see sketch). Mrs. Downs died September 6, 1855, and he was remarried April 16, 1862, to Miss Mary A. Way, daughter of Mr. Gideon, an early settler of this county, who died in 1866 in his eightieth year.

David Downs has been over fifty years a prudent, economical, straightforward and successful business man. He was a member of the Sons of Temperance, and is a republican. He is a substantial member of the Baptist church at Greensboro, Green county, of which his wife is also a member. Mr. Downs has lately retired from the cares of active business life. He stands high, wherever known, as an honest business man and a Christian gentleman.

ROBERT BRITT is a wealthy farmer of Georges township, living near Smithfield, and is now in the eighty-fifth year of his age. He is of Irish descent and the son of Robert and Mary (Lloyd) Britt.

His father was born in Philadelphia, on the 12th of January, 1772, and was a carpenter by trade. He removed to Springhill Furnace in Fayette county, in August, 1811, where he lived until he died, June 1, 1846. He was a Free Mason, and belonged to Fayette Lodge No. 228. He was an elder in the Baptist church. Mary Lloyd was the maiden name of his wife, who was born January 25, 1772, in Chester county, Pa. She was the daughter of John Lloyd, who was of Welch descent. She removed to Fayette county with her husband, and lived there till her death, May 5, 1862.

They were married October 16, 1793, and had eight children: Hannah, born December 29, 1794; John, born September 27, 1796; Elizabeth, born September 28, 1798; Levi, born December 29, 1800; Samuel, born March 1, 1803; Robert (subject), born June 4, 1805; Phoebe, born November 29, 1808, and Evan, born April 4, 1812.

DAVID R. COFFMAN, a leading farmer, was born in German township, Fayette county, Pa., February 5, 1834, and is a son of Andrew and Mary (Dunaway) Coffman, the former a native of Lancaster county, who settled near McClellandtown, the latter was born at Clarksburg, W. Va.

David R. Coffman received a plain education in the common schools of his native township. Leaving school he engaged in farming, and has continued at it most successfully up to the present time.

On October 9, 1856, he was united in marriage to Mary, a daughter of George Poundstone. Their union has been blessed with seven children, born and named as follows: Amy Ellen, October 1, 1857, wife of Winfield Johns; Larry Jasper, June 8, 1860, married Miss Lizze, daughter of Reuben Grove, of Luzerne township; George Ellsworth, February 10, 1863, died December 5, 1864; Isidore L., November 13, 1864, a machinist in Uniontown, Pa.; Ulysses W.,

November 8, 1869; Effie Verdie, April 30, 1874; Clara Oris, March 4, 1876, and Lena Dell, October 16, 1877.

David R. Coffman owns one of the most valuable farms in German township, containing 180 acres of land, and is underlaid with heavy veins of coal and limestone. He also owns a farm of 150 acres in Wharton township. He is a prominent member of the K. of P. at Uniontown, and an influential member of St. Jacob's Lutheran church. He is a democrat, a thorough-going business man, and is one of the county's most successful farmers.

ALFRED CORE, a popular justice of the peace, and the genial auctioneer of Smithfield, was born in German township, Fayette county, Pa., September 30, 1827, and is a son of Isaac and Jane (French) Core. His grandfather, Colonel Henry Core, was of German extraction and came to German township in an early day. He commanded a regiment of Pennsylvania militia. His father, Isaac Core, was born in 1790 and died in 1860. He was a farmer, and was county commissioner in 1821 and 1822. His wife was Jane French, daughter of Enoch French, the latter of Scotch-Irish descent, and a ruling elder of Dunlap's Creek Presbyterian church. Isaac Core had three sons: W. F., of Texas, Alfred and John C., of Franklin township.

Alfred Core was reared and educated in German township. His business up to the breaking out of the rebellion was farming and stock dealing. In 1863 he entered the quartermaster's department at Clarksburg, W. Va., and was afterwards transferred to Grafton, where he remained until 1865. After the war he located at Smithfield, and ran the Stentz House for eighteen months, when he engaged for three years in operating a hack line from Smithfield to Uniontown, and carried the United States mails. Relinquishing the hack line business he again engaged in stock dealing. In 1851 he was married to Miss Mary V. Sangston. They have two children: Rebecca Jane, wife of Absalom Howard, of Smithfield, and Emma R., married to James Abraham, Jr., of Greensburg, who is conductor on the Pennsylvania Central railroad. Mrs. Core's father, Hon. John A. Sangston, was born in 1803 and died is 1858. He was sheriff of Fayette county from 1829 to 1832, and a member of the Pennsylvania State senate from 1834 to 1838. He was not a speaker, but was a man of splendid natural ability. His wife was Miss Rebecca McClelland, of Uniontown. Alfred Core is a member of the I. O. of O. F., and Knights of the Golden Eagle. Before the war he was a lieutenant of a militia cavalry company and an aid-de-camp to General Ed. Swearingen. Although a republican, he has been elected for his fourth term of five years each as justice of the peace in a strong democratic township. For thirty-five years he has been a successful auctioneer. Squire Core is congenial and popular, an entertaining conversationalist, and inimitable in description of the humorous and ludicrous.

JOHN E. CRAFT, an influential citizen of Redstone township, was born on the farm which is now owned by Bashear Craft, in Redstone township, Fayette county, Pa., February 10, 1837, and is a son of John C. and Elizabeth (Colley) Craft. John C. Craft was born in Redstone township, in 1800. His wife was a daughter of John Colley who lived for many years in Redstone township, and died June 13, 1851. John E. Craft was married to Mary E. Jacobs, a daughter of William Jacobs (who died in 1868) of Redstone, June 28, 1869, at the Baptist church in Brownsville by Rev. Skinner. At the age of fourteen, he began working with a threshing machine and has followed that business continually ever since. He is known as the "king thresher" throughout Fayette county.

He is a leading member and elder in the Cumberland Presbyterian church at Pleasant View. His valuable farm in Redstone containing 130 acres, is underlaid with rich deposits of coal and limestone. He is a man of unflinching integrity and possesses fine business qualifications. In politics he is a democrat as were his father and grandfather.

ALEXANDER DEYARMAN, a retired farmer of Georges township, and ex-director of the Fayette county poor, is a son of Hugh and Isabella (Spratt) Deyarman, and was born in Georges township, Fayette county, Pa., October 12, 1801.

Hugh Deyarman was a native of County Down, Ireland, and emigrated at about the beginning of the present century to Georges township, where he engaged for a short time at Oliphant's Furnace as a common laborer. In 1812 he purchased a farm and engaged in farming. He married Isabella Spratt and their union was blessed with fifteen children.

Alexander Deyarman was reared on a farm and enjoyed the subscription-school privileges of his boyhood days. To the tillage of the soil he gave his active lifetime's interest and labor. He purchased the farm of his father, to which he has subsequently added until he now owns a farm of 135 acres of good, well-improved land. He is a democrat of the old school, has always taken an active part in politics, and has served his party in various official capacities. He was also director of the poor for three years.

Alexander Deyarman has been married three times. His first wife was Phœbe Hadden, of Georges township. They had seven children: Hugh, Louisa, Isabella, Ann, Mary J. and two that died in infancy. His second marriage was with Nancy Greenlee. The second union was blessed with the following children: William G., Alexander and Robert; John entered the Civil War and served six months, was taken sick at Cumberland and mustered out of the service; Ewing was also in the Federal service, and was captured by Mosby and held prisoner at Andersonville for six months; Julia and Fannie. Mr. Deyarman was married a third time to Martha Watt, a daughter of Samuel Watt.

He has been a member of the Presbyterian church for about fifty years, and has served for many years as elder. He is straightforward in business, and fearless and plainspoken in expressing his opinions.

Mr. Robert Britt was born June 4, 1805 in Chester county, Pa., and came to Fayette county with his father, when a little past six years old, and has made this his home ever since. He has lived here excepting two years spent in Kentucky, and eight years in Virginia, while working at his trade. He is a carpenter by trade, although for many years past he has turned his entire attention and energies to farming and to some extent raising stock. He owns 480 acres of land in Georges township, where he now resides, where he has lived for nearly forty years past.

He was married December 11, 1831, to Miss Asenath Greenlee, a daughter of William and Mary Greenlee, both residents of this county and among the oldest settlers, although the exact date of their coming to the county cannot now be ascertained. Miss Greenlee was of Irish descent, her mother was born in Ireland, and came to America when but three years old. Of this marriage were born nine children: Mary E., born September 11, 1832; Nancy M., born August 29, 1835, died June 18, 1852; Samuel G., born March 25, 1837; Ann E., born August

30, 1840, died September 3, 1844; William M., born January 13, 1842, died August 27, 1844; Frances E., born September 8, 1844; Charles R., born September 5, 1846, died June 15, 1852; John L., born April 2, 1850, died July 11, 1852, and Frank P., born April 22, 1853. Three of them are living in sight of the homestead. Frank P. is a Presbyterian minister at Corsica, Jefferson county, Pa. Mary E. was married to B. Franklin Goodwin, November 3, 1856. Samuel G. Britt was married March 11, 1860, to Caroline Miller. Frances E. Britt was married January 25, 1863, to Albert S. Miller. Rev. Frank P. Britt was married December 28, 1876, to Jennie M. Ralston.

In December, 1881, Mr. Britt and his wife celebrated their golden wedding. She died on the 17th day of June, 1882.

Mr. Britt has been a member of the Presbyterian church for many years and is a Free Mason, a member of Fayette Lodge No. 228. He has held the office of school director and some other responsible offices of the township.

JAMES POTTER CAROTHERS, one who stands high as a business man and a Christian gentleman, was born on Little Sewickley Creek, Westmoreland county, Pa., March 8, 1826, and is a son of Samuel and Ruth (Elliott) Carothers.

Samuel Carothers was born near Chambersburg, Pa., and emigrated to Westmoreland county. He was a farmer and an elder in the Presbyterian church at Sewickley. He was a democrat until Governor Ritner's election, and after that was a whig. He married Miss Ruth Elliott. They had seven children: Catherine, wife of Robert Finley, a prominent citizen of Redstone township; Ruth, wife of John Penny, of McKeesport; Matilda, William, Jane, Eliza, married the late Jasper M. Thompson (see his sketch), and James P.

James P. Carothers was brought up and educated as all farmers' sons were at that time—on the farm and in the subscription schools until sixteen years old, when he learned tanning. He was engaged in tanning at Mill Grove, Westmoreland county, until 1854, when he removed to his present residence, where he has been engaged in tanning for over thirty years, near Fairchance.

In 1848 he was married to Mary, a sister of Hon. Jasper M. Thompson. They had five children: William, Leah, wife of Robert Harvey, now of New Mexico (formerly of London), is a book-keeper and ex-reporter of the legislature for that Territory; Ruth, wife of Millard Scholl, in lumber and plaining-mill business at West Newton; Jasper, married to Flora Belles, of Ohio, and resides in Kansas, and Cyrus (deceased).

After the death of his first wife, he was married to Miss Fannie E. Smith, daughter of John and Lydia (Bedford) Smith of Georges township, both of Scotch descent and natives of New Jersey, and a niece of Rev. Dr. A. G. Fairchild.

J. P. Carothers has carefully and honestly acquired a competency of this world's goods, but has never neglected the calls of charity or suffering humanity. He is a republican, has served as school director and is recognized as an active and effective worker in the ranks of the republican party. He is a member of the Presbyterian church at Fairchance, of which he is an honored elder and trustee.

MICHAEL BAKER is of German-French extraction, and was born in what is now Nicholson township, Fayette county, Pa., February 12, 1827. He is a son of Joseph and Anna Baker (neé Larch).

Joseph Baker was the son of Michael Baker, a German Baptist minister, and early settler of Fayette county. Joseph Baker was born, reared and educated in Springhill township. He was a farmer and owned a valuable farm of 128 acres; he subsequently added to it by purchase, forty-five acres of adjoining land. He was a life-long democrat, an upright member of the Mount Moriah Baptist church, at Smithfield, and was one of the old and substantial citizens of Nicholson township, and died May 15, 1858, aged fifty-five years.

He married Miss Hannah, a daughter of Paul Larch. Their union was blessed with four children: Michael and George (twins), Josiah, cabinet-maker in Hamilton, Ohio, and Caroline, married and resides in Smithfield.

Paul Larch, maternal grandfather, as related, won his wife in rather a romantic manner. He was a native of France, emigrated to the Illinois country, and engaged as an Indian trader. He stole his wife at night from an Indian camp, where she was confined as a prisoner. She had been employed during the day in carrying wood, which the Indians intended to use in burning her during the next day. He owned four hundred acres of land where Kaskaskia, Ill., now stands. Being in fear of the Indians, he came to George's Creek, and took up four hundred acres of land, where he resided till his death.

Michael Baker grew to manhood on the farm, attended the subscription schools and read and studied during his spare moments around the fireside at home, until twenty-one years of age. Starting out in life for himself, he engaged in farming as his life-pursuit. He now owns the home farm of 128 acres, besides having an interest in a large cattle ranch in Wyoming Territory.

September 20, 1859, he was united in marriage to Miss Jane, daughter of John Dowlin, of Greene county, and sister of John Dowlin, ex-revenue collector. They have three children: Lizzie, Ella, married, and Chauncey Larch Baker.

Mr. Baker and his family, are members of the Mount Moriah Baptist church, at Smithfield.

In 1873-74-75 he served very acceptably as poor house director of Fayette county. He is a prosperous farmer, an energetic and reliable business man.

UPTON LAWRENCE CLEMMER, M. D., of Redstone (deceased). The late Dr. Upton Lawrence Clemmer, one of the most prominent and highly respected physicians of Fayette county, was the eldest son of Lewis Clemmer, and was born in Allegany county, Md., November 16, 1816. His father was a native of Maryland, where he married Miss Christina, daughter of Rev. Gideon Butler, and later removed to Pennsylvania. He was a saddler and harness-maker by trade, and after the death of his wife he married Miss Polly Lowie, of Uniontown, where he died in 1866. One of his sons is G. G. Clemmer, a banker in Iowa.

Dr. Clemmer received his early education at New Geneva, where he began the study of medicine at the age of sixteen years under the tutelage of Dr. J. J. Steele, a prominent physician of the county. He attended lectures at the Reformed Medical College, and after four years' practice graduated in medicine in 1846. He began the practice in Preston county, W. Va., thence to Grandville, Monongalia county, W. Va., and subsequently removed to Smithfield, Fayette county, where he continued successfully in the practice for eighteen years. From Smith field Dr. Clemmer removed to Brownsville, and was there engaged in the successful practice of medicine till his death, May 25, 1888. On November 14, 1839, he was married to Miss Adelia H., daughter of Wilfred Massey, of West Virginia. They had twelve children, of whom eight are living: George B., born September 20, 1842, married Fannie

Garred, April, 1875; Caroline A., born July 14, 1852; Valonia V., born November 10, 1854; Dora M., born April 19, 1858; Elizabeth W., born September 11, 1861; Pearl M., born December 30, 1862; Lawrence B., born July 31, 1865; and Adelia B., born June 10, 1869.

Dr. Clemmer served as an assistant surgeon in the Union army at Parkersburg, W. Va., in 1864, and was the inventor of the celebrated "Clemmer's Anti-Dysenteric Cordial," and the renowned "Clemmer's Little Liver Pills." He was a democrat, had been an Odd Fellow for fifty-two years, and one of the founders of Gallatin Lodge at Smithfield. He had served as coroner of Fayette county and member of the Pension Examining Board. At the time of his death he owned ten acres of valuable land heavily underlaid with lime and coal. He was a man of strictest integrity and high medical ability, and was a man who lived up to his convictions of right.

PROF. JOHN S. DAVID, one of Fayette county's prominent teachers and principal of the Uniontown public schools, is a son of Joseph M. and Mary Ann (Kildow) David, and was born at Fairchance, Fayette county, Pa., October 21, 1850.

His great-grandfather, Enoch David, was a native of Wales, emigrated to Philadelphia, and subsequently removed to Woodbridgetown, this county. His fourth and last wife, Elizabeth Harrison, was a cousin to President W. H. Harrison. One of his sons, G. W. David (grandfather), was born in Philadelphia, came to Springhill furnace, lived in Wharton township for many years, and died in German township at ninety-two years of age.

His maternal grandfather, John Kildow, was of German descent and born near Martinsburg, Va. He lived near Brownsville and was a millwright.

His father, Joseph David, was born in Wharton township, and was the youngest of a family of thirteen children; was a farmer, removed to Georges township and subsequently settled in Nicholson township. He reared a family of six children: Wells E., a teacher, enlisted in the Eighty-fifth Pennsylvania Volunteers, and died in McClellan's campaign before Richmond; James N., principal of Bridgeport schools, served in the Twenty-second Pennsylvania Cavalry, and was county superintendent of Harrison county, W. Va., for two terms; Jesse E., a farmer and stock-raiser of Oregon, previously a teacher and photographer; Sarah E.; John S., and William O., a pleasant, experienced teacher, and principal of Dunlap's Creek Academy.

Prof. J. S. David was educated in Georges Creek Academy. At eighteen years of age he began teaching, and has taught nineteen terms of school. For the last five years he has been principal of the public schools of Uniontown, and has rendered good satisfaction.

He is a republican and takes an active interest in the affairs of his political party.

He is a member of the Presbyterian church, and has been a Sabbath-school superintendent since 1875. For several years he had the superintendence of two Sabbath-schools.

Prof. David is persistent, active, thorough and successful in school work. Although unassuming and undemonstrative, yet he is abreast of the times and well conversant with the educational ideas of the present age.

JOHN DOWNEY was born in Monongalia county, W. Va., January 9, 1832; came with his parents, Darby and Lydia (Stafford) Downey, to Springhill township, Fayette county, Pa., in the spring of 1836;

is of Welsh, German and English lineage. His grandfather, John Downey, was born near Woodstock, in the Shenandoah Valley, Va., in 1778. On arriving at his majority he came to Monongalia county (now West Virginia) and engaged extensively in the business of flat-boat building, at the mouth of Scott's run on Cheat river, on what is now known as the Costello farm. The premises were then in the possession of a young widow, Gillespie, whose husband was a brother to the mother of the Hon. J. G. Blaine. The widow's maiden name was Llewellyn. John Downey was married to her in 1799. Of this union there were born three children: Nancy (inter-married with William Scott), Darby and Delilah. The elder John Downey was a man of excellent mechanical skill and well endowed mentally. He possessed indomitable push and energy, and but for the immoderate use of whisky would have been an eminent man in his day. He died at the age of fifty, leaving his widow, by improvidence, in straitened circumstances. John Downey's father, Darby Downey, was born in 1802, in Monongalia county, W. Va., was unlettered in the severest sense, was a man of fine presence, possessed of extraordinary mechanical ability and endowed with a good memory.

In 1827 he was married to Miss Lydia, daughter of James Stafford, a woman of more than ordinary intellectual capacity, and endowed, in an eminent degree, with motherly qualities. Of this union there were born five children: Mary Jane (inter-married with George Robinson), Abagail, John, James and Nancy, all of whom are living and comfortably fixed in life. Lydia, the mother, died in February, 1838. Darby Downey remained a widower two years, when he married Orpha Harvey. Of this union there were born three children: Francis M. (inter-married with Matilda Blosser), William and Elizabeth, all of whom died of consumption after reaching man and womanhood. Orpha Downey died in 1858 and Darby in 1863. John Downey, after the death of his mother, lived with Capt. James M. Oliphant, with whom he remained thirteen years. He attended the common schools a few months in the winter season and obtained only a rudimental education. In the twentieth year of his age he engaged with the Rev. Lewis Sammons to learn the cooper trade, at Smithfield. Having a natural aptitude for the mechanical arts, in less than one year he became proficient in the business, and commenced to work as a journeyman. He remained with the Rev. Sammons two years and carefully husbanded his earnings. He then went to Iowa, remained one year, working at his trade, returned to Smithfield, bought the property of his old boss, together with the shop, tools and good will of the trade and commenced what subsequently proved to be a lucrative business. On the 12th day of May, 1859, he was married by the Rev. Jesse Hull to Miss Harriet R., daughter of Zetus Linton, of Masontown, Pa. Of this union there were born four children: Ewing L., Harriet A. (inter-married with C. D. Crow), Wallace M. and Edward, the last named died in infancy. Mrs. Downey died September 5, 1874. John Downey remained a widower two years, when he married Mrs. Jane Sutton, with whom he still lives. He is a republican in politics, was elected commissioner of Fayette county in 1884, dischared the duties of the office very acceptably to the people. He is a member of the Order of Ancient York Masons, and a charter member of Gallatin Lodge 517, I. O. O. F., he is a member of of the Methodist Episcopal church at Smithfield, and adorns his profession by a correct and orderly life. He is well informed on the current topics of the day, has accumulated considerable property, is highly esteemed by his fellow citizens, lives comfortably and enjoys the society of his friends and neighbors. Ten years ago he commenced, in addition to his other business, the sale of all kinds of agricultural implements, has a large and commodious salesroom, and supplies an extensive trade.

JUSTUS DUNN, ex-county treasurer, of Fayette county, and a prominent business man, of Georges township, was born in Erie city, Erie county, Pa., June 8, 1817, and is a son of Simeon and Martha (Lewis) Dunn. His grandfather, Justus Dunn, emigrated in 1797, from New Brunswick, N. J., to Crawford county, Pa. His great-grandmother was a sister to Sir Francis Drake, the great navigator. He was a slave holder, and raised a family of six sons and two daughters. One of the daughters, Rachel, lived to be one hundred years of age. His father, Simeon Dunn, was a native of New Jersey, and died in Erie, Pa. He was a dispatch carrier in the War of 1812, and was the first to carry the news of Perry's victory to Buffalo. He married Miss Martha Lewis. They had seven children. Justus Dunn was educated in the subscription schools of Erie. His first employment was in a brick yard. He next went to Iowa and Illinois and worked as a common laborer. In 1844 he came to Georges township, where he cut cordwood at twenty-five cents per cord, and in a few years, by hard labor acquired enough to purchase his present farm of 175 acres. In 1864 he began dealing in stock, and has continued in that business until the present time. He was married to Miss Mary Ann Zearley, who was born February 12, 1825, and is a daughter of Samuel and Sarah (Griffith) Zearley. Mr. and Mrs. Dunn have eleven children: Elizabeth C., born June 18, 1854, wife of Solomon Johnson, stock dealer; Martha L., February 23, 1857, married Moses Hustead, of near Uniontown; Sarah J., September 4, 1858, wife of D. R. Anderson, merchant, Dunbar; Annie E., November 3, 1860; Emma L., August 15, 1862, wife of John Davis; Mary E., June 27, 1864, married Jefferson Smiley; Alice E., born November 27, 1866, wife of Frank Sangston; Charles J., March 14, 1869, married Amy Kyle and lives at Smithfield; Helen K., January 4, 1872; George J., November 29, 1874, and John R., born November 18, 1877.

At one time Mr. Dunn was the largest shipper of cattle in Western Pennsylvania, and engaged extensively in the huckstering business. He is a democrat, and in 1875 was appointed treasurer of Fayette county to serve out two and a half years of the unexpired term of Mr. McDonald, deceased. The Dunn family has been noted for its longevity. Oliver Dunn (an uncle), at ninety-four years of age, traveled six hundred miles to get married, and died aged 98 years For hospitality and generosity, Mr. Dunn has been noted; is just in all his dealings, and no man has a fairer character among his neighbors for honesty and integrity than Justus Dunn.

DR. THOMAS N. EASTMAN, a young and rising physician of Fayette county, was born at Merrittstown, Luzerne township, Fayette county, Pa., November 23, 1856, and is a son of Dr. Henry and Mary E. (Porter) Eastman. (For ancestry see sketch of Henry Eastman, M. D.)

Dr. T. N. Eastman was reared in Luzerne township, and received his early education in the common schools. He attended Dunlap's Creek Academy, and was graduated from Washington and Jefferson College in 1878. Choosing the medical profession for a life vocation, he entered upon its study under the tutelage of his father, Dr. Henry Eastman. After completing the required course of reading he attended lectures at Jefferson

Medical College, where he was graduated, March, 1881. After graduation he occupied the important position of resident physician in St. Mary's Hospital, Philadelphia, Pa. He was called from Philadelphia to the Asylum for the Insane, at Dixmont, as assistant physician, where he remained some time, and returned to Merrittstown and engaged in the general practice of medicine with his father, Dr. Henry Eastman. He has a large and paying practice in the western part of the county, having proved himself a worthy successor of his father, whose practice he has retained with unusual success. On June 10, 1886, he was married by Rev. A. S. Milholland, D.D., to Miss Jennie, daughter of Robert Hogsett. They have one child: Helen, born June 8, 1889.

Dr. Eastman owns a very fine residence at Merrittstown, which he erected in 1887. He is an intelligent and skillful young physician.

MICHAEL S. FRANKS, justice of the peace and a leading druggist of Fairchance, is a son of Isaac and Nancy (Morgan) Franks, and was born in Nicholson township, Fayette county, Pa., March 22, 1849.

His great-grandfather, Michael Franks, Sr., with a brother, Jacob, came from Germany to Baltimore where Michael Sr., married a German lady. Michael Sr., and Jacob came out over an Indian trail in 1760 and purchased a large tract of land near High House known as "Frankston." They were prominent in organizing St. Jacob's or the "Old Dutch Church," in 1785. In St. Jacob's cemetery, a square is left on which to erect a monument to the Franks family. (The German spelling was Fronk.) Michael Franks served in the Indian wars and his son Henry was a prisoner of the Indians for eighteen months. Michael Franks, Sr., had eleven children: Henry, Charlotte First, Mary Helmick, Abraham, Michael, Jr., John, Elizabeth First, Jacob, Dorothy Miller, George and Catherine Hatfield. Michael Franks, Jr., was born in 1773, married Amy, daughter of Jacob First and died in 1851. He had fifteen children: Jacob (dead), Elizabeth Higgins (dead), Mary Kramer (dead), Michael, (dead), James (dead), Samuel, Abraham, represented Wayne county, in Ohio legislature; George (dead), John (dead), Amy Higgins, Charlotte Trader, Christina Hess, Henry, Isaac and Phineas. Mr. Franks was an honest, prosperous farmer in what is now Nicholson township. He owned nine farms, was a democrat and was a deacon of the Baptist church for thirty-seven years. His wife died in 1872 aged ninety-one years. His son Isaac was born in 1821 and was married in 1844 to Miss Nancy, daughter of Philemon W. Morgan. (See sketch of A. Robinson.) She was an estimable woman, a member of the Baptist church and died at Morgantown, W. Va., in 1886. Isaac Franks removed to Smithfield in 1857 and engaged in merchandising and operating a foundry. In 1876 he went to Morgantown and was mail contractor until 1885, of the route from Morgantown to Fairchance. He is an honest man and a good neighbor, is firm in his convictions right; he has been a life-long democrat and of for fifty-one years a member of the Baptist church. He has two children: Lydia A. Brown, and Michael S. Lydia A., is proprietor of the Fairchance House and the celebrated "Glenmoor" summer resort, one-half mile above Ice's Ferry on the waters of Cheat, where a fine building of eighteen rooms is situated among some of the finest scenery of the United States.

Michael S. Franks educated in Georges Creek Academy and was a teacher in the common schools of West Virginia and Pennsylvania, for fifteen years. In 1884 he engaged in his present successful drug business.

In May, 1883, he was married to Miss Ella J., daughter of William Conn (deceased), of Smithfield. They have three children: William C., Annie and Edgar C.

Michael S. Franks is a regular registered pharmacist. He has a first-class drug store that is carefully fitted up and well stocked. Politically Mr. Franks is a republican and was elected justice of the peace in February, 1889. He served as postmaster from January, 1885, to November, 1887. Is an Odd Fellow and K. of G. E. He has achieved his success in life over many obstacles and maintains an excellent reputation in both public and private life.

AMADEE MELIER FRANKS, an intelligent citizen and a progressive farmer of Fayette county, is a son of Michael and Charity (Kendall) Franks. He was born in Nicholson township, Fayette county, Pa, January 13, 1848.

Jacob Franks, great-grandfather, was born in 1743, and came to Baltimore and married Miss Barbara Brandeberry. He soon removed to German township, where he bought a large tract of land called "Frankston." He helped organize the "Old Dutch Church" in 1785. One of his sons (Henry) was captured by Indians, but subsequently escaped from them. Jacob Franks died in 1802 and his descendants are numerous in the Western States, West Virginia and Western Pennsylvania. He was the father of Michael Franks, Sr., whose son Michael Franks was the father of Amadee M. Franks.

Michael Franks (father), was born October 29, 1803, and died November 26, 1879. He was a native of Nicholson township, where he owned a farm of ninety acres. In 1852 Michael Franks purchased the Nicholson farm of 200 acres; he removed to it and engaged in farming until his death. In 1879 he married Miss Charity Kendall, born March 17, 1810, and died December 6, 1879. They had seven children: Isaac K., in Mo.; Michael W., ex-county treasurer, now stamp clerk in the revenue office at Pittsburgh; Alcinda, wife of J. K. Dils; William S. (dead), John Calvin (dead), Frances Ann (dead) and Amedee M. Mr. and Mrs. Franks were prominent members of the Baptist church. He held various township offices, was a life-long democrat and was one of the old, reliable and useful citizens of Nicholson township.

Amadee M. Franks was reared on a farm and attended the common schools until nineteen years of age, when he engaged in farming with his father. After the death of the latter he purchased the home farm, which is very fertile and well improved.

He is a natural mechanic, and has pursued the trade of a carpenter, at intervals, for eighteen years.

He is a democrat, has served as road supervisor and school director, and is a member of the Royal Arcanum, and is now engaged in stock raising, having thoroughbred merino sheep and Poland China hogs.

Mr. Franks was married March 19, 1868, to Miss Nancy, daughter of Joseph and Annette (Barber) Longanecker. They have four children: Allie M., wife of A. G. Rhodes, a miller of Westmoreland county; Chauncey B., Holly W. and Vada L. Mr. and Mrs. Franks are members of the Baptist church at New Geneva, and reside in an elegant residence surrounded with all the comforts and conveniences of life.

DR. WILSON GREENE, a prominent physician of Fayette county and a resident of New Geneva, was born in Monongahela township, Greene county, Pa., December 1, 1829. He is of English and German ancestry.

William Greene (grandfather) was a native

of New England, and settled on Whitely Creek, Greene county, in an early day. He married Rebecca La Rue. They had five sons and three daughters. One of these sons, Matthew Greene, father of Dr. Greene, was born February 17, 1806, and is now in the eighty-fourth year of his age. Matthew Greene is a democrat, a member of the Baptist church and owns a valuable farm of 100 acres of first-class land in Monongahela township, Greene county. In 1828 he married Miss Rachel, daughter of Henry and Barbara (Seltzer) Sycks, the former a native of Virginia, an early pioneer of Greene county and a soldier in several campaigns against the Indians. They had four children, three daughters and one son. Mrs. Greene was born in 1796 and died in 1869.

Dr. Wilson Greene received his education in the common schools, and by teaching several winter schools was enabled to complete a liberal English education in a select school at Brownsville.

He read medicine with Dr. John A. Stone, an able physician of Greenesboro, Greene county, Pa. After five years' reading, he entered Cleveland Medical College and continued his studies there during 1858 and 1859. A diploma was granted him by the Western Reserve University, Cleveland, Ohio. In 1859 he began the practice of medicine at Bristol, Perry county, Ohio, where he remained five years in the enjoyment of a good practice. In 1864 he came to Fayette county and located at New Geneva, where he has successfully continued in the practice of medicine up to the present time. Probably no physician in Fayette county enjoys a wider practice than Dr. Greene. Extending as it does over the southern parts of Fayette and Greene counties and the adjoining counties of West Virginia.

March 23, 1859, he married Miss Pleasant M., daughter of Evan Evans and great-granddaughter of Rev. John Corbly, the pioneer Baptist preacher whose wife and children were massacred by Indians while on their way to church on Sunday morning, May 10, 1782, at Garrard's Fort, Geene county. They have two children: Isa D. and Willie W. Isa D. is the wife of O. J. Sturgis, editor of the *Republican Standard*, Uniontown, Pa., educated at Monongahela College and was graduated from Dana's Musical Institute, Warren, Ohio. She has a fine talent for vocal and instrumental music and possesses a sweet, clear and musical voice. Willie W. was educated at Monongahela College and is a graduate of Duff's Commercial Business College.

Dr. Greene has been for many years a useful and influential member of the Baptist church, of which his wife and children are also members. He is a republican in politics and takes a keen interest in public affairs, but has never sought office.

TIMOTHY HESS, a prominent republican and well situated farmer of Redstone township, was born on a farm in Menallen township, Fayette county, Pa., February 6, 1840, and is a son of John and Eliza (Dutson) Hess.

His grandfather, Martin Hess, resided in Redstone township, on property now owned by Richard Randolph, and married a Miss Wallace.

His father, John Hess, was born on a farm now owned by Lewis Hess, in about 1812. He was married to Eliza Dutson, of Washington county, who was born in 1819. They had ten children, of whom Timothy Hess was the second.

Timothy Hess received his education in the common schools of Menallen township, and turned his attention to farming until twenty-five years of age, when he went to Oil City, Venango county, Pa., and there engaged as an "oil driller." He remained two years, when he returned to Redstone, and has since been successfully engaged in farming and stock dealing.

On November 30, 1865, he was married by Rev. W. W. Hickman, to Miss Mary E., born April 26, 1847, and a daughter of Solomon and Hannah (Colley) Crumrine, the former was born July 18, 1824, in Greene county, Pa., served one term as commissioner of National road; the latter was born October 14, 1823, on the Colley homestead, four miles east of Brownsville, and died there February 13, 1871.

Timothy Hess is unswerving in his allegiance to the republican party and its fundamental principles, and is recognized as a prominent and leading member of his party.

He and wife are members of the Disciple church. He owns thirty-one acres of the Colley farm, which is productive and underlaid with limestone and coal of the best quality. He has been very successful in stock dealing as well as in farming.

GEORGE HIGGINBOTHAM, of Redstone, is an earnest republican and a thorough-going farmer. He is the fourth of a family of six children; was born at Masontown, Fayette county, Pa., October 31, 1846, and is a son of James C. Higginbotham. George Higginbotham was educated in the common and select schools. Leaving school, he engaged in his present business of farming and stock raising.

On May 15, 1869, he was married, by Rev. W. W. Hickman, to Miss Emma Colvin, daughter of William Colvin, of Redstone township. They have seven children living, born and named as follows: Minnie M., May 27, 1870; William J., April 29, 1872; Ella, September 13, 1873; Samuel F., April 11, 1875; Mary, September 29, 1876; Walter, July 5, 1878, and Robert G., Aug. 29, 1880.

Mrs. Higginbotham's father is descended from William Colvin, a pioneer settler and the ancestor of one of the old and well-known families of Fayette county. He was in Redstone township in 1766, but did not permanently locate until 1768.

Politically he is an ardent republican, and is a conspicuous worker in his party. He owns ninety-five acres of good farming land, underlaid with rich veins of coal and limestone, and well watered. Mr. Higginbotham is mainly engaged in farming, yet gives considerable of his attention to whatever is useful or advantageous to his section of country.

DR. JAMES FRANCIS HOLBERT, a prominent physician and surgeon of Fairchance, is a son of Joseph A. and Margaret P. (Stone) Holbert, and was born at Uniontown, Fayette county, Pa., November 28, 1850.

His grandfather, Joseph Holbert, was a native of Scotland, emigrated to New York City, and subsequently removed to Westmoreland county, where he died. He was a farmer, a member of the Methodist Episcopal church, served as an officer in the War of 1812, and was a very conscientious, upright man.

His father, Joseph A. Holbert, was born in Westmoreland county, Pa., in 1820. He learned the trade of tailor in Pleasant Unity, Westmoreland county, and in 1845 came to Uniontown, where he worked with John Carpenter, an extensive merchant tailor. Joseph A. Holbert was a whig, consistent member of the Methodist Episcopal church, an industrious and estimable man, a charter member of Fort Necessity Lodge, I. O. O. F., died in November, 1850, and sleeps in the old Baptist cemetry at Uniontown. He was married to Miss Margaret Priscilla Stone, a daughter of Squire Aaron and Priscilla (Black) Stone. Squire Stone was a large landholder, justice of the peace, a prominent citizen of Greene county, Pa., afterwards removed to Uniontown, where he kept the Eagle and Fulton House, and died at Smithfield. His wife was of English descent, and was a sister of Hon. Charles A. Black. Joseph A. and Margaret Holbert had two children: Aaron C., born 1847, and Dr. J. F. A. C. Holbert was engaged in teaching in Pennsylvania and the West, removed to Somerset county, Pa., married Miss Nettie Cummings, has one child, Francis Aaron, and is a promising attorney at the Somerset county bar. Mrs. Margaret P. Holbert was a woman of estimable character, a consistent member of the Baptist church, and died at Smithfield in 1869.

Dr. J. F. Holbert was reared at Smithfield, was educated in Georges Creek Academy, received a State permanent certificate, and taught twelve years in the common schools. He read medicine under Dr. B. F. Brownfield, of Smithfield, in 1782, and afterwards with Dr. John A. Stone (uncle), of Greensboro, Pa. He attended lectures at the University of New York City, and graduated with honors from that celebrated institution in 1878. He made an average of ninety-nine per cent. in his studies and won two prizes for high-class standing.

In 1879 he located at Ruble's Mills, near Smithfield, and began practice, but in one year came to his present location, Fairchance, and engaged successfully in the practice of medicine.

On April 4, 1879, he was married to Miss Sallie J. Ruble, who was educated in Georges Creek Academy and California Normal School, taught school several years, and is skilled in painting and fine art needlework.

Dr. Holbert has been for several years physician in charge of Redstone Coke Company's and Bliss Marshall's Coke Works. Is a prominent Odd Fellow, belongs to Pine Knob Lodge No. 559, is a Knight Templar in Masonry, a member of the Uniontown Commandery No. 49. He is also a member of K. of P., P. O. of Sons of America, and the Royal Arcanum. He is a democrat, has served repeatedly as school director, is president of the school board of Fairchance borough, and is the democratic nominee for coroner of Fayette county. Dr. Holbert has been a member for twenty years of Mt. Moriah Baptist church, and is thoroughgoing, energetic and successful in whatever he undertakes.

DANIEL F. HOSTETLER, a prosperous farmer of German township, is a son of George and Barbara (Franks) Hostetler, and was born in German township, Fayette county, Pa., September 23, 1839.

George Hostetler (father) was born near Sheppardstown, Va., in 1804, and died in German township in 1873. He married Miss Barbara, daughter of Michael Franks. Unto their union was born three children: Elizabeth J. (dead), Daniel F. and Lydia A. (dead). Mrs. Hostetler's grandfather, Michael Franks, Sr., came from France to Maryland in 1773. He removed to Fayette county and in 1785 assisted to build St. Jacob's church, which has been rebuilt three times. He was a devoted member of the German Reform church.

Samuel Hostetler (paternal grandfather) emigrated from Eastern Virginia in about 1815 to Fayette county, was a farmer by occupation, and died in 1861. Michael Franks (maternal grandfather) died in 1846.

Daniel F. Hostetler was reared on a farm, and was educated in the common schools. He has been engaged in farming ever since leaving schoool. In 1856 he was united in marriage to Miss Elizabeth, daughter of Jacob and Mary Leckrone. Mr. Hostetler owns a small but very productive farm of fifty acres, well-improved, and in a fine state of cultivation. He is a deacon in the Evangelical Lutheran church, and secretary of the council. Is master of German Grange, No. 743, Patrons of Husbandry, and is one of the energetic business men and reliable citizens of German township.

JOHN C. HUTCHINSON, of English-Irish descent and a prosperous farmer of Nicholson township, is a son of Samuel and Rosanna (Hagan) Hutchinson, and was born in South Union township, October 5, 1841.

Samuel Hutchinson was born near Uniontown in August, 1815, died December 29, 1882, and is interred in the cemetery at Uniontown. He was a miller in early life, but afterwards engaged in farming near Hutchinson's Mill. He owned a farm of eighty-seven acres of well improved and twenty-seven acres of heavy timber land. Mr. Hutchinson was a whig and later a republican; served one term as poor-house director, and filled the office of school director for several terms. He married Miss Rosanna Hagans, of near Walnut Hill. They were the parents of seven children: John C., James M., a prosperous farmer in Illinois; Isaac, on the home farm; Mary M., William Henry (dead); Albert B. (see his sketch in this work), and Elizabeth. Mr. Hutchinson was a Baptist, while his wife was a Cumberland Presbyterian.

His father was born in Mercer county, N. J., and came to South Union township in 1802, where he built the mill that bears his name. He was a millwright and miller; belonged to the Baptist church; was an old line whig, and enjoyed the confidence of his neighbors. Mrs. Hutchinson's father, John Hagan, came from Ireland; was a contractor on the "Old Pike," owned a farm of 250 acres of choice farming land, underlaid with coal, and now valued at $100,000 by its present owners. He was a good business man and was quite wealthy when he died.

John C. Hutchinson spent his early years on a farm and received a common-school education. In 1861 he enlisted in Company A, First Virginia Cavalry, and participated in the battles of Carnifex Ferry, South Mountain and Antietam. Afterwards at the fight of Wytheville, was taken prisoner by the Confederates, and confined in Libby prison, Belle Island, and in several other prisons. After six months' prison experience he was paroled and sent North. He rejoined his regiment after being exchanged, was with his regiment in several engagements, and was honorably discharged at Wheeling, W. Va., September 12, 1864. The year following he was a clerk in the quarter-master's department at Nashville, Tenn.

On February 17, 1867, he was married to Miss M. B. Core, daughter of William F. Core; to their union have been born two children: Jennie May, wife of John Weaver, a miller of Smithfield, and Harry Lee Hutchinson now a student in Washington and Jefferson College.

Since his marriage Mr. Hutchinson has been engaged in farming and stock raising. His farm contains over four hundred acres of well improved land and is one of the finest bodies of farming land in Nicholson township. He is an Odd Fellow and a strong republican, a member of Post No. 541, G. A. R., and was a faithful soldier in some of the severest campaigns of the Civil War.

NICHOLAS D. JOHNSON, of German and Scoth-Irish descent, and one of the substantial farmers of Nicholson township, was born October 18, 1826, in the above-mentioned township, and is a son of Peter and Barbara (Honsaker) Johnson.

His great-grandfather Johnson was a native of Scotland. At the age of fourteen, he sold several years of his time for "pass-

age money" to a German coming to America. The German paid for his passage, both came to Eastern Pennsylvania, where the young emigrant served his time and afterwards married a daughter of his German friend. One of Johnson's sons, the father of Peter Johnson, came to what is now Nicholson township at an early day. Peter Johnson (father) was born in Rockingham county, Va., and was brought to Fayette county when two years of age. He became a prosperous farmer, owned a farm of 250 acres, and operated a foundry, a saw-mill and grist-mill. He was engaged in the mercantile business in Masontown for ten years.

He married Miss Barbara Honsaker, January 1, 1825. They had thirteen children, of whom nine are living. Mrs. Johnson was born August 22, 1801, and is a devoted member of the Mennonite church. Peter Johnson was a whig and later a republican; served as school director and filled several other township offices. His death occurred April 14, 1864.

Nicholas D. Johnson was employed on a farm at an early age, and received but a limited education. January 25, 1855, he married Miss Catherine M., daughter of Michael Hayes, a farmer of Westmoreland county. To this union were born seven children: Wilfred H., Susan H., Alice E., Sarah H., Emma, Henry H.(dead) and Franklin F. (dead).

Mr. Johnson rented land and farmed until 1865, when he came into possession of his father's farm, where he now resides in a pleasant and comfortable home. He is a republican, has served as school director and inspector of elections. He is a member and deacon in the Mennonite church, to which his wife and four of his children belong. His family for four generations were also members of the same religious denomination.

WILLIAM M. LARDEN, one of the most extensive farmers and progressive business men of German township, is a son of William and Elizabeth (Miller) Larden, and was born twenty-one miles north of Pittsburgh, in Canton township, Butler county, Pa., May 24, 1840.

His grandfather, Thomas Larden, was a native of Ireland, settled in Butler county in an early day, where he secured a large tract of land for an iron dinner pot. His wife was of German descent.

His father, William Larden, was born in 1808, and is a prominent farmer and a local M. E. preacher in Butler county. An abolitionist, he is now a strong republican. His wife was Miss Elizabeth Miller, of Johnstown, who died about 1859.

William M. Larden, on leaving school, enlisted in 1861, in Company H, Ninth Pennsylvania Reserves, and was in all the battles of the peninsula campaign. He fought under Pope at the second Bull Run and was honorably discharged in September, 1862, from a hospital, on account of disability.

For seventeen years after the war he was actively engaged in the oil business, at Petrolia, Pa., which he very successfully operated. Subsequently he bought his present beautiful farm, containing 250 acres of choice farming land, richly underlaid with a nine-foot vein of coal, and has several rich deposits of lime.

On July 12, 1864, he was married to Miss Martha, a daughter of David Miller, of Masontown. Mrs. Larden was born August 19, 1843.

William M. Larden brought the first registered Short-horn cattle to Fayette county, and is one of the county's most extensive breeders of that class of stock.

He is a republican and an active member of the Methodist Episcopal church. In the Masonic fraternity he has passed through lodge, chapter and commandery, and has taken the 32d or Scottish Rite degree.

He is a man of good judgment, clear perception and quick action, and has honorably earned the competency he has acquired.

JOEL G. LEATHERMAN, one who is held in the highest esteem as an honorable and honest man by all who know him, was born on the farm where he now resides, in Georges township, Fayette county, Pa., October 20, 1804, and is a son of Joseph and Mary M. (Getzendinner) Leatherman. His grandfathers, Daniel Leatherman and Christopher Getzendinner, were born in Maryland and were farmers in that State, the latter resided all his life on the banks of the Monocacy river. His father, Joseph Leatherman, was born in Maryland and removed to Georges township where he purchased from Richard Ried a tract of land known as "strawberry ridge," on this farm; now owned by Joel Leatherman, are remains of a village founded prior to Anglo-Saxon habitation. Tradition locates it a French village in 1730, and evidences exist to warrant it an abiding-place of the dim, mysterious Mound-Builder. Joseph Leatherman was a German Baptist minister, and a democrat. He had two sons, Joel G. and one who died in infancy.

Joel G. Leatherman was raised on a farm, acquired the limited education of his boyhood days, and has spent a long and quiet life in farming and stock raising.

He was married to Miss Dianna, daughter of Joseph Showalter. She died March 27, 1866, and Mr. Leatherman now lives with his adopted son, Henry J. Daugherty, a native of Georges township.

Henry J. Daugherty was born in February, 1833, and is a son of James and Rebecca (Jennings) Daugherty. H. J. Daugherty was married to Miss Drusilla, daughter of David Field and has two children—Alvin, married Miss Emma Kerline; Florence M., married E. B. Fast, of Marion county, W. Va., and a dental student, now attending his last course of lectures. H. J. Daugherty was educated in the common schools and Waynesburg college and taught 7 terms of school. He is a charter member of Gallation Lodge, No. 517, Independent Order of Odd Fellows and a stirring republican. He lacked but 25 votes at one election of being elected treasurer of Fayette county.

He has been a republican since 1856, and is a member of the Cumberland Presbyterian church. He has always enjoyed the entire confidence of his community.

DR. WILLIAM A. LONGNECKER, of German-Irish descent, and physician of Fairchance, was born near Masontown, German township, Fayette county, Pa., April 19, 1849, and is a son of Jacob F. and Matilda (Moser) Longanecker.

He is descended from the well-known, industrious and highly-respected Longanecker family of Lancaster county, Pa. His grandfather, Joseph Longanecker, came from Lancaster county to German township in early manhood. He was strictly honest and well respected, and accumulated a large amount of property during his lifetime, and, at his death, each of his eight children received a valuable farm. One of his sons, Jacob Longanecker, the father of Dr. Longanecker, was born June 17, 1818, and died April 7, 1889. He was a farmer and stock-dealer, owning and residing, until 1882, upon the farm of 212 acres, where he was born and reared. In 1882 he bought a farm of one hundred acres, adjacent to Smithfield, where he resided till February 19, 1889, when he removed to Fairchance, and died two months later.

Jacob F. Longanecker was a republican,

and was held in such high respect as a private citizen and a capable business man, that he was elected county commissioner in 1855, when Fayette county was strongly democratic. His management of the county affairs was so acceptable to the people that many of them solicited him to offer for sheriff, but he declined to make the race. He was a faithful member of the German Baptist church and a member of the Masonic order. He was married February 24, 1842, to Matilda Moser. They had three children: Two daughters, Mary Ann and Elmira, both dead, and William A. Mrs. Longanecker was born January 5, 1819, and is a daughter of Daniel and Susanna Moser.

Dr. Longanecker was reared on a farm and educated in the common schools and Waynesburg College. Leaving college he received a professional certificate from County Superintendent Joshua V. Gibbons, and taught six terms in the common schools. In 1871 he began the study of medicine with Dr. G. W. Neff, of Masontown. In 1874 he attended lectures at Jefferson Medical College, and graduated March 10, 1876. On April 4, 1876, he formed a partnership with Dr. H. B. Mathiot, of Smithfield, with whom he continued till 1886. In 1880 he removed to Fairchance, where he is engaged in successful practice.

On October 19, 1882, he was married to Miss Ida F. Mathiot, daughter of Dr. H. B. Mathiot. (See sketch.) Their union has been blessed with two children: Ellen D., born March 10, 1887, and Carrie M., born August 3, 1889.

In politics he is a republican, and has served as school director of Georges township. In 1870 he served as assistant census marshal, and took the census of German, Nicholson, Georges and Springhill townships. He is an active worker in the Presbyterian church, while his wife is an earnest member of the Methodist Episcopal church. Dr. Longanecker, in 1882, erected his present fine residence at Fairchance, and is enjoying an extensive and lucrative practice.

ROBERT L. MARTIN, general superintendent and a stockholder of the Fairchance Furnace Company, and one of the prominent business men of Fayette county, was born in Philadelphia, July 28, 1847, and is a son of Robert L. and Adelaide (Nevins) Martin.

His paternal grandfather, Thomas Martin, was of Scotch descent, and a native of Snow Hill, Md. He was a hat manufacturer, and operated hatting establishments at Alexandria, Va., and Baltimore. He was an old line whig, served in the War of 1812, and died in Baltimore.

His maternal grandfather, Samuel Nevins, was of Irish descent, a native of Connecticut, and removed to Philadelphia, where he died. He was a banker and broker in Philadelphia.

His father, Robert L. Martin, Sr., was born in Alexandria, Va., and died in Chester City, Pa. He was engaged in cotton and woolen manufacturing at Philadelphia. He was an earnest republican and a consistent member of the Episcopal church, and an active, energetic and successful worker in the republican party. His children are: Colonel Archer N., with Post, Morton & Co., bankers, New York City; entered the Sixteenth Pennsylvania Cavalry in 1862, as second-lieutenant, was promoted to colonel, served on General Sheridan's staff, was in all the great battles of that wonderful commander; Robert L.; George S., graduate of the University of Pennsylvania and principal of a high school in Philadelphia; Mary N., married Rev. Eustace Daniel, of Frome, England, and is now pastor of the Episcopal church of that city; Harriet W., traveling in Europe, and Littleton L. (half brother of

R. L.), engaged in Kansas City in banking.

Robert L. Martin was educated by private tutors until thirteen years of age, afterward in West Chester Academy. Leaving school, he engaged for some time with his father in the cotton and woolen manufacturing business, and later, for a short period, operated a marble quarry near Philadelphia. In 1873 he engaged as assistant superintendent of the Fairchance Furnace Company; one year later accepted his present position of general superintendent, and in 1880 became a stockholder in the same company.

In 1871 he was married to Miss Annie L. Smith, of Chester, Delaware county, Pa. They have four children: Elizabeth L., Adelaide N., Robert L. and Fannie D. F. Mrs. Martin is a daughter of Thomas Smith, a lumber dealer and manufacturer of Chester. Her maternal grandfather, Judge George S. Leeper, of Delaware county, Pa., was a prominent jurist. He served in congress, and was a personal friend of Andrew Jackson and James Buchanan.

R. L. Martin is president of the Fairchance Fire-brick Company, which he assisted in organizing, and is one of the chief stockholders. He is a Master Mason and member of the Episcopal church. Politically he is a tariff democrat, takes an active part in political matters, and frequently has been solicited to act as chairman of the democratic county committee. For the last fifteen years he has intelligently supervised and successfully operated Fairchance Furnace, one of the most important furnaces in the State of Pennsylvania.

DR. HENRY BERNARD MATHIOT, an old and skilled physician and a prominent citizen of Fayette county, is a son of George and Ruth (Davies) Mathiot, and was born at Connellsville, Fayette county, Pa., August 30, 1815.

"Dr. H. B. Mathiot is descended from a French officer who, at the time of the massacre of St. Bartholomew, obeyed the voice of conscience rather than that of the king and charged on the priests with his regiments, for which he was compelled to fly from France. But the king, winking at his official misconduct, furnished him a letter intended to serve as a warrant of immunity from civil arrests, and he returned to France seeking to regain his estates. The family still found France dangerous ground on account of the priests."

Jean Mathiot, grandfather of Dr. Mathiot, came to Lancaster, Pa., in 1754. His wife was Catherine Margaret, daughter of Hon. Jean James Bernard, mayor of Dampierre, France. They were married in 1753, and had three sons: Christian, John and George, the latter the father of Dr. Mathoit. George Mathoit, born October 13, 1759, enlisted November 18, 1776, in the continental army; and was honorably discharged at the close of the war. He afterwards located at Elk Ridge Landing, Md., where he was married October 31, 1787, to an estimable Quakeress, Miss Ruth Davies, daughter of Joshua Davies of Anne Arundel county Md. In 1796 George Mathiot removed to Connellsville, and served for years as justice of the peace, was an influential member of the Methodist Episcopal church. and prominent alike in religious and secular affairs until his death, April 4, 1840. He had eleven children: Col. Jacob D., a large iron manufacturer and a member of the Pennsylvania Legislature in 1833; Eliza, wife of Col. Davidson, who refused to surrender under Hull at Detroit in 1812 and escaped with his command; Catherine; Mary; Hon. Joshua D., of Ohio, a lawyer and member of congress in 1842, and one of whose daughters married Dr. Cuyler of Brooklyn; Cassandra, John, Susan, Ann M., George F., and Dr. H. B., of whom only Ann M., widow of George W. Dorsey, and Dr. H. B., are living.

Dr. H. B. Mathiot received a limited

common-school education, and while yet a mere boy, began for himself the battle of life. He trudged forty miles on foot through the snow to engage as a clerk with his brother at Ross Iron Works. Subsequently read medicine with Dr. Anderton Brown of Newark, Ohio, for three years (1837 to 1840), when he returned to Fayette county and began the practice of medicine at Smithfield, as an undergraduate, a common custom at that time in Pennsylvania. He graduated from Jefferson Medical College in the class of 1852, and has successfully practiced medicine at Smithfield ever since. For the past year or so, however, he has been trying to retire from active practice. On March 19, 1844, he married Miss Rebecca Ruth, daughter of Col. Thomas Brownfield. They had born to them ten children, of whom four are now living: Caroline; Ida M. F., wife of Dr. Longanecker (see his sketch); Dr. Edward B., and Perie A. Dr. Edward B., graduated in 1882, from Jefferson Medical College, and practiced at West Newton, Pa., until 1888. Since 1888 has been in attendance at the celebrated medical schools of Germany and France to fit himself as a specialist.

"His domestic life has been most fortunate and happy. His wife has been a helpmeet in the grandest sense. Her husband's comfort and her childrens' happiness have been her greatest care, and to her wifely devotion he is largely indebted for the comforts of his home, the hospitable doors of which are ever open. It is proverbial that no house in the community entertains so many persons,friends and strangers, as Dr. Mathiot's. He is an earnest and persuasive public speaker, and for a quarter of a century his voice has been heard in advocacy of every moral, temperance and religious movement that has agitated the community in which he lives."

Of indomitable will and iron constitution, Dr. Mathiot has achieved a successful career in life over apparently insurmountable obstacles. He was ordained a minister of the Methodist Episcopal church by Bishop Simpson in 1872, and has given his services religiously as well as medically, freely alike to rich and poor. He was a whig and is now a republican; was twice a candidate for the legislature, running ahead of his ticket but was defeated each time. Dr. Mathiot is of that class of men who make their mark in whatever station in life to which they aspire.

WILLIAM McSHANE, a prominent farmer and a leading stock trader of German township, was born on Georges Creek, Georges township, Fayette county, Pa., February 7, 1829, and is a son of Barnabas and Elizabeth (Romyne) McShane. The former was born June 13, 1800. The latter was born in Louden county, Va. They had eleven children born to them, of whom William was the fifth child.

His father, Barnabas McShane, was a farmer and horse drover, a strong democrat, and for many years a highly respected gentleman of the county. His father, Daniel McShane, was a native of New Jersey and one of the county's pioneer settlers. Daniel McShane's wife's maiden name was probably Jane McDonald.

Barnabas McShane labored in the construction of the Pennsylvania railroad and was for some years a teamster on the National pike. His uncle, Robert McShane, was a soldier in both the War of the Revolution and of 1812.

William McShane, whose name heads this sketch, was married to Elizabeth Hurst, daughter of Nathan G. Hurst, of Fayette county, December 25, 1851. They have had born to them nine children, of whom seven are living: Mary, Arilla, Anna, William,

Julia, Martha and Porter. Mary is the wife of Hugh Cameron, now of Iowa.

William McShane, after receiving the benefit of the township schools, began life as a farmer. In 1852 he removed to Iowa, where he was extensively engaged in farming and dealing in stock, till his return to Fayette county in 1864. He purchased a farm near West Leisenring in 1865, sold it in 1881 and bought his present farm in German township and removed to it one year later. His farm of 183 acres is beautifully situated and is underlaid with two veins of coal, six and nine feet, and it also contains numerous stratas of limestone.

For the past nineteen years, he has been associated with Captain J. A. Weltner in buying and selling stock and throughout Fayette county he is known as a successful trader.

He has served as school director and held the offices of assessor, justice of the peace and tax collector, and is truly one of the leading and successful business men of the county.

GARRET MONAGHAN, one of the young and progressive business men of Nicholson township, was born March 10, 1849, in the same township, Fayette county, Pa. His parents, John and Catherine (McDonald) Monaghan were natives of Ireland. The father, John Monaghan, migrated from his native land to the United States when he was quite young. He located in New Jersey, and subsequently came to Fayette county, bought a farm of eighty acres in Nicholson township, where he was engaged as a huckster and farmer the remainder of his life. He died at the age of sixty years. He was a devoted member of the Catholic church, as was also his wife. She died May 5, 1889, at the age of sixty-nine years. They were the parents of ten children, of whom six are still living.

Garret Monaghan received a limited education in the district schools of his native township. In 1871 he was married to Miss Lavina, a daughter of Samuel Anderson. To their union was born one child, a daughter, Florence, born November 5, 1874. He owns a small but valuable farm of 22½ acres, on which he has erected a good house, and has a pleasant and comfortable home. He is a member of the Catholic church, while his wife and daughter are consistent members of the Baptist church.

GEORGE D. MOORE, deceased. The late George D. Moore, a well known and prominent man of Georges township, was a son of John and Prudence (Dearth) Moore. He was born in Luzerne township, Fayette county, Pa., November 25, 1817, and died at his residence in Georges township, this county, May 13, 1879.

John Moore was a descendant of an old and highly respectable Quaker family of New Jersey. He emigrated from the latter State to Fayette county and settled in Luzerne township, where he married Miss Prudence Dearth, to their union were born six children: William, Jesse, John, Mary, Elizabeth and George D.

George D. Moore received a farm training, and, equipped with a good practical education, began life for himself.

He was united in marriage to Miss Minerva Heaton, a daughter of Joseph Heaton of Luzerne township. Her grandfather, John Heaton, was a native of Berkeley county, Va., and came to Greene county, Pa., remained a year, then removed to Xenia, Ohio, and purchased a large tract of land. Her maternal grandfather was Colonel Henry Heaton, a native of Fayette county, who was a colonel in the War of 1812, and a member of the Pennsylvania legislature. Her father, Joseph Heaton, was a whig and republican. He always refused to run for office, and stood high in his community for integrity and honesty. His death occurred November 12, 1873, in the eighty-sixth year of his age, and which occasioned by a fall, at Uniontown, down the court-house stairs. He had had two children: Mrs. Moore, and Clarinda, wife of Alpheus Gans, of Springhill township.

Mr. and Mrs. Moore had eight children: Elmira, wife of James Hertig, of Jefferson county, Kas.; Albert G.; Clara E.; Oliver, married Susanna, daughter of Dr. Burt, of Franklin county, Ohio, went to Chase county, Kas., where he afterwards died; Nancy, married Joseph Weltner, a farmer of Monongalia county, W. Va.; John F., married Emma V., daughter of General Goe, of Redstone township; William Edgar, married Ella V., daughter of S. K. Hall, of Greensboro, Pa., and is a farmer and gardener at Fairchance.

George D. Moore was a pupil for some time under Joshua V. Gibbons, and, leaving school, was engaged for a short time in merchandising in Luzerne township.

He was a steady, thoroughgoing man, and was a consistent member of the Presbyterian church, of which Mrs. Moore is also a member.

GEORGE W. NEFF, M. D., was born in Masontown, Pa., December 19, 1845. His paternal grandfather, John Neff, was a native of Lancaster county, Pa., where he lived and died.

George W. Neff's paternal grandmother was a daughter of Major Williams, of York county, Pa.

George William Neff, M. D. (father), was born in York county, Pa., opposite Columbia; studied medicine with Dr. Bitner, of Washington, Lancaster county, and attended Jefferson Medical College at Philadelphia. He came west and was robbed of his money and a gold watch in crossing the mountain, the mode of travel being at that time by stage coach; he sought employment in Pittsburgh but found none. He was referred to Dr. Hugh Campbell, of Uniontown, and went there in 1834, and remained with him for two years. From there he went to Clarksburg, Va. Immediately after he had left Uniontown, Dr. Campbell received a letter from Dr. David B. Rhoades, of Masontown,—one of the pioneers of the medical profession of Pennsylvania,—inquiring for a suitable man as a partner. Dr. Campbell at once referred him to Dr. Neff, who came to Masontown in 1836, and formed a partnership with Dr. Rhoades, under the firm name of Drs. Rhoades & Neff.

Dr. Neff was married August 3, 1837, to Mary Ann, second daughter of Dr. Rhoades. The result of this marriage were seven children: Mary H., George W., William D., John C., Ida and Harry G. Dr. Neff died August 18, 1874. His widow, Mary A. Neff, died August 13, 1889.

Dr. David B. Rhoades (maternal grandfather) was born in Allegheny county, November 5, 1793. Married April 3, 1817, to Harriet E. Tarr, daughter of Daniel and Frances Tarr, of Westmoreland county; settled at Masontown in 1833, and died March 8, 1841, at Masontown.

Dr. Geo. W. Neff was educated at the common schools of the township and at Waynesburg. He began life as a school teacher and taught one term, then began the study of medicine with his father, attended the lectures at the Jefferson Medical College, Philadelphia, during the session of 1867-8; and practiced medicine with his father. He attended the session of 1869-70 at the same college, and graduated in the class of '70. At the time he attended lectures, Drs. Dunglison, S. D. Gross, Joseph Pancoast, Lesley Wallace and Samuel H. Dixon, were professors of the different chairs in the school. He located at Masontown, in the practice, immediately after his graduation, where he has remained to the present time, and has a very large practice.

On November 14, 1872, he was married to Miss Loretta Parshall, daughter of Elias Parshall, who resides at McClellandtown. They have four children: Hannah Matilda, born February 12, 1875; Mary Ann, born June 5, 1877; Loretta P., November 11, 1879, and Lizzie, born March 21, 1882.

Dr. Neff is a republican and was elected to the Pennsylvania legislature, session of 1887, and re-elected for the session of 1889. He was the first republican representative elected to the legislature on a straight party fight in this county. While in the legislature he was an active member, being placed on the committees of appropriations, education and committee of public health and sanitation, and was chairman of the latter He made a strong effort for the passage of a bill requiring the State to adopt an uniform series of text-books in the public schools, but the various book syndicates and monopolies lobbied the bill to defeat.

He is assistant surgeon of the Tenth National Guards of Pennsylvania.

WILLIAM R. MOORE, a descendant of Captain John Moore of Revolutionary fame, and an industrious farmer of German township, was born on the property now owned by Evans Hess, in Redstone township, Fayette county, Penn., February 21, 1824, and is a son of Rezin and Mary (Landers) Moore, the former, a native and well situated farmer of Redstone township, and the latter a daughter of Abraham Landers, an early settler (1790), of the same Township; they have three children living: John M., Mrs. Samuel Herron, and William R.

Captain John Moore (W. R. Moore's grandfather) was a prominent character in the early history of Redstone township. He was born east of the Alleghenies, emigrated to the present Evans Hess farm in 1769, made an enviable record in the Revolutionary War, was married to Miss Margaret Colvin, and died in his adopted township. His sons were: George, John, Aaron, Rezin, Ezekiel and William.

William R. Moore was reared on a farm, received a practical education for ordinary business pursuits, and has been successfully engaged in farming until the present time.

On March 5, 1846, he was married to Miss Nancy Eliza, daughter of Jesse L. Frost. Mrs. Moore died March 22, 1882, aged sixty years. They had ten children born, and named as follows: Rezin, February 1, 1847, married Miss Ann Gribble; Rachel J., May 7, 1848; Hulda A., July 12, 1849, wife of Elijah Holliday; Mary M., February 25, 1852, married G. S. Frederick, May 16, 1871; Robert F. (see his sketch in this volume); Lucy C., April 15, 1856, married Barton Keener; Jesse E., May 24, 1858, married Miss Ellen Brown; Euphemie, July 21, 1866, wife of Jesse Frost; Samuel N., July 10, 1863, married Miss Louisa Harvey. After his wife's death, Mr. Moore was re-married November 15, 1883, by Elder S. M. Cooper to Mrs. Melissa, widow of Thomas Henderson.

In politics he is a republican and adheres closely to the principles of that party. He owns 108 acres of fine farming land, which is heavily underlaid with limestone and iron ore. He also owns ten acres of valuable timber land. Is a successful farmer and highly respected both as a business man and a citizen.

JAMES NIXON, a well-known citizen of Fayette county and ex-county commissioner, was born in Georges township, Fayette county, Pa., December 3, 1828, and is a son of Judge Samuel and Hannah (Davis) Nixon.

His paternal grandfather, William Nixon, was born in New Jersey in 1745, and settled near Fairchance at what was afterwards called "Nixon's Mills." At the time of the Whiskey Insurrection he operated a distillery on the site of the present one owned by D. J. Johnson. He was a democrat of the old school, and died in 1801.

His maternal grandfather, James Davis, was a native of Georges township, and served in the Revolutionary War.

His father, Hon. Samuel Nixon, was a farmer, and in early life operated a carding machine. He was an active and influential democrat, represented Fayette county in the Pennsylvania legislature in 1828 and 1829, and was appointed Associate Judge of Fayette county by the Governor of Pennsylvania in 1828 and served on the bench until 1841. He was justice of the peace for many years, served acceptably as a judge, and was a prominent and useful man in Fayette county during his life. He was born in 1789, and died May 28, 1859. He had nine children: Jane, Keziah, Eliza, Dorcas, Mary Ann, William D., Ayres, Sarah and James.

James Nixon, son of Judge Nixon, was reared on a farm and acquired a good practical education. He has always been engaged in farming and hotel-keeping. On October 28, 1852, he was united in marriage to Miss Sarah J. Zerley, of Nicholson township, and daughter of Samuel and Keziah (Griffith) Zerley. Mr. Nixon has eight children: Dorcas, wife of Herman Custer, of Fairchance; Hannah Phebe, married to A. G. Bradley, postmaster at Masontown; Mary J., wife of Robert Goldsboro, druggist at Fairchance; William S., married Rhoda Dawson, and is a farmer in Georges township; James, Jr., of Fairchance, married Frances Nedley; Sarah K., wife of Richard Goldsboro, of Fairchance; Charles B. and Alice.

James Nixon has always been a very active worker in the democratic party. He served as county commissioner from 1885 to 1888, and while favoring strict economy in county expenditures yet advocated liberal provisions and ample appropriations where actually needed for the benefit or important for the material progress of Fayette county. Mr. Nixon is proprietor of the Nixon House at Fairchance, which was erected in 1882, and is a fine three-story frame building containing nineteen rooms and furnished throughout in a tasteful manner. He is a good citizen, a useful business man and a pleasant gentleman.

WILLIAM NORCROSS is fourth in number of eight children born to his parents. He was born in Rostravor township Westmoreland county, Pa., September 23, 1817, and is a son of Charles and Mercy Norcross. The former, who was born in Westmoreland county, Pa., March 18, 1791, was by occupation a blacksmith, and worked three miles from Fayette city. He was married to Mercy Wheatley in 1809. She was born in Fayette county, Pa., January 30, 1791. Charles Norcross died in 1844; his wife died in 1850.

William Norcross, the founder of this branch of the Norcross family, in Fayette county, was a blacksmith by trade, a native of New Jersey, and came to the county and settled near Brownsville in 1793. His wife was a Miss Taylor, also of New Jersey. William Norcross' maternal grandfather, John Wheatley, was born, lived and died in Fayette county, Pa. The subject of this sketch was reared on a farm in Westmoreland county; was first married to Louisa Snyder, June 8, 1843, who was a daughter of Nicholas Snyder, of German descent. She died, and his second wife, Rachel Mastin, was a daughter of Levi Mastin, of Washington county, Pa. Of three children, two are living. J. E. married Jane Hugh, of Brownsville, Pennsylvania.

Mr. Norcross is a substantial democrat, and a good citizen, and is a highly respected member of the Baptist church. His farm, containing about 145 acres of good land, contains rich deposits of coal and limestone. He began life poor and penniless, but by his industry and careful management, has accumulated considerable property.

ANDREW LYNN OSBORN is a native of Georges township, Fayette county, Pa., and was born December 19, 1835. He is a son of Rev. Andrew G. and Jane (Lynn) Osborn, the former a well known and patriotic minister of the Cumberland Presbyterian church, and the latter an estimable woman and native of Somerset county.

The paternal grandfather, Joseph Fowler Osborn, came from Orange county, N. J., to Fayette county, and settled in Georges township in about 1800. He was a soldier in the War of 1812, and his ancestors were natives of Kilkenny, Ireland. The maternal grandfather, Alex. Lynn, was born in Beaver county, removed to Somerset county, and served as a soldier in the War of 1812. The hatchet he carried through that war is now in the possession of A. L. Osborn.

Rev. Andrew G. Osborn was born and reared near Fairchance. His public conduct was above suspicion and his patriotism is deserving of admiration. His family consisted of twelve children: Alexander, served in Seventeenth West Virginia; Joseph; Dr. William, of Pleasant Unity, was drafted, hired a substitute and in less than a month afterward went out as a surgeon of Thirteenth Pennsylvania cavalry; Sarah A., wife of Samuel Robinson, a woolen manufacturer of Greene county, Pa.; Andrew L.; Margaret J.; Dr. Wilkins W. (see his sketch), served in Fourteenth Pennsylvania cavalry; Henry M. and Isaac B. (twins) served in Fourteenth Pennsylvania cavalry; Milton K. and Louisa, killed by an explosion of oil in 1852, and Mary Virginia, of Upper Middletown. For full history of Rev. A. G. Osborn—his fine ministerial and magnificent war record—see sketch of Dr. W. W. Osborn.

Andrew L. Osborn was educated in the common schools, and has always been engaged in farming in Georges township. He is an extensive lumber contractor for the Fairchance Furnace Company, and has acted successfully in that capacity for several years.

He enlisted in Company E, Fourteenth Pennsylvania cavalry, and was in eighteen battles besides numerous skirmishes, several daring raids and many fatiguing marches. He was mustered into the service November 23, 1862, as a corporal, and was honorably discharged as a sergeant May 30, 1865.

On December 4, 1867, he was married to Miss Mary E. Wood, daughter of John C. Wood. They have five children: William, Louisa, Ella, Presley and Arthur.

In politics Mr. Osborn and his brothers are uncompromising republicans. He has served as school director in a democratic township, and is now central committeeman of Georges township. Mr. Osborn is a member of the G. A. R. at Uniontown, a member of the Presbyterian church, and is an intelligent and upright man.

WILLIAM PARSHALL (deceased), a prominent and influential citizen of Uniontown, and for thirty-six years a well-known member of the Fayette county bar. He was born in the house now occupied by his widow, in German township, Fayette county, Pa., September 14, 1821, and was a son of Elias and Hannah Matilda (Grove) Parshall.

The founder of the Parshall family in the United States came from England, and bought Gardiner's Island (near New York City). He willed this island to his children, a son and a daughter; the latter married a Mr. Gardiner, and they bought her brother's interest in the island. This brother removed to Riverhead, on Long Island. He had three sons: John, James and Elias Parshall; the first two settled somewhere up the North river. Elias Parshall, who married Polly Young, was a sea captain, and inflicted considerable damage on British shipping during the Revolutionary War. One of the captain's sons, Elias Parshall, Sr., learned the trade of ship-builder, and removed to New Jersey, where he married a Miss Tingley, and subsequently came to Brownsville, in about 1800. He was a strong and earnest working Baptist, and died in German township. His son, Elias, Parshall, father of William Parshall, was born in Morris county, N. J., in 1797, and came to Fayette county when three years of age. He married Miss Hannah Matilda, daughter of Jacob and Mary (Brown) Grove, both natives of Shepardstown, Md.; the former was a tanner, and settled in Masontown. Elias Parshall was a farmer of German township, where he owned a large body of very fine land; was very courteous and hospitable and died in 1882.

William Parshall was reared on a farm, and educated at Rector, Va., and Washington, Pa. He studied law with Gen. Joshua B. Howell, of Uniontown, and was admitted to the Fayette county bar September 7, 1847. Mr. Parshall, however, gave a part of his attention to farming in German and Nicholson townships until 1875, when he removed to Uniontown and formed a law partnership with G. W. K. Minor. From this time until his death, July 4, 1883, he continued in the active practice of his profession.

In April, 1864, he was united in marriage to Miss Martha Hawks, a native of Orleans county, N. Y., and a daughter of Jonathan and Clarissa (Pease) Hawks, who were natives of Massachusetts and New York respectively, the former a soldier in the War of 1812, the latter a daughter of Dr. Jacob Pease, who was secreted by a Frenchman and escaped death in the Indian massacre at Detroit in 1812. To Mr. and Mrs. Parshall were born five children: William and Emily, living, and Louisa, Delafield and Vesta, deceased.

William Parshall owned the home farm of 190 acres of choice land and a Springhill farm of 192 acres. He was large and portly, and was noted for open-handed hospitality. He was an active republican, but never thirsted for public office; a constant student, and well versed in the law, he had a good practice at the time of his death.

DAVID PHILLIPS (deceased) was one of the foremost farmers of his township. He was born on the old "Phillip's homestead," in Redstone township, Fayette county, Pa. He was a son of Benjamin Phillips, an enterprising and industrious farmer of Redstone township.

Benjamin Phillips was a son of Benjamin Phillips, Sr., an ex-Revolutionary soldier. Benjamin Phillips, Sr., came from New Jersey to Jefferson township prior to 1800. He was a common laborer, but being a man of energy, he acquired means sufficient to purchase what is now the old Phillips homestead farm in Redstone township. He died in 1831, aged eighty-five years.

David Phillips was reared on a farm, and received his education in the common schools. Leaving school he engaged in farming and stock raising until his death, February 13, 1881. He was married to Miss Matilda Ann Brown, daughter of David Brown, of Menallen township. Mr. Brown was a prosperous farmer and a prominent citizen of his township. To Mr. and Mrs. Phillips were born three children, of whom two are living: Charles J., born October 25, 1862, married Harriet, daughter of John Risbeck, and Della P., born July 12, 1878.

David Phillips was a strong democrat and a successful farmer. His farm consisted of 213 acres of good land, and passed, at his death, into the hands of Newton Chalfant Mrs. Phillips now resides on the "old Ryan place" in Menallen township. During his life Mr. Phillips was held in high esteem by all who knew him.

GEORGE PORTER was born in Indianapolis, Ind., October 21, 1836. He was educated at the Dunlap's Creek Academy in Redstone township, and was engaged in farming in German township for seventeen years. In 1879 he purchased property in McClellandtown and began the mercantile business in that town and has since continued. He owns and operates a farm near to McClellandtown.

He was married to Miss Elizabeth Parshall, the daughter of Elias Parshall, who was a native of German township, and was at that time a large landowner, farmer and stock raiser of the country.

They have the following children: Elizabeth, married to George A. Hogg, of Iron Bridge, Westmoreland county, is engaged in the iron business in Pittsburgh.

Mr. Porter is a member and elder in the Presbyterian church at McClellandtown. His parents were Edward T. and Elizabeth (Wilson) Porter. Their children were named James H., now living in Indianapolis, Ind., and is engaged in farming; Edward T., deceased; and George, the subject of this sketch. His father, Edward T. Porter, was born in Chillicothe, Ohio, and removed to Indianapolis, Ind., where he engaged in merchandising until his death in 1842.

His mother's maiden name was Elizabeth Wilson; she was married a second time to Eleazer Robinson, of Uniontown, Pa. By this union she had the following children: William L., of Uniontown; and Mary E., wife of Dr. A. P. Bowie, of the same place.

Mr. Porter's paternal grandfather, George Porter, was a native of Chillicothe, Ohio, where he lived and died.

James Wilson, grandfather, was a native of Lancaster county, Pa., born in 1764, and came to Fayette county when twelve years of age. He was married twice: the first time to Miss Mary H. Robb; the second time to Miss Elizabeth Lowrie; was a large land holder, and lived on his farm near McClellandtown, till his death. He was one of the early justices of the peace of German township, having succeeded his father-in-law Andrew Robb, to that office. He served from 1807 to 1840, when he became paralyzed.

Several of his first wife's children, Dr. William Wilson, Andrew Wilson, and Sarah Yandes, were raised in Indiana. John Wilson, of German township, deceased, served as justice of the peace, and was an upright, useful citizen; was a son by the second wife. Rev. Alexander Wilson and Dr. William L. Wilson, of Washington county, Pa., are grandsons.

JAMES M. PROVANCE was born in Nicholson township, Fayette county, Pa., March 23, 1849; was reared on a farm, and attended the common schools. At the age of thirteen, he commenced to make his own living as deck sweeper on a steamboat, which he followed for one year, when he shipped as deck hand, after which he worked as a fireman for some time. He was engaged upon the river for about ten years, when he engaged in mining coal. Afterwards learned the trade of stone mason.

In 1872 he was married to Miss Mary M. Romesburg, a daughter of Adam Romesburg, who was a native of Pennsylvania, and of German descent. Mrs. Provance died September 4, 1887. To this union were born five children: Alfrida, Isa D., Della, Harry B. and James L. Alfrida is married to Daniel Davis of Fayette county.

Mr. Provance owns a comfortable little home at New Geneva.

Theron Provance, the father of the subject of this sketch, was born in Fayette county Pa., owned a small farm and had a comfortable home. His father, Joseph Y. Provance, was one of the early settlers of western Pennsylvania, and was a large land owner. He was of English birth, and came to America, and settled in Pennsylvania before the Revolution, and took part in that war. He was the father of twenty-seven children.

CAPTAIN JESSE PROVANCE is of English descent, and commanded the first steamboat that ever ascended the Monongahela river to Fairmont, W. Va. He is a son of David and Agnes (Hartly) Provance, and was born near New Geneva, in Nicholson township, Fayette county, Pa., August 13, 1819.

His grandfather, Provance, owned the celebrated "Provance's Bottoms," which are broad flats, extending along the Monongahela river, from the mouth of Jacob's creek down to the mouth of Catt's run. They are said to be the most productive tracts of land in western Pennsylvania. Mr. Provance's ancestors "were noted for their size and muscular powers, as well as love of all athletic sports."

His father, David Provance was a native of Nicholson township; he was a good farmer, and a quiet, orderly man. He had sixteen children, of whom five sons and three daughters are living.

Captain Jesse Provance was reared on a farm and attended the subscription schools then in existence. In 1839 he went on the Monongahela river and engaged as a hand on steamboats and flat-boats.

In 1864 he left the river, engaged in the hotel business in New Geneva, and has continued in that line of business up to the present time. He is now the proprietor of the Provance house, and is well prepared to accommodate the wants of the traveling public.

In 1840 he was married to Miss Hester, daughter of Benjamin Miller; she died in 1845, leaving three children: Elizabeth, Joseph (dead), Malinda (dead). In 1848 Mr. Provance married again; his second wife was Miss Nancy, daughter of John McCann. Unto this union were born twelve children, of whom seven are living: Sylvanus, Minor, Stewart, Lazier, Amadee, Frankie and Fannie.

Captain Jesse Provance has always been an industrious and hard-working man. He was the possessor of a remarkably good constitution which, has been very much impaired by excessive hard labor in early life. He has many good qualities of head and heart, and is a kind and obliging gentleman.

COL. JAMES ROBINSON, a highly respected and very worthy citizen of Fairchance, is of Scotch-Irish Presbyterian stock. He is a son of John and Mary (McClain) Robinson, and was born November 27, 1806, in what is now Nicholson township.

His paternal grandfather was born in County Antrim, Ireland, and with one sister came to Carlisle, Pa., where he served as an elder in the Presbyterian church.

John Robinson (father) was born near Carlisle in 1775, removed to Westmoreland county, and in 1780 came to Fayette county, where he settled in Georges township. He had several brothers in the frontier Indian wars, one of whom was killed. He was married, in 1805, to Miss Mary McClain, and they had two children: James, and Samuel, born May 1, 1808. His wife was a daughter of John and Margaret McClain. John McClain came from Scotland to Virginia in 1760, and afterwards settled on the Miami river near the site of Dayton. He was a strict Presbyterian.

Col. Robinson was reared on the old Robison farm, and received in the subscription schools of that day, a practical education, that fitted him for an active business career in life.

Leaving school, he engaged in farming, but soon began school teaching and continued in that avocation till 1835. In 1835 he took charge of Springhill Furnace store for J. K. Duncan. From 1836 to 1856 Col. Robinson had charge of Fairchance Iron Works, and was very popular as a superintendent, and highly respected as a gentleman.

He was married, January 27, 1857, to Mrs. Catherine Saams, of Allegheny county, Pa. She died September 9, 1863, and left three children: Margaret Ann, John Taylor and Emma Caroline. For his second wife, he married, February 15, 1866, Miss Lavina P. Caldwell, of St. Joseph, Mo. To this union two children were born, both of whom died young.

He was commissioned colonel of the State Militia in 1830, by Gov. Wolf.

Colonel Robinson and Squire Ayres were the first two school directors appointed in Georges township.

He was a director in the B. & O. railroad from Uniontown to Connellsville, and a director for a long time in two of the Uniontown banks.

He holds fast to the religious faith of his forefathers. During the last year he erected a very fine residence at Fairchance, and there, surrounded by his friends, he is living a quiet and peaceful life, with no clouds to mar the future before him and the memory of a well spent life behind him.

JOHN TAYLOR ROBINSON, one of Georges township's young business men, is a son of Colonel James and Catherine (Taylor) Saams Robinson, and was born near Fairchance, Georges township, Fayette county, Pa., June 14, 1859.

John T. Robinson (for family history see sketch of Colonel Robinson) was reared on a farm, and carefully instructed in all the details of successful farm management. He was educated in the common and select schools, and attended one year at the University of Wooster, Ohio. Leaving school, he engaged in farming, and has continued largely in that line of business ever since.

On February 15, 1888, he was united in marriage to Miss Eugenia Hampton McCormick, of Cumberland, Md. They have one child, a daughter, Jennie McCormick. Mrs. Robinson's father, Dr. William Hampton McCormick, was born near Smithfield in 1826; read medicine with Dr. Smith Fuller, of Uniontown; was graduated from Jefferson Medical College; and for many years a leading physician of Cumberland, where he has an extensive and lucrative practice.

John T. Robinson owns two hundred acres of land in Georges and Springhill townships. In religious faith he is a Presbyterian. In political opinion, he is a strong republican, and has served acceptably as school director of Georges township. Resides in a comfortable home near Oliphants, and divides his time between managing his farms and superintending his father's (Colonel Robinson) extensive business affairs. He is a conscientious and upright business man, and is one of

the directors of the People's Bank at Uniontown.

JACOB RUBLE, JR., son of Jacob and Ruth (Rhodes) Ruble, was born in Monongalia county, Va. (now W. Va.), July 6, 1824; was educated in the Virginia subscription schools, and afterwards learned the trade of a millwright, which he has since followed.

His paternal grandfather, Samuel Ruble, was born in Loudon county, Va., in 1735, and died July 11, 1799. He was a miller and farmer, and married Mary Jennings (born in 1742, died March 25, 1823), and had two children: Jacob, Sr., and George W., who was drowned. Samuel Ruble's father came from Germany.

His father, Jacob Ruble, Sr., was born in Monongalia county, Va. (now W. Va.), January 5, 1775; was a miller, and owned two mills that were far-famed in that day for doing good work. He married Miss Ruth Rhodes, daughter of William Rhodes. They had eight children: Joshua, born March 12, 1812; Samuel, born December 24, 1813, Elizabeth, born in 1816; William, born June 2, 1818; Mary, born January 21, 1821; Jacob, born July 6, 1824; Ruth, born July 18, 1828; Sarah J., born March 10, 1832.

William Rhodes (maternal great-grandfather) belonged to an artillery company in the War of the Revolution, and rendered excellent service at Baltimore.

Jacob Ruble, Jr., was married February 29, 1852, to Miss Minerva, daughter of John and Hannah (Keiser) Saddler, both natives of Springhill township and of German descent. Mr. Ruble has five children: John C., born November 30, 1852; Sallie J., born February 25, 1853; Hannah M., born April 24, 1857; William J., born April 24, 1857; Ulysses G., born August 14, 1863. He owns a valuable flouring mill near Smithfield, and also possesses thirty-two acres of good land. On the site of this mill Meshac Davis erected, in 1795, one of the first mills west of the Alleghenies. It passed to Jesse Evans and Davis' heirs, and was sold to Noah Lyon in 1835, who sold it to Nathaniel G. Hurst (1836), under whose ownership the old mill was torn down, in its stead was erected the present large and commodious mill, which afterwards passed into the hands of George T. Paul, and was next sold to its present owner, Jacob Ruble, Jr., in 1873. Ruble's mill has all the latest milling machinery, and is fitted up with all modern improvements. It has quite a reputation for manufacturing first-class flour. He is a Master Mason, is a fine workman, an experienced and skillful miller, an entertaining conversationalist and a good citizen.

WILLIAM SANDUSKEY, of Scotch descent and a highly respected citizen of New Geneva, is a son of Jacob and Sarah (Way) Sanduskey, and was born in New Geneva, Nicholson township, Fayette county, Pa., March 6, 1820.

Jacob Sanduskey was a native of Nicholson township. His people were Quakers. When a mere child, his father, mother, brothers and sisters were taken prisoners by Indians and no information was ever obtained of them afterwards. Jacob was taken after this sad affair and kindly cared for by strangers. He was raised by George Wilson, learned the trade of stone-splitting, and engaged in that business until he died, in June, 1852. His wife was a native of Eastern Virginia, a devoted member of the Presbyterian church, and died in December, 1852.

William Sanduskey was reared at the village of New Geneva, obtained the scant education of the subscription schools, and at eighteen years of age engaged with Frederick Eberhart to learn the trade of carpenter. Three years later he began business for himself and was continuously engaged in contracting and building until 1888, when he was disabled from further active work by having his hand caught and lacerated in a circular-saw.

On January 23, 1844, he married Miss Dugan. They had eight children: David D., Sarah J., Elzie, Dianna, Mary J., Elizabeth, Rachel and William, all of whom are dead except William, a carpenter and furniture dealer of New Geneva, and Rachel, wife, of Samuel Wigle. Mrs. Sanduskey was a member of the Methodist Episcopal church, and died July 16, 1865. Mr. Sanduskey married for his second wife, August 24, 1867, Miss Anna, daughter of James and Lucinda Cannon, of Mt. Morris, Greene county, Pa., the former a blacksmith, born in 1805, the latter died in 1885.

William Sanduskey owns a good house at New Geneva, and eight acres of land near that village. He is a republican, but takes no active part in political matters. He is a member of the Methodist Episcopal church, while his wife is a member of the Baptist church; but this occasions no jar for they travel life's pathway harmoniously and are highly respected by their neighbors.

MILES SCHNATTERLY, a comfortably situated farmer of Nicholson township, is a son of John and Malinda (Kendall) Schnatterly. He was born in Nicholson township, Fayette county, Pa., September 12, 1833.

His great-grandfather emigrated to Philadelphia from Holland, prior to 1775, and subsequently removed to what is now Nicholson township. Two of his brothers had preceded him, but were never heard of after leaving home, and were probably slain by Indians. He was a farmer and a devoted follower of Martin Luther.

His grandfather, John Schnatterly, was a native of Nicholson township, where he was twice married. Of the first family of eight children was John Schnatterly, Jr., father of Miles Schnatterly.

John Schnatterly, Jr., was born near New Geneva, April 17, 1805. In 1827 he married Miss Malinda, daughter of Thomas Kendall. They had nine children, of whom seven are living: Margaret (Mrs. Sturgis), Mary (Mrs. Chestler), Elizabeth (Mrs. Hartley), Miles, John C., stone mason at New Geneva; Hon. Thomas Benton, who was district attorney in 1866, member of the Pennsylvania legislature in 1870, 1877 and 1885, was State senator in 1879 and 1886, now an attorney-at-law at Uniontown; Lewis W., physician in Freeport, Pa. Mrs. Schnatterly was born in 1807, who is still living. John Schnatterly, Jr., owned a valuable farm of 111 acres of land, was engaged in farming and was a life-long democrat. He was ever ready and willing to work for his party, was elected county commissioner in 1859, and after the expiration of his term of office was justice of the peace for five years. He was a prominent member of the Baptist church at Greensborough and died July 26, 1882.

Miles Schnatterly was brought up on the farm, educated in the common schools and Georges Creek Academy and was engaged in farming with his father. He made two western trips, one in 1863 and the other in 1866, and while in the West he was engaged in mining in Montana for a short time.

On July 16, 1865, he married Miss Jane, daughter of Michael Schnatterly. They have four children: Nora B. (dead), Carson W., John M. and Otto C.

In 1870 Mr. Schnatterly removed to McDonough county, Ill., and was there engaged as a carpenter and farmer. In 1873 he returned to the home farm where he continues to reside. He is a good democrat and has filled various township offices. He was one of the organizing members and at present a deacon of the Oak Hill Baptist church. His wife and two sons are members of the same church. He is an Odd Fellow and a leading citizen of Nicholson township.

HENRY L. SHANK, D. D. S., one of New Geneva's leading citizens and a dentist of good reputation, is a son of David and Anna (Dils) Shank, and was born in Springhill township, Fayette county, Pa., October 28, 1831.

David Shank was of German extraction, born in Springhill township in 1807, and died in 1832. He was a cooper by trade, a whig in political opinion and a member of the Mennonite church. His wife was Anna Dils, who was a member of the Presbyterian church. She died January 17, 1882. Her father, Philip Dils, was a Fayette county farmer who was born in New Jersey.

Dr. Shank was reared on a farm, educated in the subscription schools and took one term at Mt. Hope Academy, Ohio. At twenty years of age, Mr. Shank began teaching school and continued in this business until 1858, when he read medicine and studied dentistry with Dr. P. L. Kramer, of Greensboro, Greene county, Pa. He practiced dentestry in 1859, at Greensboro, then for a short time at Carmichael's, and from there he removed to New Geneva, where he has since been engaged in practicing dentistry.

On March 29, 1864, he was married to Miss Fannie, daughter of Marshall Springer. To this union five children have been born: Anna L., wife of A. J. Hayden of Greensboro; David Marshall (dead); Rachel D., Emma L. and Lizzie S. (unmarried).

In 1865 he purchased property at New Geneva, where he is comfortably situated. Mr. Shank is a democrat, was elected justice of the peace in 1885, for a term of five years; is serving as justice of the peace and for nine years has held the offices of assessor and auditor of Nicholson township. He is a member of the Presbyterian church at the "Old Frame," while his wife and daughters, Mrs. Hayden and Rachel, are members of the Baptist church at Greensboro. He has been the "architect of his own fortune," is a successful dentist, and a useful man.

WILLIAM GARANNE SHARPNACK, of Masontown, was born at High House, Georges township, Fayette county, Pa., on the 15th of May, 1854, and is a son of Daniel and Mary Ann (Denny) Sharpnack.

His paternal grandfather, Daniel Sharpnack, was one of the early merchants of Greene county, Pa., and married Mary Ann Rice, a cousin of Dan Rice, the great showman. His maternal grandfather was John Denny, who used to own and operate the old Beeson mill at Uniontown.

His father, Daniel Sharpnack, a native of Jefferson, Greene county, Pa., and was born August 12, 1811, in what is now the Ingraham hotel. He came to Uniontown when twelve years old, lived with Old Ellis Bailey, and attended Madison College for five years. At seventeen he was apprenticed to Hugh Graham to learn the trade of carpenter. When he had completed his trade, he became a contractor. His first contract was repairing the old court house. He afterwards built the Dawson Law Building, Judge J. K. Ewing's residence, and the old Baptist church on Morgantown street. From 1837 to 1842 he followed merchandising at Carmichael's, Greene county, Pa. From 1842 to 1867 he engaged in farming at High House, when he came to Uniontown and entered the real estate business. The first piece of property he handled was the Weniger block that he bought and sold at a clear profit of $6,000. He successfully prosecuted the real estate business for several years. He was married December 31, 1834, to Mary Ann Denny. He was a member of the Cumberland Presbyterian church for over forty years, and died April 9, 1889. Daniel Sharpnack was a very fine mechanic, a good farmer, and a remarkably successful business man.

William G. Sharpnack attended the common schools, in 1873 entered the Iron City College, Pittsburgh, Pa., and graduated the same year. He attended Dickenson College, York, Pa., in 1875, and made penmanship a specialty. He taught a business school at Monongahela City for a few months, and then turned his attention to farming, near Brownsville, at the strong solicitation of his aged parents. In August, 1881, he began the mercantile business at Masontown, Fayette County, Pa., and has successfully continued in it until the present time.

Mr. Sharpnack was married to Miss Ida Neff, daughter of Dr. George W. Neff, Sr., and sister of Hon. George W. Neff, Jr., May 2, 1883. He is well qualified for the mercantile business that he is so successfully prosecuting; owns the handsomest residence in Masontown, which he architected and built to his own taste.

JAMES R. SHOAF, an energetic and prosperous farmer of Nicholson township, is a son of James and Malinda (Bowell) Shoaf, and was born in Georges township, March 6, 1842.

His father, James, was a son of James Shoaf, a day laborer, who lived in the mountains, and was killed by a log falling on him at the raising of a building. James Shoaf began life under very discouraging circumstances; could not read or write, but at his death left a handsome fortune, acquired by his own industry and energy. He was a farmer and democrat. He owned a valuable farm of two hundred acres of land underlaid with coal and well stocked.

He was married to Miss Malinda, daughter of Captain Bazil Bowell, who commanded a company in the War of 1812. They had nine children, of whom six are living: he was born July 26, 1814, and died July 3, 1881.

James R. Shoaf was carefully trained in farm work, and attended the common schools. Selecting farming as an occupation, he steadily devoted his time and attention to that business. On May 11, 1868, he married Miss Mary Harriet, daughter of Joseph Newcomber, an industrious farmer of Georges township. Their union have been blessed with ten children: Thomas B., Joseph N. (dead), James C., Mary Malinda, Alda Tilden, John H., Daisy D., Nancy I., Matilda R. and Frank N. Shoaf.

He is a democrat, but does not neglect his work to engage in politics. He owns two splendid farms of 203 acres in a good state of cultivation, of which one hundred acres are underlaid with coal. He recently sold a tract of sixty acres for $6,500. He is a quiet, peaceable, industrious and prosperous citizen.

DANIEL SMITH, one of the oldest and most highly respected citizens of Georges township, was born in the house he now lives in, in Georges township, Fayette county, Pa., April 1, 1806, and is a son of Henry and Margaret (Sheeter) Smith. His paternal grandfather, Philip Smith, was captain of a military organization in Germany, emigrated to Maryland prior to 1752, and removed to what is now Georges township, where he secured a patent in 1769 for what is now the Kyle, Mosier and Deffenbaugh farms. He afterwards moved to Wayne county, Ohio, where he died. His maternal grandfather, Sheeter, was born in Germany, and emigrated to Maryland, where he afterwards died. His father, Henry Smith, was born in Maryland in 1752, and came with his father (Philip) to Georges township in 1769. Henry Smith served in the Revolutionary War, was a democrat, and a member of the Lutheran church. His first wife was Elizabeth Grantstaff, by whom he had eight children. His second wife was Margaret, widow of George Stow. To the second union were born five children.

Daniel Smith received his education in the old subscription schools, and never engaged in any business but farming. He cast his first vote for Andrew Jackson, and from that day has been a democrat of the Jacksonian persuasion. He has held nearly all his township offices. Daniel Smith married Miss Elizabeth, daughter of David and Magdalena (Landis) Roderick. To Mr. and Mrs. Smith were born eight children: Henry, of Shell Rock, Iowa., married Ann Deyarman; Louisa (dead); Lydia M. (dead), married J. K. Anderson; David R., married Annie Kennison, and died in Kansas; Samuel M., married to Phebe A. Patton, and a gardener at Great Bend, Kas.; Orlando (dead); Andrew J., married Eliza J. Deyarman (dead), and lives in Iowa, enlisted in First Virginia Cavalry (federal), was at Fredericksburg, Antietam and in many other battles, and Daniel Porter Smith, married to Margaret, daughter of Henry Malaby, of Iowa. D. P. Smith was educated at Georges Creek Academy, and is a man of good general information. He is a leading and a substantial farmer, a democrat, and has served for years as school director.

Daniel Smith and his wife have been commendable members of Mt. Moriah Baptist church for over forty years. Mr. Smith has retired from active life, and in the ease and comfort of his beautiful home can calmly meditate over his long and well-spent life.

JOHN B. STEPHENS, of Redstone, the fifth of a family of eight children, was born at Lock No. 3, Allegheny county, Pa., June 7, 1843, and is a son of Nathaniel and Eliza (Parsall) Stephens.

The Stephens family is one of the oldest families in Fayette county. Nathaniel Stephens, Sr.(grandfather), was a native of Washington township, drafted in the War of 1812, but was never called into service, and died in 1868. His son, Nathaniel (father), was born June 5, 1807, married Miss Eliza Parsall, and died at California, Pa., August 1, 1886. He and his wife were consistent members of the Methodist Episcopal church. Her father, William Parsall, was one of the pioneer settlers of Ohio, and died in Cincinnati.

John B. Stephens was raised on a farm, and received a fair education in the common schools of Fayette county. He has made farming the business of his life, and has resided on his present farm for twenty-three years, although he works some at his trade, that of carpenter.

On January 3, 1865, he was married to Miss Roxanna Kelley. They have seven children, living, born and named as follows: Elmer N., June 25, 1866, at Lock No. 3; Charles A., May 12, 1868, a painter at Scottdale; Florence R., January 22, 1870; Emma E., October 2, 1871; Mary E., June 27, 1873; Joseph P., September 22, 1877, and Olive B., September 24, 1878. Mrs. Stephens' father, John Kelley, came from Westmoreland county, was a millwright, a consistent Christian and passed away April, 1877.

John B. Stephens was one of fifteen boys, of Elizabeth, Pa., who enlisted in the One Hundred and Twenty-third Regiment Pennsylvania Volunteers. Mr. Stephens participated in the great battles of Antietam, Fredericksburg and Chancellorsville. In the dreadful carnage of Fredericksburg he received a severe wound in the shoulder, and was honorably discharged May 1, 1863.

In politics Mr. Stephens is a steadfast republican. He and his wife are members of the Fairview Methodist Episcopal church in Jefferson township. His farm is two miles from Brownsville, and contains one hundred acres of good land, underlaid with coal and limestone. He is one of the successful business men of Redstone.

JAMES T. SPRINGER, an expert glass-blower and a comfortably situated farmer of Nicholson township, is a son of Marshall and Susanna (Shroyer) Springer. He was born in New Geneva, Fayette county, Pa., December 25, 1833.

In an early day his grandfather, David Springer, moved from Pennsylvania to Iowa, where he secured a tract of land under the "Homestead Act." He died in Iowa. His father, Marshall Springer, was a native of Fayette county. He learned the trade of a shoemaker, which he was engaged in during his life. His wife was Miss Susanna Shroyer, daughter of John Shroyer, and born in Greensboro July 12, 1814. They had twelve children, of whom eight are still living: J. T., J. C., C. A., D. M., W. F., Rachel, Hannah F. and Emma G. Since 1830 Mrs. Springer has been a member of the Baptist church at Greensboro. Mr. Springer was an earnest democrat and a good citizen. He died in New Geneva, February 27, 1861, aged forty-eight years.

James T. Springer was raised in New Geneva; attended school until fourteen years of age, when he entered the glass works to learn the trade of glass-blower. He served three years as an apprentice, removed to Pittsburgh in 1853, and was there engaged at his trade until 1873, when he returned to Nicholson township and bought his present farm.

On July 8, 1857, he married Miss Sarah Louisa, daughter of William Nutt, residing near Fayette City. They reared an adopted daughter, Ella Springer. She is now married, and resides on part of their farm. Mr. Springer has made extensive improvements on his farm, and built a good tenant house and put up a large barn.

Mr. Springer is a democrat, has served as road supervisor and assessor of Nicholson township. He is a man of considerable business ability, and is very pleasantly situated on his farm in Nicholson township.

LIEUT. JAMES ALEXANDER WELTNER, one of the leading farmers of German township, and an extensive wool-buyer of Fayette county, is a son of John and Elizabeth Dunaway, the former a native of Greene county and the latter of Luzerne township.

James A. Weltner was born in German township, March 3, 1839, and is of German extraction.

His father, John Weltner, was born in 1799, and died in 1877. He came to Fayette county, about fifty-one years ago, and was a justice of the peace for Nicholson township in 1856. He subsequently removed to German township, where he farmed for many years. He was a member of the Presbyterian church, and one of the building committee of the McClellandtown Presbyterian church. He married Miss Elizabeth, a daughter of Matthew Dunaway. They had nine children, eight living in Fayette county, and one in Greene county, Pa. Mrs. Weltner died in 1850.

James A. Weltner was raised on a farm, attended the common schools. He desired to enter the army in the beginning of the war, but his father objected. In 1862 he enlisted in the One Hundred and Sixty-eighth Regiment, Pennsylvania Infantry, and went to Camp Howe, where he was immediately elected First Lieutenant of Company D., and afterwards declined a captaincy on the promotion of the captain of the regiment to major. His declination was on account of not thinking himself competent, when more experienced men were members in the company. His brother, Thomas N., was in Captain Gilmore's company and saw a great deal of hard and dangerous service. Another brother was Captain John R. Weltner, who raised and was captain of Company I, Eighty-fifth Pennsylvania Volunteers, till his health failed him, when he resigned. Recuperating, he raised a company for the One Hundred and Sixteenth Regiment, serving through the war and dying afterwards from disease contracted while in the service.

After serving faithfully through the war, Lieutenant Weltner came home and persuaded his father, that he could do something besides plowing corn. After convincing him of the fact, he borrowed six hundred dollars from his father and engaged in speculation. In six months he increased his capital to twelve hundred dollars, and after this successfully branched out for nineteen years, into all kinds of stock, with William McShane as partner, of German township.

He has been for twenty years in the wool business. He buys from twenty to fifty thousand pounds every season, and sells to eastern markets.

In 1883 he was married to Miss Malzenia, daughter of James M. Allebaugh, a glass-blower by trade. Unto their union has been born two children; Robison Gray and Elizabeth Hale Weltner.

Lieutenant Weltner owns 240 acres of choice and well improved land, situated in the center of German township, which he devotes more to grazing than farming. He has a fine and tasteful residence, a first-class barn and splendid out-buildings. He is a model farmer, and owns a valuable farm.

He is a substantial member of the Presbyterian church and is emphatically one of the go-ahead farmers and business men of his township.

JOHN L. WHETSTONE descended from one of the old and respected families of Fayette county. He is of German-Irish and Welsh extraction, and was born in Springhill township, Fayette county, Pa., August 10, 1831. His father, Joseph Whetstone, was born in Springhill township in 1792. He was a farmer, owned a small farm of fifty acres, and, in connection with his farm, started and operated a fulling-mill in Springhill township. He afterwards purchased one hundred acres of land on Cheat river. Joseph Whetstone was the father of twelve children, two of whom died in infancy; the others lived to be men and women. Seven of the children are living at the present time. He was a democrat, and for many years a consistent member of the Methodist Protestant church. He died in 1852, at the age of sixty years. His wife, Eliza Whetstone (nee Louchrey), was born in Maryland, in 1808, and when very young she came with her people to Fayette county. She was a member of the same church of her husband, and died in 1874, at the age of sixty-six years.

The paternal grandfather of John L. Whetstone was one of the pioneers of Springhill township. He owned a large tract of land, but his principal occupation was boating on the Ohio and Mississippi rivers. He had five children. His death occurred after a long and well-spent life, in 1800.

The maternal grandfather, Louchrey, was an early settler in Fayette county. He was a fuller by trade, and owned a farm in Virginia.

John L. Whetstone's school advantages were limited. At the age of ten years he removed with his father to West Virginia, where he remained till 1861, when he returned to Springhill township, thence to Nicholson township, in 1862, where he has since resided. December 18, 1856, he was married to Miss Sarah A. Franks, a daughter of Samuel Franks (the latter is now in the eighty-third year of his age.) To their union were born five children: Aurelia E. (deceased), Eliza S. (deceased), William W. (deceased); the two living, Pleassie M. and Samuel F.; the latter is now in his seventeenth year. Mr. Whetstone learned the shoemaker's trade, but has followed farming most exclusively, all his life.

He owns a comfortable home and two and one-half acres of land, and superintends his father-in-law's farm of one hundred and sixty-two acres. He is a stanch democrat in politics and has filled the various township offices. He is a member of the Methodist Episcopal church at Smithfield, is one of its trustees and has held the offices of steward and class leader. His wife and daughter are members of the same church. Mr. Whetstone has a clock that has been in possession of the family for three generations and is over one hundred years old and is still a splendid time-piece.

ROBERT THOMAS WILLIAMS, of French-German descent and a very successful business man of New Geneva, was born at Millsboro, Washington county, Pa., August 9, 1852, and is a son of John P. and Sarah (Simington) Williams.

John P. Williams was born in Fayette county, in 1810, learned the trade of tailor, which he pursued for many years, and was justice of the peace for several terms at Masontown, and also at Greensboro, Greene county, Pa. He was a sober, industrious man, had a good knowledge of law, was a democrat in politics and a consistent member of the Presbyterian church. His death occurred in 1875. His wife was a daughter of Rev. Robert Simington, a Methodist minister. She was a member of that church, and died in 1856, leaving four children, of whom only Robert T. and Rachel, wife of A. Cunningham, are living.

Robert T. Williams was reared in Millsboro, and at eleven years of age, went to Ohio, where he remained eighteen months, then returned to Pennsylvania. After a short time he removed to Masontown and was engaged for one year by Benjamin Jones, a farmer of German township. After the expiration of his year on the farm, he was for a time at Fairview, and then at New Geneva. In 1869 he engaged with Littell & Co., of Greensboro, to learn the trade of potter. Upon this firm suspending business, in 1870, he completed his trade with Hamilton & Jones, and then was in their employ till 1875, when he removed to Morgantown, W. Va., and was engaged in the pottery business for three years. Leaving West Virginia, he returned to Greensboro, and worked for Hamilton & Jones until 1880, when he was engaged by John P. Eberhart & Co., of New Geneva, with whom he remained for two years. In 1882 Mr. Williams became proprietor of the New Geneva Pottery Works, and has successfully operated them ever since. His ware is in demand, and he enjoys a liberal patronage and support. In addition to his pottery business, he engaged in the mercantile business at New Geneva, March 27, 1888, and has successfully continued in merchandising till the present.

On April 13, 1876, he was married to Miss Elizabeth Sanduskey. To this union were born two children: Charles R. and William A. Mrs. Williams was a member of the Presbyterian church and died March 16, 1887.

R. T. Williams is a Jeffersonian democrat, and an active member of the Presbyterian church. He began life with no capital, but good health and strong hands, yet by industry, perseverence and careful management has acquired considerable property.

GEORGE YEAGER, of Nicholson, was born December 25, 1811, in Greensboro, Greene county, Pa. He is of German and English extraction, and is a son of George and Rhoda (Fennimore) Yeager, the former born and reared at Reading Pa. He was a hatter by trade. From Reading he removed to Morgantown and later went to Greensboro, where he engaged in making hats. He was the father of fifteen children, nine of whom grew to man and womanhood and three of the nine at present survive: Alfred, Samuel and George.

George Yeager, the father of the subject of this sketch, was a Jackson democrat, and, prior to the breaking out of the War of 1812, was commissioned colonel in the State militia. He left home with the intention of becoming a soldier in the War of 1812 and 1815, but soon after he left home, peace was declared.

He was an active member of the Lutheran church, while his wife was a member of the Presbyterian church.

The last twenty years of his life he lived retired, and at his death was possessed of considerable wealth. The grandfather of George Yeager was also born at Reading, and was a carpenter by trade.

George Yeager was educated in the ordinary subscription schools of his native town. Early in life he learned the trade of hatter with his father, and for a number of years successfully run a hatting business at Greensboro. In 1855 he removed to New Geneva and engaged in merchandising, which he continued up to 1878, when he sold out his stock. In 1863 he began the hotel business and has continued up to the present time. His hotel is known as the Yeager House.

Mr. Yeager was married May 13, 1841, to Miss Anna Maria, daughter of Benjamin Reager, of Greensboro, Pa. To their union have been born four children: James W., Flora L., Maria L. and Elizabeth E. The two first mentioned are dead. James W. was a private soldier in the Fourteenth Pennsylvania Cavalry. While out in the service he sickened and died of typhoid fever at Martinsburg, W. Va.

Mr. Yeager is one of the leading members of the Presbyterian church at Greensboro, having been a member since 1858. He is at present one of the trustees of the church and one of the teachers in the Sabbath-school. He organized the Sabbath-school at Greensboro and has accomplished much good in the Sabbath-school work. His wife has been a member of the same church of her husband since 1854.

LUZERNE, SPRINGFIELD, 

 BULLSKIN, STEWART,

AND MISCELLANEOUS SKETCHES.

GEORGE W. ACKLIN, a resident of Luzerne township, was born near Heistersburgh, Fayette county, Pa., November 17, 1850; of mingled German and British ancestry. His great-grandfather, Joseph Acklin (of English descent), was a Revolutionary soldier, and one of the two white men who first attempted to make a permanent settlement in southwestern Pennsylvania. He was born at Winchester, Va., in 1732, and died near Brownsville, Pa., in 1836. His grandfather, George K. Acklin, was born in 1803, and died in 1887. His father, Thomas J. Acklin, born near Heistersburgh, Pa., in 1827, served in the War of the Rebellion as private in Company H, Seventh Pennsylvania Cavalry, and was killed while a prisoner of war at Savannah, Ga., September 10, 1864.

On his maternal side, a great-grandfather, Peter Snyder, who was among the first settlers of Steubenville, Ohio, was killed at that place by accident in about 1805, leaving a large family of children, of whom Sarah Snyder, the grandmother of the subject of this sketch, was the eldest, who was born in 1791. She was a woman of rarest virtues, first married to Jeptha Baker, afterwards to James Pratt, and died in 1874. Among the children of her latter marriage was Mary J. Acklin, born 1831, mother of George W. Acklin- Margaret G. Acklin, now married to J. H. Ridge, and Annie Acklin; George W. and Annie are now living with their mother at her home near Davidson's Lower Ferry, Pa.

The early years of Mr. Acklin were spent in the country, where he worked as a farm hand, coal miner and country school teacher. In September, 1880, he went to Chicago, where he was enrolled as a student at law at Union College, and was graduated June 15, 1882. He remained in Chicago as a student and clerk in the offices of Sheldon & Sheldon and Daniel H. Hale & Co., until March, 1883, when he returned to his native State and was admitted to membership in the bar of Allegheny county July 5, 1884. Since that time he has pursued the practice of his profession at 402 Grant Street, Pittsburgh, where he is now enjoying a comfortable practice, especially preferring Orphans' and United States Admiralty court business. A democrat of the old school, a zealous member of the M. E. church, a steadfast friend, a self-reliant, persevering worker, always preferring success to notoriety, Mr. Acklin stands among his fellows a fair example of the self-made man.

CHARLES H. BROOKS, one of the intelligent and progressive young men of Springfield, is a son of W. H. and Lucinda)King) Brooks, and was born in Springfield township, Fayette county, Pa., October 19, 1859.

His grandfather, Joseph Brooks, was born in Fayette county, in about 1810, and Dorothea, daughter of Michael Basinger, was also a native of Fayette county. Joseph Brooks was a farmer and stock dealer by occupation, and died a highly respected citizen.

His father, W. H. Brooks, was born near the village of Springfield, Fayette county, and was married June 19, 1856, to Miss Lucinda, daughter of Charles King, by the Rev. William Shimp. Unto their union were born six children: Rebecca, Charles H., Lizzie, Maggie, Harry and Kate.

Charles H. Brooks received his early education in the common schools of Sprinfield township and attended several local normal schools of Fayette county. He began teaching at sixteen years of age in his native township, afterwards taught at New Haven and in Tyrone township. He was engaged for thirteen years in teaching, and was popular and sought after as a teacher.

In the spring of 1887, he was appointed United States gauger and store-keeper in the Internal Revenue Service. He served four months at the Gibbon's Glade distillery and resigned in order to personally superintend his business affairs at home, where he is now successfully engaged in buying and selling stock.

On August 31, 1884, he was married at Sprinfield, by Rev. J. E. McClay, to Miss Fannie B., daughter of Jacob H. and Louisa Miller, of Springfield township. They have one living child: Don Dickerson Brooks, born November 9, 1887.

His grandfather, Charles King, was born in Somerset county, Pa., in 1805. His wife, Rebecca King, was born in 1810, and died July, 1889.

Mr. Brooks is a past officer of Eylan Tribe, No. 260, Improved Order of Red Men, and a member of General Worth Lodge, No. 386, Independent Order of Odd Fellows, of Connellsville, Pa.

Mr. Brooks is an ardent democrat, an enthusiastic worker, and has addressed local political meetings during the different campaigns of the last ten years. He is considered a good political worker by the democrats.

CAPTAIN GEORGE W. BROOKS was born January 15, 1835, in Springfield township, Fayette county, Pa., is a son of Joseph and Dollie (Basinger) Brooks, and is of English and Dutch descent. He was raised on a farm and educated in the common schools of the township. He remained on the farm till the breaking out of the rebellion, when he volunteered in September, 1862, in Company B, Sixteenth Pennsylvania Cavalry, and was commissioned as second lieutenant of his company; he was afterwards promoted to the first lieutenancy, and later as captain of the same company. He was wounded twice, first in the right shoulder at the fight near Harper's Ferry; the second wound was received at the battle of Hatcher's Run, Virginia, on February 6, 1865. His final discharge was July 24, 1865. He now receives a pension of $204 a year. He married Miss Hannah King, daughter of Charles King, of Springfield township, by whom he had twelve children: Alexander, married to Lucinda Dull; Amanda, married to John Skinner; Charles K., married to Sadie Van Horn; Walter, married to Lucinda Bungard; Amy; Carrie, married to Albert Friend; Wilson married Anna Bailey; Rebecca married Levi Gilbert; John, Mary, Jennie and Dellie.

Captain Brooks is a member of the G. A. R., William T. Campbell Post, No. 375, and is past commander. He belongs to the Independent Order of Red Men, No. 260, and to the General Worth Lodge, No. 386, I. O. O. F., of Connellsville. He is a democrat, an ardent worker in his party, and delights in his party's success. He has held the local offices of constable, justice of the peace, and notary public.

GEORGE BOYLE, son of Charles E. and Mary A. (Hendrickson) Boyle was born in Uniontown, May 12, 1863.

George Boyle received his rudimentary education in the schools of Uniontown, prepared for college at Pottstown, Pa., and entered Kenyon College, Ohio, but on account of ill-health was compelled to give up his college course after attending two years.

He was thus compelled to relinquish all ideas of a professional life, and to seek work more congenial to his health; so he engaged in farming. In 1883 he took charge of a farm in Menallen township and remained on it until 1886, when he removed into what is known as "the Bend" in Luzerne township, where he had previously purchased a farm of two hundred acres of good land, upon which he has since erected a very fine house and barn on a high bluff that overlooks the Monongahela river and commands a magnificent view of the surrounding country. Mr. Boyle has a natural taste for farming, and especially interests himself in the breeding of fine stock.

In 1883 he was married to Margaret Richards, of Uniontown. Their union has been blessed with four children: Mary, Lucy, Helen and Catherine.

HON. GEORGE W. CAMPBELL. In our Republic, where offices of trust, responsibility and honor are not hereditary, men generally attain to eminence and distinction through their own efforts; among those, who are thus carving out for themselves honorable careers, is George W. Campbell, of Springfield township. He is a son of James and Rebecca (Kilpatrick) Campbell, and was born in Springfield township, Fayette county, Pa., May 18, 1853.

His father, James Campbell, was of Scotch-Irish descent, and was born at Connellsville, December 25, 1811. He learned the trade of carpenter, and removed to the pleasant little village of Springfield in 1840. He married, on November 2, 1840, Rebecca, daughter of Squire Thomas Kilpatrick, a prominent citizen of Connellsville. To their union were born eleven children, namely: John Fletcher, September 12, 1841; William Thomas (dead), October 12, 1842; Mary Elizabeth (dead), March 23, 1844; James Robison, January 22, 1846; Sarah Jane, November 3, 1848; Samuel Kilpatrick (dead), January 22, 1850; Austin Livingston (dead), March 10, 1851; George Washington, May 18, 1853; Phebe Ann, March 24, 1855; Joseph Rogers, March 14, 1856; Ellen Ethelda, January 3, 1859.

John F., and James R. Campbell enlisted in Company K, Eighty-fifth Regiment, Pennsylvania Infantry Volunteers. William T. Campbell re-enlisted, and was killed at the head of his company at Deep Bottom, Va., August 14, 1864.

George W. Campbell was reared in the village of Springfield, and received his early education in the common schools of Springfield township. When fourteen years of

age, he became a clerk in the general merchandise store of his brother, John F. Campbell, at Springfield. In 1876 he was admitted as partner by his brother, and remained as such until 1880, when he bought out his brother's interest, and has continued successfully in the mercantile business ever since. He carries a large stock of first-class goods, and has built up a large and substantial patronage. January 1, 1882, he established *The Mountaineer*, an eight-page monthly paper, which has a circulation of 1,000 copies. It is a bright, newsy and interesting sheet, welcomed and appreciated wherever it goes.

On August 11, 1880, he was married by the Rev. Samuel Wakefield, to Miss Ida M., daughter of H. L. and Helena Sparks of Indian Head, Fayette county, Pa. Their union have been blessed with the following children; Grace, born June 14th, 1881; Clyde, born November 9, 1883; Kate, born September 6, 1885, and Benjamin Harrison Campbell, born November 10, 1889.

George W. Campbell, an ardent and enthusiastic republican, is well posted on the living political issues of the day, and is an aggressive worker in his party. He has served frequently as committeeman and delegate to county conventions; was delegate to the republican State convention of 1883, and a member of the twenty-fourth district congressional conference, of 1887-88. In the November election, 1888, he was elected a member to the lower house of the Pennsylvania legislature, from Fayette county. In the session of 1888-89, he served as a member of the committee on public buildings, mines and mining, accounts and manufacturing. During this session, he introduced a "bill regulating the employment of foreign born, unnaturalized male persons, and providing a tax of fifteen cents per day on the employers of such persons. He introduced this bill in the interests of home labor, and it was the theme of much speculation and discussion in the press of the State.

JOSEPH R. CAMPBELL, postmaster at Elm, Springfield township, was born in Springfield township, Fayette county, Pa., March 14, 1856. (For ancestry see sketch of brother, Hon. George W. Campbell.) He received his education in the common and normal schools of Fayette county, and was married at Cumberland, Md., September 8, 1887, to Miss Lizzie, daughter of George F. Kimmiel, of Somerset county, Pa. In 1881, with his brother, George W. Campbell, engaged in the mercantile business at Elm, and are now doing a thriving business. Mr. Campbell is a young man full of energy and push, and is destined to make his mark in the business world. He was appointed postmaster at Elm in 1889. He is an influential republican, and is a good worker in his party.

WILLIAM B. CHALFANT, a prominent and experienced physician who is now located at Pennsville, was born on a farm in Jefferson township, Fayette county, Pa., January 17, 1835, and is a son of Walter B. and Mollie Budd (Brown) Chalfant. His father was born in Fayette county, Pa., and his mother was a native of New Jersey.

His paternal grandparents, Chads and Margaret Chalfant, as the name indicates, were of French origin, their ancestors having emigrated to this country in Penn's colony.

Dr. Chalfant was reared on his father's farm until the age of eighteen years, when he entered California Seminary (now S. W. P. Normal School). For three years he taught winter terms in the common schools and attended summer sessions at the seminary. In 1856 he entered the office of his brother, Dr.

Charles B. Chalfant, at Belle Vernon, as a student of medicine, and remained with him until November, 1859, when he attended lectures at Western Reserve Medical College of Cleveland, Ohio. He began the practice of medicine in March, 1860, at Donegal, Westmoreland county, Pa., but in October following removed to Boliver, same county, where he remained one year. From Bolivar he went to Youngstown and practiced until May, 1864, when he removed to Whitely, Greene county, Pa., and remained seven months. Leaving Whitely in December, 1864, he went to Brownsville, and was in active practice there until April, 1867, when he removed to his present location at Pennsville and where he has been engaged until the present time in the successful practice of his profession.

In June, 1860, he was married to Ellen E., daughter of John and Elizabeth Fowler, of Westmoreland county, Pa. To them were born seven children, of whom five are living: Mollie E. (Mrs. Edgar L. Boyd), Anna B., John Fowler, Ethel Winonia and Vivian Mellon.

Dr. Chalfant has belonged to several secret societies. He is a member of the Methodist Episcopal church, and since his membership in 1860 has held all the offices of that church. He is a member of the Fayette County Medical Society and also of the Fayette and Westmoreland Medical Association.

REILY D. CHRISTOPHER, one of Luzerne's useful citizens, was born in 1826, in Luzerne township, Fayette county, Pa., and is a son of Bernard and Mary (Reily) Christopher, the former a farmer, and a son of Bernard Christopher, Sr., who was also a farmer of the same township. The latter was a daughter of Dennis Reily, a farmer of Luzerne.

Reily D. Christopher was educated in the subscription schools of German township. Leaving school, he engaged in farming till 1863, when he began operating a grain threshing machine. From that time to the present he has been continuously and successfully engaged in threshing grain. Some years ago he abandoned the old horse-power machine, and now runs and operates one of the latest improved steam threshers in the country. He does a large amount of work in Luzerne and adjoining townships. His only brother, John T., enlisted in the late Civil War, and died at New Berne, N. C.

He was married to Eliza, daughter of Isaac Roberts. They have ten children: Bernard (dead); Mary F., wife of J. L. Christopher; William; Isaac N., married Hettie Ensley; Ellazan, married W. Christopher; Susanna, married Josiah Honsaker; Hettie, wife of Jacob Johnson; Hannah, wife of William Johnson; Elliott and Thomas.

Reily D. Christopher owns a valuable farm of 127 acres of land, which is among the best in Luzerne township. He is a republican, a good citizen and a successful business man, and has served as road supervisor.

WALTER S. COLBORN is a son of David L. and Julia (Dull) Colborn. He was born in Somerset county, Pa., October 6, 1860.

David L. Colborn was born in Somerset county, April 3, 1827, and is the son of Sylvester Colborn. David L. Colborn was married December 9, 1850, to Miss Julia, daughter of George Dull of Springfield township. Unto this union were born eight children: Lafayette, Lavena, Willis, George, Walter S., Jackson, Annie and Sylvester.

George Dull, maternal grandfather, was a native of Somerset county, until 1836, at which time he located in Springfield township. In 1868 came to Springfield township, this county, was educated in the common schools of Fayette county, where he learned the trade of a carpenter with William Shearer. Afterwards he engaged in the furniture business, which he has successfully pursued at Mill Run for the past three years. He also started in the same business on August 3, 1889, at Vanderbilt, Pa.

July 8, 1883, he was married to Miss Susan, daughter of George Kern, by the Rev. W. W. Hickman of Uniontown. Their union has been blessed by two children: Eva Lena, born May 9, 1884, and David L., born February 6, 1889.

Mr. Colborn is a democrat and delights in the success of his party; he also took an active part in the prohibition amendment campaign that was voted on and defeated June 16, 1889. He is a member of the Indian Creek Baptist church. Mr. Colborn is a good workman, and deserving of the liberal encouragement that he receives.

WILLIAM HENRI COLDREN (deceased). William Henri Coldren, a young lawyer of bright promise, was born on the property now owned by George Hogg, in Luzerne township, Fayette county, Pa., and is a son of Jesse Coldren, who was born in Menallen township, and is now a resident of Uniontown. William H. Coldren was reared on a farm, received his education at Dunlap's Creek Presbyterial Academy and at Kittanning. He served as assistant bookkeeper at Fairchance Furnace for a few months, but soon abandoned commercial pursuits for the legal profession. He read law under the late Daniel Kaine, of Uniontown, and was subsequently admitted to the practice of law in the courts of Fayette county. In a short time after being admitted he removed to Pittsburgh, and entered upon the active practice of his profession. He was employed as attorney for the Pittsburgh & Western R. R., and in addition to attending to the business of this railroad company, he was at the same time building up a large and paying practice in the State and county courts. After eighteen months of successful practice, he died in Pittsburgh, January 16, 1883.

On June 21, 1876, he was united in marriage in Redstone township by Rev. J. T. A. Henderson, to Miss Charlotte L. Craft, a daughter of Elijah L. Craft, of Redstone township. His widow, an excellent woman, survives him and resides in Redstone township on property once owned by J. N. Craft.

In political faith Mr. Coldren was an active, earnest and prominent worker of the republican party. In religious belief he was a zealous and useful member of the Cumberland Presbyterian church of Pittsburgh. He was an influential member of the Royal Arcanum, and was ever ready to work in lodge or church, public gathering or private enterprise. Of good personal appearance, he was courteous and affable, he was logical in argument, but brief and forcible in expression. He was cut down by death in the very opening of what promised to be a long and honorable career of usefulness and success.

JEHU CONWELL, a successful farmer and member of a family identified with the history of Luzerne township since its earliest Anglo-Saxon occupation, is a son of Yates S. and Anna (Craft) Conwell, and was born in Luzerne township, Fayette county, Pa., June 25, 1820.

One of the early pioneers of Fayette county was his grandfather, Jehu Conwell, born in Sussex county, Delaware, in 1749, O. S. Jehu Conwell with brother, Captain William, migrated to Luzerne township in 1767 and purchased 700 acres of land from James Bredin. Jehu endured many hardships and in 1772 returned to Delaware and was married by Gilbert Parker, J. P., to Miss Elizabeth, daughter of Yates Stokely.

He brought his young wife to his Luzerne home, where they endured many hardships and privations. He was instrumental in 1774 in building a fort below Merrittstown to resist Indian attacks; enlisted with his brother, Capt. William, in the Continental army in Independence year and fought throughout the war. Jehu's home was headquarters for westward-bound emigrants from Delaware. He was generous and liberal in his views, conscientious in all his deeds and was honored and respected by his neighbors and all who knew him. He built a log grist-mill, erected a distillery, and died in 1834. He left four sons: Shepard, Yates T., John and George.

Yates T. Conwell, the founder of Heistersburg, was a farmer, and was commissioned an ensign August 1, 1814, in the Eighth Regiment Pennsylvania Militia. He died Christmas, 1865. His wife was a daughter of David Craft, of Redstone township. They had five sons and two daughters.

Jehu Conwell, son of Yates T., was reared on a farm, attended Luzerne's subscription schools and Madison College. He married Miss Elizabeth, daughter of Thomas Fulton, of Redstone township. To their union have been born ten children: Thomas, dead; Emily, wife of Winfield Gilmore; Elizabeth, Margaret, dead; Annie, dead; Estelle, wife of Johnson Van Kirk; William, Annetta, dead; Nathaniel and Mary.

Jehu Conwell has been engaged since leaving school in farming and stock raising. Politically he was a whig, and on the disbanding of that political organization became a republican. His nearest approach to being a democrat was in celebrating for many years Jackson's victory at New Orleans. Mr. Conwell owns two hundred acres of fertile and productive land, and resides in the old stone mansion built by William Ewing about 1790. Mr. Conwell has been justice of the peace for fifteen years, is a member of the Presbyterian church, and is one of Luzerne's prosperous farmers.

DAVID C. CONWELL, an industrious, steady and prosperous farmer of the wealthy old township of Luzerne, is a son of Yates S. and Anna (Craft) Conwell, and was born in Luzerne township, Fayette county, Pa., September 8, 1824.

His grandfather, Jehu Conwell, was a pioneer settler of Luzerne when it was infested by wild beasts and vengeful savages. He was a Revolutionary hero and afterwards a prominent man of the township. (For his history see sketch of his grandson, Jehu Conwell.)

David C. Conwell grew up to manhood on a farm and was thoroughly trained to farm work and farm management. His educational privileges were those afforded by the subscription schools of his immediate neighborhood. His education was necessarily limited to the few branches understood by his teachers. His school (Heistersburg) was as good as any in the township, excepting Merrittstown. Leaving school he engaged in farming and stock raising, and has continued successfully in that line of business until the present time. In 1880 he married Mrs. Elizabeth (Kelly) Christopher, a daughter of Samuel Kelly, of Luzerne township.

David C. Conwell owns a fine farm of 140 acres of good land situated in an industrious and prosperous community, convenient to church and school, and near to mill and store. He is a republican, and is now serving his second term as postmaster of Heistersburg, and has repeatedly served on his township election board, but does not let political matters engage his attention from the labors of his farm or the care of his stock.

JOHN A. COX was born January 22, 1835, at Morgantown, Va. (now West Virginia.) He is the son of Levi and Mary (Myers) Cox. Levi Cox was born in 1801, in Delaware, and removed from there to Virginia in 1812, where he worked as a day laborer. He married Miss Mary Meyers, of near Grandville, Monongalia county, Va., who died in 1845, near Morgantown.

John A. Cox grew up on the farm, and was educated at the subscription schools of Virginia. He followed coal mining for ten years. He enlisted in Company A, Third West Virginia Infantry. The regiment was afterwards mounted and called the Sixth West Virginia Cavalry. Mr. Cox was in the service three years two months and thirteen days. When he came out of the army he resumed mining for a short time, and then farmed for some years. He spent two years in the West, the greater portion of the time in Minnesota. From the West he came to Broad Ford, where he had control of H. C. Frick's coal works for two years. He afterwards took charge of J. M. Schoonmaker's works for about ten years, when he settled on a farm near Mill Run, in 1881, and remained eight years. In 1889 he started a store at Mill Run, and has met with good success in the mercantile business.

He was married to Miss Julia Ann Collins, December 28, 1864, by Rev. George Westfall, of the Methodist church, a daughter of William Collins, of Prideville Iron Works, near Morgantown. He is the father of nine children, all of whom are living: Frank, born October 13, 1865, in Washington county Pa.; Eliza, born June 7, 1870, in Fillmore county, Minn.; Orline, born July 1. 1872, in Fayette county, Pa.; John A., Jr., born May 27, 1874, in Fayette county, Pa.; Leender, born June 5, 1875, in Fayette county, Pa., near Broad-Ford; Filmore, born November 16, 1876, near Broad-Ford; Signal, born March 10, 1878, near Broad Ford; Ada, born July 6, 1880, near Broad Ford, and Jannette, born August 26, 1883, at Mill Run.

Mr. Cox has held the office of school director once in Upper Tyrone township and one term in Springfield township. In the war he was severely injured in the right knee, besides receiving two other bullet wounds. He draws a pension of $360 a year.

RICHARD CROSSLAND was born at Connellsville Pa., July 17, 1823, and is a son of Richard Crossland, who was born at Poplar Springs, Md. He came to Fayette county in about 1817 and located at Connellsville.

The paternal grandfather of Richard was George Crossland, a native of England, who settled at Poplar Springs, Md., over a century ago.

Richard Crossland was reared at Connellsville and attended the public schools of that place. His main business has been that of stock drover, principally in the employ of Eli Cope and Greenberry Crossland, of Uniontown. He was married January 23, 1845, to Eliza Hisman, a daughter of Christopher Hisman, of Bullskin township. Their union has been blessed with fourteen children, twelve of whom are living: Eli, born June 1, 1846, in Bullskin township; Eliza Jane, December 16, 1847; Joseph F., May 23, 1849; Anna, February 3, 1851; Christopher S., April 23, 1853; Rebecca, April 3, 1855; George Searight, May 19, 1857; Wm. M., February 2, 1859; Ruth A., March 1, 1861; Israel P., September 16, 1863; Charles H., August 11, 1867, and James G., September 19, 1872, were all born in Bullskin township, Fayette county, Pa.

For the last forty-eight years Mr. Crossland has been a highly respected member of the I. O. of O. F., belongs to General Worth Post, No. 386, at Connellsville. He is a strong democrat and takes an active interest in the success of his party, casting his first vote for James K. Polk, and has voted for every nominee of the democratic party for president since. His sons are all democrats. His farm in Bullskin township contains eighty-four acres of well-improved land underlaid with coal.

JAMES CUNNINGHAM, deceased. The late James Cunningham was a faithful citizen of Luzerne township, as well as a trusted public officer of Fayette county. He was born at Merrittstown, Fayette county, Pa., July 26, 1812, and was a son of William and Mary (Gallagher) Cunningham.

His grandfather, James Cunningham, was a native of Ireland. Previous to 1775, with his four brothers, he came to America and settled near the site of "Little Washington," Pa., and with a "Tomahawk Claim" took up a large tract of land. He served in the War of the Revolution, and when he returned found his land in possession of other people. He then went to Chester county, where he secured a tract of land. This tract he sold for continental currency, and later exchanged the price of this depreciated paper for a horse and cow. In 1800 he removed to near Merrittstown, where he built a distillery and erected the large stone house now occupied by Armstrong Porter. One of his sons, Thomas, was a college graduate and died while young; another son, John, served with Albert Gallatin in the Pennsylvania legislature in 1794, being a member of that body from 1793 to 1805.

William Cunningham was born in 1793, died May 2, 1819. He was a whig in politics, served as county commissioner and afterwards filled the office of United States district marshal and collector of taxes. September 3, 1811, he married Miss Mary Gallagher, born July 3, 1788. One of his sons, John, was justice of the peace in Luzerne, and now lives in Iowa.

James Cunningham was raised on a farm, received his education in the subscription schools and later learned the trade of blacksmith with George Brown, of Merrittstown, but soon abandoned that trade. He taught school for a number of years in Luzerne township, when he purchased a farm and engaged in farming until his death, April 5, 1888.

In 1835 he married Miss Rosanna Muir, of Scotch descent, and to their union were born: Mary, wife of I. N. Craft; John C., merchant of Belle Vernon, Pa., married Lizzie, daughter of Dr. J. S. Van Voorhis, of that place; Martha A.; Sarah M.; Alfred H. married Laura Springer, and is a commercial traveler for a Pittsburgh house, and Annie E.

James Cunningham was an elder of the Cumberland Presbyterian church up to 1880, when he withdrew and, in the same year, joined the Presbyterian church at Dunlap's Creek, and was elected ruling elder. In politics he was a democrat, serving two terms as justice of the peace, 1840 to 1850; one term as poor house director, one term as county auditor, 1860 to 1864, and two terms as county commissioner, 1874 to 1879. He was frequently urged to offer himself as a candidate for the legislature, but never did. His services were often called in demand to settle estates and write wills. As a citizen he was highly respected. As a public official he was conscientious in the discharge of his duties.

JOHN W. DEARTH, a leading and progressive farmer of Luzerne township, is a son of Larkins S. and Mary (Williams) Dearth, and was born in the house in which he now resides in Luzerne township, Fayette county, Pa., November 3, 1833.

His great-grandfather, James Dearth, was born in 1720, in England, and died in 1797, in Luzerne township. He came to Maryland, bought slaves in 1777 and removed to Luzerne township, and ten years later patented 300 acres of land. His second wife was Miss Sophia Simmons; and a son of his, George Dearth, was born April 23, 1762, and died October, 1846, on the home farm. In 1796 he was commissioned by governor Thomas Mifflin, major of the First Battalion in the First Fayette County Brigade of the militia of Pennsylvania, for the term of seven years. And in 1800 was commissioned by governor Thomas McKean, major of the First Battalion in the Ninety-first Regiment of Pennsylvania, composed of the militia of Bedford, Fayette and Somerset counties, for seven years. He was a cotemporary, in the Pennsylvania legislature, of Andrew Stewart in 1816 and 1817, and was a democrat. He married Elizabeth Mills. They had five daughters and two sons: John, of Ohio, and Larkins S., father of John W. Dearth. Larkins S. Dearth was born October 5, 1797, and died in June, 1850. He was by occupation a farmer, in politics a democrat, and was married to Miss Mary Williams. To them were born three daughters and one son.

John W. Dearth had the advantages of a good common-school education; leaving school, he has since been engaged in farming and stock raising.

April 21, 1869, he was married to Miss Bertha Virginia Miller, daughter of Samuel Miller. They have three children: Walter L., William M. and Louise E. Mrs. Dearth is a member of the Central Presbyterian church at Hopewell. She is an amateur astronomer, owns a good telescope and takes deep interest in tracing the constellations of the northern heavens.

Mr. Dearth is a democrat and owns a farm of 250 acres of valuable land. The farm is known as "Trail Hill" on account of an Indian war trail that passed over it in early times. In the old graveyard on this farm, sleeps his paternal great-grandparents, grandfather and wife, his father, mother and one sister. Mr. Dearth is one of Luzerne's leading farmers.

JOHN S. DETWILER, a miller and extensive farmer of Bullskin township was born in the same township, Fayette county, Pa., February 24, 1831, and is a son of Henry Detwiler and Susan (Stauffer) Detwiler, daughter of Henry Stauffer, of Bucks county, Pa.

Henry Detwiler is a son of Samuel Detwiler and is of Swiss extraction. He emigrated from Bucks county to Westmoreland county, thence to Perryopolis, and from there removed to Detwiler's Mill, in Bullskin township, where he for many years followed milling.

John S. Detwiler was married to Catherine Atkinson, a daughter of Jesse Atkinson, of Bullskin township, July 20, 1854. To their union have been born eight boys, all born in Bullskin township, Fayette county, Pa.: George A., Judson B., Jacob C., Grant L., John W. G., Samuel A., Henry W. and Charles A.

John S. Detwiler has held various local offices of his township; he is a member of the "Knights of the Mystic Chain," at Moyer, and is a consistent member of the Baptist church at Pennsville. Besides owning valuable mill property in Bullskin, he owns several well-improved farms in the same township. He is a good business man, is well fixed in life and is a republican.

CALEB B. DUVALL, one of Luzerne township's steady and reliable farmers, is a son of Eli and Elizabeth (Richey) Duvall, and was born in Luzerne township, Fayette county, Pa., February 17, 1831.

His grandfather, Alexander Duvall, was a native of Fayette county and lived during the latter part of the eighteenth century. He was a hardworking farmer and resided on the Monongahela river below Brownsville.

His father, Eli Duvall, was born in Redstone township, reared on a farm and made farming his life-business. He was a whig and afterwards a republican. His family consisted of five boys and three girls: John, Eli, Caleb, Eliza, Robert, Harrison, Abigail and Rachel.

Caleb B. Duvall was trained to farming when a boy, and attended the subscription schools in the last years of their existence, ere they were succeeded by the common schools. He engaged in farming and stock raising and has continued successfully in that business ever since leaving school.

January 22, 1857, he was married to Miss Elizabeth, a daughter of Andrew Porter. They have had four children, George (dead); Eli C., a school teacher and clerk; Jennie, and Maggie, wife of John Harne, a clerk in Kansas; Haddie, Osie and Leona.

Caleb B. Duvall is a republican in political affairs, and has served acceptably as school director of Luzerne township. He owns a valuable farm and employs his time in its cultivation and improvement and stock-raising.

DR. HENRY EASTMAN is a son of Nehemiah and Anstriss B. (Woodbury) Eastman, and was born in Farmington, N. H., March 16, 1826.

His grandfather, Ebenezer Eastman, of Scotch-Irish extraction, was a son of one of the pioneer settlers of New Hampshire, and served as a captain at Bunker Hill, in the War of the Revolution, shortly after which he was accidentally killed. Hon. Nehemiah Eastman, son of Ebenezer and the father of Dr. Eastman, was born in New Hampshire, was a prominent lawyer of that State and was elected by the whigs to congress, in 1826, where he served his constituents most creditably. His son, George N. Eastman, is also a prominent lawyer of New Hampshire, and served for several years in the legislature of that State. Nehemiah Eastman married Miss Anstriss B. Woodbury, a daughter of Peter Woodbury, a prominent merchant of Francestown, N. H., whose father, James T. Woodbury, was a native of England and an officer under Gen. Wolfe at the capture of Quebec. One of her brothers was Levi Woodbury, a distinguished statesman and jurist of national reputation and at one time secretary of the navy under President Van Buren, and was afterwards appointed associate justice of the supreme court of the United States by President James K. Polk, and died while on the bench.

Dr. Henry Eastman was educated in the common schools and at Gilmanton Academy of New Hampshire. Read medicine, and graduated from Jefferson Medical College in 1847. Shortly after graduating he came to Merrittstown and entered upon the practice of his profession. His expectation was to remain only a short time, but his practice became so extensive and lucrative that he finally abandoned the idea of removal, and has since continued at Merrittstown, successfully in the practice of medicine. He is one of the most widely known and esteemed physicians in the county. In 1853 he married Miss Mary E. Porter, daughter of Moses B. and Mary (Wilson) Porter, whose ancestors were among the early settlers of the county. They have had seven children: Anstriss W., married to A. R. Struble, a prosperous farmer of Luzerne township; Thomas N., a practicing physician of Merrittstown, and a graduate of Washington and Jefferson College, read medicine and graduated at Jefferson Medical College; Anna

M. married to Dr. J. S. Hackney, of Uniontown; Martha J., dead; Henry, Ellen M., and Nora Blanche.

The Dr. and Mrs. Eastman are both respected members of the Dunlap's Creek Presbyterian church.

HENRY K. EICHER was born February 10, 1835, in Springfield, Fayette county, Pa. His grandfather, Daniel Eicher, emigrated from Germany to Lancaster county, Pa.; thence to Fayette county, in 1772. Joseph Eicher, the father of Henry K. Eicher, was born in Lancaster in 1784, and was married to Rosanna Kern, of Fayette county. To their union were born twelve children: Samuel, William, Sarah, Daniel, John, Margaret, Catherine, Elizabeth, Joseph, Henry, Abraham and Isaac.

Henry K. Eicher was educated in the common schools of Fayette county, his first teacher being David Barnes, of Connellsville. He was married at Connellsville, on December 21, 1862, to Emily Bruner, daughter of Samuel S. Bruner, of the same place. They have eight children: Charles E., Harry W., Kate V., George F., Lizzie E., Gertrude G., Lulu B. and Mary M.

In the Civil War he served in the Sixth Pennsylvania Heavy Artillery, Company K; volunteered August 22, 1864, and was honorably discharged June 13, 1865, at Fort Ethan Allen. In 1883 he was appointed postmaster at Stuarton, by President Arthur, and served four years. Mr. Eicher is a carpenter by trade, at which he is at present engaged.

ABRAM FRANKS, a well-known farmer of Luzerne township, was born in German, now Nicholson, township, Fayette county, Pa., January 19, 1816, and is a son of Abraham and Margaret (Kechler) Franks. Abram Franks, Sr., was a son of Michael Franks. The former was born on the "Core farm," near Uniontown; was a farmer, served gallantly in the War of 1812, was a Whig, afterwards republican, and died in 1860. He married Miss Margaret Kechler, and reared a family of five sons and four daugters, of whom only Abram and Eli are living. Mrs. Franks' father, Michael Kechler, left Fayette county late in life and removed to Wooster, Ohio, where he died.

Abram Franks received his education in the subscription schools of German township He engaged in steamboating on the Monongahela river, which he followed for a number of years, and then embarked in his present employment of farming and stock raising.

He was married to Miss Nancy, daughter of Martin Bolein, the latter a tailor of Greene county, Pa. To their union were born the following children: Francis M., was a soldier in the late war, served in an Illinois regiment, and now dead; William F., was in the Eighth Pennsylvania Reserves, and served from 1861 to 1865; Elihu, Jacob and Jobe served in the Eighth, were taken prisoners before Richmond; were confined in Libby prison, and afterwards removed to Saulsbury prison, where Elihu and Jacob died, and from where Jobe was carried to Danville, and died on his way home after being exchanged; Mary Ann, wife of Joseph Crago, of Greene county, Pa.; Emanuel, enlisted in the Eighth in 1863, and served to the close of the war; Abram, a farmer of German township; John N.; Eliza J., wife of Joshua Crago, of Greene county, Pa.; and Isaac, married Samantha Jane Silbaugh.

Abram Franks was an old line whig, and is a republican, and all of his sons are republicans. He owns a farm of 140 acres of good land, and is a member of the Cumberland Presbyterian church, to which his wife also belongs. He is industrious, and has reared a highly respectable family. Six of his sons fought gallantly in the famous Pennsylvania Reserves, two of whom gave their lives for the preservation of the Union.

SIMON P. HAGER, a thorough-going, stirring and successful farmer of Wharton township, is a son of Thomas and Eva (Romesburg) Hager, and was born in the same township, Fayette county, Pa., September 22, 1845.

His grandfather, Peter Hager, was of German descent and was a teamster on the "old Braddock road," when the early settlers in many places had to cover their cabins with a roof made of bark. He married Rachel Inks, conquered many of the difficulties of pioneer life in Wharton township, and purchased the Hager farms, now owned by his descendants. One of his sons, Thomas Hager, was a farmer and married Miss Eva, daughter of George Romesburg.

Simon P. Hager was raised on a farm and attended the common schools of his native township. When quite young he assumed and successfully conducted the management of his father's business affairs. Before he was nineteen years of age, he entered the Union army, enlisting in August, 1864, in Company K, One Hundredth Regiment Pennsylvania Volunteers, and served until the close of the war. He was in all of the engagements of his regiment, at the evacuation of Petersburg and Lee's surrender, and at Fort Steadman, where his company went into action thirty-eight strong, and he was one of the twelve who escaped being killed. His brother, William Hager, was a member of Company K, One Hundred and Sixteenth Regiment Pennsylvania Volunteers, fought in eleven battles and died in nine days after his return home. At the close of the war our subject returned home, resumed farming, and has devoted most of his attention to that calling ever since.

January 1, 1866, he was married to Miss Huldah A., daughter of John and Eliza (Spaw) Kemp. To them have been born the following children: Charles Milton (dead), Chauncey Alexander, Martha Ellen, William Grant, Thomas Gilbert, John Burchard, James A. Garfield, Eliza Eva and Harrison Herbert.

Simon P. Hager has made his own way in life, unaided by friends, influence or fortune. He is a member of the German Baptist church, to which his family also belong. He owns about one thousand acres of land, has some property in Uniontown and at Markleysburgh. He is never idle, always pushing, and is a thorough business man.

ABRAM GARWOOD, a leading citizen of Luzerne township, was born in Luzerne township, Fayette county, Pa., March 10, 1819, and is a son of Jesse and Lydia (Roberts) Garwood.

Jesse Garwood, son of Obed Garwood of Southwestern Pennsylvania, was born in August, 1788, in Chester county and removed to Luzerne township in early life. He was a Quaker and old line whig, and owned a valuable farm in the township where he died January 1, 1854. He married Miss Lydia Roberts, and reared a family of six sons and five daughters. Mrs. Garwood's father, Griffith Roberts, was a farmer, came from Chester county to Menallen township, but subsequently removed to Redstone township, where he died. He was an ardent and active democrat.

Abram Garwood was reared in Luzerne township, and after attending the subscription schools, engaged in farming. He continued successfully in that line of business until 1884, and then removed to Luzerne village where he is now residing in a very comfortable home. He was married to Miss Mary A., daughter of William Miller. They have had nine children: Lydia (deceased),

William M., Rebecca J., Obed, Alice, Eli, Jason H., Oliver and Edith.

Abram Garwood's people were honored members of the Society of Friends who by the simplicity and justness of their lives, beautifully illustrated the peaceful character of their religious belief, and Mr. Garwood during his long and useful life has reflected no discredit on the teachings of George Fox, William Penn and their followers.

WILLIAM HARRISON HENSHAW (deceased) was one of Luzerne's prosperous famers and stock raisers, and was born in what is now North Union township, Fayette county, Pa., October 13, 1813. He is a son of William and Ann (Parker) Henshaw, the former a farmer and a son of Nicholas Henshaw, originally of western Virginia, and afterwards a farmer of North Union township; the latter was a native of Fayette county.

W. H. Henshaw was raised on a farm and trained to farm work. His school days were passed under the old subscription school system and in the almost primitive school houses of Franklin township. He was a farmer till his death in 1886.

In 1843 he married Miss Elizabeth, daughter of John Foster, a native of Lancaster county. To their union were born five children: Mary E., married William Gaddis and died; John M., married Miss Anna, daughter of John Work; Franklin P. was educated in common schools, married January 5, 1887, Miss Hattie J. Gibbons, daughter of Elisha Gibbons, a half brother of the late Joshua V. Gibbons ex-county superintendent. Frank P. has one child, Martha J., born September 20, 1888; Anna J. (dead) and James Henry Henshaw.

W. H. Henshaw was a man who gave care and attention to his business and was a very useful and much-missed friend, neighbor and citizen. In 1881 he moved from North Union to Luzerne township where he purchased a fine farm of 330 acres of land, and engaged in farming and stock raising till his death. His sons, John M., Franklin P. and James H., reside upon the farm and are engaged extensively in farming and raising fine stock. John M. is located on the old home farm in North Union.

CLARK R. HESS, son of John and Amanda (Offord) Hess, was born in Menallen township, Fayette county, Pa., November 23, 1842.

His great-grandfather, Peter Hess, was of German descent, resided in what is now Fayette county. He died August, 1825, aged sixty-eight years, and sleeps in Moore's cemetery in Redstone township. His son George, grandfather of C. R. Hess, was a farmer of Menallen township; he died October, 1858, in the sixty-eighth year of his age; his remains also repose in Moore's cemetery.

John Hess, son of George Hess, was born in Menallen township February 8, 1812, died in German township October, 1882, and is buried at New Salem, Menallen township.

He began life without means, learning the trade of stone mason with Randolph Dearth, and after serving four years' apprenticeship, began business for himself with a capital of only $20. He worked energetically at his trade, until he had acquird enough money to purchase thirty acres of land in Menallen township. After which he still continued at his trade and was soon enabled to purchase farm after farm, until he became the owner of 750 acres of the best land in German and adjoining townships. At his death, his property was valued at between $75,000 and $100,000. He was a good financier and was universally recognized as strictly honest in all his business relations with men. He married Miss Amanda, daughter of Brooks Offord, a potter of Whitely, Greene county, Pa. His family consisted of four sons and five daughters, all living except two daughters.

Clark R. Hess was educated in the common schools of German township and was carefully trained to correct habits of business. In 1870 he removed Luzerne township and purchased a farm of 210 acres. He engaged in farming and stock-raising and has been successfully engaged in the same ever since.

October 17, 1866, he married Miss Emma, daughter of W. P. Griffin, an estimable citizen of Nicholson township. They have three children: M. Florence, born July 20, 1869, an accomplished young lady, and especially talented in music; Estella G. and Nellie G. (twins), born January 31, 1875.

C. R. Hess is a member of the Disciple church at Oak Grove, Springhill township; his wife and eldest daughter are also members of the same church. He is comfortably situated, owns a fine farm and keeps it well improved and raises some fine stock. He is a successful farmer, a careful business man and a well respected citizen of his township.

JOSEPH HALL, the grandfather of the subject of our sketch, married Mary Matthews; to them was born Garrett Hall. Garrett Hall, a native of Fayette county, married Margaret Linderman, the daughter of Henry Linderman, formerly of Somerset county, Pa. Garrett Hall and wife had nine children: Mary, Rebecca, Isaac L., Henry H., John K. (subject of our sketch), Susan E., Darrell, Barbara, Benjamin S. Garrett Hall married a second time, to Sarah Sloan; by this marriage he had two daughters: Arminda and Cascinda.

John K. Hall was born September 5, 1844, in Fayette county, Pa. He was educated in the common schools of the county. He is engaged in farming and stock raising. He served four years as constable of Stewart township, and six years as school director of the same township. He was married December 19, 1872, to Lucinda Miner, daughter of Charles Miner, of Stewart township. He served in the Civil War; volunteered in 1864 in the One Hundred and Seventh Regiment Pennsylvania Infantry, and took part in the battles of Petersburg, Hatcher's Run and Norfolk, and was in several skirmishes. He lives on Sugar Loaf, and is a member of the church.

WILLIAM W. HILLER, a highly progressive farmer and stock raiser of Luzerne township, was born in Greene county, Pa., March 28, 1822, and is a son of John and Catherine (Hughes) Hiller. His grandfather, William Hiller, was born in New Jersey, and emigrated to Greene county, Pa., where he engaged in farming until his death. His father, John Hiller, was born in about 1790. He was an extensive farmer, also engaged in the mercantile business in various parts of Greene county, and for a while conducted a hotel at Jefferson. He was a member of the Cumberland Presbyterian church, served several terms as justice of the peace and was a whig in politics. He married Miss Catherine Hughes and reared a family of ten children. Of these, Margaret married Sheriff W. R. Mulligan, of Illinois; Thomas, a merchant in Kansas, and John T. (dead), a soldier in the late war.

Mrs. Hiller was a daughter of Thomas Hughes, an old settler, and for many years a justice of the peace.

William W. Hiller attended the old subscription schools; on leaving school he engaged with his father as a clerk, and later became a pilot on the Monongahela river for four years, when he came to Luzerne township, where in 1844 he engaged in farming and raising fine sheep, and later, engaged in raising fine stock of all kind. During the few years past he has devoted his attention exclusively to raising fine and blooded horses. He owns two fine farms, aggregating about 350 acres of choice land.

He was married to Miss Mary, daughter of Henry Luce, of Greene county, Pa., and has three children: Elizabeth, wife of John M. Garrard, now in oil business at Mt. Morris, Greene county, Pa.; Artimace, wife of W B. Conwell, and Mary Alice.

W. W. Hiller is a republican and has served several terms as assessor and also as school director. He is an elder in the C. P. church at Hopewell. He is a stockholder in the Natural Gas Company at Brownsville, and is one of the substantial and advanced farmers of the county.

JOSEPH H. HUMBERSTONE, one of the young, steady and industrious farmers of Henry Clay township, is a son of Jacob and Louisa (Shaw) Humberstone, and was born in Henry Clay township, Fayette county, Pa., November 26, 1861.

His paternal grandfather, William Humberstone, was a native and resident of Frostburg, Md. He was a republican, a member of the Lutheran church, and a farmer by occupation.

His maternal grandfather, William Shaw, was born at Barton, Md., was a carpenter by occupation, a republican in politics and a Methodist in religion.

Jacob Humberstone, father of Joseph H., was born at Frostburg, Md., in 1826, and at thirty years of age removed to his present location on the National road, in Henry Clay township. He has principally been engaged in farming, and is of the same political faith and religious belief of his father. Jacob Humberstone enlisted in 1862 in the Two Hundred and Twelfth Pennsylvania Regiment of the Line (heavy artillery) and served nine months.

He owns a good property, including the old Brown wagon stand on the National road, which was established by Thomas Brown about 1798. Brown's log building was replaced in 1826 by the present large and fine two-story stone house, in which a hotel was kept as late as 1865.

Joseph S. Humberstone was one of a family of eight children, and received his education in the common schools of his native township. He has always given his time to farming, except eighteen months that he served as a telegraph operator at Marshalltown, Iowa. He was united in marriage to Miss Hattie Tharspecken, of Marshalltown, Iowa.

J. S. Humberstone is a republican, and was a delegate to the republican State Convention which met at Harrisburg on the 7th of August, 1889, and nominated Boyer for State treasurer.

Mr. Humberstone has a comfortable home, and is kept busily engaged in the management of his farm and the care of his business interests.

CAPTAIN ADAM JACOBS (deceased). The late Captain Adam Jacobs was in his day one of the most prominent and energetic business men of western Pennsylvania. He was a son of Adam and Eliza (Reiley) Jacobs, and was born at Brownsville, Fayette county, Pa., January 7, 1817.

His grandfather, Adam Jacobs, was a native of Maryland, emigrated to Lancaster county, Pa., removed to Allegheny county, and subsequently to Brownsville, in about 1794, where he was engaged in the mercantile business until his death in 1818. He sleeps in the old Episcopalian cemetery. He had one child, Adam Jacobs, the father of Captain Adam Jacobs. Adam Jacobs, the Captain's father, was born December 3, 1794, educated at Washington College, and was married January 16, 1816, to Miss Ann Reiley, of Bedford county, and died June 29 1822. He was a dry goods merchant.

Captain Adam Jacobs, while learning the trade of coppersmith with G. W. Bowman, obtained a very limited education. After two or three business ventures he engaged in the steamboat business which he followed until 1872. He commanded several and built 125 steamboats that plied upon the western waters. During this time he was interested, more or less, in milling, banking, mining, farming, merchandising and railroading. In 1865 he purchased 1,000 acres of land on the Monongahela river, eight miles southwest of Brownsville, which he named "East Riverside." Washington's birthday, 1838, he married Miss Ann, daughter of John Snowdon (see Snowdon sketch). They had ten children, of whom eight are living: Mary, wife of William Parkhill, cashier Second National Bank; Adam, captain of the James G. Blaine; Catherine, wife of S. S. Graham, superintendent P., B. and New Geneva packet line, and engaged in wholesale and retail grocery business; Carrie S., wife of J. H. Bowman, banker and real estate dealer; Annie, wife of Joseph McBurney, of Chicago, and engaged in white lead business; Martin B., a broker of Chicago; George R., farmer in Greene county, Pa., and John N., farmer in Luzerne township.

After a long and eventful career Captain Adam Jacobs died on December 18, 1883. He was for over forty years one of the prominent, active, useful and leading business men of western Pennsylvania, and whose boats plied on all the navigable waters of the Mississippi valley.

ANDREW JOHNSON, a soldier in the late Civil War and a citizen of Springfield township, was born near Columbia, Washington county, Pa., January 25, 1844. He is a son of William and Margaret (Davison) Johnson, who were born respectively in Fayette and Westmoreland. His grandfather, Joseph Johnson, was a native of Maryland.

Andrew Johnson was married October 21, 1865, to Nancy C. Stricklin, a daughter of Jesse Stricklin, of Perry township. To their marriage have been born sixteen children, ten of whom are living: Charles E., born March 31, 1870, at Brownsville, Fayette county; Frank, born November 20, 1872, in Washington county, Pa.; William, born February 5, 1875; Margaret, born March 8, 1877; Anna, born May 30, 1879; Lucretia, born May 18, 1881; Cynthia, born August 29, 1883; Andrew, born January 24, 1885; Eddie, born April 18, 1887, and Grover Cleveland, May 15, 1889, all born in Springfield township, Fayette county, Pa.

Mr. Johnson enlisted as a soldier in the War of the Rebellion August 2, 1862; he was at the battles of Fredericksburg, Chancellorsville and Gettysburg. In the battle at the latter place, he was severely wounded, July 2, 1863; and was finally discharged from the service April 16, 1865.

Mr. Johnson is a respected member and past officer of the I. O. of R. M., Tribe No. 260; member of K. of P., Lodge No. 310, at Belle Vernon, and also a member of the G. A. R., T. Campbell Post, No. 375, at Springfield. He is a member of the United Brethren church at Springfield, and is a democrat in politics.

JOSEPH F. JOHNSTON, one of the enterprising young farmers and business men of Bullskin township, was born in the same township, Fayette county, Pa., September 18, 1861, and is a son of John R., and a grandson of Alexander Johnston. The latter was born in County Tyrone, Ireland. In an early day he came to the United States and settled at Connellsville, a strict Presbyterian and was chiefly instrumental in building the first Presbyterian church at that place.

John R. Johnston was born at Connellsville, Pa., and died December 11, 1877, at Sandusky, Ohio. He was married to Elizabeth, daughter of Joseph Taylor, of New Haven. Joseph F. Johnston was married to Miss Netta Lerch, of Easton, Pa., May 28, 1885. He received his rudimentary education in the schools of his native township, afterwards attended commercial college at Eastman, Pa., and graduated in 1882. The farm where he now resides, in Bullskin township, contains 313 acres of well improved land, underlaid with coal. The McClure Coke Company have a plant of some seventy ovens erected on his farm, and are using his coal. The land also contains rich deposits of limestone and iron ore, and it is among the most valuable land in the county.

Mr. Johnston's mother died July 12, 1879, at her home in Bullskin township, at the age of fifty-two years.

THOMAS JOHNS is a son of Thomas and Mary Johns (*nee* Ross), and was born December 30, 1830, in Greene county, Pa. Thomas Johns was one of the substantial farmers of that county. He left Greene county and removed to Illinois, where he died in 1858. His wife was a daughter of Colonel Timothy Ross. Colonel Timothy Ross was a soldier in the War of 1812, at the close of which he returned to Pennsylvania. Jacob Johns, the great-grandfather of the subject of this sketch, and the founder of the Johns family in the United States, was a native of Wales. During the War of the Revolution he was forced to come to this country as a soldier in the British army. After his arrival here he deserted the British at Philadelphia, and joined Washington's army at Valley Forge; he was made lieutenant, and fought bravely until the war successfully closed.

Thomas Johns was educated in the subscription schools of Greene county, and at Carmichael's Academy, and attended three years at the Academy, completing the scientific course. In 1854 he went to Kansas, where he remained eight years, while there he was in the Kansas border wars and was personally acquainted with the famous John Brown, having slept with him under the same blanket. While in the west he acted as land agent, with headquarters at Des Moines, Iowa. Leaving there he settled in Illinois and farmed for twenty years, when he removed to Wheeling, W. Va., and operated in coal in Ohio near the West Virginia line. He successfully continued at this for seven years, when he came to Fayette county and took charge of W. J. Rainey's coal works at Moyer and has acted as superintendent of these works ever since. He was married to Sarah Rainey, of Belmont county, Ohio, a daughter of Wm. Rainey, December 29, 1875. He is a member of the Mystic Chain, No. 84, at Moyer and is a member of the National Union. He is a democrat, and while living in Illinois was chairman of the Democratic Central Committe of La Salle county.

ALEXANDER B. KEFFER, carpenter, and a prominent contractor of Bullskin township, was born in the same township, Fayette county, Pa., June 30, 1846. He received only the advantages of a common-school education in his native township. Leaving school, he engaged in coal mining, and was partly instrumental in the building of the coke ovens, in the coke regions of Connellsville. He left the mining business and went to the carpenter's trade; he is now engaged at his trade, and is a contractor for building houses. His wife was Sarah Walford, of Maryland, to whom he was married September 19, 1864. She, at the time, resided in Bullskin township. To their union have been born ten children, eight of whom are living: Eliza, born July 1, 1865; she is the wife of Benjamin F. Breakiron of the same township; Charles, born September 4, 1868, in Bullskin township; Mary, born February 15, 1870, in the same township; Albert, born May 30, 1875, in the same township; Harry, born September 8, 1881, in the same township; Roy, born September 24, 1883, in Bullskin township, and Dora, born July 22, 1885, in Bullskin township.

Alexander B. Keffer is a member of the Improved Order of Red Men of the J. O. of A. M., Lodge No. 166, at Moyer. He is a democrat in politics, and supported the prohibitory amendment to the constitution of 1889. He is a member of the Improved Order of Red Men, Moyer Tribe, and is a member of J. O. of A. M., Moyer Council, No. 166. His son Charles is also a member of the same council.

GEORGE LIVINGSTONE, the popular and leading merchant of Falls City, was born at Brownsville, Fayette county, Pa., May 29, 1847, and is a son of Austin and Phebe (Johnson) Livingstone.

Austin Livingstone (son of George Livingstone) was born in Fayette county in 1819, and was a well-known citizen of Brownsville. He married Miss Phebe Johnson, and reared a family of eight children: George, James T., Rebecca, David E., Anna J., Austin, Adam J. and Carrie J.

George Livingstone received his education in the common schools, and at an early age engaged as a clerk for J. R. Dutton, of Brownsville. His next employment was on the western waters, where he served for several years as a steamboat clerk, and then engaged in his present general mercantile business at Falls City. His store is of ample dimensions and tastefully arranged throughout. His stock of goods and wares are of first-class quality and carefully selected from the leading houses of the Eastern cities. In 1868 he was united in marriage to Miss Sarah M. Wood, of Brownsville. To their union were born four children: Dora, dead; John D. W., Brown and Mary Luella. Mrs. Livingstone died in November, 1880, and Mr. Livingstone married for his second wife Miss Ellen E. Campbell, sister of G. W. Campbell. Mr. Livingstone is a live business man, and a prominent and respected citizen of Falls City and Stewart township.

LUCIUS A. MARCHAND, an estimable citizen of Jefferson township and the founder of the village of Marchand, is a son of Dr. Louis and Sarah (Sackett) Marchand, and was born at Uniontown, Fayette county, Pa., October 5, 1838.

Dr. David Marchand, with his father, David Marchand, came to Hagerstown, Md., from the Canton of Berne, Switzerland. Dr. David Marchand was a fine physician of extended practice in Westmoreland and adjoining counties. He died July 22, 1809, in the sixty-fourth year of his age.

His children were Catherine, Elizabeth, Susanna, Judith, Dr. Daniel (a physician of Uniontown), Esther. Dr. David, Jr., settled in Westmoreland county, was twice elected to congress, was a successful physician, a man of spotless reputation, and his seven sons were all professional men.

Dr. Louis was born June 23, 1782. Dr. Louis Marchand read medicine with his father, and was graduated from the University of Pennsylvania in 1809, practiced medicine at the Marchand homestead farm for a few years and upon the death of his brother, Dr. Daniel, located at Uniontown, where he successfully practiced his profession until 1849. His death occurred January 11, 1857. He was a man in the truest sense of the word. His character was above suspicion and none knew him but to praise him for his skill as a physician and his blameless life as a man and citizen. In about 1823 he was married to Miss Sarah, daughter of Dr. Samuel Sackett, a surgeon in the Revolutionary War and a native of Connecticut. Dr. Sackett practiced his profession at Uniontown and on Georges Creek from September, 1781 to 1833, when he died. Mrs. Marchand died November 8, 1870, at the age of 73 years and left six children: Elizabeth, wife of A. J. Miller; Dr. Samuel S., a captain in the late war and died in Libby prison in 1863; Mary, wife of Thomas W. Lilly; Frances C., wife of J. W. Ward; Lucius A. and Catherine B., wife of E. W. Lilly. After four years of age, Lucius A. Marchand was reared on a farm and educated in the common and California schools. He chose farming for a life pursuit and has been a successful farmer up to the present time.

In 1866 he married Miss Minerva, daughter of Henry Van Druff, a prominent farmer and stock-dealer of Greene county, Pa. They have four children: Lewis K., Samuel V., Marion C. and Gertrude E.

Lucius A. Marchand owns the homestead farm of 130 acres (originally 400 acres) five miles below Brownsville. In 1873 he laid on this land the present thriving village of Marchand, containing fifty voters. Marchand is on the line of a projected railroad, opposite Coal Center on the P. V. & C. R. R., and is a favorable site for coke works. L. A. Marchand is a republican and school director. He is an enterprising farmer and a useful member of the Christian Brethren church at Coal Center.

JOHN McELDOWNY, a native of Bedford county, and a comfortably situated farmer of Fayette county, is a son of William and Rebecca (Gordon) McEldowny, and was born in Bedford county, Pa., January 18, 1831.

Robert McEldowny, grandfather, was a native of Baltimore, who emigrated to Bedford county and engaged in farming. His father was an early settler in western Pennsylvania and was killed by Indians.

William McEldowny was born at Bedford, Pa., in 1795, was a stone mason, democrat, and useful member of the Cumberland Presbyterian church. He removed to near Heistersburg, Fayette county, where he reared a family of three sons and six daughters; the second son, James, served in the Army of the Potomac under General Grant. Mrs. McEldowny was a daughter of James Gordon, of Bedford county.

John McEldowny, after receiving a common-school education, worked as a day laborer until twenty-five years of age, and drove stock on the "Old Pike" for Eli Cope. He was next engaged for several years in handling steamboat lumber, in the meantime, however, teaching a term of school in Greene county, Pa. Since 1863 he has been engaged in farming, at Jenning's Ferry, five years, thence to a farm near Heistersburg eight years, and afterwards removed to his present farm near Ormond. From 1857 to 1860 he ran Abel's Mill near Fairchance.

On August 16, 1856, he was married to Miss Martha, daughter of Pierce F. Vernon, of Greene county, Pa. They have six children: Thomas, of Kansas, married Miss Jennie Crawford; Jennie, wife of I. N. Heath, of Kansas; John, William, Cora and Martha.

John McEldowny owns a favorably located and desirable farm of eighty-two acres, and is conveniently situated near Ormond. He is one of the substantial citizens of his township, a member of Hopewell Cumberland Presbyterian church, is a Master Mason, and a democrat in the fullest sense of the term.

REV. JOSEPH E. McCLAY, a faithful and efficient minister of the United Brethren church, was born in Springfield township Fayette county, Pa., June 3, 1848. He is the son of Thomas and Sarah (Eicher) McClay.

His grandfather, James McClay, was born in the North of Ireland, emigated to the United States in about 1800, and settled in what is now Springfield township. He married a Miss Shuman of the same township.

His father, Thomas McClay, was born in Springfield township, and was a farmer. He married Miss Mary, daughter of Joseph Eicher.

Rev. Joseph E. McClay received his early education in the common schools and afterwards attended Madison Normal School in Westmoreland county, under Professor G. M. Bigam.

Qualifying himself for the ministry, he was accordingly licensed by the United Brethren church and first employed in 1871 on the Castleman circuit in Westmoreland county. Later he served four years on the Bedford county charge, and was then transferred to Three Springs charge in Huntingdon county, where he remained three years. From Huntingdon county he was sent to Mount Pleasant, and served one year. He was presiding elder of the Greesburgh district for some time.

On January 21, 1873, he married Mary Jane, daughter of John and Susan Eyer, of Huntingdon county. Unto this union were born three children, only one of whom, Anna Edna (born July 7, 1878), is living.

For some years he served in the Springfield charge, and then retired to a valuable farm that he owns in the township. He is at present engaged in improving his land and resting from mental labor. He is an earnest and efficient minister and an honorable gentleman.

JESSE McFARLAND, of Stewart, was born in Greene County, Pa., December 22, 1852. His grandfather, John McFarland, was born and raised in Greene county. His father, Jacob McFarland, was also born in the same county, and removed in 1870, to Ohiopyle. His wife was Susanna Brown, a daughter of John Brown, who was a native of Delaware county, Pa.

Jacob McFarland and wife had thirteen children: Rebecca, Mary A., John, Jesse, Sarah E., James L., Caroline, Minor, Malinda, Jacob, William, Alice, Thomas.

Jesse McFarland, the subject of this sketch, was educated in the common schools of Greene county, and was married November 7, 1874, to Miss Elizabeth Turney, daughter of S. G. Turney, of Preston county, W. Va. They have two children: Robert T. L. and Silva E. Mr. McFarland is engaged as book-keeper for McFarland Bros., lumber dealers. He has served as constable two terms, tax collector, two terms, and one term as school director.

LOUIS SOWERS MILLER, a prominent coal operator of the Monongahela Valley, is the only child of Augustus I. and Elizabeth K. (Marchand) Miller, and was born in Brownsville, Fayette county, Pa., March 16, 1848.

His grandfather, Israel Miller, was a very prominent business man of Brownsville, who was born April 8, 1783, and died April 16, 1871. May 6, 1810, he married Miss Anna Marie Sowers. They had five sons and six daughters. Mrs. Miller was born June 29,

1790, and died May 5, 1850. She was a daughter of Michael and Dorothy Sowers. Mr. Sowers was born October 16, 1752, and was one of the early business men of Brownsville.

His father, Augustus I. Miller, (third son of Israel Miller) was born February 2, 1821, and was married November 13, 1845, to Miss Elizabeth K., daughter of Dr. Louis Marchand. (See sketch of L. A. Marchand.) Mrs. Miller died March 18, 1848. Mr. Miller was a brave soldier and gave his life in support of tde Federal cause. He enlisted in April, 1861, in the Twelfth Regiment Pennsylvania Volunteers for three months, re-enlisted in November, 1861, for three years in Company H, Seventh Regiment Pennsylvania Cavalry, and died in Louisville, Ky., August, 19, 1863, of disease contracted in the service.

LOUIS S. MILLER attended the common schools and received his business education in the Iron City Commercial College. On November 10, 1872, he was married to Miss Mary A. Forsythe, daughter of William and Jane P. (Steele) Forsythe, of Jefferson township. They have six children: Laura, Frank, Oliver, Jennie, Lizzie and William Augustus.

Louis S. Miller, in December, 1879, became a member of the "Little Alps Coal Company, Limited," operating the Little Alps Mine on his farm, just opposite the town of California. After some changes in 1880, Mr. Miller and J. Underwood, J. S. Elliott and John W. Ailes formed a partnership and opened their present "Snow Hill Mine" in Jefferson township, opposite the village of Roscoe. The average yearly output of this mine is 1,500,000 bushels of coal, which is of very fine quality and is in great demand from Cincinnati to New Orleans. This company employs from 100 to 150 men at their coal works, and ship their coal down the Ohio and Mississippi rivers. They own a general mercantile store at Roscoe, and are proprietors of the steamer Crescent.

The beautiful home farm of Mr. Miller is opposite California, It contains one hundred acres of choice land, and is on the projected Ohio & Baltimore short line railroad. Mr. Miller is a republican, and is serving his fourth term as a trustee of the State Normal School at California. He is a member of the O. W. A. M., and is one of the enterprising and successful business men of Fayette county.

BENTON L. MILLER, is one of the leading business men of Springfield township, and is a son of Jacob A. H. and Louisa (Sherbondy) Miller, and was born in Springfield township, Fayette county, Pa., December 30, 1853.

His grandfather, Abram H. Miller, was born near Meyersdale, Somerset county, in 1787, and died at ninety-two years of age. He was a farmer, and married a Miss Long.

His father, Jacob A. H. Miller, was born in Somerset county, in 1829, and died in Springfield township, September 29, 1862. On February 14, 1853, he was married by Rev. Wakefield, to Miss Louisa, daughter of David Sherbondy. Mr. Miller owned a good farm, was engaged in mercantile business for some time and also dealt in stock.

Benton L. Miller was educated in the common schools of Springfield township, and at the Pennsville Normal School, when under the supervision of Prof. Axtell. Leaving school he engaged in teaching, which he continued for four years, when he engaged in the hotel business. Retiring from the hotel, he invested in a store, which he successfully operated until May 21, 1884, when his building and stock were destroyed by fire. After meeting with this loss, Mr. Miller engaged in farming and stock raising, in which he has continued up to the present time.

On December 29, 1880, he was married by the Rev. James Hollingshead to Miss Lina, daughter of Elias Tannehill, of Somerset county. Their union has been blessed with four children: Bernard, born December 9, 1881; Kate, born October 2, 1883; Lulu Netta, born September 11, 1885, and Archie L., born August 2, 1887.

Mr. Miller is an ardent worker in the democratic party. He was a candidate for the nomination of county treasurer in 1884, and again in 1887. In each election he ran next to the nominee. He is a general agent for farming implements, and is in the front rank of Springfield's business men. He is a member of K. of P., and also of Eylan Lodge, No. 260, I. O. R. M. He was the first sachem of his tribe, and is now its representative to the great council. He is a popular and capable citizen of his township.

LOUIS SOWERS MILLER, a prominent coal operator of the Monongahela valley, is the only child of Augustus I. and Elizabeth K. (Marchand) Miller, and was born in Brownsville, Fayette county, Pa., March 16, 1848. His grandfather, Israel Miller, was a very prominent business man of Brownsville. He was born April 6, 1783, and died April 16, 1871. May 6, 1810, he married Miss Anna Maria Sowers. They had five sons and six daughters. Mrs. Miller was born June 29, 1790, and died May 5, 1850. She was a daughter of Michael and Dorothy Sowers. Mr. Sowers was born October 16, 1762, and was one of the early business men of Brownsville. His father, Augustus I. Miller (third son of Israel Miller), was born February 2, 1821, and was married November 13, 1845, to Miss Elizabeth K., daughter of Dr. Louis Marchand (see sketch of L. A. Marchand). Mrs. Miller died March 18, 1848. Mr. Miller was a brave soldier, and gave his life in support of the Federal cause. He enlisted in April, 1861, in the Twelfth Regiment Pennsylvania Volunteers for three months, re-enlisted in November, 1861, for three years, in Company H, Seventh Regiment Pennsylvania Cavalry, and died in Louisville, Ky., August 19, 1863, of disease contracted in the service.

Louis S. Miller attended the common schools, and received his business education in the Iron City Commercial College. On November 10, 1872, he was married to Miss Mary A. Forsythe. They have six children: Laura, Frank, Oliver, Jennie, Lizzie and William Augustus.

Louis S. Miller in December, 1879, originated and became a member of the "Little Alps Coal Company, Limited," and opened the Little Alps mine on his farm, just opposite the town of California. After some changes in 1880, Mr. Miller and J. Underwood, J. S. Elliott and John W. Ailes formed a partnership and opened their present "Snow Hill Mine" in Jefferson township, opposite the village of Roscoe. The average yearly output of this mine is 1,500,000 bushels of coal, which is of very fine quality and in great demand from Cincinnati to New Orleans. This company employs from one hundred to 150 men at their coal works, and ship their coal down the Ohio and Mississippi rivers. They own a general mercantile store at Roscoe, and are proprietors of the steamer Crescent.

The beautiful home farm of Mr. Miller is opposite California. It contains one hundred acres of choice land, and is on the projected Coal Center & Connellsville railroad. Mr. Miller is a republican, and is serving his fourth term as a trustee of the State Normal School at California. He is a member of the American Mechanics, and is one of the most enterprising and successful business men of Fayette county.

ISAAC MYERS, one of the foremost business men of Henry Clay township, and a leading merchant of Markleysburg, is a son of Jacob and Hannah (Van Sickle) Myers, and was born in Preston county, Va. (now West Virginia), September 14, 1834.

His paternal grandfather, Isaac Myers, was a native of Somerset county, and removed to Fayette county where he died. He was a farmer, an old lime Whig and a devout member of the Brethren in Christ church.

His maternal grandfather, Lewis Van Sickle, was born in New Jersey and emigrated to Allegheny county, Md., where he engaged in farming. He was a member of the German Baptist church, served in the War of 1812 and was a strong and active democrat.

His father, Jacob Myers, was born in Fayette county, was a farmer, republican and a member of the Brethern in Christ church. His family consisted of four sons and nine daughters.

Isaac Myers was educated in the common schools of Henry Clay township, and for several years was engaged at carpentering and farming. He now conducts, at Markleysburg, a flouring mill, saw-mill, planing mill and a store under the firm name of Myers & Sons.

In 1864 he enlisted in the Third Maryland Infantry, Potomac Home Guards, and was in the battle of Monocacy Junction, besides numerous skirmishes.

In 1854 he was married to Miss Priscilla, daughter of Abraham Welsh, of Allegany county, Md. They have eight children: William, married Alice, daughter of G. D. Frantz; and resides in Garret county, Md.; John H.; Joshua S., carpenter and married Samantha Savage; Dora E., wife of J. B. Thomas, farmer of Garret county, Md.; Mary E., married Burbridge Thomas, of the same county; Catherine E., George W. and Laura M.

Isaac Myers is a republican, and has been chaplain and vice-grand in the Independent Order of Odd Fellows. He is a member of the Church of God and, is an elder in that church. He is one of the live, progressive men of southern Fayette county; is energetic and successful in every enterprise he has undertaken.

MARK R. MOORE, a respected citizen and ex-county commissioner of Fayette county, was born in Luzerne township, Fayette county, Pa., October 23, 1816, and is a son of Joshua and Nancy Miller) Moore.

John Moore (grandfather) was a native of New Jersey, and of English descent. He was a miller, and settled about 1783 at the old mill above Merrittstown, and afterwards removed to Bridgeport, where he was a flour inspector.

Joshua Moore (father) was brought to Luzerne at three years of age, and was a Quaker, as were all the Moores for many years afterwards. He cast his first vote for Andrew Jackson, and died at fifty-four years of age. December 25, 1809, he was married to Miss Nancy Miller, a Presbyterian. They had five sons and two daughters, and one of the former, John M. Moore served as a soldier in the late war. Mrs. Moore's father, James Miller, came from Ireland to America and located at York, Pa.

Mark R. Moore was reared on a farm and received his education in the old winter subscription schools of Luzerne township. He learned the trade of shoemaker, but was never actively engaged at it. Early in life he engaged in farming, and has continued successfully in that line of business up to the present time. He was married to Miss Hannah H., daughter of Joseph Crawford. They have five living children: George, Mary, Harriet, John G. and William.

Mark R. Moore owns the old Moore homestead of 130 acres of valuable and well improved land. He is of the same political faith as his fathers; has always voted the democratic ticket. He served as county commissioner in 1854, and has held various township offices. He is now retired from active business, and enjoys the respect of his many friends.

FRANCIS MORRISON, of Stewart township, is a man of patriotism, integrity, usefulness and marked individuality. He is of Irish descent, was born in Stewart township, Fayette county, Pa., January 15, 1845, and is a son of Francis D. Morrison, who was born in Henry Clay township, Pa., January 18, 1825. He was a soldier in the Eighty-fifth Regiment Pennsylvania Volunteers, but was discharged for disability. His maternal grandfather was born in Rahway, N. J., and was a Revolutionary soldier. His paternal grandfather, Dr. Francis Morrison, was born in Washington county, Pa., and died in Henry Clay township, this county.

Francis Morrison, the subject of this sketch, when quite a child was left to the care of strangers, and consequently saw hard times. At twelve years of age he removed west to Marshall county, Ill., and spent four years with J. G. White, who was a well-to-do farmer of that section.

At sixteen years of age he returned to the county of his nativity, and enlisted in Company H, Eighty-fifth Pennsylvania Volunteers. The old Eighty-fifth was swiftly formed to go to the front, and the record of its glorious acts is a history of which Fayette county may be forever proud. And of the part he took in the battles of that brave old regiment, Mr. Morrison may be also justly proud. He was in the battles of Williamsburg, Fair Oaks, Kenston, White Hall, Goldsboro, the siege of Fort Sumter, and Deep Bottom, Va., August 16, 1864, where he was shot through the right lung, and was discharged from White Hall Hospital, June 17, 1865, as an invalid for life. He was in many marches and expeditions besides these battles, and had many hair-breadth escapes. He served as an orderly on General Howell's staff for a considerable time.

Being unable to perform manual labor, he attended the Edinboro State Normal School to qualify himself for teaching, an avocation he successfully pursued for ten years in the common schools of the county.

In 1870 Mr. Morrison married Miss Eliza Jane Daniels, of Stewart township. They have five children: James Marshall, Laura Frances, Tabitha J., Whitelaw Reid and Alva Ethel.

As a private citizen Mr. Morrison has resided in Stewart township since the war, and devoted a portion of his time and attention to his productive farm and to stock raising.

As a public officer he has served Stewart township for fifteen years as justice of the peace; for the same length of time he has been kept almost continuously on the school board. Through his efforts every school house in Stewart township has been greatly improved, and every child in attendance has been comfortably seated.

In 1887 he was elected county auditor, and received the largest home complimentary vote of any candidate on the republican ticket. He is an occasional correspondent to some leading paper, and has the reputation of being a good public speaker.

Mr. Morrison was an industrious boy and a brave soldier. He is a good citizen, a prosperous farmer and a popular public officer.

Francis Morrison

AMOS STRAWN MURPHY, of Bullskin township, is of Scotch-Irish origin and was born in "Lazy Hollow," Franklin township, Fayette county, Pa., February 23, 1839, and is a son of Thomas and Rachel (Strawn) Murphy, who were natives respectively of Jefferson and Perry townships, Fayette county, Pa.

Thomas Murphy was born September 8, 1812, and was married by Squire Roberts, of Redstone township, September 8, 1837. John Murphy (the paternal grandfather of A. S. Murphy) was born in Philadelphia and his (A. S.'s) great grandfather, Henry Murphy, was a native of Ireland. He came to Philadelphia, thence to New Jersey; from there to Fayette county and located on a farm in what is now Jefferson township; the same farm is still in the possession of the Murphy family.

Amos Strawn Murphy received his school training in the common schools of the county; on leaving them, he attended the California Seminary, now known as the "California Normal." He soon began life as a teacher in Redstone township, and at intervals attended normal schools at Millsboro, Bridgeport, and the academy at Merrittstown. His career as a teacher began in 1859, when he taught in Redstone township. Afterwards he tauhgt three years successively at Perryopolis; two years at Connellsville and three years in New Haven. He gave up teaching to accept a position with the B. & O. R. R. Co., as car inspector, and was stationed at West Newton, Pa.; he held this position for nine months, when he was changed to the position of traveling car inspector, which he held for four years, when he was stationed at Connellsville. At the expiration of this term he was promoted to the position of general car inspector by the company, his division of work extending from Pittsburgh to Cumberland, Md., and served acceptably to the company for three years. He was then offered a still better position but refused it. He quit the railroad and went to the farm he had bought near Moyer Station.

February 26, 1866, he was married to Mary Ellen Freeman, daughter of Samuel Freeman of Connellsville, the latter died August 2, 1879. Of the seven children born to their union two are living: Katie, born April 11, 1867, at Connellsville, and Francis, born July 4, 1877.

Amos S. Murphy is a brother of Prof. D. C. Murphy, who ranks high as a teacher, author and institute instructor. A. S. Murphy owns a farm containing eighty acres of good land near Moyer and a well improved farm near Harper City, Kan. Mr. Murphy has been recording secretary of General Worth Lodge, No. 346, I. O. O. F., is a member of King Solomon Lodge, No. 386, A. Y. M., and Monarch Castle, No. 84, K. of M. C., has been councilor for two terms of Moyer Council, No. 166, Jr. O. U. A. M., and of the latter organization is representative to the State council and district deputy for a number of councils. He is justice of the peace, although a republican was elected by both parties in a township democratic by 200 majority in a total vote of about 375. Mr. Murphy is an intelligent, prominent and useful citizen.

REV. JOSHUA THOMAS NEEL, an able young minister of the Cumberland Presbyterian church, was born in Cumberland township, Greene county, Pa., January 17, 1857, and is a son of Aliff S. and Maria L. (Thomas) Neel.

Barnett Neel, his grandfather, was a blacksmith by occupation, and resided in Greene county, where he dealt in blooded stock and fine horses. His father was a soldier in the War of the Revolution.

Aliff S. Neel was born in Cumberland

township, Greene county, Pa., where he died in the prime of life. By occupation he was a farmer. He married Miss Maria L., daughter of Joshua Thomas, a Greene county farmer, and to their marriage were born the following children: Martha L., Elizabeth M. (dead), Joshua T. and Remembrance H.

Rev. Joshua T. Neel was educated in Greene Academy and Waynesburg College, and was graduated with high honors from the latter institution in the class of 1884. Leaving college he entered the United Presbyterian Seminary at Allegheny City, where he completed the course prescribed for a regular graduation. On account of the death of his father, he had to support himself, and at the same time earn the means to take his academic and professional courses in college. This he did by teaching, and taught eight terms in the common schools of Greene and one in Fayette county. Immediately after leaving the seminary he was installed as pastor of the Hopewell Cumberland Presbyterian church, one of the strongest and best supported churches of the Presbyterian faith in the county. He bears the honor of being the first regularly-installed pastor of this church since its organization in 1832. During his three years' charge of this church there have been seventy-five additions to its membership roll.

In May, 1886, he was married to Miss Rhoda Ann, daughter of Aaron Gregg, of Carmichael's, Greene county, Pa., and they have one child, Paul Vincent Neel.

Rev. Neel, in addition to his regular theological course of reading, still pursues his studies along the various lines of science and literature, and is a young and popular divine in Presbyterian circles of Fayette county.

CHARLES BERNARD NEMON was born in 1830 in Germany, and came to the United States with his parents when he was two years old. He was the son of Charles Nemon, who had the following children: Catherine, Elizabeth, Caroline, Christina and Charles B.

The subject of this sketch was raised by the father of Nicholas McCartney, until Mr. McCartney's death, and afterwards by Nicholas McCarthny, who lived in Wharton township, Fayette county, Pa. He was educated in the common schools of Fayette county. In 1856 he engaged in milling and the cattle business, in Ohio Pyle. In 1858 he went to Virginia, and was engaged in superintending furnaces, first at the Clinton furnace, and afterward at the ore mines at Franklin furnace, Preston county, Va.

He was married to Rachel Morris, daughter of Harvey Morris (deceased), of Stewart township; and they have children as follows: William, Emily, Agnes, Annie, Luther, Alva, Millie and Arthur.

He was superintendent of the Dunbar furnace for two years. From Virginia he came to Mount Braddock, as superintendent of the farm of W. & J. K. Beeson, and has been in their employ about seventeen years.

Mr. Nemon is a member of the Independent Order of Odd Fellows.

OLIVER F. M. NICOLAY was born August 4, 1853, in Springfield township, Fayette county, Pa., reared upon a farm, and was educated in the common schools of the county and at Waynesburgh College. At the age of nineteen he commenced teaching school in Fayette county, where he taught nine years, and during the summer months was engaged in farming. In January, 1876, he married Martha Williams, daughter of Daniel Williams, of Fayette county. They have five children: Minnie, Homer B., Roxana, Roy V. and Arvilda. Mr. Nicolay served as school director for one term, and was made secretary of the board.

In 1887 a new postoffice was established at the residence of Mr. Nicolay, which was named for him, and he was appointed postmaster. Mr. Nicolay still holds to his early habits as a scholar, and corresspond with the county papers. His parents were Henry and Catherine (May) Nicolay. His father was born in Somerset county, Pa., in the year 1824. His mother was of German-Irish descent, and was born in Fayette county, Pa., in 1825. Their family consisted of three children: Ellen, Oliver F. M. (the subject of this sketch) and Anna.

Mr. Nicolay is a stanch democrat, and is a zealous worker for the party in Stewart township. Mr. Nicolay's grandfather, John Nicolay, was born, lived and died in Somerset county, Pa. He was a farmer.

Mr. Nicolay is an earnest Sunday-school worker, and the schools under his supervision have always been very interesting. He is widely known for his genial hospitality.

STEPHEN RANDOLPH NUTT, an influential citizen and farmer of Jefferson township, is a son of Joseph and Ann (Randolph) Nutt, and was born in Washington township, Fayette county, Pa., Septem-24, 1828.

His grandfather, William Nutt, came from New Jersey to Fayette county, about ten or fifteen years after the close of the Revolution, in which his oldest brother, Adam, served as a scout. William Nutt married a Miss Craig; she died and left two children: Joseph and Sarah. After her death he married Miss Rebecca Cope, by whom he had one son, William.

His father, Joseph Nutt, was a blacksmith, but during the most of his adult life, was engaged in farming. He was born in Washington township in 1793, removed to Jefferson township in 1831, and went for his health to Coxe's Bar, Cal., in September, 1851, where he died in December of the same year. He was a member of the Methodist Episcopal church, and married Miss Ann Randolph. She was born in 1808 and died in 1867. Her father, Stephen Randolph, was born in New Jersey, was a boat builder, came to Fayette county and engaged in farming.

Stephen R. Nutt came with his father in 1831 to Jefferson township and attended the common schools for several winters. Attaining his majority he engaged in farming, and has continued prosperously in that line of business to the present time.

In 1850 he married Miss Sarah J., daughter of Joseph and Annie Wells. Mr. and Mrs. Nutt have seven living children: Ruth L., Rebecca W., Margaret M., Edwin J., Jennie, Paul R. and Charles H. Three and one-half miles northeast of Brownsville on the Uniontown and Greenfield road, Mr. Nutt controls 247 acres of good and well-improved land. He is a true republican, and has held several times the offices of school director, assessor and township auditor. S. R. Nutt is a member of the Redstone Presbyterian church and one of the foremost men of the township. All his methods of business are honorable, and he enjoys the respect and esteem of his neighbors.

CAPTAIN ARTHUR M. PARKER, a veteran of the War of the Rebellion and a successful and energetic business man, is a son of Orris and Mary (McKean) Parker, and was born at Stoneham, Oxford county, Maine, June 10, 1842.

Orris Parker was born at Bath, Maine, in 1809. He was a personal friend of Hon. James G. Blaine and General Neal Dow, and materially aided the latter in securing the passage of the celebrated Maine liquor law. He married Miss Mary McKean, of Irish descent. His father was Joseph Parker, of English parentage, and born at Bath, Maine. Joseph Parker was a soldier of the war of 1812, was descended from one of the earliest pioneers of the "Pine Tree State," and died at ninety-eight years of age.

Captain Arthur M. Parker was educated in the public schools of his native village. In the dark days of 1861 he and three of his brothers were among the first to respond to President Lincoln's call for 75,000 men. He enlisted in the First Maine Volunteers and served three months; re-enlisted and served two years in the Tenth Maine, when he entered the Twenty-ninth Maine Veteran Volunteers, and served until honorably discharged, June 23, 1866. Captain Parker entered the service as a private, was promoted or orderly sergeant, became lieutenant while in charge of Darlington jail, S. C., and was commissioned captain of company G, Twenty-ninth Maine, October 10, 1865. He was in twenty-seven engagements, was at second Bull Run and was with Phil. Sheridan in the valley and at Lee's surrender. While making a cup of coffee one evening he stooped down and was struck in the head by a rifle ball, which made an ugly wound. Captain Parker was one of fifty orderly sergeants who were detailed as an escort to the funeral of President Lincoln.

At the close of the war Captain Parker, after visiting his old home, emigrated west to Kingwood, W. Va., where he was married to Miss Sabina H. Beavers, October 29, 1868. After a few years he removed to near Moyer and is now actively, successfully and extensively engaged in the lumber business. In politics he is a republican. He is an honest upright citizen and is highly respected by his neighbors.

DANIEL H. PERSHING was born on the old Pershing homestead, in Bullskin township, Fayette county, Pa., May 25, 1831. His father, Abraham Pershing, was born October 21, 1796, in Derry township, Westmoreland county, Pa. He was engaged in farming which he continued to follow till his death. His wife's maiden name was Barbara Troxel, daughter of John Troxel, of Westmoreland county, who emigrated from Lebanon county, Pa., in 1806. Daniel H. Pershing is of German descent, was educated in the common schools of the county, and subsequently attended college at Mt. Pleasant, Westmoreland county, now known as the Mt. Pleasant Institute. Leaving college he engaged in teaching and taught for eight years, when he began farming in connection with the work of surveyor of land. On October 18, 1860, he was married to Amanda Miller, daughter of Isaac Miller, of Lebanon county, Pa. To their marriage has been born twelve children, nine of whom are living: Nevada, born March 14, 1863, wife of Jacob Atkinson, of the township; Louisiana, December 18, 1864, wife of John H. Seman, of Westmoreland county; Minnesota, December 31, 1866; Idaho, February 7, 1869; Missouri, April 27, 1871; Aba, March 26, 1873; Stewart, April 25, 1875; Ira Sankey, March 2, 1877, and Emerson C., May 1, 1879, all born in Bullskin township, Fayette county, Pa. Daniel H. Pershing is a prohibitionist in politics, has 370 acres of fine land in Bullskin township, and is otherwise well-fixed in life. He owns some ten houses and lots in St. Pleasant and three in Bullskin township. He is a successful business man, and is held in high esteem by his neighbors.

DR. WILLIAM R. POOLE comes of Old Virginia stock on both sides of his family. His great-grandmother was born in Loudoun county, Va., April 22, 1796. Removed to Fayette county, Pa., in 1819, settled in Georges township, thence to Franklin township, and died in 1887. Her husband John Arrison was born in 1787, and served in the War of 1812. John and Catherine Arrison were the parents of twelve children; at the time of their death they had 70 grandchildren; 140 great-grandchildren, and 25 great-great-grand-children. Samuel Arrison, grandfather of the subject of this sketch, was born in Loudoun county, Va., and was married to Margaret Minks, a native of Fayette county, Pa. They had four children: Jane, Melvina, Rachel and Matilda. His paternal grandfather, Philomen Poole, was born in Eastern Virginia. He learned the tailor's trade and served in the late war, and died of disease contracted while in the service. He had seven children: Lewis R. (father of William R.) was born March 5, 1837, learned the blacksmiths trade and came to Fayette county. He married Melvina Arrison in June, 1859. He served in the Civil War, enlisting in 1862 in the Fourteenth Regiment Pennsylvania Volunteers, and served to the close of the war. He fought in the battles of Bull Run, Antietam, Rocky Gap, and was on Salem Raid, and at the battle of Winchester, and has been practicing medicine since 1867. He and his wife were the parents of seven children: William R., Samuel, Wylie W., Charles N., Melvina, Martha L. and Margaret.

William R. Poole was born April 28, 1860, near Brownsville, was educated in the common schools of the county, and at a normal institution in Virginia, and taught school for one term. He read medicine with Dr. N. W. Truxal, of Brownsville. Attended medical lectures at Ann Arbor and graduated from American Medical College of Ohio in 1879, and has since been engaged in the successful practice of medicine. He was formerly a member of the Virginia Medical Association. On January 26, 1879, he was married to Miss Mary E. Truxal, daughter of Dr. N. W. Truxal. They have had five children: Emma L., Lewis R., Ivanora, Edgar (deceased) and Clara.

JOHN B. POTTER, one of the highly respected citizens of Stewart township, was born in Fayette county, Pa., November 30, 1828. He is a son of Samuel and Sarah (Leonard) Potter, the latter a daughter of Mahlon Leonard, who was a native of New Jersey. To their union were born the following-named children: Mary A., John B., Elizabeth, George P., Julian, Samuel, Amos, Sarah and Thomas, all living.

John Potter, the grandfather of John B. Potter, was born in New Jersey, in a very early day emigrated from that State to Pennsylvania, and settled in what is now known as "Jockey Hollow," in Henry Clay township. The maiden name of his wife was Elizabeth Callaham.

John B. Potter received the meager advantages afforded by the common subscription schools of his day. He is at the present time engaged in the milling business and has served several terms in township offices. During the war he was drafted, but upon examination he was rejected on account of the loss of three of his fingers. In 1855 he was married to Miss Tamson Harvey, of Wharton township. To them have been born eight children: Arthur F., Elmyra, Cora, Anaddo, Lorena, Erma D., Dalton and Hampton L.

JOHN F. SCHAEFER, a prominent farmer and stock raiser of Stewart township, was born at Retterod, County of Liechman, State of Hesse Cassel, Germany, November 15, 1827, where he was educated in the common schools of the county. He came to America in March, 1848, arriving at Baltimore the following May. He came at once to Pittsburg, where he was employed as a common laborer at six dollars per month. Later he went to Washington county in 1853, where he worked in a rock quarry at sixty-two cents a day. In 1856 he engaged in the coal business and remained in that business till 1871, when he removed to Fayette county and engaged in farming.

He was married in 1855 to Miss Sarah E. Williams, daughter of Samuel Williams, of Washington county, Pa. Six children have been born to their union: Samuel W., Elizabeth A., Mary E., John H. S., Sarah E. and George A.

Mr. Schaefer is a prominent member of the Lutheran church and has been for many years.

His grandfather and father, both John G., were natives of Germany. His father was a soldier in the German army against Napoleon Bonaparte in 1814-15.

He was in quite a number of battes and was at Napoleon's defeat at Waterloo.

John H. Schaefer had three brothers and two sisters: Justus, Casper, Augustus, Mary E. and Anna C.

ELIJAH SHIPLEY. Among the prominent citizens of southern Fayette county is Elijah Shipley, born near Ohiopyle Falls, in what is now Stewart township, Fayette county, Pa., July 5, 1844; and is a son of Levi and Catherine (Linderman) Shipley, both natives of Fayette county, this State.

Elijah Shipley's family is traced back to Europe, whence in 1801 Charles Shipley (Elijah's father) sailed for the United States, and afterwards settled in Fayette county. One of his sons (Levi) was born December 14, 1816. Levi Shipley was a well-to-do farmer and a highly respected citizen. He married Miss Catherine Linderman and reared a family of eleven children: Leonard, Sarah, Elijah, Everhart, Squire, Melvina, Nancy, Levi, Rebecca, George and William.

Elijah Shipley was reared on a farm and received his education in the common schools. March 25, 1864, he enlisted in the Federal service and served until the close of the war. He enlisted as corporal, was promoted to sergeant and was made assistant quartermaster and ward-master. He was captured once but succeeded in making his escape. As a soldier, he was in the battles of the Wilderness, where he was slightly injured, Cold Harbor, Chapin's Farm and in the Siege of Petersburg. Since the war, he has been engaged successfully in farming.

In 1867 he was united in marriage to Miss Mary Youtzy, of Somerset county, Pa. To their union have been born four children: Florence, Ella, Catherine and Ulysses.

In political matters, Mr. Shipley is a republican, has served twelve years as road supervisor, and nine years as school director. In 1887 he was elected as director of the poor for Fayette county, and is serving acceptably in that position at the present time. Mr. Shipley resides at Falls City and enjoys the respect and good-will of his fellow townsmen.

ABRAM H. SHERRICK is a representative of that class of men who win success in life through their own energy and individual merit. He is a prominent farmer and coke manufacturer of Bullskin township, and was born at Mt. Pleasant, Westmoreland county, Pa., March 24, 1832. He is a son of Abram and Annie (Overholt) Sherrick, who were natives, respectively, of Fayette and Westmoreland counties. His paternal grandparents, John and Annie Sherrick (née Stauffer) were among the early pioneers of Fayette county, removing here from Berks county, Pa.

Abram H. Sherrick's history is much like

that of others who, by their own efforts, have attained competence and position in this life. His early life was spent on the farm, and at the age of fifteen he went to Mt. Pleasant and attended the seminary, where he was principally educated. Some few years before he had reached his majority, he was associated with his uncle, John Sherrick, in the mercantile business at Mt. Pleasant.

At the age of twenty-two years he crossed overland to California in search of gold under the rugged crests of the "Nevadas" ere the construction of the iron-ribbed railroad which now spans the continent from ocean to ocean. He continued successfully as a gold miner for three years. From 1854 to 1858 he was engaged in the distillery business. In 1862 he removed to his farm near Pennsville, Bullskin township, where he has since resided. Besides owning a splendid and highly improved farm of three hundred acres, he is one of the most prominent and extensive stock dealers in Fayette county. He operates and is the proprietor of large coke works near Pennsville, which are supplied with coal from his own farm. He ships from these works daily about ten cars of coke.

Mr. Sherrick was married to Mary, a daughter of Samuel Dillinger. To their union have been born ten children: Frank, Samuel, Bart, Ella, Carrie, Charles, Cora, Lydia, Mollie and Edward; Frank died in 1861.

ANDREW G. CURTIN SHERBONDY was born October 13, 1863, at Springfield, Fayette county, Pa. He was educated in the public schools of Dawson, Pa. In 1876 he learned telegraphy and engaged with the B. & O. R. R., and was the agent at Dawson and Markleton and also worked at Uniontown, Mt. Pleasant, Hickman Run, Rockwood and other points. He remained in the service of the B. & O. R. R. until the spring of 1883, when he removed to Springfield and engaged in the mercantile pursuit, where he has been very successful in business. He enjoys the distinction of being the only democrat of the name of Sherbondy. He is a democrat in every sense of the word and is held in high esteem by his party, having taken an active part in politics since he was thirteen years of age. He was appointed postmaster at Elm Postoffice, Fayette county, Pa., on July 20, 1885, and resigned on February 1, 1889, to take effect 1st of last March, while his successor was not appointed and qualified until May 4, 1889. He believes in Andrew Jackson's motto "To the victors belong the spoils." He was elected congressional delegate in 1888, and is at present a member of the democratic county committee. He was married at Somerset, Pa., by the Rev. J. F. Sharer (Lutheran minister), on October 21, 1882, to Miss Aggie May Crichfield, daughter of Henry Crichfield (deceased), late of Springfield Pa. This union has been blessed by two children: Florence Belle, born July 22, 1883, and Ivan Gold, born June 6, 1889.

He is a member of Eylan Tribe, No. 260, I. O. of R. M., and is a past officer of his lodge. He is a son of John W. and Christiana (Lowry) Sherbondy, formerly of Springfield, but now of Dawson, Pa.

John W. Sherbondy (father) has been farmer, merchant and stock dealer, and held various offices: Ten years as justice of the peace for Springfield township, ten years justice of the peace at Dawson, Pa., and he was postmaster at Elm, Pa., under President Lincoln.

John W. Sherbondy was born August 13, 1822, at or near Mendon, Westmoreland county, Pa., and came to Fayette county in 1845. He has been a farmer, merchant and stock dealer, and held various offices: ten years as justice of the peace, for Springfield township; ten years as justice of the peace at Dawson, Pa; and was postmaster at Elm, Pa, under President Lincoln. Chistian Lowry is the daughter of Jacob Lowry, of Dunbar township, Pa., who died December 8, 1886, aged eighty-eight years. She was born July 18, 1827, at Dunbar, Pa. (Dunbar township).

David Sherbondy was an extensive contractor of public turnpikes in early days, having built part of Mt. Pleasant and Robston pike road from Bridgeport up Coal Hill to what is now Allentown Pittsburgh. Made several miles of turnpike up the Sciota Bottoms at Portsmouth, Ohio, and also on National, Claysville, Hillsboro, Frosburg, Md., pikes. Paved the streets of Morgantown, W. Va., and numerous other roads.

He was elected a justice of the peace for Connellsville township in 1856, and held various other offices.

David Sherbondy, the grandfather of the subject of this sketch, was born in South Huntington township, Westmoreland county, Pa., and died May 8, 1880. The Sherbondys were of German descent, and the Lowrys of Scotch-Irish. Mr. Sherbondy is one of the hard-working and energetic young men of the county, and is deserving of success in whatever he undertakes.

GEORGE W. SHOWMAN was born in Dunbar township, Fayette county, Pa., April 28, 1847, and is a son of David and Jennie (Younkin) Showman.

David Showman is a native of the town of Somerset, Somerset county. He removed to Springfield township, where he lived for fifty years. He was a farmer, and is still living. He married, in Somerset county, December, 1839, Miss Jennie, daughter of George Younkin. They had nine children: W. H., Alex., Nancy Jane, George W., Catharine, Albert, Ellen, Jeremiah and Sarah.

George W. Showman was educated in the common schools of Springfield township. For nine years he was engaged as a coal miner in Tyrone and Hutchinson mines. Leaving the mines Mr. Showman engaged in farming for six years, in Tyrone township, when he removed to Springfield township, and has continued in farming up to the present.

On November 21, 1872, he was married, at Mt. Pleasant, to Miss Frances, daughter of James Hurst, of Tyrone township. They have had four children: Alberti, born May 9, 1878, died February 11, 1879; Mary Jane, born May 29, 1874; Lida Belle, born October 9, 1876, and James G., born in Springfield September 3, 1881.

Mr. Showman is a republican, has been school director for five years, and is now president of the school board of Springfield township. He is a member of Eylan Tribe, No 260, I. O. of Red Men. He is an efficient member of the Methodist Episcopal church at Springfield, where he serves as class leader. He is a prosperous farmer and a prominent citizen of his township.

JOHN L. SHULTZ, who risked his life and lost a limb in defense of the Union, is a son of John and Sarah (Lyons) Shultz, and was born in Salt Lick township, Fayette county Pa., February 14, 1838. His father, John Shultz, was a son of Jacob Shultz, who came from Somerset county to Salt Lick township, in 1837, and located on what is now the Davis Kalp property. The Shultzs are of German extraction.

John L. Shultz was brought up on a farm and educated in the schools of the neighborhood.

On December 15, 1861, he was married, by justice Sherbondy, to Miss Mary M., daughter of Jonathan Kern, of Greene county, Pa.; three children have blessed their union: Jacob K., born May 6, 1862; Eliza

Jane, born June 15, 1867, and William K., born February 10, 1875.

In September, 1862, he left his business and enlisted in Company C, Eighty-fourth Regiment Pennsylvania Volunteers, which was afterward consolidated with Company H, Fifty-seventh Regiment Pennsylvania Volunteers. He was in the battles of the Peninsula, Fredericksburg and Chancellorsville; at the last fight he was severely wounded and unfited for duty for three months. At Hatches Run, in a charge on a skirmish line, he lost his right leg. He received his discharge from the service August 25, 1865, and returned home and is at present engaged in farming.

He is a democrat, and has held most of the various township offices. Mr. Shultz is a member of the William T. Campbell Post, No. 375, Grand Army of the Republic; is a useful member of the Methodist Episcopal church at Springfield, and has many friends.

CYRUS B. SIPE was born in Springfield township, Fayette county, Pa., September 6, 1846, and is a son of Jacob and Catherine (Corpenning) Sipe.

Peter Sipe (grandfather) was born in Somerset county, Pa., and was a farmer, and removed in an early day to what is now Springfield township, where he settled on the farm now owned by William Drill.

Jacob Sipe (father) was born in Springfield township, was reared on a farm, and received his education in the old log schoolhouses under the subscription school masters. He married Miss Catherine, daughter of John Corpenning, of Somerset county.

Cyrus B. Sipe was raised on a farm, and attended the subscription schools of Springfield township. Leaving school, he engaged in farming and stock dealing, in which he has ever since continued.

He was married by the Rev. James Wakefield, to Miss Lizzie, daughter of H. L Sparks, of Salt Lick township.

Mr. Sipe is a republican, but is no politician. He has served six years as school director, is an upright business man, and a highly respected citizen.

SQUIRE SYLVESTER SKINNER, of Stewart township, was born in Fayette county in 1819, and received only the benefit of a common-school education. He was married, January 23, 1838, to Miss Adaline Thorp, native of Fayette county, Pa., and daughter of James Thorp, Esq. They have ten children: Sarah Jane, Sabina E., James, David, John M., Abram, Tabitha, Jefferson, George, Marcellus and Ella. Rev. Skinner was a Baptist minister, and held the office of justice of the peace for ten years. His death occurred on January 17, 1870.

HORATIO L. SPARKS, one of the most influential citizens of Salt Lick township, was born in Perry Township, Fayette county, Pa., January 21, 1823. His parents, Isaac and Elizabeth (Shreaves) Sparks, were both born in Perry township, Fayette county, Pa.; the latter was a daughter of William Shreaves of the same township, who was born in about 1790.

His grandfather, Isaac Sparks, was probably born in Fayette county. He was married to Helena Hammond, a daughter of Samuel Hammond, of Westmoreland county, Pa. To their union have been born nine children, eight of whom are living: Samuel H., born in 1854, in Westmoreland county; James H., 1856, in same county; Isaac L., in the same county; Ida, in the same county, and is the wife of George W. Campbell, of Springfield; Lizzie, wife of C. B. Sipe; John, born in Bullskin township, Fayette county; Agnes, born in the same township, an

Horatio L., Jr., born in Salt Lick township, and is at present residing in Pittsburgh, Pa.

Mr. Sparks removed to Salt Lick township, in about 1863, and engaged in mercantile farming and the tanning business. He has been very successful in his business ventures and has by careful management accumulated considerable property. He owns about 1,000 acres of land in Fayette county, and is a sterling democrat, and an exemplary citizen of Salt Lick township.

JOSHUA STRICKLER, of Luzerne, a highly esteemed citizen of Fayette county, was born on Jacob's Creek, Tyrone township, Fayette county, Pa., January 28, 1821, and is a son of Jacob B. and Mary (Fiscus) Strickler.

His grandfather, Jacob Strickler, was a native of Bucks county, Pa., and married Miss Elizabeth Stewart, a relative of Hon. Andrew Stewart. Jacob Strickler owned a large tract of land in what is now Upper Tyrone township. He was a republican, an member of the Mennonite church.

His father, Jacob B. Strickler, was born in Upper Tyrone township October 30, 1791, and died August 31, 1874. He was a republican, a local preacher in the Methodist Episcopal church, and among the first farmers that drove whiskey from the harvest field by an increase of wages. He married Miss Mary, daughter of Charles Fiscus, of Westmoreland county, and she, the mother of nine children, was born October 14, 1790, and died September 12, 1868.

Joshua Strickler attended the subscription schools, until sixteen years of age, when he went upon the National road as a wagoner; but at twenty-eight years of age he left the "Old Pike" and engaged in common labor. A few thousand dollars received from home gave him a fair start in life, and in 1850 he purchased his present farm and has, by careful management and judicious investments, accumulated many thousand dollars' worth of real and personal property.

January 31, 1850, he was united in marriage to Miss Elizabeth Covert, an excellent lady, and a daughter of Benjamin Covert. They have had six children: Mary A., born December 4, 1852, married Albert Conwell, merchant of Uniontown; Jacob A., of the firm of Conwell & Strickler, of Uniontown married Miss Bowlby; Everett, born December 4, 1860, married Mary Dawson; J. Randolph, born April 20, 1869, and Frank A., born November 3, 1872, and died January 8, 1875.

Mr. Strickler is a republican and useful member of the Methodist episcopal church. He was exempted from the draft, but gave $1,000 to secure volunteers for the Union service. He is hospitable, generous, and maintains an excellent reputation in private life.

ROMULUS V. RITENOUR, a prominent educator and ex-county superintendent, of Fayette county, is sprung from good old Virginia stock, and was born in Rappahannock county, Va., April 13, 1847. His grandfather, Joseph Ritenour, was of German extraction, and was born near Gaines' Cross Roads, Va. He removed to Brandonville, Preston county, W. Va., in about 1850, where he was engaged in the hotel business until his death. John H., the father of R. V. Ritenour, came from Virginia to Fayette county, in 1856, was a farmer and stock dealer and a man who was popular in his neighborhood. He was married in 1846 to Mary Rudasill, of Rappahannock county. They had ten children born to them: Romulus V., Florence L., Mary E., Susan, Anna Belle, John Mifflin (deceased), Joseph E., George I. (deceased), Lulu B. and Elfrida C.

Romulus V. Ritenour was elected to the

office of county superintendent of schools of Fayette county in 1881, and filled the office so acceptably that at the end of his term he was re-elected and served in the office for six years. He is one of the most popular and talented educators in the county.

ADONIRAM JUDSON TANNEHILL was born July 19, 1855, near Ursina, Somerset county, Pa. He was brought up on a farm in that county, until the age of twelve years, when he was placed in the Soldiers' Orphans' School at Uniontown, in 1867, where he remained for four years, taking the complete course of study prescribed by the State in that institution. Leaving school he worked at coal mining at Valley works and Pennsylvania for two years; subsequently worked at farming for two years, when he apprenticed himself to John Cunningham to learn the trade of blacksmith (Cunningham at that time worked at Springfield, but is now a resident of Connellsville). At this time A. D. Tannehill was the only support of his orphan sisters. He commenced to work for himself at the blacksmith business in 1879, at which he has continued ever since. He owns sixty acres of land, which he has farmed, and is considered valuable mountain land, being underlaid with coal and limestone.

A. J. Tannehill was married October 5, 1882, to Miss Frances King, at Pittsburgh, by Rev. Daniel Davis. She is the daughter of Henry King, of Springfield, Pa. Three children have been born to this union: Nellie, born November 6, 1883; Mabel, July 24, 1885, and Annie Kate, February 15, 1887.

Mr. Tannehill is a member of the Methodist church. He is the recording secretary of his congregation, and represented Springfield circuit at the annual conference at New Brighton in the fall of 1887. He is a member of the Independent Order of Red Men, No. 260, at Springfield, Pa. He has held the office of treasurer of this lodge since its organization. He was elected justice of the peace, February, 1886, by the republicans, and is now holding the office.

Mr. Tannehill is the son of Eli and Eliza Jane (Graham) Tannehill. Eli Tannehill was born November 22, 1821, in Somerset county, Pa., and was married December 14, 1843, to Miss Eliza Jane Graham, daughter of John Graham, of Ligonier, Westmoreland county, Pa. He enlisted, October 27, 1862, in Company K, One Hundred and Twelfth Regiment Pennsylvania Volunteers, and he took part in all the engagements of his regiment, up to the time of his death. He was killed August 5, 1864, before Petersburg. Joseph Tannehill, an uncle of A. J. Tannehill, was killed during the war. Also two other brothers of his father served in the late war in the Union army. The great-grandfather of the subject of this sketch was a general in the Revolutionary War, taken prisoner by the British and confined in the Albany prison until exchanged, after the close of the war. He settled near Pittsburgh, Pa.; was buried at Grantshill. Tannehill street, Pittsburgh, was named after him.

CAPTAIN ISAAC C. WOODWARD, of Luzerne, president of the Pittsburgh, Brownsville and Geneva Packet Company, is a son of Levi and Mary (Chalfant) Woodward, and was born May 20, 1813, at Chad's Ford, on the old historic Brandywine Creek, Chester county, Pa.

His paternal ancestor, William Woodward, was an English Quaker, coming to America with William Penn in 1682. Woodward owned forty acres of land adjoining the newly-founded city of Philadelphia. Penn was desirous of disseminating the Quaker faith and doctrines into the interior of the colony, and accordingly offered Woodward one thousand acres of land in Chester county for forty acres near Philadelphia. Woodward accepted the offer and settled on the Chester county tract, now known as "Marshalltown." The Woodwards still own a portion of the "Marshalltown" tract, where now stands a large Quaker church, called Bradford. Captain Woodward's paternal grandfather was born at Chad's Ford, where he lived and died.

In 1816 Captain Isaac C. Woodward was brought by his parents to Chad Chalfant's, a relative of his mother, near Brownsville, and shortly after their arrival his father died. In 1819 the captain was taken by an old Quaker, by the name of Cattell, with whom he remained ten years. While with him he received his education in the subscription schools of the surrounding neighborhood. He learned the trade of carpenter, which he followed for several years. He next engaged in building steamboats, and during a period of thirty years built about twenty boats. During the Mexican War he built a boat for the United States government, which ran on the Rio Grande river. He also commanded steamboats on the Mississippi river and its principal branches. For several years he has been president of the Pittsburgh, Brownsville & Geneva Packet Company, and is one of the company's largest stockholders. At the breaking out of the Civil War, he left the western waters and purchased a fine farm of three hundred acres, near Brownsville, where he is at present engaged in farming and stock raising, making a speciality of fine sheep.

In 1846 he married Miss Maria Brashear. She died in 1853. He has two children living: Anna, educated at Mechanicsburg Seminary, and wife of Rev. Joseph J. Parks, and Mary, educated at Mechanicsburg Seminary and wife of Dr. Reichard, of Brownsville. He was married, January 1, 1880, to Miss Martha J. Woods, of near Brownsville, an only daughter of James Woods, Jr. They have no children.

Captain Isaac C. Woodward is a hospitable gentleman, a prominent citizen and one of the most intelligent farmers of the county.

HIRAM UMBEL, of Henry Clay, one of the most successful merchants of Fayette county, and a man of considerable financial standing, is a son of Daniel and Rebecca (Maust) Umbel and was born in Henry Clay township, Fayette county, Pa., May 10, 1847.

His grandfather, Isaac Umbel, came from Wales to what is now Henry Clay township, about 100 years ago. His wife was Nancy Cambell and they were members of the Brethren in Christ church. He was a democrat of the "old school."

His father, Daniel Umbel, was a native of Henry Clay township, was a farmer by occupation but was engaged in the mercantile business for a few years at Markleysburg. He was school director a number of years, a democrat and was a member of the "Brethren in Christ church."

He married Miss Sarah Meyers and they had five children. After her death he married Miss Rebecca, daughter of Jacob Maust, of Somerset county, Pa. To this second union were born two children: Nancy, wife of William Hindbaugh, and Hiram. Mr. Maust was a member of the German Baptist church and emigrated to Henry Clay township, where he afterwards died.

Hiram Umbel was raised on a farm, educated in the common schools, Grantsville (Md.) Normal School and Georges Creek Academy, and taught seven terms in the schools of Pennsylvania and Maryland. In 1863 he sought to enlist in the army but was refused on account of age. February 7, 1880, he removed to Markleysburg and engaged in his present mercantile business.

April 23, 1871, he was married to Miss Lucinda, daughter of Christian Thomas;

they have two children: Mary Alice and Isaac Walter Umbel.

Hiram Umbel is a good financier and would be an able man to handle financial affairs of any kind. He began in life without anything, yet by his energy and business ability he is now worth about $20,000.

He has two very fine business buildings in Markleysburg; one is well fitted up and heavily stocked with first-class merchandise, the other a well-furnished endertaking establishment, which was opened in 1886. In both lines of business he enjoys a large patronage.

Hiram Umbel is a member of the Church of God. He is a democrat, was postmaster ten years and is an active worker in the interests of his political party.

JOSEPH HARRISON WIGGINS, one of the foremost citizens of Wharton township, was born near Brownsville, Fayette county, Pa., August 30, 1812, and is a son of Colonel Cuthbert and Margaret (Banting) Wiggins.

Colonel Cuthbert Wiggins was a native of Bucks county, Pa., where he married Miss Margaret, daughter of Emanuel and Septema Bunting, "on the 13th day of the third month," 1799, according to the Quaker marriage certificate, in possession of J. H. Wiggins. Colonel Wiggins came to Fayette county, Pa., about 1809, and served under General George Mason in the War of 1812, in which he commanded a militia regiment, and helped launch Commodore Perry's immortal fleet on Lake Erie.

Entering the army, he relinquished the Quaker faith and afterwards united with the Cumberland Presbyterian church. Leaving the army, he removed to Uniontown, kept a hotel for four years, and thence to Wharton township and erected the Fayette Springs Hotel. His family consisted of three sons and five daughters, of whom three are living: Hannah, widow of William McMullen; Anna and Joseph Harrison.

Colonel Wiggins was a great admirer of Henry Clay and General W. H. Harrison. He was a gentleman of the "old school" and a man of commanding personal appearance. His father was a native of Philadelphia.

Joseph Harrison Wiggins was reared at Uniontown, until 1821, when he removed to Wharton township, where he received his education in an old log school house. He worked for some time on the National road, and spent one year (1839) in Iowa.

In 1840 he returned to Wharton township, and one mile east of "Chalk Hill" he opened the present popular summer resort now conducted by his son, Henry H. Wiggins. J. H. Wiggins owns 450 acres of improved land, and devotes some time to the chase, of which he is very fond. His sporting friends have named his location the "Fox-hunters' Paradise."

In 1834 he married Miss Sarah J., daughter of John and Harriet (Madden) Risler. Mr. and Mrs. Wiggins have had eight children, born and named as follows: Kate R., November 26, 1834, died December 29, 1872; Hannah M., February 20, 1837, died December 6, 1861; John R., January 16, 1839, died February 26, 1873; Henry H., April 4, 1841; Anna E., January 16, 1844, died April 23, 1846; Maggie B., March 24, 1846, died February 8, 1865; Sarah T., February 28, 1852, died May 17, 1860; Mary E., April 27, 1854, died June 21, 1867.

Mrs. Wiggins, an estimable and highly respected woman, died November 18, 1888.

Henry H. was educated in the common schools, and enlisted in the One Hundred and Twelfth Regiment Volunteers, in August, 1862, and served in the Army of the Potomac until the close of the war. October 19,

1865, he married Miss Huldah, daughter of Harvey Morris, a prominent man of Stewart township. Henry H. Wiggins was census enumerator, and since then has held various township offices. Since 1870 he has rented and conducted successfully his father's summer resort, and his son is a book-keeper with H. C. Frick & Co.

J. Harrison Wiggins has retired from active life and lives in Wharton township.

GEORGE W. WILKIN, one of the useful citizens of Marchandville, and a popular ferryman, was born at Coal Center, Washington county, Pa., January 28, 1827, and is a son of Reuben and Bethsheba (Dowler) Wilkin.

George Wilkin (grandfather) died soon after coming from Virginia to Washington county, Pa.

Reuben Wilkin (father) was a native of Hardy county, Va., was a carpenter, and died in 1879. He married Miss Bethsheba, daughter of Thomas Dowler, a farmer of Washington county. She was a member of the Methodist Episcopal church, and died in 1868, aged sixty-two years.

George Wilkin was reared at Coal Center, and learned the trade of carpenter. His first employment was boating coal down the Monongahela. After ten years spent on the river, he engaged (1855) in building skiffs and operating the ferry between Coal Center and Marchandville. In 1873 he removed to Marchandville, and has continued in the ferry business up to the present time.

In 1849 he married Miss Margaret Ann Addis, of Menallen township. She died March 31, 1865, and left four children: Angeline, Louisa D., Emma E. and John H. In 1866, Mr. Wilkin married Miss Joanna Halliday, of Dunbar. After her death he was married, in 1885, to Mrs. Annie (Dial) Hamilton, daughter of the late Isaac Dial, formerly a farmer of Tyrone township. Mrs. (Dial) Wilkin was born near the site of Everson, June 7, 1839. She accompanied her father to Ohio in 1844, and six years later removed with him from that State to Illinois. Mr. Dial was drowned in the Mississippi river near Fort Madison, Iowa, and sleeps in the cemetery at Montrose, in that State. Mrs. Wilkin's first husband was William Murray, of St. Louis, whom she married September 21, 1862. He died in 1868, and December 8, 1877, she was married to Isaac Hamilton, of Jefferson township, this county. He died in Washington county in 1883, and she was a resident of that county until her marriage with Mr. Wilkin. She has one child: Edward H. Murray, now living in Marchandville.

George W. Wilkin is one of the oldest ferrymen on the river. He is a republican, and has served as school director. He is a member of the Disciple church, a pleasant and agreeable man and an industrious citizen.

DAVID WOODMENCY was born in Fayette county, Pa., January 22, 1825. He received only the advantages of a common-school education in the schools of his neighborhood. When quite young he learned the business of tanner at the Beaver creek tannery. He afterwards bought the property known as Sugar Loaf Knob, in Stewart township, and is now a thrifty farmer and stock raiser of that township. He has been twice married; the first time, May 1, 1853, to Casinda Morrison, daughter of G. Morrison, of Fayette county. She died January 12, 1858, leaving three children: John L., Mary W. (deceased) and Ella C. He was married, the second time, October 19, 1862, to Mary A. Butler, daughter of Esquire Sylvenus Butler, of Allegany county, Md. By this marriage were born eight children: Frank, David R. W. (deceased), Anna Sabina, Andrew J., Sarah E., Lillie C., Millie F. A. (deceased) and Abraham S. (deceased). David Woodmency, the grandfather of the subject of this sketch, came from New Jersey with a colony and settled in what is now known as the "Jersey settlement," near Turkey Foot, Somerset county, Pa. He was a soldier in the Revolutionary War, and was wounded.

JOEL G. LEATHERMAN, of Georges, one who is held in the highest esteem as an honest man by all who know him, was born on the farm where he now resides, in Georges township, Fayette county, Pa., October 20, 1804, and is a son of Rev. Joseph and Mary M (Getzendanner) Leatherman. His grandfathers, Daniel Leatherman and Christopher Getzendanner, were born in Maryland; they were both farmers in that State. The latter resided and passed the most of his life on the banks of the Monocacy river.

His father, Rev. Joseph Leatherman, was born in Maryland, removed to Georges township in 1799, where he purchased from Richard Reed a tract of land known as "Strawberry Ridge." On this farm, now owned by Joel G. Leatherman, are seen traces of a village founded prior to Anglo-Saxon habitation. Tradition locates it a French village in 1730, and evidences exist to warrant that it was an abiding place of the dim, mysterious Mound-Builder. Joseph Leatherman was a German Baptist minister and a democrat. He had two sons: Joel G. and one who died in infancy.

Joel G. Leatherman was raised on a farm. He acquired the limited education of his boyhood days and has spent a long and quiet life in farming and stock raising in Georges township. In 1824 he was married to Miss Diana, a daughter of Joseph and Anne Showalter. She died March 27, 1866. Mr. Leatherman is now living with his adopted son, Henry J. Dougherty, who is also a native of the same township. He was born in February, 1833, and is a son of James and Rebecca (Jennings) Dougherty. His grandfather, James Dougherty, was a native of Ireland, and came to America at the close of the Irish rebellion of 1798, in which he was a prominent actor. H. J. Dougherty was married in 1857 to Miss Drusilla M., daughter of David and Rachel Field, and has two children: Alvin F. is married to Miss Emma Kerline, of Minnesota, and Florence M. married E. B. Fast, of Marion county, W. Va., a dental student attending his last course of lectures in Philadelphia. Mr. Dougherty was educated in the common schools and Waynesburg College, and taught seven terms of school. He is a charter member of Gallatin Lodge, No. 517, I. O. O. F. and a stanch republican. He lacked only twenty-three votes of being elected treasurer in 1887 of Fayette county. The county at that time was democratic. Mr. Leatherman has been a republican since 1856; he is a member of the Cumberland Presbyterian church, and has always enjoyed the entire confidence of his community. (A corrected sketch.)

DAVID L. WORKMAN, JR., one of the representative young farmers of Bullskin township, was born in Perry township, Fayette county, Pa., December 9, 1850. He is a son of David and Elizabeth (Wilkinson) Workman. The former, born in Fayette county in 1818, was a blacksmith by trade, removing to Bullskin township in 1867; the latter, a daughter of Moses Wilkinson of Perry township. To their union were born five children: Joseph A., born February 8, 1880; Ella Blanch, November 27, 1881; Lizzie, June 22, 1883; Harry B., June 30

1885; Howard A., August 23, 1888, all born in Bullskin township, Fayette county, Pa.

David L. Workman, Jr., was married to Catherine Biedler, a daughter of Joseph Beidler, of Bullskin township, December 27, 1877. He received his education in the common schools of Fayette and Westmoreland counties. Leaving school, he has made farming his principal business. For three terms he has held the office of school director. He is a member of the Ancient Order of Knights of Mystic Chain, Monarch Castle, No. 84, Moyer, is a member of the Baptist church at Connellsville, and holds the office of deacon. He is an ardent democrat, and stands well as a citizen in his neighborhood.

ALFRED HOWELL. "Prominent among the lawyers of Fayette county stood Afred Howell, for a period of thirty-five years identified with the interests and progress of Uniontown, where he resided. Mr. Howell was a native of Philadelphia; and was born in the year 1825, of Quaker stock, both his paternal and maternal ancestry tracing their lines through the time of William Penn back for an indefinite period among the Quakers of Wales. Benjamin B. Howell, his father, then a merchant, removed with his family to New York City in the year 1830-31, where young Howell was sent to preparatory school, and eventually, at the age of fourteen, entered Columbia College, and there continued until well advanced in the sophomore class. Meanwhile his father had quitted merchandise and entered upon the development of iron and coal industries near Cumberland, Md., having enlisted with himself several English capitalists. Having occasion to visit England on business, he took passage, in March, 1841, on board the ill-fated ocean steamer 'President,' which foundered at sea, no tidings of her or any of her human cargo having ever been had. The sudden and great calamity of the loss of his father necessitated young Howell's withdrawal from college, after which he soon entered as a student at law in the office of Graham & Sandfords, counselors-at-law and solicitors in chancery, a distinguished firm, the Sanfords afterwards having been both elevated to the bench. With these gentlemen, and their successors in partnership with Mr. Graham, Messrs. Murray Hoffman and Joseph S. Bosworth (both subsequently becoming judges), Mr. Howell remained till 1845, enjoying the good fortune of the eminent tutelage of this remakable combination of legal talent, when he migrated to Uniontown, and finished his legal studies in the office of his uncle, Joshua B. Howell, then a leading lawer, and was admitted to the bar in 1847. In 1851 he entered into partnership with Mr. Howell, and continued with him until the fall of 1861, when Mr. Howell, having raised the Eighty-fifth Regiment Pennsylvania Volunteers, and being commissioned its colonel, entered into the war of the Rebellion, wherein he became exceptionally distinguished, and was killed near Petersburg, in September, 1864, by being thrown from his horse in the night-time.

"After Col. Howell's entry into the army, Mr. Howell succeeded to the business of the partnership, and continued till his death in the practice of law, conducting a large and laborious business with conscientious fidelity to his clients, earning honorable distinction and a goodly fortune.

"He was more or less engaged in important business enterprises, among which may be mentioned the projection, in 1866, about what was then known as Dawson's Station, on the line of the Pittsburg and Connellsville Railroad, of a village, now incorporated as the borough of Dawson, on a tract of land there lying, and of which he about that time came into possession. He caused the tract to be duly surveyed and laid out into building lots, and so conducted his enterprise as in the course of a few years to erect a prosperous and desirable village, with churches, public schools, etc., upon what was before, and but for his business foresight and energy would have remained, merely an uninhabitable portion of an old farm. He has occasionally engaged in the purchase and sale of real estate, particularly dealing in coal lands, with profitable results, and taken active part with others in supplying the county with local railways, which have been the means of developing the treasures of rich coal-mines and of otherwise enhancing the wealth of the country.

"Mr. Howell became a communicant, in his early manhood, of the Protestant Episcopal church, and has ever since continued active connection therewith, and occupies the position of senior warden.

"Mr. Howell was, in the year 1853, united in marriage with Miss Elizabeth Jennings Dawson, daughter of Mr. George Dawson, of Brownsville, Fayette county. Mrs. Howell died in 1869, leaving six children, one of whom, a daughter, died in 1878. Of the five now living, the elder son, George D., is at this time a member of the senior class of Trinity College, Hartford, Conn.

JAMES ALLISON. "James Allison, without whose biography the history of Menallen township, and particularly of the village of Searight's, would be incomplete, was born near Laurel Hill, in Fayette county, Pa., December 22, 1801. His parents lived and died in that neighborhood, and their remains were buried in the Laurel Hill graveyard. In early life James Allison moved from the locality of Laurel Hill, and settled on Redstone Creek, Fayette county, Pa., and learned to be a fuller of cloth under William Searight, in whose family he ever afterwards made his home. When William Searight bought the homestead on which is the village of Searight's, James Allison moved with him to it, where he lived and died. He was born to no other inheritance than that of a noble character and good name, and was in early life thrown upon these his only resources. He held the responsible office of commissioner of the county from 1837 to 1840, and, as was the case in all his business transactions, acquitted himself creditably and honorably. He also held the office of justice of the peace for many years, and was postmaster at the village of Searight's from the time of the establishment of the office in 1845 until within a very short time of his death, having filled the longest continuous term of office of any postmaster in the State, and perhaps in the United States. So long and so very attentively did he occupy this position that he became a part of the town thought to be entirely indispensable. He was a conscientious and consistent member of the Episcopal church, and was for very many years senior warden of Grace church, Menallen. He was married in early life, and his wife died shortly after their marriage. He had no family. The life of James Allison is well worthy of imitation. It was straightforward, unfaltering, unchequered, and uneventful. His habits were extremely plain, simple, sensible, sober, temperate, and industrious. His manner was free, open, friendly, frank, and courteous. His character was a perfect lighthouse of honesty, truthfulness and uprightness. So highly was he esteemed for these qualities, it became a common saying in the surrounding community of which he was a part that 'If Jimmy Allison says it is so it must be so;' or, 'If Jimmy Allison did so it must be right.' These sayings still reverently linger in the memories of his old neighbors. He died suddenly on July 4, 1881, of a conjestive spasm, to which he was subject. His remains were interred in Grace church burial-ground on July 5, 1881. The Rev. R. S. Smith, rector of St. Peter's church, Uniontown, and Grace church, Menallen, officiated at his funeral, and in the course of his remarks said that he had known James Allison intimately for twenty years, and for that period had been his personal friend, and he knew of nothing in his life and character that he would have blotted from the book of remembrance. Notwithstanding it was mid-harvest, and the weather was extremely hot, Grace church was crowded by neighbors and friends to witness the funeral rites of James Allison—an honest man—'God's noblest work.'"

COLONEL EWING BROWNFIELD.

"Among the venerable men of Fayette county, identified particularly with Uniontown for a period extending from 1805, when, as a child of two years of age, he was brought by his parents to Fayette county, to the year of this writing (1882), a period no less than seven years more than what is commonly counted 'the allotted age of man,' stands Colonel Ewing Brownfield, in the vigor of well-preserved old age, and, if his old-time neighbors are to be credited, without a stain upon his character for general probity and uprightness in his business dealings through life. He was born near Winchester, Va., September 7, 1803, of Quaker parentage. Thomas Brownfield, his father, brought his family to Uniontown in the year 1805, and at first rented and afterwards bought the White Swan Tavern, which he conducted till he died in 1829. Ewing grew up in the old tavern, enjoyed the advantages of the common schools of that day, and when become of fitting years assisted his father as clerk and overseer of the hotel until the father's death, when, in 1830, he and his brother John, now a prominent citizen of South Bend, Ind., formed a partnership in the dry-goods business, of which more further on.

"In early manhood Colonel Brownfield conceived a great love for military discipline and display,—"the pomp and glory of the very name of war,"—and in a time of profound peace, when he was about twenty years of age, was one of the first to join a Union volunteer company at that time organized. It is one of Colonel Brownfield's proud memories that upon the occasion of General Lafayette's visit to Albert Gallatin, at New Geneva, in 1825, he, with several of his companions in arms, went on horseback, as military escort, to the residence of Mr. Gallatin, and were delightedly received by the latter gentleman and his renowned guest. About that time there came into Uniontown a certain Captain Bolles, a graduate of West Point, who formed a military drill squad, of which Brownfield was a member. Under the tutelage of Captain Bolles, Brownfield became proficient in company drill, also in battalion and field drill, etc. After the formation of the First Regiment of Fayette County Volunteers, about 1828, Colonel Brownfield, then a private, became an independent candidate for major of the regiment, and was elected over three strongly supported candidates. Holding the position for two years, he was thereafter, on the resignation of Colonel Evans, elected colonel himself without opposition, and continued in the colonelcy for five years, receiving from Major-General Henry W. Beeson, at that time a military authority of high repute, the distinguished compliment implied in the following voluntary plaudit bestowed upon his regiment, namely, 'The First Fayette County Regiment of Volunteers is among the very best field-drilled regiments in the State.'

"In 1832 he and his brother dissolved the partnership before referred to, Ewing continuing the business till 1836, when he 'went West,' and settled in Mishawaka, Ind., again entering into the dry-goods business. But owing to the malarial character of the locality in that day, he decided to leave the place after a few months, and returned to Uniontown, where, in 1837, he resumed the dry-goods business. In the same year he bought a house and lot on the corner of Main and Arch streets, tore away the old building, erected a new one, and there conducted his favorite business, continuing in the same from that date to 1862. In the latter year he disposed of his dry-goods interests, and from that time to 1872 was engaged, for the most part, in the wool business. In 1873 he was elected president of the People's Bank, which position he now holds.

"Colonel Brownfield was married in 1842 to Miss Julia A. Long, daughter of Captain Robert Long, of Springfield township, Fayette county. They have had three children: Robert L., Anna E. and Virginia E. Robert, a graduate of the Sheffield Scientific School of Yale College, New Haven, Conn., is now a prosperous merchant of Philadelphia; Anna E. graduated at the Packer Institute, Brooklyn, N. Y., and is the wife of William Huston, a wholesale merchant of Pittsburgh; Virginia died on the 14th of May, 1872."

GREENBURY CROSSLAND. "Greenbury Crossland, of Uniontown, must be ranked markedly among those worthy men generally known as 'self-made,' strong and individuate in their characteristics, and who build their own monuments of fortune and reputation. Mr. Crossland, the son of Elijah and Catherine Smith Crossland, was born at Connellsville, June 16, 1813, and moved with his parents to Uniontown in 1822, where he has ever since resided, having occupied his present domicile thirty-four years. At twelve years of age he went to work at twelve and a half cents per day with George W. Miller on a farm, where he remained a while. His literary education was obtained from three or four short terms of schooling under the tuition of William Thompson and others long before the common schools of Pennsylvania were instituted; but his father being a butcher and horse-dealer, young Crossland got his principal training in the meat-shop and by driving horses to the eastern cities.

"On the first day of January, 1833, he married Sarah Stearns, with whom he has lived happily for near half a century. In April, 1833, he commenced business as a butcher on a capital of twenty-three dollars, ten of which were furnished by his wife, and has never received a dollar by bequest, or in any way save through his labor or business transactions. At the time of his early operations as a butcher it was his custom to take a wheelbarrow at one o'clock in the morning, and wheel—his wife helping him by pulling with a rope tied to the barrow—a side of beef from the slaughter-house to the market-house, where all meat was sold in those days. The first year he made three hundred dollars, and bought a log-house and the lot on which it stood, the latter being the one on which now stands the house occupied by T. J. King.

"He continued butchering, gradually increasing in prosperity, until about 1841, when he commenced buying cattle to sell in the eastern market, a business he has followed mainly ever since. For about fourteen years he was a partner in busines with Charles McLaughlin, late of Dunbar, but did not make the business remunerative until he engaged in it alone, about 1856, since which time his march has been steadily onward in the line of fortune.

"In 1847 he bought of Charles Brown a farm of 104 acres, whereon he has since lived, the first purchase of the real estate which now constitutes him an extensive land proprietor, his domains covering over seven hundred acres in the vicinity of Uniontown, all valuable alike for agriculture and containing vast stores of mineral whealth.

"Mr. Crossland's excellent judgment of weights and measures is a matter of popular notoriety, and it is said that he can guess at any time within five pounds of the weight of a fat steer, which probably accounts for much of his success in the cattle business. His strength of purpose and moral firmness are remarkable, and he has never been led into the visionary and impracticable. His knowledge of human nature is good, he seldom erring in his judgments of men, and, it is said, never making mistakes in his investments in property.

"Mr. Crossland is in religion an ardent Methodist, and it is due to him to add that his neighbors accord to him the virtue of believing the faith he professes. He and his wife joined the Methodist church in Uniontown, January 1, 1845, and have both continued to this time active members thereof. He has been for twenty-five years past a liberal contributor to the support of the ministry and the benevolent enterprises of the church. Not only by his great liberality, but through his high character as a man of probity, is he a very pillar in the church. Desiring reliable information in regard to the chief characteristics of Mr. Crosslands, the writer, a stranger to Mr. Crossland, sought one of Mr. Crossland's long-time acquaintances, a man of high repute, and asked him for an analysis of Mr. Crossland's character, as understood by him and the public, and received, after some delay, indicative of deliberation, the following written analysis: 'Moral characteristics,—faithfulness ,honor, honesty, benevolence, and regard for the rights of others. Business characteristics,—good judgment, caution, energy, perseverance, watchfulness, combined with great shrewdness and knowledge of market values. Religious characteristics,—enthusiasm, sincerity, simplicity in manners and dress, charity, and single-mindedness.' This being accepted, particularly since it is the statement of a gentleman above suspicion on account of religious prejudice for, or fraternity with, Mr. Crossland, it is here recorded as an evidence of the high honor which simple straightforwardness, good sense, and energy may win for a man, even though not a 'prophet' among his neighbors, in these days of irreverence and carping criticism."

JAMES THOMAS REDBURN. "James T. Redburn was born in Masontown, Fayette county, Pa., May, 19, 1822, and was the son of James Tully and Rebecca Harrison Redburn. He in early life displayed an unusual aptitude for business, and during several years of his minority was connected with Zalmon Ludington in the leather trade at Addison, Pa. In 1848 he married Harriet Ann, youngest daughter of Mr. Ludington, and shortly after removed to Washington, Pa., where he embarked in the boot and shoe trade. In 1850 he came to Uniontown and reassociated himself with Zalmon Ludington in the boot, shoe and tanning business, which he carried on successfully for a number of years. In 1858 he was chosen cashier and manager of the Uniontown banking house of John T. Hogg. This soon after became the banking house of Isaac Skiles, Jr., Mr. Redburn continuing its cashier. In 1863 he became one of the incorporators of the First National Bank of Uniontown, Pa. (which succeeded I. Skiles, Jr.), which opened for business May 2, 1864. He was elected a director and cashier, to the positions of which he was unanimously re-elected year after year until his death, which occurred at his residence in Uniontown

Wednesday evening, May 23, 1877. He was also one of the originators of the Uniontown & West Virginia Railroad Company, and was its treasurer. He was also instrumental in starting the Uniontown Woolen Manufacturing Company, one of the few manufacturing establishments Uniontown could boast of, and now unluckily destroyed by fire, and was treasurer of the company.

"It was, however, as a bank officer that James T. Redburn was most widely known. To the position of cashier and director he brought tact and wisdom second to none in the county. He possessed in an eminent degree those sterling qualities of truth and justice, honor and temperance which drew to him by the most endearing ties of affection a large circle of friends, wherever he went and wherever he was known, throughout his entire life. Reserved, quiet, unostentatious, he was dearly loved and thoroughly relied upon by the numerous friends and customers that sought his advice. A statement from his lips needed no investigation to test its accuracy. Statements or rumors that found credence through current gossip he met with thorough but not effusive detestation, and those most intimately associated with him bear testimony to the silence with which he treated subjects regarding which he had only the information of rumor. He preferred to leave the impression that he had no knowledge of a subject rather than give credence to a statement he did not know to be absolutely true. In this as well as in many other particulars Mr. Redburn exerted an influence that was manly, noble, generous and self-sacrificing, and that bore most bountiful fruit through his many warm friendships throughout Fayette and adjoining counties. In his private and home life he was ever kind and watchful of the wants of others. He let not the cares or the worriment of the day follow him home to disturb the peace and quiet of his family. Never of a very rugged constitution, he was from boyhood subject to occasional periods of physical depression from that dread disease, consumption, which had carried away his four sisters and two brothers; yet he had that tenacity and will power which often held him to his desk when his strength would scarcely keep him on his feet. He was an earnest and consistent member and trustee of the Methodist Episcopal church in Uniontown, and in life followed the Master with reverence and godly fear. Possessed of a naturally kind and sympathetic heart, he was ever ready to assist the poor and destitute or impart consolation to a sorrowing soul. His funeral took place Friday evening May 25, 1877, Rev. Dr. J. J. Moffit and Rev. S. W. Davis, of the Methodist Episcopal church, conducting the services. The pall-bearers were Eleazer Robinson, Sebastian Rush, Uriah Higinbotham, Jasper M. Thompson, Charles S. Seaton, William McCleary, John Wilson and Alfred Howell. Mr. Redburn having lost his wife in December, 1860, did not marry again. Of his two children but one, Minnie L. Redburn, survives him.

ADAM JACOBS. "Capt. Adam Jacobs, of Brownsville, is of German extraction. His grandfather, Adam Jacobs, emigrated from Lancaster county, Pa., at an early day into Allegheny county, and there carried on farming on Turtle Creek, near 'Braddock's Field,' eleven miles east of Pittsburgh, for several years, and then moved to Brownsville, where he entered into merchandising, which he conducted until his death, which occurred in 1818.

"He had but one son who lived to maturity, named after himself, Adam Jacobs, and who was born in Brownsville, December 3, 1794, and was educated at the subscription schools and at Washington College, and became a merchant, and on the 16th of January, 1816, married Eliza Reiley, daughter of Martin Reiley, of Bedford, Bedford county Pa. He died June 29, 1822, leaving two children, Adam and Ann Elizabeth, long since deceased.

"Adam, the last referred to, is the subject of our sketch, and was born January 7, 1817. He received his early education in the pay schools, and at about sixteen years of age was apprenticed to G. W. Bowman to learn coppersmithing, and remained with him four years. He then went into the business for himself, and in a year or two afterwards took to steamboating on the Western rivers, and continued steamboating until 1847. He was at this time, and had been for years before, engaged also in building steamboats, and from 1847 forward prosecuted steamboat-building vigorously, at times having as many as eight boats in a year under contract. He built over a hundred and twenty steamboats before practically retiring from the business about 1872, since which time he has, however, built about five boats for the Pittsburgh, Brownsville and Geneva Packet Company, and other contracts. Capt. Jacobs was also engaged in merchandising, with all the rest of his active business, from 1843 to 1865, and may be said to be still merchandising, for he has a store at East Riverside.

"Since about 1872 he has spent his time mostly in Brownsville in the winters and at his country residence, "East Riverside," Luzerne township, on the Monongahela river, during the summer seasons.

"On the 22d of February, 1838, Mr. Jacobs married Miss Ann Snowdon (born in England in 1816), a daughter of John and Mary Smith Snowdon, who came from England and settled in Brownsville in 1818, where Mr. Snowdon soon after started the business of engine-building, and carried it on till disabled by old age. Mr. and Mrs. Snowdon both died in advanced years, and were buried in the Brownsville Cemetery, where a fine monument marks the place of their repose.

"Mr. and Mrs. Jacobs have had ten children, eight of whom are living,—Mary, wife of William Parkhill; Adam, Jr., married to Laura Myers, of Canton, Ohio; Catharine, wife of S. S. Graham; John N., married to Sarah Colvin; Caroline S., wife of John H. Bowman; Anna, wife of Joseph L. McBirney of Chicago, Ill.; Martin Reiley, now residing in Colorado; and George D."

MAJOR DAVID CUMMINGS.

"Major David Cummings, who became a citizen of Connellsville about 1820, and lived there for several years, where four of his children now reside, was born in Cecil county, Md., April 23, 1777, and was the son of James Cummings, by birth a Scotchman of distinguished family, who, coming to America, became an officer in the War of the Revolution. David Cummings was a gentleman of classical education, and in early life taught select schools. He was an officer in the army during the war of 1812, and was wounded and taken prisoner at the battle of Beaver Dam, in Canada, and with other captive American officers carried to England, where he was held for six months, until exchanged, suffering great hardships. After the war he became a mail contractor under the government, and as such first found his way into western Pennsylvania, and eventually settled at Connellsville, where he soon became a man of note. He represented Fayette county in the legislature at the sessions of 1823 and 1824, and was the first man in the legislative body who made an effort to establish a general system of education by common schools. That system being a matter of contest, he was at the next election defeated.

"Some years thereafter, leaving Connellsville, he removed to Mifflin county, where he was first engaged in the building of the Pennsylvania canal, from Huntingdon to Lewistown, he afterwards becoming superintendent of the canal, as also collector of the port of Harrisburg. He died at Lewistown, February 5, 1848, and his remains were brought to Connellsville and interred in the family burying-ground beside those of his wife, who had died some years before him.

"Major Cummings was married June 30, 1801, to Elizabeth Cathers, of Cecil county, Md., by whom he had six sons and six daughters, of whom five daughters and two sons are living: Hannah M., who married the late Thomas R. McKee; Margaret Eliza, widow of Thomas McLaughlin; Sophia, widow of Josiah Simmons, who died about 1863; Mary Ann, who first married Dr. Bresee, of New York, now dead, and as her second husband, Andrew Patterson, of Juniata county; Ellen, wife of Robert T. Galloway, of Fayette county; and Jonathan W., once a government surveyor, now of Uvalde county, Texas; and John A., who resides in Connellsville with his oldest sister, Mrs. McKee. Of the sons deceased was the late Dr. James C. Cummings, who died in Connellsville, July 28, 1872. He was born in Maryland in 1802, and moved with his parents to Fayette county about 1820, and was educated at Jefferson College, and studied medicine under Dr. Robert D. Moore, then a distinguished physician of Connellsville, where he himself afterwards became equally distinguished in his profession. He was a coroner of Fayette county for several terms, and a member of the legislature during the sessions of 1843 and 1844. He was never married."

GEORGE W. NEWCOMER, M. D.

"The medical profession, like every other profession or vocation of life, comprises men of various mental calibers, various degrees of natural adaptability and acquired equipment for its pursuit. While every practicing physician may justly, perhaps, be accorded some special merit, however slight, some valuable peculiarity which determined him in the choice of his profession, the history of medical practitioners as a craft goes to show that only now and then one is possessed of that enthusiastic love of medical science and that certain intellectual capacity to wisely apply in practice what he has learned by study which win for him the popular confidence, and not only achieve for him an extended practice, but enable him to keep it and to add to it year by year. Two things especially seem to conspire to such success, to be necessary to it in fact, namely, keen insight into the nature or cause of disease, or what medical men term scientific 'diagnosis,' and the profound forecasting of the course and event of a disease by particular symptoms (enabling the true physician to effectively apply and vary remedies from time to time as the need of them is indicated), and which they call "prognosis." The skillful diagnostician and the like excellent prognoser, or "prognostician," must unite in the one physician if he be really able, and his success for a given period of years is the best possible assurance that the two do unite in his professional character and determine his career, whoever he may be. Such a physician is Dr. George W. Newcomer, of Connellsville, who, though comparatively a young man, enjoys a very extensive practice, and stands correspondingly high in the confidence of the community, as is made evident by the fact that his 'office hours' are crowded with patients, and his town visitations and country rides out of office hours constant and laborious. Success like his is practical testimony of worth which cannot be gainsaid,—the visible crown of merit.

"Dr. George W. Newcomer is on his paternal side of German descent; on his maternal of Scotch-Irish stock. His great grandfather, John Newcomer, was born in Germany, and emigrating to America, settled in Maryland, where the doctor's grandfather, John Newcomer (Jr.), was born. The latter came to Fayette county about 1790, and settled in Tyrone township, on a farm on which the doctor's father, Jacob Newcomer, was born in 1809, and which he finally purchased, living upon it all his life, and on which the doctor himself was born.

"Jacob Newcomer, who died March 8, 1871, was the second of a family of eight children, and the oldest son. On the 21st of September, 1830, he married Elizabeth Hershey, of Allegheny county, who was born April 22, 1812. Of this marriage were ten children, of whom George W. is the seventh, and was born May 27, 1845. He was brought up on the farm till about thirteen years of age, working in summers after he became old enough to work, and attending school in the winter seasons, and devouring at home what books he could get to read. When arrived at the age above mentioned he was placed as a clerk in the store of his uncles, John and Joseph Newcomer, in Connellsville, where he remained till seventeen years of age, attending school winters. He then entered Pleasant Valley Academy, Washington county, where he passed two years, taking a partial course of classical studies.

"At nineteen years of age he commenced the study of medicine with Dr. John R. Nickel, of Connellsville, one of the most eminent physicians of the region and at one time Professor of Anatomy and Surgery in the Physio-Medical College (now Institute) of Cincinnati. He continued with Dr. Nickel during the usual period of medical office study, and in due time took the regular course of medical lectures at the Physio-Medical Institute of Cincinnati, from which institution he received his diploma, graduating February 7, 1867. He then returned to Connellsville and opened an office for the practice of medicine, which he there pursued for about five years, and then, upon the call of friends, he removed to Mount Vernon, Ohio, to take the practice of Dr. James Loar, who was about to remove farther West. Dr. Newcomer remained in practice at Mount Vernon till the spring of 1874, when, at the urgent request of his old preceptor, Dr. Nickel (who in a few weeks thereafter died), he returned to Connellsville, where he has ever since remained.

"Aside from the practice of medicine, the doctor has engaged more or less in real estate speculations with excellent result.

"Dr. Newcomer is in politics an ardent republican, and though he does not claim to have done his country great service during the war of the Rebellion, it may be mentioned here that he studied republicanism in the field for about three months in war times, being then a member of Company B of the Fifty-fourth Regiment Pennsylvania Volunteer Infantry, a three months' regiment, organized about the time of the battle of Gettysburg, but in which battle it did not participate, the company at that time being mustered in at Pittsburg and awaiting equipments. But shortly afterwards it was sent with other companies to attempt the capture of the 'Morgan raiders' in Ohio, and succeeded in cutting off Morgan at Salinesville, in that State,—a good lesson in politics, the doctor thinks."

DAVID BARNES. "Every town or borough has its distinctive 'characters,' among whom are men who seem to have been born to be publicly useful, and who could not well have gone into strictly private life if they had tried. Aside from their regular business they fill numerous offices, are known by everybody, consulted more or less by everybody about everything, are alert, smart, found apt at any business upon which they may be called to enter, wide awake,—in short, universally useful, ever willing and competent. Of this class of men is David Barnes, of Connellsville. His family has been identified with Fayette county for over eighty years. Mr. Barnes is the grandson of Zephaniah Ellis Barnes, who came to America from England and settled in Woodstown, N. J., several generations ago. There, in 1765, was born David Barnes (Sr.), father of our David, and who came to Connellsville in 1801, and built there (the first of its kind ever seen west of the mountains), what was then known as a 'go-back saw-mill.' He took a great interest in the organization of the borough, and was a member of its first council. He built the market house which now stands on the corner of Spring and Church streets, and, under Governor Simon Snyder, was appointed flour inspector for the county of Fayette. During the war of 1812 he, in company with Joseph McClurg, of Pittsburg, ran Mount Pleasant Furnace, where were made cannon, cannon-balls, and grape-shot for the government. After the war he engaged in the iron business in company with Isaac Meason and James Paull. He was a man of excellent ability to plan and execute. He died in 1832, and was buried in the Quaker graveyard in Connellsville. His wife was Sarah Proctor, a native af Old Town, Md., and born in 1785. She was a relative of the Ogles, Camerons, and Clintons of that State, and came with her parents to Perryopolis, Fayette county, in 1812. In 1818 she and David Barnes were married. At his death she was left with six children, one having previously died. Her whole time and energy were devoted to rearing and educating her children, particularly in morals and religion. She never, when in health, let an evening pass without assembling her young family and reading to them a chapter from the Scriptures. Of course she was particular to avoid such chapters as are not considered delicate and proper to be read by youthful and uninformed minds. Her selections were always judicious. After reading she always uttered a prayer for the protection of her children, mingled with earnest hopes for their future usefulness. Her family consisted of David, William, Hamilton, Joseph, Z. Ellis, Emily and Mary Bell. William was educated at Lewisburg University, and was ordained as a Baptist minster at the First Baptist church of Pittsburg. He visited the Holy Land with the view of thereby the better enabling himself to fulfill the responsible duties of his calling. He wished to see the places where Christ preached, feeling that he might gather inspiration therefrom. At the breaking out of the late war he was commissioned as chaplain of the Fifth New York Volunteer Artillery, and served until the close of the war. Hamilton has served a term in the State Senate, from Somerset county. He is a fluent and impressive speaker, and a leader in the republican party. Joseph became a carpenter, and, as a foreman of his department, helped build the Union Pacific railroad. Ellis, being a great lover of horses, has dealt extensively in them, and during the late war was quartermaster under Gen. Samuel B. Holabird. He resides at Connellsville, and carries on the livery and sale business. Emily died quite young. Mary Bell married Thomas Evans, and is the mother of a large family, all industrious and good citizens.

"David Barnes was born in Perryopolis, February 5, 1819, and attended the common schools, but regards his mother as his only real teacher and only friend in youth. At sixteen years of age he commenced teaching school, and followed the business until (he having meanwhile incurred the responsibilities of marriage) his wages would not support him, when he turned his attention to politics. In 1853 he was appointed a clerk in the State Department at Harrisburg, where he remained some sixteen years. About 1869 he resigned his office at the capitol and accepted the position of paymaster of the Pittsburg and Connellsville railroad, and thereafter resigned that to accept a position as book-keeper of the National Locomotive Works at New Haven; and on the completion of the Southwest Pennsylvania railroad, from Greensburg to Connellsville, was appointed station agent at the latter place, which position he still holds.

"Mr. Barnes is a stanch republican, and exerted considerable influence during the late war. He was the true friend of the soldiers, helping and aiding them wherever he could, visiting them in hospitals and administering to their wants. Great numbers of them made him their banker, and he judiciously invested their funds for them, often profitably refusing all fees for his services; and he still helps them in their celebrations, especially to 'fight their battles o'er,' he being a fluent and stirring speaker. Mr. Barnes is charitable to a fault, but of great determination of character, and not lacking in fiery spirit makes enemies; but, feeling that he is right, he cares not for foes, declaring that he would 'rather have one influential friend than the whole rabble of the town' at his back.

"Mr. Barnes was a popular officer at the State capital, was respected by all with whom he did business, and in war times was the confidential and trusted friend of Governor Curtin, rendering him special services, at one time carrying messages from him to all the governors of the New England States. Mr. Barnes has been somewhat of a traveler, having climbed to the top of Mt. Washington, in the White Mountains, and visited the battle-fields around Richmond, Va., and seen 'considerable of the country besides.'

"In 1848 Mr. Barnes married Mary Jane Sherman, a daughter of Samuel Sherman, of Connellsville, a native of Connecticut, and related to the family of Roger Sherman. Mr. and Mrs. Barnes have had nine children —four sons and five daughters. Two of the daughters are dead. His eldest son, Andrew Stewart Barnes, served during the late war as a soldier in the Fifth Pennsylvania Heavy Artillery. After the war he learned the machinist trade in the Baltimore & Ohio Railroad shops. Thereafter he was appointed postmaster at Connellsville, and afterwards route agent between Washington City and Pittsburgh, which position he still holds. Mr. Barnes thinks that boys should learn trades, and his son Samuel is a machinist and William a carpenter. Irwin, another son, quite young, is devoted to music. Mary Elizabeth is married, and lives in Cuba, N. Y. Jennie and Hally, his other children, are very intelligent, and likely to grow up to be excellent citizens.

"Mr. Barnes lost the use of one of his legs when he was but ten years old, and says that his misfortune was 'a godsend,' as with his vitality and energy and two good legs he 'might have become a brigand.' What is worse, he might have, and likely would have, gone into the late war, and would probably have been killed on the field. With the aid of his crutch he moves about as lively as most men on two good legs, and at the age of sixty-three is as active as ever, and looks younger than most men at fifty. His 'nerve' will probably carry him on into extreme old age, and keep him useful all the while."

SAMUEL STEELE. "Mr. Samuel Steele, of Brownsville, is of Scotch-Irish extraction. His great-grandparents came to America from the north of Ireland about 1740, and settled, it is believed, in eastern Pennsylvania. On the passage over the Atlantic Mrs. Steel presented her husband with a son, who was given the name William, and who was the grandfather of Mr.

Samuel Steele. William grew up to manhood and found his way into Maryland, where he married and resided for a period of time, the precise record of which is lost; but there several several children were born to him, one of whom, and the oldest son, was John, the father of Samuel Steele. About 1783 or 1784, William Steele removed from Maryland with his family to Fayette county, to a point on the "Old Packhorse road," about six miles east of Brownsville. where he purchased a tract of land, which is now divided into several excellent farms, occupied by Thomas Murphy, who resides upon the old Steele homestead site, and others. William Steele eventually removed to Rostraver township, Westmoreland county, where he died in 1806.

"Some years prior to his death Mr. William Steel purchased for his sons, John and William, a tract of land in what is now Jefferson township, and embraced the farms now owned and occupied by John Steele and Joseph S. Elliott. John Steele (the father of Mr. Samuel S.) eventually married Miss Agnes (often called 'Nancy') Happer, by whom he had eight children, of whom Samuel was the fourth in number, and was born June 15, 1814. Mr. John Steele died June 6, 1856, at about the age of eighty-three.

"Mr. Samuel Steele was brought up on the farm, and in his childhood attended the subscription schools. In his eighteenth year, he left home and entered as an apprentice to the tanning and currying trade the establishment of Jesse Cunningham, his brother-in law, a noted tanner of Brownsville, where he served three years in learning the business. After the expiration of his apprenticeship he entered upon the pursuit of various businesses, among which was flatboating agricultural products, apples, etc., cided, and provisions of various kinds, down the Monongahela to the Ohio and on to Cincinnati and Louisville, where he usually sold his merchandise, but sometimes made trips to New Orleans. He followed the business in springtime for some seven years, ending about February, 1843, when occurred the death of Mr. Jesse Cunningham. Mr. Steele then entered into partnership with his sister, Mrs. Cunningham, under the firm-name Samuel Steele & Co., and carried on the business at the old place till 1860, when the partnership was amicably dissolved, and Mr. Steele sank a new heard, a few blocks higher up the hill, wherein he has since that time conducted business. In 1880 he took into partnership with himself his son, William, under the firm-name of 'Samuel Steele & Son.'

"February 11, 1852, Mr. Steele married Miss Elizabeth A. Conwell, of Brownsville, by whom he has had four sons and four daughters, all of whom are living.

"In politics he was formerly an old-line whig, and is now an ardent republican. In religion he preserves the faith of his fathers, being a Presbyterian. His wife and daughters are members of the Episcopal church.

THOMAS R. DAVIDSON. "Among the distinguished men of Fayette county who have passed away, stood eminent in professional and social life, Thomas R. Davidson, who was born in Connellsville, October 6, 1814, the son of William and Sarah Rogers Davidson, both of Scotch-Irish descent. William Davidson, the father, was an old iron-master, State senator, and a man of great mental vigor. Thomas R. Davidson received his education at home and at Kenyon College, Ohio, and after being admitted to the bar, practiced law for some years in Uniontown, where he married Isabella Austin, daughter of John M. Austin, then one of the leaders of the bar in his section of the State. Of this union were two children—Mary D., now wife of P. S. Newmyer, of

Connellsville, and William A., at present practicing law at Cincinnati, Ohio. Shortly after his marriage he located in Connellsville, his old home, where he continued during the remainder of his life in the duties of his profession, and engaged in various enterprises for the advancement of the community in which he was interested. He was very cautious and reticent in business pursuits, but was quite successful and accumulated a handsome estate. He had no desire for political advancement, preferring the more congenial walks of private life, though he at once accepted the honorary office of presidential elector. Mr. Davidson died November 3, 1875.

"His appearance was very commanding, he being in stature six and one-half feet, finely proportioned, and weighing 242 pounds. Perhaps a more correct estimate of his character and standing could not be given than that expressed in the following extract from a tribute by James Darsie, who knew him long and well:

'"His departure from our midst has left an aching void which cannot be filled. No other man can take his place, do the work, and command the confidence that was reposed in him by the entire community. He was indeed the rich man's counselor and the poor man's friend, and was universally esteemed, honored and beloved as a man of lofty principle, generous and magnanimous impulses, and of spotless integrity. I have rarely met one who had so great an abhorrence of a mean, dishonorable or dishonest act as he; indeed, the love of truth and justice was in him innate. While in principle stern and unbending, even to severity, in heart and sympathy he was tender as a child. He never dissapointed the hopes and expectations of his friends, or betrayed a trust committed to his hands. He practiced his profession not so much for profit as to heal the animosities, adjust the difficulties and restore the peace and confidence of neighbors. I presume I may safely say he settled more disputes by his sagacity, wisdom and moderation than he ever did by the hard process of law, and oftentimes prevailed upon his clients to amicably settle their disputes rather than risk the vexation and uncertainty of an appeal to a legal tribunal. He was, indeed, a peacemaker in the highest sence of that term, and had a far more honest satisfaction in amicably settling a difficulty than in gaining a suit before a judge and jury. In one word, he filled the full outline of that sentiment happily expressed by one of England's noblest bards—

'An honest man's the noblest work of God.'

"The following testimonial to his great worth is quoted from resolutions by the bar of Fayette county:

'"It is with heartfelt sorrow and unfeigned regret that we are compelled to submit to the loss of one so endeared to us all by long and pleasant associations. His genial, warm and affectionate disposition, his tender regard for the feelings of others, his uniform courtesy and affability, and, above all, his high sense of honor and strict integrity secured to him the love and respect alike of bench and bar. This bar has lost a sound lawyer, an able counselor and upright man, whose honor and integrity were only equaled by his unassuming modesty and affability."'

WILLIAM H. MILLER. "William H. Miller, of Bridgeport, is of English Quaker descent on his paternal side. His great-grandfather, Solomon Miller, who was a miller by trade, was born in England, married there, and emigrated with his family to America prior to 1750, and settled in York county, Pa. Of his children was Robert Miller, who was born in York county, Pa., and in early manhood removed to Frederick county, near Frederick City, Md., and purchased a farm, and soon after married Miss Cassandra Wood, a Virginia lady, who lived near Winchester, Va. They resided upon the farm near Frederick City till 1796, when they removed to Berkeley county, Va., where they remained about three years, and then, in 1799, came into Fayette county and settled in Luzerne township, on a farm purchased of one, Joseph Briggs, and now owned by Captain Isaac Woodward. Residing there for several years, his wife meanwhile dying, Robert Miller eventually moved into Brownsville, and took up his residence on Front street, upon property now belonging to the heirs of Thomas Morehouse, and there died about 1832. He was the father of four sons and four daughters, all of whom grew to maturity. Of these was William Miller, who was born September 9, 1782, in Frederick county, Md. At the age of sixteen he became a clerk in a dry-goods store belonging to his uncle, William Wood, in New Market, Va., and in 1799 came with his father into Fayette county. He soon after took up the avocation of school-teaching, and pursued it near Perryopolis, in the old Friends' church, known as 'Redstone church,' in Bridgeport, on what was formerly called 'Peace Hill,' and elsewhere. He followed teaching until 1810, when he married Miss Rebecca Johnson, daughter of Squire Daniel Johnson, of Menallen, and at once settled on a farm in that township, near New Salem, and lived there till March, 1837. He then removed to Brownsville and purchased a woolen-factory (no longer standing) and a flouring-mill, then standing on the site whereon is located the present flouring-mill of his son, W. H. Miller. He pursued milling till 1855, when he retired from business and led a private life until his death, which occurred June 7, 1866. Mrs. Rebecca Miller died November 14, 1833, and in 1834 Mr. Miller married Ann Johnson, his first wife's half sister, who, childless herself, made a good mother for her sister's children. She is still living, nearly eighty years of age, cheerful and buoyant in spirits.

"Mr. William and Mrs. Rebecca Johnson Miller were the parents of nine children, all of whom grew to maturity, eight still living: Warwick, born December 11, 1811; Hiram, born December 31, 1813; Sarah, born September 7, 1816; Mary, born February 5, 1819; Cassandra (deceased), born March 3, 1821; Lydia, born January 14, 1823; Jane, born June 30, 1825; William H., born March 6, 1829; and Oliver, born December 13, 1831.

"William H. Miller, the eighth in the above list, was educated in the common, and the Friends' school, and learned the milling business, upon which he entered in partnership with his brother Oliver in 1855 in the mill before named, and which he and his brother inherited from their father. The partnership continued for five years, when Mr. Miller bought out the interest of his brother, who removed to a farm in Luzerne township. In January, 1866, a fire destroyed both the flouring-mill and the old woolen-factory before referred to. The buildings being uninsured the loss was total. Mr. Miller immediately put up a new and better building on the old site, and to this time conducts business therein. As is noted above, Mr. Miller's great-grandfather, Solomon, was a miller by trade, and from his day down to the present the trade has been practically and continuously represented by his descendants.

"Mr. Miller has held several town and borough offices, and was for eight years director in the Deposit and Discount Bank of Brownsville, which two years ago gave up its charter, a portion of its stockholders uniting in the organization of the National Deposit Bank of Brownsville, of which bank Mr. William H. Miller is the president, the National Bank doing business in the same house formerly occupied by the bank the place of which it took.

"May 16, 1855, Mr. Miller married Miss Margaret J. Gibson, daughter of Alexander and Mary (Hibbs) Gibson, of Luzerne township. They have two children—A. Gibson Miller, born February 7, 1861, and Sarah Helen Miller.

"Mr. Miller was brought up an Orthodox Friend, observing the faith of his fathers, but is now a member, as is also his wife, of the Cumberland Presbyterian church. In politics he is a republican."

ELEAZER ROBINSON. "Among the immigrants of Fayette county, bringing and infusing into its social and business life a then somewhat novel element, that of the 'Yankee' or New England spirit, came about 1837 Eleazer Robinson, an iron-founder. Mr. Robinson was born March 4, 1804, in Bethel, Windsor county, Vt. His parents, Eleazer Robinson and Experience Downer, were of the old New England Puritan stock. In 1810 they removed to Saratoga county, N. Y., where he enjoyed the advantages of the common schools of the times and made considerable progress in general studies. But in 1824, his parents then removing to Broome county, N. Y., young Robinson there availed himself of the opportunities offered by the academy in his neighborhood. There he devoted himself mainly to mathematics, in which he achieved marked success, leaving the academy well equipped as a civil engineer; and though he did not enter upon the profession of engineering, his studies there made have served him on many an important occasion in the avocations of life, especially in mechanical pursuits. On quitting the academy he took up the study of the law, under the direction of a leading lawyer of Binghamton, a Mr. Robinson,—not a relative, however,—and continued his legal studies until interrupted by the death of his father (who left seven children, of whom Mr. Robinson was the eldest), which threw upon him the responsible care of the family, obliging him to quit the law-office for the practical duties of the farmer, he varying these during a course of years by more or less school-teaching.

"Eventually he became largely interested in the lumber business at Owego, N. Y. But there overborne by disaster caused by a great freshet in the Upper Branch of the Susquehanna, which in a few hours swept away a fortune in lumber, he with the buoyant energy which has distinguished his whole life, moved at once to Erie, Pa., and there engaged in the drug business. At this business he continued three years, within which time he made an acquaintanceship which gave direction to the course of his life since then with a Mr. Jonathan Hathaway, the patentee of a superior cooking-stove, well remembered by the older inhabitants of Fayette county, and secured control of the manufacture of the 'Hathaway stoves,' whereupon he moved to Pittsburgh and procured their casting there. After a while, meeting with much loss through the destruction by fire of the foundry wherein the stoves were cast, he went to Uniontown in 1837, and there established a foundry, and eventually erected a branch foundry in Washington, Pennsylvania, and opened agencies at Carlisle and elsewhere, all of which were conducted very successfully for some years. Finally Mr. Robinson concentrated his business at Uniontown, there prosecuting it actively till 1867, when, having amassed a goodly fortune, he retired from business as a manufacturer, selling the foundry to one of his earliest apprentices and faithful co-workers, Mr. Thomas Jaquett.

"Since then Mr. Robinson has been engaged in various business pursuits. In 1872 he came into possession as sole owner under a private charter of the gas-works by which Uniontown is lighted. He also controls as principal owner the gas-works of Middletown, Dauphin county.

"Mr. Robinson was one of the original board of directors of the First National Bank of Uniontown, and remained a director till within a few years past. He has ever generously contributed to the upbuilding or support of such institutions in the places of his residence as commanded his respect, taking no extreme partisan cause, however, either in politics or religion, enjoying the esteem of his neighbors and the business public as a man of sterling integrity as well as clear judgment, genial sociability, and humane sentiments.

"July 12, 1837, Mr. Robinson united in marriage with Miss Cornelia Wells, of York, N. Y., who died in 1845, having borne him four children, one only of whom, Mrs. Emma R. King, now (1882) survives. On November 6, 1846, Mr. Robinson married again, being then united to Miss Mary Ann McClelland, of Uniontown, who died in September, 1850, leaving no children. Mr. Robinson married as his third wife, November 24, 1852, Mrs. Elizabeth J. Porter, daughter of James Wilson, Esq., of German township, with whom he lived twenty-nine years, she dying in May, 1881, at the age of sixty-eight years, leaving two children,—Mr. W. L. Robinson, who has mainly succeeded to his father's business, managing the gas-works, etc., and Miss Mary E. Robinson."

JUDGE THOMAS DUNCAN. "Among the venerable men of Bridgeport, highly esteemed by all who knew him, and identified with the interests of that borough and its twin-sister, Brownsville, by over half a century's residence and active business life within their limits and participating in the best measures, well performing the duties and dignifiedly bearing the responsibilities of good citizenship therein, watchful ever for the weal and social good order of the place where has so long been his home, is Judge Thomas Duncan. He is of Scotch-Irish extraction. His father, Arthur Duncan, emigrated from County Donegal, Ireland, about 1793, to America, and found his way into Fayette county as a soldier in the service of the United States among the troops sent hither by the government to suppress the Whiskey Insurrection. After the troops were disbanded he settled in Franklin township, near Upper Middletown (then known as "Plumsock"), Menallen township, and married Sophia Wharton, daughter of Arthur Wharton, of Franklin township, but a native of England, who held a large tract of land in that township, and was a man of strong individuality. Mr. and Mrs. Arthur Duncan passed the greater portion of their lives in Upper Middletown, but Mrs. Duncan died about 1845, in Pittsburgh, to which place the family had removed, and Mr. Duncan, about 1850, in Moundsville, Va., at the residence of one of his daughters, Mrs. Nancy Rosell.

"Mr. and Mrs. Duncan were the parents of ten children, the second in number of whom is Judge Thomas Duncan, who was born in Franklin township, August 22, 1807. He received his early education in the Thorn Bottom school-house, in those days often pompously or ironically dubbed 'The Thorn Bottom Seminary,' on Buck Run, in his native township. During his boyhood he wrought more or less in the Plumsock Rolling-Mill, and at eighteen years of age was apprenticed to a cabinet-maker, Thomas Hatfield, an expert mechanic, with whom he remained three years as an apprentice and three more as a partner. He then removed to Bridgeport, where he has ever since resided, carrying on as his principal business that in which he first engaged.

"Judge Duncan has always taken an active part in public affairs. He was a member of the first board of school directors in Bridgeport chosen under the present law organizing the common schools, and earnestly advocated the enactment of the law long before it was made. He has frequently been a member of the common council, and several times burgess of Bridgeport. He has also taken a prominent part as a democrat in the politics of the county, was county commissioner from 1841 to 1843, both inclusive, and was elected in 1851 associate judge of Fayette county for a period of five years, and re-elected in the fall of 1856 for a like term, and fulfilled the duties of his office throughout both terms.

"In 1837 Judge Duncan joined the Masonic order, uniting with Brownsville Lodge, No. 60, and has filled all the offices of the lodge, and is a member of Brownsville Chapter. He is also a member of St. Omer's Commandery, No. 7, of Brownsville, and has been a member of Brownsville Lodge, No. 51, of the Order of Odd-Fellows, since 1834. Judge Duncan has also been a member of the Methodist Episcopal church since the last-named year.

"In May, 1829, he married Priscilla Stevens, daughter of Dr. Benjamin Stevens, of Uniontown, whose father, Benjamin Stevens, who came to Fayette county from Maryland, was also a physician. Mrs. Duncan died in February, 1873, at the age of sixty-six years.

"Judge and Mrs. Duncan became the parents of five children, three of whom are living: Mrs. Elizabeth Worrell, Dr. W. S. Duncan, both of Bridgeport, and Thomas J. Duncan, a lawyer practicing his profession in Washington, Pa."

HON. THOMAS BENTON SCHNATTERLY. "One of the most active public men of Fayette county, and at present and for some years past a successful leading politician, and now having perhaps more promise than any other man of his party in his district, State, senatorial, or congressional, of a sure and distinguished career in the future is Senator Thomas B. Schnatterly. Mr. Schnatterly as a politician has the good sense to follow through opposition and over obloquy the dictates of his better manhood and boldly and bravely place himself upon the platform of the old-time genuine democratic principles, and wage war for the laboring classes, and consequently for the best interests of all classes at last, against the great corporations, with their unlimited exchequers at ready command for any scheme of remunerative corruption, and with their autocratic aspirations, instead of following the course of too many leading democrats, as well as republicans, who either covertly, or openly and shamelessly, sell their talents and consciences to capital in its cause *versus* righteousness among men. His political foes dedenounce his course as demagogism. That was to be expected, but the more of that kind of 'demagogism' Fayette county and Pennsylvania enjoy the better; the sooner, therefore, will the hideous wages-slavery, as base in many respects as was ever the chattel-slavery of the neighboring State of Virginia, and which has made the system practiced by many of the great Pennsylvania corporations objectionable to all right-minded thinkers, be abolished, and true republican customs be substituted therefor.

"Thomas B. Schnatterly comes of Dutch lineage on his paternal side. His great-grandfather, with a number of brothers, came from Holland prior to the Revolutionary war. A part of them settled in Eastern Pennsylvania, in Lebanon county. Two pushed westward, with the purpose of making homes near the headwaters of the Ohio, but were lost sight of and were perhaps slain by the Indians. Another, the great-grandfather of Senator Schnatterly, eventually settled in Fayette county, in what is now Nicholson township, and there married and became the father of a son named John, who was the grandfather of Thomas B. Schnatterly. John had by his first wife some eight children; by a second wife one child, a son. Of the first family of children was John Schnatterly, the father of Thomas B. He was born near New Geneva in the year 1805, and at about the age of twenty-two married Miss Malinda Kendall, daughter of Thomas Kendall, then living near Uniontown. Mr. and Mrs. John Schnatterly, both enjoying the peace of ripe old age, are the parents of nine children, seven of whom—four sons and three daughters—are living, and of whom Senator Schnatterly is the sixth in number, and was born July 13, 1841. He was brought up on the homestead farm, and was educated at the common schools and Georges Creek Academy (teaching school himself somewhat during this period of his life), and at Madison Institute and Waynesburg College.

"After leaving college, at about the age of twenty-two, he entered the office of Col. T. B. Searight, at Uniontown, as a student at law, and was admitted to the bar in December, 1864. In October, 1865, he was elected district attorney for Fayette county for the term of three years, and entered upon official duty in December of the same year, and went out of office in December, 1868. The term was an arduous one, occurring just after the war, and comprising a reign of crime. Special sessions of criminal courts were in those days held to try offenses of high degree. After the term was over he continued the practice of law in Uniontown, and at the October election of 1869 was elected by the democratic party a member of the general assembly of Pennsylvania for Fayette county, and served in the session of 1870, and was elected in that year to the general assembly of 1871, and served therein; and thereafter, while conducting the practice of law, engaged (in October, 1871) as a contractor in the construction of the Greensburg and Connellsville division of the Southwest Pennsylvania railroad, which division was completed in 1872, the charter for which he had caused to be granted in the session of 1871. In 1872 he was defeated as a candidate for the senate at the democratic primary elections by Hon. William H. Playford.

"He continued the practice of the law, and in 1876 was again elected to the general assembly for the session of 1877–78, and at the November election of 1878 was elected State senator for the Fortieth District, composed of the counties of Fayette and Greene, for the period of four years.

"In the house he served on general and local judiciary committees; in the senate, on local, judiciary, railroad and corporation committees. In both house and senate, in all legislative controversies between capital and labor, he was always on the side of the oppressed, constantly looking out for the interests of the laboring classes, and was not tenderly loved by the grasping monopolists of Pennsylvania.

"He originated the bill abolishing, under severe penalties, the odious female-waiter system then in vogue, with all its iniquities, in the cities of the State. He was also the projector of the senate bill entitled 'An act to secure to operatives and laborers engaged in and about coal-mines, manufactories of iron and steel, and all other manufactories the payment of their wages at regular intervals, and in lawful money of the United States.' In the session of 1880 this bill was passed, but was vetoed by Governor Hoyt; but it was introduced by Senator Schnatterly in the succeeding session of 1881, and again passed, and then received the governor's approval, and became the law.

"The struggle over this bill was a test fight between capital and the interests of labor in the State. The senator did brave work in pushing the bill on to recognition in law, and by a powerful array of facts convinced a senate at first in active opposition to the bill of the justice of his propositions and the necessity for the act.

"Another important fact in Senator Schnatterly's career as a legislator should not fail of record here, and it is this, that he has uniformly voted for the largest appropriations for the public schools and the public charities (a specie of 'demagogism' almost as discreditable as his legislative warfare in favor of the rights and interests of the laboring classes). He can well afford to be criticised for voting decent appropriations for the blind and the maimed. The foes who censure him for so doing are the men who also look upon the working classes of the State as unworthy a better fate than that they suffer under.

"The act above referred to, looking to the emancipation of labor is now generally evaded by those whose injustices it was intended to decrease and prevent, but in time will compel itself to be respected, when the senator, it is to be hoped, will be sustained by popular approval in all parts of the State in his efforts in the cause of humanity.

"Senator Schnatterly has of late returned to railroading as a contractor in the construction of the Pittsburgh, Virginia and Charleston road, and in that of the Southwest Pennsylvania railroad, and has just completed (March, 1882) several sections of the Redstone division of the Pittsburgh, Virginia and Charleston road.

"In 1867 he married Miss Mary Morrison, daughter of George and Anna (West) Morrison, of Uniontown."

HENRY CLAY FRICK. "Mr. Frick, of the celebrated firm of H. C. Frick & Co., manufacturers and dealers in coke, and a third owner of the business of said company, which is constituted of himself and Messrs. Edmund and Walton Ferguson, of Pittsburgh, was born in West Overton, Westmoreland county, Pa., December 19, 1849.

"Mr. Frick first engaged in active business life on any considerable scale in 1871, when he entered upon the coke business at Broad Ford, in Fayette county, Pa., and has continued to prosecute the same there and in that neighborhood to this time.

"The business at Broad Ford was started with fifty ovens, and has gradually increased till it comprises in that district over one thousand ovens.

"The firm also owns coke interests in other parts of Fayette county and in Westmoreland county."

EDWARD K. HYNDMAN. "Edward K. Hyndman, though a native of Carbon county, Pa., and present resident of Pittsburgh, resided in Fayette county for a period of about eight years, and holds large business interests therein.

"Mr. Hyndman is of Scotch-Irish descent, being the son of Hugh Hyndman, who was born in the north of Ireland in 1800, and Catharine Huff, a native of Danville, Pa., born in 1805, both still living in vigorous old age. He was born in Mauch Chunk, Pa., the great anthracite coal region, in 1844, and growing up there became a civil engineer at about eighteen years of age, and was engaged more or less in the construction and operation of railroads in their various departments until at twenty-five years of age he became the superintendent of the Lehigh and Susquehanna Railroad, from Easton to Scranton (now a part of the New Jersey Central Railroad system), in the superintendency of which he continued till 1872, when he resigned his post to take the superintendency of the Pittsburgh and Connellsville Railroad (now the Pittsburgh Division of the Baltimore and Ohio Railroad), in charge of which he remained, residing at Connellsville, for the period of eight years.

"In his official position, while living there in charge of the railroad, Mr. Hyndman enjoyed peculiar opportunities for studying the Connellsville coke business and the extent and position of the coking coal field, and was so impressed with the vast present and future importance of the business that he took measures to secure some eigth thousand acres of the best of coal lands in one body, and organized a company under the name of the Connellsville Coke and Iron Company, with Hon. John Leisenring as president, and other of his old Eastern anthracite coal friends as members, with a capital stock of one million two hundred and fifty thousand dollars, for the purpose of developing the coal property. He then resigned the superintendency of the railroad, and accepted the position of general manager of the above named company. Mr. Hyndman remained in that position until the company was thoroughly established and in working order, he finding meanwhile that his early experience in the anthracite district availed him much in the new field. He then resigned the management of the company, though still its consulting engineer, and removing to Pittsburgh, accepted (in June, 1881) the office of general manager of the Pittsburgh and Western Railroad, which office he now holds, together with that of president of the Pittsburgh Junction Railroad.

"Mr. Hyndman is also largely interested in various enterprises in and out of the State. Among these may be mentioned that of the Virginia Coal and Iron Company and the Holston Steel and Iron Company, having their center of operations in southwestern Virginia, and in which Mr. Leisenring and others of the Connellsville Coke and Iron Company are also interested. The above-named Virginia Coal and Iron Company possesses over 70,000 acres of coal and iron lands, upon the development of which they have already entered, having commenced the construction of a railroad seventy miles in length in order to reach their new fields from Bristol, Tenn. The coke to be manufactured in this field will readily supply markets not accessible from the Connellsville coke region.

"February 25, 1873, Mr. Hyndman married at Philadelphia, Miss Gulielma A. Brown, daughter of the late William Brown, Esq., of Bethlehem, Pa., and Mrs. Susan I. Brown, his widow, who now resides in Philadelphia. Mr. and Mrs. Hyndman have two sons."

COL. JAMES PAULL. "James Paull, who lived in Fayette county, from childhood to old age, and was one of its prominent and most honored citizens, was born in Frederick (now Berkeley) county, Va., September 17, 1760, and in 1768 removed to the West with the family of his father, George Paull, who then settled in that part of Westmoreland county which afterward became Fayette; his location being the Gist neighborhood, in the present township of Dunbar, which was the home of James Paull during the remainder of his long life. Judge Veech says of him that 'early in life he evinced qualities of heart and soul calculated to render him conspicuous, added to which was a physical constitution of the hardiest kind. Throughout his long life his bravery and patriotism, like his generosity, knew no limits. He loved enterprise and adventure as he loved his friends, and shunned no service or dangers to which they called him. He came to manhood just when such men were needed.'

"In the early part of his life James Paull was much engaged in military service, and in it his record was that of a brave, honorable and efficient soldier and officer. His military experience began in 1778, when, as a boy of eighteen years, he was drafted for a tour of duty in the guarding of Continental stores at Fort Burd, on the Monongahela, under Captain Robert McGlaughlin. Three years later, in 1781, he was made a first lieutenant by Thomas Jefferson, Governor of Virginia, and in that grade served with a company raised largely by his efforts, and which formed a part of the expedition which went down the Ohio under General George Rogers Clarke on a projected campaign against Detroit, as is mentioned in the Revolutionary chapters of this history. Upon the failure of that expedition he returned on foot through the wilderness from the Falls of the Ohio (Louisville, Ky.) to Morgantown, Va., and thence home, being accompanied by the men of his own command and also the officers and men of Major Isaac Craig's artillery, of Pittsburgh. In 1782 he served a short tour of duty as a private soldier at Turtle Creek, above Pittsburgh, and at its close joined (still as a private) the expedition of Colonel William Crawford against Sandusky. The story of the hardships and perils which he met in that disastrous campaign, and the manner of his almost miraculous escape from the savages, has been told in preceding pages. Again in 1783 and 1784 he was engaged in frontier service against Indian incursions along the southwest border of the State. In 1790 he served in the grade of major and lieutenant-colonel under General Harmar in the unsuccessful campaign of that officer against the Indians in the Maumee country, and in this, as in all his military service, he acquitted himself most honorably. This was the end of his military experience. Having married, he settled down to the comforts of domestic life and the pursuits of agriculture, in which he was eminently successful. He reared a large and most respectable family, seven sons: James, George, John, Archibald, Thomas, William and Joseph, and one daughter, Martha, who became the wife of William Walker. He had some concern in iron manufacture, and was occasionally, in middle life, a down-river trader. But he was a lover of home, with its quiet cares and enjoyments. He was never ambitious for office, and the only one he ever held was that of sheriff of Fayette county from 1793 to 1796. Colonel Paull was a man of perfect and unquestioned integrity and truth, and of the most generous and heroic impulses. He died in Dunbar township, July 9, 1841, aged nearly eighty-one years."

MAJ. ARTHUR B. DE SAULLES.

"Major Arthur B. De Saulles, of Dunbar, the vice-president of the Dunbar Iron Company and superintendent of its works, is the son of an English gentleman, Louis De Saulles, who is of French descent, and Armide Longer De Saulles, a Louisianian by birth, and, like her husband, of French lineage. Major De Saulles was born in New Orleans, January 8, 1840, and was instructed at home by a private tutor until ten years of age, when he was placed in a German school at West Newton, Mass., and carefully trained in the German language, as well as other studies, for two years. This period of educational discipline was followed immediately by two years at Bolmar's French-English Institute at West Chester, Pa., and the latter period by a course of study at Cambridge, Mass., in preparation for an advanced course of scientific studies, which he made at the Rensselaer Polytechnic School at Troy, N. Y., from which institution he graduated in June, 1859. During his connection with the Polytechnic School he was engaged for five months as assistant in the geological survey of Arkansas.

"After his graduation Maj. De Saulles' father sent him on a tour of inspection through the State of Pennsylvania to examine mining and metallurgical operations therein, and make report thereof to him, after which experience and report he sent him to Europe in December, 1859, and in January, 1860, De Saulles entered the Ecole des Mines, Paris, where he remained till September, 1861, when he returned to New Orleans, and three days after his arrival there entered the Confederate service, and was placed on the staff of Maj. Lovell in the engineer corps, and was put in charge of the construction of fortifications on Lake Pontchartrain and on Plaine Chalmette, south of New Orleans. With the Confederate forces he remained on active duty (with the exception of a short time when furloughed on account of a wound received in a skirmish) until the surrender of the Army of the Tennessee in North Carolina, at which time he was its chief engineer. During this period of service he was mainly employed in the construction of fortifications at various points, and in the building of pontoon trains for the Army of the Tennessee, to which he was most of the time attached, and wherein he acted as major from the fall of 1864 till the time of its surrender.

"Soon after the war he went to Europe, where he remained till April, 1866, when he returned to America and took the position of engineer of the New York and Schuylkill Coal Company's works, after a year being placed in charge, and remaining with the company till it sold out to the Philadelphia and Reading Coal and Iron Company, in October, 1871, whereupon he moved to New York City, and engaged in professional pursuits till March, 1876, when he became connected with the Dunbar Furnace Works. Aside from his connection with these works he is manager of the Percy Mining Company and one of the executive committee of the Fayette Coke and Furnace Company at Oliphant, which works in all employ about a thousand hands.

"He was one of the seven organizers (1868) of the American Institute of Mining, which now embraces about one thousand members and associates, and also one of the original members of the American Society of Mechanical Engineers, and is a member of the American Meteorological Society.

"In politics he is 'a good old-fashioned democrat,' and in religion not a 'communicant,' but takes interest in the little Episcopal church which his wife built and presented to the parish at Dunbar Furnace in 1880.

"August 19, 1869, he married Miss Catharine Heckscher, daughter of Charles A. Heckscher, of New York City, by whom he had three sons and two daughters."

SAMUEL WORK. "An excellent representative of the best class of Fayette county agriculturists, combining the instincts and culture of the gentleman with the steady industry and the muscle of the prosperous farmer, is Mr. Samuel Work, of Dunbar, who was born December 5, 1817. Mr. Work's paternal ancestors came to America from the north of Ireland. His grandfather, Samuel, whose name he bears, and who was born July 17, 1749, and died in 1833, moved from Lancaster county into Fayette county, and settled in Dunbar township about 1766, where John, the father of Mr. Work, was born in 1787, and married, in 1814, Nancy Rogers, daughter of John Rogers, of Fayette county.

"Mr. Work, the second issue of this union, attended in childhood the so called subscription school at the old "Cross Keys" schoolhouse in Dunbar until about seventeen years of age, and after that the academy at Uniontown, conducted by Rev. Dr. Wilson, till well advanced in his twentieth year, and then commenced the life of a farmer on the old homestead farm, and subsequently inherited an adjoining farm, which he cultivated with skill and profit, raising cattle, among other things, together with carrying on the business of a dealer in cattle, which he often sent in droves to the Eastern markets until 1876, when he retired from business, having previously sold the Connellsville coking coal which underlies a large portion of the farm he occupied, the surface of which he has since disposed of, he now residing in Dunbar village.

"Mr. Work is a gentleman of genial, active temperament, and in early life greatly enjoyed all kinds of athletic, manly sports, particularly that of fox-hunting with horse and hounds, and was noted as a finished horseman and bold rider; but being ever temperate and attentive to business, he never allowed his love of the chase to infringe upon important affairs. He belonged to the Fayette County Cavalry, at one time a famous organization, and took great pride in military matters. In politics he is a republican, and was formerly an old-line whig. He took great interest in the late war on the side of the Union, and contributed liberally, particularly in aid of the work of the Sanitary Commission. He is a member of the Presbyterian church, of which his wife is also a member, and to which he has belonged for about fifteen years, and enjoys an unsullied reputation for general integrity and honest dealing wherever he is known.

"On the 23d of September, 1858, he was united in marriage to Miss Jane W. Watts (born in 1837), a native of County Donegal, Ireland, and daughter of George and Jane Wilson Watts, both of Scotch descent. When about fifteen years of age, Mrs. Work, then well instructed for her years, came to America, and here continued her studies until the time of her marriage. They have no children."

COL. JAMES M. SCHOONMAKER.

"Colonel James M. Schoonmaker, though a native and resident of Pittsburgh, has large business interests in Fayette county, in the development of coal mines and the manufacture of coke, and is therefore more practically identified with the welfare of the county than are many of her own children.

"Colonel Schoonmaker is of New York 'Knickerbocker' stock, his paternal ancestors subsequent to 1660 having been born in Ulster and Orange counties, N. Y. Hendrick Jochem, one of his paternal ancestors, came to America from Holland in 1660, and settled in Ulster county.

"James Schoonmaker, the father of Col. J. M. Schoonmaker, removed from Ulster county to Pittsburgh in 1836, at the age of twenty-three years, and embarked in the drug business. In 1841 he married Mary Stockton, a daughter of Rev. Joseph Stockton, of Pittsburgh, by whom he has had nine children—five sons and four daughters—of whom James M. is the oldest. Both parents, as well as all the children, are living.

"James M. was born June 30, 1842, and was educated in private schools, and in the public schools of Pittsburgh, and attended the Western University of that city, which institution he left at the age of nineteen years, and entered the volunteer army in the War of the Rebellion, being attached as a private at first to the Union Cavalry of Pittsburgh, which joined the Army of the Potomac. With this force he served a year, being meanwhile made a lieutenant of Company A, of the First Maryland Cavalry Regiment, to which the Union Cavalry was attached. In August, 1862, he was ordered from the front to return home and take command of the Fourteenth Pennsylvania Cavalry, which was then recruiting in Pittsburgh, being partly made up of three companies from Fayette county,—Company B, under Captain Zadoc Walker; Company E, under Captain Ashbel F. Duncan; and Company F, led by Captain Calvin Springer (late sheriff of Fayette county). Many of the surviving members of these companies are now living in Fayette county.

"In November, 1862, Col. Schoonmaker received his commission as colonel, and took his regiment into the field. At that time Col. Schoonmaker, being a little less than twenty years and five months of age, was, it is believed, the youngest officer of his rank in the Federal army. He commanded the regiment till January 1, 1864, when he was assigned to the command of the First Brigade, First Cavalry Division of the Army of the Shenandoah, and remained in that command till the end of the war, after which, with his brigade still in service, he was sent by the War Department to guard the overland stage-route from the Missouri river to the Rocky Mountains, serving in that campaign till August, 1865, when the brigade was mustered out of service at Fort Leavenworth, Kans.

"During his military career Colonel Schoonmaker was constantly in the field, and participated in all the battles of the Army of the Shenandoah, under General Sheridan, the campaigns of which were especially severe. At one time his brigade was for forty-two consecutive days and nights in the saddle, engaging the enemy daily, and took part in the three decisive battles of the Shenandoah Valley, which practically ended the war by destroying the enemy's forces.

"After the mustering out of his brigade at Fort Leavenworth, Colonel Schoonmaker returned home and entered into business with his father, remaining with him until some time in 1872, when he went into business with his father-in-law, William H. Brown, in the mining of coal and manufacture of coke.

"In 1879, Mr. Brown having meanwhile died, and his business being divided or assigned among the members of his family, Colonel Schoonmaker came into possession of the Connellsville coke branch as his interest in the partnership business, and has ever since been exclusively engaged in prosecuting that. A good portion of his works are located in Fayette county, 463 coke-ovens being situated at Dawson's station, he being also chairman of the Redstone Coke Company (limited), which has 300 ovens near Uniontown, Colonel Schoonmaker owning one-third of this property. He also owns the Alice Mines, in Westmoreland county, comprising 200 ovens, and is chairman of the Morewood Coke Company (limited), of the same county, and running 470 ovens, of which property he is one-fourth owner. Colonel Schoonmaker's principal office is at 120 Water street, Pittsburgh.

"February 22, 1872, Colonel Schoonmaker married Miss Alice W. Brown, daughter of William H. and Mary Smith Brown, of Pittsburgh, and who died October 7, 1881, leaving a son."

THOMAS DUNN. "Thomas Dunn, of Franklin township, was born April 7, 1824, of Scotch-Irish stock, and was educated in the common-schools. He was married February 4, 1844, to Eleanor Scott, of German township. They have ten living children, and have lost one. Thomas Dunn was born in the house in which he lives, and which was built by his grandfather in 1796. His entire life has been spent upon the farm on which he now resides. He, his wife, and nearly all of his children are members of the United Presbyterian church.

"The children are: John A., married to Mary Junk; Agnes R., married to John Junk; Thomas S., married to Jennie Murphy; Mary C., married to Bryson Gilchrist; Samuel W., married first to Ellen Stoner, and again to

Clarissa Hanshaw; Annie E., married to Jacob Cooper; William C., married to Mary E. McClure; Harriet, deceased, unmarried; Robert C., Major E., Harry G.

"Thomas Dunn's father, John Dunn, first married Mary Smith in 1815. She died June 5, 1835. His second wife was Mary Oldham. She died in 1843. In 1844 he married Catharine Scott, who still survives him, an active woman of eighty-two years. He was a farmer, and lived upon the farm now occupied by Thomas. He was also a soldier in the War of 1812. They had eight children; Thomas was the fourth. John Dunn died October 21, 1861.

"Thomas Dunn, grandfather of the subject of this biography, was an Irishman. He married a Scotchwoman, Mary Caldwell. They came to Fayette county about 1772. Thomas patented the farm upon which his grandson Thomas now lives. He was a Revolutionary soldier, and had twelve children, each of whom raised families. They are scattered all over the United States. Thomas, Sr., died in 1799, aged fifty-five. Mary (Caldwell) Dunn was born January 20, 1746, and died 1824.

"Mr. Thomas Dunn is held in high esteem by his neighbors—an honest, genial man; and it may properly be added that the Dunn family are noted for their frankness and general good nature or affability. Mr. Dunn raised a large family in a commendable manner, and, like himself, they are good citizens."

FREDERICK JOHNSTON, of Morgan's Station, was a brave soldier during the late war, has been an extensive traveler, and is a remarkably good business man. He is a son of Thomas and Susan (Grindle) Johnston, and was born in Connellsville township, Fayette county, Pa., February 18, 1844.

Thomas Johnston (father) is of German descent, and a native of Somerset county, Pa. He came to Connellsville and engaged in farming, but soon moved to his present farm in Tyrone township. He is a republican, and is in his sixty-ninth year. His wife is a daughter of John Grindle, a Fayette county farmer. Mr. Grindle moved to Kentucky, but soon removed to West Virginia, where he died.

Frederick Johnston was reared on a farm and attended the common schools until seventeen years of age. He then learned the trade of blacksmith, and a year later he was the first man to enlist in Company B, Sixteenth Pennsylvania Cavalry. Mr. Johnston was mustered into the Federal service September 18, 1862, and was mustered out of the same at Lynchburgh, Va., June 26, 1865. He was at Chancellorsville, fought through the Wilderness, served with Phil. Sheridan in the Shenandoah valley, and then was with Grant from Petersburg to Appomattox. He was one of those veterans who by hard fighting won for the Army of the Potomac its magnificent war record. After the war Mr. Johnston resumed work at his trade, and in 1868 he opened a shop at Morgan Station. He did a paying business until 1887, when he ceased working at his trade and engaged in his present general mercantile business. He has a good storeroom, carries a large and well-assorted stock of notions, groceries, hardware and provisions, and enjoys a substantial and remunerative patronage.

Mr. Johnston has traveled in twenty-one States and six Territories of the Union, and also in Canada. He is a Free Mason, a K. of P. and an Odd Fellow and Encampment Odd Fellow and G. A. R. He is a republican, and is a trustee, steward and class-leader in the M. E. church. As a citizen and a business man he stands well with the public.

www.ingramcontent.com/pod-product-compliance
Lightning Source LLC
Chambersburg PA
CBHW060126280326
41932CB00012B/1439

* 9 7 8 0 8 0 6 3 4 7 5 0 9 *